ISBN 978-0-265-94275-8
PIBN 10913327

LIST OF ILLUSTRATIONS.

Map showing library centers .... Frontispiece

PAGE

Carnegie library, Fargo, exterior 34
Carnegie library, Fargo, interior 56
A. C. library, exterior 58
A. C. library, interior 58
Carnegie library, Grafton, exterior 60
Carnegie library, Grand Forks, exterior 62
City library, Mandan, exterior 64
Carnegie library, Valley City, exterior 66
Carnegie library, Valley City, interior 66

TABLE OF CONTENTS.

	PAGE
Frontispiece—map showing library stations	1
List of illustrations	3
Table of contents	5
Library commission directory, October 1, 1908	13
Letter of transmittal	15
Report of secretary	17
Organization of commission	17
Duties of commission	17
Work of commission	18
Traveling libraries	18
Legislative reference	18
Educational reference	18
Duties of librarian and director	19
Traveling libraries	19
Methods used	20
Sample list	27
Educational reference library	31
Aims of commission	32
Needs of the work	33
Resignation of librarian	34
Signs of progress	35
Apology	36
Conclusion	36

LEGISLATIVE REFERENCE DEPARTMENT.

PAGE

Law creating it—general provisions 38
Legislative bodies—unjust criticism 38
Department of government—procedure—
  Executive 38
  Legislative 39
  Judicial 39
Need of a reference library 40
  Charles McCarthy quoted 40
Reference work in other states 40
  James Bryce quoted 40
Aim and method 40
  List of subjects 41
Source of material—newspapers 43
  List of newspapers and periodicals received.............. 44
Practical nature of the work 43
Department non-partisan 45
Bill index—sessions of 1905 and 1907 45
Circular letter to members 46
Demands upon department 46
Work to be done 46
Debating societies 47
Bulletins of comparative legislation 47
Needs of the department 48

APPENDIX NO. I.

HISTORY OF LIBRARIES, WITH ILLUSTRATIONS.

Devils Lake Public Library .... Mrs. Frank Stoltze
Dickinson Public Library .... R. H. Johnson
Fargo Public Library .... Frank J. Thompson
Jamestown Public Library .... Mrs. A. M. Burt
Grafton High School and Public Library .... Mrs. W. L. Stockwell
Grand Forks Public Library .... Sveinbjorn Johnson
University of North Dakota Library.................... Sveinbjorn Johnson
Mandan City Library .... Mrs. Elizabeth McDonald
Minot Public Library .... Mrs. L. W. Gammons
Valley City Public Library .... Laura A. Bassett

APPENDIX NO. II.

TABLE OF STATISTICS.

Statistics of Libraries in North Dakota state institutions.
Methods of administrations in North Dakota institutional libraries.
Statistics of North Dakota public libraries.
Methods of administration in North Dakota public libraries.
List of lodge, college and academy libraries.
List of North Dakota high school libraries.
List of North Dakota public libraries.
List of North Dakota traveling library stations, November 1, 1908.

APPENDIX NO. III.

FINANCIAL REPORTS.

Report of secretary North Dakota Library Commission, March 14, 1907, to June 30, 1908; June 30, 1908, to October 31, 1908.
Table of appropriations in other states.

APPENDIX NO. IV.

Changes recommended in Library Laws.
Laws of North Dakota relating to libraries.

CHANGES IN THE LIBRARY LAW.

A year of practical work in accordance with the laws of the state has indicated to the Commission the wisdom of some changes in the laws relating to libraries.

1. The number of members on the Commission should be increased from three to five. Three scarcely suffice for suitable organization within the commission. When an emergency occurs, it is difficult to obtain a meeting to transact business from so small a number, who may be scattered by their vocations in different parts of the state.

2. If the Commission consists of five members, it is suggested that two be women appointed by the governor for four years and that the appointments be so arranged that they do not both expire in the same biennial period.

3. The law now requires libraries to report to the board of education. The transfer of the libraries to the commission and the growing interest of communities in a library tax, make it desirable that libraries be required to report to the public commission and to their city council.

4. Through an ambiguity, the printing for the commission which it was intended should be paid for outside the $1500.00 appropriation, has been charged to the commission fund.

5. It is recommended that the term of office on the commission of ex-officio members begin January first following their election to the position whose tenure qualifies them for membership in the commission.

NORTH DAKOTA PUBLIC LIBRARY COMMISSION.

MEMBERS EX-OFFICIO.

Frank J. Thompson, President Library Association,
President.

Walter L. Stockwell, State Superintendent of Public Instruction,
Vice- President.

Mrs. Minnie Clarke Budlong,
Secretary-Treasurer.

Zana K. Miller,
Librarian and Director.

Sveinbjorn Johnson, M. A.,
Legislative Reference Librarian.

Florence McPhee,
Stenographer.

Jessie M. Ramp,
Clerk.

LETTER OF TRANSMITTAL

To the Honorable John Burke, Governor of North Dakota:

I have the honor to submit herewith a report of the North Dakota Public Library Commission from its organization March 14, 1907 to November 1, 1908.

MINNIE CLARKE BUDLONG,
Secretary Public Library Commission.

NORTH DAKOTA PUBLIC LIBRARY COMMISSION

REPORT OF SECRETARY.

ORGANIZATION OF COMMISSION.

The North Dakota Public Library Commission was created by act of the Tenth legislative assembly. Its members, the president of the state library association, the state superintendent of public instruction and a third appointed by the governor, met at the capitol March 14, 1907, took the oath of office and organized by electing:

Frank J. Thompson, Fargo, President;
W. L. Stockwell, Grafton, Vice-President;
Mrs. Minnie Clarke Budlong, Bismarck, Secretary.

DUTIES OF COMMISSION.

The work outlined for the commission in the act creating it, is as follows:

"Session Laws 1907, Chapter 243.

"POWERS AND DUTIES OF COMMISSION.

SECTION 5. The state library commission on and after its creation and organization, shall take over and add to the educational reference library and the system of traveling libraries, and shall continue the same, and, as its funds permit, shall increase the number and usefulness of the libraries. * * * The commission shall catalogue and otherwise prepare said books for circulation * * *. (It) shall have power and it shall be its duty to establish a legislative reference bureau for the information and assistance of the members of the legislative assembly in the work of legislation. * * *

ASSIST FREE PUBLIC LIBRARIES.

SECTION 6. The librarian or trustees of any free public library or the trustees of any village, town or community, entitled to borrow books from said traveling libraries, may, without charge, ask and receive advice and instruction from said state library commission upon any matter pertaining to the organization, maintenance or administraton of the lbraries, and the said commission shall, as far as possible, promote and assist by counsel and encouragement the formation of libraries where none exist, and the commission may also send its members to aid in organizing new libraries or improving those already established.

REPORT.

SECTION 7. The state library commission shall keep statistics of the free public libraries of North Dakota and a record of the work done and books loaned by said commission, and shall make a full report to each general session of the legislature of all expenditures by the commission, and of such statistics and record as shall show the work done by the commission, the use made of the traveling libraries, and all other matters which they deem expedient for the information of the legislature * * *."

WORK OF COMMISSION.

October 1, 1907, Miss Zana K. Miller, visitor of libraries under the Wisconsin commission, assumed control of the work in North Dakota as librarian and director. A trip of inspection had previously been made to some of the libraries of the state including Wahpeton, Fargo, Grafton, Leeds and Minot. An office was opened in the capitol. The department of public instruction resigned to the commission the educational reference library of 3,000 volumes and the charge of the traveling libraries.

Traveling Libraries

Since 1897 the educational department had been sending libraries of 50 volumes each to county superintendents for the use of schools. Requests were sent out for the return of these libraries to be checked up by the librarian. Some books proved to be missing, many were worn out, others, having been chosen for school libraries, were not suited to the needs of traveling libraries. From the balance have been re-organized and sent out prior to November, 1908, forty-one libraries containing 1768 books, an average of forty-three volumes each. From the residue, additional libraries are being fitted out as rapidly as the other duties of the office permit. These libraries are loaned for six months, the receivers paying only the cost of transportation.

Legislative Reference Library—

Besides the re-organization of the traveling libraries, the librarian started the legislative reference bureau. Material was collected in this and other states and much of it classified before this branch of the work, in August, 1908, was placed in charge of Sveinbjorn Johnson, whose report will be found in another part of this volume.

Educational Reference Library—

It is intended that this department shall be an aid to individuals, clubs, schools or communities wishing to pursue special lines of work. Little has been accomplished so far on account of having no fund for the purchase of books. Four clubs, one school and forty-nine individuals have received a total of 375 volumes on application.

DUTIES OF LIBRARIAN AND DIRECTOR.

Besides the care of the educational reference library, the re-organization of the traveling libraries and the founding of the legislative reference library, the librarian has promoted library interest wherever possible throughout the state. The libraries of Wahpeton, Grand Forks, Fargo, Mayville, Jamestown, Casselton, Leeds, Grafton and Minot received personal visits. Others, notably Dickinson and Devils Lake, have received advice by correspondence on the planning, erecting and furnishing of library buildings. In some towns, as Jamestown and Minot, assistance has been given in awakening popular interest in a library tax. Articles explaining the work of the commission have been furnished many newspapers of the state. Aids have been sent the small libraries, also lists of books and magazines, and advice as to their selection and purchase. The first attempt has been made to locate all the libraries of the state and the statistics have been gathered which form the basis of this report. The librarian attended as a representative of the commission, a meeting of the League of Library Commissions in Chicago in January, 1908, and the A. L. A. Conference at Lake Minnetonka, Minnesota, June 22-27, 1908. Papers explaining the new system for the libraries were read before the state meeting of county superintendents at Bismarck, before the Burleigh county teachers institute and teachers' assocation, also before the summer schools at Grand Forks and Mayville. Two visits were made at Jamestown, the last one in September, 1908, to assist in the re-organization of the public library before it moved into its new quarters in the city hall.

WORK OF TRAVELING LIBRARIES.

No part of library extension is so vital to the welfare of the people as the traveling libraries. In a state consisting chiefly of farming communities, there can be no immediate prospect of many large libraries. A great proportion of the inhabitants of North Dakota must for some time depend upon the traveling library to supplement their home collection of books. A steadily increasing number of workers is pushing into the remoter districts adding yearly immense sums to the wealth of the state. In return the state owes a duty to these pioneers to see that they shall not suffer for lack of the reading to which they have been accustomed, or that their children shall not be deprived of the books and pictures needed to complete their school training. With this end in view, the work of refitting the school libraries into traveling libraries has begun, and mixed collections containing forty to fifty volumes each are sent on application.

When a community asks for a traveling library, there is sent it at once an application card accompanied by the list of rules following.

APPLICATION BLANK FOR TRAVELING LIBRARY STATION.

....

(Village or Town) (County) (Date)

To the North Dakota Public Library Commission, Bismarck, N. D:

We, the officers and members of the............................Library Association, apply for a traveling library to be used by the people of .... and the vicinity.

We hereby agree to observe strictly the Commission rules for the loan of libraries; to return each library we receive within six months of its receipt unless extension of time is given; to make no charge to patrons for its privileges; to collect suitable fines for the loss of books or undue injury to them; and to pay all transportation charges.

The libraries will be kept by..

(P. O. Address) .... in (state whether residence, store, school, etc.) .... and will be open to the public from (state hours) ....M. to ....M. on (state days of week) ....

Ship by ....R. R."

On the reverse side of the card are blank lines for the signatures of the six people agreeing to be responsible. With the card is sent these "Rules for Circulation."

"NORTH DAKOTA
PUBLIC LIBRARY COMMISSION

Traveling Libraries—How They May Be Secured.

The state law provides that the Public Library Commission shall care for the traveling libraries formerly issued from the state superintendent's office.

TO WHOM LOANED.

The libraries are not loaned to individuals, but to any village, town or community which will form a library association with not less than six members, or any school, study club, or similar organization which will act as a library association. In all cases those interested must agree to be responsible for the safe-keeping and return of the library and to manage it in accordance with the rules of the Library Commission. An application blank or agreement must be properly filled out, signed by six responsible persons and filed with the Public Library Commission at Bismarck before a library will be shipped.

A small public library may obtain a traveling library for the use of its patrons in order to encourage the use of the local library and to illustrate better selection of books.

FREE TO ALL.

No fee shall be charged for the use of these books. Arrangements should be made in advance by subscriptions or pledges for the payment of the necessary cost of transportation.

TIME LIBRARY MAY BE KEPT.

The period for which the libraries are loaned is six months, but an extension will be granted, when desired, upon application. All shipments are made from Bismarck and the libraries should be returned to the Library Commission at Bismarck.

NUMBER OF BOOKS IN EACH LIBRARY.

The libraries contain from 40 to 50 books in fixed collections adapted to both adults and children. There are no printed catalogues for distribution, but a list of the books is sent in each case.

LOCATION OF THE LIBRARY.

It is urged that the library be kept in a convenient place, open for the delivery and return of books, at such time as is determined upon by the local association, of which due notice shall be given to the public. The location of the library is important as it should be kept at a central point where people will have no hesitancy in going.

LIBRARIAN.

The local storekeeper or postmaster will often be willing to take charge of the library, but a librarian should be selected who will take an interest in the books and try to get the people to read them. The success of a traveling library depends very largely upon the librarian.

Simple directions for charging the books are sent with each library."

Upon the return of the application card properly signed a fixed collection containing 40 to 50 volumes is sent. These books are packed in a strong wooden box, so arranged that it can be used as a case for the books at the receiving station. The box is billed "From

NORTH DAKOTA

PUBLIC LIBRARY COMMISSION

The Capitol, Bismarck, N. Dak.

To ....

....

North Dakota.

Via .... Collect

Charges, including both freight and drayage, are in no case to be paid by the North Dakota Public Library Commission."

and contains for the return a shipping label as follows:

"From ....

....

TO THE

NORTH DAKOTA PUBLIC LIBRARY COMMISSION

Bismarck, N. Dak.

Via...................................... Paid.

Charges, including both freight and drayage, are in no case to be paid by the North Dakota Public Library Commission."

With it are sent three card board signs seven by eleven inches, conspicuously lettered as follows:

"NORTH DAKOTA
PUBLIC LIBRARY COMMISSION

Traveling Library.

FREE TO ALL

The Library is now located at

....

Open to the public ....
(Days of Week)

From ....M. to ....M.
(Hours)

....
Librarian.

This blank should be filled in neatly with ink and posted in several places where everyone can see them."

These signs are to be filled out and posted in places of prominence in the town.

On each book is fastened a pocket reading as follows:

"NORTH DAKOTA
PUBLIC LIBRARY COMMISSION
Traveling Library.

RULES FOR BORROWERS

Borrowers—Any person is entitled to draw books who will sign the record of card-holders after reading carefully the borrower's agreement.

Borrower's Card—Each person entitled to draw books from the library will be given a card which must be presented whenever a book is taken, returned or renewed. If this card is lost a new one will be given on seven days' notice.

Number of Volumes—One volume may be drawn at a time on one card.

Time Kept—Any book may be kept for two weeks and once renewed for the same time.

Fines—A fine of one cent a day be paid for each book kept over time, and any money thus received shall be used by the librarian of the local association for transportation and other library expenses. No books shall be lent to any one to whom a book or unpaid fine is charged.

Injuries or Loss—If a borrower loses or destroys a book, the librarian will collect the retail price; and in case of damage a fair proportion of its cost. Fines for injury or loss shall be returned to the commission.

The borrower's library card should be kept in this pocket."

In this pocket is to be kept, while the book is in the library, the book card as follows:

"(No. of Library) (No. of Book)

Author

Title."

When a borrower requests to take out the book, the date and number of the borrower are written on the book card and it is kept by the local librarian.

There is a borrower's card reading as follows:

"No.............................

Name ....

Is entitled to draw books from the

Free Traveling Library

of the

North Dakota Public Library Commission

through the

.... Library Association

and is responsible for all books taken on this card.

Loaned Returned Loaned Returned"

On this borrower's card is entered the date of loaning, this card is placed in the card pocket and must be presented by the borrower on the return of the book. When the library is returned to the commission, the borrower's cards are kept by the local association and the book cards should be in place in the pockets of the books.

The local librarian should fill out and keep the borrower's register. This register is to be returned to the commission once a year.

The commission depends upon this register and the cards for the statistics necessary to its report and therefore encloses in each library sent out:

A list of books sent,
Fifty book cards,
Fifty borrower's cards,
One borrower's register,
Two circulars of instruction for the use of librarians.
On reverse side:

"NORTH DAKOTA
PUBLIC LIBRARY COMMISSION

Free Traveling Libraries

RULES FOR CIRCULATION

Care of Books—It is especially desirable that the children should learn to use books carefully. The local librarian may absolutely refuse to loan books to any child, or to any adult who does not keep them clean or treat them carefully. The Commission reserves the right to refuse a second library where the first one has been wilfully abused.

If a borrower loses or destroys a book the librarian will collect the retail price; and in case of damage a fair proportion of its cost.

Fines for injury or loss shall be returned to the Commission.

Issuing a Card—Each person wishing to draw books should be asked to sign his name in the record of card-holders after reading carefully the borrower's agreement.

A sample is given on the two following pages of this agreement and the lines for signatures.

"NORTH DAKOTA
PUBLIC LIBRARY COMMISSION

Free Traveling Libraries

Record of Card-Holders

of the

Benson Library Association

I, the undersigned, living in Benson or vicinity hereby apply for the privilege of borrowing books from the Free Traveling Library of the Benson Library Association.

I promise to take good care of all the books I draw, to pay promptly all fines and damages charged against me, and to obey the rules of the library.

No. Name

1. James Johnson
2. Mary Smith
3. ....

The librarian should then issue to the applicant the yellow reader's card containing the applicant's name and the number of the line on which he signed the record of card-holders, as shown on the following page.

(Borrower's Card)

No. 2

Mary Smith

is entitled to draw books from the

Free Traveling Library

of the

North Dakota Public Library Commission

through the

Benson Library Association

and is responsible for all books taken on this card.

Loaned	Returned	Loaned	Returned"
3 My 05	11 My		

Loaning a Book—When a book is to be loaned, take the book card, bearing the name of the book, from the pocket and write on it the date and number of the borrower.

(Book Card)

Alcott

Rose in Bloom

3 My 05 2 11 My

Put the date in the "Loaned" column on the borrower's card, which should now be put into the book pocket. When the book is out, the book card should be kept in a tray furnished for the purpose.

Discharging a Book—Any book may be kept by a reader two weeks and once renewed for the same time. When a book is returned, the librarian should examine the dates on the book and the borrower's card to see if the book is overdue. If it is, a fine of one cent shall be charged for each day the book has been kept overtime. Any money thus received shall be used by the librarian of the local library association for transportation charges and other library expenses. Date of return should be written on the borrower's card and the book card as shown above. The book card should then be placed in the book pocket and the borrower's card returned to the borrower if he wishes to borrow another book, and if not should be kept by the librarian until wanted again.

Return of Library—When the library is returned to the Commission, the book cards should all be in the pockets. The record of borrowers and the borrower's cards should be kept by the librarian to be used with the next library. A catalog or list of the books is sent with each library and the library should be checked up before it is returned to the Commission.

The record of the borrowers should be sent to the Commission once a year.

Advertise the Library—A notice should be printed in the local papers, printing a full list of the books, better still, call attention to the different books from time to time, and give the location of the library and hours and days of opening when books may be drawn.

Change of Librarian—Kindly notify the Commission at once when a change of librarian occurs. See that the new custodian has all necessary information relative to the operation of the library before transfer is made.

Contagious Diseases—Do not receive a book from a home where there is a contagious disease. Write to the Commission for instructions.

Returning the Library—The Commission will notify the librarian ten days before the library is to be returned. The books should be called in at once and checked by the printed catalog or typewritten list.

Screw the Lid Down—Never use nails. Keep the screws carefully for use when returning the library.

Shipping label sent with the library, bears the name and address of the Commission and should be pasted on the library box when returned.

Notify the Commission of the shipment on the return addressed postal card furnished for the purpose, filling out the blank form and indicating supplies needed with next library.

Prepay freight charges."

When the library is shipped a return postal is sent as follows:

North Dakota Public Library Commission

Bismarck,...................., 190.....

To the Librarian:

Today we ship you by freight, charges collect, by way of the..............

................R. R., traveling library................containing..........

volumes with the following supplies:

..............reader's cards rules for circulation

..............signs typewritten list of books

record of card-halders shipping label

Please acknowledge receipt of shipment on the attached card, after carefully counting the books, and checking the contents of the case.

Very truly yours,

North Dakota Public Library Commission.

North Dakota Public Library Commission

The Capitol,

Bismarck, North Dakota

....

(Name of Place) (Name of Library Ass'n

I have received from the North Dakota Public Library Commission........

............volumes, (by actual count) contained in traveling library........

..............together with the following supplies:

..............reader's cards rules for circulation

..............signs typewritten list of books

record of card-holders shipping label

(Signed)......................Librarian.

Date received ...."

When the library is due a double postal is sent as follows:

"NORTH DAKOTA
PUBLIC LIBRARY COMMISSION

Bismarck,.......................190....

To the Librarian of Free Traveling Library:

This card is to remind you that your present library will be due........................and to request you to call in the books as soon as possible, unless they are still in sufficient demand to warrant extension of time beyond the six months, stating length of extension desired. This definite information, promptly given, is requisite for the best service to all our traveling library patrons. Your attention is called to the necessity for careful packing of the books in paper. Please fill out notification of shipment on attached postal and return to the Commission. Kindly see that freight charges are prepaid.

North Dakota Public Library Commission."

North Dakota Public Library Commission
The Capitol,
Bismarck, North Dakota.

.................................Place

.......................190....

I have checked the books with the list and shipped today to the North Dakota Public Library Commission traveling library No................by freight, charges prepaid, by way of the............................R. R.

Number of borrowers registered is...................

The following supplies are needed with the next library:

....
Librarian."

The above blanks cover the entire system used in the circulation of the traveling libraries.

SAMPLE LISTS OF TRAVELING LIBRARIES.

Three lists of traveling libraries are given below. These are not offered as ideal lists but as samples of libraries it has been possible to arrange from the books on hand.

TRAVELING LIBRARY NO. 4.

1. Arabian Nights .... Arabian Nights Entertainments
2. Arnold ....Stories of Ancient Peoples
3. Brown ....Ethan Allen
4. Butler .... Persimmons
5. Churchill ....The Crossing

6. Clarke .... Story of Caesar
7. Cooper .... Last of the Mohicans
8. Connor .... Sky Pilot
9 Denison .... Her Secret
10. Doubleday .... Stories of Inventors
11. Eggleston .... Running the River
12. Foley .... Prairie Breezes
13. Foster .... Stories of Minnesota
14. Grimm Brothers .... Fairy Tales
15. Hale .... Man Without a Country
16. Hemenway .... How to Make School Gardens
17. Irving .... Tales of a Traveler
18. Johnson .... The World's Discoverers
19. Kingsley .... Water Babies
20. Kipling .... Captain Courageous
21. Leighton .... Lewis and Clark
22. Longfellow .... Courtship of Miles Standish
23. McCaskey .... Lincoln Literary Collection
24. Maclaren .... Beside the Bonnie Briar Bush
25. McClintock .... The Philippines
26. Mowbray .... Journey to Nature
27. Ollivant .... Bob, Son of Battle
28. Phelps .... Successors of Mary the First
29. Pratt .... The Great West
30. Riis .... Theodore Roosevelt the Citizen
31. Roth .... First Book of Forestry
32. Sandys .... Trapper Jim
33. Schurz .... Abraham Lincoln
34. Scudder .... George Washington
35. Sewell .... Black Beauty
36. Smith .... Evolution of Dodd
37. Stockton .... Lady and the Tiger
38. Stowe .... Uncle Tom's Cabin
39. Teller .... First Book of Forestry
40. Tennyson .... Enoch Arden and Other Poems
41. True .... Iron Star
42. Van Bergen .... Story of China
43. Van Bergen .... Story of Japan
44. Ward .... Kenwick's Career
45. Whittier .... Snow-bound and Other Poems
46. Wiggin .... Bird's Christmas Carol

TRAVELING LIBRARY NO. 129.

1. Alcott .... Little Men
2. Alcott .... Little Women
3. Baldwin .... Fifty Famous Stories Retold
4. Bolton .... Girls Who became Famous

5. Bolton .... Poor Boys Who Became Famous
6. Brooks .... Abraham Lincoln
7. Brown ....Rabo and His Friends
8. Burkett and Others .... Agriculture for Beginners
9. Burroughs .... Literary Values
10. Carroll .... Alice's Adventures in Wonderland
11. Catherwood .... Heroes of the Middle West
12. Cooper .... Last of the Mohicans
13. Dana .... Two Years Before the Mast
14. Defoe .... Robinson Crusoe
15. Dodge ....Hans Brinker
16. Field .... With Trumpet and Drum
17. Franklin .... Autobiography
18. Griffis .... Brave Little Holland
19. Hale .... Man Without a Country
20. Hawthorne .... Wonder Book
21. Holmes ....Autocrat of the Breakfast Table
22. Judd .... Wigwam Stories
23. Lodge and Roosevelt....Hero Tales From American History
24. Lowell .... My Study Windows
25. Lummis...........Some Strange Corners of Our Country
26. Miller .... First Book of Birds
27. Noel .... Buz
28. Ollivant .... Bob, Son of Battle
29. Parkman .... Oregon Trail
30. Riley .... Book of Joyous Children
31. Roberts .... Kindred of the Wild
32. Schwatha .... Children of the Cold
33. Scott .... Ivanhoe
34. Scudder .... George Washington
35. Scudder .... Stories From My Attic
36. Seton .... Wild Animals I Have Known
37. Seawell.. Paul Jones
38. Seawell .... Twelve Naval Captains
39. Sewell .... Black Beauty
40. Starr .... American Indians
41. Stevenson .... Treasure Island
42. Warner ....My Summer in a Garden
43. Whittier .... Complete Poetical Works
44. Willard .... Story of the Prairies
45. Wyss .... Swiss Family Robinson

TRAVELING LIBRARY NO. 169.

1. Alrich ....Story of a Bad Boy
2. Ayrton .... Child Life in Japan
3. Bacheller .... Eben Holden
4. Bolton .... Girls Who Became Famous

5. Bolton .... Poor Boys Who Became Famous
6. Carpenter .... Africa
7. Burt .... Poems Every Child Should Know
8. Dunbar .... Folks From Dixie
9. Eastman .... Indian Boyhood
10. Field .... Little Book of Profitable Tales
11. Ford .... Honorable Peter Stirling
12. Foulk .... Braided Straws
13. Franklin .... Autobiography
14. Gordon .... The Prospector
15. Harte .... Openings in the Old Trail
16. Hemenway .... How to Make School Gardens
17. Holbrook .... Round the Year in Myth and Song
18. Hughes .... Tom Brown's School Days
19. Knapp ....Story of the Philippines
20. Leighton .... Lewis and Clark
21. Lodge and Roosevelt....Hero Tales From American History
22. London .... Call of the Wild
23. Long .... Ways of the Wood Folk
24. Long .... Wilderness Ways
25. Longfellow .... Song of Hiawatha
26. Lummis .... Some Strange Corners of Our Country
27. Matthews..Introduction to the Study of American Literature
28. Riis .... Roosevelt, the Citizen
29. Riley .... Rhymes of Childhood
30. Riley .... Sketches in Prose
31. Roberts .... Watchers of the Trail
32. Roth ....First Book of Forestry
33. Saunders .... Beautiful Joe
34. Seabury .... Porto Rico
35. Seton .... Two Little Savages
36. Smedley and Talbot .... Wizards of Ryetown
37. Tomlinson ....Winning His "W"
38. Vaile .... Truth About Santa Claus
39. Wade .... Ten Little Indians
40. Washington .... Up From Slavery
41. Wesselhoeft .... Jack, the Fire Dog
42. White .... Court of Boyville
43. Whitson .... With Fremont the Pathfinder
44. Wiggin .... Timothy's Quest
45. Winship .... Louisiana Purchase
46. Woods .... Civil Government for North Dakota
47. Yan Phou Lee .... When I Was a Boy in China

EDUCATIONAL REFERENCE LIBRARY.

There are about 3,000 volumes in this department. Besides the general reference cyclopedias, the following classification has been made:

Fine arts.
Industrial arts
Essays.
Ethics.
Drama.
Biography—Collective.
Biography—Individual.
Literature—American.
Literature—English.
Education.
Psychology.
Religion.
Sociology.
General science.
Travel.
Ancient history.
History—
  England.
  Germany.
  France.
  Russia.
  Netherlands.
  Asia.
  North America.
  United States.
  Civil war.
  Colonial period.
  Revolution and confederation.

It has been impossible as yet to catalog these works, nor is there a printed list for distribution. Schools, clubs, communities or individuals wishing to pursue a special line of study, are supplied with the best material possible from this collection on application to the librarian.

It is urged that applicants be as specific as possible in asking for books. A request for "Books on Literature" is too general to permit the librarian to make a satisfactory choice. Name the period in literature or the country, or better yet, the authors.

Signature of the following application card is the only pledge required of borrowers in this department.

"No............ Application for the use of the

Educational Reference Library

.............................190....

I, the undersigned, living in....................................., hereby apply for the privilege of borrowing books from the above library.

I promise to take good care of all the books I draw; to pay promptly all fines and damages charged against me and all transportation charges; and to obey the rules of the library.

Name..................................

Read this pledge carefully before signing. Fill out with ink."

The only expense is the express or freight on the books. Work in this department has been limited by lack of funds to purchase books. The library contains no material on many subjects sent in by clubs and individuals, and it has only been possible to give inquirers a list of titles of books and articles on their subject with addresses. It is difficult to estimate what the state loses by inability to respond to these demands. For instance, the first request to reach the secretary of the North Dakota commission was from a farmer asking for works on tree planting and dry land farming. There were no such books on the shelves and no money to buy them. Think what it would mean in the development of the state, if such information could be furnished. Similar requests have come from artisans and from professional men asking for books to pursue farther their studies into their specialties. Such an investment of state money would bring quick returns in the development of any community containing such ambitious workers and students.

AIMS OF COMMISSION.

The commission aims to continue the work begun along the lines outlined in the act by which it was created. It has not been possible to accomplish great things in any one line owing to the short time elapsing since the establishment of the work and the limited fund at disposal. The foundations of the work have been well laid in all departments. Here are samples of the letters that come in daily as winter approaches:

"Will you please give me information about the traveling school libraries? We have one school without any library. Are they free for any school district?"

Another writes:

"Can we possibly arrange for some libraries for our town this winter?"

And to all that must be sent the steretoyped reply:

"We regret to say there is no library for shipment at the present time. Your request will be filed in the order of its receipt and your application filled at the earliest possible date."

"I would like to know how a walking library works and if it is possible for me to get it to my school? Will you be so kind and give me particulars about it?"

The success of the traveling libraries is attested by the demand which exceeds the supply. The value of the legislative reference bureau will be demonstrated during the coming legislature. The success of the advisory and field work of the librarian is proven by the many letters and words of commendation received. The interest aroused wherever field work has been done points to the advisability of special development along that line of work. There is much technical work to be done, cataloging, indexing and gathering statistics. The commission aims to develop all lines of its duties to the best of its financial ability.

NEEDS OF THE WORK.

It will be impossible to continue even the work begun without a larger appropriation. The traveling libraries need books. Missouri established a library commission the same year as North Dakota. Missouri appropriated $5,000 annually for the use of its commission, which made possible the purchase of $3,500 worth of books the first year of its existence.

The educational reference department needs a book fund.

The legislative reference bureau needs suitable quarters and a competent assistant.

The field work needs a traveling fund and sufficient help in the office to permit occasional absences of the executive head of the department.

There is great need of better quarters for the office force under the commission. There is at present but one room, with not enough wall space to contain the books of the educational reference library alone. Traveling library cases must be piled in the hallways. The books from them are stored in a dark closet at a distance, difficult of access and almost impossible to sort and handle.

The legislative reference librarian has no conveniences whatever except a desk and a few shelves crowded in beside the educational books. This work alone should have at least a room with a private office for the convenience of legislators and others wishing to make use of the material prepared by the legislative reference librarian.

The North Dakota library fund of $1,500 annually is not enough to continue the work. Unless the appropriation is more than doubled it will be necessary to discontinue some of its lines of effort. It was only possible to start the departments mentioned in the bill by delaying the organization until there should be but one year's expenses to be paid from the biennial appropriation. What department under the commission can be cut off? Our workmen in all classes—farmers, artisans, office men and scholars, clubs, schools and teachers—need the educational reference helps. The state needs the added wealth that will result from their labors, aided by the best books in their specialties. The families of these workers are entitled to the education and recreation of the traveling libraries. Our lawmakers and all students interested in industrial and economic problems need the assistance of the legislative reference library. The growing library interest throughout the state needs the guidance of an experienced adviser. Must any line of commission work be cut off?

There is need of greater publicity for the work of the commission. Thanks are hereby extended to the papers in the state which have printed the articles, sent them from time to time, especially the Bismarck Tribune, the Fargo Forum, the Grand Forks Herald, the Valley City Times-Record, the Wheatland Educator, the North Dakota Magazine and the North Dakota Capitol. It is hoped other papers will follow their example and assist in making the labors of the commission and the advantages of the different library departments known to the people of the state.

RESIGNATION OF LIBRARIAN.

At a meeting of the library commission held in Fargo November 5, 1908, the following letter was read:

1069 Prospect St., Appleton, Wis., Oct. 13, 1908.

To the Members of the Public Library Commission, Bismarck, N. D.:

It is with deep regret that I find myself obliged to resign my position as your librarian, on account of ill health. I realize the embarrassment that this may cause the Commission just now and I would not think of doing it if it could in any way be avoided. For weeks and months I have deceived myself as to my own strength and now I find a sudden stop for repairs is the result. I hoped to last out until spring but my doctor forbids me to think of going back to a North Dakota winter and the hard work of a legislative session.

I hope you may be able to find the right person for the work very soon and I shall be very glad to do anything I can to help you.

Very sincerely yours,

ZANA K. MILLER.

(Per E. A.)

Miss Miller's resignation from the position of librarian and director was reluctantly accepted, and the following resolutions were adopted:

Whereas, Miss Zana K. Miller has felt compelled by failing health to resign her position as librarian and director of North Dakota public library commission work and

Whereas, The pressure of work is such that the office can not long be left without an executive head,

Resolved, That with reluctance, we accept the resignation of Miss Miller and take this opportunity of expressing our appreciation of the work she has done for all the departments under her charge.

Exterior View, Fargo Public Library.

The library interest of North Dakota will always owe a debt to the enthusiasm, discretion and technical ability of its organizer.

FRANK J. THOMPSON, Pres.,
W. L. STOCKWELL, Vice Pres.,
MINNIE CLARKE BUDLONG, Sec'y.

SIGNS OF PROGRESS

The growth of library interest in the state is most encouraging. Grand Forks, Fargo, Grafton and Valley City already have Carnegie buildings. Dickinson and Minot have plans completed to build. Devils Lake and Bottineau have voted appropriations to support Carnegie libraries.

Minot voted for a $30,000 building and passed an appropriation of $4,500 annually.

Dickinson will have a $15,000 building.

Devils Lake is preparing for a $12,500 building.

Bottineau voted to support a $10,000 library.

Park River has moved into new quarters and had $400 for furnishings.

Jamestown has completely reorganized its library and moved it into the City Hall and has been granted by the city $1,250 annually for its support.

These are only a few of the more noticeable signs of growth. It is impossible to mention all the smaller libraries that are enjoying new quarters, new books, and better service on account of their year's progress.

The report of the library committee at the state federation at Minot showed gratifying activity among the club women of the state in this important work.

The attendance from North Dakota at the A. L. A. Conference at Lake Minnetonka in June was another satisfactory indication of interest. This was the first appearance of North Dakota at an A. L. A. conference and the event was celebrated by a state dinner at which Miss Elizabeth Abbott, secretary of the state library association, presided, and Dr. J. C. Hanson, chief of catalog division, Library of Congress, was guest of honor.

The representatives in attendance at the conference were:

Miss Zana K. Miller, Librarian and Director of the North Dakota Public Library Commission.

R. A. Nestos, Secretary of the Library Board, Minot.

Miss Elizabeth Abbott, Librarian Grand Forks Public Library.

Dr. O. G. Libby, Secretary of State Historical Society.

Miss Nellie Olson, Librarian of the Normal School, Mayville.

Miss Ida Schaefer, Assistant Librarian of the Public Library, Fargo.

Mrs. Ethel McVeety, Librarian of the Agricultural College, Fargo.

Mrs. Minnie Clarke Budlong, Secretary of the North Dakota Public Library Commission.

Miss Abby Brayton, Asst. Librarian State University, North Dakota.

APOLOGY.

This first attempt of the North Dakota public library commission to tabulate the library statistics of the state is offered by its secretary with apology. There are undoubtedly errors of omission and of insertion in this report and the cooperation of all readers is requested in locating the mistakes. Had the librarian who was in charge of the work from its beginning been able to remain a few weeks longer the report would have been more complete and accurate. Miss Miller was stricken by severe illness just as the time came for preparing the report and was reluctantly obliged to return home. The remaining office force with the assistance of the secretary assumed the unexpected duty and have done what they could in the short time remaining.

Many libraries have not reported to the commission. It is hoped they may come to realize the importance of the matter that the second biennial report may contain a complete list.

The commission has not had charge of the traveling libraries long enough to furnish statistics of circulation. The book cards returned in the pockets of the books and the borrower's registers sent in once a year will furnish the basis of tables for the next report.

For the same reason it is not possible in the financial report this year to charge to each department its itemized share of expense. The work has been managed in one room by one person until August 1, 1908, and all expenses have gone into one account. Subdivisions will come later.

Hearty thanks are extended those libraries which have promptly returned their preliminary reports and made possible this first effort at tabulation, and also to those who so cheerfully responded with histories of the library movement in their respective cities.

Attention is called to the tables at the end of this report. The list collected by the librarian shows 27 public libraries, 52 high school libraries, 44 traveling libraries and 4 club, lodge and academy libraries. There are undoubtedly many libraries in the state whose existence has not come to the knowledge of the commission; also inaccuracies in the list that has been prepared, and the cooperation of the public is asked in correcting the list before the next report.

CONCLUSION.

The foregoing covers the activities of the North Dakota Public Library Commission, detailing what has been done during its brief existence, and outlining what, with the cooperation of the legislators, and people of North Dakota, it hopes to accomplish.

FRANK J. THOMPSON, Pres.
W. L. STOCKWELL, Vice Pres.,
MINNIE CLARKE BUDLONG, Sec'y.

Bismarck, North Dakota, November 1, 1908.

LEGISLATIVE REFERENCE DEPARTMENT

SVEINBJORN JOHNSON

In compliance with section 5 of Chapter 243 of the session laws of 1907 creating the Public Library Commission, the librarian and director began the collection of material on legislative subjects early in 1908. Thus was formed the nucleus of a reference library which by the gradual accession of books, pamphlets and reports has already outgrown its present quarters. As the work of assisting legislators in their difficult and important task is an innovation in North Dakota, it may not be amiss to review briefly the condition that forced the legislatures of several states to provide reference libraries for the benefit of their members.

UNJUST CRITICISM OF LEGISLATIVE BODIES.

In many states, including our own, it has been fashionable with a certain class of people to make fun of the legislature. Without regard for the seriousness of the situation when people begin to lose faith in and respect for the governing body, papers and individuals are often disposed to laugh at its work and speak lightly of its virtues. A few cases of "freak" legislation and periodic revelations of graft and corruption are made the basis of a criticism alike superficial and unjust. A study of the means and methods by which the three departments of government, the legislative, executive and judicial, discharge their several functions, justifies no such conclusion that in morals or intelligence the personnel of the legislative branch is generally speaking inferior to that of the other departments. On the contray it is difficult to escape the conclusion that though the quality of legislation is sometimes poor and often indifferent it is a compliment to the genius of Americans for lawmaking that it is no worse than we find it.

EXECUTIVE DEPARTMENT.

Inverting what would be the logical order of treatment, we find the executive charged with the duties of law enforcement. This branch is provided with numerous administrative officers who take the law as passed by the legislature and construed by the courts and apply it to the conditions that called for its enactment. Numerous devices like commissions and boards are from time to time adopted to aid this department in the performance of its duties and as a result, though it has by no means escaped adverse criticism in this country the standard of administrative efficiency has steadily risen.

JUDICIAL DEPARTMENT.

Coming to the judicial branch, which construes the law, we find a well organized system of procedure. Our courts, ever since they began to decide cases in this country, have followed the beaten path of precedent. The judge, whose library is filled with commentaries and reports, never writes an opinion until he has studied and compared the decisions of other tribunals bearing upon the question at issue. It may be that the courts of Maine or California have solved the problem the supreme court of North Dakota is called upon to disentangle. In that event North Dakota may be guided by the decision of Maine. In a word, one court takes counsel from the wisdom and experience of another.

LEGISLATIVE DEPARTMENT.

We see, then, that the courts have almost unlimited reference resources at their demand when called upon to construe the law; we provide an army of administrative and executive officers to enforce it, but what do we do for the men whose duty it is to frame this law? We are forced to admit that we do little or nothing. They are called from the farm, the office and the workshop to legislate upon the complex problems of a great commonwealth and yet the state does not provide them with means of assistance in the discharge of this extraordinary duty.These legislators are honest and intelligent men, as a rule, but they are busy men who cannot always watch the ever changing economic and sociological conditions of their state and country; they cannot, without taking much valuable time from their business, keep their information exact and up to date as to what the most progressive states are doing with the very problems their own commonwealth calls upon them to solve. They must deal with questions upon the proper solution of which great fortunes and the welfare of thousands depend, but they have no means of assistance at their command even in degree proportionate to the magnitude of the task imposed. If the legislatures had adequate means of knowing the example and experience of other states than their own and the opinions of experts and practical men of affairs, we would hear fewer complaints of laws that are dead letters or badly enforced because unwise, oppressive or unpopular. If legislation were made more scientific by providing some means of assistance to the body that makes the law we would have less need for judicial lawmaking, by broad construction, alike inconsistent with the theory of our government and in the end, disastrous to the dignity and influence of the courts. If the courts legislate the people will demand more control over them. Why it has been proposed in this country to provide a referendum of court decisions on constitutional questions.

NEED OF A REFERENCE LIBRARY.

When the legislatures of different states began to see this remarkable situation in its true light, there was neither doubt nor hesitation about the course to be pursued. The economy of employing great talent in interpreting the law and covering its defects by liberal construction without doing anything to make the process of law building scientific, seemed very unsatisfactory after a little thoughtful investigation. Men began to think that a fence at the top of the precipice was better than an ambulance at its base. The need of the reference library in the work of legislation is so well set forth by Mr. Charles McCarthy of the Wisconsin legislative library that we print an extract herewith:

"If private forces maintain bureaus of information for representatives, let us have public information bureaus, open to private and public interests alike. If it is hard to get information because of the great variety of subjects now coming before our legislators, the only sensible thing to do is to get experts to gather this material. If business interests have good lawyers to look after their legislation, the people should secure the same kind of men to help their representatives. If the business interests secure statisticians, engineers, and scientific men, then the public should do likewise. If great judges and great lawyers are constantly working upon the problems of interpretation of laws, then, surely, men of equal ability should be consulted while those laws are being constructed."

REFERENCE WORK IN OTHER STATES—MR. BRICE.

Commenting upon the work of the legislative reference library in Wisconsin and other states, Ambassador James Bryce said in his address before the New York Bar Association in February, 1908, "This shows that the legislatures are awakening to the great importance of using every device which scientific method can apply for seeing that legislation is properly conducted." The work has proved popular in Wisconsin, the legislature of 1907 appropriating $15,000 for the maintenance of the department. Reference work has also been successfully undertaken by the states of Alabama, California, Indiana, Michigan, Nebraska, Rhode Island and the city of Baltimore, Maryland. The states of Iowa and Kansas are considering the question at the present time.

AIM AND METHOD.

The aim of the department, as intimated in preceding paragraphs, is to assist the lawmaker in his work. To this end we have collected and classified laws from different states on certain topics; model laws, adopted by societies and organizations and recommended for passage; bills that have been lost in other legislatures; magazine articles by specialists and experts in various fields of work and such other literature as might be of some service to members. Except in so far as our very limited quarters have prevented, all material has been placed upon the shelves in such a way as to be most easily accessible. While the range of topics is not as yet very wide the generosity with which societies and individuals have responded to requests for material and cooperation has enabled us to make a very encouraging start.

LIST OF SUBJECTS.

To give some idea of our resources we print herewith a list of subjects on which more or less data may be found in the library:

Apportionment of Representatives.
Automobiles—laws.
Banking—
  Reports.
  Laws.
  Reserve for banks.
Bank Deposits—Guaranty.
Boards of control of state institutions.
Buildings.
Central bank.
Cities—
  Commission government.
  Civic improvements.
  Home rule.
  Lighting.
  Municipal ownership.
  Civil service.
  Model charters.
  Reports.
Child labor.
Convict labor.
Corporations—Laws.
  Public regulation.
Corrupt practices.
Currency question.
Divorce.
Drains.
Drugs—Laws.
Grain inspection.
Election—General.
  Laws.
Employers' liability.

Factory inspection.
Game—Laws.
Garbage.
Immigration laws.
Indeterminate sentence.
Industrial training in schools.
Initiative and referendum.
Injunctions.
Insurance—
Insurance—Reports.
  Casualty.
  Industrial.
  Federal regulation.
  State regulation.
Interstate commerce commission.
Irrigation.
Juvenile Courts—Laws.
  Reports.
Liquor traffic.
Legislative reference libraries.
Labor—laws.
  Reports.
Lobbying.
Monopolies.
Municipalities.
Navy.
New Zealand.
Old age pension.
Primary Election—
  General laws.
  Comments.
Public Utilities Commission—General discussion.
  Laws.
  Reports.
Parcels post.
Postal savings banks.
Proportional representation.
Public health.
Pure food—Laws.

Railroads—General.
  Reports.
  Laws.
  Rates.
  Regulation, federal and state.
  Taxation.

Recall.

Roads—General.
  Laws.
  Road building.
  State aid.

Schools—Laws.
  Reports.

Standard oil.

State constitutions.

State institutions.

State tax commissions.

Telephone—Connections.
  Competition.

Tenure of Office—Removal by governor.

Torrens system.

Taxation—General.
  Income tax.
  Inheritance tax.
  Insurance premiums.
  Single tax.

Uniform Accounting—Municipal corporations.
  Private corporations.

Waterways.

NEWSPAPERS AS A SOURCE.

One of the most valuable sources of material is the current newspaper. Through the courtesy of several publishers, within and outside the state, we receive several daily and weekly papers. These are looked over as carefully as time permits, and any valuable comment on or criticism of any law in any state in which North Dakota might be interested is clipped, mounted on cardboard and filed with the subject of which it treats. Defects in the practical operation of existing laws are often pointed out and valuable suggestions of amendments are made.

PRACTICAL WORK.

It is this newspaper material that saves the legislative reference library from the possible charge that it seeks to convert legislators into dreamers and theorists. True, we gather the opinions of experts and students, thereby enabling our lawmakers to see the law as specialists believe it should be. But—here is where the ordinary library differs radically from ours—we aim especially to collect all evidence from the actual working of the law under given economic conditions. It is our purpose to make the work as practical as possible. We believe that members should know the law of other states, not only as it is, but also as it works.

The newspaper is not only valuable because of the editorial and other criticism it contains, but also because we find in it mention of material useful to the library. A news item tells of the meeting of some association interested in some public movement and we write for its report. Or we find a reference to an address delivered by some practical man of affairs, whose work brings him in constant contact with the working of a certain class of laws, and we ask for a copy of the speech, which request is granted in the vast majority of cases. We take this opportunity to express our appreciation of the generosity of publishers who favor us with their publications. We print herewith a list of the newspapers and periodicals that come regularly to the library.

NEWSPAPERS AND PERIODICALS REGULARLY RECEIVED OCT. 31, 1908.

Donations.

Boston Evening Transcript.
Bismarck Tribune.
Daily News.
Evening Times.
Grand Forks Herald (donated by Sveinbjorn Johnson.)
Minot Optic.
Minot Reporter.
Portland Daily Journal.
Seattle Post-Intelligencer.
Devils Lake Journal.
Devils Lake Inter-Ocean.
Jamestown Weekly Alert.
LaMoure County Chronicle.
Dickinson Recorder.
North Dakota Capital.
Pioneer Express.
Valley City Times-Record.
Mayville Tribune.
Park River Gazette News.
St. Thomas Times.
Williston Herald.
North Dakota Magazine.
Westland Educator.
Public Service.

American Economist.
New York Post (donated by Z. K. Miller).
American Industries.
Freight.
Locomotive Firemen's and Engineer's Magazine.
Eastern Underwriter.
Telephony.
Economic Bulletin.
North Dakota Farmer.
Wahpeton Globe Gazette.
Success (donated by Sveinbjorn Johnson).
Minneapolis Journal (donated by Cora M. Johnson).
Railroad Trainman.
Grafton News and Times.

Subscription.

Portland Oregonian.
Chicago Record-Herald.
World's Work.
Colliers.
Yale Review.
Annals of American Academy.
Political Science Quarterly.
Outlook.
Green Bag.
Charities and Commons.
Economic Bulletin.

NON-PARTISAN WORK.

At this point a few words should be said on the attitude of the department in its efforts to compile material on a subject. Of course, it approaches this task entirely free from bias or prejudice of any kind. We seek to collect all information available on any question equally on one side as upon the other. This we believe to be the only consistent course to follow, the only method in harmony with the underlying idea of legislative reference work. It is no concern of ours what general policy the legislature may see fit to pursue. Our work is at an end when we have given members all assistance in our power which they have solicited, put into their hands whatever literature the department may have on the subjects in which they have decided to interest themselves and upon such economic problems as may from time to time arise.

BILL INDEX—SESSIONS OF 1905 AND 1907.

Owing to the pressure of work the department has not been able to index bills further back than two sessions. A card index covering the sessions of 1905 and 1907 enables anyone to find any bill on any subject introduced in our legislature since 1905 without much loss of time. No indexed record of bills had been kept, hence it was practically impossible for a member to find a bill on some particular subject. In time we hope to index all bills introduced two or three sessions further back. With such an index and the bills accessible, much unnecessary redrafting will be saved should members wish to reintroduce bills in the same or modified forms. Moreover, it will be easy to trace the history of any legislation and note every step in its evolution into the final stage of statutory law.

CIRCULAR LETTER TO MEMBERS.

Immediately after the last election, the department sent a circular letter to every member requesting him to indicate in what subjects he would be particularly interested during the coming session. The letter was in the following form:

One of the duties of the Public Library Commission, as prescribed by the legislature of 1907, is the maintenance of a reference bureau for the information and assistance of legislators. Obedient to this mandate of the law, the department has been collecting valuable discussions of subjects of legislative interest, laws, documents and reports from different parts of the country. We write you this to acquaint you with our aim and duty, and with your co-operation we hope to be of some service to you in your work.

If you will indicate in what subjects you will be most interested, we shall, to the full extent of our time and means, inform you:

1. Where valuable discussions of any subject may be found.
2. What states passed laws upon it.
3. What bills on any subject have been introduced in the last two sessions of our legislature.

We shall be pleased to send you summaries of helpful material to such extent as our means permit and if possible, answer any question the topics in which you are interested may raise.

Make your questions as specific as possible. We care nothing about your politics or on which side of a question you may happen to be. Our aim is to assist, not to influence you.

Our work is entirely free and your communications will be regarded as strictly confidential.

DEMANDS UPON THE DEPARTMENT.

During its brief period of existence, numerous demands for information have been made upon the department. Inquiries directed to the different departments of state have been referred to the reference bureau. With increasing reference facilities, the department will be in a good position to answer such requests for information. It is, moreover, one of its duties to be of all possible service to state officials in the performance of their duties.

WORK TO BE DONE.

An important work that should be undertaken as soon as time and means allow is that of indexing various state documents, governors' messages and vetoes. Many valuable documents have been printed, but are of little practical use for want of a workable index to the material they contain. With such an index in the reference library and a good storeroom, the documentary material of the state could be made available for use. Other states have allowed their printed matter to accumulate and moulder in comparative uselessness, and are only recently bestirring themselves in the direction of compiling practical reference indices to the mass of material which while representing an outlay of thousands of dollars, returns only a small per cent of the value it should yield. This task will require much time and labor and should be begun soon. Our state is yet young and its documentary resources are very limited compared with those of older states, but every year material of much value is printed and the longer the delay the greater the work will be when undertaken. The practical value of the agricultural documents, for example, to the farmers of the state, would be greatly increased were a thorough index of the same available.

DEBATING SOCIETIES.

The nature of the reference library is such as to make it especially helpful to debating societies in the various educational centers of the state. Requests for loan of material on public questions have come to the department even at this early period in its existence. It is our aim to be of such service in this connection as we may, and between sessions we shall gladly loan our material to responsible persons interested in debate. It is hoped that the department may thereby become instrumental in encouraging added interest in the art of expression by the young people of the state and at the same time a careful study of the problems of economics, government and sociology which they must help to solve as citizens and voters when they leave the schools. The department has published a small bulletin with a table of leading parliamentary motions in order of rank, convenient for the use of legislators, clubs and debating societies. This bulletin we mail upon request.

COMPARATIVE LEGISLATION BULLETINS.

Another feature of the work the department has planned which we believe will be of great practical service to members is the preparation of summaries of special legislation. In these bulletins it is aimed to set forth in clear and condensed form the law in the different states on some special subject of interest to North Dakota. These digests will be mailed to members and also exchanged for similar summaries on different subjects compiled in other states. The work of preparation will require much painstaking care in the matter of collecting and comparing the laws of the different states. To this end it will be necessary to employ a competent and trained person who has had some experience in research work, who has a liberal knowledge of economics and a grasp of a few fundamental principles of law.

NEEDS OF THE DEPARTMENT QUARTERS.

The most pressing need of the department and in fact the one that must first be considered is that of larger quarters. Our little room is already so overcrowded that material which daily comes to the library cannot be made serviceable to the full extent of its value because no more shelf room is available. The collection will continue to grow and provision must be made for the proper shelving of material which is of course of little use unless classified, but classification is of no avail if no shelf room is provided. Arrangement should also be made for a room either in or adjoining the library, with such furniture as two or three tables and chairs, wherein members who consult the library can temporarily sit and study or glance over material. At present we have barely standing room for patrons, much to the discomfort and inconvenience of members. We therefore most respectfully recommend to your attention the fact that the efficiency of the department as an aid to members will be seriously impaired unless more adequate quarters are provided.

Appendix No. I

HISTORIES OF LIBRARIES

DEVILS LAKE PUBLIC LIBRARY.

(Contributed by Mrs. Frank Stoltze.)

There are in the city of Devils Lake two women's clubs, the Shakespeare Club and the Library Club.

The library club have for several years maintained a library—some 1,500 volumes—but having no suitable place to keep it and with no reading room its usefulness was limited.

The executive board of the Shakespeare Club asked that a committee be appointed from the Library Club to cooperate with them in securing a Carnegie library.

Finding a two mill tax would maintain a $15,000 library, we waited upon the city council and asked them to give the citizens the opportunity to vote for a library at the next general election. This was granted and an active campaign inaugurated to arouse public sentiment to the crying need for some respectable place where our young men and boys might spend their evenings profitably and pleasantly. We planned to give the basement for use as a gymnasium.

We wrote to librarians of the Carnegie libraries in the state asking for letters or publications, stating the benefit of its success and the growth of interest.

Our local papers were much interested and gave us all the space we needed. We asked prominent citizens to write articles for the paper and for three weeks kept this daily before the people, besides constant agitation amounting to an almost personal canvass of all voters.

Finally just before election we obtained a complete voting list and sent a circular letter to every voter stating our great need and appealing to their patriotism to vote for the library.

The result was 343 votes for the library and 39 against it.

A library board was appointed and three lots in a most desirable location have been purchased and plans for an attractive building accepted, the erection of which will be commenced as early as possible next spring.

The board decided to ask the council for a levy of the full legal amount—four mills—the extra two mills to be used for the payment of the lots. This was granted.

BRIEF HISTORY OF DICKINSON LIBRARY MOVEMENT.

(Contributed by R. H. Johnson, Pres. Lib. Board.)

The first meeting of citizens for the purpose of securing a library was held January 20, 1908. An organization known as the Dickinson Library Association was formed and a campaign of education as to the value of a library was inaugurated assisted by the newspapers, commercial club and public meetings at which citizens spoke of the need of such an institution in Dickinson.

A committee waited on the city council and secured as a building site two lots giving a north frontage of 141 feet and 50 feet on the west.

Mr. Carnegie was asked for a donation and on April 14th he made a formal offer of $12,500 with the usual conditions as regards to site and maintenance.

The question of a library tax was voted on April 6, 1908, and by a vote of 576 to 141 the people voted in favor of it.

The library board was then appointed according to law and the following officers were elected and their first meeting held April 9, 1908.

R. H. Johnson, president; Father Rabsteineck, secretary; Dr. V. H. Stickney, librarian; W. L. Richards, Jno. F. Davis.

After looking over many plans the board decided on a general outline of kind of building wished and authorized Jos. Bell de Remer, of Grand Forks, to draw up plans and specifications for the same. After keeping the board waiting for six weeks he informed them that owing to the press of work they would do well to secure another architect.

On July 9th the board authorized W. S. Russell of this city to draw up plans and specifications.

On August 4th he submitted temporary plans and some changes being necessary the plans and specifications were not completed until September 5th.

The bids were to have been opened September 26th but some of the bidders wishing more time they were allowed until October 28th.

The bids were opened on this date and Soules & Butler of this city being the lowest bidders were awarded the contract. Work has begun on the excavating and if the weather permits the building will be enclosed before the winter sets in. The building is to be 36x48 basement and one story. The basement walls to be of stone faced with pressed brick above grade. Above basement to be brick faced with white pressed brick trimmed with Bedford limestone. Steps and damp course Kettle River sandstone. All glass to be polished plate. Roof covered with sheet copper ribbed interior trim-quarter sawed oak natural wood, basement floor, cement tile—upper floor covered with cork carpet, walls plastered–stippled and painted. Ceilings pressed sheet steel. A large ornamental brick fireplace opposite the front entrance. Low pressure steam heat with indirects for ventilation. Lighting, electric chandeliers. Plumbing, lavatory and closet. In basement to be a lecture room, boiler and fuel room, toilet room and a janitor's closet. Upper story for reading room only. The commercial club have promised to give their library of 500 volumes to the library; several smaller donations of books have been received and others promised making us feel certain of a collection of about 1,500 volumes to start with.

The State Librarian Miss Zana K. Miller has been of great service to the board in making suggestions and helping us to get a practical building.

HISTORY OF FARGO PUBLIC LIBRARY.

CONTRIBUTED BY FRANK J. THOMPSON.

Fargo has always been interested in the matter of a public library, and that interest has been apparent for a quarter of a century; yet until within the past few years no inspiration was obtained except as it was left over in remembrance by those who had come to our city from centers in which the library movement was an active factor. More than twenty years ago, a library organization was effected, and it had more or less of a spasmodic existence, and finally spread out on the surface and became mingled with the waters of doing nothing, and the books which had been gathered by this society were, we believe, turned over to the Y. M. C. A.

Through the impetus given to the library movement by the donations of Mr. Andrew Carnegie, public library affairs in Fargo again started, which resulted in the city's voting upon the proposition, and which carried. May 19th, 1900, the first library board under the state laws, was organized in the office of Mr. Thomas Baker, Jr., at which time Mr. Baker was elected president, Mrs. Ella K. Smith, secretary, and Mr. Frank J. Thompson, librarian. The other members of the board were Mrs. Alex Stern and Mr. L. Stavenheim.

No place was available to house a library, and the trustees of the Masonic Temple offered free use of one of its rooms, also furnishing light and heat. Miss May K. Stanford was elected Assistant Librarian, December 5, 1900, at the munificent salary of three dollars a week. In the meantime, the room in the Masonic Temple had been properly arranged and shelves built, the lumber for same being secured by Mr. L. Stavenheim free of cost from Mr. J. A. Chesley, Mr. A. L. Wall and the Beidler-Robinson Co., and the work done on the same terms by Mr. T. Ostbye of the firm of Schlanser & Ostbye. The first cash donation reported was from Mr. Wm. H. White. These matters were reported at the meeting of the library board, September 21, 1900. Hon. J. A. Johnson, then mayor of the city, being an enthusiastic supporter of the library movement, solicited donations of books which resulted in several hundred volumes being secured.

For two years, the library continued in the Masonic Temple. During this time, Hon. B. F. Spalding, with others, became interested in the library activities of Mr. Carnegie, and finally a donation of $20,000 was obtained from him for the erection of a library building in Fargo. It is no more than due to Mr. Spalding to say that through his efforts, more than any other one person, came the gift from Mr. Carnegie. The matter of getting the city to make the appropriations and donation of grounds, was taken up, which resulted in an annual appropriation from the city of $2,500 and the donation of a lot on the corner of Robert street and Second avenue north. In many ways, the lot donated was in an unfortunate location in that it gave no opportunity for exterior display. Its being on a part of the site of the old Columbia Hotel, which was burned June 7, 1893, made it necessary to extend its foundation far into the ground, yet there was nothing to do but to accept the location.

Architects were asked to submit plans for the library building, and Messrs. M. E. Beeve, J. Freidlander and Hancock Bros. did so, and those of the latter were accepted with some modifications. In due course of time, the building was erected by Schlanser & Ostbye, who were the lowest bidders, at the price of $15,986, the plumbing being given to Wm. D. Allen, the steam fitting to C. H. Porritt, as separate contracts.

On Monday evening, January 26th, 1903, the new library building was opened to the public by a reception. On this occasion many of the different nationalities were represented at booths, in costumes, refreshments being served, speeches being made, and a U. S. flag presented to the library by the local G. A. R., to which organization had been tendered the use of two rooms on the first floor. In this connection, it may not be amiss to say that the several women's clubs were active in promoting library interests; and to their endeavors was largely due the unique features and success of the opening night, and they also aided in the securing of books. During all of the time since, those clubs have been a potent agency for the keeping of library interests alive.

On account of the lack of opportunity for exterior adornment, efforts were made to make the interior as rich and pleasant as was possible with the money at hand. The walls of the building were constructed with the ultimate view of an addition of one or two stories. The brick of which the library is constructed was obtained from the Dickinson Pressed Brick Co. The window sills, copings and base stones are of granite. The large entrance hall is finished in marble. The woodwork of the interior is entirely of quarter-sawed oak, floors of hard maple, ceiling of steel, steel stacks from Jamestown Art Metal Co.,Jamestown, N. Y. The lower floor consists of large boiler and fuel room, janitor's room, hall and kitchen for G. A. R., commodious lecture room and storeroom. The second floor consists of entrance hall, large and well lighted general reading room, children's room, stack room and director's room. Previous to occupying the present building, all of the library board meetings, with the exception of the first few, were held in the Masonic Grand Lodge Library, Masonic Temple.

Since the library was organized, the officers have been: Mr. Thomas Baker, Jr., president from May 19, 1900, to July 6, 1903, at which time Bishop Cameron Mann was elected president and is still serving as such; the secretaries of the board have been Mrs. Ella K. Smith, May 19, 1900, to July 6, 1903, when Mr. Hubert Harrington was elected and served until December 14, 1905, at which time Miss Mary Schlanser was employed as clerk of the board to do the work of the secretary; the librarian has been Mr. Frank J. Thompson, elected May 19, 1900, and he has served continuously since that time. The assistant librarians since organization have been: Miss May K. Stanford, December 5, 1900, to July 1, 1905; Miss Lillian Mirick, September, 1905, to November, 1906; Miss Ida Schaefer, November, 1906, and still in service. The patronage of the library continuing to grow it became necessary to secure help at odd hours to aid the assistant librarian, until the present year when the Library Board felt obliged to employ an extra assistant in the library, and Miss Inga Rynning was engaged, beginning her work September, 1908.

The members of the library board have been at various times those given in the forepart of this article. Besides, Dr. Thames became a member through the resignation of Mr. Stavenheim, who left the city; and through Dr. Thames' resignation Mr. Hubert Harrington was appointed and he is at present a member of the board. Also Mrs. S. G. Roberts, Mrs. H. L. Bolley and Mrs. F. F. Grant, the two latter are now serving. Dr. J. F. Dudley was a member for a number of years, and his presence was always an inspiration, and too much credit cannot be given for his interest and assistance in the work. During his term of office, he passed away, leaving not only a vacancy on the board, but one among his fellow citizens which can hardly be filled. He was rightly named "The Grand Old Man of Fargo." A short time after the expiration of Mrs. Ella K. Smith's term as secretary, she also passed away. Her faithful service in behalf of the library was most helpful, and especially are her labors appreciated because they were given at the formative period when effort was required to awaken and push the work to consummation.

It may not be out of place to mention the humbler part of the library corps, and to whose industry and neatness much of the attractiveness of the library is due, and we refer to the janitors who have always made the Fargo Public Library the cleanest public building in the city, with no exception. Mr. Frank Cuzner served from January, 1903, to February, 1907, inclusive; Mr. Andrew Hageman, March, 1907, to February, 1908, and his son, Louis, from March, 1908, to the present.

The city has generously increased the annual appropriations until now the library receives the sum of $3,360, and yet this sum is all too small to maintain the library and furnish its patrons with the reading material for which they ask. And this can better be ap-

Partial Interior View, Public Library, Fargo, North Dakota.

preciated when it is known that the number of volumes taken out of the library for the past year was more than 25,000, and this, of course, does not include the number of volumes which have been used for reference work, and which, if the reference books were permitted to leave the library, would almost equal the circulation.

JAMESTOWN PUBLIC LIBRARY.

(Contributed by Mrs. A. M. Burt.)

Twenty-five years ago a public library was started in Jamestown and kept up for six years by a few ladies. Then it was found impossible to continue it and the books were given away.

On January 23, 1901, Mr. Alfred Dickey, a public minded citizen of Jamestown and a great reader with a phenomenal memory, called a meeting of those interested in starting a library especially as a good thing for the boys, in the Gladstone Hotel. But on that day he was very ill. The library had a sad start for the third day after the first meeting Alfred Dickey, its founder, died. His son, Alfred E. Dickey, called another meeting a month later and has since carried out his father's wishes and helped with interest and with money. At the first meeting the ladies agreed to take turns in keeping the library open, each one taking two evenings a week. Mr. Dickey gave the furniture and magazines—books were solicited from everyone in town and a room on the principal street of the city was given with heat and lights free. In about a year a librarian was engaged and paid for by Mr. Dickey. A dollar a year was the subscription price. All this money was spent for new books and for the first six years it averaged from $100 to $200 a year.

The next year the library board asked the council for $120 a year and it was put to a vote of the people and carried by a small majority.

Each year through the efforts of Mrs. Montgomery and Mrs. Glaspell, about $100 was raised by various entertainments.

In 1907 the city built a large city hall, setting aside one room 37x30 and an alcove 17x15 for library purposes. The Musical and Wednesday Clubs became interested. Through the help of the Musical Club $300 was raised with which to furnish the rooms. Through the efforts of the Wednesday Club, the question of supporting a free public library by taxation was put to vote and carried with but few dissenting votes. The council appropriated $1,500 a year with the understanding that a trained librarian should be secured. On August 8, 1908, the library was made free. On that date there were 130 cards in use. Today, October 23, 1908, there are 400 cards in use and their number is increasing at the rate of about seven a day. The library rooms are very beautiful. Both furniture and woodwork are finished in the early English finish and

Library at Agricultural College, Fargo.

Interior Views in Agricultural College Library, Fargo.

the walls are a soft green with a cream-colored ceiling. A handsome eight-day clock, magazine and newspaper rack and pictures have been given. The school children formed a line and moved the books into the new rooms with light grain pails.

These children are now constant users of the library. Just before moving into the new rooms, the library was reorganized under the direction of Miss Zana Miller of the State Library Commission, by the ladies of Jamestown and started fresh in the new rooms with a new system and new records.

GRAFTON HIGH SCHOOL AND PUBLIC LIBRARY.

(Contributed by Mrs. W. L. Stockwell.)

Grafton was the first city in North Dakota to establish and maintain a free public library. It owes its existence primarily to the Ladies' Magazine club, organized in 1895. The foundation funds were raised by a series of entertainments and voluntary contributions from public spirited citizens.

From this small beginning the Public Library association was organized, and a free public library with 400 volumes opened. The funds and property of the Library association were turned over to the city in the spring of 1897, the municipality agreeing that suitable quarters would be provided and the library maintained perpetually as a free public institution.

Through the influence of Messrs. Stockwell and Cashel the sum of $10,000 was secured from Mr. Carnegie in the spring of 1903 under the usual Carnegie provisions, viz: that the city provide a suitable site and guarantee an annual tax levy of $1,000 for maintenance. The present commodious and substantial building was erected in 1904, and formally opened to the public January 28, 1905.

The building is constructed of Dickinson pressed brick and cut stone and is most admirably adapted to the uses for which it was planned. On the ground floor is a roomy rotunda, reading room, stack room, reference room, children's room and librarian's private office; all of which are commodious, well lighted and artistically decorated. In the basement is located a large assembly room with raised platform for public gatherings—filing rooms, separate toilet rooms for the sexes and the heating plant.

The building is furnished throughout in old English oak provided by the Ladies' Library club, and made further attractive by gifts of a clock from W. L. Stockwell, president of the board, and an especially fine carbon print of the Roman forum from the Monday Night club.

The grounds were laid out by Prof. C. B. Waldron, landscape gardener of the State Agricultural College—trees, shrubs and flowering plants and substantial cement walks laid in front of and about the premises. The funds for the latter provided by the Ladies' Literary club.

At the close of the school year 1905, the school library was turned over to the library board and became a part of the public library, a separate department known as the children's room being provided.

Carnegie High School and Public Library, Grafton, N. D.

This has proved to be one of the most important and valuable features of the library. It is under the supervision of the librarian and accessible to the children at all times.

Fiction is most popular with the public, but the demand for reference works is constantly increasing. This interest has been especially fostered by the librarian.

GRAND FORKS PUBLIC LIBRARY.

(Contributed by Sveinbjorn Johnson.)

The Grand Forks public library was organized in 1899 under a state law. It is controlled by trustees chosen by the board of education. The present library building was completed in 1903, the source of the building fund being Mr. Andrew Carnegie. The book capacity is about 20,000 and the number of volumes available for reference or borrowing at the end of the year ending September, 1908, was 9,083.

The plan of the library management is to meet the needs of all classes of people. There is the general reading room with its 23 daily and weekly newspapers and a very complete collection of the most popular magazines. It is here that the laboring man among others may be found who comes between his hours of work to read the news or whatever may especially interest him.

Then there is a study room where reference works that cannot be drawn from the library are kept. The facilities of this part of the library are especially appreciated by students and others who desire to do research work.

A very spacious room in the building is set aside for children to read in. It contains a large collection of books for young people. The library is situated across the street from one of the city schools, and during part of the noon hour as well as after school this room is occupied by young and interested readers. Children may borrow books from the library on presenting a card signed by their parents.

In the basement of the building is a conveniently furnished room in which clubs and other organizations hold their meetings.

The total circulation for the past year was 23,748, while the number of borrowers was 3,576. The library is kept open week days, 10 A. M. to 8:30 P. M., and part of the year the reading room is open Sunday afternoons.

A trained librarian, Miss Elizabeth Abbott, is in charge.

Public Library, Grand Forks, N. D.

UNIVERSITY OF NORTH DAKOTA LIBRARY.

(Contributed by Sveinbjorn Johnson.)

This library was organized in 1883 and is under the control of the deans of the various colleges of the university. Up to 1908 it occupied quarters in the main building, which had for several years been inconvenient and crowded. In that year the new library building was completed at a cost of $30,000, generously contributed by Andrew Carnegie.

In recent years the growth of the library has fully kept pace with that of the university. The number of volumes has increased from 9,000 in 1904 to 27,000 (25,000 bound) in 1908. A splendid collection of nearly 2,000 volumes was donated by the widow of the late Judge John M. Cochrane and in appreciation of the fine quarters allotted this part of the library in the new Carnegie building, she has expressed her intention of making additions of books in the future.

In the spring of 1907 the university secured a gift of $3,500 from James J. Hill for a railroad library. At present this library contains over 1,000 volumes, and material additions are being made from time to time. Among the valuable books in the collection is a complete set of Poor's Manual of Railroads consisting of 32 large volumes. The first volumes are very old and only a few are left in the country. Prof. Meyers of the University of Wisconsin gave valuable advice in the selection of books and periodicals and reports from European countries are being received.

The Scandinavian collection is one of the most complete of its kind in the United States. This is mainly a contribution from the Scandinavians of the state and a large fund is still on hand with which books are being purchased. The collection of Icelandic books, secured through the efforts of Icelandic students and alumni of the university, is the most complete in the northwest and second to none in the country.

A trained librarian, Mr. C. H. Compton, is in charge. The building has a capacity of 35,000 books. There were added 1,873 volumes from July 1, 1907, to June 30, 1908, at a cost of $2,758.25.

MANDAN CITY LIBRARY.

(Contributed by Mrs. Elizabeth McDonald.)

The Mandan library had its inception in a reading circle, in 1896 The first money raised by these ladies was used in purchasing fifty books, the nucleus of the present library. Through the kindness of Mr. J. R. Clark (now deceased) part of his drug store was used for the use of the public. In 1906 a library building was erected on Third avenue northwest. The funds for this building were raised by public subscription. The library is under the management of the library association, through whose efforts it is supported —the public generously responding to the many calls made.

All regular patrons pay one dollar a year each, thus materially aiding in the purchasing of books. There are now in the library 1,800 volumes. The librarian is Miss Bessie Lanterman.

Mandan Public Library.

MINOT PUBLIC LIBRARY.

(Contributed by Mrs. L. W. Gammons.)

The question of starting a library in Minot was agitated for some time before coming to a focus. The commercial club talked it over, the woman's club talked and the ordinary citizens talked, finally the woman's club put in some substantial assistance in the shape of a little over one thousand dollars, which they had been two years raising in various ways. According to the statutes the city then gave two hundred dollars. The school board appointed a library committee of five persons, who proceeded to take action. Rooms were hired, a trained librarian appointed, and books purchased. Public sentiment was influenced and last spring the voters showed by a large majority that they were in favor of having a public library and sustaining it. By various benefits and entertainments the library was supported until Sept. 1, 1908, then a tax of $1500 was levied for this year, out of which we hope to purchase a site for our Carnegie building and run the library. Except the raising of the one thousand dollars, all this has been accomplished in less than one year. We pay our librarian $75 per month. We buy, at least, $25 worth of new books a month. We have over thirteen hundred books, besides many magazines and public documents. We consider that it is one of the best investments ever made here. The reading-rooms are very well patronized, being open every day, except Sunday, from two to six in the afternoon and from 7 to 10 in the evening.

A long correspondence with Mr. Carnegie has at last resulted in his offering us $15,000 for a building—we have thanked him and asked for $10,000 more, which we are waiting to get.

We received much valuable advice from Miss Miller, who visited Minot last winter in order to aid us.

VALLEY CITY PUBLIC LIBRARY.

(Contributed by Laura A. Bassett.)

The Valley City public library is a $15,000 Carnegie building opened in October, 1903.

It is a very pretty building of St. Louis pressed brick, is centrally located and one of the institutions of which the city is proud.

Both normal and high school students use it to a great extent for reference work. Everything on the reference shelves is new and up-to-date.

At the present time there are 1,700 borrowers and 3,000 books.

There have been no special lines of library work attempted, owing to insufficient means.

Interior Views in Carnegie Library, Valley City.

Public Library, Valley City, N. D.

Appendix No. II

TABLES OF STATISTICS

STATISTICS OF LIBRARIES IN

REPORTING TO LIBRARY COMMISSI

Name of Library	Location	Name of Librarian	Salary	No. of Ass'ts.	Salary of Ass'ts.	Date of Organization
Agricultural College.	Fargo	Ethel McVeety	$1,000	1	$600	1890
School of Forestry...	Bottineau	....	......	......	....	1907
State Historical......	Bismarck	H. C. Fish	......	......	....	1903
Industrial School	Ellendale	Carrie Tuttle	900	......	....	1904
Hospital of Insane ...	Jamestown	....	......	......	....	....
State Law Library ...	Bismarck	Mrs. N. L. Call	1,000	......	....	1894
State Educational Referance and State Traveling Libraries	Bismarck	Zana K. Miller	1,200	1	360	1907
Normal School Library.............	Mayville	Nellie A. Olson	600	......	....	1907
Normal School Library	Valley City	Mabel G. West	855	......	....	....
Penitentiary Library	Grove P. O., Burleigh Co.	....	......	......	....	....
School of Science Library	Wahpeton	Lilian Mirick	700	2	45	1903
University of North Dakota Library	Grand Forks	Chas. H. Compton	1,000	1	600	1883

NORTH DAKOTA STATE INSTITUTIONS.

·ON FOR YEAR ENDING JUNE 30, 1908.

Volumes Added, Year Ending June 30, 1908	Cost of Same	Total No. of Bound Vol.	Circulation Year ending June 30, 1908	Amt. of Income	Date	Source	BUILDINGS		
							Cost	Materials	Book Cap'ty
1,992	$663.71	20,085	4,500	$3,200	1906	Andrew Carnegie and State	$23,500	Brick with Stone Basement	$50,000
....	...	745	....	......	1908	....	......	Brick	
....	......	1,500	....	......	....	Room in Capitol			
....	....	2,000	....	500	....	Room in Main School B'ld'g.			9,000
....	....	1,000	....	......	....	Room in Hospital			
385	....	15,000	....	1,000	....	Rooms in Capitol			15,000
23	45 40	5,500	....	1,500	....	Room in Capitol			3,000
250	200.00	3,612	....	Varies	....	2 Rooms in School Building			
1,016	....	6,'31	....	......	....	Rooms in School Building			
....	....	2,100	5,200	......	....	Room in Penitentiary			
100	....	6,500	....	.. ..	....	Rooms in Main School B'ld'g			
1,873	2,758.23	25,000	....	5,211.08	1908	Andrew Carnegie	$30,000	Brick	35,000

METHODS OF ADMINISTRATION IN NORTH

Name of Library	Location	TRUSTEES			System of Classification	Charging System
		No.	Term of Office	How Chosen		
Agricultural College	Fargo	3	Indefinite	By President of College	Dewey	Cards
School of Forestry ..	Bottineau	3	....	By Governor	......	... ..
State Historical	Bismarck	16	4 years	By members S. H. S.	Dewey	......
Industrial School	Ellendale	5	....	By Governor	Dewey	Cards
Hospital for Insane ..	Jamestown	5	4 years	By Governor	None	None
State Law Library ..	Bismarck	Secretary of State			......	......
State Educational Reference and State Traveling Libraries	Bismarck	Library Commission			Dewey	Cards
Normal School	Mayville	....			Dewey	Slips
Normal School	Valley City	Control of School			D. C	Cards
Penitentiary	Grove P. O., Burleigh Co.	Control of Warden			......	......
School of Science	Wahpeton	....			Dewey	Cards
University of N. Dak	Grand Forks	6 Deans of Various Colleges			Dewey	Cards

*Library Bureau.
**State $3,102.65, Membership fees $1,198.65, Gifts $909.78, Total income, $5,211.08.

DAKOTA INSTITUTIONAL LIBRARIES.

Accession Record	Shelf List Record	Catalog	Terms of Use	No. Volumes Allowed Each Borrower at one Time	No. of Fictions Allowed	No. of Mag. and Periodicals kept	Source of Income
Book	Yes	Card	Free for Loan and Ref....	3 or 4 for special study	1	... .	State
......	.....	Card	....	....	....	37	State
......	....	Card	Free for Ref.				
A. L. A Book	Partial	Card	Free for Ref.	No fixed rule	1	....	State
None	None	Printed	Free to patients, officers and employes	....	1	....	State
Book	......	Printed	Free for Ref.	....	....	....	State
Book	{ None	None	Free for Ref.	No fixed rule	....	None }	State
	{ Yes	None	Free on application of six responsible persons	40 to 50	....	None }	State
*Book	None	Card	Free to students	No fixed rule	....	....	State
Book	Yes	Card	....	Not limited	....	....	State
......	......	Printed	Free to employes and inmates	1	1	....	Donations
Book	Yes	Card	Free for Ref. to school...	1—more for study	1	....	State
Book	Cards	Card	Free to students	....	....	....	**State

STATISTICS OF NORTH

REPORTING TO THE PUBLIC LIBRARY

Name of Library	Location	Population—Blue Book 1907	Name of Librarian	Salary	No. of Assistants	Salary of Assistants	Date of Organization
Cando Library	Cando	1,328	May Holmes	50c each opening	..	....	1902
Carrington Public Library	Carrington	1,106	Mrs. B. L. Russell	$1 each opening	..	....	1906
Casselton Public Library	Casselton	1,269	Hattie May	. ....	..	....	....
Devils Lake Public Library	Devils Lake	2,367	Mrs. O. Evans	....	..	....	1898
Fargo Public Library	Fargo	12,512	Ida Schaefer	$65 per month	2	....	1900
Fessenden Public Library	Fessenden	781	Jasephine Laderonte	$25 per annum	..	....	1900
Grafton Public Library....	Grafton	2,423	Mary Morris	$420 per annum	..	....	1897
Grand Forks Public Library	Grand Forks	10,127	Elizabeth Abbott	$900 per annum	1	$300	1899
Jamestown Public Library and Alfred Dickey Free Reading Room	Jamestown	5,093	Katherine Hager	$16 per month	..	....	1902
Langdon Public Library	Langdon	1,514	Mrs. A. A. G. McMillan	....	..	....	....
Leeds Library........	Leeds	520	Hilda Nelson	....	..	....	....
Mandan Public Library	Mandan	2,714	Rose D. Lang	$120 per annum	..	....	1895
Minot Public Library	Minot	4,125	Clara H. Kunst	$75 per month	..	....	1908
Park River Public Library	Park River	1,435	Bessie I. Robbins	....	..	...	....
Valley City Public Library	Valley City	4,059	Mrs C F. Mudgett	No salary	..	....	1900
			Mrs. Laura Basset	$40 per month	..	....	....
Mayville Public Library	Mayville	1,212	R. S. Wilson	....	..	....	....

DAKOTA PUBLIC LIBRARIES.

COMMISSION FOR YEAR ENDING JUNE 30' 1908.

Volumes added Year ending June 30, 1908	Total No. of Bound Volumes	Circulation for Year ending June 30, 1908	Source and Amount of Income	BUILDINGS				
				Date	Cost	Source	Materials	Book Cap'ty.
......	1,745	......	Membership fees $1 per annum..........	....	Room in Town Hall		....	2,000
......	957	75	Subscript'n and funds raised by Woman's Club	....	Rented Rooms		....	......
......	1,200	......	$250 per year from city; some help from Woman's Club	....	In City Hall		....	......
......	1,650	......		....	... .		....	......
......	8,000	24,207	City Tax $3,000	1903	$20,000	Andrew Carnegie	Brick and Stone	25 000
200	1,200	......	Gifts and entertainments	....	Pub. School Bldg.		....	......
......	4,500	18,172	City Appropriation Board of Education	1905	$10,000	Andrew Carnegie	Brick	5,000
......	9,083	23,748	City Appropriation ..	1603	$31,000	Andrew Carnegie	Brick and Limestone	20,000
......	1,400	4,850	City tax $125; Endowment from A. E. Dickey $78; Membership fee $1.......	....	2 Rented Rooms		....	......
......	780	......	$200 per yr. from city; $100 from other sources	....	....		....	......
30	1,560	......	....	....	Library kept in Club Room		....	......
......	1,745	2,223	Membership fee $1 yearly	1906	$1,500	...	Frame	6,000
......	1,147	5,078	City Appropriation					
......	2,000	......	$200 for 6 months, Gifts $1.578.01.......	....	2 Rented Rooms		....	......
......	2,956	8,714	$400 annually from city	....	....		....	......
......	......	......	City Tax $1,500	1903	$15,000	Andrew Carnegie	Brick and Stone	4,000
......	1,407	......	City Tax $700.........	....	......	....	....	......

METHODS OF ADMINISTRATION IN

REPORTING TO PUBLIC

Name of Library	Location	TRUSTEES			System of Classification	Charging System	Accession Record
		No.	Term	How Chosen			
Cando Library	Cando	5	1 year	By stockholders	Yes	Cards	Card
Carrington Public Library	Carrington	Woman's Literary Club			Dewey	Cards	Yes
Casselton Public Library	Casselton	6	......	....	....	....	......
Devils Lake Public Library*	Devils Lake	The Library Board, a Woman's Club of 12 members			....	....	......
Fargo Public Library	Fargo	5	2 years	By Board of Education	Dewey	Cards	Book
Fessenden Public Library	Fessenden	..	....	....	Dewey	Cards	Book
Grafton Public Library	Grafton	5	2 years	By Board of Education	Dewey	Cards	Book
Grand Forks Public Library	Grand Forks	5	2 years	By Board of Education	Dewey	Cards	Book
Jamestown Public Library	Jamestown	5	2 years	By Board of Education	Yes	Cards	Yes
Langdon Public Library	Langdon	7	....	....	....	....	......
Leeds Library........	Leeds	Alfredian Club			....	....	Yes
Mandan City Library	Mandan	Association			Dewey	Cards	Yes
Minot Public Library	Minot	5	2 years	By Board of Education	Dewey	Cards	Book
Park River Public Library........... .	Park River	3	....	....	....	....	......
Valley City Public Library	Valley City	5	2 years	By Board of Education	....	Cards	Yes
Mayville Public Library	Mayville	....	....	....	....	....	.....

*Six to Teachers and Students.

NORTH DAKOTA PUBLIC LIBRARIES.

LIBRARY COMMISSION

Shelf List Record	Catalog	Terms of Use	No. of Volumes allowed such borrower at one time	No. of Fictions allowed	No. of Magazines and Periodicals kept	How Organized	Hours Kept Open
Yes	Card	Free for Reference Loans by Subscription	One	1	....	....	Wednesday and Saturday Evenings
Yes	Card	Free for Reference Loans by Subscription.—Free to Children's Circle	One	1	....	Woman's Literary Club	Tuesday and Saturday Afternoons and Saturday Evenings
.....	......	Free except Rental for new novels	......	..	....	Booklovers' Club	Saturday, 10 to 12 a. m., and 2 to 6:30 p. m.
......	.....	Subscription $1.00 per year	......	..	....	....	Wednesday and Saturday Afternoons and Evenings
Yes	Card	Free	One or more	1	42	State Law	Open for lending afternoons and evenings; for reading, forenoons, Sunday and holidays
Yes	None	Free	One	1	....	....	Three afternoons from 4 to 5
Yes	Card	Free	Two	1	15	....	Morning and Afternoon, 6 days; 3 Evenings
Card	Card	Free	*Two	1	75 Mag. and Per. and 23 Newspapers	State Law	All day and evening
No	Typewritten	Free for reference $1 Subscription for Lending	One	1	25 Mag. donated by A. E. Dickey	State Law	Open Saturday and Sunday afternoon and evenings
......	......	Subscription	......	..	....	Women's Club	Wednesday and Saturday Afternoons; Saturday evening
......	......	Subscription	......	..	....	Alfredian Club	Wednesday, Saturday and Sunday afternoons
......	Card	Subscription	Two	2	8	....	Saturday afternoons, Tuesday, Thursday and Saturday evenings
Yes	Card	Free	One	1	19	State Law	Afternoons and evenings
......	......	Free	......	..	....	Private Subscription	Saturday afternoons; Wednesday and Saturday evenings
Yes	Card	Free	Two	1	22	State Law	Afternoons and evenings
......	......	Free	......	..	....	....	Evenings and Tuesday and Wednesday afternoons

CLUB, COLLEGE, ACADEMY

REPORTING TO THE PUBLIC

Name	Location	Name of Librarian	Salary	No. of Assistants	Salary of Assistants	Date of Organization	Vols. Bought Year ending June 30, 1908
Fargo College	Fargo	Bertha Vittum	$200	2	Tuition	1888	119
Sheyenne River Academy	Harvey	N. W. Lawrence, Principal	....	..	....	....	......
Masonic Grand Lodge	Fargo	Frank J. Thompson	200	1	....	1893	206
Booklovers' Club	Lakota	J. S. Cole	....	..	....	1906	......

AND LODGE LIBRARIES

LIBRARY COMMISSION.

Cost of Same	Total No. of Bound Volumes	Amount of Income	Circulation Year ending June 30, 1908	System of Classification	Charging System	Accession Record	Shelf List Record	Catalog	Building
$220.00	5,000	Interest of Endowment of $15,000	1,400	Dewey	Cards	Yes	Yes	Card	Rooms in College
......	200	....	......	......	......	....	....	.....	....
579.74	5,251	10c per capita upon lodge members of state	Ref., Lib.	Dewey	......	Book	Yes	Card	Masonic Temple
......	500	By subscription	......	......	......	....	....	Yes	Court House

LIST OF HIGH SCHOOL LIBRARIES IN NORTH DAKOTA.

NO.	LOCATION	NO. OF VOLUMES
1	Bathgate	400
2	Bismarck	600
3	Caledonia	350
4	Cando	800
5	Carrington	600
6	Casselton	256
7	Cavalier	170
8	Cooperstown	985
9	Devils Lake	369
10	Dickinson	1,100
11	Drayton	469
12	Edgeley	200
13	Ellendale	1,000
14	Enderlin	65
15	Fairmount	60
16	Fargo	1,627
17	Fessenden	1,700
18	Grand Forks	879
19	Hankinson	450
20	Harvey	985
21	Hillsboro	275
22	Hope	700
23	Hunter	650
24	Inkster	523
25	Jamestown	1,500
26	Lakota	2,750
27	La Moure	52
28	Langdon	537
29	Larimore	1,500
30	Leeds	2,150
31	Lidgerwood	1,252
32	Lisbon	500
33	Mandan	553
34	Mayville	355
35	Michigan	454
36	Minot	422
37	Minto	850
38	New Rockford	450
39	Northwood	340
40	Oakes	1,300
41	Page	600
42	Park River	700
43	Pembina	600
44	Reynolds	373
45	Rolla	600

NO.	LOCATION	NO. OF VOLUMES
46	St. Thomas	540
47	Tower City	1,450
48	Valley City	400
49	Velva	40
50	Wahpeton	1,200
51	Webster	100
52	Williston	1,378
	Total	37,659

NORTH DAKOTA PUBLIC LIBRARIES.

NO.	NAME AND PLACE OF LIBRARY	LIBRARIAN
1	Barlow, Barlow Public Library	
2	Bismarck, State Historical Library	Mr. H. C. Fish
3	Bismarck, State Law Library	Mrs. Nellie Call
4	Cando, Public Library	Miss Holmes
5	Carrington, Public Library	Mrs. Lulu Russell
6	Casselton, Public Library	Miss Hattie May
7	Devils Lake, Public Library	Mrs. O. Evans
8	Dickinson, Public Library	
9	Fargo, Agricultural College	Mrs. Ethel McVesty
10	Fargo, Public Library	Miss Ida Schaefer
11	Fargo, Masonic Grand Lodge Library	Mr. F. J. Thompson
12	Fessenden, Public Library	Miss Josephine Laderoute
13	Grafton, High School and Public Library	Miss Mary Morris
14	Grand Forks, Public Library	Miss Elizabeth Abbott
15	Grand Forks, State University Library	C. F. Compton
16	Jamestown, Public Library	Katherine Hager
17	Lakota, Book-lovers Club	J. S. Cole
18	Langdon, Public Library	Mrs. A. A. G. McMillan
19	Leeds, Public Library	Hilda Nelson
20	Mandan, City Library	Rose D. Lang
21	Mayville, Public Library	Mr. R. S. Wilson
22	Mayville, Normal School	Miss Nellie Olson
23	Minot, Public Library	Miss Clara Kunst
24	Park River, Public Library	Miss Bessie I. Robbins
25	Valley City, Public Library	Mrs. Laura A. Bassett
26	Valley City, Normal School	Miss Mabel G. West
27	Wahpeton, North Dakota Science School	Miss Lillian Mirick

LIST OF TRAVELING LIBRARY STATIONS

NOVEMBER 1, 1908.

No.	Location	Date of Shipment	Name of Signers
1	Barton	June 24	Grace L. Pulver Viola Gilmore Geo. H. Gilmore A. J. Erickson M. M. Miller John Turney
2	Berg.............	July 17	Christine Erickson Mrs. O. I. Berg Ingelborg H. Isaacson Charlie Erickson W. H. Beeley Antone Anderson
3	Berg.............	October 24	Edward Von Eschen Louis Evenson W. E. Jones R. F. Strong H. J. Lovaas C. L. Dailey J. L. Stevens G. W. Loomer
4	Bordulac	August 8	R. P. Groves A. H. Wentland M. C. Murphy W. H. Sutherland E. A. Roach Angus Ferguson
	Bowman.........	October 8..........	Mrs. John Hudson Marie Hovick John Hudson Joseph Silha C. V. Townsend Ella Lombard H. C. Lee A. Sletten Henry Roen Myrtle Hudson
6	Bucyrus	October 1..........	Mabel Milliren Mrs. Ella Mahon Gunder Houge Lars Larson Chas. Fahy Wm. A. Stagen
7	Churches Ferry..	May	Maud D. Whitney Amy O. Kirkpatrick G. M. Steig James McCormick B. L. Wilson Joseph G. Nichol S. K. Hansen C. W. Whitney Jas. A. Dow Lottie Riley J. G. Jacobson

LIST OF TRAVELING LIBRARY STATIONS (Continued)

NOVEMBER 1, 1908

No.	Location	Date of Shipment	Name of Signers
8	Crosby	October 13	Geo. P. Hommes Togstad Bros. J. H. Phelps Krank Korster S. O. Nelson John O. Kuoph
9	Donnybrook	June 28	C. W. Graves J. P. Dunn W. E. Freeman Thos. O'Brien E. Galehouse Geo. W. Offatt S. O. Chase
10	Doyon	October 24	Adale B. Collins C. H. Doyon F. S. Chamberlin P. C. Vernon J. H. Blaufuss W. P. Retillard
11	Emerado	September 8	Will Hancock Prof. C. C. Stoliker L. F. Waruken A. A. Hood H. B. Lemvillican S. J. Hancock
12	Fairdale.........	April 29	Ada Sylvester Helen Green Ralph Silvester J. Emerson Shaw Chas. Green John Schostead
13	Fergus	October 8	Geo. A. Fisher Geo. O. Espeland B. E. Yahma A. B. Knapton M. M. Slawson H. G. Johnson
14	Gackle........ ..	July 25	R. A. Werner E. G. Bleedow Jacob Knopp H. B. Huntley G. M. Noyes Emil Peterson
15	Gladys...........	March 24	J. H. Ulsrud Carl E. Rustad Lillie Bailey P. C. Pederson Olaf Heier W. E. Bailey P. F. Myre

LIST OF TRAVELING LIBRARY STATIONS (Continued)

NOVEMBER 1, 1908

No.	Location	Date of Shipment	Name of Signers
16	Grandin	February 26	Clarence Record
			Willard Bell
			James Bell
			A. Bell
			Emil Hansen
			Mrs. Emil Hansen
			W. J. Connor
			Mrs. W. J. Connor
17	Hamilton	August	Pearl Connell
			H. E. Kellar
			Alex. Strusky
			F. Hoesley
			Geo. L. Paxman
			A. E. Thacker
			H. P. Wood
			Jas. A. Wright
			D. L. Spring
			H. Fernnell
			H. Gerger
18	Hazelton	August 14	Mrs. Lester Briggle
			Mrs. Nellie C. Riley
			Frank P. Simpkins
			Mrs. Sylvia R. Graham
			Mrs. Lena Appert
			John Schneider
19	Heaton	July 10	C. E. Harding
			C. I. Turner
			E. E. Sanders
			H. C. Barber
			C. M. Brace
			R. Prang
20	Heart............	January 20	Gainer P. Moore
		August 11	A. L. Elder
			Charles Cryderman
			N. H. Whitcomb
			W. A. Butler
21	Hurdsfield	January 28	Maud Outram
		August 19	Mrs. Lillie Bowers
			W. C. Miller
			M. G. Blaha
			J. P. Heald
			O. P. Jordal
			C. G. Heminger
			Emma Rosberg
22	Kathryn.........	January 14.........	L. B. Conroy
		September 12	K. O. Abrahamson
			Louis Larson
			G. T. Simmons
			W. Reinck
			L. W. Michelson
			E. Michelson

LIST OF TRAVELING LIBRARY STATIONS (Continued).

NOVEMBER 1, 1908

No.	Location	Date of Shipment	Name of Signers
23	Kramer.........	January 27........	H. S. Tupper
		August 14.........	S. W. Ronning
			W. G. Bowen
			C. T. Kretschman
			Helen C. Laughlin
24	Leal.............	March 31........	Olivia Wagle
			M. E. McCurdy
			A. E. Lundy
			F. B. Smith
			Alpha Smith
			Mary Carr
			Howard Wilson
25	Leads—Wheatland District No. 10.........	June 4............	W. J. Carnahan
			Ivia Hinkle
			Mrs. R. M. Stair
			Mrs. O. A. Nestegard
			F. O. Anderson
			Carl E. Johnson
26	Linton..........	October 1..........	Mrs. J. N. Peterson
			E. E. Martin
			Gus Daffinrud
			A. W. Sims
			W. J. Marchant
			G. A. Herolz
			J. G. Pitts
			J. L. Owens
			Ethel Pravitz
27	Max.............	October 22.........	Thos. A. Moran
			P. D. Podhola
			O. J. Pleven
			S. H. Thorpe
			F. Malloy
			F. M. Hunt
			F. E. Whitney
			Chas. W. Morton
28	Maxbass.........	July 19...........	Lea H. Hamilton
			W. H. Sears
			C. J. Smith
			W. A. Myers
			R. A. McBrayne
			N. P. Blycken
			Will Freeman
			Andy Wall
			A. O. Smith
29	Medora..........	June 28...........	Mrs. Orrin Kendley
			Lorena King
			P. E. Burgess
			A. D. Ferris
			Mrs. N. D. Nichols
			Mrs. J. W. Fol[illegible]

LIST OF TRAVELING LIBRARY STATIONS (Continued)

NOVEMBER 1, 1908

No.	Location	Date of Shipment	Name of Signers
30	Napoleon	January	R. A. McCalmont
		September 26	Mrs. A. D. Hillard
			Herbert Brown
31	New Salem	October 24	Daisy Thompson
			Arne Vinje
			Chas. F. Peterson
			Jacob Rohs
			Martin Larson
			Jay Wilder
32	Pekin	October 29	Benj. H. Cooley
			C. O. Moen
			Albert Larson
			E. C. Brekken
			Ingvald Nymoen
			Otto Sletten
33	Reeder	August 6	Mabel Howard
			Fannie Muller
			Mrs. Herbert Lewis
			Miss Hazel Pierce
			Anna Heig
			Margrethe Langlie
			H. S. Leavell
34	Sawyer	July 21	Everett Bunken
			C. S. Beighle
			F. W. Long
			R. W. Beighle
			M. M. Beighle
			F. B. Pitkin
			G. G. Rielly
35	Shrewood.	October 21	D. Ray Gregg
			C. R. Hamilton
			V. B. McGuire
			W. F. Lowe
			H. Parting
			P. E. Johnson
			E. L. Penn
			P. M. Jenks
			M. J. Keys
			J. B. Switzer
36	Souris	September 12	John F. Haskel
37	Turtle Lake	January 0	John L. Brekken
			Mary Thompson
			E. Lindquist
			C. G. West
			Christ Thompson
			H. O. Barnes
			E. J. Jones
			James Hanson

LIST OF TRAVELING LIBRARY STATIONS (Continued)

NOVEMBER 1, 1908

No.	Location	Date of Shipment	Name of Signers
38	Uxbridge	May 8	Cassie Simpson Katherine V. Sherry G. B. Simpson F. L. Widdifield C. Christ T. E. McMillan
39	Velva	February 26	Martin B. Slatton Miss Hettie M. Clough Mrs. C. B. Ward C. B. Ward J. A. Clough Wm. Julian Mrs. Geo. Simons Geo. Simons
40	White Earth	October 13	J. P. Smerud L. H. Oliver J. C. Hangan C. E. Shepard Chas. M. Muns C. Hansen.
41	Wimbledon	September 2	Mrs. H. M. Stroud M. S. Mallough Mrs. W. O. Joos J. J. Feckler A. Y. More H. M. Stroud Mrs. A. M. Henson H. George Mrs. M. E. Coleman W. H. Stevens M. E. Coleman
42	Winchester	October 24	Mrs. W. H. Ross B. M. Richardson T. E. Lawler Thos. Yetter T. J. Richardson
43	Winona	August 6	Theo. Meppen C. O. Putman Jennie Grover Anton Naader J. D. Umber R. H. Coonen J. B. Paine
44	York	July 10	E. D. Read Nellie R. Sieber John Brager P. O. Brager N. S. Lotvedt I. E. Garveck

Appendix No. III

FINANCIAL REPORT

FINANCIAL REPORT OF SECRETARY OF NORTH DAKOTA PUBLIC LIBRARY COMMISSON

FROM MARCH 14, 1907 TO JUNE 30, 1908.

Date: Month	Date: Day	Date: Year		Receipts	Expenditures	Transportation of Books	Books Purchased	Periodicals and Membership Fees	Stationery and Postage	Printing	Aids to Libraries	Supplies	Commission Expenses	Salaries and Extra Clerical Work	Office Furniture
Mch.	2	1907	Balance Educational Library Fund	$ 194.52	$	$	$	$	$	$	$	$	$	$	$
Mch.	2	1907	Balance Traveling Library Fund	1,878 41											
Nov.	1	1907	Expenses 1907 to November 1	....	123 95	......	......	......	......	......	......	......	48.55	75.40	......
Dec.	1	1907	Expenses for November, 1907	....	180.78	.60	......	......	......	61.50	......	18.68	......	100.00	......
Dec.	31	1907	Expenses for December, 1907	....	106.00	......	......	6.00	......	......	......	......	......	100.00	......
Jan.	31	1908	Expenses for January, 1908	....	324.71	11.37	......	29.75	87.64	......	......	12.30	......	101.15	82.50
Feb.	29	1908	Expenses for February, 1908	....	164.68	6.89	32.00	12.42	......	......	10.87	2.50	......	100.00	......
Mch.	31	1908	Expenses for March, 1908	....	190.00	......	......	......	20.00	......	......	......	......	100.00	70.00
April	30	1908	Expenses for April, 1908	....	219.90	......	......	2 00	75.00	......	......	22.50	......	120.40	......
May	31	1908	Expenses for May, 1908	....	304.55	3.99	......	12.00	......	6.00	17.73	28.45	......	130.00	106.38
June	30	1908	Expenses for June, 1908	....	158.30	3.60	......	......	10.00	......	......	......	14.70	130.00	......
			Total Expenditures to June 30, 1908	....	$1,772.87	$26.45	$32.00	$62.17	$192.94	$67.50	$28.60	$84.43	$63 25	$956.95	$258.88
			Credit Balance, June 30, 1908	....	$ 300.06										
				$2,072.93	2,072.9										

FINANCIAL REPORT OF SECRETARY OF NORTH DAKOTA PUBLIC LIBRARY COMMISSION

FROM JULY 1, 1908 TO OCTOBER 31, 1908.

Date: Month	Day	Year		Receipts	Expenditures	Transportation of Books	Books Purchased	Periodicals and Membership Fees	Stat. and Postage	Printing	Aids to Libraries	Supplies	Commission Expenses	Salaries and Extra Clerical Work	Office Furniture
July	1	1908	Credit Balance..............	$ 300.06	$	$	$	$	$	$	$	$	$	$	$
July	1	1908	Biennial Appropriation......	3,000.00											
July	31	1908	Expenses for July, 1908......	....	231.00	......	......	......	......	......	......	10.00	86.70	130.00	4.30
Aug.	31	1908	Expenses for August, 1908....	....	377.20	18.24	5.00	11.50	10.00	109.70	1.25	......	......	213.25	8.26
Sept.	30	1908	Expenses for September, 1908	....	343.30	9.24	8.40	......	20.00	3.00	......	37.00	......	265.66	.....
Oct.	31	1908	Expenses for October, 1908...	....	288.38	6.47	3.26	......	......	......	......	.20	......	277.00	.75
			Total Expenditures July 1 to November 1, 1908............	....	$1,239.88	$33.95	$16 66	$11.50	$30.00	$112.70	$ 1.25	$47.90	$86.70	$885.91	$13.31
Nov.	1	1908	*Credit Balance..............	....	$2,060.18										
				$3,300.06	$3,300.06										

*It was deemed necessary by the commission to keep this balance to meet the heavy expenses unavoidable from November 1, 1908 to March 1, 1909.

AMOUNT APPROPRIATED ANNUALLY IN VARIOUS STATES FOR LIBRARY COMMISSION WORK.

Figures taken from 1907 year book of League of Library Commissions.

Name	Date Establ.	Amount	How Spent	
California	1903	$20,000.00		
Connecticut ..	1893	11,500.00		
Idaho.........	1901	5,500.00		
Indiana......	1899	7,000.00		
Iowa..........	1900	8,820.00		
Kansas	1889	6,000.00		
Minnesota	1899	12,500.00		
Missouri	1907	5,000.00		
Nebraska	1901	3,000.00		
New Jersey ...	1899	4,000.00		
New York	1892	47,200.00	Grants to Libraries	$28,000.00
			For Pictures and Traveling Libraries	6,000.00
			For Salaries	13,200.00
Ohio	1896	10,100.00	For Traveling Libraries	9,600.00
			For Expenses	500.00
Oregon	1905	6,000.00		
Pennsylvania .	1899	12,500.00		
Virginia		7,500.00		
Wisconsin	1895	23,500.00	For Admin. Traveling Libraries and Field Work	12,000.00
			For Library Schools ...	7,000.00
			For Legislative Reference.................	4,500.00
North Dakota .	1907	1,500.00		

Appendix No. IV.

NORTH DAKOTA LAWS RELATING TO LIBRARIES

LAWS RELATING TO LIBRARIES.

PUBLIC LIBRARIES

REVISED CODES OF 1905

TAXES.

Section 2972. The city council of each city, not exceeding in population fifty thousand inhabitants, and each village or township board of every village and township containing over five hundred inhabitants, shall have power to establish and maintain a public library and reading room, and for such purposes may annually levy and cause to be collected, as other taxes are collected, a tax not exceeding four mills on each dollar of the taxable property of such city, village or township, to constitute the library fund, which fund shall be kept separate from the other money of the city, village or township, by the treasurer thereof, and the same shall be used exclusively for such purpose; provided that no library shall be so established without first receiving the approval of the majority of the electors of such city, village or township, voting on such question at any general election at which it may be submitted to vote.

BOARD OF DIRECTORS—APPOINTMENT.

Section 2973. For the government of such library and reading room there shall be a board of five directors appointed from the citizens of such city, village or township, including both males and females, who shall be appointed by the board of education or school board of such city or village, or where there is no incorporated city or village then by the board of supervisors of such township; and there shall be one member of such board of education or school board or board of supervisors appointed as one of the directors of such library and reading room.

Such directors shall hold their office for two years from the first day of July in the year of their appointment and until their successors are appointed, but upon their first appointment they shall divide themselves at their first meeting by lot into two classes, and two of such directors shall hold for one year and the remaining three for two years, and thereafter there shall be appointed in each year the requisite number to fill the vacancies caused by the expiration of the terms of those going out of office in such year. All vacancies shall be immediately reported to and filled by such board of education, school board or board of supervisors, and if for an unexpired term.

for the residue of the term only. No compensation whatever shall be paid or allowed any director in such official capacity.

BOARD OF DIRECTORS—DUTIES—POWERS.

Section 2974. Said directors shall immediately after their appointment meet and organize by electing from their number a president, secretary and librarian. They shall make and adopt such by-laws, rules and regulations relating to the duties of officers and for the management of the library and reading room as may be expedient, not inconsistent with this article. They shall have the exclusive control of the expenditures of all moneys collected for or contributed to the library fund, and the supervision, care and custody of the library property, rooms or buildings constructed, leased or set apart for that purpose; and such money shall be drawn from the treasury by the proper officers upon vouchers of the board of directors without being otherwise audited. They may with the approval of the board of education or school board, or board of township supervisors aforesaid, without which no lease, purchase or contract therefor shall be valid, build, lease or purchase an appropriate building and purchase a site therefor, not however, employing in such purchase or building more than one-half of the income in any one year.

REGULATIONS GOVERNING USE OF LIBRARY.

Section 2975. Every library and reading room established under this article shall be forever free for the use of the inhabitants of the city, village or township where located, always subject to such reasonable rules and regulations as the board of directors may deem necessary to adopt and publish to render the use of said library and reading room of the greatest benefit, and the board may exclude from the use of said library and reading room any and all persons who shall wilfully violate such rules.

ANNUAL REPORT.

Section 2976. The board of directors shall make an annual report to the said board of education or school board or board of supervisors stating the condition of the library and property, the various sums of money received from all sources, and how much money has been expended and for what purpose, the number of books and periodicals on hand, the number added by purchase or gift during the year, the number lost and loaned out, the character and kind of books contained in the library, with such other statistics, information and suggestions as they may deem of general interest.

DONATIONS.

Section 2977. All persons desirous of making donations of money, books, personal property or real estate for the benefit of such library shall have the right to vest the same in the board of directors, to be held and controlled by such board when accepted for the use of such library and reading room, and as to such property said board shall be held and considered by the special trustees.

CITY COUNCIL—APPROPRIATE FUNDS.

Section 2978. To aid and facilitate the organization of a library in any city, village or township as in this article provided, where the same is required by the people thereof, and where in any city the sum of four hundred dollars or more shall have been donated and deposited with the city treasurer for that purpose, and to any village or township where the sum of one hundred and fifty dollars or more shall have been donated and deposited with the village or township treasurer for the benefit of such library, and also where such amount shall prior to the passage of this code have been donated and expended for the purchase of a library existing in any such city, village or township, the city council of such city is authorized and it shall be its duty to appropriate two hundred dollars from the general fund of such city for such library, for which amount a warrant shall be drawn on the city treasurer; and the board of trustees of such village or the board of supervisors of such township are authorized and it shall be their duty to appropriate one hundred dollars from the general fund of such village or township for such library, for which amount a warrant shall be drawn on such village or township treasurer; provided, that in the case of any library associations now existing it shall first agree to turn over to the library and reading room thus established all books, periodicals and other property. The treasurer of such city, village or township shall accept such warrant and apply the proceeds from the sale of the same to the library fund, which, together with the amount donated, shall be held subject to the order of the board of directors for such library; and the payment of such warrants shall be provided for in the next assessment of taxes in such city, village or township, and such library may be organized without submitting the same to a vote as provided in section 2972.

NORTH DAKOTA PUBLIC LIBRARY COMMISSION.

Session Laws 1907, Chap. 243—How Constituted.

Section 1. There is hereby created a state public library commission consisting of three members.

MEMBERS.

Section 2. The president of the North Dakota Library association and the superintendent of public instruction are hereby constituted ex-officio members of the said state public library commission; and the governor of the state shall appoint as soon as practicable after the passage and approval of this act one suitable person within the state as a member of the said state public library commission, which appointment shall be confirmed by the senate. The commission shall elect its own officers from among its own members, and shall also have power to select a competent person as librarian, who shall have control and be in charge of the library work of the commission.

MEMBERS—TERM OF OFFICE.

Section 3. The member appointed by the governor shall be appointed for a term of two years from April 1, 1907, and until his successor is appointed and qualified. In case of appointment to fill a vacancy caused by resignation, death or removal, the appointment shall be made for the unexpired term of the member whose death, resignation or removal caused the vacancy.

MEMBERS—COMPENSATION.

Section 4. No member of said state library commission shall ever receive any salary or per diem or compensation of any kind for services as such commissioner. Members of the state library commission shall be allowed and paid necessary traveling expenses in attending meetings of the commission or in visiting or establishing libraries, and other incidental and necessary expenses connected with the work of the commission.

POWERS AND DUTIES OF COMMISSION.

Section 5. The state library commission on and after its creation and organization, shall take over and add to the educational reference library and the system of traveling libraries, and shall continue the same, and, as its funds permit, shall increase the number and usefulness of the libraries. Any city, town, village, school district or community within the state of North Dakota may borrow books under the rules and regulations of the state library commission. The commission shall catalogue and otherwise prepare said books for circulation and shall make rules and regulations according to which the business of the commission shall be done; and also such rules and regulations as shall insure the care, preservation and safe return of all books loaned. The state libray commission shall have power and it shall be its duty to establish a legislative reference bureau for the information and assistance of the members of the legislative assembly in the work of legislation. The legislation of other states and information upon legal and economic questions shall be classified and catalogued in such a way as to render the same easy of access to members, thereby enabling them better to prepare for their work. It shall be the duty of the librarian of the state library commission to assist in every way possible the members of the legislative assembly in obtaining information and the preparation of bills.

ASSIST FREE PUBLIC LIBRARIES.

Section 6. The librarian or trustees of any free public library or the trustees of any village, town or community, entitled to borrow books from said traveling libraries, may, without charge, ask and receive advice and instruction from said state library commission upon any matter pertaining to the organization, maintenance or administration of the libraries, and the said commission shall, as far as possible, promote and assist by counsel and encouragement the formation of libraries where none exist, and the commission may also send its members to aid in organizing new libraries or improving those already established.

REPORT—PRINTING.

Section 7. The state library commission shall keep statistics of the free public libraries of North Dakota and a record of the work done and books loaned by said commission, and shall make a full report to each general session of the legislature of all expenditures by the commission, and of such statistics and records as shall show the work done by the commission, the use made of the traveling libraries, and all other matters which they deem expedient for the information of the legislature, and the printing of which, and all other printing coming within the purview of the library commission, shall be paid for by the state.

PLACE OF MEETING OF COMMISSION.

Section 8. There shall be provided in the office of the superintendent of public instruction a place of meeting and also office room for the librarian of the state library commission.

APPROPRIATION.

Section 9. There is hereby appropriated for the use and purposes of the state library commission any unexpended balances in the funds appropriated for the educational reference library and traveling libraries, and also an annual appropriation of fifteen hundred dollars out of any moneys in the state treasury not otherwise appropriated.

REPEAL.

Section 10. All acts and parts of acts in conflict with the provisions of this act are hereby repealed, especially any acts or parts of acts carrying any appropriation for the so-called educational reference library and traveling libraries.

EMERGENCY.

Section 11. Whereas, an emergency exists in that there is now no provision for a state library commission, this act shall take effect and be in force on and after its passage and approval.

Approved March 2, 1907.

PUBLIC DOCUMENT NO. 24

SECOND BIENNIAL REPORT

OF THE

North Dakota Public Library Commission

1909-1910

BISMARCK:
TRIBUNE, STATE PRINTERS AND BINDERS
1910.

This report as originally prepared contained 32 pages, of which the first 13 and last 2 are printed by the commissioners of public printing. The contents omitted are:

III. Reports from libraries.

IV. List of traveling library stations.

V. Personal mention:

In memoriam, Frank J. Thompson.
Changes in library commission.
Changes among librarians.
Extracts from letters.

VI. Illustrations:

Carnegie library, Devils Lake.
Carnegie library, Dickinson.
Portrait, Frank J. Thompson.

١

SECOND BIENNIAL REPORT

OF THE

North Dakota Public Library Commission

1909-1910

BISMARCK:
TRIBUNE, STATE PRINTERS AND BINDERS
1910.

TABLE OF CONTENTS.

	PAGE
Frontispiece, map showing library stations.	
Table of contents	3
Library commission directory, June 30, 1910	4
Letter of transmittal	5
I. Report of secretary	7
Statistics	7
Traveling libraries	7
Farmers' liabraries	8
Educational library	9
Publicity	10
Office work of the commission	10
II. Report of legislative reference librarian	13
III. Financial report	14-15

NORTH DAKOTA PUBLIC LIBRARY COMMISSION.

Directory June 30, 1910.

MEMBERS EX-OFFICIO.

O. G. Libby, Secretary State Historical Society, University, President.

W. L. Stockwell, State Superintendent of Public Instruction, Bismarck, Vice President.

Max Batt, President State Library Association, Agricultural College

Appointed by the Governor.

Mrs. Clara L. Darrow, Fargo,
Term expires March 10, 1913.

A. E. Sheets, Lakota.
Term expires March 10, 1915.

Mrs. Minnie Clarke Budlong,
Secretary and Director.

Julia A. Robinson,
Acting Secretary.

Sveinbjorn Johnson,
Legislative Reference Librarian.

Florence McPhee,
Stenographer.

Jessie M. Ramp,
Clerk.

LETTER OF TRANSMITTAL.

To the Honorable John Burke, Governor of North Dakota:

I have the honor to submit herewith a report of the North Dakota Public Library Commission from July 1, 1908, to June 30, 1910.

(MRS.) MINNIE CLARKE BUDLONG,
Secretary Public Library Commission.

NORTH DAKOTA STATE PUBLIC LIBRARY COMMISSION.

REPORT OF SECRETARY.

	July 1 1908	July 1 1910
Number of traveling library stations.........	19	138
Number of traveling libraries	19	117
Number of books in traveling libraries	851	6158
Number of farmers' libraries		25
Number of books in farmers' libraries		365
Number of educational reference books		2425
Number of public and institution libraries	27	33
Number of Carnegie library buildings	6	8

TRAVELING LIBRARIES.

Traveling libraries are fixed collections of books sent out in a wooden case containing shelf for holding the books while at the library station. The books in a case cannot be varied but there are eighteen different collections, which permits the adjusting to special needs of school or community to which sent.

Each case contains from forty to fifty books, twenty-five of which are fiction, fifteen for adults and ten for children; the remaining fifteen or twenty volumes are made up of several books on travel and biography, a few on problems of home and society, on recent discoveries and inventions, on aids in self improvement and selections in history and literature. There were nineteen of these libraries July 1, 1908, and nineteen stations. July 1, 1910, there were one hundred thirty-eight stations and one hundred seventeen libraries.

As the libraries are kept six months in a place each library serves two stations a year. During the two years sixty new libraries have been purchased at a cost of $3,105.39. The remaining additions have been made from the books received from the department of public instruction at the time the library commission was organized. Many of these libraries are kept in schools, others are stationed in post offices, stores, banks, club rooms, residences. The commission places them wherever six people agree to be responsible for their safe keeping and appoint one of their number to keep records of their circulation. The only expense is the transportation and the payment of cost price for books lost. A glance at the map used as frontispiece shows the distribution of these libraries.

FARMERS' LIBRARIES.

At the beginning of the period which this report covers there were no farmers' libraries circulated by the Commission.

Five duplicates of a list containing fifteen titles were purchased in December, 1909, and the work brought to the attention of the farmers at the Tri-State Grain Growers' convention held in Fargo January, 1910. The secretary had on exhibition a set of the books and called attention to them at a general session held in the opera house. The advice and co-operation of the farmers was solicited in the selection and circulation of these books and as a result of the encouragement received ten more copies of the first set were ordered and a second list was selected of which ten additional sets were purchased. The books were received too late in the season to be available for that winter's reading, but are ready for the winter of 1910-1911. Acknowledgements are due the professors in the Agricultural College, who have given so freely of their time and knowledge in the selection and introduction of these books. The supply of farmers' libraries will be increased as rapidly as the demand necessitates and funds permit, as this is an important factor in the upbuilding of the weath of the state. These boxes of books are sent free to any three responsible farmers who agree to circulate them in their vicinity. The only expense is the cost of transportation. As they are usually sent by freight, this is a very small item.

The lists of books available July 1, 1910, were:

List 1.

Austin—The Flock.
Card—Farm Management.
Craig—Judging Live Stock.
Davidson—Farm Machinery and Motors.
Edgar—The Story of a Grain of Wheat.
Harwood—New Creations in Plant Life.
Hunt—Cereals in America.
Mayo—Diseases of Animals.
Parloa—Home Economics.
Shaw—Animal Breeding.
Streeter—The Fat of the Land.
Smith—Profitable Stock Feeding.
Hunt—Forage and Fibre Crops in America.
Lipman—Bacteria in Relation to Country Life.
Lock—Variation, Heredity and Evolution.

List 2.

Bailey—Training of Farmers.
Bruncken—N. A. Forests and Forestry.
Green—Popular Fruit Growing.
Gurler—The Farm Dairy.

MacDonald—Dry Farming.
Massey—Practical Farming.
Maynard—The Small Country Place.
Michels—Dairy Farming.
Powell—Hedges, Windbreaks, etc.
Sardo—American Poultry Culture.
Shaw—Feeding Farm Animals.
Shepperd—Elements of Agriculture.
Van Norman—First Lessons in Dairying.
Plumb—Types and Breeds of Farm Animals.

Since July 1, 1910, there have been added the following:

LIST 3.

Burkett—Farm Stock.
King—Physics of Agriculture.
Taylor—Agricultural Economics.
Snyder—Human Foods.
Wilkinson—Practical Agriculture.
Smith—Economic Entomology.
Roberts—The Fertility of the Land.
Hunt—Choosing a Farm.
Burkett—Soils.
Roberts—Farmer's Business Handbook.
Shaw—Clovers.
Wing—Alfalfa.
Dietrich—Swine Husbandry.

LIST 4.

Wilcox—Farm Animals.
Collins—The New Agriculture.
Hopkins—Soil Fertility and Permanent Agriculture.
Cobleigh—Handy Farm Devices.
Burkett—Farmers' Veterinarian.
Publow—Questions and Answers on Milk.
Publow—Questions and Answers on Butter Making.
King—Ventilation.
Smith—Our Insect Enemies and Friends.
Green—Vegetable Gardening.
Spillman—Grasses.
Fletcher—Soils.
Harwood—The New World.
Shaw—Forage Crops.

EDUCATIONAL REFERENCE LIBRARY.

This department consisted July 1, 1908, of encyclopedias and reference books in history and literature received from the department of public instruction when the commission was organized. The collection has been increased by the purchase of 107 volumes, costing $211.31, and numbered July 1, 1910, 2,445 volumes. The entire collection has been classified and catalogued, groups have been made up for study club work, notably in art, music and North Dakota history and literature. Any club sending in its program of study may receive books on that line to be kept as long a part of the club year as need may be.

Individuals preparing papers on special topics receive assistance. Advanced students are sent works in their specialty.

Debaters receive aid from the mounted clippings taken from the Legislative Reference Department.

PUBLICITY.

There is great need that the work of the commission be better understood by the people of the state. Comparatively few realize that books, information and assistance in study will be furnished practically free on application.

To aid in the dissemination of accurate knowledge on the subject there have been several methods adopted. Folders and leaflets are widely distributed. Especial effort has been made to present the subject to the teachers in their state meetings and some trustees meetings and county institutes have been reached. The exhibits held at the Tri-State Grain Growers' Convention in Fargo, January, 1910, and at the State Fair July, 1910, reached many farmers. The meeting of the State Library Association held September 30th and October 1st in Fargo and Moorhead in conjunction with the librarians of Northwestern Minnesota, awakened much interest and enthusiasm. The better farming train that traveled from Fargo to Beach in June, 1910, and stopped at two or three places each day carried a library exhibit in charge of a member of the commission, who distributed literature and explained the benefits to many thousands of farmers.

These and other publicity methods should be continued until the nature and advantages of the work are understood throughout the state.

OFFICE WORK OF THE COMMISSION.

The work in a Library Commission office is manifold. Most of the records are kept on cards typewritten. Each traveling library must have seven cards, as follows:

An application card filed in order of receipt. Application filled after libraries are sent, filed alphabetically by station.

A station card, containing name of station, county, shipping station, postoffice, railroad, population of town or village, number of library, date sent, date returned, condition when sent and returned, readers, circulation, name of librarian, filed alphabetically by name of town.

Two sets of library cards, each containing history of library, its number, kind, whether school or community, source, number

EXHIBIT PUBLIC LIBRARY COMMISSION, STATE FAIR, 1910.

of volumes, name of place, date sent, date returned, condition, readers and circulation; one filed numerically by the number of the library and one alphabetically by month in which library is due.

A card acknowledging receipt, filed alphabetically by station.

A card for a library over due, filed alphabetically by name of station.

Every book in each library must have an author card, containing full name of author, name of book and numbers of the traveling libraries in which it is contained. Each book should also have a title card. These cards are filed alphabetically in card cabinets for convenience in consultation. Each library returned to the office must be checked with its list, all missing or damaged books reported back to the station, every book examined minutely and the covers of most of them scrubbed with soap and water and then shellaced and the pages cleaned by erasers or pumice stone—slow processes. Many of the books require skillful mending. They are then repacked, new lists and supplies for the borrowers inclosed and the library is ready to start again. Farmers' libraries receive the same treatment, but must be kept in separate records, as they circulate in different collections and under different rules.

Books in the Educational Reference are shelved by subjects and must be classified and catalogued before they can be of use. This requires a card catalog with two to five or more cards for each book. These books are loaned to clubs and individuals throughout the state, which requires another system of loan records.

The circulation of books in the capital and vicinity necessitates another charging system, such as city libraries maintain.

The Legislative Reference Library, consisting largely of cuttings from papers and periodicals, means much work in the selecting, mounting and distributing of these clippings.

The demands of the publicity department require preparation of materials for folders, pamphlets and newspapers and also, when requested, talks on library subjects by members of the staff.

The reference questions contained in a single letter sent the department often requires hours and occasionally days of time in research. There is also the growing correspondence needed to keep in touch with the traveling library stations in the state and to give the counsel and advice to public libraries, and to prepare the statistics, called for by law.

The growing demand for traveling, farmers' and club libraries necessitates the selection, purchase and preparation for circulation of many books. Recent publications must be watched and the needs of many individuals, schools and communities studied. Before a book is ordered, a card is made containing author, title, series, number of volumes, date, edition, publisher, price, by whom recommended and where reviewed, also date ordered and from what firm. If it is a book for the classified part of the library, the class number, book number and Library of Congress, card number must be looked up and entered on the card. When the book is received, it must be entered in the accession book with date, author, title, publisher and price, and the accession number and date received and cost price must be entered on the card to complete the record of the book. These cards are filed and form a complete history of every book in the library. The book must next have its leaves cut, the pocket inserted, the card for the pocket typed, the call number inked on its back, and the catalog cards made and filed. Not until all these processes (and others omitted for the sake of brevity) are completed is a book ready for circulation. This is not a complete list, but gives some idea of the complex and numerous details of work in a commission office and the amount of clerical assistance needed. There is also the growth of the library activities throughout the state to be fostered and often active field work and assistance in organization to be given.

STATISTICS.

In compliance with the requirements of section 7, chapter 156, of the laws of 1909, statistics of administration, finances, books purchased and circulation have been collected and classified from thirty-two public and institutional libraries. Records of one hundred seventeen traveling library stations with the work done have been listed. A brief history of the changes in the library commission, due to the amendment of the library law, in 1909, and of the changes among librarians in the state, due to death or resignation, has been prepared. These records are on file in the office of the library commission at Bismarck.

(Mrs.) Minnie Clarke Budlong,
Secretary and Director Public Library Commission.

Bismarck, North Dakota, December 1, 1910.

LEGISLATIVE REFERENCE WORK.

During the past two years the legislative reference department has enlarged its collection of material on public questions likely to come before the legislature or which may be of interest to citizens and public officials generally. It is the aim of the workers to get together in condensed and classified form information on public questions, legal and economic, that will be of practical service to the members of the legislature in their work. To this end laws of other states have been obtained, reports of judicial decisions construing them, discussions of their practical operation by the boards or officials who administer or enforce them, as well as information relating to the economic conditions under which these laws are enforced and which they were designed to meet.

The department has prepared two bulletins, Permanent State Tax Commissions and Good Roads, which were published by the Commission.

At the request of the State Railroad Commission, much material was obtained pertaining to express rates in this state and elsewhere.

In addition, briefs have been prepared on various questions of interest to legislators or public officials in the state.

A complete file of bills introduced in the sessions of 1903, 1905, 1907 and 1909, has been indexed and bound for convenient reference by members and others interested.

Between sessions we find that our reference material is in much demand for the use of high school and other debating societies.

The existence of this library, containing as it does references on public questions not available elsewhere in the state, we hope will have a tendency to bring about a selection of practical subjects for debate, rather from the field of government and sociology than from the old and threadbare lists of little or no educational importance.

SVEINBJORN JOHNSON,
Legislative Reference Librarian.

REPORT OF SECRETARY AND TREASURER OF NORTH DAKOTA PUBLIC LIBRARY COMMISSION.

July 1, 1908—June 30, 1909.

Date	Expenditures	Transportation of Books	Books Purchased	Periodicals and Membership Fees	Stationery and Postage	Printing	Aids to Libraries	Supplies	Commission Expenses	Salaries	Office Furniture	Miscellaneous
1908—												
July	$ 231.00	$	$	$	$	$	$	$ 10.00	$86.70	$130.00	$4.30	$
Aug.	377.20	18.24	5.00	11.50	10.00	109.70	1.25			213.25	8.26	
Sept.	343.30	9.24	8.40		20.00	3.00		37.00		265.66		
Oct.	288.38	6.47	3.26					.90		277 00	.75	
Nov.	301.66	6.86		1.00			4.50		43.30	246.00		
Dec.	504.85	16.33	61.92	5.00	7.50	13.50		34.85		350.00		15.75
1909—												
Jan.	231.90	2.80				29.10				200.00		
Feb.	562.00	8.50	169.07	19.00			7.61	.75	57.07	300.00		
March	438.00		84.95	38.80	8.00			4.25		300.00	2.00	
April	478.24	2.50	1.99	5.00	106.20			1.55	26.00	335.00		
May	933.60	7.45	520.89	7.25	10.00		14.51		3.20	335.00		35.30
June	431.80	7.75	65.84		10.00					235.00	18.41	94.80
	$5121.93	$86.14	$921.32	$87.55	$171.70	$155.30	$27.87	$89.30	$216.27	$ 91	$33.72	$145.85

REPORT OF SECRETARY AND TREASURER OF NORTH DAKOTA PUBLIC LIBRARY COMMISSION.

July 1, 1909—June 30, 1910.

Date	Expenditures	Transportation of Books	Books Purchased	Periodicals and Membership Fees	Stationery and Postage	Printing	Aids to Libraries	Supplies	Commission Expenses	Salaries	Office Furniture	Miscellaneous
1909—												
July	$ 854.31	$ 36.83	$ 310.95	$	$	$	$12.50	$	$	$ 458.88	$	$35.15
Aug.	408.77	5.00	36.24	7.00			1.03	10.50		335.00	14.00	
Sept.	545.90	4.25	190.37	10.85	10.00			.90	74.40	255.13		
Oct.	522.59	10.18	68.86					8.45	25.10	410.00		
Nov.	540.47	4.33	41.44	1.00		7.00		30.50		270.00	186.20	
Dec.	399.34	29 95		1.00	31.84	3.00	3.00		45.55	285.00		
1910—												
Jan.	709.73	12.44	90.45	17.00				52.63	127.21	410.00		
Feb.	1025.36	35.74	640.74	22.00	6.00		5.00		23.75	292.13		
Mch.	561.91	11.43	214.30	2.20	11.00			22.33	1.90	298.75		
Apr.	958.35	19.00	539.68	17.00			1.00	7.10	32.85	304.00	37.72	
May	638.16	11.77	279.99	11.70	25.00			11.95	2.75	295.00		
June	379.87	22.90	13.82	2.00	5.00			7.60	33.55	295.00		
	$7544.76	$203.82	$2426.84	$91.75	$88.84	$10.00	$22.53	$151.96	$367.06	$3908.89	$237.92	$35.15

PUBLIC DOCUMENT NO. 28

THIRD BIENNIAL REPORT

OF THE

NORTH DAKOTA PUBLIC LIBRARY COMMISSION

1911-1912

KNIGHT PRINTING COMPANY
STATE PRINTERS
FARGO

THIRD BIENNIAL REPORT

OF THE

North Dakota Public Library Commission

1911-1912

FARGO
KNIGHT PRINTING CO.
PRINTERS

TABLE OF CONTENTS

Frontispiece—map showing library stations

	Page
Table of contents	3
Library Commission directory	4
Letter of transmittal	5
Report of Secretary—	
Summary of statistics by departments	6
Traveling library system	7
School libraries	7
Community libraries	7
Farmers' libraries	8
Foreign books	8
Expense of traveling libraries	8
to borrowers	8
to the state	9
Circulation	9
Indefinite loan	10
Libraries—where kept	10
Report school and community library stations	11
Report farmers' library stations	22
Educational reference department	26
Field and publicity work	26
Public libraries—	
Carnegie buildings	29
Memorial buildings	29
Statistics, financial	30
Statistics, circulation	31
Comparative statistics	32
Libraries in state institutions	34
College and club libraries	34
Publications	35
Report of Legislative Reference Librarian	37
Financial report	38

LIST OF ILLUSTRATIONS
(Between pages 20 and 21)

Carnegie Library	Devils Lake
Carnegie Library	Dickinson
Carnegie Library	Minot
James Memorial Library	Williston

REPORT OF SECRETARY

NORTH DAKOTA PUBLIC LIBRARY COMMISSION.

Directory June 30, 1912.

Members Ex-Officio.

O. G. Libby, Secretary State Historical Society.

E. J. Taylor, Superintendent of Public Instruction.

R. A. Nestos, President State Library Association.

Members Appointed by the Governor.

Mrs. Clara L. Darrow, Fargo.—Term expires March 10, 1913.

A. E. Sheets, Lakota.—Term expires March 10, 1915.

OFFICERS:

O. G. Libby, President.

Mrs. Minnie Clarke Budlong, Secretary and Director.

STAFF.

I. A. Acker, Legislative Reference Librarian.

Florence MacPhee, Chief Traveling Library Department.

Haldora Peterson, Stenographer.

Elsie Smith, Clerk.

LETTER OF TRANSMITTAL.

To the Thirteenth Legislative Assembly:

Gentlemen:

As required by Chap. 156, Sec. 7, Laws of 1909, the report of the North Dakota State Public Library Commission for the period July 1, 1910 to June 30, 1912, is herewith submitted.

O. G. Libby,
President Public Library Commission.

NORTH DAKOTA STATE PUBLIC LIBRARY COMMISSION

Report of Secretary

Summary of Statistics by Departments

	1908	1910	1912
Traveling Library Department			
Number of traveling libraries	19	117	*151
Number of books in traveling libraries	851	6,158	7,165
Number of traveling library stations	19	138	356
Number of farmers' libraries	....	25	95
Number of books in farmers' libraries	....	365	1,270
Educational reference department			
Number of educational reference books	....	2,425	3,175
Number of books loaned from educational reference library	....	....	4,570
Number of pamphlets and clippings loaned	....	....	1,542
Indefinite loan	....	....	1,190
Field work			
Number of public libraries in state	27	33	37
Number of Carnegie buildings	6	8	10
Number of Memorial buildings	1	1	5
Number of trips of organizer	....	....	12
Number of library visits	....	....	22
Publicity			
Number of addresses given	....	....	12
Number of advertising trips and exhibits	....	....	8

Legislative reference department

The work of the legislative reference department cannot be summarized in statistics. For an account of that work see the report of the Legislative Reference Librarian page 37.

*15 traveling libraries were withdrawn in 1911, worn out. 105 of these collections are suited to community use, and 46 to school use.

TRAVELING LIBRARY SYSTEM.

The traveling library system consists of fixed collections of books sent out in wooden cases for three to six months' loan, wherever in the state responsible people will agree to care for them, to circulate them free of charge and to return them to Bismarck with freight both ways paid. The selection of books varies, some cases containing a larger proportion of reading for adults, and some being better adapted to children or young people. Some are largely composed of books for recreation and inspiration. Others are technical books for clubs and students. The demand for these libraries exceeds the supply. **In the winter of 1911-1912, there were on file over fifty applications which could not be filled for want of books.**

The 2500 books taken over from the department of Public Instruction are wearing out and must soon be replaced.

$5,000.00 could be wisely spent in increasing the number and variety of the traveling libraries.

There are three different kinds of traveling libraries, known as school libraries, community libraries and farmers' libraries.

SCHOOL LIBRARIES.

These consist of forty to fifty supplemental books in history, travel, literature and science and contain some juvenile fiction. They are intended principally for use in schoolhouses, although they contain much reading of interest to homes and communities. At present they are deficient in books for primary and intermediate work. There is special need of small boxes of twenty to twenty-five books suited to the first five grades of the country schools. Teachers write some school-houses in the state are without a single book and they find pupils who have never seen any book but a text-book.

COMMUNITY LIBRARIES.

These are boxes containing forty to fifty books, suited to all ages and conditions. Usually, fifteen books are adult fiction and ten juvenile. The remainder consists of classed books—history, literature, sociology, travel, biography and other up-to-date works of general interest. These libraries are popular in stores, club rooms, residences, offices and other central locations. A list of the places where traveling libraries have been kept will be found on another page.

FARMERS' LIBRARIES.

Farmers' libraries are made up of technical books on farming, stock-raising, machinery, gardening, poultry, dairying and related subjects. They are in great demand among the farmers during the winter months and in the schools teaching agriculture. It is impossible to show in figures the use made of these books as there is no librarian such as the traveling libraries have to keep a record of circulation. The cases containing twelve to fifteen books are sent wherever three men sign an application card, and may be kept three months if freely circulated in the community. In schools they are used as text and reference by classes in agriculture. The Bankers' Association was quick to see the financial benefit to the state of the circulation of these books and through their committee on agriculture has been active in introducing them. Nineteen per cent of the farmers' libraries sent out have been kept in banks. This method of agricultural education was one item which helped win the cup for North Dakota at the Bankers' and Educators' conference in St. Paul. July, 1912. A letter from the librarian of the American Bankers' Association, Aug. 6, 1912, says, "North Dakota seems to be the only state where stations (Farmers' library) have been established in banks."

FOREIGN BOOKS.

A few German and Norwegian books have been purchased, and may be included with the English books in a traveling library whenever a station so requests.

These are not books for children, but are standard works in fiction, travel and other subjects, suited to the older members of the household who can not be expected to learn to read English.

EXPENSE OF TRAVELING LIBRARIES.

To Borrowers—The heaviest boxes weigh less than a hundred pounds, and often the freight is not over twenty-five cents. If there are transfers, the expense is greater. A library shipped from Bismarck to Hope costs ninety cents each way for freight. After six months' use, the station reported 186 readers, making the total expense less than one cent to each reader. For that expenditure of one cent, each patron had the opportunity of reading all of the 48 books contained in the library. The records showed that many of the volumes were loaned twelve to eighteen times.

To the State—Books differ greatly in wearing qualities. Some editions, particularly illustrated books, fall to pieces in a dozen to twenty readings, others remain in good condition after more than twice that number of recorded loans. If a book, costing the state fifty to ninety cents to purchase, is circulated twenty to thirty times, as often occurs, in these traveling libraries, how trifling is that expense compared with the cost to an individual of the purchase at retail of the same book, and the waste involved in the disuse of the book after the purchaser has read it.

The cost of books purchased for traveling libraries varies greatly according to titles and editions chosen. The average cost of each book in a few series, selected to show the extreme range of prices, is given below.

Series number	No. of books in series	Total cost of library	Average cost of each book
220-224	48	$24.57	$ .51
210-214	46	29.70	.64
225-229	48	32.99	.68
215-219	43	30.83	.71
180-184	50	50.79	1.01
185-189	50	55.00	1.10

In 100 libraries, containing 4960 volumes, bought in this biennium, the average cost per book was 90 cents. Some of these copies have already been to four or five different stations and have a recorded circulation of twenty or more readers without being worn out. With a little mending, they will reach thirty or more readings before being placed in the "Indefinite Loan" collection—a cost to the state for purchase of not over three cents for each borrower.

CIRCULATION.

It is difficult to count circulation. A book is carried home and read by the whole family, and still the records show only one reader—the name of the borrower. Books kept in schools are used in the building by many pupils, and yet only the loans made for home use are recorded. In some cases books returned to the Commission showed so much more use than the reports indicated, that letters of inquiry were sent and elicited replies like the following: "My wife, my son and myself read every book in the case, but did not think it worth while to put it down." "The library was used in the high school as a reference library, and in the building in connection with the preparation and recitation of lessons. This accounts for the fact that there was no circulation list."

Other library commissions estimate that every book taken home is perused by three to five readers. In these traveling library statistics only recorded borrowers are counted, which is probably not one-fifth of the actual number using the books. In 414 libraries in which records were kept, 5616 borrowers were reported with a circulation of 35,797. 15,000 readers and a circulation of 100,000 would be nearer the facts in the case. A few of the stations reporting the largest number of readers for each library are:

Fairdale	95
Hope	186
Sykeston	95
Williston	108

Fairmount reports the largest average circulation—over ten books to each reader. Loraine reports a circulation of 1040 for four libraries.

Perhaps the greatest usefulness of these libraries is not where the number of readers is largest, but where a few families, far from town and neighbors, find in the entertainment and sociability these books promote, the principal recreation available through the winter months.

What expenditure of state money gives more pleasure or profit to a greater number of inhabitants or reaches to the same degree the isolated districts especially in need of encouragement?

INDEFINITE LOAN.

Books in the traveling libraries are cleaned and mended after each trip, but there comes a time when the book is so worn, the cost of repairing approximates the price of a new volume. The book is then placed in the "Indefinite Loan" collection and sent to some institution or school that can profit by its remaining usefulness. In 1911-12, 1190 books were thus disposed of, most of them being sent to country schools. Trustees and teachers are glad to receive them, even though soiled and worn, as there is transportation only one way to be paid and the books are allowed to wear out in the school.

LIBRARIES—WHERE KEPT

	Traveling libraries	Farmers' libraries	Total
Residence	84	54	138
School	187	9	196
Post Office	13	5	18
Business Office	13	6	19
Newspaper Office	3	1	4
County Superintendent's Office	6	1	7
Bank	13	20	33
Store	27	9	26
Club Room	4	2	6
Church	2	....	2
Hotel	4	....	4
Fort	1	....	1
Library	1	2	3

REPORT OF SCHOOL AND COMMUNITY LIBRARY STATIONS TO JULY 1, 1912

Name of Station—Date Established	No. of libraries	Average No. of readers	Total circulation	Library Where Kept	Name of Librarian
Abercrombie—Mar. 1910	1	10	....	Residence	Th[illegible] Flaa
Absaraka—Jan. 1911	1	22	79	School	L. J. Hanson
*Alta—Sept. 1911	2	34	132	Post office	Jno. [illegible]
[illegible]rose—Jan. 1910	1	42	....	Office of Ambrose Pub. Co.	Ray J. [illegible]
Aneta R. R. No. 5—Apr. 1909	2	25	[illegible]	School	J. A. [illegible]
Aneta—Jan. 1910	1	15	52	Law office	Halvard Norskog
*Antler—Apr. 1912	1	...	....	Com. club room	H. N. [illegible]
Aplin—Jan. 1911	1	22	46	Residence	Carl Stephens
[illegible] Creek—Oct. 1911	1	21	132	Schoolhouse	Gertrude [illegible]
Arena—Dec. 1911	1	52	....	Schoolhouse	Jenett Purdy
Bantry—Feb. 1911	1	6	32	Schoolhouse	Emma Bartel
[illegible]—Oct. 1911	1	...	....	School	M. Arveson
[illegible] Feb. 1910	2	42	306	Post office	A. S. McMillan
*Barlow—Dec. 1911	1	....	....	Post office	J. H. Kilmer
Barton—June 1908	2	...	94	Schoolhouse	Grace [illegible]
*Beach—Sept. 1911	2	17	62	Cong. Church	E. W [illegible]
*Beach—June 1912	1	..	....	Office	Hazel Chrysler
Belfield School No. 1—Aug. 1909	1	17	90	Schoolhouse	F. Speedling
*Belfield Twp. 141—Apr. 1912	1	....	....	Residence	L. O. [illegible]
*Belfield—Mar. 1911	2	21	160	Residence	D. E. McLeod
Belfield—Jan. 1911	1	....	77	Tryberg school	Ruth Smith
Benedict—Jan. 1912	1	31	171	School	K. Christenson
Bentley—Oct. 1911	1	27	75	School	G. C. [illegible]
Berg (Blue Butte)—July 1908	2	25	40	Residence	Mrs. O. I. Berg
Berg—Oct. 1908	1	10	38	Residence	Louis Evenson
Bergen—Feb. 1911	1	..	....	Residence	O. Moxness
Bi[illegible]—Oct. 1910	1	19	31	Grant Hotel	Mary Brost
Bisbee—Jan. 1910	1	.	....	[illegible]ol	Wells [illegible]
Bismarck—Feb. 1910	....	....	....	Library Com'n office	
Bismarck—Oct. 1910	2	25	90	Y. M. A. Reading Room	[illegible]est Wright
Bordulac—Aug. 1908	2	28	138	Bank	A. H. Wentland
*Bostonia—Apr. 1911	2	24	67	Residence	T. A. [illegible]
*Bowdish—Oct. 1911	1	...	....	Schoolhouse	John L. Cass
*Bowdon—May 1912	1	...	....	Bank	H. F. Konichek
[illegible]ct. 1911	1	45	130	Office Bldg.	Geo. A. Totten

REPORT OF SCHOOL AND COMMUNITY LIBRARY STATIONS TO JULY 1, 1912—Continued

Name of Station—Date Established	No. of libraries	Average No. of readers	Total circulation	Library Where Kept	Name of Librarian
Bowman—Oct. 1908	1	....	....	School	Marie Hovick
Braddock—Oct. 1910	1	17	61	School	H. N. Fitch
Braddock—Feb. 1909	2	27	103	School	Mrs. O. M. Vie
Brinsmade—Oct. 1910	1	32	100	Office	F. H. Bowman
*Brittin—June 1912	1	....	....	School	Mabel Carlson
Brittin—Feb. 1911	2	26	156	Residence	Mrs. L. A. Couch
*Brocket—June 1912	1	....	....	Store	H. Svoboda
Buchanan—Nov. 1909	1	24	112	School	V. Keating
Bucyrus—Oct. 1908	2	27	....	Restaurant	Mrs. E. Mahon
Buford—Nov. 1909	1	18	70	Residence	B. E. Ellerick
*Burnstad—Mar. 1911	2	63	114	Bank	Chas. Hernett
Burt—Dec. 1911	1	19	50	School	Bernice Bysom
Cando—Jan. 1910	1	30	....	Co. Supt's office	John Gang
Canfield—Nov. 1910	1	11	66	Residence	M. Fjelde
Carlson—Sept. 1910	1	27	98	Residence	E. M. Carlson
Carlyle—Dec. 1909	3	30	266	Residence	E. L. Wiley
Carson—Dec. 1911	1	30	67	School	E. E. Boyden
Cathay—Oct. 1909	1	40	151	Pub. sch.	Alvilda Johnson
*Cathay—Dec. 1908	6	18	173	Residence	M. Josund
Cavalier—Sept. 1910	1	24	96	Office	E. H. Gunderson
Center—Nov. 1908	1	11	24	Bank	H. H. Kenyon
Christine—Oct. 1910	1	15	70	School	Inger Skindrud
*Church's Ferry—May 1908	6	43	716	Hotel	C. E. Harding
Cleveland—Mar. 1911	1	16	91	Residence	C. G. Foye
Cleveland—Feb. 1911	1	12	....	Residence	Y. C. Sund
Cleveland—May 1909	1	....	....	School	Mrs. L. B. Christopher
Clifford—Oct. 1909	1	47	470	School	J. A. [illegible]
Clyde—Mar. 1910	2	34	193	School	H. [illegible]
Coal Harbor—Nov. 1909	1	....	....	School No. 2	Anna Norrdin
Coal Harbor—Dec. 1911	1	20	94	School	Rhoda [illegible]
Columbia—Nov. 1910	2	23	202	School	M. McIntosh
Columbus—Oct. 1911	1	24	70	School No. 3	R. L. Lingeman
Columbus—Jan. 1910	1	18	29	School	T. L. Thorkildson
Conway—May, 1910	1	22	58	School Dist. No. 41	Mina Sellstad
Conway—Oct. 1909	1	30	78	School	J. L. Lawrence

REPORT OF SCHOOL AND COMMUNITY LIBRARY STATIONS TO JULY 1, 1912—Continued

Name of Station—Date Established	No. of libraries	Average No. of readers	Total circulation	Library Where Kept	Name of Librarian
Cooperstown—Nov. 1911	1	10	37	Residence	Elisa Brosten
Coteau—Feb. 1911	1	18	35	School	elga Trovaten
*Coulee—Apr. 1912	1	....	....	Store	E. L. Evenson
*Courtenay—Aug. 1911	2	64	206	Bank	Loran Nichols
Courtenay—Oct. 1909	1	....	....	School	A E. Ross
*Crary—Feb. 1912	1	....	....	School	Marion Knowles
*Crary—Feb. 1912	1	....	....	Odessa Twp. school	Marion S. Kirk
Crosby—Oct. 1908	3	58	215	Store	C E. Rice
Crosby—Oct. 1910	1	48	117	School	Teresa O'Reilly
rystal—Jan. 1912	1	37	171	School	Beatrice Watson
Crysta—May 1912	1	....	....	School Dist. No. 86	Julius Puppe
aglum—July 1909	1	27	....	Residence	Mrs. D. M. Hart
Davenport—Feb. 1911	1	35	84	School	LaDelle Briggle
Dawson—Oct 1911	1	....	....	School	Celia A. Miller
Dawson—Jan. 1909	1	18	35	School	A. E. Ross
Dazey—May 1911	2	49	144	Editor's office	Leo Ratcliffe
Deering—Feb. 1910	1	....	74	School	E. D. Sylvester
Dickey—May 1911	1	11	11	Com. club rooms	H. D. Mack
Dickinson—Aug. 1910	2	22	153	Residence	Mrs. A. Shipley
ogden—Feb. 19 0	3	37	244	School	Julia Poroth
Do nybrook—June 1908	4	25	212	Store	C. M. Graves
*Doyon—Oct. 1908	4	82	416	Post office	S. A. Chase
Drake—Dec. 1911	1	21	42	Residence	Gust Berndt
Drake—Dec. 1911	1	14	23	School No. 3	E. I. Jacobson
Drake—Feb. 1910	1	26	86	Office	W E. Blatherwick
Drake—Oct. 1910	1	26	214	School	L. F. Guthrie
Driscoll—Nov 1909	2	32	152	School	L. D. Burgess
Driscoll—Nov 1910	1	....	....	School	Emma Bartel
rbin—Feb. 1912	1	30	40	School	E. Baumgarten
Dwight—Dec. 1911	1	....	....	School	Inger Skindrud
Dwight—Dec. 1909	1	56	....	School No. 3	Andrew Soule
Eckman—Feb. 1911	1	17	27	Residence	Inez Tweidt
Edgar—Nov. 1910	1	....	....	Residence	Amy Zabel
Edinburg—Nov. 1910	2	7	30	Residence	S. Thordarson
Edinburg—Jan. 1911	2	40	304	Bank	A. C. Thompson

REPORT OF SCHOOL AND COMMUNITY LIBRARY STATIONS TO JULY 1, 1912—Continued

Name of Station—Date Established	No. of libraries	Average No. of readers	Total circulation	Library Where Kept	—Name of Librarian
Edinburg—Feb. 1910	1	....	....	School	A. T. Green
*Edmore—June 1911	1	....	....	School No. 19	Margaret Baker
*Edmore—June 1911	1	....	....	School	Agnes Connor
Edmunds—Jan. 1912	1	12	54	Residence	J. W. Tangney
Egeland—Dec. 1910	1	....	....	School	Amy Brightbill
*Elbowoods—July 1909	5	33	405	Residence	Deborah Hall
Elgin—Sept. 1911	1	31	110	Residence	Mrs. G. Hoffman
Elmgrove—Feb. 1910	3	9	104	Residence	Una C. Fleek
*Elsworth—Feb. 1912	1	....	....	School	Gertrude Stevens
Emerado—Sept. 1908	1	....	154	School	C. E. Stoliker
*Enderlin—Mar. 1912	1	....	....	Store	Mrs. E. Bangert
Englevale—Apr. 1911	2	25	200	Store	C. G. Carlson
Enloe—Jan. 1911	1	19	54	Residence	O. Bolme
Fairdale—Dec. 1911	1	95	172	School	A. G. Strand
Fairdale—Apr. 1908	3	36	110	Residence	H. F. Davis
Fairmount—Dec. 1911	1	23	50	Bank	W. H. Cox
Fairmount—Jan. 1912	1	15	102	School No. 3	Clara Wagner
Fairmount—Jan. 1912	1	21	215	School No. 4	Anna Pechacek
Fairmount—Nov. 1910	1	....	....	School	Clara Wagner
Fallon—Nov. 1910	1	....	....	School	Adeline Wilson
Fayette—Nov. 1911	1	21	59	Store	Anna Fisher
*Fergus—Oct. 1911	2	40	124	School	Marion E. Feir
*Fergus—Sept. 1911	2	40	192	School	Earl E. Feir
Fergus—Oct. 1908	2	36	326	Residence	Geo. O. Espeland
*Fertile—Dec. 1911	1	....	....	Post office	Jno. L. Sorenson
Finley—Feb. 1910	1	....	....	Residence	Jno. Birkland
*Forbes—Mar. 1910	1	15	....	Residence	T. R. Shimmin
*Ft. Clark—Mar. 1912	1	....	....	Store	E. W. Chamberlain
Ft. Lincoln—Nov. 1911	1	....	....	Post hospital	J. A. Dailey
Ft. Ransom—Sept. 1910	2	32	264	Store	C. G. Carlson
*Fullerton—June 1912	1	....	....	Residence	Mrs. J. W. Julian
Fullerton—Mar. 1910	4	15	245	Residence	Mrs. W. H. Church
Gackle—July 1908	2	....	....	Bank	E. G. Blodeu
Galchutt—Jan. 1911	1	19	128	School No. 7	A. Skindrud
Gardena—Nov. 1911	1	23	48	Pub. sch.	Marie L. Stack

REPORT OF SCHOOL AND COMMUNITY LIBRARY STATIONS TO JULY 1, 1912 Continued

Name of Station—Date Established	No. of libraries	Average No. of readers	Total circulation	Library Where Kept	Name of Librarian
Gardner—Nov. 1911	1	19	103	School	Matilda Aasen
Gardner—Nov. 1910	2	35	310	School	P. M. Paulson
Garrison—Dec. 1911	1	20	46	School	Michael Rosen
Garrison—Nov. 1910	1	26	110	Drug store	J. M. Boyd
Gascoyne—Jan. 1910	3	39	267	Store	H. G. Fischbein
*Gascoyne—Dec. 1911	1	....	....	School	Della Langen
Gem—Apr. 1910	1	....	....	Residence	G. M. Anderson
*Gem—Dec. 1910	1	....	....	School	Louise Ross
*Giese—Jan. 1912	1	....	....	Residence	Mrs. K. Cahill
Gladstone—Nov. 1910	1	....	....	School	L. F. Green
Gladstone—Jan. 1912	1	26	94	School	Otto Pippin
Gladstone—Jan. 1911	2	18	49	Residence	J. M. Turner
*Gladys—Jan. 1911	2	24	109	Residence	F. Marshal
Gladys—Mar. 1908	2	29	111	Residence	Lilly Bailey
Glen Ullin—Oct. 1910	1	38	94	School	A. C. Culve
Grafton R. F. D. No. 5—May 1909	1	10	18	Farm house	Geo. K. Dike
Grandin—Jan. 1911	1	....	36	Residence	Agnes Bradis
Grandin—Feb. 1908	1	....	....	School	Willard Bel
Granville—Nov. 1910	2	34	159	Law office	Leo McLaughlin
Guelph—Jan. 1912	1	27	118	School	C. B. Amley
Gwyther—Mar. 1911	2	44	263	Store	J. Gwyther
Hamar—Feb. 1910	1	....	....	Residence	O. E. Hanson
Hamilton—Aug. 1908	1	16	37	Store	C. L. Spring
Hampden—Apr. 1911	1	12	46	Residence	E. E. Bergren
Hankinson—Mar. 1910	1	....	....	School	Hazel Hubbard
Hankinson—Dec. 1910	1	16	50	School	Sina Romerein
Hannaford—Oct. 1909	1	....	....	School	E. Frederickson
Hannah (R. D.)—Apr. 1911	1	....	....	Residence	O. R. Daniels
Hannah—Nov. 1911	1	25	....	Bank	Belle McKnight
Hastings—Dec. 1908	4	28	430	Store	Len S. Reitan
Haynes—Dec. 1908	1	....	....	Residence	Mrs. . Pressfield
*Hazelton—Aug. 1908	8	48	808	Residence	Mrs. L. Briggle
Hazelton—Jan. 1912	1	....	34	School	R. M. Ralston
Hazelton—Oct. 1910	1	47	239	School	M. E. Watkins
Heart—Jan. 1908	3	22	109	School	G. P. Moore

REPORT OF SCHOOL AND COMMUNITY LIBRARY STATIONS TO JULY 1, 1912—Continued

Name of Station Date Established	No. of libraries	Average No of readers	Total circulation	Library Where Kept	Name of Librarian
*Heaton—July 1908	6	39	693	Bank	C. I. Turner
Hebron—Mar. 1911	2	32	189	Office	Geo. L. Landon
Hensel—Oct. 1911	1	16	70	School	Ella Olafson
Hensel—Oct. 1910	1	20	145	Store	Fred Johnson
*Hensler—Apr. 1911	2	51	162	Store	Mrs. R. A. Kyser
Hensler—Jan. 1909	1	16	35	Residence	Ruth McCone
*Homen—Apr. 1912	1	....	....	School	Julia Torgerson
Hoople—Dec. 1911	1	58	214	School	O. Voge
Hoople—Nov. 1911	1	25	57	School	Arthur Fedje
Hoople—Feb. 1910	1	11	30	School	Tessa Walker
*Hope—Nov. 1909	3	131	414	Drug store	Jno. J. Wamberg
Horace—Jan. 1912	1	34	135	School	N. H. Johnson
Howard—Jan. 1912	1	11	45	Residence	M. D. Boardman
*Howe—June 1912	1	....	....	School	Theo. Hanson
*Hunter—May 1912	1	....	....	Residence	M. J. Nelson
*Hurdsfield—Jan. 1908	5	62	413	Store	H. F. Miller
Jamestown—Apr. 1912	1	6	....	School	M. Kupferschmidt
*Jollette—Jan. 1910	3	28	121	Residence	Fred Shannon
*Jud—Mar. 1911	2	21	68	Drug store	W. L. Sackett
Kaiser—Aug. 1911	1	32	116	Residence	O. B. Whisler
Kaiser—Nov. 1910	2	32	128	Residence	O. B. Whisler
Kathryn—Jan. 1911	1	21	113	School house	Emma Knudtson
Kathryn—Jan. 1908	4	35	273	Store	K. O. Abrahamson
Kensal—Feb. 1910	1	42	145	Post office	Agnes D. Thompson
Kindred—Feb. 1910	2	14	96	School	R. E. Ulness
Kintyre—Oct. 1910	3	....	....	School	Anna Stanley
*Kintyre—Feb. 1912	1	....	....	School	Mildred Lane
Kramer—Jan. 1908	3	20	61	School	H. S. Tupper
*Lakota—Sept. 1911	1	....	....		Mrs. B. O. Skrivseth
Lamoine—Jan. 1911	1	26	60	Post office	Emma Virgin
*Langdon—Sept. 1910	3	29	157	Schulke Block	Marie H. Harlan
Langdon—May, 1910	1	....	....	School	Belle A. Hanson
Langedahl—July 1909	1	3	3	Residence	G. W. Whitehead
Lansford—Nov. 1909	3	48	432	High school	Jessie Middaugh
Larimore—Oct. 1911	1	14	28	School	L. M. Evans

REPORT OF SCHOOL AND COMMUNITY LIBRARY STATIONS TO JULY 1, 1912 Continued

Name of Station—Date Established	No. of libraries	Average No of readers	Total circulation	Library Where Kept	Name of Librarian
*Lark—Oct. 1911	2	26	69	Residence	L. A. Havens
*Lark—Feb. 1912	1	....	....	Residence	Gleun H. Roberts
Larson—Apr. 1912	1	....	....	School	Clara Holmlie
Leal—May 1908	2	40	233	School	Katherine Sherry
Leal—Oct. 1910	1	10	27	School	Clifford Wilson
Leal—Mar. 1908	1	27	131	School	M. E. McCurdy
Leeds R. F. D. No. 1—May 1911	1	....	....	School	Gladys Mowry
Leeds—June 1908	2	6	11	School No. 2	W. H. Carnahan
*Leith—Apr. 1912	1		...	Residence	Edith Jones
Lidgerwood—Nov. 1911	1	8	9	School No. 2 and 4	E. H. Webster
*Linton—Mar. 1912	1		...	High school	Helen J. Evenson
Linton—Dec. 1910	1		...	School	E. A. Kling
Linton—Oct. 1908	1	5	12	Office of Co. Supt.	Mrs. J. N. Peterson
Lisbon—Sept. 1911	1		...	School office	W. B. Simcox
Lisbon R. No. 3—Dec. 1909	1	12	45	School house	Clara Olson
Logan—Dec. 1910	1	....	....	Residence	Oliver Sangstad
*Loraine—Nov. 1908	5	45	1,040	Post office	Pearl Robertson
*Lostwood—Nov. 1910	2	29	175	Bank	C. E. Burdick
*McClusky—Mar. 1912	1	....	....	Residence	J. I. Oldaker
*McHenry—Feb. 1909	1	....	....	School No. 2	John Knox
*McKenzie—Aug. 1910	2	14	54	Residence	Judd Porter
McKenzie—Dec. 1910	1	23	26	Residence	C. F. Roth
*McLeod—Mar. 1911	2	36	106	School house	Florence Sours
McLeod—Apr. 1910	2	20	151	Residence	E. Ketcheson
Maddock—Dec. 1910	2	28	300	Residence	L. A. Westad
Manfred—Oct. 1911	1	20	69	Residence	Anna Nertrost
Manfred—Feb. 1910	2	42	122	Post office	A. L. LeGrand
Mannhaven—Oct. 1911	1	....	....	Residence	Peter Bohrer
Marmarth—Feb. 1909	1	38	81	School	Leona Forrest
Marstonmoor—Nov. 1909	1	10	25	School	Geo. Conry
Max—Oct. 1908	1	....	....	Real estate office	P. D. Podhola
Max—Dec. 1911	1	20	23	School	Grace Bentley
Max—Feb. 1910	1	33	118	School	Lee V. Brinton
Maxbass—July 1908	6	60	902	Post office	G. J. Getschel
*Medora—June 1908	3	24	61	School	Mrs. Lorena Will

REPORT OF SCHOOL AND COMMUNITY LIBRARY STATIONS TO JULY 1, 1912 Continued

Name of Station—Date Established	No. of libraries	Average No of readers	Total circulation	Library Where Kept	Name of Librarian
Melville—Nov. 1909	1	26	86	School	Leon Fried
Menoken—Jan. 1912	1	20	48	School	Emelia Olson
Menoken—Nov. 1910	1	....	80	School	Anna L. Slater
Menoken—Nov. 1910	2	20	205	Residence	Mrs. H. B. Moffitt
Mercer—Nov. 1908	1	30	80	School	Olga Natwick
*Milnor—July 1909	3	19	110	Residence	Y. M. Ytrehus
Milnor—Feb. 1911	1	....	....	School No. 1	Anny Mattson
Milnor—Nov. 1909	2	21	246	School	Josie Johnson
Milnor—July 1909	2	20	74	School	Miss Cross
Milton—Oct. 1910	1	32	112	Residence	Olivia Johnson
Moffit—Mar. 1912	1	5	26	School	Lola N. Welch
Mohall—Mar. 1911	1	6	17	Office (News)	L. M. Rockne
Mohall—Dec. 1909	2	55	427	School	Bernard Larson
Napoleon—Jan. 1908	4	51	355	School	Herbert Brown
Napoleon—Oct. 1910	1	28	43	School (Foster)	Ethyle White
Napoleon—Nov. 1911	1	21	98	School (Starkey)	Ethyle White
Napoleon—Dec. 1910	1	....	....	Residence	A. E. Eggleston
Napoleon—Mar. 1912	1	41	121	School	Glenn V. Dill
Newburg—Apr. 1911	1	16	35	Drug store	Harry R. Van Voorlise
*New England—Dec. 1910	1	....	....	Residence	Marie Ackerman
New England—Jan. 1910	2	18	183	Residence	Mrs. D. M. Hart
New Salem—Oct. 1908	3	24	189	School	Arne Vinje
Niagara—Dec. 1910	1	....	....	Town Hall	Ernest Kirk
Northwood—Nov. 1910	1	8	31	Residence	Theo. Kaase
Northwood—Jan. 1911	2	21	80	Club rooms	P. P. Glasrud
*Northwood—Jan. 1911	2	17	65	School No.	Mrs. T. O. Mandt
Northwood—Dec. 1911	1	12	31	School	Mandius Bridstone
*Odessa—Apr. 1912	1	....	....	Hotel	G. W. Pollard
Orr—Sept. 1910	1	17	....	Residence	L. H. Raymond
Oscar—Jan. 1909	2	9	77	Residence	Peter Romsass
Page—Oct. 1910	1	24	112	School No. 2	Agnes Brownlee
Page—Oct. 1911	1	33	105	School	Belle McDonald
*Page—Jan. 1912	1	....	....	School	Georgia D. Kelly
*Paoli—Dec. 1911	1	....	....	School	Lucy Doescher
Paoli—Oct. 1908	2	28	100	School	Bertha Havick

REPORT OF SCHOOL AND COMMUNITY LIBRARY STATIONS TO JULY 1, 1912—Continued

Name of Station—Date Established	No. of libraries	Average No of readers	Total circulation	Library Where Kept -Name of Librarian
Pekin—Oct. 1908	1	14	22	Post office ....C. O. Moen
Pembina—Dec. 1911	1	38	91	School ....C. D. Curtis
Perth—Jan. 1910	1	28	114	School ....Henry Berkner
Petersburg—Oct. 1911	1	....	....	Residence ....Mrs. W. G. McCrae
Pisek—Jan. 1911	1	15	47	Bank ....C. J. McKean
Plaza—Nov. 1910	1	42	120	School ....R. P. Graves
Portal—Oct. 1910	1	31	85	School ....Jeanette Mathews
Pretty Rock—Nov. 1911	1	35	174	School ....Elma Johnson
*Purcell—Mar. 1912	1	....	....	School ....Mrs. F. S. Atkinson
Reeder—July 1908	1	....	....	Store ....Fannie Muller
*Richardton—Apr. 1912	1	....	....	School ....H. M. Pippin
*Rock Lake—Jan. 1912	1	....	....	School No. 3 ....Ruth Hunt
Rock Lake—Oct. 1910	1	....	....	School ....R. L. Calvin
Rolette—Nov. 1909	1	74	384	School ....N. D. Frodd
Rolette—Feb. 1909	1	28	73	Jewelry store ....M. Stageberg
Ross—Dec. 1909	1	20	160	School ....M. E. Kaniut
Ryder—Apr. 1911	2	20	124	Implement office ....S. A. Olsen
St. Thomas—Jan. 1909	1	36	146	School ....Lena Watson
*St. Thomas—Feb. 1912	1	....	....	School ....Elma Baldwin
*Sandlie—Oct. 1909	3	47	547	School ....Mrs. H. Isaacson
Sawyer—July 1908	1	17	43	Residence ....C. S. Beighle
*Sentinel Butte—Apr. 1909	5	19	272	Office ....J. A. Kitchen
Sharon—Sept. 1909	2	42	276	Public school ....G. F. Simmons
*Sheldon—Oct. 1911	2	28	41	School ....Marie Kemp
Sheldon—Jan. 1912	1	14	27	Residence ....J. R. Adams
Sheldon—Feb. 1912	1	25	48	School ....P. M. Arntson
Sherbrooke—Jan. 1909	1	....	....	Office of Co. Supt. ....A. G. Miller
Sherwood—Oct. 1908	1	42	128	Drug store ....C. R. Hamilton
*Souris—Sept. 1908	2	24	70	Store ....Chas. A. Wales
Spring Brook—Nov. 1910	1	....	....	School ....A. M. Watkins
*Stady—Nov. 1909	3	39	573	School ....Mrs. Alice Olsen
Stady—Oct. 1909	2	27	206	School ....Nina Douglas
Stanley—Feb. 1910	1	....	....	Office of Co. Supt. ....Mrs. H. J. Linde
*Stanton—Apr. 1912	1	....	....	Office of Co. Supt. ....E. W. Thomas
Steele—Jan. 1911	3	65	550	Office of Co. Supt. ....Lydia Hinman

REPORT OF SCHOOL AND COMMUNITY LIBRARY STATIONS TO JULY 1, 1912—Continued

Name of Station—Date Established	No. of libraries	Average No of readers	Total circulation	Library Where Kept—Name of Librarian
Sterling—Mar. 1910	2	....	....	School ... Mrs. J. F. Chaffin
Sterling—Apr. 1909	1	....	66	School ... O. Simonson
Stevenson—Feb. 1912	1	11	49	Post office ... Mrs. E. J Reed
Surrey—Mar. 1910	1	37	57	High school ... L. H. Purdy
*Svold—Feb. 1912	1	....	....	School No. 2 ... B. Eastman
Sykeston—Oct. 1910	1	54	264	Public school ... Leva Smith
*Sykeston—Apr. 1911	2	95	245	Drug store ... C. W. Smith
*Tappen—Mar. 1912	1	....	....	Residence ... Mrs. L. Cooper
*Taylor—Oct. 1911	1	51	186	School ... H. N. Hem
Tolley—Dec. 1908	1	31	90	School ... Kathryn Daly
Tower City—Nov. 1910	1	....	....	School ... R. B. Murphy
Turtle Lake—Jan. 1908	4	45	338	School ... W. E. Earlson
Tyler—Nov. 1911	1	17	60	School No. 4 ... Margare Schiller
Tyler—Mar. 1910	1	....	49	School No. 5 ... Thomas Larson
Underwood—Jan. 1910	2	32	139	School ... H. J Putnam
Underwood—Sept. 1910	1	....	....	School ... A. H. Gleason
Underwood—Feb. 1912	1	23	93	School ... Verna Folsom
Upham—Apr. 1911	1	12	38	Residence ... C W Whipple
*Valley City—Mar. 1912	1	....	....	School ... E. G. Getchell
Velva—Feb. 1908	1	....	....	Residence ... Hattie Clough
Velva—June 1909	1	5	12	Residence ... Hattie Clough
*Voltaire—Apr. 1912	1	....	....	Residence ... S. I. Knutson
Wahpeton—Nov. 1910	1	....	....	School No. 5 ... Bessie Stewart
Walcott—Jan. 1911	2	53	364	School ... Chas. Hanson
Walhalla—July 1911	1	15	94	School ... C. I. Peterson
Washburn—Sept. 1909	1	53	166	School ... W. P. Dean
*Wheatland—Jan. 1911	2	9	45	Residence ... Mary D. Madson
Wheelock—Jan. 1911	1	16	....	Residence ... A W Widlund
White Earth—Oct. 1908	1	....	....	School ... L. H. Oliver
White Earth—Jan. 1910	1	23	107	School ... J. B. Hauglie
Williams—Nov. 1909	1	25	60	School ... G. C. Snow
Williams—Nov. 1910	1	30	126	School ... S. I. Doefler
Williston—July, 1909	1	108	271	Library ... Miss McMillan
Williston—Mar. 1910	1	....	....	School ... Zella Francis
Williston—Oct. 1911	1	33	173	School ... L. F. Guthrie

Carnegie Library, Minot.

James Memorial Library, Williston

Carnegie Library, Devils Lake

Carnegie Library, Dickinson

REPORT OF SCHOOL AND COMMUNITY LIBRARY STATIONS TO JULY 1, 1912 - Continued

Name of Station—Date Established	No. of libraries	Average No of readers	Total circulation	Library Where Kept	Name of Librarian
Williston—Oct. 1909	1	....	....	School	Jno. McGrath
Wilton—Nov. 1909	1	....	....	School	M. A. Barnes
Wilton—May 1910	1	11	27	School No. 5	C. Ersland
*Wimbledon—Sept. 1908	6	58	1,003	Crowley's drug store	Mrs. M. S. Mallough
Winchester—Oct. 1908	1	....	....	School No. 2	B. Richardson
Winona—Aug. 1908	1	17	48	School	Jennie Crover
*Wiprud—Nov. 1910	2	....	....	Store	Marie Berg
Wyndmere—Nov. 1910	1	12	44	School	E. Huxford
York—July 1908	1	....	....	Residence	Jno. Broger
Ypsilanti—Dec. 1911	1	21	98	Bank	E. A. Hoff

*One library still at station, record of which is not included in readers and circulation.

Total libraries sent	531
Total number of libraries reporting	414
Total number of borrowers in 414 libraries	5,616
Total circulation in 414 libraries	35,797
Average number of readers where records were kept	13.56
Average number of books to a reader where records were kept	6.3

If records had been returned from all stations, computing on average readers and circulation, 531 libraries would show 7,194 readers and 45,322 circulation.

REPORT OF FARMERS' LIBRARY STATIONS TO JULY 1, 1912

Name of Station—Date Established	No. of libraries	Average No of readers	Total circulation	Library Where Kept—Name of Librarian
Abercrombie—Jan. 1911	1	7	9	Residence ....Olaf O. Sveam
Agate—Jan. 1911	1	6	6	Store ....J. J. Fichtinger
Akra—Apr. 1911	1	....	....	Residence ....S. T. Olafson
Almont—Mar. 1911	1	....	....	Residence ....Jon. Pederson
*Aneta—Apr. 1911	2	....	....	Residence ....O. J. Kjorvestad
Antler—July 1911	1	7	9	School ....S. B. Mills
Antler—Jan. 1912	1	....	....	Com. club ....Helga N. Anderson
Aplin—Jan. 1912	1	7	9	Residence ....Carl Stephens
Barnes—Feb. 1912	1	3	7	Residence ....L. M. Stolberg
*Bathgate—Feb. 1910	1	....	....	Residence ....Alex Morrison
Belfield—Feb. 1911	1	....	....	Residence ....A. C. Gibbons
Bergen—Jan. 1911	1	12	14	Post office ....Postmaster
Bergen—Jan. 1911	1	13	21	Post office ....Postmaster
Bismarck—Nov. 1910	2	....	....	High school ....Bessie Johnson
Blanchard—Feb. 1910	1	2	4	Residence ....A. R. Sheritt
*Burnstad—Jan. 1911	2	....	16	Bank ....Chas. Hernett
Cando—Mar. 1911	1	3	....	Office of Co. Supt. ....Mamie Sorenson
Cleveland—Jan. 1911	1	....	8	Residence ....A. Y. C. Sund
Clyde—Dec. 1911	1	8	11	School ....Mamie Kurck
Cooperstown—Jan. 1911	1	....	12	School ....W. H. Sansburn
*Courtenay—Aug. 1911	2	17	20	Bank ....Loran Nichols
Crosby—Feb. 1911	1	5	11	Residence ....A. Ellergodt
Cuba—Dec. 1910	1	6	8	Residence ....V. E. Grant
Dazey—Apr. 1911	1	2	3	Editor's office ....Leo Ratcliff
Dickinson—Nov. 1910	3	16	63	Residence ....O. E. Foote
Doyon—Mar. 1912	1	....	....	Store ....J. H. Blufas
Drady—Dec. 1911	1	15	23	Store ....Tom Drady
Drake—Feb. 1911	1	10	....	Residence ....Martin B. Olson
Drayton—Apr. 1911	1	6	12	Store ....F. N. Wallace
Dwight—Feb. 1910	1	15	23	Office ....Joel A. Larson
Edinburg—Dec. 1911	1	12	26	Bank ....A. C. Thompson
*Fairmount—Mar. 1911	3	12	23	Bank ....W. H. Cox
Fallon—Nov. 1910	1	....	....	School ....Adeline Wilson
Fergus—Nov. 1911	1	....	....	Residence ....Joseph Yahna
Fergus—Jan. 1910	1	5	7	Store ....H. G. Johnson

REPORT OF FARMERS' LIBRARY STATIONS TO JULY 1, 1912 - Continued.

Name of Station—Date Established	No. of libraries	Average No of readers	Total circulation	Library Where Kept	Name of Librarian
Ft. Rice—Feb. 1911	1	2	2	Residence	Chester Dutton
Gayton—Feb. 1912	1	9	14	Post office	Mrs. Tessa Casey
*Giese—Nov. 1911	1	....	....	Residence	Mrs. K. Cahill
Grafton—Mar. 1910	1	....	9	Residence	Geo. K. Dike
Grand Forks—Nov. 1910	1	....	....	Residence	W. H. Hall
*Gwyther—Feb. 1912	1	....	....	Residence	W. L. Caddell
*Gwyther—Apr. 1912	1	....	....	Residence	Peter Holberg
Hampden—Mar. 1911	1	2	....	Residence	Ernest G. Berggren
Hannah—Oct. 1911	1	2	3	Bank	Belle McKnight
Hannah—Feb. 1911	1	....	....	Residence	O. R. Daniels
Hatton—Mar. 1911	2	....	....	Residence	Jno. L. Thompson
Haynes—Dec. 1910	1	6	11	Residence	Chas. O. Wright
Hazelton—Nov. 1911	1	9	19	Bank	G. A. Lenhart
Hazelton—June 1910	1	17	53	Residence	Mrs. L. Briggle
*Hazelton—Mar. 1911	3	12	55	Residence	Chas. H. Soule
Hensler—Mar. 1911	1	....	....	Store	R. A. Kyser
*Hettinger—Apr. 1912	1	....	....	Residence	G. N. Keniston
*Homen—Feb. 1912	1	....	....	Residence	Julia Torgerson
*Hoosier—Mar. 1911	2	4	10	Residence	D. P. Abbey
Hope—May 1911	1	2	8	Bank	M. B. Cassell
Hope—May 1911	1	4	5	Bank	M. B. Cassell
Hope—Apr. 1911	1	13	20	Bank	M. B. Cassell
Hope—Apr. 1911	1	13	16	Bank	M. B. Cassell
Hope—Apr. 1911	1	3	3	Store	J. J. Wamberg
*Kramer—Mar. 1911	1	....	....	Residence	John Dinius
*Landa—Feb. 1911	2	11	12	Residence	Otto Finstad
*Landa—Jan. 1912	1	....	....	Residence	Otto Finstad
Larimore—Feb. 1910	2	15	43	Office	J. Dexter-Pierce
Lark—Dec. 1911	1	4	....	Residence	Gainer P. Moore
Leal—Mar. 1911	2	15	35	Bank	P. A. Pickett
Lee—Mar. 1912	1	5	9	Post office	P. J. Hanson
Logan—Nov. 1910	1	....	22	Residence	Oliver Sangstad
Lostwood—Nov. 1910	1	11	13	Bank	C. E. Burdick
McKenzie—Mar. 1911	1	4	4	Office	C. W. Malmquist
Mandan—Feb. 1912	1	2	6	Residence	S. W. Unkenholz

REPORT OF FARMERS' LIBRARY STATIONS TO JULY 1, 1912—Continued.

Name of Station Date Established	No. of libraries	Average No of readers	Total circulation	Library Where Kept	Name of Librarian
Mandan—Feb. 1912	1	2	10	Residence	E. C. Johnson
*Mandan—Feb. 1912	1	....	....	Residence	P. A. Fristad
*Mandan—Feb. 1912	1	....	....	Residence	Joe Klesalek
Mayville—Apr. 1911	1	2	5	Residence	B. R. Cleveland
Max—Jan. 1912	1	....	....	Residence	P. Sveum
Mohall—Jan. 1911	1	....	....	Residence	Walter Deitz
Monango—Mar. 1911	1	2	....	Store	DeWitt Warren
Mott—Mar. 1912	1	....	....	Library	Mrs. P. J. Washer
New England—Nov. 1910	1	....	....	Residence	C. R. Ackerman
Niagara—Dec. 1910	2	7	11	Residence	Ernest Kirk
Northwood—Nov. 1911	1	4	7	Residence	Theo Kaase
Northwood—Oct. 1911	1	10	....	School No. 1	Mandius Bridston
Pollock—Jan. 1912	1	7	47	Store	A. Jager
Reeder—Oct. 1911	1	7	14	School	J. G. Thorson
Rhame—Nov. 1911	1	2	7	Residence	G. A. Branson
Richardton—May 1911	1	....	....	Bank	J. Muggli
Richardton—Mar. 1911	1	....	....	Bank	J. Muggli
Richardton—Mar. 1911	1	....	....	Bank	J. Muggli
Richardton—Mar. 1911	1	....	....	Bank	J. Muggli
Ruso—Oct. 1910	1	2	12	Residence	Thos. Dildine
Ryder—Mar. 1911	1	5	11	Implement office	S. A. Olsen
Sarles—Oct. 1911	2	....	....	Bank	S. M. Mowry
Sentinel Butte—Nov. 1910	1	....	....	Residence	P. S. Kitchen
*Stanley—Mar. 1911	2	7	50	Residence	Jos. Huff
Stella—Nov. 1911	1	....	....	Residence	H. E. Stoskoff
Stevenson—Dec. 1911	1	....	....	Post office	E. J. Reed
Tower City—Nov. 1910	1	12	28	Bank	S. F. Sherman
Underwood—Nov. 1911	1	4	11	Residence	Chas. Stroh
Valley City—Jan. 1912	1	....	....	School	G. W. Hanna
Valley City—Mar. 1911	1	5	11	Residence	Levi Getchell
Valley City—Mar. 1911	1	....	....	Normal school	M. C. James
Voltaire—Jan. 1911	1	4	6	Farmers' club hall	C. P. Byers
Walhalla—May 1911	1	....	....	Office	St. A. Andrews
Washburn—Mar. 1911	1	....	....	Office	Joseph Mann
Williston—Jan. 1912	1	9	20	Library	B. R. Baldwin

REPORT OF FARMERS' LIBRARY STATIONS TO JULY 1, 1912—Continued.

Name of Station	Date Established	No. of libraries	Average No. of readers	Total circulation	Library Where Kept	Name of Librarian
Wimbledon	Feb. 1911	1	5	15	Residence	C. W. Sherwin
Wimbledon	Mar. 1911	1	...	17	Bank	H. M. Strand
Wimbledon-	Feb. 1911	1	...	9	Bank	H. M. Strand
Woodworth	Mar. 1911	1	14		Residence	M. Anderson

*No records returned.

Total number of farmers' libraries sent	127
Total number of libraries reporting	76 *
Total number of farmers' library readers recorded	466
Total circulation recorded	999
Average number of readers where records were kept	6
Average number of books to a reader where records were kept	2
Total number of readers computed on average records returned	779
Total circulation, computed on average records returned	1,635

EDUCATIONAL REFERENCE DEPARTMENT.

From this department books are loaned singly or in groups to any individual or club in the state agreeing to pay transportation both ways and to be responsible for their safe return.

In the two years ending June 30, 1912, 4570 books were loaned individuals. Complete club statistics were not kept in 1910-11. In the year ending June 30, 1912, 1382 pamphlets and mounted clippings on 60 subjects were sent to 132 clubs and 63 individuals.

For the use of clubs studying North Dakota laws and conditions, special digests were made by the Legislative Reference Librarian as follows: "Laws for Women and Children," "Juvenile Courts, and "Board of Control." These digests have not been granted publication by the Commissioners of Public Printing.

In two years 750 books have been added to the reference collection, making a total of 3175 volumes. These volumes are accessible to the public and are consulted many times daily; of this use no record is kept. The demands on this department by students, debaters, and others, are increasing so rapidly that there is great need of an assistant to take charge of the cataloging and reference work.

FIELD WORK.

Sec. 6, Chap. 156, Code 1909, reads as follows: "The librarian or trustees of any free public library or the trustees of any village, town or community, entitled to borrow books from said traveling libraries, may, without charge, ask and receive advice and instructions from said library commission upon any matter pertaining to the organization, maintenance or administration of the libraries, and said commission shall, as far as possible, promote and assist by counsel and encouragement, the formation of libraries where none exists, and the commission may also send its members to aid in organizing new libraries or improving those already established."

The discharge of the duties outlined in this section of North Dakota library law is known as "field work."

Little has been accomplished in this department. The Board of Audit has questioned the legality of such trips and has deferred payment of such expenses from the Library Commission fund until opinions were obtained from the Attorney General. By the time decisions were received on all the points raised, it was too late to plan or to execute many visits to library stations. According to the decisions, field work comes within the provisions of the North Dakota library law, and in the future visits for organization will be made to the towns in the state that are interested in library extension. Kenmare, Hatton, Hillsboro, Wahpeton, Enderlin, Fessenden, Hannah, Leonard, Lisbon, Bowman, Rugby, Mott, Crosby, Antler, Carrington, Sykeston, Park River, and others, have shown interest in such work. The library at Kenmare was visited in May, 1912, the books were classified and systematic records started. Other libraries have been assisted by correspondence until such time as a visit can be made.

PUBLICITY.

In any new undertaking, private or public, publicity must be an important factor in development. Especially is this true when the aim of the work is to offer the greatest benefit to the most isolated portions of the state. For this purpose many addresses, trips and exhibits are necessary, and much printed matter must be distributed before the desired results are obtained. Through addresses at state and county teachers' meetings, institutes and summer schools, the traveling libraries have been brought to the notice of the rural schools. By means of exhibits at grain growers' conventions, at state fairs, at expositions and on better farming trains, the attention of the farmers has been called to the traveling library system. Through the State Federation of Women's Clubs, the Library Commission keeps in touch with the study clubs of the state. Through correspondence, it reaches as many individual students as possible. The press of the state has been of great assistance in publicity work. Many thousands of leaflets have been distributed by mail, at exhibits, by extension lecturers and on better farming trains. Similar work has been performed by the Bankers' Association, by county superintendents, and by others who believe in the financial, educational and inspirational value of library extension work.

FIELD AND PUBLICITY WORK

Date	Place	Nature of Work	Time Occupied	Expense	Persons Employed
1910					
July	Fargo	Exhibit at State Fair	1 week	$ 26.00	Sec. of Com.
				26.10	Leg. Ref. Lib'n.
July	Mackinac Island	Delegate A. L. A.	1 week	49.64	Sec. of Com.
Aug.	Dickinson	Visit to Pub. Lib.	1 day	9.45	Sec. of Com.
Sept. 26	Jamestown	Visit to Jamestown P. L., Insane Asylum Lib. and Jamestown College Lib.	1 day	....	Sec. of Com.
Sept. 27	Fargo & Casselton	Fargo and Casselton Public Libraries	1 day	....	Sec. of Com.
Sept. 28	Grand Forks	Grand Forks P. L. and University Lib.	1 day	....	Sec. of Com.
Sept. 29	Fargo	Arranged for State Lib. Ass'n meeting	1 day	38.00	Sec. of Com.
Sept. 30	Fargo	Attended State Lib. Ass'n. meeting	1 day	....	Sec. of Com.
Oct. 1	Fargo	Attended State Lib. Ass'n. meeting	1 day	....	Sec. of Com.
Oct. 1	Fargo	Attended State Lib. Ass'n. meeting	1 day	14.45	Leg. Ref. Lib'n.
Oct. 11-14	Bismarck	State Federation of Women's Clubs	4 days	....	Entire staff
Oct. 18-21	Bismarck	State Teachers' Ass'n.	3 days	....	Entire staff
1911					
Jan.	Fargo	Tri-State Grain Growers' Conv.	Evening address	....	Member of Commission
Feb.	Fargo	Fargo College Lib. organization	2 days	14.55	Sec. of Com.
May.	Normal School (Valley City)	Arranging for summer school	2 days	10.50	Sec. of Com.
May	Mandan	Attending meeting of Lib. Board	2 days		
July	Grand Forks	Exhibit at State Fair	1 week	42.00	Sec. of Com
				30.00	Leg. Ref. Lib'n.
Sept. 26-Oct. 14	Bismarck	Exposition Exhibit	3 weeks	39.25	Entire staff
Oct. 10-13	Devils Lake	State Federation of Women's Clubs	4 days	37.10	Sec. of Com.
Oct. 20-21	Jamestown	State Library Ass'n. meeting	2 days	10.70	Sec. of Com.
				7.35	Leg. Ref. Lib'n.
				.30	Sec'y. of Com.
1912					
Feb. 15	Mandan	Address to State Dairymen's Conv.	1-2 day	....	Sec'y. of Com.
Feb. 15	Bismarck	Address to Public Library meeting			
Apr.	Bismarck	Address to state meeting of county superintendents		....	Sec'y. of Com.
May 20-26	Valley City	Arranging for summer school	1-2 day		
	Kenmare	Classifying public library	4 days	30.45	Sec'y. of Com.
	Minot	Visit to Public Library	1-2 day		
June	Bismarck	Address to Burleigh Co. Teachers' Inst.		....	Sec'y. of Com.
June	Better Farming Train	6 Farmers' libraries and 3 traveling libraries		....	No attendant
				$ 386.44	

CARNEGIE LIBRARIES IN NORTH DAKOTA—JULY 1, 1912

Name	Date	Cost	Librarian
Agricultural College	1906	$ 23,500	Mrs. Ethel McVeety
Devils Lake P. L.	1910	15,000	Anna Sprung
Dickinson P. L.	1909	12,500	Josephine Hargrave
Fargo College	1910	......	Edithe A. Conn
Fargo P. L.	1903	20,000	Amy G. Bosson
Grafton P. L.	1905	10,000	Mary Morris
Grand Forks P. L.	1903	31,000	Adah Durand
Minot P. L.	1911	17,000	Margaret Greene
University	1908	30,000	C. W. Sumner
Valley City P. L.	1903	15,000	Mrs. Laura Bassett

MEMORIAL LIBRARIES IN NORTH DAKOTA—JULY 1, 1912

Name	Date	Cost	By whom given—In whose memory	Librarian
Jamestown College	1912	$ 18,000	Not made public	Alice M. Paddock
Jamestown P. L.*	......	20,000	A. E. Dickey—Alfred Dickey	Alice M. Paddock
Leonard P. L.	1911	......	E. Watts—Mrs. E. Watts	
Mayville P. L.	......	......	Grandin	Miss Ylvisaker
Williston P. L.	1911	20,000	James estate—Willis James	Bessie R. Baldwin

*Building not yet started.

FINANCIAL STATISTICS PUBLIC LIBRARIES JULY 1, 1910—June 30, 1912—Continued

Place	Population	Date organized	Source of Income	Total Income 1910-11	Total Income 1911-12	Expenditures: Books, Period. and Binding 1910-11	Expenditures: Books, Period. and Binding 1911-12	Expenditures: Total 1910-11	Expenditures: Total 1911-12	Librarian
Cando	1,332	1902	Gifts; fees	*						
Carrington	1,217	1906	Gifts; fees	$ 203.81	219.07	$ 131.07	103.32	391.79	294.62	Mrs. B. L. Russell
Casselton	1,553		City, $200	......	338.73	......	30.78	......	321.03	Emir D. Morton
Devils Lake	5,157	1910	4-mill tax	2,943.27	2,837.16	399.94	263.50	2,391.57	2,148.86	Anna Sprung
Dickinson	3,678	1908	City, $1,250	3,982.70	3,384.66	517.15	437.60	2,138.45	1,627.37	Josephine Hargrave
Enderlin	1,540	1912	Gifts	......	292.72	......	175.38	......	240.16	Mrs. E. Bangert
Fargo	14,331	1900	Tax, $3,984	5,389.01	5,225.45	848.56	426.65	4,269.05	3,639.21	Amy G. Bosson
Fessenden	713	1900	Gifts	*						Sara M. Belseker
Grafton	2,229	1897	City, $700							
			Sch. Brd. $300	1,401.11	1,452.75	168.19	163.52	1,108.16	1,141.45	Mary Morris
Grand Forks	12,478	1899	Tax	3,399.47	4,867.05	605.77	951.06	2,915.36	4,185.75	Adah Durand
Hannah	500	1911	Fees	51.00	37.50	46.70	31.97	51.00	37.50	Belle McKnight
Jamestown	4,358	1902	Tax	2,068.87	3,453.10	698.13	688.91	1,899.61	1,627.09	Alice M. Paddock
Langdon	1,214		City, $200	258.50	272.40	21.50	60.00	177.50	216.70	Marie H. Harlan
Leeds	682		Fees	21.00	265.45	......	29.05	......	244.25	Theo Gronbeck
Mandan	3,873	1895	Fees	*						Olivia M. Draper
Minot	6,188	1908	Tax	9,011.01	9,386.80	587.41	686.48	7,044.52	5,496.99	Margaret Greene
Park River	1,008		City, $400	537.00	418.00	200.00	175.00	402.00	380.00	Bessie I. Robbins
Rugby	1,630	1912	Gifts	......	150.00	......	......	......	......	Hattie S. Sikes
Valley City	4,606	1900	Tax	2,679.29	4,211.86	429.23	401.19	2,003.00	2,659.35	Mrs. Laura Bassett
Wahpeton	2,467	1912	Gifts	......	168.98	......	91.53	......	147.13	Mrs. J. G. Forbes
Williston	3,124	1910	Tax, $2,500	2,506.36	3,764.00	85.90	368.13	1,736.22	3,277.38	Bessie R. Baldwin

*No report

CIRCULATION STATISTICS PUBLIC LIBRARIES—JULY 1, 1910—June 30, 1912—Continued

Place	Population	Date organized	Volumes Owned June 30, 1910	Volumes Owned July 1, 1912	Borrowers 1910-1911	Borrowers 1911-1912	Circulation 1910-1911	Circulation 1911-1912	Librarian
Cando	1,332	1902							
Carrington	1,217	1906	1,396	1,696	626	822	3,901	3,485	Mrs. B. L. Russell
Casselton	1,553		1,245	1,544	250	461	2,906	4,115	Emir D. Morton
Devils Lake	5,157	1910	2,495	3,204	1,009	1,484	19,154	16,331	Anna Sprung
Dickinson	3,678	1908	2,365	3,177	644	1,038	23,824	20,400	Josephine Hargrave
Enderlin	1,540	1912	80	325		214		2,150	Mrs. E. Bangert
Fargo	14,331	1900	9,491	9,871	5,935	*6,867	26,069	33,492	Amy G. Bosson
Fessenden	713	1900	....	....	....	265	....	1,608	Sara M. Beiseker
Grafton	2,229	1897	2,618	3,136	1,258	1,452	18,109	10,747	Mary Morris
Grand Forks	12,478	1899	5,903	6,240	1,246	**1,247	24,932	28,391	Adah Durand
Hannah	500	1911	61	109	....	....	....	....	Belle McKnight
Jamestown	4,358	1902	3,045	4,244	1,591	1,958	17,381	17,596	Alice M. Paddock
Langdon	1,214		1,050	1,110	25	52	....	1,500	Marie H. Harlan
Leeds	682		921	1,515	47	35	....	....	Theo Gronbeck
Mandan	3,873	1895	2,172	2,608	....	....	....	....	Olivia M. Draper
Minot	6,188	1908	2,489	3,001	1,722	2,091	16,965	18,898	Margaret Greene
Park River	1,008		1,300	1,721	462	505	8,201	8,925	Bessie I. Robbins
Rugby	1,630	1912	....	353	....	105	....	....	Hattie S. Sikes
Valley City	4,606	1900	3,544	3,731	2,100	2,346	9,940	11,528	Mrs. Laura Bassett
Wahpeton	2,467	1912	....	629	....	....	....	....	Mrs. J. G. Forbes
Williston	3,124	1910	....	3,509	....	397	....	15,840	Bessie R. Baldwin

*Re-registered. Total number of borrowers June 30, 1912—3,224.
**Re-registering.

COMPARATIVE STATISTICS OF PUBLIC LIBRARIES, N. D. JUNE 30, 1910—JULY 1, 1911

	Devils Lake	Dickinson	Fargo	Grafton	Grand Forks	Jamestown	Minot	Valley City
Population, 1910	5,198	3,678	14,331	3,000	12,478	4,358	6,188	4,606
Number of borrowers July 1, 1910	1,009	644	5,935	1,258	1,246	1,591	1,722	2,100
Gain in borrowers to June 30, 1911	475	343	932	242	980	461	438	253
Present number of borrowers in each 100 population	28	27	48	50	18	34	32	57
Cost of each borrower including purchase of books	$ .16	2.17	.62	.85	1.31	.92	3.09	.85
Number of books loaned each borrower	13	24	3.8	12.	11.2	8.4	8.1	4.2
Cost to circulate each book	$ .103	.099	.131	.051	.092	.068	.106	.15
Number of non-fiction in each 100 books circulated	18	21	19	.013	22	17	25	14
Total number of books owned July 1, 1911	2,962	2,725	9,820	2,784	6,299	3,569	2,799	3,757
Number of times each book circulated	6.5	8.7	2.5	6.5	4.	4.8	6.	2.7
Number of books owned to each resident	.57	.74	.68	.92	.50	.59	.45	.81
Number of books loaned to each resident	3.7	6.48	1.8	6	2.	2.89	2.7	2.16

COMPARATIVE STATISTICS OF PUBLIC LIBRARIES IN TOWNS OVER 3,000. JUNE 30, 1911-JULY 1, 1912

	Devils Lake	Dickinson	Fargo Re-registered	Grafton	Grand Forks	Jamestown	Mandan	Minot Re-registered	Valley City	Williston
Population	5,157	3,678	11,331	2,229	12,478	4,358	3,873	6,188	4,606	3,124
Number of borrowers July 1, 1911	1,484	1,038	6,867	1,452	1,247	1,958	....	2,091	2,346	397
Gain in borrowers to June 30, 1912	382	329	1,188	115	1,054	020	....	516	216	586
Present number of borrowers in each 100 population	36	37	22	70	18	56	....	12	53	31
Cost of each borrower including purchase of books	$ 1.25	1.25	1.12	.73	1.82	.66	....	3.79	1.22	3.48
Number of books loaned each borrower	9.5	15	10.3	6.9	12	7.1	....	6.1	5.3	16.8
Cost to circulate each book	$ .11	.058	.09	.091	.114	.053	....	.116	.141	.16
No. of non-fiction in each 100 books circulated	27	22.6	21	2.1	40	20	....	27	13.3	20.6
Total number of books owned July 1, 1912	1,696	3,204	9,871	3,136	6,240	4,244	*2,608	3,001	3,731	3,509
Number of times each book circulated	5	6	3.4	3	4.5	4.1	2.5	6.2	3	4.5
Number of books owned to each inhabitant	.6	.8	.6	1.4	.5	.97	.7	.5	.8	1.1
Number of books loaned to each inhabitant	3.1	5.5	2.3	1.9	2.3	4	1.7	3	2.5	5

LIBRARIES IN STATE INSTITUTIONS

Name of Library—City	No. vols. July 1		Books Period. and Binding		Total Expenditures		Librarian
	1910	1912	1910-11	1911-12	1910-1911	1911-1912	
Agricultural College—Fargo	22,301	23,436	$ 1,550.14	$ 2,969.84	$ 3,778.64	$ 5,344.84	(Mrs.) Ethel McVeety
Institution for Feeble-minded—Grafton	......	100	......	......	......	......	Alice B. Scott
Normal School—Mayville	5,272	5,573	......	......	......	......	Nelle A. Olson
Normal School—Valley City	7,540	8,110	......	......	......	......	Phebe Parker
Normal Industrial School—Ellendale	......	2,875	......	......	500.00	500.00	Carrie Tuttle
School of Forestry—Bottineau	......	1,500	......	......	......	......	Teachers
School of Science—Wahpeton	......	1,143	437.59	209.94	......	......	Lilian Mirick
State Historical Society—Bismarck	......	*250	......	......	......	......	H. C. Fish
State Hospital for the Insane—Jamestown	......	916	......	......	......	......	......
State Law—Bismarck	16,388	20,055	1,527.91	1,364.01	......	......	E. P. Wing
State Educational Reference—Bismarck	2,425	3,175	1,006.67	387.84	2,266.14	1,422.55	M. C. Budlong
State Penitentiary—Grove	......	2,930	......	......	......	......	J. E. Remington
University of North Dakota—University	37,086	44,390	3,845.38	4,628.86	9,936.71	5,472.00	C. W. Sumner

*Added 1912.

COLLEGE AND LODGE LIBRARIES

Name of Library—City	No. of Vols.		Librarian
	1910	1912	
Fargo College—Fargo	5,605	6,089	Edithe A. Conn—1910. Carnegie Building.
Library Hall Jamestown College—Jamestown	......	*900	1912. Gift of building costing $18,000.00.
Masonic Grand Lodge—Fargo	2,397	2,629	W. L. Stockwell—Purchased books and bulletins in 1911-12, $413.60 Total expenditures, $696.45.

*Added 1912.

PUBLICATIONS.

Budlong (Mrs.), Minnie Clarke.
First Biennial Report of North Dakota Library Commission, 1908.
Suggestive list of books for school libraries, 1909.
Plan of organization for small libraries; methods of work; lists of supplies and aids, 1910.
Second Biennial Report of North Dakota Library Commission. 1910.
Third Biennial Report of North Dakota Library Commission, 1912.

Johnson. Sveinbjorn.
Parliamentary motions in order of rank.
Permanent state tax commissions, 1910.
Good roads. An outline of state road systems, 1910.

Robinson, Julia A.
Papers and Proceedings of the Fourth Annual meeting of the North Dakota Library Association. 1909.

INFORMATION AND PUBLICITY LEAFLETS.

North Dakota Public Library Commission. 1908—No. 1.
North Dakota Public Library Commission revised. 1909—No.2.
North Dakota Public Library Commission. revised 1910—No.2
North Dakota Public Library Commission. revised 1911—No. 7
Facts about traveling libraries 1909—No. 3.
Facts about traveling libraries. reprint 1910—No. 3.
Facts about traveling libraries. reprint 1911—No. 3
Are you getting your share of free books? 1910—No. 4.
Are you getting your share of free books?, revised 1911—No. 4.
Aims—Results Needs 1910—No. 5.
Aims—Results—Needs, revised 1911—No. 9.
Farmers' libraries 1911—No. 6.
Farmers' libraries. revised 1911—No. 8.
New Year's Greetings 1910.

AWAITING PUBLICATION.

Budlong, (Mrs.) Minnie Clarke.
Papers and Proceedings of the Fifth Annual meeting of the North Dakota Library Association, 1910.
Statistics traveling and public libraries excluded from Second Biennial Report, 1910.
Publications in North Dakota Educational Reference library by North Dakota authors, or concerning North Dakota, 1912.

Johnson, Sveinbjorn.
North Dakota laws relating to women and children, 1911.
Acker, Iver A.
State Board of control law, 1911.
State juvenile court law, 1911.
State uniform accounting laws, 1912.
State laws relating to tuberculosis, 1912.
Budget laws, domestic and foreign, 1912.

LEGISLATIVE REFERENCE DEPARTMENT.

The legislative reference librarian has endeavored to keep this department up to the high standard maintained by his predecessor. The laws of other states, judicial decisions, reports of state departments and boards and material of economic and sociological value have been collected and placed on file so as to be conveniently accessible to legislators, public officials and all persons interested. Digests of state laws have been prepared as follows:

(1) State board of control law.
(2) State juvenile court law.
(3). State uniform accounting laws.
(4) State laws relating to tuberculosis.
(5) Budget laws, domestic and foreign.

A complete file of bills introduced in the sessions of 1903, 1905, 1907, 1909 and 1911 has been indexed and bound for ready reference.

This department has been of great assistance to the high schools of the state. In the school year 1911-12 all the high schools in the debating league were furnished material. It is anticipated that the demand for such material will be even greater during the present school year.

State officials have frequently requested information and assistance.

Municipal officials have also been assisted. Many requests for information relating to the work and problems of cities have been received. When the proposed state municipal league has been organized, this department will be of great value to city officers.

I. A. ACKER,
Legislative Reference Librarian.

ANNUAL REPORT OF TREASURER OF N. D. PUBLIC LIBRARY COMMISSION—JULY 1, 1910 TO JUNE 30, 1911

Year	Month	Expenditures	Transportation of Books	Books Purchased	Periodicals and Membership Fees	Stationery and Postage	Field Work	Aids to Libraries	Supplies
1910	July	$ 432.28	24.53	7.40	....	....	....	....	29.18
	August	418.55	5.50	....	6.50	....	32.10	....	....
	September	534.44	5.00	102.94	....	....	....	....	65.10
	October	569.21	1.10	215.84	....	11.00	....	....	5.00
	November	635.13	16.76	113.62	1.00	6.00	....	....	1.75
	December	1,325.64	16.76	425.08	39.50	106.20	....	5.00	66.00
1911	January	1,303.55	15.13	691.82	24.20	10.00	....	19.80	....
	February	977.82	22.16	180.93	3.00	....	14.55	11.50	202.22
	March	1,005.81	18.63	387.87	14.00	....	....	....	80.45
	April	2,054.46	38.14	1,578.46	1.00	23.00	....	....	10.03
	May	667.71	22.94	172.68	....	....	....	....	3.25
	June	518.49	17.19	31.54	4.00	....	10.50	....	15.15
		$ 10,443.09	$ 203.84	$ 3,908.18	93.20	156.20	77.15	36.30	478.13

ANNUAL REPORT OF TREASURER OF N. D. PUBLIC LIBRARY COMMISSION—JULY 1, 1910 TO JUNE 30, 1911—Continued.

Year	Month	Commission Expenses	Salaries	Office Furniture	Miscellaneous	Total Traveling Libraries	Total Educational Library	Total Legislative Reference	Total Miscellaneous Expenses
1910	July	88.64	282.53	....	....	111.86	146.58	65.03	108.81
	August	....	345.00	....	9.45	210.00	....	192.60	15.95
	September	....	359.40	....	2.00	288.51	57.78	174.40	13.75
	October	....	271.50	....	64.77	147.60	228.24	111.50	81.87
	November	69.55	412.00	....	14.45	146.98	163.15	241.00	84.00
	December	....	521.10	146.00	....	348.17	348.86	389.68	238.93
1911	January	30.35	510.00	2.25	....	635.45	290.46	305.21	72.43
	February	....	510.00	19.00	14.46	489.94	130.20	293.82	63.86
	March	50.15	424.96	....	29.75	577.49	136.51	206.91	84.90
	April	....	388.08	....	15.75	1,597.39	206.86	202.26	47.95
	May	....	375.94	60.90	32.00	311.41	154.87	108.53	92.90
	June	....	440.11	....	....	271.01	163.90	73.08	10.50
		238.69	4,840.62	228.15	182.63	5,135.81	2,027.41	2.364.02	915.85
									$ 10,443.09

ANNUAL REPORT OF TREASURER OF N. D. PUBLIC LIBRARY COMMISSION—JULY 1, 1911 TO JUNE 30, 1912

Year	Month	Expenditures	Transportation of Books	Books Purchased	Periodicals and Membership Fees	Stationery and Postage	Field Work	Aids to Libraries	Supplies
1911	July	$ 630.30	11.58	91.90	....	....	57.85	....	13.00
	August	459.63	16.87	32.20	8.50	....	14.75	....	7.47
	September	448.24	9.93	7.98	....	....	....	2.00	5.50
	October	461.08	9.83	38.72	....	....	.75	....	10.70
	November	585.45	....	....	....	....	27.00	....	152.90
	December	428.61	15.00	....	2.00	....	....	....	....
1912	January	537.02	1.15	3.85	20.00	....	....	10.00	5.50
	February	783.38	10.98	252.73	11.00	20.00	47.80	....	10.50
	March	500.84	18.91	17.64	47.95	....	....	....	....
	April	581.59	33.89	76.74	9.50	....	....	....	....
	May	542.75	18.29	74.04	....	30.00	30.45	....	2.25
	June	556.65	3.04	100.90	1.35	....	....	....	....
		$ 6,515.54	149.47	696.70	100.30	50.00	178.60	12.00	207.82

ANNUAL REPORT OF TREASURER OF N. D. PUBLIC LIBRARY COMMISSION—JULY 1, 1911 TO JUNE 30, 1912—Continued

Year	Month	Commission Expenses	Salaries	Office Furniture	Miscellaneous	Total Traveling Libraries	Total Educational Library	Total Legislative Reference	Total Miscellaneous Expenses
1911	July	....	455.97	....	....	331.14	167.98	73.33	57.85
	August	....	379.84	....	....	263.82	74.71	98.53	22.57
	September	....	397.83	....	25.00	180.65	96.76	163.33	7.50
	October	....	401.08	....	....	187.46	104.04	168.83	.75
	November	....	405.55	....	....	332.62	60.00	165.83	27.00
	December	....	411.61	....	....	200.28	60.00	165.83	2.50
1912	January	50.30	446.22	....	....	205.71	85.85	180.16	65.30
	February	14.50	414.12	1.75	....	238.42	298.75	175.66	70.55
	March	....	416.34	....	....	191.61	99.12	210.11	....
	April	....	416.46	....	15.00	266.35	86.58	183.66	45.00
	May	....	417.72	....	....	251.86	83.00	177.44	30.45
	June	35.20	416.16	....	....	261.74	84.20	175.51	35.20
		100.00	4,978.90	1.75	40.00	2,911.66	1,300.99	1,938.22	364.67
									6,515.54

Public Document No. 9

SIXTH BIENNIAL REPORT

OF THE

Public Library Commission

of the State of North Dakota

1916-1918

TRIBUNE PRINTING CO.
Bismarck, N. D.

SIXTH BIENNIAL REPORT

OF THE

North Dakota

Public Library Commission

of the State of North Dakota

1916-1918

TRIBUNE PRINTING CO.
Bismarck, N. D.

CONTENTS

Table of Contents
Library Commission Directory
Letter of Transmittal
Duties of Library Commission
Report of Secretary .... ;

Educational Reference Department 7

Traveling Library System 8
Reorganization 9
School libraries 9
Community libraries 10
Farmers' libraries 11
Circulation 11
Expense 12
Indefinite loan 12
Table showing stations 13

Legislative Reference Bureau 14

Field Work 15
Bismarck Public Library 15
Statistics—public libraries containing over 3,000 volumes 16
Statistics—public libraries containing less than 3,000 volumes..17
Statistics—institutional libraries 16

Notes on Libraries 18-20
Changes of Librarians 21
War Work ....;...22
Bequests 23
Publications 23
Criticism and Commendation....................................24-26
Summary 26
Needs 27
Financial Report 28

LIST OF ILLUSTRATIONS

Frontispiece—Map showing all traveling library stations, July 1, 1916 to June 30, 1918.

Carnegie Library, Bismarck 15

NORTH DAKOTA STATE BOARD OF REGENTS

July 1, 1916

L. F. Crawford............................Sentinel Butte, President
Frank White ....Valley City, Vice-President
J. D. Taylor....................................Grand Forks
Emil Scow..Bowman
J. A. Power...Leonard

June 30, 1918

L. F. Crawford............................Sentinel Butte, President
J. D. Taylor...........................Grand Forks, Vice-President
Charles E. Vermilyea..................................Bismarck
George A. Totten......................................Bowman
Robert T. Muir...Sarles

PUBLIC LIBRARY COMMISSION

Mrs. Minnie Clarke Budlong..................Secretary and Director

STAFF

July 1, 1916

Florence MacPhee ....Chief Traveling Library Department
Earl H. Davis.......................Legislative Reference Librarian
Haldora Peterson ....Stenographer
Elsie Smith ....Clerk

June 30, 1918

Charlotte Matson........Deputy and Legislative Reference Librarian
Helen Frances Carleton..........Chief Traveling Library Department
Mary Ethel Fleming..............................Stenographer
Mrs. S. Sloan...Clerk

LETTER OF TRANSMITTAL

To the State Board of Regents:

Gentlemen:—The report of the North Dakota State Public Library Commission for the period July 1, 1916 to June 30, 1918, is herewith submitted.

(MRS.) MINNIE CLARKE BUDLONG,
Secretary and Director,
Public Lilbrary Commission.

DUTIES OF THE PUBLIC LIBRARY COMMISSION

Chapter 156, Laws of 1909, outlines for the North Dakota Public Library Commission the following duties:

1. Charge of educational reference library.

2. Charge of traveling libraries and increase in their number and usefulness.

3. Establishment and care of legislative reference bureau.

4. Free aid, advice and instruction to public libraries.

5. Assistance in formation of libraries where none exist.

6. Preparation of statistics of public libraries and record of work done by commission.

REPORT OF SECRETARY

The work of the North Dakota Public Library Commission is organized under the following divisions:

I. Educational reference department.
II. Traveling library system.
III. Legislative reference bureau.
IV. Field work.

The offices of the Commission are in the Capitol at Bismarck. The secretary of the Commission is director of all departments of work. There are department heads for the traveling library system and the legislative reference bureau. Educational reference work and field work are performed by the secretary assisted by the staff. The Library Commission together with the University, Agricultural College, Normal Schools, School of Science, Industrial School, and School of Forestry is supervised by the State Board of Regents.

EDUCATIONAL REFERENCE DEPARTMENT

Invoice taken May, 1918, shows the educational reference department to consist of 4,879 books and 19,507 pamphlets and clippings, representing all classes of literature. These may be borrowed by any club or individual in the state who will pay the cost of transportation, and agree to be responsible for their safe return. No guarantee is required.

This collection contains very little fiction and no juvenile books. It is strong in history, biography, travel and sociology, and is especially intended as an aid to individuals, to clubs and to debating societies. Books are loaned for a month and renewed if requested, and an effort is made to supply students with books in their special line of research. Clippings, cut from magazines and newspapers, and mounted for circulation, keep this collection up to date. When the legislature is not in session, this department lends material from the collection of the legislative reference bureau.

From June 30, 1916, to July 1, 1918, 12,564 pamphlets and clippings and 5,473 books were sent from this department, besides 825 programs loaned 129 clubs. This makes a total of 18,863 pieces sent in answer to 5,232 applications. The requests came from 396 postoffices reaching every county. In the first six months of 1918, requests were received from 57 postoffices not previously on the mailing list, which shows the rapid extension of the demands on this department.

As every piece sent generally serves a group varying in size from a small study club or a school class to a community league, the real good accomplished can not be indicated by figures. The total is surprising when one considers that these figures cover only the period of war activity in which many clubs have reduced study outlines to the simplest form and High School classes have been materially decreased in numbers. Also the circulation of fiction and children's books from this office to the city of Bismarck, which in 1916 averaged 164 volumes a month, has been discontinued since the opening of the Bismarck Carnegie library 1917. This correspondence service is one of the most popular and practical departments of the Library Commission work, and will continue to grow in importance until public libraries are established in each county to reach all students.

The use of this department to supplement school resources is shown by the fact that in the spring of 1918, 55 requests from 37 students and teachers in one High School (Grafton) were received. To them were sent 20 books and 368 pamphlets and clippings. In May alone material was sent to 127 people in 70 towns. This reached many more than the 127 patrons. For instance one teacher at Forbes requested material on 22 subjects for her school, receiving 4 books and 79 pamphlets. Grafton received the most material of any town for the month of May, 3 books and 125 pamphlets and clippings being sent to 17 patrons on 19 subjects. Many of these requests served many more than the one individual writing the letter, altho the material is all entered in the one name. For instance, it is not unusual for the secretary of a club to request material for a number of members in one letter. In May one club letter from Mercer asked material for nine papers. Of the 127 people to whom material was sent in May 37 were legislators, club women and public speakers, and 90 were teachers and High School students.

The books in the educational reference department are consulted many times daily by the public and of this use no record is kept. The work of this department is hampered by having no department head, as have the traveling library system and the legislative reference bureau, whose special work it shall be to keep all the material up to date, to answer at length reference questions and to keep records of the work done. A trained chief for this department is the next addition that should be made to the Library Commission staff.

TRAVELING LIBRARY SYSTEM

The traveling libraries serve many purposes in the development of the state. They are of great help to teachers in schoolhouses where few, if any, books are found. They furnish supplemental aid to textbooks in history, literature, geography, agriculture and other subjects, and with their illustrations in color broaden the outlook of pupils who have not yet traveled beyond the home environment. They supply individuals and clubs with an incentive and a means of study. They furnish reading for improvement and recreation to all in the community. They aid social life by providing the center around which groups gather for study and discussion. They promote community life and spirit and are proving a powerful factor in the betterment of farm conditions.

The traveling library system consists of fixed collections of books sent out in wooden cases for three to six month's loan, wherever in the state responsible people will agree to care for them, to circulate them free of charge and to return them to Bismarck with freight paid both ways. There are three kinds of these libraries:—Farmers' libraries—12 to 15 technical books on farming; School libraries—20 to 25 books selected for use in schools; and Community libraries—40 to 50 volumes for general reading of interest to adults and children. The selections of books varies, some cases containing a larger proportion of books for adults and some being better adapted to children or young people. Some are largely composed of books for recreation and inspiration. Others are technical books for clubs and students. The demand for these libraries exceeds the supply, and application for community and school libraries should be filed early in the summer to insure prompt shipment in the fall. The Library Commission owned June 30, 1918, 324 traveling libraries, containing 10,606 books.

REORGANIZATION

During this biennium the traveling library system has been completely reorganized. Lack of libraries to supply the demands has necessitated dropping many stations. In this report only stations that have received boxes July 1, 1916 to June 30, 1918, are included.

In ten years of service many books have worn out. In this biennium 69 libraries containing 3,194 books have been withdrawn. For this reason lists have been revised, new editions substituted, new titles added, and additional libraries prepared. For all departments of Commission work there have been purchased in these two years 5,163 books costing approximately $4,300.00.

School libraries formerly varied from boxes containing 20 to 25 books for the lower grades to collections of 40 to 50 books suited to all grades. Henceforth the name "school library" will be used for the small collections only and the larger collections will be classed with community libraries. Under this classification the Library Commission owned June 30, 1918

74 School libraries containing	1,797	books.
161 Comunity libraries containing	7,618	books.
89 Farmers' libraries containing	1,191	books.
Open shelf collection	2,103	books.
	12,709	

SCHOOL LIBRARIES

School libraries consist of 20 to 25 books in history, literature, biography, science and juvenile fiction. They are intended primarily for use in the first five grades of school, but contain also reading of interest in homes and communities. There were 58 of these collections at the beginning of the biennium and 112 requests were filled, each library serving two stations. They are loaned on request of teacher and school board or to six responsible people who agree to care for them and to insure their safe return. They may be kept six months and renewed if requested, and the only expense to borrowers is freight both ways. They are usually kept thru the school year and must then be returned to the Library Commission office where they are thoroly cleaned and repaired before being shipped to another station.

The service rendered by school libraries can not be recorded in figures since their first use is as reference in class or in preparation of lessons. When taken home by pupils they reach families and often groups of families while the entry on the card records only one reader—the borrower. A more accurate indication of their usefulness is found in letters of appreciation from patrons. A few extracts from such letters are given on page 25.

Thirty-five school libraries have been purchased in this biennium, containing 895 books and costing $609.13.

COMMUNITY LIBRARIES

Community libraries are boxes containing 40 to 50 books suited to all ages and conditions. Usually 15 books are adult fiction and 10 juvenile fiction. The remainder includes history, literature, travel, sociology, biography, war books and other recent books of general interest. These libraries may be borrowed by groups of six responsible people and kept at any place convenient of access. 339 community libraries containing 15,278 books were loaned in this biennium and were distributed among 131 schools, 81 residences, 30 banks, 13 offices, 20 country stores, 10 drug stores. 7 clubs, 6 postoffices, 5 courthouses, 5 libraries, 4 churches, 3 city halls, 2 hotels, 2 Odd Fellows' halls, 1 farm, 1 fort, and 1 restaurant.

The distribution by counties is as follows:

In	1	county	are	21	stations	that	have	had	32	libraries
"	1	"	"	16	"	"	"	"	27	"
"	2	counties	"	15	"	"	"	"	37	"
"	2	"	"	14	"	"	"	"	49	"
"	1	county	"	12	"	"	"	"	17	"
"	1	"	"	11	"	"	"	"	19	"
"	3	counties	"	10	"	"	"	"	49	"
"	1	county	"	9	"	"	"	"	19	"
"	2	counties	"	8	"	"	"	"	28	"
"	6	"	"	7	"	"	"	"	67	"
"	7	"	"	6	"	"	"	"	67	"
"	3	"	"	4	"	"	"	"	28	"
"	3	"	"	4	"	"	"	"	21	"
"	5	"	"	3	"	"	"	"	22	"
"	8	"	"	2	"	"	"	"	23	"
"	7	"	is	1	station	"	has	"	15	"
	—			—					—	
	53	counties		322	stations				518	libraries

64 community libraries containing 3,006 books have been withdrawn in this period. Many of these books had been in circulation over 10 years. 75 libraries containing 3,340 books, costing $2,840.13 were purchased. The Library Comission owns, June 30, 1918, 161 community libraries containing 7,618 books.

FARMERS' LIBRARIES

Farmers' libraries consist of technical books on farming, stockraising, machinery, gardening, poultry, dairying and related subjects. They are in great demand among the farmers during the winter months and in the schools teaching agriculture. It is impossible to show in figures the use made of these books, as there is no librarian such as the traveling libraries have to keep record of circulation. The cases containing 12 to 15 books are sent wherever three men sign an application card and may be kept three months if freely circulated in the community. In school they are used as text and reference by classes in agriculture and in clubs as material for papers and discussions. They are also used as texts for individual consultation and study. The Commission has 89 of these collections and 261 stations to which one or more has been sent. The collections were started in 1909 and circulated thru the cooperation of the Agricultural College, farmers' institutes, and bankers' associations. The Agricultural College thru its extension department now furnishes information on agricultural subjects. It is the policy of the Library Commission not to dissipate its funds and energies in the duplication of work in fields which can be occupied to better advantage by some other state agency. Consequently, no attempt has been made to add to the number of these libraries. They are still sent to schools and clubs on request. The following extract from a letter written by a principal of schools is typical in its statement of what is accomplished by farmers' libraries: "I am returning the farmers' library today * * * we have used the books as reference for our class in High School agriculture. There are 11 members in the class, and the books were very helpful. The children often took them home for their parents."

CIRCULATION

The record of circulation for traveling libraries can, at best, be only approximate, since some libraries are returned with only the evidence of much usage to record how many times books have been read. The highest recorded circulation in this biennium for one use of a traveling library is from Mott where 23 patrons read 301 books. This is an average of 13 books read by each patron in six months. The largest number of readers recorded for one shipment is at Center where 125 borrowers drew books from one traveling library. Often the greatest usefulness of these libraries is not at a populous station, which can record a large number of readers or of circulation but at some sparsely settled point where a few families are opening new territory and find in these libraries a nucleus for the winter's reading, recreation and sociability. They are proving a valuable aid in the development of rural community life.

EXPENSE OF TRAVELING LIBRARIES

To Borrowers: The heaviest boxes weigh less than a hundred pounds and often the freight is not more than 25c. If there are transfers, the expense is greater. A leaflet has been prepared, giving freight rates from

Bismarck to a number of stations from which borrowers can estimate to their own station. While no charge can be made at the library station for the use of books, it is permissible to assess a fine for overdue books, and at some stations this sum proves sufficient to pay freight. At others, the six signers of the card contribute the few cents apiece necessary to raise the amount. The freight on school libraries is often paid from the school fund.

To the State: In no way can good reading be furnished citizens with so little expense to the state as thru a traveling library system. The Library Commission has the advantage of purchasing books in large quantities. The waste of purchasing thru agents and middlemen is eliminated. It has expert aid in book selection so that no money is spent in undesirable titles or worthless editions. The loss from books standing idle on a shelf after a few readings is minimized. Only books well recommended are found in its collections and they are constantly in use until worn out. To the state the cost of a reading of a book by each borrower is less than two cents, and the reader has no capital tied up in a book rapidly becoming out of date.

INDEFINITE LOAN

Books too worn to be longer included in traveling libraries are sent to schools or camps under the title "indefinite loan," since there is no time set for their return. They usually wear out in the place to which they are sent. as the Libray Commission asks for no report upon them after acknowledgement of their receipt. 801 books were thus distributed thru rural teachers who called at the Library Commission office.

The opening of the Carnegie library in Bismarck relieved the traveling library department from further local circulation of fiction and juvenile books which had been conducted for the accommodation of Bismarck patrons. 104 books were "indefinitely loaned" the Bismarck public library.

While the State Militia was encamped at Fort Lincoln, N. D., 797 volumes of "indefinite loan" were sent to the soldiers.

When books were being collected by the American Library Association for soldiers' use in camps and cantonments, 980 were contributed by the Library Commission.

This makes a total of 2,682 volumes distributed thru "indefinite loan."

TABLE SHOWING NUMBER OF STATIONS FOR TRAVELING LIBRARIES IN EACH COUNTY AND NUMBER OF LIBRARIES SENT EACH COUNTY

Counties	Stations	No. Libraries
Adams	1	2
Barnes	16	27
Benson	9	19
Billings	3	5
Bottineau	10	12
Bowman	3	4
Burke	1	1

Counties	Stations	No. Libraries
Burleigh	15	17
Cass	14	29
Cavalier	6	10
Dickey	7	10
Divide	6	10
Dunn	7	9
Eddy	4	4
Emmons	12	17
Foster	6	7
Golden Valley	2	4
Grand Forks	6	7
Grant	14	20
Griggs	1	4
Hettinger	7	10
Kidder	5	8
LaMoure	6	10
Logan	1	2
McHenry	7	10
McIntosh	2	2
McKenzie	8	16
McLean	11	19
Mercer	1	1
Mountrail	10	24
Morton	21	32
Nelson	15	20
Oliver	7	14
Pembina	6	12
Pierce	1	2
Ramsey	3	7
Ransom	2	3
Renville	4	13
Richland	1	1
Rolette	2	2
Sargent	4	4
Sheridan	2	3
Sioux	3	3
Slope	3	3
Stark	5	15
Steele	2	4
Stutsman	10	13
Towner	5	5
Traill	2	3
Walsh	2	2
Ward	7	14
Wells	8	12
Williams	6	11
Total	322	518

LEGISLATIVE REFERENCE BUREAU

The work of the Legislative Reference Bureau is primarily the collection of material for use of law makers and state officials and aid in the preparation and drafting of bills. The bureau contains 852 books and 19,121 pamphlets and mounted clippings. This increase in the number of pamphlets and clippings does not represent the actual increase in material the department has received, as owing to lack of space in the library it is continually necessary to discard old or duplicate material to make room on the shelves for what is new and up to date. The material of the department when not needed during sessions is loaned thru the Educational Reference Department to clubs and individuals in the state—much of the debate work for schools being handled by the Legislative Reference Bureau. February, 1918, was the record month of the biennium, so far as circulation statistics were concerned, the department sending out 45 books, 156 pamphlets, 22 typed manuscripts, 11 bills and 597 clippings, a total of 631 articles in answer to 110 questions.

An important part of the regular work of the Legislative Reference Bureau consists in reading and clipping magazines and papers. 12 weekly, 10 daily and 2 semi-weekly newspapers; 10 weekly, 1 biweekly, 12 monthly, 1 bimonthly, and 7 quarterly magazines are indexed, clipped, marked for future clipping or filed away for use with the periodical indexes. The collections of the department must be kept up to date, and this necessitates sending many requests for material each month to departments of other states and of the government. The latest compilation of laws of all the states on such subjects as labor, banking, taxation, corporations, insurance, education, highways, health, fish, and game, etc., have been collected. Special attention has been paid to the subject of the liberty loan, taxation and other matters relating to war finance.

During the biennium there have been two sessions of the Legislature, the regular session of 1917, and the short special session of 1918. 444 bills were introduced in the House and 323 in the Senate during the regular session, and of these 329, or almost half passed thru the Legislative Reference Bureau, some for amendment and others for complete drafting. No bill drafter was employed for the special session as the preliminary work on the bills had been done for the most part before the session began, but many bills were copied. The bills of both sessions have been indexed. In preparation for the meeting of the special session letters were sent to all the states asking for copies of existing or proposed laws on the subjects of seed grain and war moratoriums, and the information received was tabulated for use of Legislators. The principal work done during the session was reference work, among the questions on which information was furnished being the following: Absent voters laws for soldiers; laws relating to home guards; government policy in renting Indian lands; seed grain laws; state laws establishing councils of defense; moratory laws.

FIELD WORK

The demands of office and correspondence prevented the secretary from undertaking much field work. Visits were made including 24 towns and many addresses were given before state and district associations, educa-

Carnegie Library, Bismarck.

tional and club meetings, schools, Red Cross societies, and other gatherings.

Addresses, sometimes as many as five, were made in practically all the towns visited. School and public libraries were visited in all these towns not previously inspected. Work on the school library at Steele was finished and work at LaMoure, Page, and Cando begun. The towns included in field work were: Baldwin, Bismarck, Cando, Devils Lake, Dickinson, Egeland, Ellendale, Fargo, Garrison, Grand Forks, LaMoure, Leeds, McClusky, Mandan, Minot, Mott, Napoleon, New Salem, Oakes, Page, Steele, Stewartsdale, Valley City, Williston.

The only trips outside the state in this biennium were one to Chicago, January, 1917, to attend the annual meeting of the League of Library Commissions in which the secretary is first vice-president, and one to St. Paul, August, 1917, where the United States Bureau of Education was holding a conference on rural school problems and invited the secretary to discuss library extension from consolidated schools.

At the 1917 meeting of the North Dakota Educational Association an exhibit was conducted to acquaint teachers with the aids to be obtained from the Library Commission.

The Fifteenth Legislative Assembly included in the budget for the Library Commission an appropriation which will permit the employment of an organizer after July 1, 1918. The much needed work with schools and public libraries can then be systematically undertaken.

BISMARCK'S LIBRARY BUILDING

The $25,000.00 library building that Carnegie gave Bismarck has been erected on a lot 75x100 ft. facing the courthouse square.

It is in Colonial design with ground dimensions of 46x64 ft., having one story and finished basement. It is built of dark red brick and hollow tile and trimmed with Bedford limestone. With shingles of asphalt and crushed green slate, it will resist all kinds of weather and fire from outside sources. Special care has been taken to prevent the penetration of the walls by either dampness or frost. It is steamheated from its own plant.

The library proper is on the main floor. This is one room, 44x62 ft., with a ceiling 15 ft. high. It is divided by floor book stacks, into general reading room, children's room, reference room, stack room and librarian's office. Bookcases and magazine racks line the walls of all rooms. The finish of all woodwork in the library proper is ivory enamel with shelves of birch mahogany. Walls are tinted a soft warm gray. The woodwork of lobby is white oak finished in a gray stain with walls to match the library. The lighting fixtures are semi-indirect of a design to harmonize with the Colonial treatment of the room. The entire floor is covered with heavy cork carpet.

The basement contains a Community room, 26½x43½ ft. with a lecture platform. In addition there are a staff room, work room, janitors room, and the boiler and fuel rooms. The finish in the basement is Douglas fir stained a rich brown and the walls are a deep buff. The main entrance lobby is on the north and the basement entrance on the east. Adjoining stairs connect the two floors and are so enclosed that communication between the floors can be stopped at will. The basement story is 10 ft. 6 in. high. The architect is Frederick W. Keith.

STATISTICS FOR PUBLIC LIBRARIES of 3,000 OR MORE VOLUMES, JULY 1, 1916—JUNE 30, 1918.

Place	Population State Census, 1915	Date of Organization	Volumes Owned June 30, 1918	Borrowers June 30, 1918	Circulation July 1, 1916 to June 30, 1918	Name of Librarian
*Bismarck	6,344	1917	4,680	506	2,063	Mrs. Florence Davis
Devils Lake	4,525	1898	4,879	1,939	39,016	Marie O'Brien
Dickinson	4,120	1908	5,017	1,724	44,070	Zenka [redacted] Trinka
Fargo	20,549	1900	13,030	7,932	125,947	Winnie Bucklin
Grafton	2,474	1897	4,702	2,141	29,466	Mary Morris
Grand Forks	13,554	1899	8,245	44,076	61,822	Lillian Cook
Jamestown	5,516	1902	7,078	4,051	33,669	Alice M. Paddock
**Mandan	4,142	1895	3,019	190	3,391	Mrs. Ada a[redacted]tt
Minot	10,053	1908	6,646	3,818	62,067	Margaret Greene
Valley City	4,783	1900	5,296	2,172	33,491	Edna Hackett
Williston	4,678	1910	5,029	1,492	34,614	Bessie R. Baldwin

* Report covers eight months.
**Subscription library. Report for one year only.

STATISTICS OF COLLEGE AND INSTITUTIONAL LIBRARIES, JULY 1, 1916 TO JUNE 30, 1918.

Name of Library	Location	New Books 1916-1918	Total No. of Books Owned July 1, 1918	Name of Librarian
† Agricultural College	Fargo	1,454	26,683	Mrs. Ethel McVeety
Fargo College	Fargo	702	8,327	F. E. Stratton
*Historical Society	Bismarck	2,858	17,858	Edna L. Rupp
Industrial School	J[redacted]lle		3,800	Carrie [redacted]le
†† Institution Feeble-Minded	Grafton			A. R. T. Wylie
†† Insane Asylum	Jamestown			W. M. Hotchkiss
Jamestown College	Jamestown			F. B. Taylor
Law Library	Bismarck	600	16,100	J. H. Newton
Library Commission	Bismarck	5,163	17,840	Mrs. M. C. Budlong
Masonic Library	Fargo	322		Clara A. Richards
Normal School Library	Mayville	635	6,840	Nelle A. Olson
Normal School Library	Valley City	2,598	14,401	Helen M. Crane
† Penitentiary	Bismarck	120	3,638	Frank Davis
School of Forestry	Bottineau	25	861	[redacted]bel Rosel
School of Science	Wahpeton	315	1,959	Lillian [redacted]ck
†University	Grand Forks	2,847	65,125	Blanche Hedrick (Acting Librarian)

* Report covers 15 months. †† No report this [redacted]nn. † Report covers 1 year.

STATISTICS FOR PUBLIC LIBRARIES OF LESS THAN 3,000 VOLUMES. JULY 1, 1916 TO JUNE 30, 1918.

(In this list are included only those libraries which have sent the Library Commission a report in this biennium. This does not necessarily mean those dropped from previous list have ceased to exist or have diminished their activity, but only that their Board has not realized the importance of stopping its war work long enough to send the annual report.)

Place	Population 1915 Census	Date of Organization	Volumes Owned July 1, 1918	Borrowers July 1, 1918	Circulation July 1, 1916 to June 30, 1918	Source of Income	Total Income	Name of Librarian
Alexander	274	1917	450			Gifts		Mrs. Edwin Johnson
Antler	294	1912	950	125	1909	City Appropriation	$ 338.01	Mrs. Geo. C. Brown
Bathgate	376	1916	275	190	1,335	Gifts	92.71	Mrs. J. J. Manning
Beach	1,542	1915	1,175	187	6,832	†Subscription	695.14	Isabelle S. Whitaker
Bowman	744	1913	1,938	704	1,770	††Gifts	1,427.12	Mrs. Jas. Touhey
Cando	1,177	1902	2,431	30	540	Subscription		Mrs. Jas. V. Brooks
*Carrington	1,328	1906	2,663	753	10,[illegible]	City Appropriation	774.81	Edna E. Parker
Casselton	1,564	1906	1,882	848	9,740	City Appropriation	629.40	Caroline E. Newton
Edgeley	718	1912	447	47		Subscription	49.50	Mrs. [illegible] F. Schaper
*Ellendale	1,361	1911	1,982	521	7,469	††City Appropriation	466.79	Mrs. Fred [illegible], Jr.
*Langdon	1,150	1912	1,320	130	2,500	City Appropriation		Mrs. J. H. Harlan
*Leeds	631		1,851	80	1,060	Gifts		[illegible] Wardrope
*Leonard	437	1913	1,629	223	3,621	City Appropriation	254.00	Susie E. Nystul
Mott	738	1912	1,212	490	8,233	City Appropriation	507.86	Louise Wagner
Oakes	1,403		1,875	598	6,384	City Appropriation	1,053.36	Anna B. Fay
*Rugby	1,458	1912	1,068	30	882	††City Appropriation	256.27	Grace B. Fox
*Sanborn	412	1903	788	28	780	Subscription	13.63	Katherine [illegible]
Wahpeton	2,814	1912	2,381	314	19,187	City Appropriation	800.15	Mrs. Jessie C. Searing
Washburn	622	1915	1,298	260		Gifts		Mrs. C. A. Rice

* Report for one year only.
† Made free to the public 1917.
††Voted city tax 1918.

NOTES ON LIBRARIES

Public Libraries

It is interesting to note the effect of war conditions on the ten larger libraries of the state. Eight have added over 500 new books each, Jamestown adding 1,398, Minot 1,745 and Fargo 2,632. Jamestown increased its number of borrowers 23 per cent with a slight decrease in circulation. Minot increased borrowers 40 per cent and circulation 33 per cent. Three libraries show a decrease in circulation, but these towns were very active in Red Cross work. Valley City increased its borrowers 50 per cent with a very slight increase in circulation. Practically all libraries show a marked increase in amount of non-fiction circulated. Evidently in these cases the libraries are reaching an increasing number of patrons, and borrowers are reading fewer and better books. Dickinson doubled its number of borrowers and increased circulation 40 per cent. The notable increase in number of borrowers is as follows: Williston 18 per cent, Jamestown 23 per cent, Fargo 36 per cent, Minot 40 per cent, Valley City 50 per cent, Dickinson 100 per cent. The increase in circulation is as follows: Williston 9 per cent, Mandan 11 per cent, Devils Lake 12 per cent, Fargo 32 per cent, Minot 33 per cent, Dickinson 40 per cent.

It is easy to see in these figures the widening usefulness of public libraries and their growing influence in the more serious affairs of community life.

Alexander reports the Woman's Club has started a library in a room under the State bank with 450 bound volumes.

Bathgate with only 275 books in its library sent 38 of them to the soldiers.

Beach which has had a subscription library made it free to the public January 1, 1917.

Bowman in 1917 took a complete inventory and classified according to the Dewey Decimal system. In May 1918 the city voted to organize under state law.

Buxton requested aid in classifying its school library of 1,000 volumes.

Center is starting a library movement by buying a few books to use in connection with the traveling library until such time as a permanent library association can be organized.

Columbus has a public library committee which is accessioning 500 books according to the plan recommended by Public Library Commission.

Courtenay reports that Red Cross work has affected library progress.

Dickinson doubled its non-fiction circulation by display of "Better books for children" before Christmas and by new shelves centrally placed on which were arranged groups of books with attractive posters, such as: "Books for business men," "How to entertain," "Books boys like best," etc.

Edgeley reports not so many new borrowers as in previous years but great activity in collecting books for soldiers, conducting food campaigns, and other war work.

Ellendale added reading table and chairs for children, and blackboard for publicity work and distributed literature at weekly Red Cross meetings. It secured a city appropriation of $400.00.

Fargo mad a gain in 1916-7 of 5,329 in adult circulation and of 1,802 in juvenile. The total circulation of 62.399 was slightly increased in 1917-8 in spite of war activities, giving a total circulation for the biennum of 125,947—the largest in the state. The librarian conducted the Food Administration Publicity Campaign among librarians of the state.

Forman. The Literary Club secured a room in the court house free of charge and started a library in June, 1917, to be kept open one day in the week.

Grand Forks was active in A. L. A. war work, sending 800 books to Camp Dodge and 8.000 to France. On this library fell a heavy share of the volunteer work in collection and preparation of books for soldiers not only for the city but also for the northeastern part of the state.

Hope. The Woman's Club conducts a library to which it has recently added 50 new books.

Jamestown secured new borrowers thru printing book marks with special lists of books for school children. It collected 2,000 books for soldiers and $238.15 cash for books.

Lakota. The Civic League started a small library in connection with their rest room. November 21, 1917, it was formally opened under the management of a city library board of five members, which cooperates with the school library. An attractive feature of their opening night was the exhibit of "100 master pieces from French galleries," and F. Hopkinson Smith's "Venice" loaned by the Library Commission.

Marmarth. The Study Club planned to start a library, but decided to postpone it while war work is so pressing. The school has small library used by pupils only.

Minot. Growth in children's work necessitated fitting of basement in Auditorium for children's room. In 1918 children's books were 56 per cent of the circulation. The librarian conducted the spring book drive for the state started by the A. L. A. to secure books for soldiers.

Mott reports, "Distributing recipes, food pamphlets, collecting money and books for the soldiers, putting up food posters, Liberty Bond and book posters, sending to Agricultural College and University for material on food conservation and farming and distributing the same."

Oakes library moved into a new room with new equipment of shelves, chairs, tables, magazine rack and card file. The library has been used by class in surgical dressings.

Rugby in March, 1918, reorganized under state law.

St. Thomas had the use of a room given free for library purposes and the Study Club, Civic League and other interested parties began keeping it open one day a week in 1917. They report approximately 250 books.

Sanborn reports, "The same ladies who keep this library are keeping their Woman's Club together during these difficult times. Said club took the instruction in Red Cross work and every member is active in Red

Cross work. Not one of the members has a maid, which means 'keep the home fires burning.' "

Valley City cooperated with food administration and with A. L. A. War Council, collecting and preparing over 1,000 books. The increase in number of borrowers from 1,430 to 2,172 in this biennium is notable.

Wahpeton reports Red Cross meetings held in library and 1,670 magazine clippings, and pamphlets, circulated during 1918 in addition to books.

Williston specialized in reference instruction to High School students and experimented with a branch library at Springbrook. Reading room attendance for one year was 8,741 and reference work 1,728.

Wildrose. The Woman's Club organized a library in 1917 in connection with rest room, sending to the Library Commission for its "Plan of organization."

Institutional Libraries

The Agricultural College librarian conducts a course of instruction in library methods consisting of twelve lectures for freshmen. About two hundred students have satisfactorily completed the work.

Fargo College library set apart two rooms which are in use nearly every day and evening by various Red Cross organizations.

Ellendale Normal library shows especially good use of library as reference and study room for students.

Mayville Normal library added clipping and picture cabinet file, collected books in Mayville and sorted and prepared shipments from Devils Lake, Pekin, Sarles, Portland, and Park River.

Minot Normal library reports $1,744.76 spent for 1,244 books in this biennium and a daily use of reading room of 300 to 500.

State Historical Society library is in process of reorganization. A logical arrangement of books alphabeted under states is being made. A reading room has been provided and special attention is paid to collections from Minnesota, Montana, Canada, and the Northwest. Works of North Dakota are being collected and early North Dakota imprints. A genealogical division has been opened. Arrangements have been made to deposit the four volumes of the Historical Society reports and collections with any school so requesting.

Valley City Normal library collected 594 books and prepared 2,454 for camp libraries.

Wahpeton School of Science library in cooperation with Public library prepared books from Wahpeton and surrounding country for camps.

Miscellaneous

Bismarck has now enough trained librarians to form a Library Science Club which meets regularly for the discussion of library news. At present the membership contains representatives from the following schools: Wisconsin Library School; Simmons College; Pratt; Library School of New York City Public Library; Syracuse University.

Libraries having trained librarians have acted as city and regional centers for collection of money and books and for distribution of government material and for American Library Association service and publicity. There are employed in the state at present 15 graduate librarians, and 12 with partial training. They are located in 9 counties. In the remaining 44 counties the support of libraries and creation of interest therein lies largely with club women.

These are a few of the more important news notes. Practically every library did war and publicity work. In fact the notes from Mott and Sanborn are typical of all the smaller libraries. In only a few instances did circulation decrease while there was great gain everywhere in library activity in community life. One library reports a decrease of one-third in circulation, but as this circulation was novel reading the time and energy are well transferred to war work. Libraries keeping their circulation steady show a decided gain in per cent of non-fiction reading. A few of the smallest libraries report " Putting their money in the bank," "Packing up the books" or "Locking the door until the demands of the Red Cross become less insistent."

Few new libraries have been established in North Dakota this biennium, but the notable increase in civic usefulness, in dignity, and importance as social centers of those already established marks this as one of the most progressive periods of library development.

CHANGES OF LIBRARIANS

The changes which war conditions have brought in business have been duplicated in the library world. The value of assistants with training or experience in card systems, and other details of library science has been recognized by tempting offers from business houses which have depleted library staffs.

Public Library Commission

The entire staff of the Library Commission has been changed. Florence MacPhee after nine years of service in building up the traveling libraries resigned as chief of that department, to accept a position of chief bookkeeper for the Overland-Doyle Co., Fargo. Haldora Peterson, stenographer to the commission since 1911, November 1917, was promoted to a position in the office of the State Engineer, and in August, 1918, was called to a position in the headquarters office of the A. L. A. War Service Library of Congress, Washington, D. C. Elsie Smith for five years clerk in the traveling library department accepted a position with the Burleigh County Abstract Co. Stewart S. Williams, who succeeded Earl H. Davis as legislative reference librarian, was called to service in France, where he is sergeant in Quartermaster Corps, American P. O. 705. Earl H. Davis is with the Medical department, 12 Engineers Railway, Headquarters, A. E. F.

Charlotte Matson came October, 1917, from the Municipal branch of the Minneapolis public library to be legislative reference librarian. She was trained in the Library School of New York Public Library. Helen Carleton, graduate Simmons College and former librarian at Dickinson, accepted the position as chief traveling library department, November, 1917. Ethel Fleming, graduate Bismarck Business College, became stenographer, November, 1917.

Grand Forks Public Library

Adah Durand, librarian Grand Forks public library, became Mrs. Lester Chidlaw and resigned to accept a position in Minneapolis public library in order to be near her husband at Fort Snelling. Lillian Cook, formerly librarian at Valley City, was called to the vacancy in Grand Forks library. Her place at Valley City was temporarily filled by the assistant, Edna Hackett.

University Library

Clarence W. Summer, librarian at University, resigned September, 1917, to accept the librarianship of the Sioux City, Ia., public library. The University library has since been in charge of Blanche Hedrick, acting librarian.

WAR WORK

Money Drive

By virtue of office the secretary of Library Commission is state director of American Library War Service.

A campaign was conducted in September, 1917, thru librarians and county chairmen of Federated clubs to raise money for books for soldiers.

In the report published by the national chairman of War Finance committee in Library Journal, March, 1918, North Dakota is credited with having paid $5,539.01 toward this fund. Subsequent contributions have increased the amount to $5,928.28 and it will approximate $6,000.00 when all pledges are paid, as some counties, notably Pierce, give to this fund 5 per cent of all war money raised prior to September 1, 1918. Concerning this contribution the Divisional Director wrote the State Director, "North Dakota has certainly done its share and I should think you would be very proud of it."

At the time of the money campaign, no special effort was made to collect reading matter, but 5,341 books and 12,943 magazines were sent thru the Library Commission from numerous towns in the state to various camps.

Book Drive

In the spring of 1918 a campaign for books was pushed thruout the state. Charge of this work was given to Margaret Greene, librarian Public library, Minot. She reports 131 towns responding out of the 222 asked to cooperate and 28,246 books collected. These were assembled at Grand Forks, Mayville, Valley City, Wahpeton, Jamestown, Williston and Minot to be sorted and prepared for circulation before shipment to camp libraries. 10,630 books were sent to Camp Dodge and 14,300 volumes to ports of embarkation. $44.50 cash contributed in place of books was forwarded to treasurer of A. L. A. War Council. The expense of the campaign—about $50.00—was borne by the Minot Public library.

Miss Greene reports, "The enthusiasm and interest shown by school teachers, club women and librarians in helping to carry out the work have been most sincerely appreciated and have made possible the results as noted. Especially do I want to mention the work of the librarians at the assembling points, for theirs has been by far the greatest task and with not a word of complaint, but always readiness and willingness to do whatever was needed. Most of them have sorted and made ready thousands of volumes."

Publicity

The publicity campaign among North Dakota Libraries was conducted by Miss Winnie Bucklin, librarian of Fargo public library, in cooperation with the Agricultural College, which has in charge food administration for the state.

Many letters, leaflets, and posters were distributed thru this agency and conspicuously displayed in the libraries and played an important part in educating public opinion to conformity with Hoover regulations.

Scrapbooks

A special appeal was made to club women and school children to prepare scrapbooks of cheerful contents and bright pictures for hospital use. The response was enthusiastic and 158 clubs, schools, and societies sent a total of 598 scrapbooks.

The variety and beauty of these scrapbooks was a revelation of what can be done with inexpensive materials in furnishing sanitary reading and satisfactory recreation for convalescents. Most of them were sent direct to the Public library at Boston for immediate shipment to hospitals in France. 142 were first sent to the Biennial meeting of Federated clubs at Hot Springs, Arkansas, as a North Dakota exhibit and were then forwarded to hospitals.

BEQUESTS

The principal bequest this biennium is the Public library at Bismarck, for which $25,000.00 was given by the Carnegie corporation.

In 1915 $500.00 was given to the Langdon public library by Robert Watson.

In 1917 the Dorcas Society of Wyndmere donated the library $100.00 for books.

PUBLICATIONS

Publications have been chiefly revisions of earlier leaflets.

Revised Editions

"Facts concerning traveling libraries," 1917
(Revision of circular of information No. 3)

"What are farmers' libraries," 1917
(Abridgement of circular of information No. 17)

"The Public Library Commission and club women," 1918
(Revision of leaflet No. 14)

A revised edition of "Plan of organization for small libraries," formerly published by the Library Commission was issued 1917 by the Boston Book Company as No. 19 of its "Useful reference series."

New Publications

"Maps showing farmers', school, and community libraries circulated in rural communities, North Dakota," 1916.

"Lists of books in community libraries," 1918.

"The American sword," Lewis F. Crawford, president State Board of Regents, reprinted by consent of the Quarterly Journal of the University of North Dakota."

"Sixth biennial report of the North Dakota Library Commission 1916-18."

The Library Commission had planned the printing, beginning 1918 of a quarterly publication devoted to library news, but the changes due to war conditions made a postponement advisable.

CRITICISM AND COMMENDATION

Criticism

The secretary invites frank statements of complaints, which will enable the Library Commission better to understand conditions in the field and thus to improve this service. So far as such criticisms have reached the secretary, they are based on lack of sufficient libraries to fill requests promptly, and delay in freight shipments. The first mentioned complaint should be made by individuals and school board directly to representatives and senators who are in a position to see that appropriations for additional libraries are made as rapidly as financial conditions permit.

Slow freight shipments are hard to remedy, but investigation shows that traveling libraries occasionally lie for weeks unclaimed at destination thru some trifling oversight or misunderstanding. Thoro and persistent inquiry should be continued at the receiving station until a library ordered has been received, as well as notice sent the Commission.

A third complaint refers to selection of books in traveling libraries. In the ten years the Library Commission has been circulating these collections five objections to books have reached the secretary. A minister objected to Harold Bell Wright's "Calling of Dan Matthews," as belittling the ministry. A county superintendent thot Lynde's "Taming of Red Butte Western" demoralizing with its pictures of cowboys and pistols. A prospective borrower looking over lists of books in the various libraries commented on Butler's "Pigs is Pigs," "we burn that in our town." A priest thot Gunsaulus' "Paths to Power" contained in one page statements historically incorrect. A mother objected to a modern novel found in a school. In this case investigation showed that a community library has been borrowed and placed in a school house. In such cases the books should always be examined by a competent judge, who will remove from the box any books that should not be placed in the hands of children. In sending community collections advertised to contain "books suited to all ages" with 25 volumes of fiction, there will inevitably be some works on which school children should not be spending their time. Since this objection was made it has been possible to purchase small school libraries of 25 books which contain no adult fiction. Some of the new books are examined in the offices of the Library Commission before purchase, but more of them are selected from lists recommended by expert readers and employees of the American Library Association, and large libraries or commissions, which make a practice of examining lists for the guidance of small libraries. With the utmost care and judgment, opinions are bound to vary, as the books objected to in one station will in another have the largest circulation.

Commendations

The correspondence files of the Library Commission contain many words of appreciation for the good work accomplished. A few extracts are given to show the extent and variety of usefulness of these books.

Farmers' Libraries

"I should like to keep the library a little longer unless you have a call for it * * * I am particularly interested in Professor Coburn's book on alfalfa and being that we are endeavoring to raise more and more alfalfa, this is a handy guide." A. H. Teigen, stock farmer, Marshall.

"These libraries have been of great value to us. We have used the farmers' library as source material for farm club discussions during the winter months. The community library has been circulated thruout the neighborhood and has been used in connection with the Pupils' Reading Circle work in which we hold first rank in the county. We have also made use of some of the books for individual report work in English and book reviews." G. R. Ingram, principal consolidated school, Brockett.

School Libraries

"The library has proved a great aid to the children in mastering their reading at school, as it gave them a definite motive for learning to read better and more rapidly." Eva Sandberg, teacher, Portal.

"We are returning library and we are thanking you very kindly, for it was much enjoyed. We want another right away." Dora Wasdahl, teacher, Verona.

"Library 230 we used in connection with our school work for references and also for reading to the pupils. The reading in most of the books in library 230 is quite heavy. Under supervision they got considerable out of the books." Lena C. Nelson, teacher, Flasher.

Community Libraries

"I wish the appropriation committee realized what the traveling library means to these little North Dakota towns in winter. We shall be more than glad to get any books you can send us." Lydia Hinman, county superintendent, Steele.

"Our people are very anxious for the new library and are calling every day to see if it has arrived. I don't know what they will do with me for I had promised them according to your card that it ought to be here. It is not easy to get around now, as we have some snow and this morning it is 26 below zero. Mr. M—— went in yesterday (16 miles), but it was not at the depot." Mrs. Jennie Matteson, Fryburg.

"I want to thank you for the literature sent me at Mrs. H's. * * * Mrs. H. is greatly pleased with the prospect of having a traveling library. It will make a great difference with their winter. * * * I wish all the people in the state who would enjoy a library might know about it * * *

Some of the people I have talked with are *intellectually hungry* and one woman told me sadly that she had never been within reach of a circulating library! When the children do not go to school in winter, it would make a great difference to them if they could have your books." Florence Merrian Bailey, Rolette.

Educational Reference Department

"I regret having kept our book and pamphlets longer than we should, but they have been so eagerly read it has been hard to deny them to others wanting." Mrs. H. E. Harris, presidentof Civic Club, Belfield.

"Your reference library has been of great help in teaching history." Rose O'Brien, teacher, Napoleon.

"I wish to thank you for use of the books. I have used them most every evening in writing my oration and also essays and explanations, which I have written for other people." Elsei J. Brandt, High School, Carrington.

"Will you please send me what material you can spare on the life and works of Henry Van Dyke and George Eliot? I would like magazine clippings and any other good material you can send. I wish to use it in the English IV. class." Mildred Grey, High School, Hettinger.

"Am returning today all the valuable reference material you sent me. We are indeed fortunate to have a library that will put so much time and effort on finding just what we need for our papers and reports. I assure you the club women all over the state realize this too." Mrs. Geo. P. Homnes, Crosby.

"I might say that I have gained considerable information on library science from the material you sent me. In fact I did not even know what cataloging a library meant. If it is possible to secure the A. L. A. Booklist, I would appreciate receiving it, as I shall endeavor to add to my library good books." Gilbert A. Engen, Finley.

"Your little pamphlet on the organization of a small library was ever so helpful and we are using the order cards you gave us to very good advantage." Mrs. R. C. Chisholm, Lakota.

SUMMARY

This biennium has witnessed a complete reorganization in the office at the Capitol. The Library Commission completed in 1917 ten years of existence and found its growth in all departments necessitating changes in method.

The duties in each department have been systematized and separated. The addition to the staff of two graduate librarians with an appropriation in the budget for a third after July 1, 1918, makes possible the appointment of chiefs for three of the four departments of work outlined by law for the Library Commission. Educational reference and field work can not be clearly divided until a fourth chief is added to the staff.

Owing to the cramped quarters in which work must be done it is not possible for the library to expand naturally. Shelves are full. There is no room for more cases. Consequently, old books, magazines and clippings must be continually discarded to make room for the new. A few are packed away. Some were sent to camps, others went to rural schools, and others were destroyed. Therefore, the seeming gain in number of books from 14,468 to 17,840 does not at all represent the real strengthening of the collection, which has resulted from the substitution of new material for that becoming out of date.

Complete invoice of all books, furnishings, and other property has been taken preparatory to this report. The Commission purchased 5,163 books in this biennium and now owns in all departments 17,840 books and 38,638 magazines and clippings. These are distributed by departments as follows:

		Books	Pamphlets and Clippings
Educational Reference		4,879	19,507
Traveling library			
School libraries	1,797		
Community libraries	7,018		
Farm libraries	1,191		
Open shelf collection.........	2,103		
	12,109	12,109	
Legislative Reference		852	19,121
		17,840	38,628

In this biennium 54 books are not accounted for. This is a very small proportion considering the number circulated. Most of these are lost in the mail. Some of them will probably yet be found and returned to this office.

It has been an important period for the Library Commission in addition of new libraries, growth of extension work, increase in staff and appropriation, and progress in professional standing.

NEEDS

Space in which to grow.

Fireproof housing for valuable collections.

An amendment to the law to provide for county libraries.

Increase in salaries in proportion to cost of living so that valued assistants may be retained.

An appropriation for books that will replace worn titles and add needed new ones.

FINANCIAL REPORT

Of Secretary of North Dakota Public Library Commission

July 1, 1916—June 30, 1918.

Books, periodicals, and membership fees	$ 5,236.81
Postage	690.24
Office supplies	328.76
Salaries	11,418.68
Furniture	334.11
Printing	571.82
Freight, drayage, and miscellaneous expense	550.54
Aids to libraries	194.88
Traveling expense	254.31
Total	$19,580.15

SEVENTH BIENNIAL REPORT

and

EIGHT BIENNIAL REPORT

of the

STATE LIBRARY COMMISSION

of

NORTH DAKOTA

1918-1920

and

1920-1922

SEVENTH BIENNIAL REPORT

and

EIGHT BIENNIAL REPORT

of the

STATE LIBRARY COMMISSION

of

NORTH DAKOTA

1918–1920

and

1920–1922

NORMANDEN PUBLISHING CO.
STATE PRINTERS
GRAND FORKS, N. DAK.

NORTH DAKOTA STATE BOARD OF REGENTS.

July 1, 1918.

L. F. CRAWFORD, President. - - - - - - - - - Sentinel Butte
J. D. TAYLOR, Vice President. - - - - - - - - Grand Forks
CHARLES E. VERMILYEA, - - - - - - - - - - - Bismarck
GEORGE A. TOTTEN, - - - - - - - - - - - - - Bowman
ROBERT T. MUIR, - - - - - - - - - - - - - - Sarles

BOARD OF ADMINISTRATION

July 26, 1919.

GEORGE A. TOTTEN, Chairman - - - - - - - - - Bowman
ROBERT T. MUIR, - - - - - - - - - - - - - - Sarles
P. M. CASEY, (to Dec. 16, 1920) - - - - - - - - Lisbon
J. I. CAHILL, (from Dec. 16, 1920) - - - - - - - - Leith
MINNIE J. NIELSON, - - - - - - - - - - - Valley City
JOHN N. HAGEN, - - - - - - - - - - - - - - - - - Deering
CHARLES LIESSMAN, Secretary, - - - - - - - - Bismarck

BOARD OF ADMINISTRATION

July 12, 1921.

ROBERT T. MUIR, Chairman, - - - - - - - - - - Sarles
GEORGE A. TOTTEN, - - - - - - - - - - - - - Fargo
J. I. CAHILL, (to March 14, 1922) - - - - - - - - Leith
R. B. MURPHY, (from March 14, 1922) - - - - - Grafton
MINNIE J. NIELSON, - - - - - - - - - - - Valley City
JOHN N. HAGEN, (to Nov. 28, 1921) - - - - - - - Deering
JOSEPH A. KITCHEN, (from Nov. 28, 1921) - - - - Sentinel Butte

LETTER OF TRANSMITTAL.

TO THE STATE BOARD OF ADMINISTRATION:

Lady and Gentlemen:

As no report of the State Library Commission has been printed since 1918, it seems best to include the Seventh Biennial Report for 1918-1920 left by Miss S. Blanche Hedrick, with the Eighth Biennial Report for 1920-1922 herewith submitted. Attention may be called also to references to the work of the State Library Commission in reports of the State Board of Administration for 1919, 1920, 1921 and 1922.

MARY ELIZABETH DOWNEY,

Librarian and Director,

State Library Commission.

SEVENTH BIENNIAL REPORT OF THE NORTH DAKOTA PUBLIC LIBRARY COMMISSION:

Report covering period July 1, 1918, to June 30, 1920:

The report of the Public Library Commission for the above period must, of necessity, be very brief, since there is no one on the present staff who was connected with the Commission during any portion of the period covered by this report. We have not been able to find, in the rooms of the Commission, any records which would aid materially in compiling a statistical record of any absolute value.

During the first year of this period the staff in charge of the work was as follows:

MRS. MINNIE CLARKE BUDLONG, ... Secretary & Director
MISS CHARLOTTE MATSON, ... Legislative Reference Librarian
MISS FRANCES CARLETON, ... Chief of Traveling Library Dept.
MISS FLORENCE FISHER, ... Field Organizer
MRS. S. SLOAN, ... Clerk
MISS ETHEL FLEMING, ... Stenographer

In August, 1919, Mrs. Budlong, who had been in charge of the Commission for ten years, resigned and her resignation was accepted to take effect September 1, 1919. Also, during the months of August and September, 1919, all of the other members of the staff resigned and left the Commission.

Miss Ethel Lane was appointed as stenographer and began work on August 18, 1919. Miss Anne Peterson was later appointed Deputy Librarian and arrived November 17, 1919, to take up the work in the capacity of Acting Director. Miss Lane, who had been appointed stenographer in August, 1919, resigned February 1, 1920, and Miss Edyth Moore was appointed to take her place. Miss Peterson also resigned from the position of Deputy Librarian June 30, 1920, and the Commission was left in charge of Miss Moore, the stenographer, until the present Director arrived the latter part of August. During this period From Sept. 1, 1919, to Sept. 1, 1920, there were two or three appointments of inexperienced assistants who each remained only a few months.

The present Librarian and Director was appointed to take charge of the Commission August 15, 1920, and Miss Inez Spicer was appointed cataloguer to begin work September 1, 1920.

It will be obvious, that owing to the many changes which occurred in the personnel of the Commission from June, 1919, to September, 1920, the work became much confused and disarranged and the present staff found it rather difficult to pick up the threads of the work and get things back into systematized running order. We have found it necessary to go back over the work of the past three or four years in order to complete some of the records. To do this and at the same time keep up with the work of the present day has been a considerable task taking into account the small number on the staff at present.

So far as I am able to ascertain, from figures found in the Commission rooms, the collections contained on June 30, 1920, the following:

Educational Reference Collections:	
Books	5,767
Pamphlets	22,421
Legislative Reference Collection:	
Books	1,045
Pamphlets	22,557
Traveling Library Department:	
Books	13,886

The rooms of the Commission are very much crowded and it is impossible to properly arrange the material in a way to make the work easy to handle. This condition must, of course, exist until the Commission can be moved into new quarters. The present staff is also inadequate to properly take care of the work which is increasing constantly. We have at present, besides the Librarian and Director, only one trained assistant on the staff. I would suggest that there should be, besides the trained cataloguer which we now have, two other library trained assistants, one as head of the Traveling Library Department, and the other as a general assistant. With a staff of three trained workers and a stenographer the Librarian could be able to direct the work to the best advantage. It is my understanding that the Legislative Reference work is no longer handled by the Library Commission.

Respectfully submitted,

S. BLANCHE HEDRICK,

Librarian & Director.

EIGHTH BIENNIAL REPORT OF THE NORTH DAKOTA STATE LIBRARY COMMISSION,

For the period July 1, 1920, to June 30, 1922:

The eighth biennial report commemorates fifteen years existence of the North Dakota State Library Commission.

This report includes one year of administration under Miss S. Blanche Hedrick with its second year under the present director and secretary. The staff for the biennium has included the following persons:

Miss S. Blanche Hedrick, Director, July 1, 1920 to September 1, 1921; Miss Mary E. Downey, September 15, 1921 to date; Mrs. Edythe Herbert to date; Mrs. Mary Candee, November 1, 1921, to April 1, 1922; Miss Ellen Hedrick, half time service from November 1, 1921, to May 30, 1922; Miss Caroline F. Gates, May 1, 1922, to date and Mrs. Sadie B. Calkins, July 1 to August 30, 1922.

The duties of the State Library Commission are set forth in the State law and have been outlined in previous reports so there is no need to repeat them. It will be our purpose to show what has been done to fill the requirements and something of the vision for the future.

So far as the Library itself is concerned, the last year has been a time of reconstruction, reorganization, re-arranging collections; preparing the mass of material, books and pamphlets that had accumulated, for the shelves; gathering and arranging a periodical file for reference, spending the sum available for books and preparing them for service, cleaning, mending and renewing traveling libraries and making up new ones, checking old records and starting new ones, and circularizing the service of the Commission to every part of the State. New circulars have been compiled, old ones revised and reprinted, and thousands of them mailed or distributed over the State with application cards for reference and traveling libraries. A good beginning of all has been made which will take some time fully to accomplish.

Along with this necessary work has been the desire to build on what already has been done and hold the vision had by those in the beginning and through the years the Commission has existed to this time.

ACCESSIONS.

The accession records show 2,143 books added since June 30, 1920, making a total of 21, 796 books in the Library according to previous records.

Pamphlets are in process of classification and arrangement and records of this work will be completed for the next report.

An indefinite loan of Thwaites "Early Western Travel," subject to the call of the Director, was made to Mr. L. F. Crawford and such loans of duplicates and discards to the Dickinson State Normal, State Training School, State Penitentiary, and to schools asking for them.

A good deal of gift material had accumulated which belonged to the Historical Society and Law Collection and was sent to those libraries.

Assistance was given to the Governor's office and to the Department of

Agriculture in re-arranging and sorting books and pamphlets and those not needed were turned over to the State Library Commission, the Law Library and Secretary of State. We have been asked to go over other state department collections which will be done as time permits.

REFERENCE SERVICE.

While no record can be made of the persons using the literature sent out because of being used by such groups as clubs, schools and various organizations, the number of requests and pieces of literature and where they are sent make interesting records.

There were 1,680 books and 4,039 pamphlets and clippings loaned in answer to 2,854 requests from July 1, 1920, to June 30, 1921, and 3,617 books and 2,790 periodicals, clippings and pamphlets loaned in answer to 4,315 requests from July 1, 1921 to June 30, 1922, making a total for the biennium of 12,126 pieces of literature filing 7,169 requests. Pamphlet use evidently is much greater in legislative years.

A great deal of reference work is done by visitors directly in the Library, however, of which no account is kept. This is true of reference collections generally. The Library is swamped with requests to supply material outlined in the Public School Course of Study. While this provision should be met primarily by each school locally, if funds were available no greater service could be rendered from the State Library Commission. County libraries also would solve this problem adequately for the rural community.

But with the present limitations such service can be only very limited. The book fund should be so increased as to afford purchase of many books needed in all classes of literature to do more effective reference service.

While the legislative reference work is now legally connected with the Law Library, the pamphlet material is still in the State Library Commission and every effort will be made to cooperate in meeting the needs of the coming session of Legislature. A great deal of material is yet to be classified and arranged for this purpose.

The individual circulation of fiction and children's books has been discontinued again to Bismarck as this material is so limited, demand in the traveling libraries so great, and the local supply of this demand is the province of the Public Library. Class books and reference material, however, are served locally as far as the limitations of the Library provide.

TRAVELING LIBRARIES.

Traveling library books like money in a bank have a reason for being only when in circulation.

Schools, clubs and other organizations were circularized through the fall of 1921 and the response was so great that every traveling library was out on the last day of February 1922. With the publicity now being given to the use of traveling libraries and the thorough reorganizing they are having to make them so desirable, it is safe to predict that there will not be one in the Department by the New Year when there will be a waiting list. The work that could be developed in this department as well as that of reference is limited only by the material that can be provided and by the staff to take care of the work.

Beginning with June 1, 1922, the records are all started new; every library as it returns thoroughly renovated, books cleaned and mended, worn out books discarded, enough new ones put in to fill the cases, lists revised and alphabeted, and a re-registration of borrowers and places developed. Fifty cases were mended and repainted in the carpenter shop and sixty-three new libraries made up. According to the records the State Library Commission now has 483 traveling libraries. A complete inventory will result through the process of record revision.

So long as space for work and shelving books is so limited, it will be necessary to use fixed collections as heretofore for the most part. This crowded condition may be relieved by moving into the new Memorial Building. The ideal method is to have all the books shelved by grade for the schools, and class for other books and make up each collection according to individual request, which is done as far as limitations make possible. This arrangement would make both the reference work and traveling libraries more satisfactory as much more material would be available for both.

The farmers' collections have been thoroughly advertised but there seems to be very little demand for them per se. This may be accounted for by the special work in agriculture through the schools in recent years for which their own books are provided. Farmers are interested in more general collections and it seems best to reorganize these libraries and put a few books on farming in each community library. So long as the fund for books is so small it would seem best also to use it for books of general interest to the schools and communities, to create the reference and reading habit than to specialize in subjects met by other agencies. There is an occasional request for a few Norwegian and German books to be added to the collection of English books to be sent some station, but these are exceptional and require but few books to meet the demand.

It is interesting to note that although the traveling library books show wear and usage they have better care among patrons than that shown by the average public library use of books.

Records from July 1, 1920, to June 30, 1921 show 169 traveling libraries sent out, and from July 1, 1921 to June 30, 1922, 311 libraries containing 12,533 books. Eighty new stations were added the latter year.

FIELD WORK.

The greatest library need of the State is field work. When staff and traveling funds are provided more and more should be done. There are only 17 tax supported libraries in the State and most of them are in need of State aid in organization and development. Funds for them have been cut in the last few years and until the State law is changed must continue to be so. This means depletion of staff and books. To help relieve the need for books and to stimulate interest, book drives have been instituted through the public schools.

Book and magazine drives have been held in Bismarck, Dickinson and Devils Lake, and will continue till most of the libraries of the State have replenished their shelves in so far as this method can be of service. Thousands of good books have been obtained in each of these towns. If the county library bill passes the next session of Legislature most of the libraries no doubt will change automatically to county libraries and so have their funds, efficiency and service greatly augmented.

Aside from building up reference files for the public library, the Bismarck magazine collection greatly assisted the State Library Commission in starting a reference file and the surplus will be used by the State Historical Society Library and others to complete their files.

Visits made from July 1, 1921 to June 30, 1922 have included libraries of the following towns, a few of them visited more than once, Beach, Bismarck, Devils Lake, Dickinson, Fargo, Grand Forks, Hankinson, Jamestown, Mandan, Minot, Valley City, Wahpeton. Aside from the public libraries, visits were made to the libraries of the State University, State Normal Schools at Dickinson, Minot and Valley City, State Agricultural College, State School of Science, Fargo College, Jamestown College, Fargo Masonic Temple, State Historical Society, State Law Library, State Penitentiary, State School for the Deaf, State Hospial for the Insane and State Training School.

A great deal of advisory work has been accomplished through correspondence and visits. A resume of what field work fully accomplished should mean to the libraries of the state is as follows: to arouse interest in starting a library; speak before various organizations; urge book and magazine drives and contributions of money; find a room in which to start a library; arrange for an organizer to take charge of the library; tell people how to start a reading room, get periodical subscriptions, and make a book collection; talk about the library law, voting a tax, and the Carnegie building; look for a suitable site; urge the use of local building materials, if possible; go over plans for building with architect and board; confer with architects as to detail of plans for service; when population and tax warrant more than the building fund procured, urge the board to ask Mr. Carnegie for more; discuss furnishings with the board; to help organize the library; classify, accession, shelf list, and catalog books and put in a proper loan system; to divide the library into proper departments, reference, reading room, children's room, fiction and classed books; to suggest partitioning the library into departments by book stacks; to stimulate a reference collection especially of bound periodicals; to urge the collection of old magazines from the homes to help the local and other libraries; to teach a proper use of the library, especially to academy, college and high school students; where the town has had a library for some time without the tax levy, to urge it, and to ask for a Carnegie building; to see if the tax levy is being granted and used, and the balance on hand is not too great; to see if the book collection is properly selected;

to see if the librarian and board are performing their duty to the public; to urge the librarian to attend summer school and ask the board to send her; to inspect the building as to janitor service; when shelving is lacking, to develop such cooperation between library and school that the manual training department will make shelving and furniture for the library; when the library is crowded, to ask that the children's room be moved to the auditorium; to suggest plans for shelving, furnishings and administering the children's room; to bring about proper co-operation between the library and the schools; to urge the circulation of books from the library through the grades by letting each teacher have as many books suited to the age and grade as there are children in the room; to inquire into the use of the library; compare the annual circulation with the population and, if the circulation is not what it should be, to find the cause and set it right; to inspect the borrower's register and find out what proportion of the population is using the library and, if small, to suggest methods of increase; to make suggestions as to the binding and mending of books and peridicals; to suggest ribbon arrangement of fiction when feasible; to explain Poole and Readers' Guide to periodical literature and urge their purchase when not in the library; to urge the combination of several libraries in a town into one; when trouble is found between librarian and board, to clear the air, if possible; and where there is rivalry between nearby towns, to use it in helping the library.

The staff of the State Library Commission should be comprised of such efficient workers that every member would be able to be effective work and the staff should have enough members to permit sufficient field work to meet the needs of the State.

Aside from the 17 tax supported libraries there are some 40 non-tax supported libraries in the State started and fostered by the women's clubs, still unorganized and undeveloped for the most part. With activity on the part of the Library Commission and cooperation with the women's clubs the material and efficiency of these libraries can be greatly increased. The great thing, however, is to get tax support for them, as the permanency of no library can be assured without it. If the county library bill passes many of them will become county libraries while every effort should be made to get municipal tax support for others. Much field work also is needed to develop and organize them. From one to three weeks could be spent profitably with each one. High School and Junior High School libraries also are in need of being built up and organized.

LIBRARY SCHOOL EDUCATION.

Comparatively few librarians in the State have had any systematic library school education. Special training for the work is sadly needed to bring up the library efficiency of the State. A great deal can be done through short course work to which many of the states ranking high in the library world owe much. A short course school would accomplish a great deal for North Dakota in a comparatively short time and if there is sufficient response from library workers over the state, one will be held this coming year.

COUNTY LIBRARY LAW.

It is hoped and expected to bring a county library bill through the next session of the legislature. Such a provision for county libraries effectively put over will mean state wide library service. Every effort is now being made to give understanding of what a county library is and what it will do, so that when the bill goes through it will begin to go into effect at once. It is as great a thing to put a law into operation as to get it passed. To this end the library conditions and needs of the State are being studied from every angle, so that the best bill possible, and particularly adapted to North Dakota, may be presented to the legislators. The Director has spoken on the county library movement before groups of people over the State on every opportunity afforded, and the newspapers have published the following thirty-three points which she has developed on "What a County Library Law will do for North Dakota": give equal reading facilities to every man, woman and child in North Dakota; stimulate the library movement and reading habit in the State as nothing else can do; make every library already established render greater service; create libraries in county seat towns now without them; stimulate the establishment of a library in every town of North Dakota; place a deposit of books in every hamlet of the State; send books in answer to letters or telephone by parcels post to the most isolated person in the county; lend books to all residents of the county on the same conditions as to residents of the town in which the library is located; make rural life more desirable. especially to young people; increase the value of property; attract homeseekers to increase the population; promote business and industrial enterprises; give the same reading advantages to the country child which are now enjoyed by the city child; supplement the public school course of study with material for general reading and reference; provide a book to a child suited to his grade in every schoolroom of North Dakota; create a generation of readers of the children now passing through the public schools of the State; raise the standard of appreciation of the later studies of students in our schools of higher education because of opportunity for a foundation of general reading; supply the demand for books which the schools create; give the people something *to read* after they have been *taught* how to read; offer opportunity to continue education after leaving school; stimulate home education; aid study clubs; provide adequate reference material; develop greater community intelligence; bring thousands of dollars more money for library buildings into the State than ever can be had without a county law; give a county building to county seat towns too small to have them under the municipal plan; provide more efficient library service in the most economical way possible; save duplicating many of the expensive reference books; give county supervision of libraries which naturally follows county supervision of schools; supplement the work of all other county agencies with literature; give to each county as good a library as the State Library Commission now provides for the State as a whole; add North Dakota to the twenty-five progressive states in the Union now operating under the county library system; and place North Dakota on the library map of the United States.

Thousand of copies of these points will be printed as a broadside and distributed through the State Educational Association, Federation of Women's Clubs, District Teachers Associations, County Teachers Institutes, Parent-Teachers Associations, Granges, County Commissioners, Members of the Legislature and officials generally. There would seem to be no opposition but there must be the greatest activity to produce the bill, get it passed and then put into effect. The State has marvelous opportnuity for library development when proper conditions are brought about to accomplish it.

The library connected with the State Library Commission is quite typical of what any county in the State might soon develop as a fair county library, for example such a county as Burleigh, where the Capital is located, but would be meager for such a county, with so large a population as Cass, including Fargo. So one sees how very limited the Commission Library is for a state the size of North Dakota.

At the North Dakota Federation of Women's Clubs meeting in October, 1921, a resolution was passed inviting the Director to speak before the spring district meetings on "The County Library for North Dakota." She was able to attend and speak before six of the meetings, thus visiting Minot, Dickinson, Grace City, Hankinson, Kulm and Jamestown. The club women are enthusiastic in regard to library work in general and especially for the county movement. Reports of the district chairmen show a great deal of library activity on the part of the club women of the State.

Addresses on various subjects also have been made before the North Dakota Library Association at Bismarck; the North Dakota Educational Association, Fargo; Southeastern Educational Association, Mandan; county teachers' institutes at Steele and Hillsboro; Fargo Business Women's Club; Bismarck High School and every grade of the public schools; Dickinson State Normal; Devils Lake Junior High School; Beach public school teachers; State Training School and State School for the Deaf.

PUBLICITY.

There has been a great deal of library publicity in the newspapers throughout the State. To express thanks adequately would mean naming practically every newspaper in the State. Reporters have done splendid work which has had state wide effect. Library publicity also has been given through the school people of the state, the club women and state officials, all of which is greatly appreciated.

In addition to the North Dakota Library Association the Director also attended the midyear meetings of the American Library Association in Chicago, the annual meeting of the American Library Association held in Detroit and the meeting of the General Federation of Women's Clubs at

Chautauqua, N. Y., where she represented the library part of the program speaking on "Library Extension."

PUBLIC LIBRARY ANNUAL REPORTS.

Effort has been made to obtain the June 30th Annual Report required by law from librarians of the State. Lists of libraries are appended to this report with such tabulation of statistics as is possible to make from the return of blanks sent out. There is appended also a report made up of excerpts from correspondence which shows something of the activity of libraries in the last year.

Respectfully submitted,

MARY E. DOWNEY, Director.

Statistics of Tax Supported Public Libraries in Towns of 2,000 Population and Over, June 30, 1922.

Population	City	Number books	Books per capita	Circulation	Circulation per capita	Hours open daily	Number staff	Salaries	Salary cost per book circulated	Tax levy	Rate per capita	Librarian
7,122	Bismarck	5,975	.8+	19,726	2.7	5	2	$2,220.00	11.2 ct.	$3,500.00	.48+	Mrs. Florence H. Davis
5,140	Devils Lake	6,219	1. +	31,445	6.1	6 1-2	1	1,102.00	3.5 ct.	2,551.00	.49+	Marie O'Brien
4,122	Dickinson	5,593	1. +	18,681	4.5	6 3-5	1	1,500.00	8 ct.	3,000.00	.72+	Mrs. Sadie B. Calkins
21,961	Fargo	17,140	.8	88,548	4.	12	4	4,524.96	5.1 ct.	5,102.08	.23+	Inga Rynning, Acting
2,512	Grafton	5,015	2	9,151	3.6	3 1-2	1	440.00	4.8 ct.	1,460.00	.54+	Mary Morris
14,010	Grand Forks	9,114	.6+	55,958	3.9	11	2	3,194.96	5.7 ct.	6,500.00	.46+	Jessie M. Budge
6,627	Jamestown	6,077	1	27,448	4.1	6 1-2	1	1,790.75	6.5 ct.	4,580.23	.68+	Gertrude M. Edwards
10,476	Minot	8,222	.8	35,006	3.3	12	2	2,688.55	7.6 ct.	7,510.39	.71+	Ingeborg Reishus, Acting
4,686	Valley City	8,240	1.5	25,836	5.5	6	1	1,226.76	4.7 ct.	3,675.70	.78+	Harriet Anfinson, Acting
4,178	Williston	5,877	1.4	25,636	6	6	1	1,794.16	7 ct.	3,160.84	.75+	Bessie R. Baldwin

Statistics of Public Libraries Reporting From Other Towns With or Without Tax Support.

Population	Town	Volumes	Borrowers	Circulation	Income	Librarian
1,172	Bottineau	703	302	......	....	Mrs. C. A. Leonard
1,420	Carrington	4,140	1,464	8,887	$1,264.19	Hazel A. Johnson
1,538	Casselton	1,733	492	4,790	620.74	Emir D. Scott
200	Center	1,000	300	4,000	70.25	Mrs. M. Jennings
490	Courtenay	581	100	1,000	32.05	Mrs. R. A. McBroom
200	Hamilton	410	.....	......	129.05	Mrs. D. T. Park
1,477	Hankinson	1,065	505	3,924	168.35	Mrs. Kate R. Spottswood
500	Hannah	215	105	......	....	Mrs. A. B. Miller
959	Lakota	1,145	.....	3,262	....	Mrs. Ellen Hullett
1,228	Langdon	1,950	180	4,815	680.17	Mrs. D. W. Barker
704	Leeds	2,245	250	5,029	178.00	Nora Jacobson
175	Leonard	1,629	235	1,714	....	Alma Roney
1,855	Lisbon	3,276	1,251	14,156	1,815.46	Mrs. H. S. Oliver
416	Mott	1,611	813	5,734	361.26	Louise Wagner
1,637	Oakes	4,041	697	1,284	906.53	Anna B. Fay
1,114	Park River	3,101	909	6,654	433.60	Mrs. Bertha B. Farup
1,424	Rugby	1,258	477	3,133	501.26	Eva D. Crockett
836	Velva	810	230	......	78.75	Mrs. C. K. Relstice
3,069	Wahpeton	3,525	625	10,771	1,582.26	Mrs. Jessie Searing
521	Wimbledon	464	106	80	12.96	(Woman's Study Club)

Correspondence Reports From Non-tax Supported Libraries.

ASHLEY—The Ashley Public Library was started some ten years ago by the Ashley Woman's Club. For a while it had a steady growth, then there came a time when it had to be moved and as no suitable place could be found we packed and stored all the books for a couple of years. Last June the library was reopened in the basement of the new court house and we hope to be able to keep it open from now on. Since reopening the library last June we have added by gift and purchase (mostly purchase) about two hundred books—and hope soon to have more to add.

BATHGATE—The Study Club got some new books last spring and planned on getting more this fall. But the bank the money was in went broke and settled the book question for us for the time being.

CANDO—Our library is supported by the F. D. L. Club. It is open twice a week in the evening. Cards are one dollar a year. We usually have about one hundred subscribers. The books for the most part are late fiction, of which we have a very good assortment. We have histories and encyclopedias but a good general reference collection is so expensive that we have not been able to support one.

CASSELTON—I think our library holds a pretty fair list of books. We are open only Friday afternoons but in that time check out from 100 to 150 books. We occupy a room in the High School building, not very large so we cannot have a reading room, just a plain library.

CAVALIER—The Civitas Club has charge of the library here.

CENTER—Our shelves of books consist of one set of Standard Reference books. Close to 700 other books. We have used the traveling library for the past five years also. We saw the demand for reading facing us five years ago, and started a library for the entire public. The different ones who helped me organize have moved away, some few are here and are willing to help. During the World War I kept steadily on with my library work, as people demanded reading just the same. We give one corner of the drug store for this purpose of handling the books and I have acted as Librarian. This was better as I was always at home to attend to the wants of the public. Our reading territory is large, it extends to Fort Clark, Yucca, Hanover and numerous other places. Of course Center is the largest territory to draw from. What we need is a small building for our books in connection with a reading room. I know we could get a few ladies to care for the library each week or day. Everything depends on the work, of these different women. If we get a crop this fall we possibly may see our way to obtain a building. I am very much interested in this work as I know the number of foreigners who are taking an interest in reading. The young Russian boys are calling for books and it surely gives me a great deal of pleasure to wait on them.

COLUMBUS—We just added $40 worth of new books. Find it hard to get our patrons interested in anything but novels. Wish we could get them to like the better literature. No certain one has charge of our library. Each member of the Club takes their turn alphabetically in keeping it open every Friday P. M., for two hours. We consider this the most economical way of taking care of it. We have added about 25 new books this last year. It is in good condition at the present time.

EDGELEY—The library here in the last year has grown rapidly. We have about 1,500 volumes and have both town and country patronage, open only one afternoon each week, as all services are given free. I mean Librarian and assistant draw no salary. We charge for library ticket one dollar which provides one book each week for reader, additional book to those holding ticket 10c. Have privilege of two weeks on book, over that time; if not renewed, 2c for each day.

FESSENDEN—At present our library is undergoing complete renovation along the line of mending, relabeling, etc. New books to the number of about 105 volumes have just been ordered. We are also planning a book shower, that is, to secure books by donation. At present we have no librarian but expect that one of our local teachers will act as soon as the library is ready to open. Members of the Saturday Club are in active charge of the library. There are about 1,606 books in the library, 768 for juveniles, and 838 for adults. Now as to the condition of these books, they have been given a general overhauling, relabeling and indexing, during the past two weeks, so the library is now in good condition.

FORT CLARK—Fort Clark wants a library. They have a purse of enough to get a start for books and one of the ladies, has decided to care for the books. She and her husband are book lovers and when we get them in charge of library work we are going to have a success of our efforts.

HARVEY—By spending a great deal of time and energy upon the library last year, it is pretty thoroughly organized and classified under the Dewey Decimal system, though some public documents are still untouched. One of the needs of the library is more of the books given on the state school list for outside reading. This is especially true of biography, books about girls, and books of local state interest.

HEATON—Just began purchasing books last fall, have about 50 late books on hand, mostly fiction. We also have one of the traveling libraries from the Commission and are very well patronized.

HETTINGER—Our library is a very small one of about 500 books. At present the town hall is the home of our collection of a most curiously mixed assortment of books. We would gladly welcome a place for regular library and reading rooms. Hettinger really needs such a place badly, especially for the young folks. But hard times prevent any extensive move in that direction. If we could have books sent from the "Traveling Library" we would be very glad to get them. Also we will greatly appreciate the book lists and gift of books from book drives that you mention.

HOPE—We have about 400 volumes which belong to the Woman's Club besides the set belonging to the traveling library. Library is kept open Saturday afternoons and continues during the club year. The average number of books loaned for a period of four months was 17 plus, so you see there is a demand for good reading. At the present time we are conducting a "Book Drive" by canvassing the homes and asking for donations of books. So far we have about forty volumes to add to our number.

KENMARE—The Library in Kenmare is owned and controlled by the public schools. The library at present is in very bad condition. Steps are now being taken to increase the number of books and make the library of greater value not only to the school but to the entire community. The Parent-Teachers Association is cooperating in this matter and have appointed a committee to make a study of the library situation.

LAKOTA—One can give no better proof to the public of the growing interest and appreciation of our City Library than by its monthly reports. They demonstrate as nothing else a spirit of harmony between citizens and city library or the contrary. The following is our Library report since New Year 1922, and it speaks highly for Lakota.

Books loaned out and returned	947
Books added by purchase	25
Books given to the library	105
Cash from 1 cent a day books	$18.40

We have only about 20 "one cent a day books." They are the very best in latest fiction, hence expensive. The one "When Winter Comes" is just now very much read in Lakota. So is "The Gray Angels" and also "Galushia the Magnificent." Library hours from 3 o'clock until 5:00 Saturday. Everybody welcome. Our City Library is doing splendid work, averaging nearly 100 volumes a week loaned out and returned. We are also accumulating books both by purchase and donation. More than 100 volumes of worth have been given to the Library since New Year. We now have nearly eleven hundred volumes cataloged.

LARIMORE—The public library of Larimore is in the school building.

LEEDS—We have about 2,500 volumes and an average circulation of 500 books per month. We are catalogued under the Dewey Decimal classification, and open two afternoons a week. *I believe our Library is the only privately owned one in the State that is absolutely free to the public. It is owned by the Alfredian Club of this city.* We are very anxious to make our library the very best possible, and would appreciate very much any help from the Commission. I might add also that we cooperate with the schools in providing reading matter for silent reading periods, book reviews, etc.

MANDAN—The Mandan Public Library is maintained and managed by the Mandan Library Association, an organization of twenty-five women. Through the efforts of its members the library building has been built and furnished and about 3,400 volumes accessioned to date, including fiction, history, art, essays, classic poetry and prose, juvenile books, biography, travel and a few mechanical books. Although not free for circulation a subscription card may be secured for one dollar a year. The free reading table furnishes the best magazines and daily papers, and there is an average of about twenty readers each evening. There are 135 taking books by the year and many quarterly, while many more take books on the 5 cent plan; there being about 45 books taken each evening, three times a week, and Saturday afternoons.

The work of foundling this library began almost twenty years ago and each year a growing sense of appreciation on the part of the public is seen. The Mandan Library Association is trying to make the Library a definite part of our educational system in aiding and supplementing the work of the local schools. There are many readers among boys and girls, between ages of 12 and 17, who choose healthy, juvenile reading.

NEW ENGLAND—Our library at school may be used by any of the public so desiring, although at the present time there are no community borrowers. The only additions which have been made in recent years have been reference books for school purposes and supplementary English classics. The Woman's Club upon turning the books over to the school intended it to be used both as a public and school library.

NEW ROCKFORD—We have on the shelves something over 1,000 books. We have a room in the city hall, and are open to the public Friday, and Thursday evenings, and Saturday afternoon. The library is owned by the Minerva Club. But the city voted a small mill tax, and for several years have had help from that source. For dues and fines for 1921, I received something over $300, and we bought about $275 worth of books, mostly the late fiction. We have about

1,200 books for circulation besides several reference books. A fee of 5 cents is charged for each book that goes out and a fine of 1 cent a day for each day over two weeks if it is not returned. It has done well this winter but in the summer there is not nearly so much reading done. A number of people from the country have been reading this winter.

PEMBINA—The library is open one afternoon a week, when we give out at least a hundred books. I have full charge and am given fifty dollars a year by the city for running it. Any money we need for books or anything I have certain persons to help me get up some sort of entertainment. Last month we had six card parties in the library room, which were very successful. The Legion of Honor put on a dance, from the proceeds of which we got about eighty books. Have about 900 books on hand as up-to-date fiction, children's books and a lot of good reading along historical and advertising lines. Would be glad of any donations at any time. We had a book shower not long ago, which was most pleasant. We had a reception when our last shipment of books arrived. Had our Mayor and city council invited.

RUGBY—Our library, supported by a small city appropriation, is open only two afternoons a week. We could do great things if we had more money. The library is in the teachers examination room in the court house, so we do not have to pay rent. Will you please suggest a good way to take care of newspaper files? How do you file them? Would it be possible to get some one from the Library Commission to come and help classify our books? What would it cost?

TOWER CITY—It is the policy and intention of the Board to make the library for the use of the entire community. However, very few books leave the library except as drawn by the student body. This may be due to the fact that the community as a whole do not know that it is for public use. It is my intention to bring the matter of the library before the Parent-Teachers Association; encourage them to cooperate with the drive to put new fiction into the room; and awaken the community as to its supposed services. I am quite sure that public interest can be revived, and that the community would desire that it be retained as a public library.

VAN HOOK—Up to the present time we have simply ordered about $100 worth of books, through our local book dealer, who gets wholesale prices for us through his company giving us about 20 per cent discount. Have secured room in the First National Bank, and sectional book cases are promised by the same firm. Library supplies for cataloging have been ordered. We have also quite a donation of used books from local parties. It will be a mixed library, juvenile and up through the grades, including high school books, some reference works, also fiction. We plan to have a member of the club each Saturday take charge of the library.

VELVA—Velva now has a library of nearly 1,000 volumes open to all citizens and school students of the city, which is the result of five years' work by the Velva Woman's Club. The books, including fiction, prose, poetry, classics and scientific and historical works, have all been donated by members of the club and local citizens. The members of the club volunteer their services without pay. The library is open every Wednesday afternoon.

WIMBLEDON—We have several late books in our library and have ordered more. An everage of one hundred books are taken out each week.

WYNDMERE—We have a public library purchased and cared for by the Wyndmere Civic club, containing about 150 volumes. We keep our Library open each Tuesday afternoon from 3:00 o'clock to 5:00 and each club member cares for it one month usually in alphabetical order.

SCHOOL AND INSTITUTIONAL LIBRARIES.

Town Library Librarian*

Bathgate, School for the blind, B. P. Chapple, Supt.
Bismarck, State Library Commission, Mary E. Downey.*
Bismarck, State Historical Society.
Bismarck, State Law Library, Joseph Coghlan.*
Bismarck, State Penitentiary, L. L. Stair, Warden.
Bottineau, School of Forestry, Vernon L. Mangum, Pres.
Dickinson, State Normal School, S. T. May, President.
Devils Lake, School for the Deaf, Burton W. Driggs, Supt.
Dunseith, Tuberculosis Sanitorium, J. G. Lamont, Supt.
Ellendale, State Normal Industrial School, Carrie Tuttle.*
Fargo, Florence Crittenden Home.
Fargo, Fargo College, F. E. Stratton.*
Fargo, N. D. Agricultural College, Mrs. Ethel McVeety.*
Fargo, Grand Lodge N. D. A. F. of A. M., Clara A. Richards.*
Grafton, Institution for Feeble Minded, A. R. T. Wylie, Supt.
Grand Forks, University of North Dakota, A. D. Keator.*
Grand Forks, Wesley College.
Jamestown, Hospital for the Insane, Mrs. A. W. Guest.*
Jamestown, Jamestown College, Dean F. B. Taylor.
Lisbon, Soldier's Home, Dr. H. G. Rowe, Supt.
Mandan, State Training School, W. F. McClelland, Supt.
Mayville, State Normal School, Edith V. Davis.*
Minot, State Normal School, Huldah L. Winstad.*
Valley City, State Normal School, Helen M. Crane.*
Wahpeton, State School of Science, Lillian Mirick.*

NINTH BIENNIAL REPORT

OF THE

State Library Commission

OF

NORTH DAKOTA

1922-1924

BOARD OF ADMINISTRATION

June 30, 1924

R. B. Murphy .... Chairman

H. P. Goddard

F. E. Diehl

Minnie J. Nielson

Joseph A. Kitchen

STATE LIBRARY COMMISSION

Lillian E. Cook .... Secretary and Director

Bessie R. Baldwin .... Traveling Library Chief

Margaret Welch .... Reference Librarian

Mary Williamson .... Clerk

LETTER OF TRANSMITTAL

To the State Board of Administration,

Bismarck, North Dakota.

Herewith is submitted the Ninth Biennial Report of the North Dakota State Library Commission, covering the period from July 1, 1922 to June 30, 1924.

—Lillian E. Cook, Secretary and Director.

The Ninth Biennial report of the State Library Commission covers the period from July 1, 1922 to June 30, 1924; sixteen months under the direction of Mary E. Downey and eight months under the present secretary and director.

The work of the Library Commission is organized along three general lines: (1) The development of library service thruout the state, (2) the operation of the traveling library department, and (3) the direction of the reference department. The varied activities carried on under these three heads are shown on the graf on page 340.

In addition to the state work a considerable amount of reference work is done locally, supplementing the Bismarck and Mandan collections. The Commission also serves the staffs of the various state departments for reference and recreational reading.

ABSTRACT OF REPORT

I. Office Work

1. Correspondence
2. Preparation of special book lists
3. Publicity circular letters
4. Collection and compilation of records
5. Filling library vacancies

II. Field Work

1. Public Libraries
   (a) 26 visits paid
   (b) 8 mending demonstrations
   (c) 17 board meetings
   (d) 4 open publicity meetings
   (e) 2 libraries organized
2. School Libraries
   (a) 26 libraries visited
   (b) 8 libraries organized
   (c) 12 instructional talks to assemblies, etc.
   (d) 16 mending demonstrations
3. Clubs
   13 club talks on books and reading

III. Clubs

1. 3 district meetings attended
2. Special club library service started

IV. Aids to Libraries

1. Subscriptions to book buying guides and book lists
2. Preparation of general book lists
3. Furnishing standard library supplies
4. Lending professional literature

V. County Library Bill

Educational work being carried on but bill not to be introduced this year

VI. Traveling Library Department

1. Circulated 30,274 volumes thru 674 libraries, a gain of 194 libraries over last biennial period
2. 305 traveling library collections
3. 263 new applications
4. 426 active stations
5. Needs—More children's books

VII. Reference Department

1. Circulated 12,231 books and pamphlets
2. Collection badly in need of recent books of current interest
3. Service rendered to:
   (a) Teachers
   (b) School pupils
   (c) Private citizens
   (d) Club women

VIII. Needs
 1. To extend field work
 2. Addition of books
 3. Revision of salary schedule

IX. State Work
 1. Normal growth in most libraries
 2. State average tax three-fourths A. L. A. minimum standard
 3. Wahpeton has a $43,000 building given by Mayor and Mrs. Leach.

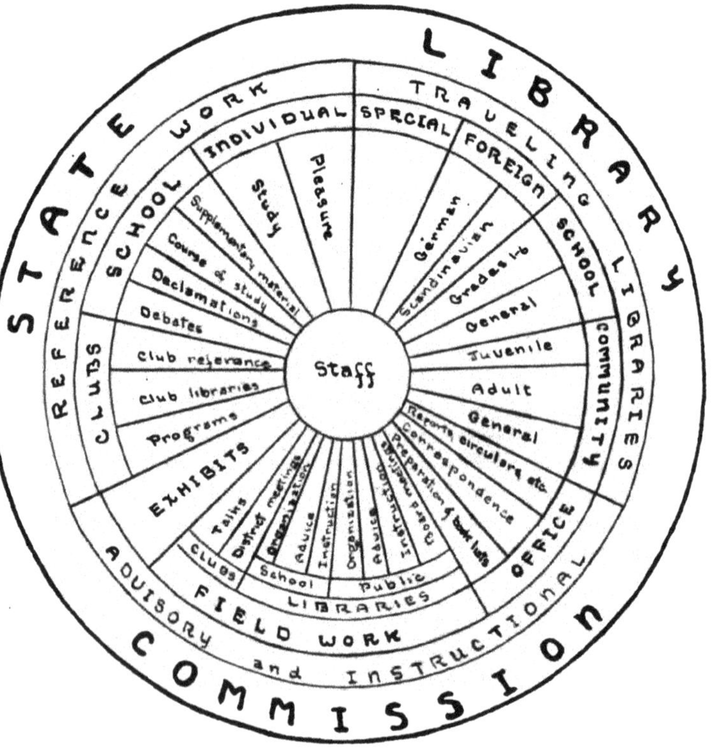

OFFICE WORK

There are no statistics which show the office work but it represents many busy hours. Some work which could (more effectively) be done in person must of necessity be done by correspondence, and librarians, public library boards and school officers write us for help and information along various lines. The library turn-over in the state is small but the Commission aids in filling vacancies; book orders are made out for small libraries and reading lists suggested; and lists of books for various other purposes are compiled. There is no regular state library publication so circular letters are sent out occasionally for the purpose of publicity and "keeping-in-touch"; reports are gathered from all the libraries in the state and statistics compiled from them. A directory of North Dakota libraries and librarians is being carefully compiled and an information file in regard to librarian's formal education, professional training, hours of service, salary, etc., is well started. Thru correspondence as close contact as possible is kept with the persons and localities which it is impossible to visit in person.

FIELD WORK

The small boy who was not satisfied to stay alone in a dark room with only the angels there to care for him because he wanted someone with "skin on," may be used as an illustration of what our field work means—it gives us a chance to become a person, and not a signature nor a department to the various club, school and library people of the state. The maintenance of friendly personal relations between the Commission and the state at large seems to the director the best basis for effective service, and the personal contacts as important as the actual field work done. It is impossible to make a detailed report of the field work for the first eighteen months of the period, but the following work has been done during the past six months. Visits were paid to 26 public libraries, 26 school libraries, and 7 state school libraries in 35 towns in 25 counties. Ten libraries were organized, 24 mending demonstrations were given, 12 instructional talks given to school assemblies and teacher training classes, 17 public library board meetings attended, talks on reading to 13 clubs and 4 open publicity meetings held. The greatest need for service is, of course, where the library resources are the least, so the field work is largely confined to the smaller towns. Out of the 33 places visited, 15 have less than 1,000 population, and six others between 1,000 and 1,500.

CLUB

Any service which the Library Commission can give the club women of the state is but a partial return for all they have done and are doing for the libraries. Special effort is made to help them in the preparation of club programs, by supplying reference material for individual papers and furnishing club libraries which are groups of reference books adequately covering a year's course of study. The director or a representative attended three club district meetings and greetings were sent to all, outlining the ways in which the Commission could aid the club in the small town and urging them to make use of this service.

AIDS TO LIBRARIES

Aside from the help which is given thru correspondence and field visits, the Commission aids the small libraries in the following ways: (a) subscriptions to Standard Catalog Bi-monthly, a guide for book selection, (b) subscriptions to a series of selected book lists to be used in buying and publicity, (c) furnishing at cost library supplies which the small library might have difficulty in securing, thus insuring standard grades at a reasonable price, (d) occasional multigraphed book lists from this office, (e) where buying in quantities means a considerable saving, ordering material on the celebration of special weeks, as Children's Book Week, and (f) the lending of current professional literature of all kinds, which the librarian of the small library cannot be expected to own, but which she must see. This reading helps her to keep in touch with modern library thought, achievement and methods, to accomplish the routine with efficiency and to have vision and inspiration in her work; without which any library work becomes mechanical and thus ceases to be true library service.

COUNTY LIBRARY BILL

The County Library Bill on which a great deal of publicity work was done last year, did not get out of committee and so never reached the Legislature. The bill will not be introduced to the Legislature next session as those who are most closely in touch with North Dakota conditions believe that no county is financially ready to function under it. Meanwhile the educational campaign is being carried on and it is believed that the people of the small towns and open country will so thoroughly recognize the advantages of the larger taxing unit in building up a library system, that their demand will insure the passage of the bill when introduced.

The Library Commission is anxious to work for and support in every way possible a county library bill, sponsored by the North Dakota Library Association or other group of interested citizens.

TRAVELING LIBRARIES

The circulation of the traveling libraries for the year ending June 30, 1923, amounted to exactly 312, of which 109 were placed in homes or places of business, while 203 were at school houses.

In the fall of 1923, in cooporation with the Department of Public Instruction, a traveling library was exhibited at each County Teachers' Institute, and left for use in the county. Considerable attention was thus directed to the teachers' use of them. As a result 290 libraries were sent to schools during the year ending June 30, 1924, while 72 were placed in homes or places of business,—a total of 362 libraries circulated during this year and a gain of 50 over the previous year.

There are only 305 traveling libraries available, and less than half of these are made of books useful in a school library. With the steadily increasing demand from the schools the Traveling Library Department finds itself in great need of a book fund with which to buy more books for juvenile reading. Thirteen years of experience in public library work in this state have convinced the head of this department that there is no phase of library work more important than furnishing the right kind of reading for boys and girls.

The Traveling Libraries consist at present of three kinds: (1) Community, (2) School and (3) Special. Tht Community libraries are made up of about one-third adult fiction, one-third adult non-fiction and one-third children's books. The School libraries are entirely juvenile, except for books supplementing the teacher's supply of reference books. The Special libraries consist of foreign books usually, which are made up on demand from Scandinavian or German titles. Another type of Special library has just been inaugurated, consisting of titles for grades one to six, about twenty in a box. These will be very popular and as yet are far too few to meet the demand.

With the Community libraries using about fifteen children's books each, the School libraries using thirty to forty juvenile, and the Special Lower Grades Libraries using twenty to twenty-five titles each, the crying need of the Traveling Library Department is more children's literature.

No attempt has been made in the School libraries to follow the school list for library purchase sent out by the Department of Public Instruction. The individual schools must use their own library purchase money for these books and add them to their permanent collections.

For the present the libraries must remain in fixed collections, instead of being made up at the request of various communities, to suit their individual needs and desires, but if these needs and desires are indicated, the library will be chosen to fit them as nearly as possible, and a few books can be added to the fixed collection to meet requests.

THE REFERENCE DEPARTMENT

The reference department circulated 3,119 books and 2,161 magazines, pamphlets and clippings during the year July 1, 1922—June 30, 1923, as compared with 3,647 books and 3,304 magazines, pamphlets, and clippings circulated during the period July 1, 1923—June 30, 1924. This represents an increase of circulation during the past year amounting to 1,671 pieces of literature. The reference collection consists of about 6,800 books and 15,000 pamphlets and clippings.

The borrowers to whom this material was loaned may be divided into five classes: (1) Teachers, who call upon us for books along educational lines, for material to supplement their texts, and particularly for selections prescribed in the course of study. (2) High school students who need material to supplement their texts and, most especially, debate material. (3) The private citizen whose school days are over but who needs us to provide him either with books for pleasure reading, or texts to aid him in serious study—often a correspondence course, or material to assist him in preparing speeches for special occasions. (4)The club women whom we serve in three ways—either by providing them with a club library covering the subject of their year's study, or by sending them each month a package containing material to cover their papers for the month; or, lastly, in case they do not care for regular service, by helping from time to time the individual members in the preparation of their papers. (5) The heads of departments and employees in the capitol building who bring their reference questions to us and who depend upon us largely to provide the books which they read for pleasure.

In order to serve our large and varied clientele satisfactorily, we must have an increased book fund so that we may strengthen the weak spots in our reference collection, duplicate the material most often demanded, and add the new titles which will contribute most fully to the pleasure and profit of our patrons. We can neither continue to meet the needs of the borrowers who have learned to depend on us for service, nor can we hope to extend our service to those who need us just as badly but have not learned that their wants can be supplied by an agency within the state, unless we are provided with the funds which will make possible an adequate reference collection.

STATE LIBRARY COMMISSION STATISTICS—JUNE 1923—JUNE 1924

New applications	263	
Active stations	427	
Number traveling libraries	305	
Volumes in traveling libraries		13,525
Volumes in foreign collections		155
Open shelf collections		6,800
Total number volumes		20,480
Pamphlets and clippings	15,000	

TRAVELING LIBRARY LOANS

	1923	1924	Total
Traveling Libraries	312	362	674
Volumes in traveling libraries	14,278	15,996	30,274

REFERENCE LOANS

	1923	1924	Total
Books	3,119	3,647	6,766
Pamphlets and magazines	2,161	3,304	5,465
			12,231

NEEDS

The Library Commission has a triangle of needs, the base of which is more books; one side, extension of field work, and the other the means to hold an efficient staff. If this triangle a b c can be made to coincide with the triangle a' b' c' whose periphery is an "adequate-working-appropriation," these needs can be met.

The first need of more books is easily demonstrated. Sixteen counties having 22% of the population, have no library service except that which is furnished by the state. About 15% of the population has access to a library supported wholly or in part by municipal appropriation, but many of these libraries are so small as to need supplementing from the Commission. About 4% of the population lives where libraries are supported by the women's clubs, and these libraries also, often borrow boxes of books from the Commission. Some of these libraries furnish books to the people living outside the city, either free or at a small cost, but a very small percent of the country population is served in this way; 2,244 persons, according to the libraries which report.

This means that practically 80% of the population is dependent upon the Commission for books. The present appropriation allows us to spend about fifteen hundredths of a mill per person per year—which will not go far toward buying a book. Because many of the school districts have been unable to buy new books, the demand upon the Commission for supplementary material and references to cover the course of study has been especially heavy and we have been able to meet it only in part.

The reference department needs new and up-to-date material. The work with the individual is as important as the work with the group, and a line of activity for which the Commission is as responsible as for the community service. Our most direct contacts are, of course, with the individual, and meeting a specific need is as necessary as supplying a general demand. This legitimate function of the Commission is one which must not be lost sight of in the endeavor to supply community reading.

This report has already indicated the need for field work in that the director was in the field almost constantly for six months, and still has many libraries listed which have asked for help. The emphasis in all field work is for more practical and economical ways of accomplishing work and the extension and strengthening of local library service.

Books which are kept mended wear much longer, so the mending demonstrations save the library money as well as add to the appearance of the collection, for a book in need of repairs is always untidy. Most young people get their first training in civic responsibility in the library as it is here they first use public property. If a respect for this public property is to be instilled in them the books must be kept in good condition. Here, also, is where the child receives his first training in recognition of the rights of others. The books belong to John as well as to William and keeping them overtime, or abusing them, becomes an infringement on John's rights and is an unsocial act.

The library boards often need help in questions of local administration, sometimes legal problems need solving, and always a personal conference helps both the board and the Commission director to a better understanding of local problems and the service which the Commission is in a position to render. There is no aggressive state library extension program, but a well established attempt to strengthen and make more effective the lines of service already established, for it is believed that only on this foundation can a larger permanent library structure be built. Adequate library service in a community is its own best justification for the library appropriation and for county extension.

The scale of salaries thruout the Library Commission is lower than for other departments. The scale should be raised so that efficient people with educational and professional training may be induced to stay on the staff.

If the Library Commission can keep a trained staff, and have sufficient funds to do the necessary field work and buy the books needed to meet the immediate demand, it will function as it was intended it should, and will bring to those people living in isolated districts the library advantages of those living in the cities. North Dakota does not want any of her residents to suffer lack of intellectual or inspirational opportunities because of living in rural communities, and the Library Commission is one of the agencies thru which the state can supply those opportunities.

STATE WORK

Reports have been received from forty libraries and indicate a healthy growth in the work in the state. A few libraries report a smaller circulation for 1924 than 1923, but in almost every case the cause may be found in a smaller book appropriation. The state as a whole read 21,500 more books in 1924 than in 1923, over 19,000 thru the public libraries and over 2,200 thru the Library Commission.

Twenty-six of the libraries reporting have some municipal appropriation and fifteen are wholly supported by taxation. The average tax per capita in these libraries is 75 cents which is just three-fourths the minimum standard set by the American Library Association as an adequate income. Attaining this standard will mean greater usefulness on the part of each library to each man and woman, girl and boy in North Dakota.

Out of seventeen libraries for which figures are available for two years, eleven report an increase in income for 1924 which is very encouraging. However, running expenses have increased also and if libraries are to continue to give service they must have an appropriation which will be comparable with expenses.

Wahpeton has a fine new $43,000 library building, the gift of Mayor and Mrs. Leach. A library has been maintained for years by the club women of Wahpeton and now the city has voted an annual tax of $4,000 and with this the administration in the attractive and spacious building affords a larger book collection and increased hours of service.

Mrs. Jessie Searing, to whom much of the credit for library interest in Wahpeton belongs, will continue as librarian.

North Dakota believes in education and is willing thru local and state taxation to maintain those agencies thru which each citizen may achieve that education which Lowell says is the best—that which he gives himself.

DIRECTORY OF NORTH DAKOTA LIBRARIES

T—Tax Supported A—Association or Club S—Special

Place	Size	Name of Library	Kind	Volumes	Librarian
Ashley	1009	Public	A	4386	Mrs. H. D. Piper
Bathgate	352	Public	A		Margaret Brown
Beach	1106	Public	A		Mrs. John Keohane
Bismarck	7122	Public	T		Mrs. Florence Davis
		State Historical	S	50000	Corrinne Kittleson
		State Law	S	35000	E. J. Taylor
		State Library Commission	S	20325	Lillian E. Cook
		State Penitentiary	S	1200	John Lee, Warden
Bowman	787	Public	T	2797	Mrs. E. E. Hogoboom
Cando	1111	Public	A	2500	Mrs. C. J. Lord
Carrington	1420	Public	T	4342	Hazel Johnson
Casselton	1538	Public	A	1518	Mrs. E. D. Scott
Cavalier	819	Public	A	903	Edna P. Ralston
Center	200	Public	A	1000	Mrs. M. Jennings
Columbus	332	Public	A	400	Mrs. G. C. Keup
Courtenay	490	Public	A	665	Mrs. A. A. Hoffman
Devils Lake	5140	Public	T	6389	Marie O'Brien
		State Deaf School	S	2437	Burton W. Driggs
Dickinson	4122	Public	T	6292	Minnie M. Orr
		State Normal	S		Pres. S. T. May
Drake	517	Public	A	350	Mrs. H. B. Parmenter
Edgeley	803	Public	A	1328	Mrs. Mary F. Cornwell
Ellendale	1334	Public	T	2797	Mrs. V. D. Coleman
		Normal & Industrial Normal	S	5300	Carrie Tuttle
Fargo	21961	Public	T	19081	Inga Rynning
		Agricultural College	S	37448	Mrs. Ethel McVeety
		Fargo College	S		Dr. Stratton
		Masonic	S		Clara Richards
Fessenden	731	Public	A		Ella Marie Speiser
Glenburn	228	Public	A	750	Mrs. Edward Simpkins
Grafton	2512	Public	T	5080	Mary Morris
		School Feeble Minded	S	98	Dr. A. R. T. Wylie
Grand Forks	14010	Public	T	9840	Mrs. Lulu Hart
		University	S	80652	Alfred Keator
Hamilton	200	Public	A	700	Amanda Larson
Hankinson	1477	Public	T	1005	Mrs. Kate R. Spottswood
Heaton	200	Public	A	95	C. I. Turner
Hettinger	817	Public	A	700	Mrs. J. G. Johns
Hope	699	Public	A	560	Mrs. Katie Gumb
Jamestown	6627	Alfred Dickey	T	7129	Gertrude Edwards
		Jamestown College	S		Dean F. B. Taylor
		Insane Asylum	S	1219	Mrs. A. W. Guest
Lakota	969	City	A	1864	Mrs. Frank Pierce
LaMoure	1014	Public	A	1997	Mrs. Paul Adams
Langdon	1228	Public	T	2216	Mrs. D. W. Barker
Leeds	704	Public	A	2549	Nora Jacobsen

Leonard	175	Watts Free (Twp.)	T	1227	Alma Roney
Lidgerwood	1065	City	T	2961	Elizabeth Kings
Lisbon	1855	Public	T	2391	Mrs. H. S. Oliver
Maddock	557	Public	A		Mrs. B. G. Anderson
Mandan	4336	Public	A	3212	Mrs. J. A. Biggs
		State Training School	S		W. F. McClelland
Marmarth	1318	Public	A	385	Cleo Dixon
Mayville	1218	Public	T	2324	Cora Ames
		State Normal..	S	9470	Mary Deaver
Milton	393	Community	A	590	Mrs. J. H. McCullock
Minot	10476	Public	T	9224	Catherine McSherry
		State Normal..	S	5294	Mrs. Alice P. Morris
Mott	416	Inez Hendrickson	T	1862	Louise Wagner
New Rockford	2111	Public	A	1755	Mrs. Roy Stitzel
Oakes	1637	Public	A	4233	Mrs. G. B. Fay
Park River	1114	Public	T	2519	Mrs. J. C. Overbye
Pembina	802	Public	A		Mrs. George Morris
Rugby	1424	Public	T	1448	Mrs. Seldon Crockett
Sanborn	391	Myosotis Club	A	625	Mrs. H. J. Malm
St. Thomas	576	Public	A	932	Mrs. E. T. Thompson
Tioga	320	Masonic Lodge	A	401	W. E. Berg
Valley City......	4686	Public	T	9021	Harriet Anfinson
		Teacher's College	S	20322	Mary Buffum
Van Hook	331	Women's Civic League	A	505	Mrs. E. A. Nelson
Velva	836	Public	A	855	Mrs. S. S. Ritchie
Wahpeton	3069	Leach Public ..	T	5456	Mrs. Jessie Searing
Wahpeton	3069	Science School	S	2579	Lilian Mirick
Watford City..	260	Public	A	170	Ruby Thomas
Williston	4178	James Memorial	T	6255	Marian Goss
Wimbledon	521	Public	A	500	Mrs. W. O. Joos

STATISTICS OF LIBRARIES WITH MUNICIPAL APPROPRIATION JULY 1, 1924

Place	Receipts				Expenditures				Circulation							
	Population	Tax	Extra	Total	Salaries	Heat Light Rent	Books and Periodicals	Total	Volumes	Borrowers	1923	1924	Total	Hours Open	Terms of Lending	County Borrowers
Over 2,500																
1 Fargo	21,961	8889	*$1,000.00	$12,871.00	$5,075.16	$897.53	$2,326.14	$12,093.73	19,081	12,395	91,945	92,595	184,540	72	Free	....
2 Grand Forks ..	14,010	6500	....	10,812.00	4,628.58	710.18	1,123.49	6,987.59	9,840	4,617	66,571	70,500	137,071	63	Free	20
3 Minot	10,476	8359	....	11,669.00	3,876.00	629.82	1,687.63	7,625.41	9,224	5,927	41,106	48,093	89,209	72	Free	50
4 Bismarck	7,122	4000	....	4,104.00	2,220.00	729.63	532.45	4,104.00	7,186	2,759	24,372	31,235	55,607	49	Free	1
5 Jamestown	6,627	5803	....	8,060.00	2,865.35	857.71	1,785.78	7,774.74	7,129	3,303	33,958	41,068	75,026	46½	Free	....
6 Devils Lake ..	5,140	3945	....	5,185.00	1,636.00	680.28	908.53	4,167.19	6,389	2,731	29,727	33,037	62,765	36	Free	6
7 Valley City ..	4,686	2601	....	4,792.00	1,629.00	426.27	453.37	3,460.09	9,021	4,990	25,503	24,536	50,039	36	Free	....
8 Williston	4,178	4659	....	7,016.00	1,677.18	615.78	598.22	4,911.14	6,255	2,231	23,842	25,539	49,381	36	Free	270
9 Dickinson	41,22	3000	....	3,000.00	1,996.36	389.48	654.85	3,322.52	6,292	287	18,675	17,271	35,946	36	Free	15
10 †Wahpeton	3,069	2634	....	3,878.00	300.00	14.28	21.90	3,038.59	5,456	599	14,736	5,154	19,890	10	Free	23
11 Grafton	2,511	500	* 600.00	1,507.36	540.00	193.05	18.25	880.78	5,080	......	......	......	....	22	Free	....
Under 2,500																
12 Bowman	787	1000	....	....	540.00	....	....	....	2,797	144	......	5,391	....	21	Free	....
13 Carrington	1,420	487	Room	1,342.43	600.00	33.46	276.16	1,021.05	4,342	1,347	11,346	8,843	20,189	33	Free	261
14 Ellendale	1,334	525	Room	673.69	339.00	....	155.11	581.87	2,797	700	5,891	5,023	10,114	15	Free	150
15 Hankinson	1,477	120	Room	257.02	120.00	....	....	137.00	1,005	704	......	2,440	....	4	....	....
16 Langdon	1,228	400	....	1,281.16	150.00	329.90	155.08	805.27	2,216	73	4,601	6,585	11,186	15	Charge	6
17 Leeds	704	......	Room	225.91	40.50	Free	79.34	225.91	2,649	250	4,499	5,054	9,553	6	Free	....
18 Leonard	175	§250	....	250.00	125.00	10.00	....	332.35	1,227	256	......	1,285	....	6	Free	....
19 Lidgerwood ..	1,065	1500	....	2,114.40	968.00	116.54	174.47	2,074.40	2,961	933	16,356	15,907	32,263	35	Free	353
20 Lisbon	1,855	1729	....	2,467.21	375.65	300.00	150.92	1,826.22	2.391	1,101	12,807	11,806	24,613	18	Free	119
21 Mayville	1,218	1000	....	....	400.00	436.86	35.00	934.27	2,324	415	......	2,324	....	12	Free	....
22 Mott	416	400	Room	422.58	185.00	Free	....	379.16	1,862	573	6,433	4,490	10,923	6	Free	....
23 New Rockford	2,111	100	Room	371.00	178.50	Free	19.00	132.45	1,755	250	......	3,000	....	8	Charge	....
24 Park River ..	1,114	400	Room	416.40	180.00	Free	33.10	225.49	2,519	1,021	7,068	8,177	15,245	8	Free	...
25 Rugby	1,424	483	....	788.75	126.00	250.00	....	417.50	1,448	497	2,827	3,185	6,002	4	Free	58
26 Velva	836	50	....	223.00	Free	Free	100.00	225.49	835	385	......	925	....	2	Free	100
27 Oakes	1,637	675	....	858.63	240.00	316.49	171.48	777.46	4.233	600	......	1,384	....	15	Charge	50

* From School Board.
† Report covers 4 months only.
§ From Township.

STATISTICS OF ASSOCIATION LIBRARIES

		Population	Receipts	Expenditures	Volumes	Borrowers	Circulation	Hours Open	Terms of Lending	County Borrowers
1	Ashley	1009	$133.77	$111.59	3197	281	4386	6	Charge	......
2	Bathgate	352	No Report							......
3	Beach	1106	207.15	125.87	1710	500		5	Free	......
4	Cando	1111	......	......	2500	50			Charge	......
5	Casselton	1518	681.21	362.69	1518	450	4180	5	Free	......
6	Cavalier	819	......	......	903	800	1560	3½	......	100
7	Center	200	......	......	1000	150	......	....	Charge	......
8	Columbus	332	......	......	400	285	......	2	......	......
9	Courtenay	490	51.39	25.86	665	512	......	2	Charge	......
10	Drake	517	......	......	350	150	936	....	Charge	......
11	Edgeley	803	116.49	103.24	1400	75	......	....	Charge	35
12	Enderlin	1919	No Report							
13	Fessenden	731	No Report							
14	*Glenburn	228	110.08	70.31	1029	12	1003	5	Charge	......
15	Hamilton	200	47.40	45.50	700	......	2000	2	(Adults pay)	......
16	Hannah	500	No Report							
17	Heaton	200	25.76	25.59	95	......	......	....	Charge	22
18	Hettinger	817	No Report							
19	Hope	699	......	......	500	52	560	1	......	6
20	Lakota	969	348.45	279.76	1864	150	5574	3	......	......
21	LaMoure	1014	269.11	152.08	1997	351	......	6	Free	......
22	Maddock	557	No Report							
23	Mandan	4336	104.55	......	3212	80	4989	12	Charge	......
24	Marmarth	1318	71.25	29.00	385	80	1285	2	Free	......
25	Milton	393	......	......	590	265	......	4	......	87
27	Pembina	802	No Report							
28	Sanborn	391	35.00	35.00	625	50	500	....	Charge	......
29	St. Thomas	576	111.00	23.60	932	155	1283	3	Charge	......
30	Van Hook	331	160.00	123.60	505	228	......	2	......	85
31	Watford City	260	12.38	70.75	170	197	......	5	Free	98
32	Wimbledon	521	......	......	500	......	......	....	Free	......

* 1923 Report.

STATE OF NORTH DAKOTA

TENTH BIENNIAL REPORT

Of The

State Library Commission

For the Period

July 1, 1924-June 30, 1926

BOARD OF ADMINISTRATION

June 30, 1926

R. B. Murphy..Chairman

F. E. Diehl

W. J. Church

Minnie J. Nielson

Joseph A. Kitchen

STATE LIBRARY COMMISSION

Lillian E. Cook..Secretary and Director

Bessie B. Baldwin..Traveling Library Chief

Margaret Welch..Reference Librarian

Bertha Severtson..Stenographer

LETTER OF TRANSMITTAL

To the State Board of Administration,

Bismarck, North Dakota.

Herewith is submitted the Tenth Biennial Report of the North Dakota State Library Commission, covering the period from July 1, 1924, to June 30, 1926.

LILLIAN E. COOK, Secretary and Director.

The Tenth Biennial report of the State Library Commission covers the period from July 1, 1924, to June 30, 1926.

The work of the Library Commission is organized along three general lines: (1) The development of library service throughout the state, (2) the operation of the traveling library department, and (3) the direction of the reference department.

SUMMARY

New libraries	[illegible]
Total tax supported libraries	25
Association libraries	35
Association libraries opened	4
New library buildings	1
Advisory visits to libraries	102
Addresses	67
Exhibits	4

'olumes added to Commission library:

Reference Department	1,910
Traveling Library Department	1,100

REPORT OF THE SECRETARY AND DIRECTOR

The North Dakota Library Commission was established in 1907 to (a) maintain an education reference library and a system of traveling libraries; (b) to give advice and instruction upon any matter pertaining to the organization, maintenance or administration of libraries; (c) to promote and assist the formation of libraries where none exist.

The organization has varied from time to time and at present the Commission is under the direction of the Board of Administration. In 1919 the Legislature transferred the work of the Legislative Bureau from the Library Commission to the State Law Library; therefore there is no mention of the work of this bureau in this report. An account of the activities of the Commission along the other lines indicated by law constitutes this report.

FIELD AND OFFICE WORK

To "advise" and "instruct," to "promote" and "assist" are largely the work of the director since there is no organizer. This work can be done partly by correspondence, but can be done much better, and has been done largely, through field work. The contacts made in the field and the information gained have been of great value to the Commission, and there is also the worth while by-product of publicity. The growth in office and reference work will practically necessitate the discontinuance of field work during the next biennial period, but we hope to add a cataloger and organizer to the staff next year, which will again make field work possible.

The field work is naturally most largely done in the small towns which must depend on the state for all library help. The following work was done in sixty-five towns of varying size, in forty counties:

Less than 500 population	19 towns
500 to 1,000	18 towns
1,000 to 1,500	12 towns
1,500 to 2,500	6 towns
2,500	10 towns

Visits	39	public libraries
	49	school libraries
	14	State schools and institutions
	102	
Organization	22	school and library collections
Mending demonstrations	30	
Conferences	59	
Library board meetings	29	
Talks	16	public schools
	14	state schools
	17	clubs
	9	Parent Teachers Associations
	11	state and district meetings
	67	

The secretary and director attended (1) the annual state meetings of the N.D.L.A., N.D.F.W.C., N.D.E.A., P. T. A. and the county superintendents; (2) twenty-four county institutes and ten club district meetings; and (3) the annual mid-winter meetings of the League of Library Commissions at Chicago. At each of the mid-winter trips, visits were paid to the Wisconsin and Minnesota Commissions and conferences held.

Office work includes correspondence, conferences, preparation of book lists for small libraries or criticism of lists already prepared, helping libraries to get librarians or librarians to get libraries; suggestions for and revision of organizing work where visits cannot be made, gathering statistics, "advising, instructing and assisting" in every way possible.

LIBRARY NOTES

A new venture of the Commission during the last biennial period has been the issuing about every six weeks of a two or three-page mimeographed publicity sheet which we have called "Library Notes." Eight numbers of "Library Notes" have been issued and it has proved valuable as a means of publicity and interchange of ideas. Most Commissions print a monthly or bi-monthly bulletin which we have not been able to afford. Until our appropriation will cover printing a news sheet, we shall try to continue the mimeographed sheet, which has proved useful enough to justify the time and expense it takes to issue it in its present form.

EXHIBITS

The Commission held an exhibit of traveling libraries and reference material at the state fair at Fargo, July, 1924. An exhibit of club libraries and club program material was held at the meetings of the N. D. F. W. C. at Minot in 1924 and Valley City in 1925. An exhibit of graphs, etc., representing the work of the Commission, was sent to Sioux City for the regional meeting.

NORTH DAKOTA LIBRARY ASSOCIATION

The 1924 meeting was held at Minot and was a joint meeting with the State Federation of Women's Clubs.

In 1925 North Dakota joined with Iowa, Minnesota, Missouri, Nebraska and South Dakota in a joint regional library meeting at Sioux City. This larger meeting, bringing as it did an opportunity to meet with other workers and hear and see some of the prominent library workers in the United States, was much enjoyed. One day was set aside for local meetings and the N.D.L.A. elected the following officers:

President	Catherine McSherry	Minot
Vice President	Ethel Fleming	Fargo
Secretary and Treasurer	Nora Jacobsen	Leeds
Directors	Christian Dick	University
	Bessie R. Baldwin	Bismarck
Council Member	Lillian E. Cook	Bismarck

NEEDS

Graphs, like actions, speak louder than words. Unfortunately, complete statistics have not been kept, but the accompanying graph will show the circulation of reference and traveling library departments by biennial periods, also the number of books circulated for each dollar spent for books.

The second graph shows the growth of the circulation in the reference department and the relation between it and the total appropriation.

The law requires that the books be cataloged; this has not been done for many years: need one is for a cataloger and field worker. The circulation of the traveling libraries has fallen off the past biennium because the collections are worn, shabby and out of date: need two is for funds to get new books of current interest. The work of the reference department is growing very rapidly—almost trebling the circulation of the preceding biennium and almost quadrupling that of two periods previous. The work is well started and we can only continue to do effective and helpful work for the state if we have the books with which to do it; need three is for more money for refernce books, magazines, and a part time cataloger to make them of greater service.

TRAVELING LIBRARIES

Circulation figures for the biennium show 329 libraries sent out up to July, 1925, and 296 in the following year. Of these the type of library used appears as 161 community, 162 school and 6 special libraries in the first year, and 122, 170 and 4, respectively, in the second.

These figures are significant in the following respects: School libraries, collections of from 20 to 50 books made up especially for children's reading, show a gain, while the community libraries, adult titles in the main, show a falling off. This is a natural result of the policy adopted by the department. Attention has been concentrated on buying books for the school collections, bringing them into as nearly adequate a number and quality as funds permitted. No school in 1925-6 was obliged to take a community library because there were not enough school libraries to go around. If one was sent it was a matter of choice. There were enough school libraries to meet the requests, though they were often small. Many of them, at least, were fresh and attractive.

Community libraries, on the other hand, were increased by a small amount only—seven in 1925-6 and fewer than that the year before. To build up an adequate collection of fifty books in a community library costs, nowadays, $75 to $80 at the least. Children's titles can fortunately be purchased for less cost per volume. One does not expect to arouse enthusiasm or response over out-of-date and worn-looking collections of books.

In the fall of the first year nearly every Teachers' Institute was visited and the opportunity to take out application blanks for traveling libraries was brought directly to the attention of the rural teachers. In the second year the libraries had to depend largely on an established reputation as funds did not permit the personal contact at the Institutes. The number of repeat orders from the schools was gratifying and the number of satisfied letters which accompanied the return of the libraries this spring even more so.

Arrangement of circulation for the two years by counties shows Burleigh naturally in the lead, with 37, McLean with 30, while Morton and Grant each have 27. With one exception these counties are not supplied with public library service. That neither transportation expense nor population entirely determine the number, however, shows up in 10 in Pembina County and 13 in Golden Valley. An interested county superintendent can do a great deal to further the cause of good reading in his county.

REFERENCE DEPARTMENT

The statistics for the reference department for the biennium, July 1, 1924, to July 1, 1926, show an increase in circulation of 250 per cent as compared with the circulation of the former biennial period. This considerable increase in circulation has been accomplished with no increase in staff.

The clientele of the reference department for the past two years has been similar to that of the preceding biennium except that many borrowers have been added to those who were already depending on the reference departmnt for service. The borrowrs may still be divided into five groups: (1) teachers, (2) pupils, (3) club women, (4) heads and staffs of state departments, and (5) a large group of people who are not required to study, but who read for their own personal pleasure and profit.

Every effort has been made to serve this varied clientele effectively. About 2,000 new books have been added during the biennium. In buying these books it was the aim of the reference librarian to strengthen the weak spots in the reference collection, notably along the lines of sociology, economics, and Bible study; to provide the best of the current fiction, and to add from time to time new books of travel, biography, literary criticism and scientific books of a popular nature.

The pamphlet and clipping file was completely revised and transferred from unwieldy wooden boxes to metal files. Many new pamphlets and clippings were added and all old material which was either out-of-date or useless for other reasons was discarded. The collection now consists of some 10,000 pieces of usable, up-to-date material. Of this collection, many of the publications are government documents. These have been shelf listed. Especial attention has been given to collecting pamphlets and clippings on North Dakota. This material is in constant demand.

In addition to providing schools with material for debates, contests and special day programs, a special effort has been made to lend the books required for outside reading to those schools whose libraries were inadequate. Another activity of the reference department has been the building up of a large collection of good plays which are borrowed freely by the schools and various community groups.

A complete file of P.T.A. publicity and reference material is kept and lent to many places which are considering organizing, or lent to individuals for reference purposes. An effort has been made to secure many of the books on the "Parent's Book Shelf," to lend to P.T.A. members who wish to do this reading.

The work of the reference department with the clubs has grown appreciably. Programs have been obtained from every conceivable source covering a wide range of subjects, and many special programs have been prepared to meet special needs. During the year 1924-25 ten clubs depended entirely on the Commission for material and during 1925-26 twenty clubs were either using club libraries prepared by the reference department or were receiving regular service.

With the individual reader in mind a large number of reading courses covering many subjects have been collected. These courses are lent to persons who wish to do consistent, constructive reading.

STATISTICAL REPORT, 1924-26

Books

Traveling library:	
Number of traveling libraries	321
Number of libraries added during period	45
Number of books in libraries	11,332
Reference department:	
Number of books	8,510
Number of books added during period	1,910
Number of pamphlets	10,000

Circulation

Traveling library	24-25	25-26	Total
Number of libraries circulated	329	296	625
Number of stations			366
Number of books circulated	13,958	11,529	25,487
Reference Department:			
Number of requests	4,204	5,287	9,491
Number of club libraries sent	10	20	30
Number of books in club libraries	147	391	538
Number of reference books circulated	7,873	11,219	19,092
Number of pamphlets	5,171	6,429	11,600
Total circulation	29,149	29,568	56,717

Appropriation, 1925-27

Books and periodicals	$3,000.00
Binding	500.00
Salaries	14,440.00
Furniture and fixtures	200.00
Stationery and supplies	300.00
Printing	300.00
Postage	200.00
Total	$20,840.00

STATE WORK

The libraries in the state report some variation in circulation, with Minot topping the list with an increased circulation of 35,000 volumes, 1925-26.

There are no new publc library buildings, but the club women of St. Thomas, who maintain without help a library for that place, bought a building which they have made into a very attractive library.

Libraries have been started or reopened at Washburn, Rolla, Brantford and Tolna, all of them under the auspices of the women's clubs except Brantford, where the P.T.A. is sponsoring it.

There have been several librarians' resignations in public libraries and some changes among the club women who are administering libraries for their communities, Bismarck, Bowman, Dickinson and Jamestown being the libraries with municipal support which have changed librarians this year. A corrected list of librarians will be found in the directory.

A study of the reports of six of the larger libraries for the past five years shows almost uniformly a direct relation between the book purchases and the circulation. The graph "Comparative Statistics" shows this. Where circulation has been maintained without a corresponding book expenditure it indicates a librarian of unusual ability. The first need for any library is a trained librarian of ability, secondly, a representative collection of books, and thirdly, working conditions which enable her to accomplish the greatest amount of service with the least loss of time and effort.

The following tables outline the work of the various libraries for past two years.

STATISTICS OF ASSOCIATION LIBRARIES, 1924-26

Place	Population	Income		Expenditures Books		Total		Volumes	Borrowers	Circulation			Hours Open Per Week	Terms of Lending	County Borrowers	Place
		25	26	25	26	25	26			25	26	Total				
1. Ashley	962	......	199	......	......	......	188	4,159	113	......	3,353	......	6	Fee	......	Ashley
2. Bathgate	828	......	50	......	......	......	50	500	73	......	1,200	......	1½	Free	......	Bathgate
3. Beach	1,148	......	62	......	50	62	62	1,700	696	......	9,360	......	5	"	46	Beach
4. Cando	1,055	200	500	......	200	200	500	2,300	75	......	2,840	......	4	Fee	......	Cando
5. Cavalier	810	101	48	57	......	101	2	737	407	788	1,336	2,119	2½	Free	47	Cavalier
6. [illegible]er	200	......	52	60	50	52	5	1,050	270	2,640	1,000	3,640	......	Fee	50	[illegible]er
7. Columbus	471	65	69	49	50	65	69	481	100	879	715	1,594	2	Free	......	[illegible]us
8. Courtenay	328	55	40	24	25	40	85	691	79	870	837	1,707	2	Fee	11	[illegible]y
9. Drake	636	......	......	......	75	......	......	275	85	......	......	......	2	"	15	Drake
10. Edgeley	735	78	108	78	......	78	65	1,588	45	3,640	......	......	3	"	4	Edgeley
11. Enderlin	1,824	......	......	......	......	......	......	3,857	800	......	8,320	......	4	Free	10	Enderlin
12. Fessenden	757	188	......	112	......	184	......	......	......	......	......	......	......	......	......	Fessenden
13. [illegible]rn	248	......	......	......	33	......	48	800	22	......	1,144	......	3	Fee	5	[illegible]rn
14. Hamilton	179	......	......	......	35	......	......	......	600	......	......	......	2	Adult fee	......	Hamilton
15. Heaton	200	......	......	......	6	......	8	152	85	250	884	1,134	Bank	Free	20	Heaton
16. Hettinger	1,009	76	58	50	38	76	58	580	217	......	1,000	......	2	Free	......	Hettinger
17. Hope	577	......	17	......	18	......	......	628	40	314	4,756	5,060	2	Fee	......	Hope
18. Lakota	869	291	290	188	95	275	170	2,156	......	5,306	......	......	23	Free	......	[illegible]keta
19. [illegible]re	994	223	604	121	299	265	428	2,399	550	3,004	3,900	6,904	6	"	......	LaMoure
20. Leeds	668	174	94	98	75	174	94	2,820	272	4,591	4,599	9,190	6	"	5	Leeds
21. Maddock	383	......	......	......	80	......	90	660	330	572	2,000	2,572	3½	"	35	Maddock
22. [illegible]an	5,068	......	......	......	......	......	......	4,500	......	......	5,500	......	8	"	......	Mandan
23. Milton	370	......	......	......	70	......	70	850	440	......	8,000	......	2	Fee	300	Milton
24. Pembina	802	......	......	......	65	......	65	800	150	......	2,500	......	4	Free	20	Pembina
25. Rolla	686	......	......	......	22	......	54	385	140	......	......	......	4	Fee	......	[illegible]lla
26. St. Th[illegible]mas	576	......	......	......	52	......	550	1,208	201	1,100	5,220	6,320	3	Free	......	St. [illegible]mas
27. [illegible]born	391	29	10	22	15	23	25	877	22	50	500	550	1	Fee	4	Sanborn
28. [illegible]ga	320	48	68	33	75	40	76	583	......	450	1,479	1,929	......	Free	......	Tioga
29. Tolna	192	......	......	25	25	......	......	111	......	......	520	......	3	"	......	[illegible]na
30. Turtle Lake	395	......	......	......	......	......	......	472	......	......	1,560	......	2	Fee	......	Turtle Lake
31. Van Hook	331	8	11	80	64	120	78	618	252	......	3,120	......	2	Free	70	Van Hook
32. Velva	836	......	......	......	......	......	......	1,200	200	......	5,000	......	2	"	......	[illegible]va
33. Washburn	558	......	......	......	......	......	7	......	......	......	......	......	4	"	......	Washburn
34. Wimbledon	521	5	7	46	28	52	33	700	30	......	......	......	1	"	......	Wimbledon

STATISTICS OF LIBRARIES WITH TAX SUPPORT, JULY 1, 1924-JUNE 30, 1926

PLACE	Popula-tion	Receipts				Expenditures							
		Tax		Total Income		Salaries		Heat, Rent Light		Books Bind Magazines		Total Expenditures	
Over 2,500		1925	1926	1925	1926	1925	1926	1925	1926	1925	1926	1925	1926
1. Fargo	24,921	10,674	10,860	14,535	12,796	5,441	6,072	876	1,000	2,682	2,456	13,670	12,124
2. Grand Forks	15,168	6,500	7,000	7,459	8,031	4,003	4,153	817	862	1,827	1,435	7,453	7,447
3. Minot	12,245	8,320	8,892	8,787	9,387	4,091	4,205	582	580	1,870	4,110	8,034	10,228
4. Bismarck	9,150	4,000	4,970	4,093	4,970	1,850	1,612	429	500	437	2,326	3,700	4,960
5. Jamestown	7,230	4,908	4,476	5,967	5,546	1,704	3,309	809	922	1,490	1,996	6,096	7,482
6. Devils Lake	5,409	4,656	4,930	4,927	5,264	1,622	1,676	689	754	1,558	1,005	4,633	4,646
7. Valley City	4,695	3,152	5,940	3,414	6,209	785	1,591	450	540	457	1,622	3,194	5,605
8. Dickinson	4,467	3,000	3,000	3,129	3,133	2,056	2,040	335	360	475	449	3,542	3,363
9. Williston	3,948	5,183	5,160	5,876	5,515	2,529	2,641	566	502	1,331	1,776	5,160	5,573
10. Wahpeton	3,187	3,940	3,973	4,149	4,104	720	780	176	....	202	2,040	1,400	5,503
11. Grafton	2,913	1,700	1,352	2,065	1,412	557	597	228	150	418	185	1,333	1,072
Under 2,500													
12. Bowman	775	1,014	1,219	1,098	1,895	620	620	124	130	116	211	1,175	982
13. Carrington	1,315	755	1,078	785	1,452	530	650	140	188	137	277	731	1,008
14. Casselton	1,416	300	280	826	281	123	104	....	....	226	148	362	272
15. Ellendale	1,094	325	450	439	591	310	300	....	....	143	164	510	476
16. Hankinson	1,390	....	200	....	....	....	....	....	....	....	....	....	....
17. Langdon	1,239	....	425	489	651	153	120	192	277	110	80	516	656
18. Leonard	541	250	250	252	270	125	125	14	8	....	110	160	281
19. Lidgerwood	1,009	1,600	1,400	2,032	1,585	955	924	75	89	101	182	2,069	1,589
20. Lisbon	1,626	2,000	2,000	2,071	2,063	375	379	305	300	307	259	1,649	2,058
21. Mayville	1,345	800	1,000	876	1,245	400	350	299	122	89	195	883	852
22. Mott	810	400	400	466	431	180	180	180	180	18	1	397	395
23. New Rockford	2,050	90	100	375	....	176	....	....	....	242	....	427	....
24. Oakes	1,509	975	989	1,043	1,068	500	380	54	....	156	812	716	1,142
25. Park River	1,044	400	400	416	445	180	190	....	....	97	106	292	315
26. Rugby	1,509	318	300	334	318	48	....	....	276	54	102	387	449

STATISTICS OF LIBRARIES WITH TAX SUPPORT, JULY 1, 1924-JUNE 30, 1926—Continued

PLACE	Volumes		Borrowers		Circulation			Hours open per week	Terms of Lending	County Borrowers		PLACE
Over 2,500	1925	1926	1925	1926	1925	1926	Total			1925	1926	
1. Fargo	19,990	20,598	13,550	14,334	103,242	111,479	214,721	72	Free	445	530	Fargo
2. Grand Forks	10,346	10,880	5,126	4,919	67,934	62,951	130,885	63	"	60	....	Grand Forks
3. Minot	9,751	11,678	7,692	7,309	58,953	94,384	152,337	72	"	186	206	Minot
4. Bismarck	6,568	7,281	3,473	3,359	31,218	19,436	50,754	42	"	3	....	Bismarck
5. Jamestown	7,887	8,813	3,528	3,871	42,815	51,771	94,585	48	"	....	75	Jamestown
6. Devils Lake	6,898	7,224	2,617	2,654	27,490	26,266	53,756	36	"	....	2	Devils Lake
7. Valley City	9,201	9,413	1,611	2,054	18,861	20,484	139,345	36	"	....	....	Valley City
8. Dickinson	6,506	6,688	....	....	10,888	14,005	24,893	36	"	....	....	Dickinson
9. Williston	6,927	7,264	2,208	2,360	23,906	26,844	50,750	36	"	224	220	Williston
10. Wahpeton	6,060	6,626	887	1,013	15,679	15,090	30,769	13	"	....	30	Wahpeton
11. Grafton	5,607	2,292	564	730	6,080	7,460	13,540	16	"	11	4	Grafton
Under 2,500												
12. Bowman	3,009	3,170	98	161	5,310	6,352	11,862	16	Free	....	....	Bowman
13. Carrington	4,274	4,520	1,016	1,130	8,598	11,950	20,548	27½	"	....	340	Carrington
14. Casselton	1,075	1,040	470	583	4,080	4,060	8,140	5	"	....	....	Casselton
15. Ellendale	2,850	2,945	775	886	8,497	9,479	17,976	14	"	....	246	Ellendale
16. Hankinson	1,192	1,332	725	811	2,440	1,221	3,661	8½	"	....	11	Hankinson
17. Langdon	2,440	2,561	102	56	7,246	5,307	12,553	8	Fee	....	....	Langdon
18. Leonard	899	1,095	272	150	1,297	1,302	2,599	6	Free	....	....	Leonard
19. Lidgerwood	3,025	3,286	727	704	15,889	13,858	29,247	35	"	354	....	Lidgerwood
20. Lisbon	2,582	2,608	1,195	1,127	10,638	13,427	24,065	18	"	93	97	Lisbon
21. Mayville	2,456	2,967	468	530	2,965	3,148	6,113	12	"	50	....	Mayville
22. Mott	1,918	2,006	138	140	4,266	3,864	8,130	6	"	15	....	Mott
23. New Rockford	1,472	1,500	128	....	....	5,000	....	8	Fee	....	....	New Rockford
24. Oakes	3,464	3,663	485	674	7,983	12,382	20,365	16	"	54	105	Oakes
25. Park River	2,604	2,729	1,032	923	6,485	6,765	13,885	8	"	63	....	Park River
26. Rugby	1,585	....	642	665	5,120	5,290	10,510	4	....	....	....	Rugby

STATE INSTITUTIONAL LIBRARIES

Place	Name	Volumes	Employees Full	Employees Part	Amount Spent for Books	Librarian
Bismarck	Historical society	24,001	1	0		Mrs. Florence Davis
Bismarck	Law	20,000	1	0	2.000	E. J. Taylor
Bismarck	Library commission	19,842	4	1	2,500	Lillian E. Cook
Bismarck	Penitentiary		1	1		Warden John Lee
Bottineau	Forestry school	1,500	....	4		L. M. Minkle
Devils Lake	School for the deaf	2,361	....	1		Burton Driggs
Dickinson	Normal	3,000	....	....	1,000	E. O. Purtee
Ellendale	Normal and industrial school	5,910	1		500	Carrie Tuttle
Fargo	Agricultural college	40,248	4	2	3,700	Mrs. Ethel McVeety
Grafton	School for the feeble-minded	202	....	1	50	Maud Stewart
Grand Forks	University	84,729	5	9	7,500	Alfred Keator
Jamestown	Insane hospital	1,700	1	1	150	Mrs. A. W. Guest
Mandan	Training school	....	....	....	200	W. F. McClelland
Mayville	State teachers college	11,496	1	4	1,869	Mrs. Hazel Webster Byrnes
Minot	State teachers college	8,548	2	1	....	Mrs. Mable W. Etheridge
Valley City	State teachers college	22,222	3		1,817	Mathilde Maier
Wahpeton	State science school	2,791	1	1	323	Lilian Mirick

DIRECTORY OF NORTH DAKOTA LIBRARIES

T—Tax Supported A—Association or Club S—Special

Place	Size	Name of Library	Kind	Volumes	Librarian
Ashley	962	Public	A	4159	Mrs. H. D. Piper
Bathgate	342	Public	A	500	Annie Slagerman
Beach	1148	Public	A	1700	Mrs. John Koehane
Bismarck	9150	Public	T	7281	Pauline Rich
		State Historical	S	24001	Mrs. Florence Davis
		State Law	S	20060	E. J. Taylor
		State Library Commission	S	19842	Lillian E. Cook
		State Penitentiary	S		Warden John Lee
Bottineau	1067	Forestry School	S	1500	L. M. Minkle
Bowman	775	Public	T	3170	Mrs. Emil Scow
Cando	1055	Public	A	2300	Mrs. C. J. Lord
Carrington	1315	Public	T	4520	Edna Parker
Casselton	1416	Public	T	1040	Mrs. E. D. Scott
Cavalier	810	Public	A	737	Mrs. Fred Harris
Center	200	Public	A	1050	Mrs. M. Jennings
Columbus	471	Public	A	481	Mrs. P. J. Broen
Courtenay	328	Public	A	691	Mrs. A. A. Hoffman
Devils Lake	5409	Public	T	7224	Marie O'Brien
		State Deaf School	S		Burton W. Driggs
Dickinson	4467	Public	T	6688	Gertrude Voldal
		State Normal School	S		E. O. Purtee
Drake	636	Public	A	275	Mrs. A. B. Parmenter
Edgeley	735	Public	A	1588	Mrs. Ralph Stevens
Ellendale	1094	Public	T	2945	Mrs. V. D. Coleman
		Normal and Industrial School	S	5910	Carrie Tuttle
Enderlin	1824	Public	A	3857	Mrs. E. T. Danielson
Fargo	24921	Public	T	20598	Inga Rynning
		High School	S	3768	Esther C. Goudy
		Agricultural College	S	40248	Mrs. Ethel McVeety
		Masonic Library	S		Clara Richards
Fessenden	757	Public	A		Ella Marie Speiser
Glenburn	248	Public	A	800	Mrs. Edward Simpkins
Grafton	2913	Public	T	2292	Ruth Nollman
		School Feeble Minded	S	202	Maud Stewart
Grand Forks	15168	Public	T	10880	Ruth O. Brown
		University	S	84729	Alfred Keator
Hamilton	179	Public	A	600	Mrs. Robert Kippen
Hankinson	1390	Public	T	1332	Mrs. George Schuett
Heaton	200	Public	A	152	C. L. Turner
Hettinger	1009	Public	A	580	Mrs. F. T. Lembke
Hope	577	Public	A	628	Mrs. Katie Gumb

Jamestown	7230	Alfred Dickey	T	8831	Margaret Mueller
		Insane Hospital	S		Mrs. A. W. Guest
		Jamestown College	S		Dean F. B. Taylor
Lakota	869	Public	A	2045	Mrs. Frank Pierce
LaMoure	994	Public	T	2399	Mrs. D. A. Martens
Langdon	1239	Public	T	2569	Mrs. D. W. Barker
Leeds	668	Public	A	2820	Nora Jacobsen
Leonard	541	Watts Free (Twp.)		1095	Agnes Roney
Lidgerwood	1009	Public	T	3286	Mrs. Elizabeth Kings
Lisbon	1626	Public	T	2608	Mrs. H. S. Oliver
Maddock	583	Public	A	660	Leila Anderson
Mandan	5068	Public	A	4500	Mrs. John Biggs
		Training School	S		Mrs. W. F. McClelland
Mayville	1345	Public	T	2967	Cora I. Ames
		State Teachers College	S	11496	Mrs. Hazel W. Byrnes
Milton	370	Community	A	850	Mrs. J. H. McCulloch
Minot	12245	Public	T	11678	Catherine McSherry
		State Teachers College	S	8548	Mrs. Mable W. Etheridge
Mott	810	Inez Hendrickson	T	2006	Louise Wagner
New Rockford	2050	Public	T	1500	Mrs. E. R. Davidson
Oakes	1509	Public	T	3663	Alice Craig
Park River	1044	Public	T	2729	Priscilla Overbye
Pembina	665	Public	A	800	Mrs. Pauline Brennan
Rolla	636	Public		385	Mrs. C. Jacobsen
Rugby	1509	Public	T	1757	Hattie S. Sikes
St. Thomas	443	Study Club	A	1203	Mrs. E. T. Thompson
Sanborn		Mysotis Club	A	877	Mrs. Robert E. Kee
Tioga	365	Masonic Lodge	A	583	W. E. Berg
Tolna	192	Public	A	111	Mrs. C. J. Hand
Turtle Lake	472	Public	A	472	Mrs. L. J. Vonderheide
Valley City	4695	Public	T	9413	Harriet Anfinson
		State Teach-College	S	22222	Mathilde Maier
Van Hook	368	Women's Civic League	A	618	Charlotte Stenshoel
Velva	872	Public	A	1200	Mrs. I. A. Beebe
Wahpeton	3187	Leach Public	T	6626	Mrs. Jessie Searing
		State Science School	S	2791	Lilian Mirick
Washburn	618	Public	A		Mrs. G. M. Wallbrecht
Williston	3948	James Memorial	T	7264	Mrs. Ethel H. Kuenning
Wimbledon	447	Public	A	700	Mrs. W. O. Joos

STATE OF NORTH DAKOTA

Eleventh Biennial Report

OF THE

State Library Commission

For the Period

July 1, 1926—June 30, 1928

BOARD OF ADMINISTRATION

June 30, 1928

R. B. Murphy..Chairman

F. E. Diehl

W. J. Church

Bertha R. Palmer

Joseph A. Kitchen

STATE LIBRARY COMMISSION STAFF

Lillian E. Cook ....Secretary and Director

Bessie R. Baldwin ....Traveling Library Chief

Mahala Saville ....Reference Library

Metella Williams ....Cataloger

Ellen Davis ....Stenographer

Thelma Liessman ....Clerk

LETTER OF TRANSMITTAL

To the State Board of Administration,

Bismarck, North Dakota.

Herewith is submitted the Eleventh Biennial Report of the North Dakota State Library Commission, covering the period from July 1, 1926, to June 30, 1928.

LILLIAN E. COOK,

Secretary and Director.

SUMMARY

New libraries	9
Total tax supported libraries	28
Association libraries	39
New library buildings or quarters	6
Advisory visits to libraries	46
Addresses	49
Exhibits	11

REPORT OF THE SECRETARY AND DIRECTOR

Covering the biennial period July 1, 1927—June 30, 1928, this report marks the "Coming of age" of the State Library Commission, which, established in 1907, has served the state for twenty-one years.

The governing organization has differed from time to time and the staff personnel has had many changes, but the purposes of furnishing worth while reading to the residents of the small towns and the open country, and of aiding and encouraging the small libraries of the state, have remained constant.

The work of the Commission falls roughly into three classes, (a) office work, (b) field work with the state-at-large and state organizations, and (c) book service to communities, schools and clubs, and to individuals, given through the Traveling Library and Reference Departments.

OFFICE WORK

The Commission has never kept track, as some commissions do, of the number of letters and circulars written, lists compiled, programs made out, and packages handled, during a biennial period. This work has been heavier the last two years because of the greater bulk of work and because there has been less field work done, necessitating more letter writing. When the Commission staff includes a field worker, much more efficient and concrete help can be given in the field.

Cataloging. Because, during disorganized years, the reference collection was not completely cataloged, reference work has been very difficult. The legislature of 1927 made an appropriation for a cataloger who began work August first of that year. Since then the regular cataloging has been done, the pamphlets and mounted clippings "headed," shelf list and catalog checked for about two-thirds of the collection, and 1500 books cataloged.

North Dakota Teacher. Through the courtesy of the editor, the Commission has had a page in the North Dakota Teacher each issue, which has been devoted to school library helps, suggestions, and information.

Bulletin No. 5 is the buying list for grade school libraries and is published by the State Department of Public Instruction, although, the selection of books, the preparation of copy and the reading of proof is largely done in this office. An attempt is made to fit the books for each grade into the course of study for that grade, and each grade list is checked carefully that it in itself may be a balanced collection and appeal to the tastes of the various pupils.

Library Notes is a mimeographed sheet of North Dakota library news and helps issued about every two months. To keep twenty-five of the small libraries of the state informed of national library activities, to bring them some of the best library papers and addresses, and to furnish them with lists of books especially selected for small libraries, the Commission subscribes for the Wisconsin Library Bulletin (monthly), which is a much more pretentious publication than the Commission can afford.

Children's Book Week. Because the Secretary and Director of the Commission happened to be also the State Club Federation chairman of library extension, through cooperation with the Federation state literature chairman, all of the Children's Book Week activity has been headed up by the Commission. In the larger towns the public libraries took over the work, the Commission furnishing some of the supplies. In the smaller towns where there were public or association libraries, the Commission cooperated with the libraries, furnishing posters, lists and publicity material. In the towns where there was a Federated club and no library, similar supplies were furnished and suggestions of the Week's observance made. Thanks to the whole-hearted help and interest of librarians and club women, some very effective and worth while "Weeks" have been developed.

Circulars. We find that in spite of being twenty-one years old, there are many who still do not know of our book service. To call attention to it, circular letters were sent out to the editors, lawyers, doctors, bankers and ministers of the small towns. In these circulars, the service was explained and a short list of books enclosed, a different list for each group, made up with their interests and preferences especially in mind.

FIELD WORK: STATE AND STATE ORGANIZATIONS

The field work of the Commission staff during the past four years was in twenty-two towns as follows:

Less than 500 population	6 towns
500 to 1,000	8 towns
1,000 to 1,500	7 towns
1,500 to 2,500	5 towns
2,500	9 towns

Visits	46	public libraries
	10	school libraries
	18	state schools and institutions
	74	
Organization	75	school and library collections
Conferences	20	
Library board meetings	32	
Talks	6	public schools
	11	state schools
	3	clubs
	5	Parent-Teacher Associations
	35	state and district meetings
Exhibits	11	
Fairs	3	
	201	

League of Library Commissions annual meeting was held in Chicago December 28-31, and the Secretary and Director went. The mid-winter meeting of the American Library Association is held at the same time, so general as well as league conferences were attended. On this trip, visits were made to the various libraries and book stores at Chicago, St. Paul and Minneapolis, and to the Wisconsin and Minnesota Commissions. Time was spent in the Hennepin County Library headquarters and a field trip was made with the librarian.

Clubs. A close and friendly relation is always maintained between the women's clubs and the Commission. During the spring of 1927, the Secretary attended all but one of the eight district meetings and during 1928, attended all of them. Literature in regard to Commission service and county libraries was distributed at each meeting and a short explanatory talk made.

P. T. A. The Commission offers program help and reference material to all P. T. A's. A special effort has been made to strengthen the collection along the lines of P. T. A. interests and the books on the lists recommended by the National Congress and those reviewed in Child Welfare are usually bought. The Secretary has attended the state meetings, having exhibits of books and program helps.

San Haven. A new library project of the state is one undertaken by the Federation of Women's Clubs, which has started and is developing a library for the new children's building at San Haven. The Library Commission secretary has been a committee of one to select the books. One hundred twenty-two clubs contributed $174.45 and 135 books have been bought since January, 1928, with a small balance on hand toward the next purchase.

BOOK SERVICE

Reference Department

The reference work shows growth during the last biennial period. This department has worked under something of a handicap, for there has been a different librarian each year, but in spite of this, old borrowers have been satisfied and new ones secured, and the work has grown.

The only change in the work with individuals, clubs, P. T. A's and schools, has been in volume and not in kind. The needs of the club women and teachers have been kept constantly in mind and have determined, largely, the book selection for the reference department. Lists of pamphlets and government documents are carefully checked and much of the "live" reference material is furnished through them. These pamphlets, with mounted clippings, constitute the "vertical file" which is constantly weeded out that it may contain the latest and most up-to-date information. As in the past, special attention has been paid to the preservation of North Dakota material.

The work with the club women has grown, the monthly service for program helps being the most popular. Schools are more and more depending on us for special topic, theme, debate, and special day material, and the grade and high school demand for required and credited outside reading books is heavy.

The working capital of the reference department is about 9,000 books and 16,000 pamphlets and mounted clippings, and this collection during the past biennial period, had a circulation of 35,918.

TRAVELING LIBRARY DEPARTMENT

Two features mark the progress of the work in the last biennium: the addition of package library service and the purchase of community libraries designed to aid the clubs doing library work in small communities.

The package library grew out of two needs—that of supplying books to a family or individual where securing the five signers necessary to obtain a traveling library was not feasible, and where a small collection, changed more frequently, worked to a better advantage than a large collection kept six months. Over a thousand books have been sent out in this way since the service was started a year ago, and repeat orders have come from twenty-three of these borrowers. One shut-in, has had nine of these packages, which contain about a dozen books and can be kept two months.

The traveling libraries, planned to supplement small community libraries, have been so useful that the demand is greater than the supply. Repeat orders have come back from these in almost every instance. Towns taking advantage of this opportunity include Kay, Wishek, Sheyenne, Towner, La Moure, Cooperstown, Tioga, Rolla, Bowbells, Beach, Carrington, Hettinger, Van Hook and Windsor. These in addition to stations of long standing like Heaton, Loraine, and Medora, appreciate opportunity to get fresh reading material, and the traveling library longs for larger resources with which to meet the demand.

Fortunately the children's books do not go out of fashion and the school libraries, to which the department gave first emphasis in previous years, are now sufficient to supply the demand. The result of the new features has been a gain of over three thousand in circulation in the last two years. One hundred and nine package libraries do not appear in the healthy advance of 660 traveling libraries over 625 previously. Of the 660, the school libraries still hold the majority of 429. That service is well established and seems to be much appreciated by the rural and small town schools.

The total circulation of 27,623 books against 25,847 of the last report is encouraging. The map showing the distribution of the libraries is easier to comprehend than a written description.

STATISTICAL REPORT, 1926-1928

Books

Traveling Library:	
Number of traveling libraries	350
Number of libraries added during period	50
Number of books added during period	1,587
Number of books in libraries	12,450
Reference Department:	
Number of books	9,000
Number of books added during period	1,301
Number of pamphlets	16,000

Circulation

Traveling Library:			
Number of libraries circulated	26-27	27-28	Total
School	214	215	429
Community	120	111	231
Package	....	109	109
Number of books circulated	13,174	14,457	27,631
Number of stations	....	....	312
Reference Department:	26-27	27-28	Total
Number of requests	5,672	5,478	11,150
Number of club libraries sent	5	9	14
Number of books in club libraries	171	202	373
Number of reference books circulated	11,241	13,644	24,885
Number of pamphlets	4,899	5,761	10,660
Total reference circulation	16,311	19,607	35,918
Total commission circulation	29,485	30,064	63,549

Appropriation, 1927-29

Books and periodicals	$ 3,000.00
Binding	500.00
Salaries	17,440.00
Furniture and fixtures	200.00
Stationery and supplies	500.00
Printing	300.00
Postage	200.00
Miscellaneous	2,000.00
Total	$24,140.00

NORTH DAKOTA LIBRARY ASSOCIATION

The 1926 meeting was held at Jamestown in October, Catherine McSherry of Minot presiding. The problems of the very small library were discussed. Clarence B. Lester of Wisconsin was the national speaker.

In 1927 the meeting was held in Dickinson. No speaker of national fame was present, but the central theme of the meeting was a better knowledge of our own state. North Dakota authors, books and pamphlets about North Dakota, North Dakota wild life and its conservation, were presented by speakers whose familiarity with their subjects gave particular zest to their contributions. Two of North Dakota's authors were present for evening addresses,— Mr. George Will and Mr. P. E. Byrne of Bismarck. The post-conference trip to Peaceful Valley and a first-hand acquaintance with the Bad Lands made a fitting close to this session.

Bessie R. Baldwin was the presiding officer at this session. The officers elected for 1928 were Harriet Pearson, president, and Gertrude Voldal, secretary.

LIBRARY FACTS

Of the seven states without county library laws and service, North Dakota ranks highest in rural population (which county libraries serve most) and third in assessed valuation.

The United States Census Bureau and the American Library Association furnish the following population and public library figures for the whole United States.

	Illiteracy	% population rural	% population without library service	Assessed valuation per capita	Book expenditure per capita	Book supply per capita	Book reading per capita
High for United States	18.1	86.6	85	$3,106	1.08	2.22	7.33
Low for United States	1.1	2.5	3	252	.02	.06	.13
Average for United States	6.0	48.6	43	1,280	.33	.62	2.13
North Dakota	2.1	86.4	80	2,022	.12	.23	.77

COUNTY LIBRARIES

North Dakota is still interested in county library legislation and several meetings in its behalf have been held. Interest has been general wherever the matter has been presented and it is hoped that a permissive amendment, allowing county library work, may be secured at the 1929 legislative session. This amendment has been endorsed by the North Dakota Federation of Women's Clubs, the North Dakota Library

Association, the North Dakota Educational Association and the North Dakota Congress of Parent-Teacher Association. The accompanying cut shows the status of county library service in other states. According to figures compiled by the American Library Association, North Dakota ranks about one-third of the average for the United States for books provided through public libraries, funds expended for such books, and amount of reading done from them

SCHOOL

The Commission is very happy in its close association with the schools. Both institutions are part of the educational system of the state and the cooperation is for mutual advantage and service. The lines of association are briefly indicated.

Reference. Books, magazines and clippings supplying reference material for reports, themes, debates, special days.

Books for required and credit outside reading for both high school and grades.

Traveling Libraries through which books for general reading are furnished for rural and small town schools.

Organization of school libraries by a staff member when possible, and printed and correspondence help when personal help cannot be given.

North Dakota Teacher: A page of school library help and information in each issue.

Bulletin No. 5: The Department of Education list of library books for grade schools, selected, copy prepared and proof read. The books listed in Bulletin No. 5 are collected at the Commission where they may be borrowed for examination or seen at the office by superintendents making up booklists.

Librarians' Section North Dakota Educational Association: The Commission has cooperated with the institutional librarians in arranging programs, and securing this section.

High School library service has been fostered by the Commission by cooperation with superintendents and board members. Mr. Frank Walter, librarian of the University of Minnesota, spoke on the general program of the N. D. E. A. in 1927 and Mr. Tighe, principal of Fargo High School, led a round table discussion on "The Place of the library in the high school program" in the high school section in 1928.

Normals and State Teachers Colleges: An attempt is made to visit each regular session and each summer school, to present to the students the help the Commission offers the teacher and the school.

STATE WORK

The final summary of public library work for the period 1926-28 shows progress. More attention has been paid to careful book selection, especially for juveniles, book appropriations have been cut only in a few places, and gains in circulation have been made. The biennial report shows that 247,172 more books were circulated through libraries with municipal support in 1926-28 than in 1924-26. The total circulation for such libraries was 1,393,161 and for association libraries 130,302, making a total of 1,523,463.

Buildings: Lakota (gift of A. M. Toftehagen,) and Lidgerwood (bought by the library board) have moved into new library buildings; Rugby and Edgeley have pleasant rooms in new city halls; Enderlin has a large ground floor room in the community building; Sanish bought a building for club and library purposes and the university library is to be moved into the old commons building which has been renovated and remodeled for its use.

New Libraries: Lakota became a tax supported library when it moved into the new building. The new association libraries are, Amidon, Bisbee, Bowbells, Goodrich, Hansboro, Ray, Sanish, Towner, and Wishek.

New Librarians are serving at Bismarck Public Library, Dickinson State Normal, Drake, Edgeley, Enderlin, Fargo High School, Jamestown Public Library, Lakota, La Moure, Oakes, Park River, Valley City State Teachers College and Van Hook. The directory gives a full list of all the librarians of the state and the statistical tables outline the work of the libraries.

State Library Commission

PLACE	Population	Receipts Tax 1927	Receipts Tax 1928	Receipts Total Income 1927	Receipts Total Income 1928	Salaries 1927	Salaries 1928	Heat, Rent Light 1927	Heat, Rent Light 1928	Books, Binding, Magazines 1927	Books, Binding, Magazines 1928	Expenditures Total 1927	Expenditures Total 1928
Over 2,500													
1. Fargo	24,921	11,448	11,464	15,383	13,169	6,171	7,069	728	755	3,918	5,318	12,406	14,882
2. Grand Forks	15,168	8,200	6,300	9,484	7,422	3,927	3,727	947	1,116	1,903	1,524	9,045	7,714
3. Minot	12,245	10,538	8,289	11,458	8,762	4,623	5,251	753	603	3,921	2,019	1,386	8,762
4. Bismarck	9,150	5,000	5,337	5,429	5,854	2,460	3,035	662	595	1,125	922	5,415	5,705
5. Jamestown	7,230	5,167	5,889	8,276	6,464	2,785	2,709	887	798	1,458	1,579	7,978	8,954
6. Devils Lake	5,409	5,031	4,730	7,233	5,163	1,653	1,724	643	661	2,073	1,959	4,810	4,915
7. Valley City	4,695	3,151	3,412	5,546	3,673	1,413	1,639	506	527	488	1,147	3,225	4,361
8. Dickinson	4,467	3,000	4,000	3,602	4,239	2,115	2,081	223	270	1,004	1,327	3,584	4,199
9. Williston	3,948	4,240	4,058	8,019	5,509	2,980	3,158	518	591	1,307	1,362	4,123	6,089
10. Wahpeton	3,187	3,646	3,798	5,922	3,892	1,509	1,723	675	552	1,991	482	4,301	3,140
11. Grafton	2,913	1,600	1,100	2,617	1,296	647	645	184	146	338	187	1,275	1,044
Under 2,500													
12. Bowman	775	652	957	1,253	1,163	627	613	112	114	412	171	1,199	1,050
13. Carrington	1,315	1,120	1,384	1,564	1,499	650	600	42	36	426	368	1,260	1,004
14. Casselton	1,416	250	300	254	321	150	150	....	....	88	144	254	321
15. Ellendale	1,094	450	450	754	578	360	295	....	....	305	227	735	596
16. Hankinson	1,390	120	420	120	537	120	120	....	....	....	400	120	587
17. Lakota	869	....	1,200	259	1,200	52	280	....	....	183	250	259	761
18. La Moure	994	473	600	682	647	300	300	3	....	148	239	504	595
19. Langdon	1,239	600	500	787	500	153	150	275	272	127	235	562	686
20. Leonard	541	250	250	250	250	125	140	....	....	125	139	250	250
21. Lidgerwood	1,009	1,400	1,400	1,551	2,137	955	912	104	124	122	160	1,458	1,770
22. Lisbon	1,626	2,000	1,906	4,125	1,960	378	381	300	300	176	240	3,399	2,581
23. Mayville	1,345	750	1,000	876	1,128	369	360	391	256	72	135	1,293	998
24. Mott	810	400	560	400	597	185	180	....	180	17	16	213	401
25. New Rockford	2,050	100	100	360	774	200	208	....	....	125	360	361	774
26. Oakes	1,509	1,172	774	1,612	1,129	604	791	....	....	361	281	1,581	1,186
27. Park River	1,044	300	300	449	362	185	185	....	....	247	62	449	305
28. Rugby	1,509	300	220	361	282	....	....	....	....	65	72	361	282

State Library Commission

PLACE	Volumes		Borrowers		Circulation			Hours open per week	Terms of lending	County Borrowers		PLACE
Over 2,500	1927	1928	1927	1928	1927	1928	Total			1927	1928	Over 2,500
1. Fargo	22,417	23,962	7,000	7,841	125,741	141,818	267,059	76	Free	186	296	1. Fargo
2. Grand Forks	11,490	12,025	5,091	5,294	69,960	66,405	135,365	67	Free	67	97	2. Grand Forks
3. Minot	13,827	14,201	9,467	10,867	132,710	127,386	260,096	75	Free	250	250	3. Minot
4. Bismarck	8,199	8,722	2,800	3,511	32,056	44,768	76,824	45	Free	8	....	4. Bismarck
5. Jamestown	9,195	9,734	2,740	3,492	60,011	69,910	121,921	45.7	Free	....	....	5. Jamestown
6. Devils Lake	7,669	8,259	1,983	2,432	30,128	30,499	60,627	40	Free	4	3	6. Devils Lake
7. Valley City	9,742	10,068	2,364	3,876	27,070	30,791	58,861	40	Free	....	....	7. Valley City
8. Dickinson	6,319	7,004	1,862	2,616	25,194	28,270	53,464	54.5	Free	12	19	8. Dickinson
9. Williston	8,104	8,773	2,384	3,484	30,641	34,169	64,810	40	Free	....	314	9. Williston
10. Wahpeton	7,931	9,525	1,317	1,500	21,745	22,837	44,582	18	Free	32	50	10. Wahpeton
11. Grafton	2,605	2,714	307	....	7,482	9,558	17,040	16	Free	6	9	11. Grafton
Under 2,500												Under 2,500
12. Bowman	3,353	3,530	....	....	6,170	6,413	12,683	21	Free	....	....	12. Bowman
13. Carrington	4,680	4,724	1,265	1,331	14,262	14,151	28,413	27.5	Free	395	445	13. Carrington
14. Casselton	1,000	1,005	355	385	4,420	4,940	9,360	4	Free	....	....	14. Casselton
15. Ellendale	3,021	3,133	888	868	7,119	9,271	16,390	17¼	Free	175	200	15. Ellendale
16. Hankinson	1,192	2,025	440	300	2,820	2,041	4,861	4	Free	....	....	16. Hankinson
17. Lakota	2,157	3,500	142	....	4,672	9,880	14,450	18	Free	....	....	17. Lakota
18. La Moure	2,467	1,797	615	646	5,106	6,290	11,396	6	Free	160	188	18. La Moure
19. Langdon	2,348	2,652	65	59	5,251	4,368	9,619	10	Free	....	16	19. Langdon
20. Leonard	1,328	1,510	150	165	2,340	2,340	4,680	6	Free	....	....	20. Leonard
21. Lidgerwood	3,388	3,407	767	850	19,839	14,968	29,807	29	Free	....	....	21. Lidgerwood
22. Lisbon	2,730	2,938	948	933	12,943	10,539	23,482	18	Free	....	82	22. Lisbon
23. Mayville	3,055	3,167	578	627	3,077	2,790	5,867	12	Free	....	....	23. Mayville
24. Mott	2,057	2,242	808	567	2,912	2,958	5,870	6	Free	120	87	24. Mott
25. New Rockford	1,800	2,000	200	200	4,369	4,500	8,869	8	Free	....	....	25. New Rockford
26. Oakes	3,939	4,102	804	986	11,545	13,832	25,377	3	Free	146	182	26. Oakes
27. Park River	2,889	2,949	1,012	1,082	4,940	4,628	9,568	8	Free	....	....	27. Park River
28. Rugby	1,901	2,028	672	729	5,310	5,510	10,820	4	Free	36	22	28. Rugby

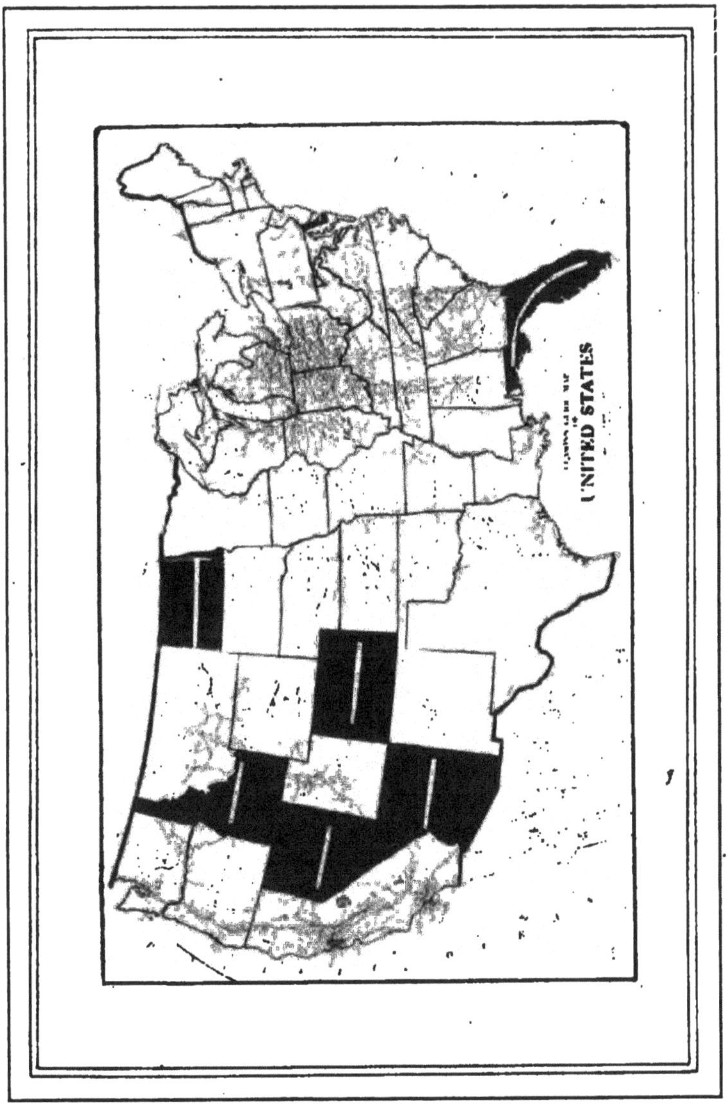

State Library Commission

STATISTICS OF ASSOCIATION LIBRARIES, 1926-1927

PLACE	Population	Expenditures: Books 1927	Expenditures: Books 1928	Expenditures: Total 1927	Expenditures: Total 1928	Volumes	Borrowers	Circulation 1927	Circulation 1928	Circulation Total	Hours Open Per Week	Terms of Lending	County Borrowers	PLACE
1. Amidon	......	......	......	......	......	......	......	......	......	......	......	......	......	1. Amidon
2. A[illegible]ey	962	72.87	124.20	152.07	202.95	4,228	287	4,420	4,680	9,100	6	Fee	......	2. A[illegible]ey
3. Bathgate	342	......	......	70.00	......	700	55	600	......	......	2	......	......	3. [illegible]ate
4. Beach	1,148	50.00	50.00	50.00	50.00	3 000	600	4,420	4,420	8,840	5	Free	......	4. [illegible]ch
5. Bisbee	449	......	......	......	......	[illegible]	35	......	247	247	......	......	......	5. [illegible]ee
6. Bowbells	615	......	......	......	......	155	184	......	......	......	4	Free	......	6. [illegible]lls
7. Cando	1,055	100.00	200.00	100.00	700.00	3,000	100	4,000	4,160	8,160	4	Fee	......	7. [illegible]do
8. Cavalier	810	29.00	15.00	69.00	15.00	810	83	......	520	......	2.5	Fee	......	8. [illegible]er
9. [illegible]r	200	80.00	50.00	80.00	50.00	1,100	105	6,760	4,940	11,700	......	[illegible]	20	9. [illegible]ter
10. [illegible]lumbus	471	50.00	......	61.50	......	531	325	750	......	......	2	......	......	10. [illegible]us
11. Courtenay	328	......	31.12	18.24	44.98	739	100	728	1,300	2,028	2	Fee	......	11. Courtenay
12. Drake	636	......	......	97.00	......	425	242	11,024	......	......	3	Free	......	12. Drake
13. Edgeley	735	52.00	100.00	117.68	147.21	1,778	50	1,260	1,075	2,335	3	[illegible]	......	13. Edgeley
14. Enderlin	1,824	......	72.58	......	145.09	1,971	770	......	5,966	......	8	Free	15	14. Enderlin
15. Fessenden	757	......	......	......	120.00	[illegible]	200	17,160	......	......	......	......	......	15. Fessenden
16. Goodrich	454	......	27.00	......	47.00	372	125	......	624	624	2	Free	......	16. Goodrich
17. Hamilton	179	......	25.00	25.00	25.00	700	50	1,500	2,500	3,000	2	Free	......	17. Hamilton
18. Hansboro	204	......	20.00	......	30.00	200	......	......	325	......	3	Free	......	18. Hansboro
19. Heaton	200	2.31	14.69	3.16	14.00	[illegible]	60	......	......	......	42	Fee	......	19. [illegible]on
20. Hettinger	1,009	25.00	32.00	45.00	67.00	675	180	[illegible]	2,080	4,636	2	Fee	......	20. [illegible]er
21. Hope	577	20.00	25.00	20.00	25.00	720	46	1,300	676	1,976	1	Fee	......	21. Hope
22. Leeds	668	......	85.00	......	85.00	2,890	250	3,650	3,000	6,500	6	Free	......	22. Leeds
23. Maddock	583	88.85	87.07	119.25	117.41	864	483	4,000	3,380	7,380	3.5	Free	4	23. [illegible]k
24. Mandan	5,068	......	......	......	......	5,168	......	......	......	......	8	[illegible]	......	24. Mandan
25. Milton	370	37.04	25.00	44.69	25.00	947	117	1,765	2,860	4,625	2.5	Fee	......	25. Milton
26. Pembina	665	60.00	65.00	60.00	65.00	975	75	4,680	4,500	9,180	3	Free	......	26. Pembina
27. Ray	557	......	......	......	50.00	......	50	......	1,300	......	2	Free	......	27. Ray
28. Rolla	636	......	......	......	......	......	......	......	......	......	......	......	......	28. Rolla
29. St. [illegible]mas	443	51.16	119.92	4 .32	301.78	1,368	64	5 088	6,240	11,328	2.5	Fee	......	29. St. [illegible]as
30. S[illegible]orn	323	8.48	......	8.48	......	888	21	262	......	......	1	Fee	5	30. Sanborn
31. S[illegible]h	296	......	30.00	......	130.00	300	50	......	1,810	......	3	Free	......	31. Sanish
32. [illegible]ga	365	30.00	45.00	30.00	45.00	775	150	3,120	2,057	5,177	66	Free	......	32. Tioga
33. [illegible]a	192	10.00	25.00	20.00	35.00	200	150	......	4,650	......	3	Free	......	33. Tolna
34. Towner	531	......	......	......	......	211	77	......	572	......	4	Free	......	34. Towner
35. T[illegible]rtle Lake	472	90.41	71.63	98.91	71.63	736	51	1,525	4,004	5,529	2	Fee	......	35. Turtle Lake

36. Van Hook	868	28.50	125.00	28.50	125.00	800	380	4,732	5,200	9,932	2	Free	......	36. Van Hook
37. Velva	872	......	100.00	115.00	100.00	1,300	250	......	8,840	......	2	......	......	37. Velva
38. Wimbledon	447	......	43.00	7.50	53.00	700	......	3,900	4,160	8,060	1	Free	......	38. Wimbledon
39. Wishek	1,016	......	222.00	96.42	104.00	500	125	2,600	......	......	4	Free	......	39. Wishek

STATE INSTITUTIONAL LIBRARIES—1927-1928

Place	Name	Volumes	Employees Full	Employees Part	[illegible]t Spent for Books	Librarian
Bismarck	Historical society	25,080	1	0	1,000	Mrs. [illegible]ce Davis
Bismarck	Law	20,500	1	0	2,500	E. J. T[illegible]lor
Bismarck	Library Commission	21,450	5	1	2,500	Lillian E. [illegible]k
Bismarck	Penitentiary	7,000	5	1	633	Warden John Lee
Bottineau	Forestry school	1,500	..	4	....	L. M. [illegible]e
Devils Lake	School for the deaf	2,372	..	1	577	Burton Driggs
Dickinson	Normal	5,498	..	..	....	[illegible]a Stoxen
Ellendale	Normal and industrial sch'l	6,773	1	..	500	Carrie Tuttle
Fargo	Agricultural college	44,058	4	2	4,714	Mrs. [illegible]el McVeety
Grafton	School for the feeble-minded	202	..	1	50	[illegible]d Stewart
Grand Forks	University	95,215	5	9	7,536	Alfred Keator
Jamestown	Insane hospital	5,416	1	1	100	Mrs. A. W. [illegible]est
Jamestown	College	8,971			....	F. B. Taylor
Mandan	Training school	....	..	..	200	W. F. [illegible]land
Mayville	State teachers college	13,379	1	4	1,869	Mrs. Hazel Webster Byrnes
Minot	State teachers college	11,071	1	3	....	[illegible] [illegible]le W. [illegible]ge
Valley City	State teachers college	24,336	4	..	2,486	[illegible]de [illegible]er
Wahpeton	State science school	3,232	1	2	606	[illegible] Mirick

Place	Names of Library	Librarian
Amidon	Public Library	Mrs. C. P. Brownlee
Ashley	Public Library	Mrs. H. D. Piper
Bathgate	Public Library	Annie Slagerman
Beach	Public Library	Mrs. John Koehane
Bisbee	Clionian Club	Mrs. B. J. LaRue
Bismarck	Public Library	Helen Kennedy
Bismarck	State Historical Library	Mrs. Florence Davis
Bismarck	State Law Library	E. J. Taylor
Bismarck	State Library Commission	Lillian E. Cook
Bismarck	State Penitentiary	Warden John Lee
Bottineau	Forestry School	Marguerite Walter
Bowbells	Study Club	Mrs. M. B. O'Rourke
Bowman	Public Library	Mrs. Emil Scow
Cando	Public Library	Mrs. C. J. Lord
Carrington	Public Library	Edna Parker
Casselton	Public Library	Mrs. E. D. Scott
Cavalier	Public Library	Mrs. Fred Harris
Center	Public Library	Mrs. M. Jennings
Columbus	Public Library	Mrs. A. L. Tennis
Courtenay	Public Library	Mrs. A. A. Hoffman
Devils Lake	Public Library	Marie O'Brien
Devils Lake	State Deaf School	Burton W. Driggs
Dickinson	Public Library	Gertrude Voldal
Dickinson	State Normal School	Matilda Stoxen
Drake	Public Library	Mrs. B. Magnuson
Edgeley	Public Library	Mrs. Mary Cornwell
Ellendale	Public Library	Mrs. V. D. Coleman
Ellendale	Normal & Industrial School	Carrie Tuttle
Enderlin	Public Library	Mrs. J. S. Sanders
Fargo	Public Library	Inga Rynning
Fargo	High School	Anabelle Smith
Fargo	Agricultural College	Mrs. Ethel McVeety
Fargo	Masonic Library	Clara Richards
Fessenden	Public Library	Ella Marie Speiser
Glenburn	Public Library	Mrs. Edward Simpkins
Goodrich	Public Library	Mrs. R. S. Troyer
Grafton	Public Library	Emma Cobb
Grafton	School Feeble-Minded	Maud Stewart
Grand Forks	Public Library	Ruth O. Brown
Grand Forks	University	Alfred Keator
Hamilton	Public Library	Mrs. Robert Kippen
Hankinson	Public Library	Mrs. George Schuett
Hansboro	Public Library	Mrs. R. T. Lymburn
Heaton	Public Library	C. I. Turner
Hettinger	Public Library	Mrs. F. T. Lembke
Hope	Public Library	Mrs. Katie Gumb

Place	Name of Library	Librarian
Jamestown	Alfred Dickey	Agnes Hassell
Jamestown	Jamestown College	Dean F. B. Taylor
Jamestown	Insane Hospital	Mrs. A. W. Guest
Lakota	Public Library	Mrs. Ellen Hullett
La Moure	Public Library	Mrs. E. F. Coyne
Langdon	Public Library	Mrs. D. W. Barker
Leeds	Public Library	Nora Jacobsen
Leonard	Watts Free	Agnes Roney
Lidgerwood	Public Library	Mrs. Elizabeth Kings
Lisbon	Public Library	Mrs. H. S. Oliver
Maddock	Public Library	Leila Anderson
Mandan	Public Library	Mrs. John Biggs
Mandan	Training School	Mr. W. F. McClelland
Mayville	Public Library	Cora I. Ames
Mayville	State Teachers College	Mrs. Hazel Webster Byrnes
Milton	Community	Mrs. J. H. McCulloch
Minot	State Teachers College	Mrs. Mable W. Etheridge
Mott	Inez Hendrickson	Louise Wagner
New Rockford	Public Library	Mrs. E. R. Davidson
Oakes	Public Library	Mrs. Edgar Christianson
Park River	Public Library	Margaret Kohnen
Pembina	Public Library	Mrs. Pauline Brennan
Ray	Public Library	Mrs. S. E. Markel
Rolla	Public Library	Mrs. C. Jacobsen
Rugby	Public Library	Hattie S. Sikes
St. Thomas	Study Club	Mrs. E. T. Thompson
Sanborn	Mysotis Club	Mrs. G. D. Dysart
Sanish	Public Library	Mrs. C. A. Pickering
Tioga	Masonic Lodge	W. E. Berg
Tolna	Public Library	Mrs. C. S. Hawkins
Towner	Public Library	Mrs. Elizabeth Gieseler
Turtle Lake	Public Library	Mrs. E. J. Vonderheide
Valley City	Public Library	Harriet Anfinson
Valley City	State Teachers College	Mathilde Maier
Van Hook	Woman's Civic League	Mrs. G. E. Yonkers
Velva	Public Library	Mrs. I. A. Beebe
Wahpeton	Leach Public	Mrs. Jessie Searing
Wahpeton	State Science School	Lilian Mirick
Williston	James Memorial	Mrs. Ethel H. Kuenning
Wimbledon	Public Library	W. O. Joos
Wishek	Public Library	Mrs. George Grant

TWELFTH BIENNIAL REPORT

OF THE

State Library Commission

TO THE

State Board of Administration

FOR THE PERIOD

JULY 1, 1928—JUNE 30, 1930

TWELFTH BIENNIAL REPORT

OF THE

State Library Commission

TO THE

State Board of Administration

FOR THE PERIOD

JULY 1, 1928—JUNE 30, 1930

BOARD OF ADMINISTRATION

June 30, 1930

J. E. Davis .... Chairman

R. B. Murphy

W. J. Church

Bertha R. Palmer

Joseph A. Kitchen

STATE LIBRARY COMMISSION STAFF

Lillian E. Cook .... Secretary and Director

Bessie R. Baldwin .... Traveling Library Chief

Mary Maynard .... Reference Library

Metella Williams .... Cataloger

Ellen Davis .... Stenographer

Thelma Liessman .... Clerk

LETTER OF TRANSMITTAL

To the State Board of Administration,

Bismarck, North Dakota.

Herewith is submitted the Twelfth Biennial Report of the North Dakota State Library Commission, covering the period from July 1, 1928 to June 30, 1930.

LILLIAN E. COOK,

Secretary and Director.

REPORT 1928-30.

State Library Commission Program
State Library Commission Activities
1. Professional
    a. General
    b. Field
2. Book Service
    a. Traveling Library
    b. Reference Department
3. Statistical report
4. Needs and growth
Organizations and Meetings
1. North Dakota Library Association
2. North Dakota Education Association: Library section
3. Institutes
4. Parent Teacher Association
5. League of Library Commissions
6. American Library Association
7. Library Conference
The State at Large
Statistical Library Report
Directory of Librarians

REPORT OF THE SECRETARY AND DIRECTOR, 1928-1930

The last report marked the coming of age of the State Library Commission and it was remarkable to note the growth and expansion of kinds of service the Commission is rendering. Sensing the complexity of the work it has seemed wise to make something of a survey and see just where we stand, what things if any can now be dropped, what emphasized and what initiated. Therefore this report will be brief on what has been done and will try to present what the Secretary and Director feels are the responsibilities of the Commission and what the objectives are toward which we are working and building. Therefore a program has been outlined and is here presented, not as Utopian nor for immediate achievement, but as a constructive adequate program possible of attainment.

COMMISSION PROGRAM

It is assumed that the library is a public educational institution, through which all the people of the state, regardless of age are served. Therefore the state library agency has a definite responsibility in securing:

1. EQUALIZATION OF LIBRARY OPPORTUNITY FOR ALL RESIDENTS OF THE STATE, WITH DIRECT STATE AID. The figures show the following local library service:

Urban with	82,559
Urban without	None
Rural with	40,585
Rural without	518,048

Equalization must be attained through development of local service under the county library system, increased appropriation for Library Commission that book demands on it may be met, and by some form of state or national aid.

2. CONSTRUCTIVE AND FLEXIBLE LEGISLATION ESPECIALLY FOR COUNTY LIBRARIES.

   Legislation which will make possible the adequate support of libraries, and permissive county library legislation allowing "county option" on establishing the most effective and economical form of library service. North Dakota is one of the few states not allowing such service.

3. ESTABLISHMENT AND EXPANSION OF LIBRARIES.

   Not the establishment of a library in a town too small to support it, but where it has a reasonable chance to live, Libraries should grow through better and greater service and this will come with better trained librarians and better selected books. Library institutes should be held for librarians unable to attend library school.

4. DEVELOPMENT OF PROPER STANDARDS OF PUBLIC AND SCHOOL LIBRARY SERVICE.

   North Dakota ranks 66 and 2/3 per cent below the average of the United States in public library service and is reported the lowest state in the North Central Association in school library service. This means there is much to do and one factor in the solution is a full time field library worker.

5. PROMOTION AND DEVELOPMENT OF LIBRARY PERSONNEL UNDER CERTIFICATION STANDARDS.

   Each profession has realized that certification of its members is necessary if standards are to be maintained. North Dakota must join other states in a certification scheme for her librarians if progressive work is done.

6. UNIFIED PROGRAM OF LIBRARY EXTENSION.

   This requires a survey of agencies offering books and reference extension service, that the state work as a whole may be strengthened and duplication avoided.

7. SERVICE TO STATE LEGISLATORS, OFFICIALS, EMPLOYEES AND WARDS.

   The legislative reference department should be reestablished, more work along professional lines done for state officials and employees, and a specially trained library worker available for field work for the following state institutions: penitentiary, training school, insane hospital, and the schools for the deaf, blind, and feeble minded.

8. COOPERATION WITH STATE DEPARTMENTS AND INSTITUTIONS.

The professional knowledge and skill of the Commission staff should be at the disposal of state departments and institutions for such cooperative library and bibliographical work as will increase and strengthen the work of each department. This may be as simple as suggestions on the arrangement of a pamphlet file, or it may be as elaborate as the entire selection and editing of state school library lists.

9. COOPERATION WITH ALL STATE AGENCIES AND EFFORTS WORKING TO INCREASE THE EFFECTIVE READING OF GOOD BOOKS.

This means working with the Federation of Women's Clubs, the P. T. A., the farm groups, and individuals who are interested in reading for the purpose of being better educated, of being more sensitive to fine and beautiful things and of being at home in the world of books and men.

COMMISSION ACTIVITIES.

1928-1930

It is not enough however to present what should be done and we are happy to record the accomplishments and activities of the past two years.

THE COMMISSION.

Professional Activities.

The following professional activities are largely the responsibility of the Secretary and Director: giving advice and help on general state library problems; helping to secure librarians for public and school libraries; gathering and publishing state library statistics; making contacts with national organizations; gathering and circulating to boards and librarians professional literature; preparing general book lists; selecting the books and editing the school library lists for the State Department of Public Instruction; publishing each month an article on school libraries in the North Dakota Teacher; selecting the books for the Dunseith juvenile library (financed by the Federated Women's Clubs); cooperating with state institutions and helping with book selections, building and personnel problems; cooperating with Good Book Week observance in the state; cooperating with state organizations such as the Parent Teacher Association, Federated Women's Clubs, etc.; giving information about library schools and about subscription and reference sets; preparing the occasional mimeographed publicity sheet, "North Dakota library news"; suggesting books for individual buying; planning and conducting institutes; talking on reading and libraries to clubs, farm groups and schools; attending conferences, institutes and organization meetings; and generally directing the Commission staff. The field work is done mostly by the Secretary and Director although the following figures include the field work done by the secretary and staff for the biennium.

Field Work

Because some trips could be made by auto at comparatively small cost field work was done in more towns during this biennium than in the last in spite of a reduced travel fund. There have been many requests for organization of school libraries which could not be met because of expense, but the public libraries have been visited. As usual we try to help the smaller towns but as they are increasingly finding it harder to start and maintain libraries the calls are not so frequent as formerly. The following work was done in the following towns.

Towns

Less than 500	4
500-1000	8
1000-1500	6
1500-2500	3
2500-up	8

Public libraries

29 board meetings
3 organized
1 building planned

School libraries

2 organized
4 assembly talks
11 State Teachers College and Normal school visits
2 University

Institutes	2
Exhibits	18
Fairs	5

State Meetings

Federated, State 2. District	2
North Dakota Library Association	2
North Dakota Education Association	2

Rural Groups

Farm boys and girls
Master home makers
Homemakers club camp at H. T. Ranch

Conferences

Out of state 4

Parent Teacher Association meetings 9

State institutions

Dunseith

Devils Lake

Mandan

Book Service.

The book service is given through the traveling library and reference departments and figures will be given in the statistical report.

Traveling Library Department.

The traveling library circulation has increased to 36,255 for the biennium, in contrast to 27,631 of the last biennial report. To meet this increased demand we have added only 12 community libraries of about 50 books each and 20 school libraries of varying sizes. The department could do a much bigger business than it reports if it only had the books to work with. Each year of this past period we have had to turn down new applications that came in after the holidays and say: Get your requests in early next fall, and we hope then to be able to serve you. The added attractiveness of the collections of the past 4 years accounts in part for the continued demand from established stations. Old borrowers have had to wait until libraries out in circulation were returned, some requests being held two months. This is true of the service to schools. Community libraries have been sent more promptly as they do not swing with the school year but come and go at any time.

The package library, containing about a dozen books suited to a family or small group, started out with a circulation of 109 packages in its first year (1927-28). The next year saw it reduced to 98 and last year it totalled 53. This is not because the package idea is not popular but because we have been compelled to make them up of old books. It is largely an adult demand and could be made the ideal way to serve the isolated family, or individual.

Though we try to help the small library in the town where the women's club or a similar organization is promoting a library project our major work continues to be with the school and our major interest continues to lie in getting good reading into the hands of boys and girls. More and more we are convinced that the county library idea is the only one that will solve this problem. Of the 842 libraries shipped in the biennium, 581 served schools and 261 served communities. The total of the last biennium was 660 libraries circulated.

We are doing an increased business of 8,264 books and 182 libraries. And we are not meeting the demand.

Reference Department.

Through the reference department individuals and study groups rather than communities are served. This includes the preparation of club programs and all the service given study groups: Federated Women's Clubs, Parent Teacher Associations and farm organizations. It includes the work with the schools: required reading, debate, declamatory, special days, projects, long themes, etc. It includes meeting individual needs for recreational and purposeful reading, preparation of reading lists, and suggestions for courses of reading.

The book service is limited to persons without adequate local libraries; it is extended to state employees; it includes service through a very limited supply of foreign books.

STATISTICAL REPORT, 1928-30.

Books.

Traveling Library:

Number of traveling libraries	307
Number of libraries added during period	32
Number of books added during period	1,671
Number of books in libraries	12,820

Reference Department:

Number of books	9,595
Number of books added during period	1,295
Number of pamphlets	14,000

Circulation.

Traveling Library:

	1928-29	1929-30	Total
Number of libraries circulated	427	415	842
School	301	280	581
Community	126	135	361
Package	98	53	151
Number of books circulated	18,314	17,941	36,255
Number of stations			362

Reference Department:

Number of requests	6,600	8,087	14,687
Number of reference books circulated	18,408	27,395	45,803
Number of pamphlets and magazines	5,359	5,931	11,290
Total reference circulation	23,767	33,326	57,093
Total Commission circulation	42,081	51,267	93,348

Appropriation, 1929-31

Books and periodicals	$ 3,000.00
Binding	500.00
Salaries	16,380.00
Furniture and fixtures	200.00
Stationery and supplies	400.00
Printing	300.00
Postage	500.00
Miscellaneous	1,725.00
Total	$23,005.00

Needs and Growth

The needs of the Commission are:

1. More books to meet an existing and constantly increasing demand
2. A travel fund which will allow the Commission staff to meet some of the calls from small public and school libraries for organization help
3. Eventually a field worker to care for these requests
4. The salary schedule equalized with other technically trained state workers.

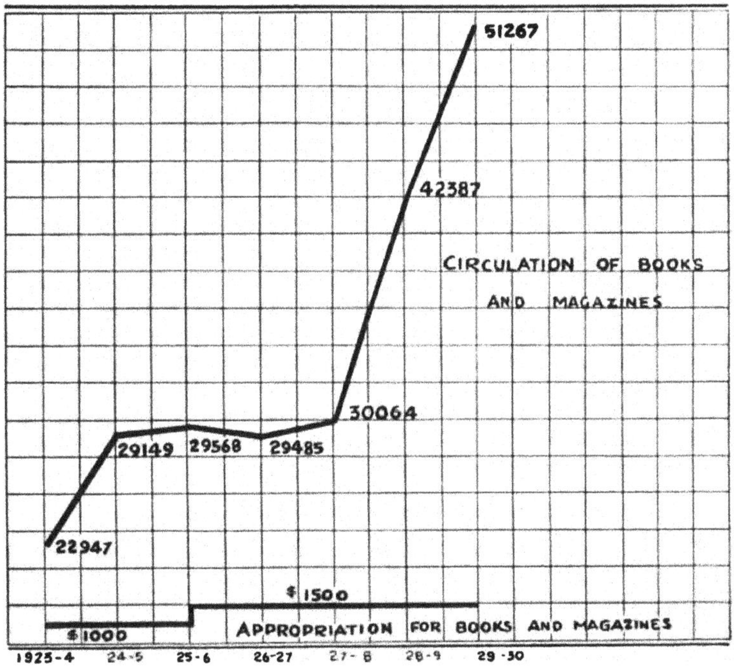

Because of the disorganized condition of the Commission during 1919-20 exact figures are not available, so instead of making a ten-year comparison it seems wise to show the growth of the work under the present secretary and director and the head of the traveling library department.

ORGANIZATIONS AND MEETINGS.

North Dakota Library Association.

In 1928 North Dakota held a joint session with Minnesota at Fargo. Miss Harriet Pearson of the Agricultural College library presided for North Dakota. Dr. Locke of Toronto, president of the American Library Association, was the leading speaker. County librarians from St. Paul and Minneapolis gave to us of their rich experience in this line to which North Dakota is looking forward.

In 1929 we met at Devils Lake. Mrs. Ethel Kuenning of the James Memorial Library at Williston was the presiding officer. Contact with Miss Gratia Countryman who came from the Minneapolis Public Library to add to our conference from her wisdom was a liberal education. Again the emphasis was laid on County Library service.

LIBRARY SECTION

North Dakota Education Association.

The Library sections held meetings at the 41st and 42nd annual meetings of the North Dakota Education Association. At the Grand Forks meeting Mrs. Hazel Webster Byrnes, who was elected secretary the year previous, presided as president in the absence of Mr. Minkle. Librarians from the State Teachers Colleges of Minot and Valley City, and from the Fargo and Grand Forks High Schools, contributed to the discussion and the outstanding event was having Dr. Solandt of Toronto, Canada, as our guest. Dr. Solandt was chief speaker at the joint session of the English and Library sections and at their luncheon.

Mrs. Byrnes was elected president and presided at the Minot meeting. Again the English and Library sections shared one session, with Mr. Carlson of the University Library and Duane Squires representing the library. The next day the librarians met separately to discuss problems directly relating to school libraries. It was voted that the president should appoint two committees to develop school library score cards suited to the normal and high schools of the state. Mrs. Mabel W. Etheridge was elected president for 1929-30.

Library Institutes.

The librarians of the northeastern corner of the state met for two institutes, one at St. Thomas in 1929 and one at Pembina in 1930. Mending demonstrations were held at each meeting, and administrative problems considered. Book selection and book discussions took up the major portion of the time, with emphasis on drama at the 1929 meeting and biography at the 1930 meeting. The combined registration for the two years was 49 librarians, and board members representing six libraries.

Parent Teacher Association.

While neither of the state meetings was attended, several county council meetings and two district instruction meetings were attended. Exhibits were held at all of them covering all or some of the following: children's books; program suggestions and help; books of interest to Parent Teacher Association leaders and county library service. The secretary and director has resigned her state chairmanship of the three committees; Children's Reading, Home Education and Standards in Literature, but is still intensely interested in the Parent Teacher Association work and anxious to be of service personally and through the Commission.

League of Library Commissions

The secretary attended the League of Library Commissions meetings at Chicago in December 1928, and Washington, D. C., in May 1929, where the problems of the state library extension agency were discussed from national viewpoints. Adult education was discussed and the ways in which Commissions could develop this form of service considered. The other emphasis was on ways in which Commissions can cooperate to mutual advantage, and the following lines suggested: bulletins, professional papers, book lists and information about furniture and equipment.

American Library Association.

The 1929 American Library Association was held at Washington, D. C., and immediately following it was the meeting of the American Association of Adult Education at Chapel Hill, N. C., and the secretary attended both meetings. Because every phase of library work is of interest to a state worker there was much value in the meeting where every type of service was considered. The opportunity to have national leaders who are influencing thought and educational policies and to see the offerings of the book publishers were benefits added to the professional help and knowledge gained.

Summer Library Conference.

Miss Baldwin of the Traveling Library Department attended the Madison, Wisconsin, conference of 1929 during the weeks of July 1-14. The conference brought together librarians from 23 states and the exchange of ideas was stimulating. The course in book selection under Miss Mary K. Reely of the Wisconsin Library School was outstanding. She directed our attention to the tendency to "Humanize" knowledge and put it in popular form. A leading authority along the line of biography, philosophy, history, science and literature led the hour's discussion each day.

Those of us interested in rural book service attended the Rural Sociology courses conducted by Dr. Kolb and Dr. Colbert for the group of ministers from rural parishes. We librarians "listened in" to our great edification at these University sessions which have been going on for several years, gathering rural pastors of all denominations.

THE STATE AT LARGE

The reports for the biennial period indicate it has been a busy two years for librarians, for almost universally the use of the library has increased. The problems of finance have been present in all libraries and acute in some. As library buildings grow older and need more extensive and expensive repairs; as book collections wear out and must be replaced; as school service grows and the demands on the book collection and the librarian's time increase; as the library idea spreads and more people depend on the public library for purposeful as well as recreational reading, this will be increasingly true.

The little library is finding it increasingly hard to maintain itself and while the club women of Garrison and St. John, and the community of Crosby with county cooperation, have started libraries, Amidon, Bisbee, Center, Columbus, Glenburn, Maddock, Ray, and Sanborn have discontinued or have turned the library over to the school. These "straws" indicate the need of a windbreak in the form of county library service.

There is one new library building "in the making" at Ellendale for the Normal and Industrial School. The public library at Lisbon has been entirely rebuilt, more than doubled in size, redecorated and made most attractive. Their increase in circulation naturally accompanies the pleasanter and more commodious quarters. Several librarians report extensive repairs and renovations of buildings.

As the secretary of the Library Commission sees the public library needs of the state they are primarily,

1. Equalization of library service, through
2. County library systems
3. New buildings or enlarged buildings to relieve present congestion
4. More funds for books for replacements in the juvenile collection and to keep up to date the technical and sociological books in the adult collection.
5. Books, especially in the small libraries, selected only from accredited lists.

STATISTICS OF LIBRARIES WITH MUNICIPAL APPROPRIATIONS*

	Place	1925 Population	Receipts: Tax	Receipts: Total	Expenditures: Total Salaries	Expenditures: Heat, Rent Light	Expenditures: Books Magazines	Expenditures: Total	Volumes	Borrowers	Circulation 1928-30	Hours Open Per Week	Rural Borrowers
	Over 2,500												
1.	Fargo	24,921	13,441	20,973	8,663	785	3,773	20,531	26,699	12,075	341,221	72	555
2.	Grand Forks	15,168	8,400	10,123	4,695	1,288	1,593	9,744	13,637	5,596	135,139	66	93
3.	Minot	12,245	8,801	9,454	5,305	692	1,868	9,454	17,316	7,903	303,302	72	200
4.	Bismarck	9,150	6,690	7,357	3,419	784	1,864	7,187	8,296	3,968	99,895	42	0
5.	Jamestown	7,230	6,999	11,286	3,194	570	2,189	10,094	10,941	4,707	124,907	51	419
6.	Devils Lake	5,409	2,856	5,707	1,728	600	1,772	5,605	8,329	2,593	64,423	36	4
7.	Valley City	4,695	3,752	7,075	2,205	94	491	6,633	10,785	3,450	74,167	36	0
8.	Dickinson	4,467	4,000	4,843	2,409	256	950	4,809	8,181	3,742	67,429	36	49
9.	Williston	3,948	5,071	8,447	3,375	521	887	5,874	9,784	3,345	81,852	42	487
10.	Wahpeton	3,187	3,816	5,780	1,200	878	683	3,817	11,038	1,905	56,336	21	167
11.	Grafton	2,913	2,200	8,391	787	187	404	1,616	3,086	899	36,441	30	3
	Under 2,500												
12.	Ashley	962	150	833	120	......	171	333	4,745	316	10,650	6	......
13.	Bowman	775	1,515	1,788	621	189	225	1,158	3,972	350	5,658	21	......
14.	Carrington	1,315	1,146	1,495	600	25	478	1,271	5,503	1,320	28,075	27.5	451
15.	Casselton	1,416	350	305	150	......	197	305	860	375	7,750	4	
16.	Ellendale	1,094	600	758	430	......	192	752	3,288	1,015	21,303	15	275
17.	Hankinson	1,390	......	......	120	......	150	270	4,000	350	10,084	8	......
18.	Lakota	869	800	879	350	90	123	701	3,970	500	14,446	20	......
19.	La Moure	994	600	659	300	......	267	652	2,349	700	13,527	6	226
20.	Langdon	1,239	420	......	150	252			2,280	148	10,150	8	......
21.	Leonard	541	......	......	140		......		1,612	200	3,600	6	......
22.	Lidgerwood	1,009	1,900	2,435	974	135	154	2,432	3,839	944	25,075	27	447
23.	Lisbon	1,626	1,944	4,765	629	192	382	4,162	3,317	1,039	26,404	22.5	94
24.	Mayville	1,345	750	882	395	390	68	1,082	3,281	510	9,189	12	......
25.	Mott	810	400	433	180	180	26	410	2,203	827	5,463	7.5	......
26.	New Rockford†	2,050	100	774	200	......	860	774	2,000	200	4,500	8	......
27.	Oakes	1,544	1,056	2,151	950	......	520	1,553	4,618	1,037	38,485	36	220
28.	Park River	1,044	......	306	180	......	100	306	3,082	520	14,300	8	......
29.	Rugby	1,509	200	......	......	......	159	178	3,805	963	15,733	8	......
30.	Wishek	1,016	100	150	50	......	100	150	400	260	6,000	4	......

* 1929-30 only.
† Fiscal Year 1929-30.

STATISTICS OF ASSOCIATION LIBRARIES

	Place	Population	Expenditures		Volumes	Borrowers	Circulation			Hours Open Per Week	Free to Grades	
			Books & Magazines	Total			1929	1930	Total			
1.	Bowbells	615	—	53	440	360	1,500	2,250	3,750	4	Free	1.
2.	Cando	1,055	50	—	2,700	61	2,250	—	2,250	4	Fee	2.
3.	Cavalier	810	55	67	1,017	245	1,950	2,650	4,600	2.5	Fee	3.
4.	Crosby	1,147	700	900	1,114	190		3,450	3,450	12	Fee	4.
5.	Courtenay	828	—	16	769	162	1,250	1,000	3,500	2	Fee	5.
6.	Drake	636	80	80	641	475	4,500	5,850	10,350	1.5	Free	6.
7.	Enderlin	1,824	139	154	1,718	6,929	8,600	8,200	16,800	5	Free	7.
8.	Fessenden	757	90	150	1,696	295	5,000	4,500	9,500	4	Free	8.
9.	Garrison †	714	—	—	903	61	—	1,250	1,250	10	Fee	9.
10.	Goodrich †	454	66	—	500	67	—	3,000		2	Free	10.
11.	Hamilton	179	25	30	838	—	2,500	1,250	3,750	2	Free	11.
12.	Hansboro †	204	15	20	216	85		2,000		3	Free	12.
13.	Heaton	200	24	24	251	65	—	—	—	—	Free	13.
14.	Hettinger	1,009	124	154	730	195	2,000	2,100	4,100	3	Free	14.
15.	Hope	577	80	—	902	25	900	600	1,500	1	Fee	15.
16.	Leeds	668	68	127	2,085	257	6,500	5,750	12,350	6	Free	16.
17.	Mandan	5,068	—	—	5,000	—	7,226	5,591	13,817	8	Free	17.
18.	Milton	870	25	25	1,042	71	2,550	1,900	4,450	2	Fee	18.
19.	Rolla †	636	25	68	676	150	—	2,100	—	2	Fee	19.
20.	St. John §	460	50	—	214	—	—	—	—	2	Free	20.
21.	St. Thomas *	443	146	224	1,513	201	—	—	—	3	Fee	21.
22.	Tioga	365	40	45	1,100	350	1,050	2,000	3,050	—	Free	22.
23.	Towner	531	—	—	336	290	1,750	2,150	3,200	4	Free	23.
24.	Turtle Lake	472	94	100	1,003	124	4.400	11,650	16,050	2	Free	24.
25.	Van Hook †	368	60	—	754	395	—	3,750	—	2	Free	25.
26.	Velva †	872	150	150	1,800	235	—	13,650	—	45	Free	26.
27.	Wimbledon	447	—	4	50	60	3,000	2,800	5,800	1	Free	27.

The following libraries are functioning but have not sent in reports for either year of the biennial period: Bathgate, Beach, Edgeley, Hansboro, Pembina, Sanish, Tolna.

§ Opened June 1930.

* Report 1928-29.

† Report 1929-30

SCHOOL AND COLLEGE LIBRARIES

Place	Name	Volumes	Book Budget	Staff Full	Staff Part	Librarian
Bottineau	Forestry School	2,818	212		One	Marguerite Lee Walter
Dickinson	Normal	6,603	1,630		Several	Mathilda Stoxen
Ellendale	Normal & Industrial School	6,950	1,000	One		Carrie Tuttle
Fargo	Agricultural College	47,292	3,666	Five		Ethel McVeety
Grand Forks	University	68,752	6,973	Seven	Several	Wm. H. Carlson
Jamestown	College	15,000	1,424		One	F. B. Taylor
Mayville	Teacher's College	14,386	1,497	One	Several	Hazel W. Byrnes
Minot	Teacher's College	13,317		One	Three	Mabel W. Ethridge
Valley City	Teacher's College	27,350	1,880	Two	Several	Lulu Ruth Reed
Wahpeton	Science School	3,524	462	One	One	Lillian Mirick

STATE SPECIAL AND INSTITUTIONAL LIBRARIES

Place	Name	1929-31 Book Appropriation	Librarian or Superintendent
Bismarck	Historical Society	750	Mrs. Florence Davis
Bismarck	Law	5,000	E. J. Taylor
Bismarck	Library Commission	3,000	Lillian E. Cook
*Bathgate	School for the Blind	2,000	B. P. Chapple
Bismarck	Penitentiary	......	C. C. Turner
Devils Lake	School for the Deaf	1,000	B. W. Driggs
Dunseith	Tuberculosis Sanatorium	......	Dr. Charles McLachlan
†Grafton	School for the Feeble Minded	91	Dr. A. R. T. Wylie
Jamestown	Hospital for the Insane	50	Dr. J. D. Carr
Mandan	Training School	......	W. F. McClelland

Books and Musical Instruments*
Amount Spent†

DIRECTORY OF NORTH DAKOTA LIBRAR.

Place	Name of Library	Librarians
Ashley	Public Library	Mrs. H. D. Piper
Bathgate	Public Library	Annie Slagerman
Beach	Public Library	Mrs. John Koehane
Bismarck	Public Library	Ruth King
Bismarck	State Historical	Mrs. Florence Davis
Bismarck	State Law Library	E. J. Taylor
Bismarck	State Library Commission	Lillian E. Cook
Bottineau	Forestry School	Marguerite Walter
Bowbells	Study Club	Mrs. Clyde Bohn
Bowman	Public Library	Rhoda A. Wilker
Cando	Public Library	Mrs. H. C. Barber
Carrington	Public Library	Edna Parker
Casselton	Public Library	Mrs. E. D. Scott
Cavalier	Public Library	Mrs. Fred Harris
Courtenay	Public Library	Mrs. A. A. Hoffman
Crosby	Public Library	Mrs. L. R. Murray
Devils Lake	Public Library	Marie O'Brien
Devils Lake	State Deaf School	Burton W. Driggs
Dickinson	Public Library	Gertrude Voldal
Dickinson	State Normal School	Matilda Stoxen
Drake	Public Library	Mrs. E. W. Phillips
Edgeley	Public Library	Mrs. J. E. Kipp
Ellendale	Public Library	Mrs. V. D. Coleman
Ellendale	Normal & Industrial Sch.	Carrie Tuttle
Enderlin	Public Library	Mrs. R. L. Long
Fargo	Public Library	Inga Rynning
Fargo	Agricultural College	Mrs. Ethel McVeety
Fargo	Masonic Library	Clara Richards
Fessenden	Public Library	Mrs. A. E. Southard
Garrison	Public Library	Mrs. H. T. Holtz
Goodrich	Public Library	Mrs. J. R. Doering
Grafton	Public Library	Mrs. Emma Cobb
Grafton	School Feeble Minded	Maud Stewart
Grand Forks	Public Library	Ruth O. Brown
Grand Forks	University	William H. Carlson
Hamilton	Public Library	Mrs. Robert Kippen
Hankinson	Public Library	Mrs. George Schuett
Hansboro	Public Library	Mrs. William Wilson
Heaton	Public Library	C. I. Turner
Hettinger	Public Library	Mrs. F. T. Lembke
Hope	Public Library	Mrs. Katie Gumb
Jamestown	Alfred Dickey	Anne Procter
Jamestown	Jamestown College	Dean F. B. Taylor
Jamestown	Insane Hospital	Dr. J. D. Carr
Lakota	Public Library	Mrs. Ellen Hullett
LaMoure	Public Library	Mrs. Carl Neverman
Langdon	Public Library	Mrs. M. A. Jensen
Leeds	Public Library	Mrs. George Gylnquist
Leonard	Watts Free	Mrs. Agnes Roney
Lidgerwood	Public Library	Mrs. Elizabeth Kings
Lisbon	Public Library	Mrs. H. S. Oliver
Mandan	Public Library	Mrs. John Biggs
Mandan	High School	Myrtle Sliper
Mayville	Public Library	Sophia Springer

Mayville	State Teachers College	Mrs. Hazel Webster Byrnes
Milton	Community	Mrs. R. T. Wait
Minot	Public Library	Catherine McSherry
Minot	State Teachers College	Mrs. Mabel Etheridge
Mott	Inez Hendrickson	Louise Wagner
New Rockford	Public Library	Vannie Hall
Oakes	Public Library	Mrs. Edgar Christianson
Park River	Public Library	Margaret Kohnen
Pembina	Public Library	Mrs. Pauline Brennan
Rolla	Public Library	Mrs. J. O. Einerson
Rugby	Public Library	Hattie S. Sikes
St. John	Public Library	Anna M. Butts
St. Thomas	Study Club	Mrs. E. T. Thompson
Sanish	Public Library	Mrs. C. A. Pickering
Tioga	Masonic Lodge	George E. Mueller
Tolna	Public Library	Mrs. C. S. Hawkins
Towner	Public Library	Grace Bennett
Turtle Lake	Public Library	Mrs. C. E. Paulson
Valley City	Public Library	Harriet Anfinson
Valley City	State Teachers College	Lulu Ruth Reed
Van Hook	Womans Civic League	Mrs. E. A. Nelson
Velva	Public Library	Mrs. I. A. Beebe
Wahpeton	Leach Library	Mrs. Jessie Searing
Wahpeton	State Science School	Lilian Mirick
Williston	James Memorial	Mrs. Ethel Kuenning
Wimbledon	Public Library	Mrs. H. M. Stroud
Wishek	Public Library	Mrs. T. H. Reque

THIRTEENTH BIENNIAL REPORT

OF THE

State Library Commission

TO THE

STATE BOARD OF ADMINISTRATION

FOR THE PERIOD

JULY 1, 1930—JUNE 30, 1932

BOARD OF ADMINISTRATION

June 30, 1932

Nelson Sauvain .... Chairman

Laura B. Sanderson

Robert M. Rishworth

Bertha R. Palmer

Joseph A. Kitchen

STATE LIBRARY COMMISSION STAFF

Lillian E. Cook .... Secretary and Director

Bessie R. Baldwin .... Traveling Library Chief

Margaret Fulmer .... Reference Library

Frances Heath .... Stenographer

Ruth Johnson .... Clerk

Leona Jordan .... Clerk

LETTER OF TRANSMITTAL

To the State Board of Administration,

Bismarck, North Dakota.

Herewith is submitted the Thirteenth Biennial Report of the North Dakota State Library Commission, covering the period from July 1, 1930 to June 30, 1932.

LILLIAN E. COOK,

Secretary and Director.

REPORT OF THE SECRETARY AND DIRECTOR, 1930-32
THE LIBRARY COMMISSION

The biennial period saw the inception of no new policies or lines of service, but a rather remarkable growth in volume of work, a growth which has absorbed the staff's time and the Commission's appropriation. Briefly the two years' work may be summarized as follows:

Aim

1. To make existing library service more effective.

2. To provide worth-while books in communities without local collections.

3. To assist and advise with small communities endeavoring to establish local service.

4. To cooperate with all state agencies and groups in the interests of better and of purposeful reading.

5. To be allied with national groups and movements fostering reading and the advance of library interests.

Accomplishment

1. Established libraries have been helped through constant keeping-in-touch through correspondence; through visits to 33 libraries where 14 board meetings were held; through a special book service designed to strengthen local collections in small towns; through a subscription to a professional periodical for the small libraries; through the occasional circulation of a mimeographed sheet serving the purpose of a Commission Bulletin. For the small libraries of the northeastern section a library institute was held at Grafton.

Time and thought were devoted to the County Library Bill, introduced by Representative Northridge of Barnes which passed the House but was killed in Senate committee. Obviously this legislation must now wait for better times.

2. The demand for books in committees without local service has taxed the resources of the Commission which has less money to meet state demands than some North Dakota libraries have to meet the needs of the town. Careful buying stretches the appropriation to cover the absolute need and no more. We do not have the resources to meet the enlarged demands and so cannot advertise nor expand the service.

3. As a matter of policy in view of the difficulties the State Library Commission does not encourage the establishment of local service in very small communities. Many have attempted to "start a library" and have had to abandon the effort. However, when the community

itself is determined to offer some form of local library service, the Commission gives every possible help. Conferences were held at New England and Killdeer where libraries were established.

4. In cooperation with other state agencies and groups, visits were made to five state institutions; two state North Dakota Educational Association meetings were attended; two state and seven district Federated Women's Club meetings; 3 P. T. A. district or special meetings; 5 high school assembly talks were given. Special lines of cooperation have been carried on with the Extension Division of the Agricultural College, the Training School at Mandan and the children's department at Dunseith, the two latter consisting of selecting and ordering library books to build up the institutional libraries.

5. The national contacts include attendance at the Rural Library Institute held at Madison, Wisconsin, a regional library meeting of six states at St. Paul, the midwinter meeting of the American Library Association at Chicago, serving on various national American Library Association, Parent and Teachers Association and Federation of Women's Clubs committees and membership in national organizations such as the American Association of Adult Education, National Education Association, etc.

6. Miscellaneous activities include gathering and publishing state library statistics, preparation of general and professional booklists, a monthly page in the North Dakota Teacher, promotion of Good Book Week, attendance at the dedication of the new library building at the Ellendale Normal and Industrial School, meeting with the rural leaders at Mayville when an exhibit was held, attendance at two 4-H camps and one meeting of Master Home Makers.

BOOK SERVICE

Traveling Libraries

With decreased appropriations for school and small town buying throughout the individual communities, the Traveling Library Department is finding a steadily increasing demand on state resources. The statistics for the last biennium show a circulation of 39,467 which is an increase of 3,212 over the previous period. We simply fill requests as long as the supply lasts in the fall, and then file the others to be filled whenever possible.

21 libraries have been added during this period, with a heavier emphasis on the community type. An experiment has been tried with the school service in an effort to make the books go faster and farther. Instead of putting 45 new books into one large freight case, they have been divided into two mailing cases and sent out separately for three months instead of six. For the inland rural school this service has proved very satisfactory.

Of the 986 libraries shipped, 704 have gone to schools and 282 to communities. The total for the previous biennium was 842. A steady demand comes from established stations, 495 of them having repeated orders.

REFERENCE DEPARTMENT

The individual library service of the State Library Commission is done through the Reference Department. This includes the preparation of program outlines for club study and the supplying of the books and reference material. Women's clubs, Parent Teacher Associations and farm groups receive this service. Books on the required reading lists are sent to the schools, also reference material for debates, declamations, themes and other special school projects. Individual borrowers may receive a package of books each month for recreational and purposeful reading. Booklists and reading courses are available.

The book service is limited to persons without adequate local libraries; it is extended to state employees; it includes service through a very limited supply of foreign books.

STATISTICAL REPORT 1930-32

Books

Traveling Library:	
Number of traveling libraries	338
Number of libraries added during period	21
Number of books added during period	405
Number of books in libraries	13,182
Reference Department:	
Number of books	9,336
Number of books added during period	1,036
Number of pamphlets	18,200

Circulation

	1930-31	1931-32	Total
Traveling library:			
Number of libraries circulated	464	522	986
School	330	374	704
Community	134	148	282
Number of books shipped	18,605	20,862	39,467
Number of new stations	110	100	210
Reference Department:			
Number of requests	10,791	11,471	23,682
Number of books circulated	29,181	36,134	65,315
Number of magazines and pamphlets	6,727	8,240	14,967
Total Reference circulation	35,908	44,374	80,282
Total Commission circulation	54,513	65,236	119,749

TRENDS

The increased use of the State Library Commission may be seen from the following. The causes are various—reduced amounts spent for personal buying of books and magazines; reduced amounts spent for commercial amusements; increased leisure. To these certainly must be added a group of satisfied borrowers who not only repeatedly send for material, but tell others of the service. The State Library Commission is proud of the loyal friends it has made.

One year 1920-21 12,479 books circulated.

One month Oct. 1932, 10,313 books circulated.

Two years 1926-28, 63,549 books circulated.

One year 1931-32, 65,236 books circulated.

Five years 1922-27, 128,707 books circulated.

Five years 1928-32, 243,151 books circulated.

Ten years apart 1921-22 average monthly circulation 1577.4.

1931-32 average monthly circulation 5435.

Appropriation 1930-32

Salary	$ 5,000.00
Clerkhire:	
Chief Traveling Librarian	3,600.00
Reference Librarian	3,000.00
Stenographer	2,400.00
Clerk	1,800.00
Clerk(part time)	600.00
Postage	700.00
Office Supplies	400.00
Furniture and Fixtures	200.00
Printing	300.00
Miscellaneous	600.00
Travel Expense	600.00
Aids to Libraries	200.00
Books	3,500.00
Preparation of Books	200.00
Binding	500.00
Total	$23,600.00

THE LIBRARIES OF THE STATE

The library reports show increased use in spite of reduced budgets. During a period when people have more leisure and less money to spend for commercial amusements they turn to the public libraries for their reading. A study of the following tables shows the growth in circulation.

PLACE	1930 Population	RECEIPTS: Tax 1930–31	Tax 1931–32	Total 1930–31	Total 1931–32
Over 2,500					
1. Fargo	28,619	14,248	14,382	19,686	20,116
2. Grand Forks	17,112	7,000	9,100	8,548	10,830
3. Minot	16,099	7,119	10,245	7,914	10,965
4. Bismarck	11,090	7,497	7,670	8,144	8,258
5. Jamestown	8,187	7,000	5,750	9,261	6,806
6. Devils Lake	5,451	5,480	3,120	6,007	4,832
7. Valley City	5,268	4,276	4,447	7,014	5,892
8. Dickinson	5,025	4,000	4,000	4,305	4,362
9. Williston	5,106	3,720	3,500	6,493	6,523
10. Wahpeton	3,176	3,914	3,820	6,021	6,472
11. Grafton	3,136	......	1,100	2,552	2,850
Under 2,500					
12. Ashley	1,033	150	50	268	129
13. Bowman	888	......	......	......	......
14. Carrington	1,717	1,507	1,843	1,731	2,311
15. Casselton	1,253	......	300	......	......
16. Ellendale	1,264	550	550	747	767
17. Garrison	......	......	191	......	......
18. Hankinson	1,400	......	120	......	70
19. Lakota	860	800	722	1,163	883
20. LaMoure	889	600	600	664	663
21. Langdon	1,221	......	......	......	614
22. Leonard	......	150	150	200	150
23. Lidgerwood	1,029	1,900	1,900	2,017	2,036
24. Lisbon	1,650	2,036	1,487	2,870	1,020
25. Mayville	1,199	700	700	1,020	946
26. Mott	1,036	400	240	421	263
27. New Rockford	2,195	100	100	......	......
28. Oakes	1,709	1,130	1,063	1,858	1,750
29. Park River	1,131	......	......	......	......
30. Rugby	1,512	200	200	239	......
31. Wishek	1,146	......	50	......	60

PLACE	EXPENDITURES: Salaries 1930–31	Salaries 1931–32	Heat, Rent Light 1930–31	Heat, Rent Light 1931–32	Books Magazines 1930–31	Books Magazines 1931–32	Total 1930–31	Total 1931–32
Over 2,500								
1. Fargo	8,825	8,866	828	741	3,990	2,976	18,821	18,134
2. Grand Forks	4,472	4,707	1,204	1,199	1,515	2,313	8,207	10,467
3. Minot	4,575	3,914	458	410	2,127	535	7,914	10,900
4. Bismarck	4,014	3,947	606	615	2,011	1,784	8,116	8,244
5. Jamestown	2,990	3,371	502	452	1,760	1,507	9,253	6,398
6. Devils Lake	1,833	1,800	747	404	1,128	1,050	4,766	3,922
7. Valley City	2,323	2,201	870	741	1,307	668	6,819	3,901
8. Dickinson	2,370	2,313	255	248	1,202	1,091	4,238	4,292
9. Williston	3,250	2,551	570	359	1,017	624	5,665	4,393
10. Wahpeton	1,760	1,701	685	538	694	760	6,021	6,472
11. Grafton	867	907	179	178	474	494	1,666	2,850
Under 2,500								
12. Ashley	120	120	......	......	141	96	268	129
13. Bowman	......	......	......	......	......	......	......	......
14. Carrington	650	690	28	24	550	374	1,263	1,144
15. Casselton	140	150	......	......	116	175	256	......
16. Ellendale	420	430	......	......	196	211	730	747
17. Garrison	60	60	120	120	......	......	180	180
18. Hankinson	120	120	......	......	73	50	73	70
19. Lakota	396	396	67	78	136	94	777	795
20. LaMoure	300	300	......	......	253	178	664	529
21. Langdon	150	150	......	......	214	......	614	614
22. Leonard	100	90	......	......	......	......	116	140
23. Lidgerwood	918	1,106	108	149	181	92	2,017	1,988
24. Lisbon	662	537	161	129	350	216	1,578	1,020
25. Mayville	380	381	116	172	58	180	855	946
26. Mott	180	180	180	......	7	......	385	......
27. New Rockford	216	200	......	......	75	50	318	......
28. Oakes	870	871	......	......	371	258	1,308	1,214
29. Park River	......	180	......	......	......	104	......	......
30. Rugby	76	52	......	......	83	92	177	173
31. Wishek	39	52	......	......	......	......	40	......

PLACE	CIRCULATION			Volumes	Borrowers	Hrs. Open Per Week	Rural Borrowers
	1930–31	1931–32	Total				
Over 2,500							
1. Fargo	187,216	197,237	384,453	29,702	15,510	72	829
2. Grand Forks	67,558	77,503	145,063	15,126	5,989	45	......
3. Minot	173,361	152,232	325,593	16,507	7,254	72	300
4. Bismarck	66,442	81,543	148,085	9,948	4,865	42	......
5. Jamestown	76,721	84,449	161,170	11,970	5,818	42	600
6. Devils Lake	39,697	43,990	83,687	7,896	2,538	36	25
7. Valley City	42,405	46,905	89,310	11,963	2,230	42	10
8. Dickinson	38,892	44,706	83,798	9,415	2,605	30.5	156
9. Williston	46,101	45,340	91,441	10,343	3,923	42	105
10. Wahpeton	30,475	32,549	63,024	12,440	2,216	30	......
11. Grafton	18,920	24,152	43,072	3,923	1,162	22	10
Under 2,500							
12. Ashley	5,200	4,868	10,068	....	....	....	......
13. Bowman	....	....	....	....	....	....	......
14. Carrington	19,544	20,852	40,396	6,238	1,527	27.5	566
15. Casselton	5,720	4,000	9,720	750	400	4	......
16. Ellendale	12,326	12,533	24,859	3,435	1,162	15	325
17. Garrison	2,250	1,350	3,600	1,192	12	10	......
18. Hankinson	3,956	8,700	12,656	3,100	350	4	50
19. Lakota	8,929	8,977	17,806	4,450	....	15	57
20. LaMoure	8,111	9,306	17,417	2,579	849	6	......
21. Langdon	11,492	....	....	....	....	....	......
22. Leonard	2,750	2,759	5,509	1,632	210	6	......
23. Lidgerwood	13,406	11,617	25,023	4,095	981	29	......
24. Lisbon	12,236	12,417	24,653	3,515	830	19.5	42
25. Mayville	4,747	5,977	10,724	3,616	568	8	......
26. Mott	3,298	4,088	7,386	2,309	685	7	......
27. New Rockford	5,000	....	....	3,000	400	8	......
28. Oakes	24,292	27,877	52,169	5,037	1,093	36	263
29. Park River	....	10,150	....	1,400	395	8	4
30. Rugby	8,553	11,354	19,907	3,685	727	8	30
31. Wishek	5,200	4,500	9,700	750	....	....	......

PLACE	Population	EXPENDITURES Books and Magazines	EXPENDITURES Total	Vols.	Borrowers	CIRCULATION 1931	CIRCULATION 1932	CIRCULATION Total	Hours Open Per Week	Free to Grades
1. Bathgate	292	52	101	1,000	60	....	2,250	....	2	Free
‡2. Beach	1,263	25	57	1,500	260	5,750	4,350	10,100	4	Free
3. Beulah	913	106	106	793	49	6,500	3,000	9,500	3	Fee
4. [illegible]	1,164	75	75	4,000	94	....	3,650	....	2	Fee
*5. Carson	356	......	16	....	......	....	....	....	3	Free
6. [illegible]	850	32	38	1,247	158	....	2,850	....	3.5	Fee
‡7. Courtenay	350	2	13	786	609	1,950	1,350	3,300	2	Fee
‡8. Crosby	1,271	15	20	1,692	423	4,000	4,200	8,200	8	Free
*‡9. Dawson	306	......	......	550	......	....	....	....	2	Free
‡10. Drake	644	69	112	848	558	6,750	6,250	12,900	4	Free
‡11. Edgeley	821	99	......	1,680	55	....	3,600	....	2	Fee
‡12. Enderlin	1,839	196	231	2,623	1,245	12,500	12,750	25,250	5	Free
‡13. Fessenden	738	36	109	2,020	457	5,600	4,250	9,850	2	Free
‡14. Goodrich	468	......	19	557	60	2,750	3,000	5,750	2	Free
15. Hamilton	151	25	30	765	50	1,000	1,650	2,650	2	Free
16. Hansboro	176	15	......	260	37	1,050	....	....	2	Fee
17. Heaton	....	21	22	312	140	....	....	....	7.5	Free
‡18. Hettinger	1,292	15	57	670	195	2,500	2,600	5,100	3	Free
‡19. Hope	535	......	12	1,009	84	1,750	2,700	4,450	2	Fee
*20. Killdeer	495	......	......	21	36	....	800	....	2	Free
‡21. Leeds	704	35	191	1,506	260	....	3,250	....	2	Free
22. Mandan	5,037	......	......	5,121	......	4,050	....	....	8	Fee
*23. New England	911	......	......	....	....	....	....	....	....	
‡24. Pembina	551	45	97	1,350	110	....	5,000	....	..	Free
‡25. Rolla	852	25	30	1,000	213	4,000	4,900	8,900	2	Fee
‡26. St. John	372	110	161	325	125	1,800	3,500	5,300	3	Free
‡27. St. Thomas	595	69	[illegible]	1,690	208	6,350	5,500	11,850	4	Free
28. Sanish	463	9	29	378	50	....	2,100	....	1	Free
29. Tioga	435	......	15	1,200	450	1,800	5,000	6,800	12	Free
‡30. Towner	622	......	5	336	580	....	2,500	....	4	Free
‡31. Turtle Lake	579	......	20	1,110	150	1,250	....	....	2	Fee
32. Wimbledon	121	2	16	590	65	2,250	2,750	5,000	1	Free

No Report—Bowbells, Milton and Tolna.
*Opened 1932.
‡Housing expense paid by some city agency.

SCHOOL AND COLLEGE LIBRARIES

Place	Name	Vols.	1931-32 Bk. Budget	Staff Full	Staff Part	Salaries
*Bottineau	Forestry School	....	....	..	..	....
Dickinson	State Teachers College..	8,751	1,978	2	..	3,572
Ellendale	State Normal & Ind. Sch.	8,733	....	1	1	1,900
Fargo	N. D. Agricultural Col...	51,275	5,216	6	..	9,848
Grand Forks	University	73,057	6,031	7	8	16,092
*Jamestown	College	....	....	..	..	....
Mayville	State Teachers College..	15,602	1,667	1	9	4,343
*Minot	State Teachers College..	19,427	....	2	2	4,788
Valley City	State Teachers College..	30,003	1,099	3	5	6,000
Wahpeton	Science School	3,772	269	2	1	1,700

*No report.

STATE SCHOOL AND SPECIAL INSTITUTIONAL LIBRARIES

Place	Name	Vols.	1931-32 Bk. Budget	Librarian or Superintendent
Bathgate	School for the Blind	....	....	Dr. B. P. Chapple
Bismarck	Historical Society	31,000	375	Mrs. Florence Davis
Bismarck	Law Library	21,000	2,500	E. J. Taylor
Bismarck	Library Commission	22,519	1,750	Lillian E. Cook
Bismarck	Penitentiary	5,771	....	C. C. Turner
Devils Lake	School for the Deaf	....	....	B. W. Driggs
Dunseith	Tuberculosis Sanatorium	....	....	Dr. Chas. McLachlan
Grafton	School for Feeble Minded	649	....	Maud Stewart
Jamestown	Hospital for Insane	2,100	200	Dr. J. M. Carr
Mandan	Training School	364	750	W. F. McClelland

Place	Name of Library	Librarian
Ashley	Public Library	Mrs. H. D. Piper
Bathgate	Public Library	Annie Slagerman
Beach	Public Library	Elinor Lovell
Beulah	Public Library	Mrs. Frank Marshall
Bismarck	Public Library	Ruth King
Bismarck	State Historical	Mrs. Florence Davis
Bismarck	State Law Library	E. J. Taylor
Bismarck	State Library Commission	Lillian E. Cook
Bottineau	Forestry School	L. Naomi Aplund
Bowbells	Study Club	Mrs. Clyde Bohn
Bowman	Public Library	Mrs. Mertie Pond
Cando	Public Library	Mrs. H. C. Barber
Carrington	Public Library	Edna Parker
Carson	Public Library	Mrs. Joel E. Stokes
Casselton	Public Library	Mrs. E. D. Scott
Cavalier	Public Library	Mrs. Fred Harris
Courtenay	Public Library	Mrs. A. A. Hoffman
Crosby	Public Library	Mrs. L. R. Murray
Dawson	Public Library	Mrs. C. A. Cross
Devils Lake	Public Library	Marie O'Brien
Devils Lake	State Deaf School	Burton W. Driggs
Dickinson	Public Library	Gertrude Voldal
Dickinson	State Teachers College	Matilda Stoxen
Drake	Public Library	Mrs. E. W. Phillips
Edgeley	Public Library	Mrs. J. E. Kipp
Ellendale	Public Library	Mrs. V. D. Coleman
Ellendale	Normal and Industrial School	Carrie Tuttle
Enderlin	Public Library	Mrs. R. L. Long
Fargo	Public Library	Inga Rynning
Fargo	Agricultural College	Mrs. Ethel McVeety
Fargo	Masonic Library	Clara Richards
Fessenden	Public Library	Mrs. A. E. Southard
Garrison	Public Library	Cecelia Behles
Goodrich	Public Library	Mrs. J. R. Doering
Grafton	School for Feeble Minded	Maud Stewart
Grafton	Public Library	Mrs. Emma Cobb
Grand Forks	Public Library	Ruth O. Brown
Grand Forks	University	William H. Carlson
Hamilton	Public Library	Mrs. Robert Kippen

Place	Name of Library	Librarian
Hankinson	Public Library	Mrs. George Schuett
Hansboro	Public Library	Mrs. William Wilson
Heaton	Public Library	C. I. Turner
Hettinger	Public Library	Mrs. F. T. Lembke
Hope	Public Library	Mrs. Katie Gumb
Jamestown	Alfred Dickey	Anne Procter
Jamestown	Jamestown College	Dean F. B. Taylor
Jamestown	Insane Hospital	Dr. J. D. Carr
Killdeer	Public Library	Mrs. I. L. Aaser
Lakota	Public Library	Mrs. Ellen Hullett
LaMoure	Public Library	Mrs. Carl Neverman
Langdon	Public Library	Mrs. M. A. Jensen
Leeds	Public Library	Mrs. George Gylnquist
Leonard	Watts Free	Mrs. S. A. Magnuson
Lidgerwood	Public Library	Mrs. Elizabeth Kings
Lisbon	Public Library	Mrs. H. S. Oliver
Mandan	Public Library	Mrs. John Biggs
Mayville	Public Library	Cora Ames
Mayville	State Teachers College	Mrs. Hazel Webster Byrnes
Milton	Community	Mrs. R. T. Wait
Minot	Public Library	Catherine McSherry
Minot	State Teachers College	Mrs. Mabel Etheridge
Mott	Inez Hendrickson	Louise Wagner
Napoleon	Public Library	Mrs. J. F. Wagner
Neche	Public Library	Mrs. Herbert Briggs
New England	Public Library	Geneva Hagen
New Rockford	Public Library	Vannie Hall
Oakes	Public Library	Mrs. Edgar Christensen
Park River	Public Library	Mrs. Averil Gillespie
Pembina	Public Library	Mrs. Pauline Brennan
Rolla	Public Library	Mrs. J. O. Einerson
Rugby	Public Library	Hattie S. Sikes
St. John	Public Library	Anna M. Burts
St. Thomas	Study Club	Mrs. E. T. Thompson
Sanish	Public Library	Mrs. C. A. Pickering
Tioga	Masonic Lodge	George E. Mueller
Tolna	Public Library	Mrs. C. S. Hawkins
Towner	Public Library	Grace Bennett

Place	Name of Library	Librarian
Turtle Lake	Public Library	Mrs. C. E. Paulson
Valley City	Public Library	Mrs. Helen Tracy
Valley City	State Teachers College	Lulu Ruth Reed
Velva	Public Library	Mrs. I. A. Beebe
Wahpeton	Leach Library	Mrs. Jessie Searing
Wahpeton	State Science School	Lilian Mirick
Westerheim	Public Library	Mrs. A. H. Allen
Williston	James Memorial Library	Mrs. Ethel Kuenning
Wimbledon	Public Library	Mrs. H. M. Stroud
Wishek	Public Library	Mrs. Kattie M. Wilson

FIFTEENTH BIENNIAL REPORT

OF THE

State Library Commission

TO THE

State Board of Administration

FOR THE PERIOD

JULY 1, 1934-JUNE 30, 1936

FIFTEENTH BIENNIAL REPORT

OF THE

State Library Commission

TO THE

State Board of Administration

FOR THE PERIOD

JULY 1, 1934-JUNE 30, 1936

BOARD OF ADMINISTRATION

June 30, 1936

J. D. Harris....................Chairman

Jennie Ulsrud

Robert M. Rishworth

Arthur E. Thompson

Theo. Martell

STATE LIBRARY COMMISSION STAFF

June 30, 1936

Lillian E. Cook....................Secretary and Director

Bessie R. Baldwin....................Traveling Library Chief

Doris L. Hidde....................Reference Librarian

Arlene Wagner....................Stenographer

Helen Targart....................Clerk

Marian Morton....................Clerk

LETTER OF TRANSMITTAL

To the State Board of Administration

Bismarck, North Dakota

Herewith is submitted the Fifteenth Biennial Report of the North Dakota State Library Commission, covering the period from July 1, 1934 to June 30, 1936.

LILLIAN E. COOK,
Secretary and Director.

REPORT OF THE SECRETARY AND DIRECTOR, 1934-36

State Library Commission

Happily after a period generally designated as "Depression" the State Library Commission has some positive gains to record. These include a biennial gain in circulation; new juvenile book service to the small libraries of the state; the organization of a state wide book repair project; cooperation with the State Department of Public Instruction in the new ruling in regard to trained librarians in high schools; and the rearrangement of the State Library Commission office and working space and book stacks. The period reflects the unusual economic and social conditions which have affected established activities and progress, stimulating some, retarding some, and inaugurating others. The State Library Commission has been glad to continue to cooperate with state departments and to associate also with the new federal departments which have had so large a part in North Dakota's history the past two years.

Throughout the state there has been a great interest in local libraries, with the American Legion Auxiliary especially active. The federal recreational directors in the various counties have also been interested, and many new collections have been assembled and opened to the public. The Commission regrets that the introduction to community borrowing of books has had to come through untrained service, but is counting on the new readers to support more adequate library service when it is possible.

The completion of the new capitol building released space in the Liberty Memorial building which had been assigned to the State Library Commission when the building was planned but which for various reasons had never been available. In the distribution of space by the Board of Administration, the State Library Commission was given the rooms south of the stairway on the ground and first floors, and the stacks on the first floor and its mezzanine. A doorway was cut between the two first floor west rooms, both were redecorated, and they provide a much needed office for the secretary, a commodious room to house the files for the clippings and pamphlets, the play collection, a reading table, and shelving for professional books. The former office has the desks for the stenographer and reference librarian; the main floor stacks accommodate the clerks' desks; the office of the Traveling Library Department has been moved to the ground floor in a room adjacent to the storage room for the Traveling Library collections when they are not in the field. The Traveling Library suite contains a supply closet, a combined work and office room, and a small typewriting room.

This arrangement eased the hampering congestion in office and shelving space, and has made working conditions much better.

Staff changes caused by low wage scale were numerous and are outlined below.

Reference Librarian
- July, 1934-October 15, 1935........Elizabeth Gieseler
- November 23, 1935-March 19, 1936........Leona Christensen
- May 15, 1936-date........Doris Hidde

Stenographer
- July, 1934-April, 1935........Frances Heath
- April, 1935-November, 1935........Chrissie Budge
- December, 1935-date........Arlene Wagner

Clerk
- July, 1934-January, 1936........Marion Jordan
- February, 1936-date........Marian Morton

A comparison of the directories in this report and that of 1932-34 will show many changes in librarians, two association libraries no longer functioning, and service established in thirteen towns.

ADMINISTRATIVE DEPARTMENT

The Secretary-director has had to devote considerable time to other than Commission administrative duties. The organization of federal library projects required many hours while the program was getting started, and because of personnel changes much of the reference work of 1935-36 had to be done by the secretary and the head of the Traveling Library Department. Field work was reduced to a minimum partly because of press of office work and partly because of lack of travel funds. During 1934 three district library meetings were held, but none were scheduled in 1935. Attendance at two state library meetings, two North Dakota Educational Association meetings, one of the Federation of Women's Clubs, the organization of the Wahpeton Indian School Library, and conferences and board meetings at twelve towns completed the Secretary's field work.

We have always felt that the small public libraries of the state were entitled to more help that it has been possible to offer them. Unfortunately the things they need most, money for supplies and new popular books to supplement the local collection are just the things the Commission's small budget will not provide. This lack was partially supplied as far as juvenile books are concerned through the generous cooperation of book publishers who donated sample copies of their new publications. These books were sorted, graded, and sent to the public libraries first as book week or special exhibits and later for circulation purposes. A collection of juvenile books was borrowed in the spring of 1936 from a lending agency in Philadelphia, and these have been sent in groups of about twenty-five to small libraries to help meet the summer demand.

Preliminary work has been done on a new edition of Bulletin No. 5 (the list of books for grade school libraries) but because the Department of Public Instruction could not finance its printing, its completion and distribution must wait a later date.

TRAVELING LIBRARY DEPARTMENT

The number of books purchased has been limited, and many have gone to replace worn-out copies in older libraries so that the actual number of new libraries is smaller than ever before—24 as against 27 during the previous biennium. And yet we have met an increase in circulation of 2,063 over the previous period. 1934-35 was the best year the Traveling Library Department has known. Always the circulation could have been larger if there had been more books to meet the peak of the winter demand.

It is gratifying to note that satisfied borrowers have returned to ask for more service, 321 of them in the second half of the period as against 286 in the first half. Some stations have been served continuously for nearly thirty years. The bank at Heaton began in 1908 under Mr. C. I. Turner, and since his death his son Howard Turner has continued this fine piece of community service.

The schools continue to be the heaviest borrowers. These lean years have seen many communities unable to supply books for the school libraries and they have been grateful for a central state agency to turn to. Superintendents of high schools increasingly ask for help in supplying the necessary outside reading for their English students. Both Traveling Library and Reference Departments have contributed to this.

Federal aid under FERA and WPA has made possible increased efficiency in Traveling Library service. Light wooden shipping cases were made by the carpenters for small collections of 20-25 books. These go by parcel post, and the durable cases, instead of pasteboard boxes, have been making the shipping more convenient and much safer. The average amount of postage has been thirty-five cents each way, and these small libraries have been very popular. Circulating for three months only they have doubled the turnover, in comparison with the heavy freight cases which go for six months.

Aid in book-mending under WPA has been another outstanding help. One woman has been kept busy through the year, and three during the summer when all the traveling libraries are gathered in to be renovated.

REFERENCE DEPARTMENT

The Reference Department is the branch of the Library Commission that serves directly the persons of the state and its employees in Bismarck. Of necessity about 90% of the requests for specific books, information, or collections of books is received by mail. By this means library service is made available to persons in isolated communities. The Library Commission also supplements from its collection material found in the small library units. Assistance is given to clubs throughout the State by means of program suggestions, outlines, and collections of material. Forty-five clubs were registered for regular service last year, and a number of others requested material for their programs from time to time. Schools are served by sending books for required reading, debate material and declamations at their request. Every effort is made to serve the inhabitants of this state with worthwhile up-to-date material for serious study and books in a lighter vein for recreational reading. For this purpose reading lists are compiled with a view to aid people in selecting their books, and bibliographies on special subjects are prepared upon request.

FEDERAL

The reports of many state departments for the past two years must include not only those activities financed by the regular state appropriation but also those carried out in cooperation with federal funds. The State Library Commission has worked with the federal agencies on various library projects which during this period have emphasized staff help rather than renovation of buildings.

FERA

The Federal Emergency Relief Administration succeeded the Civil Works Administration in the spring of 1935. Fortunately most of the librarians who had been employed under CWA were continued on FERA library projects, were transferred to other projects or secured private employment.

The largest project developed under FERA was a county wide plan for mending and cleaning the books in public and school libraries which was tried out in four counties. Workers were trained at the State Library Commission, supplies paid for by FERA funds were selected and bought by the Commission and sent to the various counties. Supervision and checking were not provided for, but the project was so successful that it was expanded and continued under WPA.

WPA

In the fall of 1935 projects were submitted providing for the cleaning and repairing of library and text books in rural and small town schools and the public libraries of the state, clerical help for all libraries and a supervisory staff. Owing to various federal complications the work was not really started until January, 1936 after which it was established rapidly.

Clerical and staff help was given in most of the public libraries, some in combination with county wide book mending projects, but fifteen with one or more full time workers. Eighty-four other groups of relief women were trained and organized to clean and mend text and library books in public schools, special emphasis being placed on small town and rural schools. On these various projects 415 persons were employed, and up to June 30, 58,623 books were mended at an average cost of .033 cents a volume, exclusive of wages. Hospital work was continued at Bismarck and established at Williston. Back work was cleaned up in many libraries and much necessary mending done. Some professional organizing was done in public and school libraries.

STATISTICAL REPORT 1934-36

Books

Traveling Library:	
Number of traveling libraries	388
Number of libraries added during period	24
Number of books added during period	787
Number of books in libraries	15,180
Reference Department:	
Number of books	17,888
Number of books added during period	740
Number of pamphlets	18,200

Circulation

Traveling Library:	1934-35	1935-36	Total
Number of libraries circulated	623	567	1,190
School	469	449	918
Community	154	118	272
Number of books shipped	23,177	20,701	43,878
Number of new stations	129	117	246
Reference Department:			
Number of requests	11,348	9,104	20,452
Number of books circulated	53,068	42,901	95,969
Number of magazines and pamphlets	9,343	9,658	19,001
Total Reference circulation	62,411	52,559	114,970
Total Commission circulation	85,588	73,260	158,848

PLACE	1930 Population	RECEIPTS			
		TAX		TOTAL	
		1934-1935	1935-1936	1934-1935	1935-1936
Over 2,500					
1. Fargo	28,619	13,237	13,447	16,182	14,450
2. Grand Forks	17,112	4,600	6,000	5,701	7,166
3. Minot	16,099	4,834	6,396	5,490	7,132
4. Bismarck	11,090	7,400	8,200	8,403	9,170
5. Jamestown	8,187	2,500	4,200	4,200	5,834
6. Devils Lake	5,451	3,707	3,598	4,078	4,036
7. Valley City	5,268	3,577	2,089	3,824	2,285
8. Dickinson	5,025	4,000	4,000	4,272	4,262
9. Williston	5,106	1,698	4,147	1,995	8,147
10. Wahpeton	3,176	3,000	3,000	3,472	3,100
11. Grafton	3,136	1,100	1,084	1,662	1,640
Under 2,500					
12. Ashley	1,033	25	25	153	237
13. Bowman	888	389	393	623	670
14. Carrington	1,717	1,287	690	1,287	705
15. Casselton	1,253	300	300	300	...
16. Ellendale	1,264	350	350	611	590
17. Garrison	1,024	190	...	210	...
18. Hankinson	1,400	377	40	12	45
19. Lakota	860	377	360	444	400
20. LaMoure	889	500	500	546	500
21. Langdon	1,221	...	...	...	...
22. Lidgerwood	1,029	515	650	565	837
23. Lisbon	1,650	967	1,182	1,631	1,324
24. Mayville	1,199	584	...	714	...
25. Mott	1,036	360	360	379	381
26. Oakes	1,709	828	883	999	1,169
27. Park River	1,131	400	400	408	415
28. Rugby	1,512	100	100	161	164
29. Velva	870	50	50	67	95
30. Wishek	1,146	...	75	...	80

PLACE	EXPENDITURES							
	SALARIES		HEAT, RENT, LIGHT		BOOKS, MAGAZINES		TOTAL	
	1934-35	1935-36	1934-35	1935-36	1934-35	1935-36	1934-35	1935-36
Over 2,500								
1. Fargo	7,279	7,199	709	779	2,591	2,766	13,513	14,392
2. Grand Forks	3,826	3,773	898	1,006	869	767	6,026	6,745
3. Minot	2,892	2,501	435	394	1,285	1,408	5,407	5,001
4. Bismarck	4,127	4,454	743	640	1,421	2,087	8,409	9,182
5. Jamestown	1,383	2,144	541	510	993	1,551	3,864	5,350
6. Devils Lake	1,492	1,440	390	344	501	710	2,758	4,134
7. Valley City	1,851	1,800	365	424	536	730	2,955	3,500
8. Dickinson	2,075	1,984	309	318	1,297	1,560	4,420	4,241
9. Williston	1,710	1,831	441	485	1,168	1,143	2,699	4,187
10. Wahpeton	1,530	1,585	484	548	417	634	2,099	3,323
11. Grafton	947	947	...	84	490	406	1,529	1,574
Under 2,500								
12. Ashley	120	120	...	...	62	104	182	224
13. Bowman	326	325	66	62	239	100	628	671
14. Carrington	600	600	22	18	442	223	973	1,062
15. Casselton	150	150	...	...	138	104	290	264
16. Ellendale	370	370	...	...	183	155	610	591
17. Garrison	60	...	10	...	44	...	177	...
18. Hankinson	...	40	...	...	8	5	15	45
19. Lakota	216	216	...	...	44	36	398	401
20. LaMoure	305	300	...	...	182	159	528	550
21. Langdon	150	150	...	...	186	218	...	268
22. Lidgerwood	342	374	57	175	87	96	587	773
23. Lisbon	482	475	142	180	174	189	1,105	1,332
24. Mayville	345	240	192	...	98	144	711	794
25. Mott	180	300	15	...	21	39	430	349
26. Oakes	636	608	...	...	160	392	855	1,077
27. Park River	180	180	...	...	88	74	268	320
28. Rugby	78	51	...	...	58	120	143	214
29. Velva	...	...	...	...	23	78	26	101
30. Wishek	52	52	...	...	10	5	120	71

PLACE	CIRCULATION			Volumes	Borrowers	Hours Open Per Week	Rural Borrowers
	1934-35	1935-36	Total				
Over 2,500							
1. Fargo	205,949	202,053	408,022	34,125	19,288	72	421
2. Grand Forks	76,862	75,423	152,285	14,350	5,948	42	93
3. Minot	185,046	148,151	333,197	17,680	7,178	72	...
4. Bismarck	151,031	162,241	313,272	13,752	7,088	54	...
5. Jamestown	69,315	74,259	143,574	13,017	6,004	36	807
6. Devils Lake	32,047	28,217	60,264	8,741	2,724	40	34
7. Valley City	37,985	38,179	76,174	13,290	2,806	36	203
8. Dickinson	52,571	50,351	102,922	12,185	3,857	51	239
9. Williston	28,492	30,222	58,714	10,772	3,801	42	26
10. Wahpeton	26,191	26,858	53,049	10,297	2,414	33	...
11. Grafton	27,050	25,868	52,918	5,316	1,458	24	6
Under 2,500							
12. Ashley	5,460	4,836	10,296	8,915	340	6	...
13. Bowman	6,333	6,021	12,354	6,706	704	14	...
14. Carrington	23,100	18,768	41,868	6,980	2,475	25	956
15. Casselton	5,200	4,420	9,620	900	150	4	...
16. Ellendale	15,538	15,300	30,838	4,005	1,076	15	350
17. Garrison	1,820	.....	.....	1,156	.....	8	...
18. Hankinson	5,720	3,264	8,984	4,300	500	4	50
19. Lakota	7,386	12,020	19,406	4,733	.....	9	...
20. LaMoure	11,870	9,530	21,400	3,215	1,092	9	459
21. Langdon	10,814	12,000	22,814	5,110	275	8	...
22. Lidgerwood	11,503	7,915	19,418	4,130	827	24	...
23. Lisbon	12,577	10,622	23,199	3,783	1,079	27	225
24. Mayville	3,515	4,732	8,247	4,003	567	8	8
25. Mott	2,914	3,715	6,629	2,881	1,090	9	...
26. Oakes	29,255	25,844	55,099	6,127	1,144	20	318
27. Park River	5,830	7,540	13,370	2,636	780	8	125
28. Rugby	7,280	13,000	20,280	2,257	1,114	8	300
29. Velva	9,100	9,880	18,900	5,715	425	6	...
30. Wishek	5,200	5,200	10,400	1,271	90	6	...

TOWN	Population	EXPENDITURES		Volumes	Borrowers	Total Circulation	Hours Open Per Week	Free to Grades
		Books & Magazines	Total					
1. *Barney	...	...	...	120	...	.....	1	Free
2. Bathgate	292	42	64	1,000	250	3,060	2	Free
3. Beulah	913	24	41	1,237	22	4,263	2	Free
4. Bowbells	695	...	10	773	340	2,700	4	Free
5. Cando	1,164	50	126	3,485	70	5,460	2	Fee
6. Carson	356	2	...	519	167	.....	4	Free
7. Cavalier	850	43	50	1,534	346	8,112	3½	Fee
8. *Cogswell	426	15	20	857	126	.....	3	Free
9. Courtenay	350	2	7	826	108	1,352	1½	Free
10. Crosby	1,271	...	...	1,535	714	10,140	11	Free
11. Dawson	306	6	8	700	87	5,924	2	Fee
12. Drake	644	64	88	1,195	685	5,230	3	Free
13. Enderlin	1,839	124	135	2,944	1,125	21,424	13	Free
14. Fessenden	738	54	60	3,256	.....	9,708	4	Free
15. *Finley	587	...	...	194	.....	.....	12	Free
16. *Flaxton	423	12	12	481	62	.....	5	Free
17. *Gackle	493	17	34	156	86	583	4	Free
18. Hamilton	151	18	18	862	...	2,808	2	Free
19. Hansboro	176	6	...	355	40	6,136	2	Fee
20. Heaton	.....	9	10	520	120	3,920	44	Free
21. Hettinger	1,292	17	60	762	280	12,427	3	Free
22. *Hillsboro	1,317	...	...	151	...	.....	..	Free
23. Hope	535	45	45	1,423	100	4,836	15	Free
24. Leeds	704	50	...	.....	...	13,676	6	Free
25. Leonard	.....	...	14	1,950	...	5,752	6	Free
26. *Linton	1,192	175	320	341	105	3,848	4	Free
27. *McHenry	219	...	...	120	50	.....	3	Free
28. Mandan	5,037	...	...	7,214	...	13,354	7	Fee
29. New England	911	19	...	1,156	375	5,040	3	Free
30. New Rockford	2,195	35	...	3,000	400	.....	7	Fee
31. Pembina	551	35	35	1,800	105	.....	4	Free
32. *Portal	512	10	...	1,132	248	2,116	6	Free
33. *Regent	308	20	60	625	90	2,860	3	Free
34. Rolla	852	50	89	1,270	1,324	2,860	2	Fee
35. St. John	372	10	15	521	500	2,641	3	Free
36. St. Thomas	595	142	185	2,185	...	11,180	3	Fee
37. Sanish	463	20	23	445	570	1,976	1	Free
38. Tioga	435	...	...	763	48	2,247	42	Free
39. Towner	622	32	72	654	217	5,556	15	Free
40. Turtle Lake	579	16	...	1,228	10	2,236	2	Free
41. Velva	870	77	101	5,715	425	11,980	6	Free
42. *Verona	222	...	...	77	47	1,560	2	Fee
43. Wimbledon	421	10	...	800	60	.....	1	Free

The following Libraries are functioning but have not sent in reports for either year of the Biennial period: Beach, Edgeley, Goodrich, Lansford, Milton, Mohall, Neche, New Salem, Tolna.

**Libraries open less than two years.*

Place	Name of Library	Librarian
Ashley	Public Library	Mrs. H. L. Woll
Barney	Public Library	Mrs. James Little
Bathgate	Public Library	Mrs. Herbert C. Thomson
Beach	Public Library	Marian Wallace
Beulah	Public Library	Mrs. F. C. Worch
Bismarck	Public Library	Ellen B. Lawin
Bismarck	State Historical Library	Mrs. Florence Davis
Bismarck	State Library Commission	Lillian E. Cook
Bismarck	State Law Library	Mr. E. J. Taylor
Bottineau	Forestry School	L. Naomi Aplund
Bowbells	Study Club Library	Claire Buskrude
Bowman	Public Library	Mrs. Mertie Pond
Cando	Public Library	Mrs. Mai Riggs
Carrington	Public Library	Mrs. Ella Mae Hargrave
Carson	Public Library	Mrs. C. N. Harmon
Casselton	Public Library	Mrs. Emir D. Scott
Cavalier	Public Library	Mrs. Fred Harris
Cogswell	Public Library	Mrs. Paul G. Hample
Courtenay	Public Library	Mrs. A. A. Hoffman
Crosby	Public Library	Mrs. H. Covell
Dawson	Public Library	Mrs. C. A. Cross
Devils Lake	Carnegie Library	Marie E. O'Brien
Devils Lake	State Deaf School	Burton W. Driggs
Dickinson	Public Library	Gertrude Voldal
Dickinson	State Teachers College	Matilda Stoxen
Drake	Public Library	Mrs. E. Van Horn
Edgeley	Public Library	Mrs. J. E. Kipp
Ellendale	Public Library	Mrs. V. D. Coleman
Ellendale	Normal & Industrial School	Dorothy Aronsson
Enderlin	Public Library	Mabel I. Smith
Fargo	Public Library	Inga Rynning
Fargo	Masonic Library	Clara Richards
Fargo	Agricultural College	Mrs. Ethel McVeety
Fessenden	Public Library	Mrs. W. W. Barr
Finley	Public Library	Thelma Sund
Flaxton	Public Library	Mrs. Kenneth A. Nicolson
Gackle	Public Library	Mrs. N. S. Johnson
Garrison	Public Library	Arlena Youngberg
Goodrich	Public Library	Mrs. J. R. Doering
Grafton	Public Library	Mrs. Emma Cobb
Grand Forks	Public Library	Ruth O. Brown
Grand Forks	University Library	William H. Carlson
Hamilton	Public Library	Mrs. Andrew Knutson
Hankinson	Public Library	Mrs. Corrine Stack
Hansboro	Public Library	Mrs. O. R. Anderson
Heaton	Public Library	Howard I. Turner
Hettinger	Public Library	Mrs. Milo C. Richardson
Hillsboro	Public Library	Mrs. Clara Sarles
Hope	Public Library	Mrs. D. J. Gumb

Place	Name of Library	Librarian
Jamestown	Alfred Dickey Library	Mercedes Muenz
Jamestown	Jamestown College Library	Pearl Carlson
Jamestown	Insane Hospital	Dr. J. D. Carr
Kulm	Public Library	Mrs. C. O. Fergusson
Lakota	Public Library	Mrs. Helman Hullett
LaMoure	Public Library	Mrs. Carl Neverman
Langdon	Public Library	Mrs. E. J. Donovan
Lansford	Public Library	Mrs. Anne Olrich
Leeds	Public Library	Mrs. Albert Johnson
Leonard	Watts Free Library	Mrs. S. Qualley
Lidgerwood	Public Library	Mrs. Elizabeth Kings
Linton	Public Library	Mrs. L. E. Koeppen
Lisbon	Public Library	Berniece Johnson
Mandan	Public Library	Mrs. John A. Biggs
McHenry	Public Library	Mrs. R. J. Leahy
Mayville	Public Library	Cora Ames
Mayville	State Teachers College	Mrs. Hazel W. Byrnes
Milton	Community Library	Mrs. R. T. Wait
Minot	Public Library	Jean Taggert
Minot	State Teachers College	Mrs. Mabel Etheridge
Mohall	Public Library	Vivian Movius
Mott	Inez Hendrickson Library	Louise Wagner
Neche	Public Library	Mrs. Herbert Briggs
New England	Public Library	Edith Fox
New Rockford	Public Library	Vannie Hall
New Salem	Public Library	Mrs. Goldie Schreiber
Oakes	Public Library	Mrs. Edgar Christensen
Park River	Public Library	Mildred Ferguson
Pembina	Public Library	Mrs. Pauline Brennan
Portal	Public Library	Mrs. Albert Charbonneau
Regent	Public Library	Mrs. H. C. Bowers
Rolla	Public Library	Mrs. A. R. Beardsley
Rugby	Public Library	Frances Frydenlund
St. John	Public Library	Carolyn Wells
St. Thomas	Study Club Library	Mrs. E. T. Thompson
Sanish	Public Library	Mrs. H. C. Helvey
Tioga	Masonic Library	Marian Koolmo
Tolna	Public Library	Mrs. C. S. Hawkins
Towner	Public Library	Mrs. J. H. Van Deusen
Turtle Lake	Public Library	Mrs. W. N. Harris
Valley City	Public Library	Mrs. Helen Tracy
Valley City	State Teachers College	Loretta Swift
Velva	Public Library	Mrs. Blanche Crawford
Verona	Public Library	Mrs. W. J. Tiedeman
Wahpeton	Beach Library	Dorothy Hohler
Wahpeton	State Science School	Lillian Mirick
Westerheim	Public Library	Mrs. A. H. Allen
Williston	James Memorial Library	Mrs. Ethel Kuenning
Wimbledon	Public Library	Jessie Watne
Wishek	*Public Library*	Mrs. E. D. Lowers

Sixteenth Biennial Report

OF THE

State Library Commission

TO THE

State Board of Administration

FOR THE PERIOD

JULY 1, 1936 - JUNE 30, 1938

Sixteenth Biennial Report

OF THE

State Library Commission

TO THE

State Board of Administration

FOR THE PERIOD

JULY 1, 1936 - JUNE 30, 1938

BOARD OF ADMINISTRATION

June 30, 1938

Jennie Ulsrud .... **Chairman**

J. D. Harris
R. A. Kinzer
John N. Hagan
Arthur E. Thompson

STATE LIBRARY COMMISSION STAFF

June 30, 1938

Lillian E. Cook .... **Secretary and Director**
Bessie R. Baldwin .... **Traveling Library Chief**
Doris L. Hidde .... **Reference Library**
Arlene Wagner .... **Stenographer**
Wilda Sebastian .... **Clerk**
Viola Hess .... **Clerk**

LETTER OF TRANSMITTAL

To the State Board of Administration,

Bismarck, North Dakota.

Herewith is submitted the Sixteenth Biennial Report of the North Dakota State Library Commission, covering the period from July 1, 1936, to June 30, 1938.

LILLIAN E. COOK,
Secretary and Director.

REPORT OF THE SECRETARY AND DIRECTOR, 1936-38
STATE LIBRARY COMMISSION

North Dakota as a whole finds itself having outgrown its library garment. Most inadequate is the state library law which has no provision for regional library service, thus putting us quite out of line in library advance in the United States. The law should be rewritten to provide for a more modern approach to an enlarged field of library administration.

A second great handicap is in outgrown buildings. WPA grants have helped Dickinson to a new wing, and Grand Forks to a revamped basement room, for the children's and youth's collections, but most of our public library buildings are too small, often inconvenient and badly in need of modern lighting, ventilating, etc. Several of the larger towns need entirely new buildings, and all should be cleaned, repaired, and modernized.

Another legal need is a provision for certification of the professional staff of the public and school libraries to insure the hiring of trained workers as vacancies occur.

And finally there must be an appropriation adequate to provide for the necessary services the library is constantly called on to contribute to the educational, cultural, and recreational program of the community.

The emphasis on library work by the American Legion Auxiliary is responsible for several of the new libraries organized during the period, and a few are the result of the WPA recreational program and activities. Both WPA and NYA workers are helping in these new libraries.

A comparison of the directories for the last and present biennial periods show only four libraries discontinued, of which one was never firmly established, two were turned over to the schools, and one just died. Offsetting the four discontinued are five inaugurated, resulting in a net gain of one.

THE LIBRARY COMMISSION

A diagram of State Library Commission activities for the biennial period, 1936-38, would show a slightly reduced total area if measured by book circulation, and an irregular outline indicating bulges of advance or hollows of reduction in certain phases of work.

The State Library Commission is a busy place with a staff of three trained and three clerical workers trying to meet the library needs of a state largely rural and largely without professional book help, except as it is given from the state agency. As the schools become more and more conscious of the part books take in the educational field and aroused to the necessity of having these books used efficiently, the demands for professional organization of local collections go hand in hand with a greater demand for books, and the Commission finds itself unable to adequately meet either demand. Were it not for the help supplied through WPA, the Commission would find itself critically handicapped in clerical and book-mending help.

The appropriation is very inadequate in several particulars—salaries, money for books, and travel fund which allows the Secretary to keep in personal touch with library conditions throughout the state. The cuts in various administrative salaries amounting to almost 40% for the Secretary have never been restored, and the schedule for the professional group is much too low. The service that can be given depends on the books available to meet the demands. The present supply results in empty shelves and all-too-long waiting lists of reserves.

A brief report of the three divisions of the State Library Commission follows—the administrative, or the work of the Secretary and Director; the Traveling Library Department, through which book service is offered to communities and schools as units, and the Reference Department, which serves individuals and organizations.

ADMINISTRATIVE DEPARTMENT

Heavy office work with some field work, combining supervision of WPA library projects and visits to public libraries, comprised the work of two years. District meetings were held, and the Secretary attended such state and national meetings as she could, and gave book talks at local gatherings. In addition the field work is:

Visits to Public Libraries	23
Visits to WPA Projects	20
Visits to High School Libraries	8
Visits to State Schools	7
District Meetings (With attendance of 132)	6
State and national meetings	5
Special meetings	1
Talks to groups or state meetings	5

The Secretary has prepared for each issue of the NORTH DAKOTA TEACHER a list of free and inexpensive material; has issued at irregular intervals the mimeographed sheet, "North Dakota Library Notes"; did the editorial work on a new edition of Bulletin No. 5 and read proof on it; has made numerous comparative studies of reference books; has prepared many special book lists and secured through correspondence with publishers, juvenile books which were reviewed, graded, listed, sorted, and sent as special exhibit material to the libraries of the state. These books eventually become the property of the State Library Commission, and constitute a most welcome addition to the juvenile collection.

TRAVELING LIBRARY

The most successful experiment the Traveling Library has undertaken is the half-size library of juvenile books for a three month loan.

All of the new juvenile books are put in these collections—330 this biennium—and the fact that they go to the rural school by parcel post brings the gratifying thought that these children away from railroad centers have the attractive books while they are fresh and new. Of course a large number of the older libraries of the parcel post size go to them, too.

There is a steady demand for the community libraries from the small club or little town library. Ten of these were added during the biennium. We try to choose the books carefully enough so that they do not lose their attraction when they are not "hot off the press." The traveling libraries contain the "best sellers" of the moment only when they show enduring qualities.

During this biennium about twenty community libraries that had served for fifteen years were retired. Thanks to the perennial quality of children's books, these could be salvaged and rejuvenated by the WPA menders and used to replace wornout books in grade libraries partially worn but still in circulation. This meant that all new books could go into new libraries and not be used for replacement.

Under the supervision of the state carpenter, an NYA boy made twenty-five wooden packing cases for parcel post libraries—a great help. And to Federal help thanks are due for the continual supply of freshly mended books. It has been possible to keep several women employed on the mending from both Reference and Traveling Library Departments.

One of the pleasant duties of the Traveling Library Department has been the loaning of fresh juvenile books to Camp Grassick each summer. These are arranged according to cottages and remain in camp during the full season. Other ideas for the use of the newer juveniles during the idle summer are welcome.

THE REFERENCE DEPARTMENT

Library service for persons of the state who do not have access to a local library who have definite reading wants, both for recreation and for study, is extended by the Reference Department of the State Library Commission. Reading lists on various subjects are compiled from time to time to aid the patron in his selection of books. In many cases selection is left to the reference librarian of the Commission.

Clubs are continuing to use the library service offered, not only for material to prepare papers, but for suggestions in program building. Forty-five study clubs are registered for regular service and more request information at various times.

Because of the extremely limited finances of the rural and elementary schools in some localities of the state, these schools have come to depend almost entirely on the resources of the Library Commission for reading material for their pupils. During 1937-38, 400 rural and elementary teachers used this service regularly.

High school libraries are supplemented from the State Library Commission book collections and are supplied with up-to-date reference material for term papers.

In each group served—individual, club, and school—requests far exceed the supply. Because of this demand, reserve lists become long. Patrons must wait as long as ten months before their turn comes. In the case of GONE WITH THE WIND, seventy names were on the list with a supply of only six copies. Many times if material is out when the request comes, it cannot be sent at a later date because the time for its usefulness is past. An adequate book budget is necessary if the residents of the state without local library service are to be satisfactorily supplied with reading material.

WPA

The State Library Commission's sponsorship and supervision of the statewide WPA library project has continued throughout the period and we are very proud of what has been accomplished. The friendly reception of the project on the part of school and library boards we feel was largely because of the confidence they had in the Commission. The fact that many of the projects have continued since January, 1936, and that projects were welcomed wherever we felt the type of worker available justified establishing it shows how effective the service has been. Because there were no professionally trained people on relief, the projects have had to offer largely service covering, cleaning and mending of books; picture and pamphlet mounting; magazine reinforcement; repair of maps and record books, and the binding of Braille books. In public and school libraries where there are trained librarians, clerical help has been provided and has been trained to do much routine library work.

Library and school administrators have come to depend very much on this service, and we wonder with dismay what adjustment can be made when the Government no longer offers it. During the biennial period, approximately 496,000 hours of service have been given, which resulted in the rehabilitation of 428,102 books. In addition to the hours spent on cleaning and repairing books, 80,812 hours have been given for library service, either under the supervision of a trained librarian or in a small town by an especially capable worker.

STATISTICAL REPORT, 1936-38

Books

Traveling Library:	
Number of traveling libraries	376
Number of libraries added during period	23
Number of books added during period	780
Number of books in libraries	14,920
Reference Department:	
Number of books	18,380
Number of books added during period	1,745
Number of pamphlets	18,000

Circulation

Traveling Library:	1936-37	1937-38	Total
Number of libraries circulated	526	529	1,055
School	409	426	835
Community	117	103	220
Number of books shipped	19,348	19,012	38,360
Number of new stations	113	128	241
Reference Department:			
Number of requests	9,316	10,752	20,068
Number of books circulated	36,665	43,922	80,587
Number of magazines, pamphlets	9,839	10,469	20,308
Total Reference circulation	46,504	54,391	100,895
Total Commission circulation	65,852	73,403	139,255

Appropriation:	
Salary	$ 1,600.00
Clerkhire	6,380.80
Postage	700.00
Office Supplies	500.00
Furniture and Fixtures	300.00
Printing	350.00
Miscellaneous	500.00
Travel Expenses	250.00
Aids to Libraries	150.00
Books	2,750.00
Preparation of Books	200.00
Binding	450.00
TOTAL	$14,130.80

Public and Association Libraries with Municipal Help

	PLACE	1930 Population	RECEIPTS Tax 1936-37	RECEIPTS Tax 1937-38	RECEIPTS Total* 1936-37	RECEIPTS Total* 1937-38
	Over 2,500					
1.	Fargo	28,619	$ 14,661.52	$ 19,939.09	$ 18,286.05	$ 24,292.12
2.	Grand Forks	17,112	7,900.00	9,700.00	10,064.69	11,613.86
3.	Mot	16,099	5,917.66	6,846.73	11,058.83	11, [illegible]26
4.	Bismarck	11,090	8,200.00	9,499.46	9,501.18	11,739.13
5.	Jamestown	8,187	4,000.00	4,000.00	5,697.50	5,519.46
6.	Devils Lake	5,451	3,647.08	3,826.99	5,529.25	6,826.46
7.	[illegible]ley City	5,268	3,418.10	3,526.13	5,799.54	[illegible]
8.	[illegible]on	5,025	4,000.00	4,[illegible]0.00	4,524.68	4,683.89
9.	[illegible]on	5,[illegible]6	1,735.18	2,604.23	6,379.30	5,533.47
10.	Wahpeton	3,176	4,000.00	4,000.00	5,986.37	6,154.42
11.	[illegible]on	3,136	1,100.00	1,033.83	2,741.25	2,558.99
	[illegible]der 2,500					
12.	[illegible]ley	1,033	....	50.00	102.00	145.95
13.	[illegible]an	888	219.62	600.00	491.54	1,083.35
14.	[illegible]on	1,717	1,473.14	1,214.12	1,844.98	1,996.01
15.	[illegible]selton	1,253	300.00	250.00	300.00	337.75
16.	Ellendale	1,264	375.00	375.00	589.65	597.71
17.	Hankinson	1,400	....	60.00	45.00	63.00
18.	[illegible]ata	860	382.00	345.22	383.00	567.08
19.	[illegible]re	889	600.00	600.00	628.22	600.00
20.	[illegible]on	1,221	....	....	498.92	479.99
21.	Lidgerwood	1,029	675.00	775.00	876.76	992.57
22.	[illegible]on	1,650	1,009.82	1,300.28	2,157.91	2,220.08
23.	Mayville	1,199	700.00	650.00	820.70	828.84
24.	Mott	1,036	360.00	360.00	395.81	382.36
25.	Oakes	1,709	463.00	609.81	1,167.05	1,024.74
26.	Park River	1,131	400.00	400.00	408.95	400.00
27.	Rugby	1,512	100.00	100.00	152.30	124.40
28.	Velva	870	50.00	50.00	101.33	60.50
29.	Wishek	1,146	75.00	50.00	105.00	111.50

* Includes Balance

EXPENDITURES

Place	Salaries 1936-37	Salaries 1937-38	Heat, Rent, Light 1936-37	Heat, Rent, Light 1937-38	Books and Magazines 1936-37	Books and Magazines 1937-38	Total 1936-37	Total 1937-38
Over 2,500								
1. Fargo	$7,802.25	$8,184.50	$ 747.76	$ 852.26	$3,305.35	$3,469.46	$14,861.15	$17,389.58
2. Grand Forks	3,901.38	4,827.38	897.36	662.76	1,482.70	3,093.33	9,260.49	10,201.03
3. Mot	2,526.88	3,057.54	432.48	436.47	3,085.37	1,871.77	7,262.91	6,808.30
4. Bismarck	4,087.95	4,848.30	636.38	841.53	2,030.04	3,940.00	8,398.88	11,535.66
5. Jamestown	2,400.16	2,369.10	523.42	557.13	1,224.90	1,219.88	5,382.49	4,987.92
6. eDils Lake	1,440.00	1,550.00	477.92	414.70	1,052.96	1,392.63	3,367.93	4,698.54
7. aMley City	1,850.00	1,861.00	352.87	391.66	913.18	627.47	3,446.43	4,219.79
8. Dickinson	1,933.25	2,071.50	302.05	296.67	1,492.09	948.82	4,069.05	3,607.74
9. Williston	1,827.45	1,837.69	448.47	522.84	655.58	263.40	2,747.43	3,178.65
10. Wahpeton	1,607.51	1,638.00	464.52	489.73	1,185.15	920.52	3,994.99	3,875.31
11. Grafton	990.85	947.50	240.17	224.11	396.60	509.10	1,758.80	1,933.34
Under 2,500								
12. Ashley	90.00	....	....	....	81.44	23.32	182.19	145.95
13. Bowman	324.00	324.00	65.63	69.56	47.80	121.86	711.16	1,009.21
14. Carrington	600.00	600.00	22.75	19.79	239.18	189.74	1,116.11	858.41
15. Casselton	150.00	150.00	....	....	146.68	87.75	332.29	245.75
16. Ellendale	370.00	370.00	....	....	150.52	186.84	589.25	593.62
17. Hankinson	....	60.00	....	....	....	3.00	....	63.00
18. Lkata	216.00	216.00	....	....	50.00	17.86	382.00	567.08
19. LaMoure	300.00	300.00	34.83	46.30	107.39	172.84	628.22	600.00
20. Langdon	150.00	150.00	....	....	142.50	132.12	448.92	179.99
21. dgd	546.00	543.50	70.68	165.16	87.08	117.08	842.11	902.75
22. Lisbon	498.00	515.50	136.19	177.22	298.71	199.60	1,301.11	1,181.75
23. Mayville	420.00	375.00	275.02	280.86	139.65	129.32	860.22	828.84
24. Mott	300.00	300.00	....	....	75.00	70.00	395.81	452.36
25. Oakes	605.00	633.00	....	....	288.51	79.12	931.92	794.11
26. Park River	260.00	270.00	....	....	61.48	21.75	408.95	325.58
27. Rugby	51.00	52.00	....	....	135.00	....	201.00	....
28. Ita	....	....	....	....	48.54	47.83	82.64	59.50
29. Wishek	52.00	49.00	....	....	1.38	61.50	78.63	118.33

Place	1936-37	Circulation 1937-38	Total	Volumes	Borrowers	Hrs. Open Per Week	Rural Borrowers
Over 2,500							
1. Fargo	[illegible]	205,333	413,621	35,927	19,040	72	416
2. Grand Forks	76,085	79,163	155,248	15,173	8,526	66	75
3. Minot	109,076	84,541	193,617	7,595	4,981	65	54
4. Bismarck	165,120	183,312	348,432	[illegible]	7,114	65	....
5. Jamestown	69,828	68,782	138,610	3,688	5,822	54	651
6. Devils Lake	28,215	30,140	58,355	10,240	3,308	36	23
7. Valley City	35,646	33,128	68,774	14,255	3,399	36	277
8. Dickinson	59,260	61,132	120,392	3,278	3,016	36	218
9. Williston	30,387	31,837	62,224	0,211	3,914	42	186
10. Wahpeton	31,804	27,594	59,398	9,502	1,649	30	352
11. Grafton	22,665	23,807	46,472	6,056	1,447	24	3
Under 2,500							
12. Ashley*	4,992	5,525	10,517	3,404	549	6	....
13. Bowman	5,555	4,666	10,221	6,781	591	30	....
14. Carrington	19,594	5,636	35,230	6.516	2,921	27	985
15. Casselton	4,500	5,200	9,700	925	175	4	....
16. Ellendale	14,413	14,864	29,277	4,472	993	14	350
17. Hankinson	1,264	1,525	2,789	4,400	500	4	50
18. Lakota	5,840	5,203	11,043	5,098	....	8	....
19. LaMoure	8,220	7,221	15,441	3,420	1,097	6	467
20. Langdon*	13,000	10,400	23,400	6,471	175	8	....
21. Lidgerwood	5,416	5,844	11,260	4,398	730	26	346
22. Lisbon	0,437	11,176	21,613	4,001	1,170	20	....
23. Mayville	3,905	3,724	7,629	4,403	661	8	....
24. Mott	3,889	4,554	8,443	3,453	1,071	7	....
25. Oakes	25,394	26,081	51,475	6,501	1,205	30	342
26. Park River	7,696	7,000	14,696	2,495	588	20	154
27. Rugby	3,780	14,040	27,820	1,815	400	4	....
28. [illegible]	820	9,500	19,120	5,765	425	6	....
29. Wishek	3,750	5,200	8,950	1,159	176	5	....

* Charge for use of books.

ASSOCIATION LIBRARIES—NO MUNICIPAL HELP

	Place	Population	Expenditures: Books & Magazines	Expenditures: Total	Volumes	Borrowers	Total Circulation	Hours Open Per Wk.	Free to Grades	Free to Public
1.	Barney	....	None	None	120	38	350	2	Free	Free
2.	Bathgate	292	100.00	304.00	1,200	80	2,250	4	Free	Free
3.	Beulah	913	2.70	25.10	1,458	17	1,050	1	Fee	Fee
4.	Bottineau	1,322	....	45.00	546	850	1,450	5	Free	Free
5.	Bowbells	695	None	8.37	783	310	850	2	Free	Free
6.	Cando	1,164	50.00	98.00	5,000	104	5,200	2	Fee	Fee
7.	Cavalier	850	25.56	66.61	1,797	281	4,300	4	Free	Fee
8.	Cogswell	426	9.90	20.97	1,550	177	1,000	3	Free	Fee
9.	Courtenay	350	None	2.39	527	108	400	1½	Fee	Fee
10.	Crosby	1,271	None	11.00	1,618	509	1,800	8	Free	Fee
11.	Dawson*	306	8.42	9.96	700	70	2,100	3	Fee	Fee
12.	Drake	644	65.70	76.96	1,485	520	3,600	3	Free	Free
13.	Enderlin	1,839	132.35	154.87	4,786	1,322	9,600	19	Free	Free
14.	[illegible]	493	1.85	7.01	508	142	3,700	3	Free	Free
15.	Goodrich	468	None	27.50	818	37	1,850	2	Free	Free
16.	Halliday	305	4.50	30.00	607	81	3,888	22	Free	Free
17.	Hamilton	151	17.99	17.99	914	520	600	2	Free	Fee
18.	Heaton	1,292	None	1.70	564	50	300	45	Free	Free
19.	Hillsboro	1,317	124.16	124.16	480	110	11,500	11	Free	Free
20.	Hoople	325	60.00	70.00	950	250	3,750	1½	Free	Free
21.	Hope	535	44.62	44.62	987	30	1,750	6	Fee	Fee
22.	Leeds	725	35.00	82.50	....	....	1,028	6	Free	Free
23.	Linton	1,192	112.05	112.05	752	178	4,500	5	Free	Free
24.	McHenry	219	None	None	200	40	2,500	2	Free	Free
25.	Mandan	5,037	....	....	6,045	100	5,950	6	Fee	Fee
26.	Mohall	676	15.00	15.00	1,325	830	600	15	Free	Free
27.	New England	911	44.00	46.00	1,300	130	2,500	4½	Free	Free
28.	New Rockford	2,195	55.30	310.29	3,500	40	2,000	8	Free	Free

29.	New Salem	804	23.00	33.00	1,400	479	7,500	25	Fee	Fee
30.	Pembina	551	21.00	61.00	1,650	226	3,350	3	Free	Free
31.	Portal	512	21.35	45.38	579	190	2,250	3	Free	Free
32.	Regent	308	10.00	40.00	825	40	3,000	3	Fee	Fee
33.	Rolla	852	72.54	138.57	1,136	146	1,100	2	Fee	Fee
34.	St. Thomas	595	99.55	147.37	2,394	100	591	3	Fee	Fee
35.	Sanish	463	4.00	4.00	501	64	828	1	Free	Free
36.	Towner	622	35.00	42.96	978	566	3,929	17½	Free	Free
37.	Turtle Lake	579	25.00	25.00	1,300	25	3,000	2	Fee	Fee

*Report covers 4 months.

The following libraries are functioning but have not sent in reports for either year of the Biennial Period: Garrison, Beach, Carson, Edgeley, Flaxton, Hansboro, Hettinger, Lansford, Leonard, Milton, Neche, Selfridge, Tioga, Tolna, Verona, and Wimbledon.

Place	Name of Library	Librarian
Ashley	Public Library	Mrs. H. L. Woll
Barney	Public Library	Mrs. James Little
Bathgate	Public Library	Mrs. Herbert C. Thomson
Beach	Public Library	Marian Wallace
Beulah	Public Library	Mrs. F. C. Worch
Bismarck	Public Library	Erana Stadler
Bismarck	State Historical Library	Mrs. Florence Davis
Bismarck	State Library Commission	Lillian E. Cook
Bismarck	State Law Library	Mr. E. J. Taylor
Bottineau	Forestry School	Ruth Clausen
Bottineau	Public Library	Mrs. Archie Crandall
Bowbells	Study Club Library	Claire Buskrude
Bowman	Public Library	Mrs. Mertie Pond
Cando	Public Library	Mrs. Mai Riggs
Carrington	Public Library	Mrs. Ella Mae Hargrave
Carson	Public Library	Mrs. C. N. Harmon
Casselton	Public Library	Mrs. C. W. Cotant
Cavalier	Public Library	Mrs. Fred Harris
Cogswell	Public Library	Mrs. L. A. Dodge
Courtenay	Public Library	Mrs. A. A. Hoffman
Crosby	Public Library	Mrs. Wanda W. Berg
Dawson	Public Library	Mrs. C. A. Cross
Devils Lake	Carnegie Library	Marie E. O'Brien
Devils Lake	State Deaf School	Burton W. Driggs
Dickinson	Public Library	Gertrude Voldal
Dickinson	State Teachers College	Matilda Stoxen
Drake	Public Library	Mrs. E. Van Horn
Edgeley	Public Library	Mrs. J. E. Kipp
Ellendale	Public Library	Mrs. V. D. Coleman
Ellendale	Normal & Industrial School	Ruth McCarthy
Enderlin	Public Library	Mabel I. Smith
Fargo	Public Library	Inga Rynning
Fargo	Masonic Library	Clara Richards
Fargo	Agricultural College	Mrs. Ethel McVeety
Flaxton	Public Library	Mrs. Chas. Carter
Gackle	Public Library	Mrs. E. A. Nisser
Garrison	Public Library	Arlena Youngberg
Goodrich	Public Library	Mrs. J. R. Doering
Grafton	Public Library	Mrs. Emma Cobb
Grand Forks	Public Library	Irma Walker
Grand Forks	University Library	Della Mathys
Hamilton	Public Library	Mrs. Andrew Knutson
Hankinson	Public Library	Mrs. Corrine Stack
Hansboro	Public Library	Mrs. O. R. Anderson
Harvey	Public Library	Mrs. A. B. Hannes
Heaton	Public Library	Howard I. Turner
Hettinger	Public Library	Mrs. Milo C. Richardson

Place	Name of Library	Librarian
Hillsboro	Public Library	Mrs. Beatrice Nedland
Hoople	Public Library	Mrs. J. O. Wallum
Hope	Public Library	Mrs. D. J. Gumb
Jamestown	Alfred Dickey Library	Mercedes Muenz
Jamestown	Jamestown College Library	Pearl Carlson
Jamestown	Insane Hospital	Dr. Lorenzen
Kulm	Public Library	Mrs. C. O. Fergusson
Lakota	Public Library	Mrs. Helman Hullett
LaMoure	Public Library	Mrs. Carl Neverman
Langdon	Public Library	Mrs. E. J. Donovan
Lansford	Public Library	Mrs. B. B. Bussie
Leeds	Public Library	Mrs. Albert Johnson
Leonard	Watts Free Library	Mrs. S. Qualley
Lidgerwood	Public Library	Mrs. Elizabeth Kings
Linton	Public Library	Alice Stewart
Lisbon	Public Library	Berniece Johnson
McHenry	Public Library	Mrs. R. J. Leahy
Mandan	Public Library	Mrs. John A. Biggs
Mayville	Public Library	Cora Ames
Mayville	State Teachers College	Mrs. Hazel W. Byrnes
Milton	Community Library	Mrs. R. T. Wait
Minot	Public Library	Jean Taggert
Minot	State Teachers College	Mrs. Mabel Etheridge
Mohall	Public Library	Dorothy J. Robinson
Mott	Inez Hendrickson Library	Margaret Mooney
Neche	Public Library	Mrs. Herbert Briggs
New England	Public Library	Mrs. J. L. Boucher
New Rockford	Public Library	Vannie Hall
New Salem	Public Library	Lily Geiss
Oakes.	Public Library	Mrs. Edgar Christensen
Park River	Public Library	Mrs. L. N Gullickson
Pembina	Public Library	Mrs. Pauline Brennan
Portal	Public Library	Mrs. W. H. McCauley
Regent	Public Library	Mrs. H. C. Bowers
Rhame	Public Library	Mrs. L. G. Bertschy
Rolla	Public Library	Martha Marchland
Rugby	Public Library	Julia Schneider
St. Thomas	Study Club Library	Mrs. E. T. Thompson
Sanish	Public Library	Mrs. M. J. Olson
Selfridge	Public Library	Mrs. J. A. Caddell
Tioga	Masonic Library	Marian Koolmo
Tolna	Public Library	Mrs. C. S. Hawkins
Towner	Public Library	Mrs. L. Miller
Turtle Lake	Public Library	Mrs. W. N. Harris
Valley City	State Teachers College	Loretta Swift
Valley City	Public Library	Mrs. Helen Tracy
Velva	Public Library	Mrs. Blanche Crawford

Place	Name of Library	Librarian
Verona	Public Library	Mrs. S. G. Felti
Wahpeton	Beach Library	Elizabeth Hoge
Wahpeton	State Science School	Lillian Mirick
Williston	James Memorial Library	Mrs. Ethel Kuenning
Wimbledon	Public Library	Jessie Watne
Wishek	Public Library	Mrs. T. A. Alexander

Seventeenth Annual Report

OF THE

State Library Commission

TO THE

State Board of Administration

STATE LIBRARY COMMISSION STAFF

June 30, 1940

Lillian E. Cook	Secretary and Director
Bessie R. Baldwin	Chief, Traveling Library
Doris L. Hidde	Reference Librarian
Chrissie E. Budge	Stenographer
Wilda Sebastian	Clerk
Clara Graves	Clerk

FOR THE PERIOD

JULY 1, 1938 - JUNE 30, 1940

Biennial

Seventeenth ~~Annual~~ Report

OF THE

State Library Commission

TO THE

State Board of Administration

STATE LIBRARY COMMISSION STAFF

June 30, 1940

Lillian E. Cook	Secretary and Director
Bessie R. Baldwin	Chief, Traveling Library
Doris L. Hidde	Reference Librarian
Chrissie E. Budge	Stenographer
Wilda Sebastian	Clerk
Clara Graves	Clerk

FOR THE PERIOD

JULY 1, 1938 - JUNE 30, 1940

To the State Board of Administration: M. I. Forkner, Chairman, J. D. Harris, R. H. Sherman, Math Dahl, and Arthur E. Thompson, Bismarck, North Dakota.

Herewith is transmitted the Seventeenth Biennial Report of the North Dakota Library Commission, covering the period from July 1, 1938 to June 30, 1940.

REPORT OF THE SECRETARY AND DIRECTOR,

STATE LIBRARY COMMISSION

1938-40

The biennial period shows on the credit side closer cooperation with the public libraries of the state; more service to the residents of the state who are without libraries, as proved by the 3000 additional requests and an increase in circulation of 21,923, to mark an all time high; a slight increase in legislative appropriation (later more than offset by the Commission, in common with other state departments, voluntarily making an 18 per cent cut in its total budget to help bring the state budget within the income); and most welcome additions to the book collection through WPA purchase of 2800 titles, and publishers' gifts of recent juveniles, sent out primarily for exhibit purposes but eventually added to the Commission's collection.

ADMINISTRATION

The Secretary and Director was glad to visit several small libraries which had not been contacted for several years. Both the Commission and the libraries would gain from closer association than has been possible with the travel budget, and it is one thing to work for.

Twice it looked very hopeful that regional service could be established; in the fall of 1938, under the sponsorship of WPA in the western part of the state, and in the Spring of 1940 in Benson County, with the Fort Totten Indian Agency, WPA and the State Library Commission cooperating. Book lists were made out, plans for bookmobiles developed, and a week spent in Minneapolis and St. Paul taking field trips on the county bookmobiles there. The service did not materialize, but the books bought in 1938 by WPA were turned over to the State Library Commission, and plans for regional service may again be renewed.

The monthly lists of inexpensive material for schools, published in the North Dakota Teacher, has been continued; books have been selected to be transcribed into Braille by the North Dakota WPA projects; purchase lists have been checked or made out for institutional, school or small public libraries; traveling exhibits (about 800 books in all) of juvenile books sent to the Commission by publishers, have been sent each spring and fall to the public libraries of the state; help has been given in planning the programs and arranging for district library meetings; time and thought and conferences were devoted to consideration of the possibilities of enlarged library service if federal aid became available; and, in the absence of a reference librarian from January to July, 1940, club programs were developed and, with the help of the staff, the regular reference work carried on.

ADMINISTRATIVE

The administrative work for 1938-40 outlines as follows:

MEETINGS

County Superintendents, January 27, August 11-13, 1938; North Dakota Education Association, October 28, 1938, October 25, 1939, North Dakota Library Association, April 5, 1939, May 11, 1939, May 10, 1940.

District Library meetings at Grafton, Carrington, Ellendale and Flaxton in 1938, and at Leeds, Grafton, Casselton, Ashley and Goodrich in 1939.

Pacific Northwest Library Association, August 1938 (at own expense).

Minnesota Library Association, September 1938, to visit bookmobiles (paid own travel).

American Library Association, Chicago, December 27-31, 1938 (paid half of travel).

Plans for library rooms or buildings: Grand Forks, October 11, 1938; Minot high school library, October 13, 1938; Fargo, January 6, 1939; Mandan, March 10, 1939; Harvey, August 1, 1939; Lisbon, June 10, 1940.

Library and board meeting visits: Lakota, Minot State Teachers College Training School, Jamestown, Dickinson and Valley City in 1938; Drake, Rugby, Leeds, New Rockford, Wishek, Bottineau, Rolla, Mohall, Bowbells, Flaxton, Crosby, Portal, Williston, Dickinson, Beach, New Salem, Hebron, Wahpeton, Lisbon, Fargo and Minot in 1939.

Special meetings: Dunseith, October, 1938. WPA Institutes at Bismarck, June and July, 1940.

REFERENCE DEPARTMENT

For eighteen months, from June, 1938 to January, 1940, Miss Doris Hidde was Reference Librarian and served club women, schools, individuals and various organizations through a constantly increasing circulation. Again it must be noted that only the size of the collection and lack of opportunity of the librarian to contact residents of North Dakota needing books, limits the service. February 1940 marked the largest circulation in the history of the Commission for any single month, with 8,841 books (or about 385 per day), and represents efficient work on the part of librarians and clerks to select, wrap, address and make the records for this volume of service by mail.

New lines of service during the biennium were: (1) the students enrolled with the Department of Correspondence Study and College Extension Classes of the North Dakota Agricultural College; (2) to the music lovers of the state through a loan collection of sheet music. The music service was inaugurated in 1939 with the gift of a collection of piano music from Karl W. Peterson and later supplemented by gifts from Mrs. P. E. Byrne, and collections of octavo vocal music (part songs for women's voices, mixed choruses and male quartets) from the Schumann Club of Minot and the Thursday Music Club of Bismarck. (3) Through the facilities of the State Library Commission, about 800 volumes in Braille were lent to the blind of North Dakota.

TRAVELING LIBRARY DEPARTMENT

The Traveling Library Department has been glad to prepare material for school use in grades one to eight, for the county declamation contests. Suitable prose material has been difficult to obtain, particularly for the lower grades. With the almost prodigal outpouring of children's books these days the task of selecting an incident belonging to the child's level of experience, cutting it to dramatic briefness but leaving the literary value, has been a pleasant one. The collection now numbers 78 prose cuttings and 140 poems. It has an author and title index and is divided into upper and lower grade prose, and upper and lower grade poetry.

It has taken long, steady and persistent effort to win a place for this type of prose declamation, which has no melodramatic appeal and no showiness before an audience, but the steady demand for it has been proof of its worth. These declamations bring freshness and wear well.

For the adult readers "Necessity was the mother of invention." With the aid of the WPA Mending Project, still interesting though not of recent publication, was made physically attractive with bright covers and thorough cleaning. Letters were sent to a number of places using community libraries suggesting the use of this additional fiction during the winter. Repeat orders have proved the success of this experiment. One order asked for one of our "rehabilitated libraries," which perhaps describes them pretty well.

The gain in circulation over the last biennium is gratifying, a gain of 5,985 books. Circulation for the traveling libraries is counted by the number of books in each box as it is shipped, not the number of people who read the book while it stays in the community.

THE STATE

Growth

Reports are on file from eight new libraries: Forman, Hebron, Milnor, Oberon, Petersburg, Rhame, Selfridge, and Zeeland. The Bowbells library is closed while seeking new quarters; the collections at Garrison, McHenry and Tioga were turned over to the school libraries, leaving a net gain of four libraries. To these may be added 15 libraries which, after a lapse, have sent in their reports to the State Library Commission for the period 1938-1940; Beach, Edgeley, Flaxton, Hansboro, Harvey, Hettinger, Kulm, Leonard, Milton, Sanish, Sheyenne, Tolna, Verona, Watford City and Wimbledon.

Advance

Another type of growth is shown in Mandan, where library service has been made free to all city borrowers; in Rugby, where the library board was reorganized according to the state library law and a working appropriation secured; in Bismarck, which has its first full-time cataloger; in Grand Forks, where hospital service was inaugurated; in Jamestown, where branch service is now offered at Washington School; in Minot, which has its first trained children's librarian, and at Mayville State Teachers College, which established rural adult circulation.

Buildings

Fargo Public Library has been entirely made over under PWA; Dickinson doubled its size with the completion of a new wing with WPA help, and has a most attractive children's room; Mandan moved into the Community Building, selling its old, outgrown building; Beach moved into the new City Hall, with pleasant and permanent quarters; fire destroyed the building and most of the contents of the Lisbon Public Library. The library board is now working on plans for a new building to be erected on the lot which they already had; McHenry also suffered loss by fire, but the books were saved; Harvey moved into the new school building.

Federal

For another two years the libraries of the state are indebted to government agencies for much help. The WPA has provided many hours of labor by women in both public and school ilbraries, and has rehabilitated buildings and furniture. The NYA-in-school students have worked some in public libraries but largely in school systems. The excellence of the work done has resulted in old projects being continued and new ones started in the following towns during the biennium:

Mending and Library Service. Beulah, Bismarck, Bottineau, Bowbells, Bowman, Carrington, Devils Lake, Dickinson, Fargo Public Library and Agricultural College Library, Grafton, Grand Forks Public Library and University Library, Hoople, Lakota, Langdon, Lidgerwood, Lisbon, Mandan, Mayville, Minot, Mott, New Rockford, Portal, Tioga, Towner, Valley City Public Library and State Teachers College Library, and Wahpeton.

Acting Librarian: Ashley, Crosby, Enderlin, Gackle, Halliday, Mohall, New Salem, Towner and Oberon.

Work on Library Building: Bismarck, Dickinson, Fargo Public Library and the Agricultural College Library, Grand Forks, Valley City. The Fargo Public Library was remodeled by PWA.

N. Y. A. Workers: Flaxton, Halliday, Hettinger, Hillsboro, Linton, Oakes, Selfridge and Velva.

Braille Books: The books transcribed into Braille by WPA workers have been bound by the Library Project workers and are on deposit at the State Library Commission, where they are circulated throughout the state. About 800 volumes have been circulated in the past two years.

During the past two years the records show 130,935 hours of book mending, 40,807 of library service, and 116,999 books mended.

The book situation at the State Library Commission would have been much more drastic during these months of reduced buying had it not been for the volumes purchased by the WPA for Commission use. The initial purchase for the proposed bookmobile, with many Reading Circle titles, and the subsequent monthly purchases have been responsible to a large extent for the Commission's ability to meet book demands in the state as fully as it has. The only current adult books added to the Commission's collection at this time are those purchased by WPA.

LILLIAN E. COOK,

Secretary and Director
State Library Commission.

STATISTICAL REPORT, 1938-40

Books

Traveling Library:

Number of traveling libraries	414
Number of libraries added during biennium	38
Number of books added during period	680
Number of books in libraries	15,290

Reference Department:

Number of books	19,207
Number of books added during biennium	924
Number of pamphlets in collection	18,860

Circulation

Traveling Library:

Number of libraries circulated:	1938-39	1939-40	Total
School	511	474	981
Community	124	134	258
Number of books shipped	22,112	22,233	44,345
Number of new stations			215
Reference Department:			
Number of requests during biennium	11,060	11,837	22,897
Number of books circulated	44,381	51,666	96,047
Number of magazines and pamphlets	10,514	10,272	20,785
Total Reference circulation	54,895	61,938	116,833
Total commission circulation	77,007	84,171	161,178

PUBLIC LIBRARIES

Town	Date established	1940 population	RECEIPTS: Tax Appropriation 1938-39	RECEIPTS: Tax Appropriation 1939-40	RECEIPTS: Total 1938-39	RECEIPTS: Total 1939-40
Bismarck	1914	15,141	$ 9,750.00	$10,250.00	$11,120.95	$11,581.83
Bowman	1916	965	406.63	470.48	543.87	556.34
Carrington	1906	1,850	1,200.00	1,200.02	2,337.15	2,443.55
Casselton	1906	1,367	261.82	279.78	294.67	308.50
Devils Lake	1898	5,902	3,636.58	1,479.02	6,155.54	6,757.30
Dickinson	1908	5,836	1,750.00	1,750.00	....	5,306.65
Ellendale	1912	1,515	375.00	375.00	611.22	599.09
Fargo	1900	32,571	19,223.50	21,670.26	[illegible]751.69	31,312.64
Grafton	1895	4,064	1,100.00	3,200.00	2,272.18	4,339.02
Grand Forks	1899	20,186	12,000.00	9,924.26	14,239.36	12,275.42
Jamestown	1901	8,784	1,000.00	4,000.00	5,787.46	5,371.31
Lakota	1906	908	335.00	....	361.31	....
LaMoure	1924	989	600.00	600.00	655.20	[illegible]61
Leonard	1913	....	120.00	125.00	....	128.13
Lidgerwood	1913	1,043	700.00	725.00	[illegible]18	902.97
Lisbon	1915	1,994	1,123.69	1,387.13	2,298.02	7,889.83
Mayville	1900	1,350	650.00	750.00	[illegible]40	862.45
Minot	1908	16,569	5,951.47	7,713.83	11,642.62	11,742.84
Mott	1912	1,219	360.00	360.00	384.73	373.88
Oakes	1905	1,666	924.49	1,254.09	[illegible]04	1,851.89
Park River	1900	1,406	400.00	308.59	453.84	308.59
Rugby	1912	2,171	185.60	603.76	221.41	767.76
Valley City	1900	5,910	3,000.00	4,443.54	1,959.73	5,072.97
Wahpeton	....	3,707	4,000.00	1,000.00	6,451.03	5,809.15
Williston	1910	5,713	2,089.41	8[illegible]2.19	1,385.42	4,107.74
Wishek	1926	1,112	100.00	100.00	105.42	103.00

PUBLIC LIBRARIES

EXPENDITURES

Town	Salaries		Maintenance		Books-Periodicals		Totals	
	1938-39	1939-40	1938-39	1939-40	1938-39	1939-40	1938-39	1939-40
Bismarck	$ 5,565.02	$ 5,986.26	$ 931.77	$ 1,055.49	$ 2,553.63	$ 2,505.64	$ 10,852.17	$ 11,439.48
Bowman	300.00	300.00	79.27	67.39	79.27	82.25	518.47	503.95
Carrington	630.00	666.00	86.58	39.02	203.59	305.84	1,098.03	1,070.53
Casselton	29.00	96.00	....	....	200.96	197.21	250.92	318.50
ls Lake	1,320.00	1,320.00	915.39	590.48	1,528.36	1,416.82	4,416.11	4,394.91
Dickinson	1,817.50	1,938.25	420.75	440.51	702.80	995.28	10,335.04	5,042.88
ile	370.00	370.00	3.28	2.30	154.97	152.93	559.98	577.12
Fargo	[illegible]	8,253.75	936.15	1,463.70	2,554.05	3,628.82	27,032.84	24,190.18
Grafton	780.00	780.00	373.68	1,545.68	381.62	414.13	1,862.28	2,042.78
Grand Forks	4,703.08	5,620.46	1,761.82	823.31	2,557.90	2,251.40	12,828.19	11,502.79
Jamestown	2,402.35	2,392.17	789.32	694.25	1,131.16	1,168.01	5,302.09	4,995.79
Ldta	18.00	312.00	133.00	76.00	29.06	29.50	319.56	419.50
LaMoure	300.00	315.00	52.54	40.16	172.88	191.97	565.61	614.31
Leonard	75.00	75.00	....	....	50.00	.88	124.00	75.88
Lidgerwood	420.00	490.00	151.46	78.26	130.21	118.05	867.63	770.89
on	437.50	437.50	323.90	359.99	239.07	352.88	1,226.34	1,169.51
Mayville	240.00	240.00	333.81	213.71	100.65	107.73	810.40	676.53
Mot	3,080.00	3,918.20	484.44	431.49	2,285.08	2,319.97	8,443.42	7,270.56
Mott	300.00	300.00	....	....	86.25	66.88	382.55	373.88
aes	630.00	630.00	....	....	210.21	403.78	878.44	1,115.34
Park River	280.00	210.00	....	....	[illegible]	40.94	423.02	338.40
Rugby	52,.00	390.00	....	....	101.94	80.03	173.11	593.39
alley City	1,448.00	1,451.00	1,747.35	1,018.40	626.22	619.38	1,499.01	4,080.36
Wahpeton	1,307.77	1,294.90	1,266.38	532.18	1,146.00	1,220.41	4,832.59	4,275.84
Williston	1,560.06	1,250.75	544.45	547.80	[illegible]	99.25	3,273.08	2,816.59
Wishek	56.00	53.00	....	....	....	....	80.32	64.26

PUBLIC LIBRARIES

Town	Circulation 1938-39	Circulation 1939-40	Total	Volumes	Borrowers	Hours Open Week	Rural Borrowers
Bismarck	184,064	173,809	357,873	17,928	7,016	63	....
Bowman	4,392	4,629	9,021	6,868	570	30	....
Carrington	18,073	15,236	33,309	6,356	1,093	30	210
Casselton	2,418	2,750	5,168	1,067	200	4	....
Devils Lake	34,041	32,435	66,476	11,219	1,740	30	28
Dickinson	60,415	58,058	118,473	13,897	3,356	42	274
Ellendale	16,103	17,431	33,534	4,810	1,015	14	350
Fargo	203,059	199,878	402,937	35,998	12,860	72	342
Grafton	24,077	24,472	48,549	6,647	1,509	24	3
Grand Forks	78,308	92,877	171,180	20,066	6,688	66	106
Jamestown	80,656	75,833	6,489	,384	5,529	54	686
Lakota	5,573	4,743	10,316	6,041	220	9	6
LaMoure	6,386	6,739	13,125	3,789	1,022	6	427
Leonard	1,550	1,150	3,241	2,091	137	6	....
Lidgerwood	7,359	6,617	13,976	4,521	720	31	392
Lisbon	13,317	14,024	27,341	887	1,200	27	165
Mayville	3,786	4,361	8,147	4,457	601	12	....
Minot	90,824	96,103	6,927	1,973	8,085	72	60
Mott	3,876	4,269	8,145	3,726	1,232	6	428
Oakes	22,965	22,688	45,653	6,932	1,197	30	366
Park River	3,750	4,500	8,250	2,490	421	20	140
Rugby	5,041	11,193	16,234	4,924	890	31	254
Valley City	36,041	8,305	74,346	4,985	3,236	36	368
Wahpeton	27,521	33,732	61,253	0,168	2,373	30	491
Williston	33,821	27,468	1,889	9,816	3,542	42	459
Wishek	....	5,200	....	1,314	412	4	....

ASSOCIATION LIBRARIES GIVING FREE SERVICE

Town	Date Estab-lished	1940 Popu-lation	Munici-pal Help	Hours per Week	Vol-umes	Bor-rowers	Circula-tion	1938-1940 Expenditures Books	Total
Barney	1937	....	Room	2	120	25	300	....	....
Bathgate	1916	314		2	1,501	152	5,050	$ 64.54	$ 92.82
Beach	1912	1,174	Room $120	6	2,146	411	5,900	124.50	265.51
Bottineau	1915	1,679	Room	2	596	115	600	....	....
Crosby	1930	1,403	Room $35	13	2,853	1,022	17,091	105.61	133.44
Drake	1920	653	Room	3	1,789	700	8,200	146.28	168.89
Enderlin	1912	1,596	Room	5	4,145	518	7,100	334.36	348.98
[illegible]	1935	358	Room	6	1,115	130*	6,350	106.30	118.30
Forman	1939	502		6	415	65	1,400	....	8.00
Gackle	1936	537	$15	2	538	154	696	5.31	5.31
Goodrich	1926	426	Room $25	2	970	45	2,274	28.00	43.15
Halliday	1937	396	$10	22	716	200	4,400	20.00	75.50
Hankinson	1907	1,420	Room $60	4	4,400	544*	2,845	20.00	140.00
Heaton	1915	110		30	585	75	850	13.81	18.37
Hebron	1938	1,268		48	510	388	4,625	11.80	194.89
Hager	1912	1,150	Room	12	900	80	2,350	14.50	14.50
Hillsboro	1936	1,334	Room	10	1,050	150	5,000	210.00	235.00
Hoople	1937	346	Room $50	1½	1,040	....	3,750	61.00	76.00
Kim	1937	735	Room	2	360	85	3,850	29.25	44.85
Leeds	1902	780	Room $50	6	2,279	248	7,641	75.00	176.45
Lion	1936	1,602		6	1,025	265*	6,750	190.00	190.00
McHenry	1936	250	Room	2	200	140	1,800	....	....
(Destroyed by fire, [illegible], 1939)									
Mandan	1896	6,722	Room	10	5,014	850	14,450	207.33	464.85
Minor	1939	678	Room Mtce.	7	600	190	450	....	....
Mill	1937	687	Room $6.75	15	1,555	153*	300	80.42	164.86
New England	1931	891	Room	3	1,480	160	499	36.42	60.80
New Salem	1935	875	Room	24	1,900	150	5,000	40.00	59.00
Pembina	1916	702			1,735	86	6,650	56.00	136.00

ASSOCIATION LIBRARIES GIVING FREE SERVICE (Con't)

Town	Date lished Estab-	1940 lation Popu-	Munici- pal Help	Hours per Week	Vol- mes	Bor- rowers	Circula- tion	1938-1940 Expenditures Books	1938-1940 Expenditures Total
Petersburg	1938	284		2	546	95*	1,850	$ 73.73	$130.95
Portal	1935	499	Room	2	766	100	3,500	32.50	69.32
Sanish	1928	453		1	619	66	3,200	38.34	642
Selfridge	1938	329	Room	48	290	139	2,460	....	....
Sheyenne	1928	431	Room	1½	1,100	125	2,400	41.89	57.00
Tolna	1926	171	Room	2	605	150	6,750	43.00	70.00
Towner	1927	920	Room	10	1,135	185	5,327	2.67	60.87
Velva	1921	1,013	Room Me.	15	5,700	525	17,500	50.00	60.00
Verona	1925	200	Room $50	2	145	60	3,750	....	60.00

*Serves county also.

ASSOCIATION LIBRARIES CHARGING FOR SERVICE

Town	Date Estab-lished	1940 Popu-lation	Munici-pal Help	Hours per Week	Vol-umes	Bor-rowers	Circula-tion	1938-1940 Expenditures Books	Total
Ashley	1913	1,345	Room $50	18	3,905	485	13,677	$246.53	$329.28
Beulah	1931	939	Room	1½	1,501	29	2,850	41.72	62.39
Cando	1902	1,277	$48	2	4,550	104†	3,450	75.00	200.00
Cavalier	1915	1,105	Heat	6	2,050	386*	3,350	108.57	140.97
Cogswell	1935	431		3	2,030	60	3,500	....	45.00
Courtenay	1916	297	Room	2½	534	108	1,040	....	6.04
Dawson	1932	263	Room	3	1,000	108*	4,000	27.13	34.66
Edgeley	1912	802	Room $50	2	2,400	52*	3,940	84.60	90.60
Hamilton	1916	255		2	973	90*	1,560	30.00	30.00
Hansboro	1928	195		2½	524	41	1,450	....	8.79
Harvey	1909	1,948	Room	3	904	556	2,350	82.91	108.90
Hope	1910	472	Room	3	1,128	85	3,950	82.91	92.74
Langdon	1912	1,542	Room $150	8	6,615	350*†	31,250	285.12	572.54
Milnor	1940	678	Room Me.	13	575	340	450	....	....
Milton	1923	309	Room	2	958	42	2,350	20.45	20.45
New Rockford	1907	2,023	Room $216	6	3,600	40	7,360	82.00	598.49
Oberon	1938	......		6	500	325	1,500	20.00	26.00
Regent	1935	308	Room	3	801	63	2,100	....	51.16
Rhame	1938	281		4	500	40*	700	20.00	60.00
Rolla	1924	1,006	Room	2	1,283	75	2,670	130.22	179.14
St. Thomas	1917	502	$84.02	2½	2,504	310	11,691	172.02	257.69
Turtle Lake	1926	635	Room	2	1,425	41†	6,150	49.50	....
Watford City	1924	1,165		4	1,765	165	9,051	147.00	291.00
Wimbledon	1915	357	Room	2	1,239	44	1,250	34.15	42.35
Zeeland	1937	489	Room	1	175	28	2,000	....	....

*Free to grades.
†Serves county also.

STATE DIRECTORY

Town	Name of Library	Librarian
Ashley	Public Library	Mrs. Viola H. Wishek
Barney	Public Library	Mrs. James Little
Bathgate	Public Library	Mrs. H. G. Thomson
Beach	Public Library	Mrs. R. E. Arnold
Beulah	Public Library	Mrs. F. C. Worch
Bismarck	Public Library	Erana Stadler
Bismarck	State Library Commission	Lillian E. Cook
Bismarck	State Historical Library	Mrs. Florence Davis
Bismarck	State Law Library	Mr. E. J Taylor
Bottineau	School of Forestry	Ruth Clausen
Bottineau	Public Library	Mrs. C. P. Russell
Bowman	Clara Lincoln Phelan Memorial Library	Mrs. Mertie Pond
Cando	Public Library	Mai Riggs
Carrington	Public Library	Mrs. Ella Mae Hargrave
Casselton	Public Library	Mrs. L. E. Correll
Cavalier	Public Library	Mrs. A. Harris
Cogswell	Public Library	Olive M. Bartlett
Courtenay	Public Library	Mrs. A. A. Hoffman
Crosby	Public Library	Mrs. J. H. Phelps
Dawson	Public Library	Mrs. J. A. Kooker
Devils Lake	Carnegie Library	Marie E. O'Brien
Dickinson	Public Library	Gertrude Voldal
Dickinson	State Teachers College	Matilda L. Stoxen
Drake	Public Library	Mrs. E. Van Horn
Edgeley	Public Library	Mrs. G. J. Lee
Ellendale	Public Library	Mrs. V. D. Coleman
Ellendale	Normal & Industrial School	Ruth McCarthy
Enderlin	Public Library	Mrs. G. H. Flynn
Fargo	Public Library	Inga L. Rynning
Fargo	Masonic Library	Clara Richards
Fargo	Agricultural College Library	Mrs. Ethel McVeety
Flaxton	Public Library	Mrs. A. H. Buckwitz
Forman	Public Library	Mrs. W. C. King
Gackle	Public Library	Mrs. J. M. Hummel
Goodrich	Public Library	Mrs. J. R. Doering
Grafton	Public Library	Mrs. Emma B. Cobb
Grand Forks	Public Library	Irma Walker
Grand Forks	University Library	Della Mathys
Halliday	Public Library	Mrs. Malcolm Pippin
Hamilton	Public Library	Mrs. Andrew Knutson
Hankinson	Public Library	Esther Spreckles
Hansboro	Public Library	Mrs. L. C. Agarand
Harvey	Public Library	Mrs. A. B. Hannes
Heaton	Public Library	Howard I. Turner
Hebron	Public Library	Mrs. A. E. Funk
Hettinger	Public Library	Mrs. J. O. Wigen
Hillsboro	Public Library	Emogene Anderson
Hoople	Public Library	Mrs. J. O. Wallum
Hope	Public Library	Mrs. D. J. Gumb
Jamestown	Alfred Dickey Free Public Library	Mercedes Muenz
Jamestown	Jamestown College Library	Pearl Carlson
Jamestown	State Hospital for Insane	Dr. A. M. Fisher
Kulm	Public Library	Mrs. C. O. Ferguson

STATE DIRECTORY

Town	Name of Library	Librarian
Lakota	Public Library	Mrs. Ellen Hullett
LaMoure	Public Library	Mrs. Carl Neverman
Langdon	Public Library	Mrs. E. J. Donovan
Leeds	Public Library	Mrs. Albert Johnson
Leonard	Watts Free Library	Mrs. Maymie Peterson
Lidgerwood	Public Library	Mrs. Elizabeth Kings
Linton	Public Library	Alice Stewart
Lisbon	Public Library	Berniece Johnson
Mandan	Public Library	Mrs. J. A. Biggs
Mayville	Public Library	Cora I. Ames
Mayville	State Teachers College Library	Mrs. Hazel W. Byrnes
Milnor	Public Library	Jeane Hanson
Milton	Public Library	Mrs. M. McCullough
Minot	Public Library	Barbara Williams
Minot	State Teachers College Library	Mrs. Mabel Etheridge
Mohall	Public Library	Eliza A. Paris
Mott	Inez Hendrickson Library	Margaret Mooney
New England	Public Library	Mrs. J. L. Boucher
New Rockford	Public Library	Vannie A. Hall
New Salem	Public Library	Mrs. Adelaide Schwartz
Oakes	Public Library	Mrs. Edgar Christensen
Oberon	Public Library	Mrs. O. C. Haskin
Park River	Public Library	Mrs. Lloyd N. Gullickson
Pembina	Public Library	Mrs. Pauline Brennan
Petersburg	Public Library	Mattie Leite
Portal	Public Library	Mrs. Madeleine Swenson
Regent	Public Library	Mrs. George Trunkill
Rhame	Public Library	Mrs. Mae Oien
Rolla	Public Library	Mrs. Martha Marchand
Rugby	Public Library	Mrs. Elsie M. Fagan
St. Thomas	Public Library	Mrs. E. T. Thompson
Sanish	Public Library	Mrs. H. E. Helvey
Selfridge	Public Library	Max Erker
Sheyenne	Public Library	Mrs. G. Moe
Tolna	Public Library	Mrs. C. A. Porter
Towner	Public Library	Mrs. William Leach
Turtle Lake	Public Library	Mrs. E. Melby
Valley City	Carnegie Public Library	Mrs. Helen H. Tracy
Valley City	State Teachers College Library	Loretta Swift
Velva	Public Library	Mrs. Walter Hobbs
Verona	Public Library	Mrs. V. A. Myrah
Wahpeton	Leach Public Library	Helen Lincoln
Watford City	Masonic Library	R. M. Christensen
Williston	James Memorial Library	Mrs. Sylvia R. Monson
Wimbledon	Public Library	Mrs. E. H. Neiss
Wishek	Public Library	Mrs. J. W. Hofer
Zeeland	Public Library	Mrs. A. E. Boschee

Eighteenth Biennial Report

of the

State Library Commission

to the

State Board of Administration

For the Period July 1, 1950—June 30, 1952

Eighteenth Biennial Report

of the

State Library Commission

to the

State Board of Administration

STATE LIBRARY COMMISSION STAFF

June 30, 1942

Lillian E. Cook	Secretary and Director
Lois Waldron	Librarian
Mildred Lippert	Assistant Librarian
Chrissie E. Budge	Stenographer
Wilda Sebastian	Clerk
Clara Graves	Clerk

FOR THE PERIOD

JULY 1, 1940 - JUNE 30, 1942

TO THE STATE BOARD OF ADMINISTRATION: M. I. Forkner, Chairman, J. D. Harris, R. H. Sherman, Math Dahl, and Arthur E. Thompson, Bismarck, North Dakota.

Herewith is transmitted the Eighteenth Biennial Report of the North Dakota State Library Commission covering the period from July 1, 1940 to June 30, 1942.

REPORT OF THE SECRETARY AND DIRECTOR, NORTH DAKOTA STATE LIBRARY COMMISSION — 1940-1942

The regular activities of the State Library Commission were carried on during the 1940-42 biennium. These are not mentioned, but certain activities are presented in outline.

Library Visits

Public libraries were visited, WPA library projects inspected, and conferences held at:

Barney	Grand Forks	New Rockford
Beach	Halliday	Oakes
Bottineau	Jamestown	Oberon
Carrington	Killdeer	Pembina
Casselton	Lakota	Portal
Crosby	Leonard	Sanish
Dickinson	Lidgerwood	Sheyenne
Ellendale	Lisbon	St. John
Fargo	Minot	Stanley
Flaxton	Mohall	Wahpeton
Forman	Mott	Watford City
Goodrich	New England	Williston

Institution and special libraries were visited at:

Belcourt Indian School	Teachers College, Dickinson
Elbowoods Indian School	Teachers College, Minot
Ft. Totten Indian School	Teachers College, Valley City
Dunseith Sanitarium	State Agricultural College, Fargo
Harvey High School	University of North Dakota, Grand Forks
Minot High School	State Science School, Wahpeton

Meetings Attended

The secretary and director attended the following meetings and appeared on the programs of most of them:

District library meetings at Edgeley, Forman, Grafton, Harvey, Hope, and Rugby.

North Dakota Education Association, Grand Forks, 1940.

North Dakota Education Association, Minot, 1941.

North Dakota Library Association, State Program Committee, Fargo, March 22, 1941, Minot, May 22, 1941, Bismarck, May 14, 1942.

WPA Adult Education Conference, July 10, 1940.

WPA Vocational Education Conference, July 25, 1940.

WPA Library Institute, Bismarck, June 24-26, 1941.

Forum Leaders' Training, Bismarck, November 1940 and May, 1941.

Citizens' Morale Conference, Bismarck, February 7, 1942.

Dairy Council, Bismarck, April 22, 1942.

Women's Defense Council, Bismarck, May 9, 1942.

American Library Association, midwinter meeting at Chicago, December, 1941, and the Annual Convention, Milwaukee, as the Governor's representative, June, 1942.

Special

Institute for all WPA library workers of North Dakota, planned and held in Bismarck, June, 1941.

Supplement to Bulletin No. 5, the elementary school book-list, prepared for the State Department of Public Instruction.

DRAWBACKS

Loss of WPA library workers throughout the state.

Withdrawal of 3,896 WPA books from the collection of the State Library Commission.

Rising costs along all lines, resulting in budget shortages.

Advance in travel and book postage rates.

Drop in circulation, for the first time since 1924.

Libraries closed in Barney, Courtenay, Milnor, Milton, Pembina, Selfridge, Towner and Zeeland.

Failure of bookmobile plans at Ft. Totten and Minot to materialize.

GAINS

State:

Libraries opened in Elbowoods, Killdeer, Lehr, and Northwood.

Municipal support secured by the Mandan Public Library.

Campaigns for municipal support in Forman and Turtle Lake.

Commission:

Closer cooperation with the State Department of Public Instruction, with our book-lists and library helps going out with their bulletins.

More successful fall and spring traveling book exhibits, with a larger number of books exhibited and a larger attendance.

LILLIAN E. COOK
Secretary and Director
State Library Commission

STATISTICAL REPORT, 1940-42

BOOKS

Traveling Library Department

Number of traveling libraries	432
Number of libraries added during this biennium	28
Number of books added during the period	525
Number of books in traveling libraries	15,425

Reference Department

Number of books in this department	16,944
Number of books added during this biennium	1,273
Number of pamphlets in collection	19,000

CIRCULATION

Traveling Library Department

Number of Libraries Circulated	1940-41	1941-42	Total
Schools	469	808	1,277
Communities	88	163	251
Number of books circulated	19,338	14,469	33,807
New T. L. stations	124	127	251

Reference Department

Number of requests filled	11,749	9,144	20,893
Number of books circulated	54,499	51,060	105,559
Magazines & pamphlets sent out	9,274	5,829	15,103
Total reference dept. circulation	63,773	56,889	120,662
TOTAL CIRCULATION OF COMMISSION	83,111	71,358	154,469

PUBLIC LIBRARIES

Town	Date Established	1940 population	RECEIPTS Tax Appropriation 1940-41	1941-42	Total Receipts 1940-41	1941-42
Bismarck	1914	15,496	$10,650.00	$11,650.00	$11,930.06	$12,749.34
Bowman	1916	967	261.11	[illegible]	329.95	921.70
Carrington	1906	1,850	1,200.00	1,200.00	1,280.28	1,200.00
Casselton	1906	1,358	303.46	307.94	332.46	328.99
Devils Lake	1898	6,204	3,733.26	4,141.48	4,298.14	4,696.02
Dickinson	1908	5,839	4,750.00	4,750.00	5,112.30	5,118.47
Ellendale	1912	1,517	375.00	375.00	580.30	564.96
Fargo	1900	32,580	21,026.56	20,735.21	22,422.08	21,763.24
Grafton	1895	4,070	1,200.00	1,200.00	1,820.38	1,763.43
Grand Forks	1899	20,228	10,750.00	10,500.00	11,629.03	11,408.12
Jamestown	1901	8,790	3,950.00	4,000.00	5,084.97	4,699.90
Lakota	1906	907	722.04	464.91	749.40	499.03
LaMoure	1924	990	600.00	600.00	631.33	618.74
Leonard Township	1912	465	125.00	125.00	128.83	126.42
Lidgerwood	1913	1,042	650.00	755.00	811.06	856.93
Lisbon	1915	1,997	1,279.52	1,330.19	1,392.03	1,435.63
Mayville	1900	1,351	750.00	750.00	914.86	890.02
Minot	1908	16,577	7,692.04	8,387.97	8,524.14	9,219.14
Mott	1912	1,220	335.00	360.00	363.00	347.80
Oakes	1905	1,665	1,050.92	797.35	1,145.96	1,002.84
Park River	1900	1,408	....	[illegible]	....	417.28
Rugby	1912	2,215	600.00	1,400.00	689.14	1,494.82
Valley City	1900	5,917	3,270.70	4,508.44	3,390.37	4,640.64
Wahpeton	....	3,747	4,500.00	4,000.00	4,758.24	4,193.08
Williston	1910	5,790	2,560.85	4,341.70	2,764.55	4,465.94
Wishek	1926	1,112	100.00	150.00	107.58	157.46

PUBLIC LIBRARIES

Town	EXPENDITURES Salaries 1940-41	Salaries 1941-42	Maintenance 1940-41	Maintenance 1941-42	Books-Periodicals 1940-41	Books-Periodicals 1941-42	Total 1940-41	Total 1941-42
Bismarck	$ 6,236.48	$ 6,706.25	$ 2,923.75	$ 3,187.20	$ 2,506.32	$ 2,849.54	$1 [illegible]55	$12,742.99
Bowman	300.00	300.00	288.66	409.00	101.91	107.06	690.57	816.06
Carrington	676.00	672.00	84.27	164.14	477.43	280.87	1,237.70	1,117.01
[illegible]on	104.00	104.00	59.18	12.00	137.45	102.00	300.63	218.00
D[illegible]ls Lake	1,320.00	1,320.00	1,713.18	1,274.49	1,937.35	1,849.62	4,970.53	4,444.11
Dickinson	2,075.00	2,116.25	965.61	1,138.30	3[illegible]2.64	1,275.80	4,403.25	4,530.35
Ellendale	370.00	370.00	31.07	24.31	185.81	170.33	586.88	564.64
Fargo	9,878.00	10,104.25	3,653.24	4,420.30	1,600.55	3,392.17	18,131.79	17,916.72
Grafton	780.00	780.00	658.96	656.22	122.76	328.06	1,861.72	1,764.28
Grand Forks	5,658.91	5,437.91	3,154.67	3,837.63	1,908.05	2,346.41	10,721.63	11,799.63
Jamestown	2,477.94	2,489.85	1,563.82	1,173.95	736.73	820.54	4,778.49	4,484.34
Lakota	216.00	216.00	159.91	211.38	45.85	36.62	421.76	464.00
LaMoure	300.00	300.00	71.77	135.79	182.58	195.48	554.35	631.27
Leonard	75.00	75.00	....	....	24.00	....	136.35	102.46
Lidgerwood	472.00	461.00	264.39	267.38	136.04	153.78	872.84	882.16
Lisbon	437.50	437.50	466.83	1,280.66	365.07	390.16	1,269.40	2,108.32
Mayville	240.00	240.00	542.03	521.87	194.84	194.47	976.87	521.87
Minot	3,600.00	4,030.75	2,108.79	1,730.41	2,463.10	2,915.99	8,171.89	8,677.15
Mott	300.00	275.00	....	....	63.00	71.75	371.00	347.25
Oakes	699.00	750.00	112.01	130.77	456.53	394.05	[illegible]54	1,274.82
Park River	270.00	270.00	20.90	9.70	174.62	85.50	[illegible]52	365.20
Rugby	460.00	705.50	95.14	106.97	112.86	302.81	668.00	1,114.28
Valley City	1,465.00	1,477.25	1,280.32	1,263.63	864.09	534.28	3,609.41	3,358.62
Wahpeton	1,448.54	1,582.11	1,691.24	1,337.43	1,360.76	[illegible]57	4,500.54	3,631.11
Williston	1,125.07	1,441.81	[illegible]16	1,587.70	85.03	373.97	2,868.26	3,403.48
Wishek	52.00	53.00	12.21	21.49	12.56	39.43	76.78	113.92

PUBLIC LIBRARIES

Town	Circulation 1940-41	Circulation 1941-42	Total	Volumes	Borrowers	Hours Open Week	Rural Borrowers
Bismarck	151,106	144,147	295,253	19,572	6,967	63	....
Bowman	3,879	3,772	7,601	6,818	541	30	....
Carrington	14,467	11,690	26,157	6,869	1,185	30	245
Casselton	3,450	4,042	7,492	1,934	313	4	....
Devils Lake	28,852	30,814	59,666	12,154	3,863	36	30
Dickinson	54,756	48,743	103,499	15,882	3,066	42	278
Ellendale	14,741	14,463	29,204	5,176	950	15	325
Fargo	214,666	205,804	420,470	41,210	17,111	72	438
Grafton	22,078	16,366	38,444	6,882	1,527	24	4
Grand Forks	94,530	85,019	179,549	20,900	6,521	66	133
Jamestown	73,549	67,016	140,565	14,509	4,451	54	511
Lakota	4,290	3,946	8,236	5,242	171	9	17
LaMoure	6,650	5,405	12,055	4,062	979	6	425
Leonard Township	1,300	1,409	2,709	1,881	120	6	30
Lidgerwood	7,202	7,004	14,206	6,189	853	39	503
Lisbon	13,022	14,234	27,256	1,990	780	27	210
Mayville	4,987	4,757	9,744	4,786	605	8	....
Minot	89,647	83,907	173,554	19,565	6,202	54	73
Mott	5,850	4,083	9,933	3,885	1,033	6	188
Oakes	24,460	23,084	47,544	7,490	1,379	36	396
Park River	5,700	7,500	13,200	2,823	255	16	131
Rugby	12,271	14,138	26,409	6,132	2,307	33	103
Valley City	37,164	31,661	68,825	15,217	3,4[illegible]0	36	406
Wahpeton	30,744	27,201	57,945	9,649	1,959	27	271
Williston	18,355	16,882	35,237	10,180	3,659	36	391
Wishek	5,000	6,250	11,250	1,409	410	4	125

ASSOCIATION LIBRARIES GIVING FREE SERVICE

Town	Date Established	1940 Population	Municipal Help	Hrs. Per Week	Volumes	Borrowers	Circulation	1940-1942 Expenditures Books	Total
Bathgate	1916	312	None	2	1,313	312	2,800	$ 73.57	$131.50
Beach	1912	1,178	Room $120	6	2,461	580	6,650	177.31	414.31
[illegible]h	1931	942	Room	4	1,603	285	3,350	41.93	64.67
Bottineau	1915	1,739	Room	2	791	167	2,450	91.06	95.00
Cogswell	1935	430	None	3	2,213	121	2,[illegible]00	40.00	98.53
Crosby	1930	1,404	Room $50	15	4,012	997	18,050	344.86	491.03
Dawson	1932	263	Room	3	1,125	131	2,800	7.64	12.96
[illegible]ake	1920	654	Room	3	1,872	500	6,700	148.52	182.29
[illegible]lds	1941	......	None	9	1,600	[illegible]41	7,250	25.00	45.00
Enderlin	1912	1,593	Room	4	3,118	511	6,000	343.96	434.18
Flaxton	1935	362	Room	3	1,620	203	3,550	60.00	82.00
Forman	1939	500	$138	6	876	65	5,500	73.22	78.22
[illegible]e	1936	537	None	2	577	158	2,212	16.30	20.32
[illegible]h	1926	476	Room $50	2	670	80	5,250	None Reported	
Halliday	1937	395	$60	13	849	209	6,550	35.00	[illegible]00
Hamilton	1916	255	None	2	956	46	1,550	45.00	45.00
Hankinson	1907	1,420	Room $60	4	2,370	175	2,477	7.60	127.60
Heaton	1915	110	None	30	577	......	......	10.89	10.89
Hebron	1938	1,267	Room $104	5	772	282	5,550	9.97	83.18
Hettinger	1912	1,138	Room	3	910	80	2,550	25.00	75.00
Hoople	1937	346	Room	1½	......	109	1,500	68.70	108.70
Killdeer	......	650	None	2	493	50	1,850	15.18	23.51
Kulm	1937	734	Room	2	461	199	2,200	34.27	59.21
Leeds	1902	782	Room $50	5½	2,176	398	[illegible]00	82.50	196.00
Lehr	1941	458	Room	2	71	......	[illegible]00	None Reported	
Linton	1936	1,602	Room	13	1,309	261	5,000	90.00	[illegible]2.00
Mandan	1896	6,685	Room $200	10	4,480	[illegible]00	21,350	603.79	1,314.77
Mohall	1937	687	Room $120	15	2,079	[illegible]94	3,900	61.30	118.78
New Salem	1935	875	Room	26	2,972	340	6,500	34.00	65.18
Northwood	1941	1,063	None	5½	376	199	1,500	35.17	50.21

ASSOCIATION LIBRARIES GIVING FREE SERVICE—(Continued)

Town	Date Established	1940 Population	Municipal Help	Hrs. Per Week	Volumes	Borrowers	Circulation	1940-1942 Expenditures Books	Total
Berg	1938	285	None	2	571	95	1,350	11.31	40.31
Portal	1935	499	Room	2	820	212	1,900	30.00	72.53
Sanish	1928	455	None	1	688	40	1,800	81.01	135.24
Tolna	1926	172	Room	1½	714	85	2,250	19.80	51.30
Turtle Lake	1926	62	Room	2	1,447	54	9,700	48.50	....
Velva	1921	1,013	Room $200	35	4,500	585	15,750	210.00	290.00
Verona	1925	201	Room	2	[illegible]	42	1,200	None	6.00
Milton	1915	357	Room	2	950	33	2,150	19.00	19.20

ASSOCIATION LIBRARIES CHARGING FOR SERVICE

[illegible]	Date Established	1940 Population	Municipal Help	Hrs. Per Week	Volumes	Borrowers	Circulation	1940-1942 Expenditures Books	Total
[illegible]	1940	22	Room	1½	750	26	Not Reported		
[illegible]	[illegible]	1,345	[illegible] $50	6	4,072	333	12,600	[illegible]1.57	$294.45
Cando	[illegible]	1,282	None	2	4,300	64	2,400	102.29	435.32
Cavalier #	[illegible]	1,105	[illegible] $25	6½	2,472	327	7,050	169.25	361.91
Edgeley	[illegible]	[illegible]	Room $50	2	2,084	30	2,[illegible]	105.00	....
Hansboro	[illegible]	[illegible]	[illegible]	3	698	45	1,050	24.17	45.31
Harvey	[illegible]	1,851	Room	3	986	459	4,300	101.92	101.92
Hope *	[illegible]	[illegible]	Room	3	600	105	3,000	109.07	[illegible]6.07
Langdon	[illegible]	1,546	Room $250	8	6,[illegible]94	273	30,[illegible]	209.59	435.91
[illegible] England	[illegible]	[illegible]	Room	2	1,621	148	3,200	63.34	65.08
[illegible] Rockford	1907	2,017	Room $240	8	3,690		Not Reported		
Oberon	[illegible]	....	[illegible]	6	549	98	2,400	41.22	143.70
Reg[illegible]ert	[illegible]	[illegible]	Room	2	817	42	1,900	Not Reported	
Rhame	[illegible]	[illegible]		4	683	59	750	18.34	82.21
Rolla	[illegible]	1,008	Room	2	1,170	[illegible]	2,350	130.13	388.41
St. Thomas	[illegible]	[illegible]	Lt., Heat, $50	1½	2,781	60	9,150	[illegible]	284.07

Library service free to school children.
* Library was destroyed by fire, January 1942.

Ashley	Public Library	Mrs. Max A. Wishek
Bathgate	Free Public Library	Mrs. Henry Kane
Beach	Public Library	Mrs. R. E. Arnold
Beulah	Public Library	Mrs. F. C. Worch
Bismarck	Public Library	Erana M. Stadler
Bismarck	State Historical Library	Mrs. Florence Davis
Bismarck	State Library Commission	Lillian E. Cook
Bottineau	Public Library	Mrs. C. P. Russell
Bowman	Clara Lincoln Phelan Library	Mrs. Mertie Pond
Cando	Public Library	Mrs. Mai Riggs
Carrington	City Library	Mrs. Ella Mae Hargrave
Casselton	Public Library	Mrs. Martha B. Correll
Cavalier	Public Library	Mrs. Clark Brown
Cogswell	Public Library	Olive M. Bartlett
Crosby	Divide County Library	Mrs. J. H. Phelps
Dawson	Public Library	Mrs. Jos. A. Kooker
Devils Lake	Carnegie Library	Marie E. O'Brien
Dickinson	Public Library	Gertrude Voldal
Dickinson	State Teachers College	Mathilda L. Stoxen
Drake	Public Library	Mrs. E. Van Horn
Edgeley	Public Library	Mrs. George Lee
Elbowoods	Public Library	Alice M. Watson
Ellendale	Public Library	Mrs. V. D. Coleman
Ellendale	Normal & Industrial School	Audrey Graff
Enderlin	Public Library	Mrs. G. H. Flynn
Fargo	Public Library	Inga L. Rynning
Fargo	State Agricultural College	Mrs. Ethel McVeety
Flaxton	Public Library	Mrs. E. A. Anderson
Forman	Public Library	Mrs. O. W. Petterson
Gackle	Public Library	Mrs. J. M. Hummel
Goodrich	Public Library	Mrs. J. R. Deering, Sr.
Grafton	Public Library	Mrs. Emma B. Cobb
Grand Forks	Public Library	Irma Walker
Grand Forks	State University Library	Della Mathys
Halliday	Public Library	Mrs. Malcolm Pippin
Hamilton	Public Library	Mrs. Andrew Knutson
Hankinson	Public Library	Esther Spreckles
Hansboro	Public Library	Mrs. Leonard Graetz
Harvey	Public Library	Mrs. A. B. Hannes
Heaton	Public Library	Howard I. Turner
Hebron	Public Library	Mrs. C. E. Gilbertson
Hettinger	Public Library	Mrs. Theodore Lokken
Hoople	Public Library	Mrs. J. O. Wallum
Hope	Public Library	Mrs. D. J. Gumb
Jamestown	Alfred Dickey Free Library	Mercedes Muenz
Jamestown	Jamestown College	Pearl G. Carlson
Killdeer	Public Library	Mrs. J. O. Severtson
Kulm	Public Library	Mrs. Otto Gackle
Lakota	The A. M. Tofthagen Library	Mrs. Inga Ferris
LaMoure	Public Library	Mrs. Carl Neverman
Langdon	Public Library	Mrs. E. J. Donovan
Leeds	Public Library	Mrs. Benjamin Baglien
Lehr	Public Library	Mrs. Arnold Jenner
Leonard	Leonard Township Library	Mrs. Harold C. Peterson

LIBRARY DIRECTORY

Town	Name of Library	Librarian
Lidgerwood	City Library	Mrs. Elizabeth Kings
Linton	Public Library	Alice Stewart
Lisbon	Public Library	Berniece Johnson
Mandan	Public Library	Mrs. J. A. Biggs
Mayville	Public Library	Cora I. Ames
Mayville	State Teachers College	Mrs. Hazel W. Byrnes
Minot	Public Library	Barbara Williams
Minot	State Teachers College	Mrs. Mabel Etheridge
Mohall	Public Library	Mrs. Eliza A. Paris
Mott	Inez Hendrickson Library	Mrs. E. H. Trousdale
New England	Public Library	Mrs. Vivian Schnitker
New Rockford	Public Library	Vannie Hall
New Salem	Public Library	Mrs. Adelaide Schwartz
Northwood	Public Library	Mrs. H. G. Webster
Oakes	Public Library	Mrs. E. C. Christensen
Oberon	Public Library	Mrs. O. C. Haskin
Park River	Public Library	Mrs. L. N. Gullickson
Petersburg	Public Library	Dagny Reiten
Portal	Public Library	Mrs. W. H. McCauley
Regent	Public Library	Mrs. Geo. Trunkill
Rhame	Public Library	Mrs. A. K. Dahl
Rolla	Public Library	Mrs. Martha Marchand
Rugby	Public Library	Helen Marie Fay
St. Thomas	Public Library	Mrs. E. T. Thompson
Sanish	Public Library	Mrs. Albert Brevig
Tolna	Public Library	Mrs. C. A. Porter
Turtle Lake	Public Library	Mrs. Elmer Melby
Valley City	Carnegie Public Library	Mrs. Helen H. Tracy
Valley City	State Teachers College	Loretta Swift
Verona	Public Library	Mrs. Fred Isley
Wahpeton	Leach Public Library	Lydia A. Simonson
Wahpeton	State Science School	Mildred Oelke
Watford City	Public Library	Mary Ann Thompson
Williston	James Memorial Library	Mrs. Sylvia R. Monson
Wimbledon	Public Library	Mrs. Albert Lewellyn
Wishek	Public Library	Mrs. J. W. Hofer

Nineteenth Biennial Report

of the

State Library Commission

to the

State Board of Administration

STATE LIBRARY COMMISSION STAFF

June 30, 1944

Lillian E. Cook	Secretary and Director
Gunn J. Bakken	Librarian
Martha S. Wanner	Stenographer
Wilda Sebastian	Clerk
Bertha Kallenberger	Clerk

FOR THE PERIOD

JULY 1, 1942 — JUNE 30, 1944

Nineteenth Biennial Report

of the

State Library Commission

to the

State Board of Administration

STATE LIBRARY COMMISSION STAFF
June 30, 1944

Lillian E. Cook	Secretary and Director
Gena J. Bakken	Librarian
Martha S. Wanner	Stenographer
Wilda Sebastian	Clerk
Bertha Kallenberger	Clerk

FOR THE PERIOD
JULY 1, 1942 — JUNE 30, 1944

TO THE STATE BOARD OF ADMINISTRATION: M. I. Forkner, Chairman, R. H. Sherman, O. A. Braseth, Math Dahl and Arthur E. Thompson, Bismarck, North Dakota.

Herewith is transmitted the Nineteenth Biennial Report of the North Dakota State Library Commission covering the period from July 1, 1942 to June 30, 1944.

REPORT OF THE SECRETARY AND DIRECTOR, NORTH DAKOTA STATE LIBRARY COMMISSION—1942-1944

As in every other line of service and activity the regular routine work of the State Library Commission has been vitally affected by the war. Briefly the effect has been: less use of general books; an increased demand for specialized books; delay and difficulty in obtaining books and supplies; a great shortage and turnover in personnel; cancellation of professional meetings; and a critical budget-complicating increase in prices and salaries.

To meet the requirements for a condensed report because of printing and paper restrictions the work of the secretary is presented in outline form.

Library visits, Public Libraries:

Beach, December 1943
Devils Lake, June 1943
Dickinson, September 1943
Edgeley, January 1944
Ellendale, October 1942
Fargo, October 1942
Forbes, January 1944
Grafton, June 1943
Grand Forks, June 1943
Jamestown, May 1943
LaMoure, January 1944
Lidgerwood, January 1944
Lisbon, June 1943
Mayville, June 1943
Mott, June 1942
Oakes, January 1944
Rugby, July 1943
Valley City, May 1943
Wahpeton, June 1944

Library visits, Special and Institutional:
State Teachers College, Dickinson
State Teachers College, Ellendale
State Teachers College, Mayville
State Teachers College, Valley City
University of North Dakota, Grand Forks
State College, Fargo
Normal and Industrial, Ellendale
Jamestown College, Jamestown
Crippled Children's Home, Jamestown

Meetings attended:

Library

North Dakota Library Association, Fargo, May 1944
Regional Library Association, Minneapolis, Minnesota

Special

N. Dak. Federated Womens Clubs, Valley City, May 1943
N. Dak. Federated Womens Clubs, Jamestown, May 1944
N. Dak. Educational Association, Fargo, October 1942
N. Dak. Educational Association, Bismarck, November 1943
Leadership Training Institute, Bismarck, April 1943
Missouri River Valley Association, Bismarck, August 1943
Board Meeting, Leadership Training, Fargo, November 1943
County Superintendents, Bismarck, February 1943
County Superintendents, Dickinson, October 1942
Regional Library, Grand Forks, June 1943

Talks: North Dakota Library Association, North Dakota Federated Women's Clubs, County Superintendents, Library Training Classes State Teachers College, Valley City, Dickinson, Grand Forks, Mayville; Teachers Institute, Ellendale, Community meetings for beginning libraries, Cooperstown and Forbes; North Dakota-Minnesota regional library meeting, Grand Forks.

STATE LIBRARY COMMISSION

Because of the great turnover in personnel the Secretary has had to devote most of her time to routine work. The administrative activities have been carried in a limited way, the outline report shows the field work. The "Library Notes" have been issued irregularly; book exhibits have been sent each spring and fall to the Public Libraries of the state; a column of free and inexpensive material useful for schools has been prepared each month for the North Dakota Teacher; book lists, library planning, positions, problems as usual.

The chief of the Traveling Library Department left in September 1942 and the Secretary and Director has largely had charge since then. The collections have been almost entirely revised, made over and brought up to date. Material past salvaging went to the "paper drive" and hundreds of old, shabby out-of-date books have been withdrawn, leaving only usable collections. Rural and small town schools continue to make the greatest use of collections suited to grade and high school ages, while the small public libraries use the adult and mixed collections.

REFERENCE DEPARTMENT

The country-wide characteristic of decreased library circulation due to the war has been noted by the Reference Department also. However, during the past year there has been a heartening upward trend. Through the Reference Department, individuals of the state who are without available or adequate library facilities are served, and their recreational and informational needs are taken care of by selection of up-to-date and tested material. Book lists of recent additions or bibliographies for individual study courses are sent on request. Forty-five registered, and a dozen or more non-registered women's clubs continue to use the program suggestions, outlines, and material available from the Library Commission. These clubs reflect the serious consideration that is being given to post-war planning and present-day problems. School collections are being supplemented by books from this department—500 rural teachers used the Reading Circle monthly collections, declamations and special day material; high schools continue to call for themes, debates, plays and outside reading; the State Agricultural College refers its correspondence students to us for books they need. Over sixty carefully selected periodicals are obtainable as well as a continuous addition of approved books.

The Reference Department has supplied Camp Trenton, the camp for conscientious objectors, with books and reference material. This service has also been given to individual borrowers from the camp for prisoners of war at Fort Lincoln.

We are grateful to the WPA for the gift of 3,500 books left with us when that project was discontinued. Such a substantial gift has aided greatly in the satisfactory service it is our aim to give.

The STATE AT LARGE shows the following gains: the public library at Towner reopened and a new library opened at Forbes under the sponsorship of the PTA; Wahpeton is sending collections of books to nearby small towns; Mandan, since January 1943, has had municipal support and an appointed library board; Turtle Lake and Forman are having municipal financial help; Fargo purchased land which makes future expansion possible; Bismarck sponsored a very successful series of open forums. Renovation and new equipment are reported from Carrington, Casselton, Devils Lake, Dickinson, Ellendale, Fargo, Grafton and Wahpeton; Cooperstown, one of the few county seats in North Dakota without a public library, has plans so nearly complete that the library will open in July; most of the libraries helped in the Victory Book Drive and a satisfactory number of books were shipped from North Dakota. All libraries are cooperating with government war work, information centers, government projects, such as canning, salvage, etc.

LILLIAN E. COOK
Secretary and Director
State Library Commission

STATISTICAL REPORT, 1942-45

BOOKS

Traveling Library Department

*Number of traveling libraries	133
Number of libraries added during this biennium	78
Number of books added during this period	1,990
*Number of books in traveling libraries	5,004

Reference Department

Number of books in this department	21,868
Number of books added during this biennium	4,392
Number of pamphlets in collection	24,000

CIRCULATION

Traveling Library Department

Number of Libraries Circulated	1942-43	1943-44	Total
Schools	276	285	561
Communities	79	56	135
Number of books circulated	11,360	9,832	21,192
New T. L. stations	71	74	145

Reference Department

Number of requests filled	6,937	6,976	13,913
Number of books circulated	39,960	43,050	83,010
Magazines and pamphlets sent out	4,617	5,854	10,471
Total reference dept. circulation	44,577	48,904	93,481
TOTAL CIRCULATION OF COMMISSION	55,937	58,736	114,673

* Only new and revised libraries, cleaned, mended and ready for circulation July 1, 1944 are included in this count.

PUBLIC LIBRARIES

Town	Date Established	1940 population	RECEIPTS Tax Appropriation 1942-43	RECEIPTS Tax Appropriation 1943-44	RECEIPTS Total Receipts 1942-43	RECEIPTS Total Receipts 1943-44
Bismarck	1914	15,496	$11,975.00	$12,000.00	$13,355.77	$13,874.41
Bowman	1916	967	233.78	279.99	89.06	697.09
Carrington	1906	1,200	1,200.00	1,200.00	2,618.10	2,667.09
[illegible]	1906	1,358	310.41	333.25	87.50	591.21
Devils Lake	1898	6,204	4,197.21	3,472.70	6,348.66	7,041.92
Dickinson	1908	5,839	4,750.00	5,750.00	5,254.69	6,320.11
[illegible]dale	1912	1,517	475.00	650.00	61.66	854.66
Fargo	1900	32,580	20,196.62	21,844.73	36,610.50	32,938.45
Grafton	1895	4,070	1,600.00	2,700.00	1,839.10	4,286.41
Grand Forks	1899	20,228	12,030.00	10,500.00	12,909.61	13,745.26
[illegible]	1901	8,790	4,000.00	4,500.00	5,574.47	5,820.66
Lakota	1906	907	398.82	23.39	1,077.08	68.99
LaMoure	1924	990	600.00	60.00	645.97	63.12
Leonard [illegible]ship	1912	465	125.00	25.00	25.00	29.57
[illegible]	1913	1,042	685.00	85.00	745.79	81.14
[illegible]	1915	1,997	1,403.25	1,577.15	2,808.83	3,485.07
[illegible]	1896	6,685	599.71	3,000.00	23.25	3,156.95
[illegible]ville	1900	1,351	750.00	55.00	1,065.16	917.36
[illegible]	1908	16,577	9,168.93	9,389.88	15,329.41	17,483.07
[illegible]	1912	1,220	380.00	28.24	26.12	63.70
Oakes	1905	1,665	1,000.00	85.95	1,667.75	1,635.69
[illegible] River	1900	1,408	300.00	80.00	397.26	83.17
Rugby	1912	2,215	1,000.00	40.00	1,649.12	1,227.83
Turtle Lake	1926	632	160.00	60.58	105.74	66.58
Valley [illegible]	1900	5,917	3,967.76	5,349.69	6,424.89	8,225.71
[illegible]	....	3,747	4,000.00	4,000.00	7,096.99	6,096.50
[illegible]	1910	5,790	3,308.32	4,069.57	5,587.82	5,212.99
Wishek	1926	1,112	200.00	50.00	346.02	396.96

PUBLIC LIBRARIES

EXPENDITURES

Town	Salaries 1942-43	Salaries 1943-44	Maintenance 1942-43	Maintenance 1943-44	Books-Periodicals 1942-43	Books-Periodicals 1943-44	Total 1942-43	Total 1943-44
Bismarck	$ 7,693.30	$ 7,894.01	$ 1,040.95	$ 850.37	$ 2,377.34	$ 2,932.02	$12,553.78	$12,667.51
Bowman	324.00	324.00	77.32	69.84	127.74	150.54	529.06	697.09
Carrington	670.00	665.00	75.23	21.86	315.86	265.20	1,115.00	2,667.10
[illegible]	114.00	116.00	164.01	....	164.09	158.45	451.79	300.94
Devils Lake	1,551.15	1,845.00	657.39	649.71	759.58	812.05	3,464.14	3,495.50
Dickinson	2,553.40	2,938.00	518.22	584.42	1,043.81	1,079.56	5,085.62	5,591.34
Ellendale	370.00	494.80	9.50	....	141.24	250.03	636.81	854.66
Fargo	11,913.98	12,871.58	3,518.99	1,897.50	3,711.87	3,565.57	29,960.21	19,242.90
[illegible]	1,021.30	1,165.15	302.56	331.70	359.75	293.40	1,714.04	1,791.96
Grand Forks	6,327.06	7,168.20	1,038.17	667.11	2,076.37	2,452.89	10,543.15	11,144.61
Jamestown	2,377.21	2,710.61	936.05	1,196.51	1,144.37	1,035.51	5,195.21	5,523.05
Lakota	312.00	264.00	156.98	140.67	58.84	27.61	678.26	459.36
LaMoure	332.94	324.50	7.04	80.01	144.10	170.57	564.98	663.12
Leonard Twp.	75.00	75.00	4.25	11.68	25.18	1.97	124.29	96.15
Lidgerwood	416.00	588.00	142.41	46.48	123.65	128.13	725.22	851.66
Lisbon	617.50	617.50	664.85	571.15	331.19	369.27	1,735.28	1,654.10
Mandan	663.88	1,464.50	11.84	57.60	109.80	519.22	723.25	2,122.65
Mayville	370.00	329.80	395.95	196.91	183.61	231.96	1,037.51	842.84
Minot	4,568.87	5,339.60	405.30	1,021.30	2,596.57	2,442.13	8,102.24	9,782.24
Mott	188.40	180.00	1.08	....	126.19	105.81	347.64	288.57
Oakes	807.40	812.10	....	....	445.50	326.88	1,287.52	1,182.51
Park River	270.00	270.00	....	8.09	102.25	5.79	379.87	309.38
Rugby	735.25	720.03	....	....	139.51	176.08	977.11	945.40
Turtle Lake	....	35.00	....	....	14.39	11.25	39.42	46.25
Valley City	1,997.00	2,195.50	584.06	465.29	612.07	588.66	3,539.86	3,457.21
Wahpeton	2,458.71	2,603.06	477.82	597.83	1,493.03	942.12	5,295.93	4,429.83
Williston	2,290.50	2,553.32	525.56	510.56	1,261.13	393.10	4,478.59	3,665.23
[illegible]	52.50	52.00	....	....	55.83	137.82	115.81	197.45

PUBLIC LIBRARIES

Town	[illegible]tion 1942-43	1943-44	Total	[illegible]	Borrowers	Hours Open Week	Rural Borrowers
[illegible]k	28,[illegible]0	122,075	250,985	20,284	5,894	66	....
Bowman	3,[illegible]88	2,889	6,277	6,918	551	30	....
Carrington	15,[illegible]65	11,263	26,928	6,216	838	33	261
[illegible]h	4,[illegible]21	3,772	7,993	2,397	294	4	12
Devils Lake	31,[illegible]28	25,457	56,685	12,612	3,988	36	27
Dickinson	[illegible]0,497	36,001	76,498	16,830	2,704	36	236
[illegible]e	11,[illegible]28	11,978	23,906	5,511	1,028	30	325
Fargo	[illegible]6,[illegible]2	173,723	360,525	44,266	18,678	76	481
Grafton	12,[illegible]6	9,923	22,079	6,562	1,821	24	6
Grand Forks	75,[illegible]05	65,443	140,448	22,526	5,864	66	106
[illegible]n	54,[illegible]0	50,369	104,719	14,831	4,795	52	531
Lakota	3,[illegible]3	2,205	5,908	5,238	170	9	....
[illegible]e	4,215	4,038	8,253	4,370	929	12	435
Leonard To[illegible]nship	1,040	1,040	2,080	1,980	37	37	12
Lidgerwood	8,[illegible]70	12,030	20,800	6,371	901	30	548
[illegible]n	9,[illegible]0	11,396	21,326	2,555	1,006	19	339
[illegible]an	3,[illegible]6	8,885	12,851	4,939	1,040	28	1
[illegible]ville	4,[illegible]3	3,372	7,555	4,986	394	24	....
[illegible]	61,667	60,530	122,197	19,801	7,617	60	97
Mott	2,144	2,858	5,002	3,040	367	6	45
[illegible]s	17,[illegible]5	17,145	34,240	7,557	1,509	28	426
Park River	8,[illegible]0	8,580	16,900	2,945	287	16	85
Rugby	[illegible],[illegible]4	11,829	18,983	6,425	2,665	30	215
Turtle Lake	1,[illegible]80	1,820	3,700	1,463	210	2	3
[illegible]y [illegible]y	23,[illegible]5	19,851	42,986	15,784	2,532	36	438
Wahpeton	18,[illegible]35	17,656	35,991	10,379	3,512	33	370
[illegible]n	18,[illegible]8	19,522	37,560	10,353	4,215	36	370
Wishek	4,[illegible]0	2,600	6,760	1,532	423	4	80

ASSOCIATION LIBRARIES GIVING FREE SERVICE

Town	Date Established	1940 Population	Municipal Help	Hrs. Per Week	Volumes	Borrowers	Circulation	1942-44 Expenditures Books	1942-44 Expenditures Total
[illegible]te	96	32	None	2	1,513	48	3,432	$ 53.71	$ 61.67
e[illegible]h	92	1,178	Room $310	6	2,436	1,112	3,790	228.11	461.07
[illegible]h	91	92	Room	½	1,735	89	2,100	121.38	126.33
[illegible]	95	1,739	Room	2	90	20	1,300	70.00	75.00
Cogswell	95	80	Room	5	2,305	86	3,380	24.90	39.47
Crosby	1 90	1,404	No report	....	....	....	....	....	....
Dawson	92	83	Room	3	1,188	98	3,585	16.69	25.86
Drake	90	64	Room	3	2,037	80	3,500	123.47	192.37
[illegible]woods	1941	....	Room	[illegible]	1,563	61	8,892	[illegible]ne	20.00
Enderlin	92	1,593	Room	4	3,268	50	2,800	222.46	233.46
t[illegible]h	95	62	Room	3	1,630	36	80	6.00	48.00
Forman	99	60	Room	4	1,310	81	3,952	58.48	331.83
[illegible]e	96	537	Room	2	85	....	2,704	10.21	12.95
Goodri[illegible]h	96	476	Room	2	81	71	2,704	93.02	120.53
[illegible]alliday	1937	85	Room	7	934	125	5,460	14.00	125.10
[illegible]amil t[illegible]n	96	85	Room	2	1,116	32	56	35.68	35.68
[illegible]ki [illegible]n	1907	1,420	Room	4	1,590	247	2,496	2.00	122.00
Hebron	98	1,267	Room	4	837	89	1,612	[illegible]d 1944	
[illegible]er	92	1,138	Room $25	3	1,305	89	1,456	[illegible]e	53.50
Hoople	1937	346	Room	2	85	....	3,120	[illegible]e	30.00
e[illegible]r	....	60	None	2	98	....	4,277	97.95	155.38
Kulm	1937	34	Room	2	65	796	1,768	[illegible]e	29.08
Leeds	1902	82	Room $50	5½	2,187	798	2,600	[illegible]t Given	

Lehr	1941	458	Room		2	171	1,033	1,924	16.05	33.53
Linton	1936	1,602	Room		7	1,875	254	4,776	20.00	299.79
Mohall	1937	687	Room	$141.75	15	679	298	3,203	52.26	79.20
New Salem	1935	875	Room		7			No Report		
Northwood	1941	1,063	None		4	520	458	3,848	63.59	107.76
Petersburg	1938	285	None		2	632	40	1,612	100.03	145.98
Portal	1935	499	Room		2	767	193	2,900	23.51	88.62
Sanish	1928	455	....		1	803	136	3,224	92.83	180.67
Towner	....	....	Room	$80	4	1,910	175		Incomplete	
Vernon	1925	201	Room		1½	137	77	2,600	None	39.75
Wimbledon	1915	357	Room		1	1,000	40	1,952	1.80	2.00

ASSOCIATION LIBRARIES CHARGING FOR SERVICE

Town	Date [illegible]	[illegible]	Municipal Help	Hrs. Per Week	Volumes	Bor-rowers	Circu-[illegible]	1942-44 Expenditures Books	Total
Ashley	1913	1,345	Room	6	4,254	500	7,072	$183.07	$370.32
[illegible]	1902	1,282	None	2	3,500	75	7,200	251.04	413.04
[illegible]	1915	1,105	Room $25	6	2,668	242	5,200	192.24	213.46
Edgeley	1912	[illegible]	Room	2	2,514	35	7,280	82.84	....
*Forbes	1944	....	Room	6	530	79	3,536	None	44.09
Hansboro	1928	196	$10	2	717	44	1,456	35.44	52.81
Harvey	1909	1,851	Room	3	1,108	....	....	61.04	72.32
Hope	1910	474	Room	3	750	78	3,500	139.17	168.17
Langdon	1912	1,546	Room & $250	8	6,348	169	18,200	189.83	588.73
New England	1931	895	Room	2	1,737	110	3,305	41.47	41.47
New [illegible]	1917	2,017	Room & $300	8	3,670	....	3,000	139.53	769.03
Oberon	1938	....	None	4	609	67	[illegible]	39.84	127.87
Regent	1935	261	Room	2	834	71	2,486	None	45.59
[illegible]	1938	283	$15	2	950	85		Incomplete	
Rolla	1924	1,008	Room	2	1,251	58	4,940	48.72	59.63
St. Thomas	1917	503	$50 and light, heat and ins.	2½	2,850	51	5,460	119.36	176.18
Watford City	1924	1,073	None	10	2,400	200	2,080	....	144.00

* Free to children.

LIBRARY DIRECTORY

Town	Name of Library	Librarian
Ashley	Public Library	Mrs. Max A. Wishek
Bathgate	Free Public Library	Mrs. Henry Kane
Beach	Public Library	Grace Houck
Beulah	Public Library	Mrs. F. C. Worch
Bismarck	Public Library	Erana M. Stadler
Bismarck	State Historical Library	Mrs. Florence Davis
Bismarck	State Library Commission	Lillian E. Cook
Bottineau	Public Library	Mrs. E. M. Ertresvaag
Bowman	Clara Lincoln Phelan Library	Ruth Stewart
Cando	Public Library	Lucile Harris
Carrington	City Library	Mrs. Ella Mae Hargrave
Casselton	Public Library	Mrs. Martha B. Correll
Cavalier	Public Library	Mrs. Clark Brown
Cogswell	Public Library	Olive M. Bartlett
Crosby	Divide County Library	Mrs. J. H. Phelps
Dawson	Public Library	Mrs. Joseph A. Kooker
Devils Lake	Carnegie Library	Inez Serumgard
Dickinson	Public Library	Gertrude Voldal
Dickinson	State Teachers' College	Mathilda L. Stoxen
Drake	Public Library	Mrs. John Haldi, Sec.
Edgeley	Public Library	Mrs. Florence Lee
Elbowoods	Public Library	Alice M. Watson
Ellendale	Public Library	Mrs. V. D. Coleman
Ellendale	Normal & Industrial School	Lois Bailey
Enderlin	Public Library	Mrs. E. B. McLeod
Fargo	Public Library	Inga L. Rynning
Fargo	State Agricultural College	Elliot L. Hardaway
Flaxton	Public Library	Mrs. E. A. Anderson
Forbes	Public Library	Mrs. Isabel Vick
Forman	Public Library	Mrs. J. W. Carlen
Gackle	Public Library	Mrs. J. M. Hummel
Goodrich	Public Library	Mrs. J. R. Doering, Sr.
Grafton	Public Library	Mrs. Ella Myers
Grand Forks	Public Library	Irma Walker
Grand Forks	State University Library	Della Mathys
Halliday	Public Library	Mrs. Elmer Goetz
Hamilton	Public Library	Mrs. Andrew Knutson
Hankinson	Public Library	Bernice Spreckles
Hansboro	Public Library	Mrs. J. O. Funk
Harvey	Public Library	Mrs. A. B. Hannes
Hettinger	Public Library	Mrs. Beulah De La
Hoople	Public Library	Audrey Heder
Hope	Public Library	Mrs. D. J. Gumb
Jamestown	Alfred Dickey Free Library	Mercedes Muenz

LIBRARY DIRECTORY

Town	Name of Library	Librarian
Jamestown	Jamestown College Library	Mrs. Florence Summers
Killdeer	Public Library	Mrs. J. O. Severtson
Kulm	Public Library	Mrs. E. E. Orth
Lakota	The A. M. Tofthagen Library	Mrs. Inga Ferris
LaMoure	Public Library	Mrs. James A. Frank
Langdon	Public Library	Mrs. E. J. Donovan
Leeds	Public Library	Mrs. J. B. Kinneberg
Lehr	Public Library	Mrs. Eugene Grenz
Leonard	Watts Free Library	Mrs. Elsie Greuel
Lidgerwood	City Library	Mrs. Elizabeth Kings
Linton	Public Library	N. S. Sheffield
Lisbon	Public Library	Dorothy Thompson
Mandan	Public Library	Mrs. Eleanor Trzcinski
Mayville	Public Library	Cora I. Ames
Mayville	State Teachers College	Mrs. Hazel W. Byrnes
Minot	Public Library	Mrs. Arthur Schempp
Minot	State Teachers College	Marion Grady
Mohall	Public Library	Mrs. Eliza A. Paris
Mott	Inez Hendrickson Library	Mrs. J. W. Hoye
New England	Public Library	Mrs. Vivian Schnitker
New Rockford	Public Library	Mrs. Vannie Hall
New Salem	Public Library	Mrs. Max Buckman
Northwood	Northwood City Library	Mrs. S. C. Sampson, Sec.
Oakes	Public Library	Mrs. E. C. Christensen
Oberon	Public Library	Mrs. W. A. Burgstahler
Park River	Public Library	Mrs. Vera H. Warner
Petersburg	Public Library	Carrie Barnum
Portal	Public Library	Mrs. W. H. McCauley
Regent	Public Library	Mrs. E. A. Reitan
Rhame	Public Library	Mrs. A. K. Dahl
Rolla	Public Library	Mrs. Clara R. Jacobsen
Rugby	Public Library	Mrs. P. E. McMahan
St. Thomas	Public Library	Mrs. E. T. Thompson
Sanish	Public Library	Mrs. Arvid Olson
Towner	Public Library	Mrs. Kathryn Stiehm
Turtle Lake	Public Library	Mrs. John Frey
Valley City	Carnegie Public Library	Mrs. Helen H. Tracy
Valley City	State Teachers College	D. W. Ferguson
Verona	Public Library	Mrs. Fred Isley
Wahpeton	Leach Public Library	Phyllis Pope
Wahpeton	State Science School	Mildred Oelke
Watford City	Masonic Library	R. M. Christensen
Williston	James Memorial Library	Mrs. Sylvia R. Monson
Wimbledon	Public Library	Mrs. W. B. Wanner
Wishek	Public Library	Irene Frank

Twenty-first Biennial Report

of the

State Library Commission

to the

State Board of Administration

FOR THE PERIOD
July 1, 1946 - June 30, 1948

Twenty-first Biennial Report

of the

State Library Commission

to the

State Board of Administration

STATE LIBRARY COMMISSION STAFF
June 30, 1948

Lillian E. Cook........Secretary and Director
Gena J. Bakken........Librarian
Wilda Sebastian........Chief Clerk
Mrs. Arlene Stocker........Stenographer

FOR THE PERIOD
July 1, 1946 - June 30, 1948

1—66651

TO THE STATE BOARD OF ADMINISTRATION: R. H. Sherman, Chairman, O. A. Braseth, F. A. Foley, Math Dahl, and Garfield B. Nordrum, Bismarck, North Dakota.

Herewith is transmitted the Twenty-first Biennial Report of the North Dakota State Library Commission covering the period from July 1, 1946 to June 30, 1948.

REPORT OF THE SECRETARY AND DIRECTOR, NORTH DAKOTA STATE LIBRARY COMMISSION—1946-1948

When the war was over reading in all libraries fell off, but there is now an upward trend, and the Commission and the public libraries of the state show an increase in book circulation. A measurement of this kind is easily made, and often a period is considered successful simply on the basis of numbers, but this leaves unrecognized the intangible factors in library service which are more important than the volume of books read; such factors as the type of books read, progress in reading ability, planned and purposeful reading, and books introduced to individuals and groups not using them before. The State Library Commission believes it and other libraries in the state have made an advance along these lines also; although there are no statistics to prove it.

The problems which bothered during the last biennial period are still bothersome: constantly increasing prices for books and all supplies and materials needed in library work; salaries to hold personnel that tax the budget; a national shortage of trained librarians that makes staff replacements or enlargement impossible.

The social security law passed in 1947 makes a slight security provision for the members of the State Library Commission staff, and, as city employees covers the librarians of tax supported public libraries.

The LIBRARY DEMONSTRATION BILL which passed the Senate in the spring of 1948 failed to clear from the House committee and was lost in the press of business at the close of the session. This is the second session in which failure came because of press of "must" legislation and not because of criticism of the bill. Undoubtedly it will again be reintroduced in the 81st Congress, and it is to be hoped will clear both houses early in the session. The lost bill carried an appropriation for the demonstration of necessary library service of $25,000 for each state for each of five successive years, where acceptable plans were developed within the state.

Surplus commodities were not of benefit to the libraries of North Dakota. Much time was spent in circularizing and compiling data from various forms sent out by the government, but quantities were too large or plans for distribution just seemed to evaporate.

12-14-48

STATE LIBRARY COMMISSION

GENERAL AND ADMINISTRATIVE

The 1946-48 budget was sufficient in the main to hold the staff even in competition with other departments, and the turn over in personnel has been smaller than in recent years. We have been unable to secure a much needed additional professional worker, but competent untrained help has made possible handling the volume of work. Because of congested conditions it was necessary to rearrange the shelves and sort and weed material. Books and magazines past their usefulness were disposed of, certain collections moved to other floors, and the general reference collection rearranged for greater convenience.

The Secretary and Director did less field work than usual, but an effort was made to visit the libraries where problems were pressing. A tabulation of library visits follows.

Public libraries	23
School and Institutional libraries	7
State library meetings	2
State educational meetings	2
District library meeting	1
Organization visits	2
Trips for county library promotion	4

Through an insurance plan worked out locally, group insurance has been provided for all members of the State Library Commission staff, with quarterly premium deductions made from the pay roll.

Much needed supplementary work on the state list of approved books for grade schools was done along two lines, a mimeographed supplement published early in 1947, and three supplementary lists with a cumulative index published in the February-May issues of the NORTH DAKOTA TEACHER. It is hoped that a provision for a real revision may be made at the next legislature.

Former lines of service have been continued, there has been cooperation with many state departments and state organizations, with the State Library Commission endeavoring to be of service to all residents of North Dakota with reading and book problems.

REFERENCE DEPARTMENT

Each month the Reference Department progresses a little beyond the corresponding month of the previous year. That is as it should be, and we are happy that it is so. Part-time assistance has eased the load of the reference librarian whose work it is to catalog the ever-increasing book collection in addition to answering the numerous and varied reference questions upon which correspondents seek information.

Cataloging is the process by which books, pamphlets, and clippings are made available and usable to the public. 1,428 books of the present collection of 24,046 were processed during this biennium, and that figure does not include the great number of replacements of shabby copies made possible by our larger book appropriation. We have also withdrawn 432 books that had outgrown their usefulness. The pamphlet and clipping collection (Vertical File) is intended as a subject file of information of current import. We are ever alert on the job, and off the job, for that elusive information necessary, and so hard to obtain, on live issues of the day.

We continue to subscribe to sixty-eight periodicals, carefully chosen for their reference value.

Our contact with the clubwomen of our state is very close. Many libraries, directly or indirectly, originated through the efforts of clubwomen. The Secretary and Director prepared lists of program suggestions and developed outlines for each of the Year and Part-year topics. These are mailed to more than one hundred and twenty-five clubs. The majority of these clubs are given assistance in planning their yearbooks. Eighty-three clubs depend on us altogether or in part for study material. The reference librarian attended two conventions of the Federated Woman's Clubs: a district meeting at Turtle Lake and the state convention at Grafton.

A popular type of book service is that given through the "Books a Month" file where a record is kept of the reading interests of families and individuals who get books mailed to them directly upon return of their previous package without having to make a written request each time. Over seventy are registered in the "Books a Month" file.

There is much bustle and activity during the school year. Students and teachers call upon us for information related to themes, debates, special days, plays, and elementary grade declamations. Last, but not least, is the assistance given to schools through the Reading Circle. The Secretary and Director compiles a list of standard books upon which the Department of Public Instruction bases its requirements for Reading Circle credit. 7,500 volumes make up the part of our collection devoted to the Reading Circle. In our statistical report these are included in the total figure for the Reference Collection. The chief clerk is in charge of the circulation of the Reading Circle books. As more than seven hundred teachers use this special service to the schools, one can easily realize the bulk of work handled.

We would also like to mention that a representative of the Library Commission attended the convention of the American Library Association at San Francisco in 1947 and at Atlantic City in 1948. The Secretary and Director and the Reference Librarian attended a Regional Library Association meeting held in Minneapolis in October, 1947. At the convention at Atlantic City, North Dakota was placed in the newly created Trans-Mississippi Region of the American Library Association.

TRAVELING LIBRARY DEPARTMENT

Schools continue to make the greatest use of the Traveling Libraries, but small public libraries avail themselves of this relatively inexpensive way of supplementing their local collections. One hundred sixty-one more libraries were sent out than in the last biennium, or a total of 780. Sixty-five new libraries were added made up of new and attractive books. The book selection is still being done by the Secretary and Director with a clerk handling the lending, but when professional help is available, there should be a trained person in charge of this department to make possible the maximum service to rural districts.

THE STATE AT LARGE

County service has been continued in Divide County on a small scale, which cannot be increased until an adequate appropriation is secured. Interest in such type of library coverage is growing in Barnes, LaMoure and Richland counties.

In Barnes county, after preliminary meetings, a county-wide meeting was held May 10, 1948 at which time a committee was appointed to carry on through the summer and promote an active educational campaign during the fall, looking forward to submitting the question for vote in the general fall election.

With the emphasis on larger units of service, only one new library has been established. Steele and Mercer are interested and a public meeting was held at Mercer to discuss the possibilities. Rolette has the new library.

The long-range plans for library progress and service in the State as seen from the level of the State Library Commission are:

1. More book help for small local libraries; buying suggestions and book loans from the State Library Commission.

2. Library workshops for untrained librarians.

3. An educational campaign to have counties and regions understand the value of regional library service and establish it.

4. Eventually, when trained personnel is available, a certification law which will require full, or summer school, library training for librarians of tax supported libraries.

5. The State Library Commission needs more professional help and a budget making possible service to all rural residents.

LILLIAN E. COOK
Secretary and Director
State Library Commission

STATISTICAL REPORT 1946-48

BOOKS

Traveling Library Department

Number of Traveling Libraries	367
Number of libraries added during this biennium	65
Number of books added during this period	1,711
Number of books in traveling libraries	11,101

Reference Department

Number of books in this department	24,046
Number of books added during this biennium	1,460
Number of pamphlets in collection	21,300

CIRCULATION

Traveling Library Department

Number of Libraries circulated	1946-47	1947-48	Total
Schools	336	332	668
Communities	54	58	112
Number of books circulated	10,784	10,522	21,306
New Traveling Library stations	83	95	178

Reference Department

Number of requests filled	7,411	6,986	14,397
Number of books circulated	52,204	53,648	105,852
Magazines and pamphlets sent out	6,711	7,040	13,751
Total Reference Department circulation	58,915	60,688	119,603
TOTAL CIRCULATION OF COMMISSION	69,699	71,210	140,909

PUBLIC LIBRARIES

Town	Date Established	1940 Population	RECEIPTS Tax approp[illegible] 1946-47	[illegible] 1947-48	Total 19[illegible]6-47	[illegible] 1947-48
B[illegible]k	1914	15,496	$15,500.00	$18,250.00	$17,771.52	$20,746.00
Bowman	1916	967	1,202.76	1,271.61	1,385.97	2,660.57
Carrington	1906	1,200	1,200.00	1,200.00	2,787.82	1,255.00
[illegible]h	1906	1,358	319.87	30.92	846.13	907.58
Devils Lake	1898	6,204	3,243.23	5,397.50	7,932.91	9,065.89
[illegible]in	1908	5,839	5,000.00	5,000.00	6,145.12	6,087.76
e[illegible]e	1912	1,517	[illegible]0.00	[illegible]0.00	1,221.65	1,384.70
Fargo	1900	32,580	19,915.09	21,665.14	32,409.00	38,873.18
Grafton	1895	4 070	2,400.00	1,200.00	4,462.67	3,871.81
Grand Forks	1899	[illegible]28	10,750.00	18,000.00	[illegible]7	21,166.84
Jamestown	1901	8,790	5 [illegible]6.63	5,916.74	7,645.02	8,581.65
Lakota	1906	907	[illegible]3.09	1, 00.00	[illegible]8.46	1,221.44
LaMoure	1924	90	[illegible]0.00	[illegible]0.00	[illegible]0.91	803.50
Leonard Township	1912	465	[illegible]5.00	[illegible]0.00	[illegible]9.86	156.76
Lidgerwood	1913	1,042	1,112.00	1, [illegible]0.00	1,135.08	1,109.77
Lisbon	1915	1,997	1,385.31	1, [illegible]0.98	4,771.12	4,681.69
M[illegible]n	1896	6,685	2,555.02	2, [illegible]3.00	3,971.50	5,297.80
[illegible]e	1900	1,351	[illegible]0.00	[illegible]0.56	1,248.11	1,179.80
M[illegible]t	1908	16,577	12,292.74	12, [illegible]9.32	22,165.83	22,889.[illegible]8
M[illegible]tt	1912	1,220	[illegible]0.00	[illegible]6.89	545.82	[illegible]1.98
Oakes	1905	1,665	1,200.00	1,112.28	2,214.22	2,335.50
Park Ri[illegible]er	1900	1,408	[illegible]0.00	400.00	725.29	[illegible]6.15
Rugby	1912	2,215	1,351.06	1,537.50	1,709.29	1,894.79
Turtle Lake	1926	62	[illegible]0.00	100.00	124.10	16.10
Valley [illegible]y	1900	5,917	4,465.48	....	13,556.57	9,005.[illegible]9
[illegible]n	....	3,747	2,000.00	4,384.37	6,364.58	5,279.82
[illegible]n	1910	5,790	5,999.26	5,511.35	6,023.00	5,544.00
[illegible]k	1926	1,112	200.00	200.00	454.49	473.93

PUBLIC LIBRARIES
EXPENDITURES

Town	Salaries 1946-47	Salaries 1947-48	Maintenance 1946-47	Maintenance 1947-48	Books-Periodicals 1946-47	Books-Periodicals 1947-48	Total 1946-47	Total 1947-48
Bismarck	$11, 54.15	$11, 66.03	$1,772.69	$2,382.86	$3,235.01	$4,680.84	$16,361.80	$18,099.73
Bowman	69.00	60.60	75.04	87.32	193.25	403.59	977.29	1,694.51
[illegible]	80.00	91.00	03.78	40.82	391.32	269.00	1,315.10	1,280.82
[illegible]	21.00	22.00	10.41	10.32	190.06	167.76	321.47	80.08
[illegible] Lake	2,069.60	2,094.00	1,443.48	1,501.92	1,005.95	771.09	4,518.53	4,452.90
Dickinson	3,646.40	3,908.79	66.75	26.75	1,148.27	1,067.04	5,391.42	5,759.12
Ellendale	87.70	67.50	31.58	19.44	618.56	429.47	1,137.84	1,016.41
Fargo	16,255.73	19,313.84	2,069.63	4,666.72	4,422.84	5,096.17	22,648.20	36,832.74
Grafton	1,333.00	1,335.06	298.39	62.36	326.82	239.92	1,958.21	2,077.34
Grand Forks	8,977.99	10,185.66	3,894.37	4,154.51	2,290.10	3,128.04	14,840.36	[illegible]
[illegible]	3,523.83	4,106.56	1,061.04	2,255.55	1,774.97	1,531.77	6,359.84	8,214.57
Lakota	428.75	25.70	462.59	192.90	25.20	448.70	[illegible].54	1,067.30
LaMoure	386.00	87.00	107.94	144.88	336.44	270.91	830.38	803.29
Leonard Twp.	96.00	96.00	20.10	40.05	25.00	....	141.10	133.65
[illegible]	714.00	60.00	24.67	221.96	86.64	72.55	1,125.31	1,074.51
[illegible]	757.50	94.69	62.11	886.04	69.50	40.75	1,819.11	2,140.58
[illegible]	1,684.65	1,770.70	31.10	1,062.49	81.46	29.11	2,867.21	3,562.33
Mayville	80.00	30.00	20.61	431.31	24.81	62.41	1,045.42	963.73
[illegible]ot	6,699.37	8,623.33	2,200.32	1,781.14	3,921.04	3,973.41	12,820.72	12,356.88
[illegible]	90.00	20.00	53.26	96.77	227.89	253.46	491.15	590.23
[illegible]	63.90	855.20	45.02	88.56	382.20	434.22	1,231.12	1,377.98
Park [illegible]	20.00	20.00	54.54	75.58	01.74	174.27	576.28	694 85
Rugby	97.00	1,080.00	141.43	102.99	98.51	489.94	1,396.94	1,672.93
Turtle Lake	50.00	50.00	....	....	18.00	27.70	68.00	77.70
Valley [illegible]	3,114.30	3,155.94	741.16	972.60	80.14	1,125.53	4,805.60	5,331.90
[illegible]	2,709.62	2,772.21	1,976.37	548.34	1,014.86	837.41	5,700.85	4,157.96
[illegible]	2,983.55	3,046.50	908.43	875.08	2,060.02	1,920.66	5,952.00	5,975.14
[illegible]	65.00	74.75	28.58	9.41	96.48	126.22	90.06	210.38

PUBLIC LIBRARIES

Town	Circulation 1946-47	Circulation [illegible]-48	Total	Volumes	Borrowers	Hours Open a Week	Rural Borrowers
Bismarck	101,490	109,770	211,260	23,547	5,959	66	......
Bowman	3,250	3,269	6,519	7,068	566	14	......
Carrington	10,261	10,050	20,311	5,861	723	19½	150
Casselton	4,[illegible]0	4,455	8,965	2,[illegible]91	357	4	37
Devils Lake	18,668	19,665	38,333	13,[illegible]22	1,923	36	15
Dickinson	38,935	35,735	74,670	18,[illegible]27	2,777	42	258
Ellendale	12,213	15,778	27,991	6,[illegible]61	[illegible]44	[illegible]½	126
Fargo	175,987	167,478	343,465	50,[illegible]83	20,250	72	553
Grafton	8,602	7,792	16,394	7,[illegible]01	2,376	19	4
Grand Forks	61,838	57,605	119,443	31,[illegible]23	7,032	63	63
Jamestown	50,290	49,039	99,329	15,801	[illegible]4	50	516
Lakota	3,269	2,449	6,118	5,122	131	9	......
LaMoure	7,327	6,228	13,555	5,386	1,135	6	563
Leonard Township	64	....	....	2,140	85	6	15
Lidgerwood	16,576	12,629	29,205	6,776	843	30	473
Lisbon	12,240	10,144	22,384	3,399	710	27	219
Mandan	13,671	15,242	18,913	5,306	1,485	48	122
Mayville	3,374	2,847	5,221	5,620	....	8	......
[illegible]t	73,296	79,373	152,669	22,137	5,386	54	166
[illegible]t	3,220	3,736	6,956	3,385	361	6	127
[illegible]s	22,331	21,502	43,833	7,737	1,100	28	206
Park River	9,658	7,124	16,782	3,257	588	20	102
Rugby	16,928	13,569	30,497	6,184	1,168	33	225
Turtle Lake	347	357	704	1,456	55	2	......
Valley City	22,454	23,228	45,682	17,217	2,806	36	386
[illegible]n	24,117	22,809	46,926	11,762	2,138	27	408
[illegible]h	9,418	8,234	17,652	11,605	4,225	36	528
[illegible]k	2,325	2,414	4,739	2,351	582	4	134

ASSOCIATION LIBRARIES GIVING FREE SERVICE

Town	Date Estab-lished	1940 Popu-lation	Municipal Help	Hours Open Week	Volumes	Borrowers	Circulation	1946-1948 Expenditures Books	Total
Ashley	1913	1,[illegible]5	None	6	4,903	591	6,[illegible]0	$187.05	$ 427.05
Bathgate	1916	[illegible]32	None	2	1,297	87	[illegible]0	63.50	105.58
Beach	1912	1,[illegible]78	Room $300	5½	3,015	638	3,500	288.05	462.68
Beulah	1931	[illegible]2	Room	2	1,931	284	1,300	28.12	81.62
Bottineau	1915	1,[illegible]9	None	2	1,296	325	2,750	66.27	....
Cavalier	1915	1,[illegible]5	Room $[illegible]0	4½	2,636	434	2,450	203.45	401.23
Cooperstown	1945	1,[illegible]7	$5.00	6	568	....	1,392	296.88	610.88
Crosby	19[illegible]	1,[illegible]4	Room	37	5,250	790	11,850	848.50	2,302.42
Drake	1920	[illegible]64	Room	3	2,232	296	4,[illegible]0	96.23	96.23
Drayton	1946	[illegible]68	Room	3½	985	355	1,900	189.76	283.01
Flaxton	1935	[illegible]62	Room	2	2,147	30	[illegible]0	....	....
Forbes	1944	[illegible]88	Room	6	1,007	118	3,250	98.46	190.34
Goodrich	[illegible]6	[illegible]46	$50.00	2	2,085	150	[illegible]0	....	26.40
Halliday	[illegible]7	[illegible]95	Room	2½	850	80	50	40.94	71.60
Hankinson	[illegible]7	1,[illegible]0	Room	2	650	35	1,300	....	60.00
Hebron	[illegible]8	1,267	Room $100	3	1,081	251	3,650	28.89	117.68
Hettinger	[illegible]2	[illegible]8	$700.00	8	1,822	175	2,500	278.76	532.65
Hoople	[illegible]7	[illegible]6	Room	2	558	120	1,500	43.25	63.25
Hope	[illegible]0	[illegible]4	Room	....	1,633	....	1,[illegible]0	109.67	135.00
Kulm	[illegible]7	734	None	2	1,073	120	3,250	56.45	106.[illegible]7
Linton	[illegible]6	1,602	Lib. salary	11	3,039	....	2,400	72.00	682.00
[illegible]	[illegible]7	687	[illegible] $[illegible]0	6	2,359	442	1,950	54.40	364.40
Northwood	[illegible]1	1,063	Room	2	633	55	1,250	74.16	76.05
Oberon	[illegible]8	225	None	4	704	120	[illegible]0	39.50	48.65
[illegible]	1946	123	No activity to report						
[illegible]	1947	460	Room	4	345	131	....	158.77	400.51
St. Thomas	19[illegible]7	503	$50.00	2½	2,756	....	1,500	....	71.00
[illegible]	[illegible]8	455	$25.00	1½	1,134	105	1,500	39.65	126.97

ASSOCIATION LIBRARIES CHARGING FOR SERVICE

Town	Date Established	1940 Population	Municipal Help	Hours Open Week	Volumes	Borrowers	[illegible]	1946-48 Expenditures Books	Total
[illegible]o	1902	1,282	None	2	4,270	103	10,300	$ 72.65	$641.65
Edgeley	1912	803	Room $50	2	2,543	30	1,500	35.00	59.00
Enderlin	1912	1,593	Room	4	6,746	807	3,100	281.70	301.77
Forman	1939	500	Room $ [illegible]0	4	1,451	110	1,250	16.24	88.24
Hamilton	1916	255	None	2	1,108	32	200	....	....
Hansboro	1928	196	$[illegible]0	3	[illegible]2	16	200	38.42	....
[illegible]	1909	1,851	Not [illegible]ing temporarily						
Killdeer	....	650	None	2	1,640	....	1,600	74.01	93.75
[illegible]	1912	1 [illegible]6	Room Lib. salary	8	6,807	118	10,000	77.95	391.35
L[illegible]s	1902	[illegible]2	Room $100	3	2,457	166	1,150	....	52.00
Lehr	1941	[illegible]8	Room	1 ½	[illegible]8	....	1,400	....	13.50
N[illegible]w England	1931	[illegible]5	Room	2	1,774	135	1,150	30.72	33.32
New Rockford	1917	2,017	Room Lib. salary	8	3,126	97	2,100	118.80	160.34
Regent	1935	[illegible]1	Room	2	[illegible]8	27	850	15.00	54.33
[illegible]a	1924	1,008	Room	2	2,469	69	1,250	65.31	70.91
Zeeland	1946	[illegible]9	Room	1	[illegible]5	40	2,400	....	6.31

STATE OF NORTH DAKOTA
LIBRARY DIRECTORY

Arnegard	Public Library	Mrs. Clifford Sovig
Ashley	Public Library	Mrs. Ione Huether
Bathgate	Free Public Library	Mrs. O. S. Spuhmann
Beach	Public Library	Mrs. Grace Houck
Beulah	Public Library	Mrs. W. H. Esterly
Bismarck	Public Library	Erana Stadler
Bismarck	State Historical Library	Mrs. Florence Davis
Bottineau	Public Library	Mrs. E. M. Ertresvaag
Bottineau	State Forestry School Library	Geo. P. Hynes
Bowman	Clara Lincoln Phelan Library	Mrs. Mertie Pond
Cando	Public Library	Lucile Harris
Carrington	City Library	Mrs. Ella Mae Hargrave
Casselton	Public Library	Delores C. Ries
Cavalier	Public Library	Mrs. Robert Thacker
Cogswell	Public Library	Olive M. Bartlett
Cooperstown	Public Library	Mrs. S. H. Larson
Crosby	Divide County Library	Mrs. J. H. Phelps
Devils Lake	Carnegie Library	Mrs. James Barrett
Dickinson	Public Library	Gertrude Voldal
Dickinson	State Teachers College Library	Matilda L. Stoxen
Drake	Public Library	Mrs. E. T. Rhode
Drayton	Public Library	Mrs. Willis J. Devlin
Edgeley	Public Library	Mrs. Florence Lee
Elbowoods	Public Library	Alice M. Watson
Ellendale	Public Library	Maude B. Blumer
Ellendale	Normal & Industrial School Library	Mrs. Cecil Purcell
Enderlin	Public Library	Mrs. Thomas Pierce, Jr.
Fargo	Public Library	Inga Rynning
Fargo	State Agricultural College Library	H. Dean Stallings
Flaxton	Public Library	Dora L. Kundiger
Forbes	Public Library	Merle Borgen
Forman	Public Library	Betty Sofstrom
Gackle	Public Library	Mrs. J. M. Hummel
Goodrich	Public Library	Helen Martin
Grafton	Public Library	Mrs. Glenna M. Dooley
Grand Forks	Public Library	Helen E. Garnaas
Grand Forks	State University Library	Della Mathys
Halliday	Public Library	Mrs. Elmer Goetz
Hamilton	Public Library	Mrs. Andrew Knutson
Hankinson	Public Library	Mrs. Geo. Schuett
Hansboro	Public Library	Mrs. J. O. Funk
Harvey	Public Library	Mrs. A. B. Hannes

Hebron	Public Library	Mrs. Nick Bingert
Hettinger	Public Library	Mrs. Mabel Tommerson
Hoople	Public Library	Mrs. Elmer Gryte
Hope	Public Library	Mrs. A. E. Dolezol
Jamestown	Alfred Dickey Free Library	Mrs. Anna P. Bensch
Jamestown	Jamestown College Library	Marian Hemmings
Killdeer	Public Library	Mrs. Wm. Cickburn
Kulm	Public Library	Mrs. E. E. Orth
Lakota	The A. M. Tofthagen Library	Mrs. Inga Ferris
LaMoure	Public Library	Mrs. James A. Frank
Langdon	Public Library	Mrs. E. J. Donovan
Leeds	Public Library	Mrs. Ben Baglien
Lehr	Public Library	Mrs. Roy Bittner
Leonard	Watts Free Library	Mrs. Elsie Greuel
Lidgerwood	City Library	Mrs. Elizabeth Kings
Linton	Public Library	N. S. Sheffield
Lisbon	Public Library	Pauline M. Billing
Mandan	Public Library	Eleanor Trzcinski
Mayville	Public Library	Sophia Springen
Mayville	State Teachers College Library	Mrs. Hazel Webster Byrnes
Minot	Public Library	Mrs. Lois A. Ronning
Minot	State Teachers College Library	Nellie R. Swanson, Acting
Mohall	Public Library	Mrs. Orville P. Witteman
Mott	Inez Hendrickson Library	Virginia Mehrer
New England	Public Library	Mrs. E. M. Boucher
New Rockford	Public Library	Mrs. James Donnelly
Northwood	Northwood City Library	Mrs. West Mutchler
Oakes	Public Library	Jessie M. Robinson
Oberon	Public Library	Mrs. Hazel Carlson
Omemee	Public Library	Mrs. Willis Watson
Park River	Public Library	Vera H. Warner
Petersburg	Public Library	Carrie Barnum
Pembina	Public Library	Mrs. Pauline Brennan
Portal	Public Library	Mrs. W. H. McCauley
Regent	Public Library	Mrs. C. J. Bowers
Rolette	Public Library	Mrs. Vesper Lewis
Rolla	Public Library	Mrs. Clarence Jacobsen
Rugby	Public Library	Mrs. P .E. McMahon
St. Thomas	Public Library	Mrs. E. T. Thompson
Sanish	Public Library	Mrs. A. L. Brevig
Turtle Lake	Public Library	Mrs. John Frey
Valley City	Carnegie Public Library	Mrs. Helen H. Tracy
Valley City	State Teachers College Library	D. W. Ferguson
Verona	Public Library	Mrs. Louise Laney
Wahpeton	Leach Public Library	Mrs. M. Kachelhoffer
Wahpeton	State Science School Library	Carol Anderson
Williston	James Memorial Library	Mrs. Sylvia R. Monson
Wimbledon	Public Library	Mrs. Henry Fehr
Wishek	Public Library	Mrs. Herbert Ottmar
Zeeland	Public Library	Lucille Maier

Twentieth Biennial Report

of the

State Library Commission

to the

State Board of Administration

FOR THE PERIOD

July 1, 1944 - June 30, 1946

Twentieth Biennial Report

of the

State Library Commission

to the

State Board of Administration

STATE LIBRARY COMMISSION STAFF

June 30, 1946

Lillian E. Cook.....Secretary and Director
Gena J. Bakken.....Librarian
Wilda Sebastian.....Chief Clerk
Martha S. Wanner.....Stenographer

FOR THE PERIOD

July 1, 1944 - June 30, 1946

TO THE STATE BOARD OF ADMINISTRATION: M. I. Forkner, Chairman, R. H. Sherman, O. A. Braseth, Math Dahl and Arthur E. Thompson, Bismarck, North Dakota.

Herewith is transmitted the Twentieth Biennial Report of the North Dakota State Library Commission covering the period from July 1, 1944 to June 30, 1946.

REPORT OF THE SECRETARY AND DIRECTOR, NORTH DAKOTA STATE LIBRARY COMMISSION—1944-1946

North Dakota took an important forward step in library progress during the biennium in the passage at the 1945 legislature of an amendment to the state library law making possible the establishment and maintenance of county and regional library service. Divide County has already taken advantage of this permissive legislation and at the June 25th primaries voted for such a tax. The question is being considered in other sections of the state.

Otherwise the State Library Commission and public libraries of the state have been "reconverting" and adjusting to peace time conditions. These conditions affect 1. the choice of books, emphasis changed from books about war to books on the peace, the United Nations, the problems of the returned soldier; 2. the price of books which has gone up tremendously; 3. adult reading, ("I don't want anything about the war"); 4. children's books, giving a new demand for life in other lands, tolerance and understanding of other peoples. This period has produced the highest standard of book publication in juvenile literature, the best physical makeup, the best authors, the best illustrators, and the highest prices. It has also produced (in an attempt to hold the price down) worthwhile books so cheaply made and bound, many in spiral bindings, that they will not serve library uses.

Personnel is still a problem, with professional help practically impossible to secure and constant changes in the clerical positions. A desperately needed increase in State Library Commission salaries was allowed by the 1945 legislature which has helped in the personnel problem.

Because of changing library personnel in the libraries of the state and because of new library legislation there were many requests for field help not all of which have been met. The following libraries were visited and meetings attended:

Public Libraries:

Beach	Flaxton	Mayville
Carrington	Grafton	Minot
Cooperstown	Grand Forks	Park River
Crosby	Hope	Pembina
Devils Lake	Jamestown	Valley City
Dickinson	Lakota	Wahpeton
Edgeley	LaMoure	Williston
Fargo	Lisbon	

Institutions:
- University, Grand Forks
- Agricultural College, Fargo
- State Teachers Colleges, Dickinson, Mayville, Minot and Valley City
- State Science School, Wahpeton

State and national and special meetings:
- North Dakota Library Association board meeting at Valley City;
- North Dakota Library Association state meeting at Fargo;
- North Dakota Education Association state meeting, Fargo;
- American Library Association meeting at Chicago;
- County Superintendents, Bismarck (2 meetings);
- Library section, NDEA (2 meetings);
- Parent Teachers Association state meeting, Bismarck.

STATE LIBRARY COMMISSION GENERAL AND ADMINISTRATIVE

While the Public Library reports for the state for the past two years show in general a falling off in circulation, the State Library Commission has a net gain for the period of 13,601 books or 6,800 a year. An increased appropriation available July 1, 1945 with more money for salaries and books has made it possible to hold the professional staff and recruit new clerical help as resignations came in.

The Secretary devoted a great deal of time and effort to the legislative program which secured for the Commission its most adequate budget and for the state at large the county library law. Time also was devoted to helping Divide County secure favorable action when the question was submitted to vote at the primary. Time and effort were given to the larger nationwide movements for the extension and improvement of library service as incorporated in the two movements, the Library Development Fund and the Library Demonstration bill.

Thru the wholehearted cooperation of all public and school libraries an educational campaign in regard to the American Library Association Library Development campaign was put on, and eventually the North Dakota quota of $400 was oversubscribed. With the amount pro-rated to the state from publishers' contributions the final figure is $483 or 121%, a percentage only exceeded by five other states.

The Federal Library Demonstration bill which as finally approved carried an appropriation of $37,500 for each of five successive years for each state for a demonstration of some form of service vitally needed in that state. The bill was reported out favorably by the Education Committee of both Senate and House of Representatives but too late for Congressional action at the last session. The bill will be reintroduced early in the 1947 session.

Field work, publication of Library Notes and a monthly page in North Dakota Teacher; semi-annual book exhibits for the small libraries; board meetings and conferences with both school and public libraries, cooperation with the State Department of Public Instruction on various publications; regular office and administrative work more than fill the working hours of the Secretary and Director.

REFERENCE DEPARTMENT

There has been a gratifying and steady upward trend in the demand for library service through the Reference Department during the past biennium. Whether this would have come about anyway, or whether it is due to the publicity given libraries through recent library legislation, is a matter of conjecture.

Through the reference department "qualified" borrowers who wish selective packages of books are served. By "qualified" we mean all residents of North Dakota who do not have adequate library service available in their communities. State employees may, and do, avail themselves of the services of the Library Commission.

Besides supplying individuals with books to meet recreational and informational needs, schools are supplied with supplementary books for outside reading. The Reading Circle collection, composed of books recommended by the Department of Education, is used heavily by rural and village schools. Approximately six hundred schools have registered for this type of service. The reference department also provides declamations for the grades, "special day" program suggestions, and plays for the grades and high school. The high schools are supplied with up-to-date books that meet the standards for outside reading for book reviews and themes on a variety of subjects.

About the same number of registered clubs as formerly (forty-five) make use of the specialized service given them. The director prepares suggested programs and developed outlines for them based on material available through the Library Commission. An ever increasing number of unregistered clubs are using our club program suggestions and material.

Through the "Book a Month" plan, individuals who borrow may have books mailed to them as soon as they return books borrowed without a written request each time. Fifty-eight make use of this privilege. We are glad to note more children among our regular borrowers.

Until this year, the Agricultural College referred its correspondence students to us for books and other information. However, due to a larger appropriation having been allowed them by the legislature, this service from us is no longer necessary.

With the abandonment of the camps for conscientious objectors and internees, our service to them was ended.

With a larger book appropriation and somewhat less trouble in getting the books we order, about double the usual number of books per year have been added to the reference collection. Preparation of the books through cataloging is done by the reference librarian. Although we do not have a complete catalog of books in our collection to mail out, attempts are made to supply lists of new books from time to time. Booklists on specific subjects are made up and sent on request.

Over sixty carefully selected periodicals, some twenty thousand pamphlets and clippings, and a book collection of 22,734 are at our disposal. The staff is on the alert for usable material whether in books, magazines, pamphlets, or clippings. During the past year reference material in regard to the Garrison Dam project has been popular. The reference questions that come to us are as varied and as seriously asked as any that come to the attention of reference librarians in city libraries.

TRAVELING LIBRARY DEPARTMENT

The secretary is still carrying the professional work of the Traveling Library Department with changing clerical help. In spite of the fact that school districts have more funds and are building up local school libraries, and small public libraries are spending more for books, the circulation from this department is practically the same as for the war years 1942-44. This is probably because the libraries which are being sent out are recent ones or have been remade and are more attractive, physically and in subject matter.

THE STATE AT LARGE

New libraries opened at Cooperstown, Drayton, Omemee and Zeeland. Libraries reopened at Hebron and Wimbledon. Libraries closed at Beulah, Portal, Towner and Watford City. New library buildings at Ashley and Northwood.

Resignation after long service: Mrs. Ethel McVeety, Agricultural College, after 48 years; Miss Vannie Hall, Public Library, New Rockford, after 38 years. Many libraries were able to secure labor and materials for extensive redecoration and repairs and at least two institutions have funds earmarked for a new building. The Agricultural College and Jamestown College. Construction must await changed building conditions.

COMMISSION NEEDS

1. MORE PROFESSIONAL HELP. There are now only two trained people on the staff, the secretary and the reference librarian. A cataloger who can help with field work will be requested in the next budget. The second need is for trained head for the Traveling Library department.

2. MORE BOOKS. Changing conditions mean that books go out of date quickly and new science (atomic power) and political movements (United Nations) mean that a whole new collection must be built up. Advancing prices necessitate more money for the same number of books.

3. CLOSER TOUCH WITH SMALL PUBLIC LIBRARIES which experience the changes and do not have experienced staff to meet them and depend on the State Library Commission for help and suggestions.

STATE NEEDS

1. Library recruiting to build up a group of trained librarians interested in North Dakota.

2. SOCIAL SECURITY. Librarians are not included in Federal Social Security and only school librarians can benefit from the Teachers Retirement Fund. Some system of retirement annuity or pension should be secured.

3. More librarians with full or summer school library training to give more efficient service.

4. State wide educational campaigns to inform rural residents of the benefits and possibilities of regional library service.

LILLIAN E. COOK
Secretary and Director State
Library Commission

STATISTICAL REPORT—1944-46

BOOKS

Traveling Library Department

Number of Traveling libraries	206
Number of libraries added during this biennium	73
Number of books added during this period	1,910
Number of books in traveling libraries	6,764

Reference Department

Number of books in this department	22,734
Number of books added during this biennium	1,066
Number of pamphlets in collection	21,150

CIRCULATION

Traveling Library Department

Number of Libraries circulated	1944-45	1945-46	Total
Schools	302	317	619
Communities	79	70	149
Number of books circulated	10,701	10,316	21,017
New T. L. stations	30	67	97

Reference Department

Number of requests filled	6,638	7,430	14,068
Number of books circulated	46,551	49,528	96,079
Magazine and pamphlets sent out	4,815	6,363	11,178
Total reference department circulation	51,366	55,891	107,257
TOTAL CIRCULATION OF COMMISSION	62,037	66,207	128,244

PUBLIC LIBRARIES

Town	Date [illegible]	1940 population	RECEIPTS Tax appropriation 1944-45	1945-46	[illegible] Receipts 1944-45	1945-46
Bismarck	1914	15,496	$12,000.00	$15,500.00	$14,225.70	$18,442.57
Bowman	1916	967	468.34	1,538.14	681.46	1,682.54
Carrington	1906	[illegible]	1,200.00	1,200.00	2,823.58	2,740.41
Casselton	1906	1,358	345.81	323.29	698.52	786.80
Devils Lake	1898	[illegible]	3,391.00	4,561.84	7,395.86	7,681.72
Dickinson	1908	5,839	[illegible]	5,000.00	6,034.79	6,[illegible]96.23
Ellendale	1912	1,517	650.00	750.00	978.76	1,108.92
Fargo	1900	32,580	20,791.63	20,844.60	36,882.50	31,[illegible]97.98
Grafton	1895	4,070	1,200.00	600.00	5,431.18	3,452.67
Grand Forks	1899	20,228	12,510.00	[illegible]	13,449.56	16,086.48
Jamestown	1901	8,790	4,500.00	[illegible]541.63	6,511.81	6,880.73
Lakota	1906	907	139.81	51.07	468.25	782.57
[illegible]	1924	990	[illegible]	750.00	678.91	819.79
Leonard [illegible]	1912	465	125.00	125.00	129.43	133.65
Lidgerwood	1913	1,042	720.00	1,050.00	779.97	1,070.26
Lisbon	1915	1,997	1,591.78	1,525.84	5,921.99	6,[illegible]94.81
Mandan	1896	6,685	1,873.98	2,265.66	4,316.44	3,968.00
Mayville	1900	1,[illegible]51	750.00	750.00	968.59	1,179.79
Minot	1908	16,577	11,054.42	10,952.19	19,522.35	20,470.12
Mott	1912	1,220	380.00	380.00	500.03	544.53
Oakes	1905	1,665	920.32	1,079.68	1,595.74	1,846.89
Park River	1900	1,408	[illegible]	400.00	601.21	688.18
Rugby	1912	2,215	817.76	1,285.00	1,320.43	1,672.77
[illegible] Lake	1926	632	[illegible]	100.00	131.33	133.95
Valley City	1900	5,917	4,781.44	6,658.91	9,843.64	13,062.31
Wa[illegible]		3,747	5,000.00	6,000.00	6,994.79	8,389.39
Wil[illegible]	1910	5,790	6,484.33	4,694.49	[illegible]	7,486.50
Wishek	1926	1,112	[illegible]	200.00	352.66	431.45

PUBLIC LIBRARIES

EXPENDITURES

Town	Salaries 1944-45	Salaries 1945-46	Maintenance 1944-45	Maintenance 1945-46	Books-Periodicals 1944-45	Books-Periodicals 1945-46	Total 1944-45	Total 1945-46
Bismarck	$ 8,069.70	$ 9,785.38	$ 1,993.18	$ 1,701.01	$ 2,836.73	$ 4,211.70	$12,900.31	$16,348.80
Bowman	484.00	586.50	79.49	130.27	152.82	220.75	716.31	[illegible]
Carrington	723.00	720.00	199.82	47.28	360.35	385.91	1,283.17	1,154.19
[illegible]n	106.00	118.00	28.00	71.38	151.01	130.16	285.01	314.54
Devils [illegible]ke	2,615.50	1,823.66	999.66	922.37	[illegible]	590.29	4,624.22	3,336.26
Dickinson	3,077.35	3,219.95	664.53	717.11	1,545.48	1,549.83	5,287.26	5,486.89
Ellendale	485.30	491.48	23.44	14.63	339.67	338.04	848.41	871.15
Fargo	[illegible]	14,344.25	6,087.04	5,096.12	2,692.33	3,594.71	22,495.69	23,035.08
Grafton	1,220.00	1,334.85	304.14	472.37	364.42	417.28	1,888.56	2,224.50
Grand Forks	6,592.95	8,729.45	1,720.70	2,088.43	2,012.36	2,267.10	10,326.01	[illegible]
[illegible]wn	2,850.99	3,042.72	1,515.58	1,732.29	1,334.03	1,238.47	5,720.60	6,013.48
[illegible]ta	373.00	427.50	180.03	369.41	45.59	51.07	598.42	847.98
LaMoure	322.73	385.25	72.61	96.81	271.93	327.88	667.27	809.94
Leonard [illegible]hip	75.00	96.00	22.90	22.81	30.62	....	128.52	118.81
Lidgerwood	510.00	660.00	122.45	266.99	139.87	139.41	772.32	1,066.40
[illegible]on	617.50	617.50	240.68	1,045.46	429.07	369.75	1,287.25	2,032.71
[illegible]an	1,368.66	1,703.25	749.40	150.89	794.27	984.60	2,912.33	2,838.74
Mayville	341.00	300.00	369.44	358.05	257.02	226.46	967.46	985.51
[illegible]ot	5,516.00	5,694.90	2,507.60	1,881.52	2,787.75	3,920.60	10,811.35	[illegible]
[illegible]tt	180.00	180.50	7.87	2.76	212.15	74.90	400.02	258.16
Oakes	829.65	803.70	33.93	54.69	225.43	278.25	1,089.01	1,136.64
Park River	320.00	420.00	28.41	54.38	196.98	89.47	545.39	563.85
Rugby	749.60	883.80	102.97	137.14	327.39	241.18	1,179.96	1,262.12
Turtle Lake	70.00	50.00	5.00	31.10	30.38	34.65	105.38	115.75
Valley City	2,185.00	2,655.20	797.20	850.62	841.44	848.01	3,823.64	4,353.83
Wahpeton	2,442.00	2,529.98	1,720.10	[illegible]	[illegible]	965.01	4,979.54	4,525.01
[illegible]on	2,590.10	2,805.50	1,313.88	754.45	1,441.44	1,919.83	5,345.22	5,479.78
[illegible]ek	59.50	68.75	6.61	9.49	67.95	107.30	134.06	185.54

PUBLIC LIBRARIES

Town	Circulation 1944-45	Circulation 1945-46	Total	Volumes	Borrowers	Hours open per week	Rural Borrowers
Bismarck	120,525	109,099	229,624	2[illegible]208	5,872	77	136
Bowman	5,173	3,507	8,680	6,896	577	14	......
Carrington	8,898	10,367	19,265	5,837	916	33	310
Casselton	4,036	4,002	8,038	2,684	316	4	15
Devils Lake	23,588	20,692	44,280	13,138	1,381	36	26
Dickinson	38,323	40,659	78,982	17,934	2,658	45	278
Ellendale	11,894	13,285	25,179	5,854	366	30	100
Fargo	181,475	175,433	356,908	46,925	19,356	49	501
Grafton	9,832	8,745	18,577	6,836	2,125	42	3
Grand Forks	49,250	52,363	101,613	21,808	6,715	42	220
Jamestown	46,000	48,783	94,783	14,410	4,480	52	520
Lakota	2,152	2,508	4,660	5,112	120	9	......
LaMoure	4,443	6,257	10,700	4,806	988	18	463
Leonard Township	....	....	....	2,081	50	6	15
Lidgerwood	12,159	11,650	23,809	6,540	773	32	563
Lisbon	11,076	11,613	22,689	3,103	894	18	194
Mandan	12,403	12,254	24,657	5,255	1,131	....	20
Mayville	3,594	3,146	6,740	5,265	....	24	....
Minot	58,317	60,194	118,511	20,688	5,103	46	116
Mott	3,077	2,621	5,698	3,407	452	5	68
Oakes	18,846	19,593	38,439	7,458	1,556	6	428
Park River	15,000	7,991	22,991	3,105	370	24	90
Rugby	19,081	17,324	36,405	6,676	1,462	30	165
Turtle Lake	50	988	1,038	1,416	85	2	......
Valley City	24,687	22,736	47,423	16,514	3,060	36	326
Wahpeton	17,086	23,143	40,229	11,020	2,868	24	443
Williston	16,680	8,461	25,141	11,121	4,441	36	539
Wishek	2,500	1,552	4,052	1,886	450	4	65

ASSOCIATION LIBRARIES GIVING FREE SERVICE

Town	Date Established	1940 population	Municipal help	Hours per week	Volumes	Bor- [illegible]s	Circulation	1944-46 Expenditures Books	Total
Arnegard		222	Room $10	2	303	......	......	$ 10.00	$ 15.00
Ashley	1913	1,345	None	4	4,384	733	5,180	62.52	552.05
Bathgate	1916	312	None	2	1,766	......	2,107	29.79	60.08
Beach	1912	1,178	Room $300	5½	2,557	605	3,688	183.15	424.57
Beulah	1931	942	Room	2	1,894	......	2,044	116.38	135.03
Bottineau	1915	1,739	None	2	1,159	312	2,786	66.00	73.00
[illegible]er	1915	1,105	Room $75	4	2,908	......	4,028	269.78	286.84
Cogswell	1935	430	None	5	2,974	423	3,500	....	....
[illegible]wn	1945	1,077	None	6	353	200	....	227.59	333.93
Crosby	1930	1,404	Room	6	4,281	550	13,482	228.00	494.71
Drake	1920	654	None	3	2,096	516	7,200	123.70	128.55
Drayton	1946	688	Room	2½	789	172	2,288	....	....
Elbowoods	1941	....	Room	all	1,331	100	3,500	....	....
Flaxton	1935	362	$50	2	1,480	156	3,230	7.00	41.50
Forbes	1944	268	$75	6	795	102	3,300	128.45	288.88
Goodrich	1926	476	Room $50	2	2,020	190	2,860	65.00	78.50
Hamilton	1916	255	None	2	1,185	8	500	....	....
Hankinson	1907	1,420	$60	2	1,603	88	1,554	15.05	135.05
Hebron	1938	1,267	Room $100	4	982	276	5,500	65.68	201.07
o[illegible]le	1937	346	None	1	777	6	3,604	100.00	130.00
Killdeer	....	650	Fuel	2	1,453	......	4,236	156.50	225.09
Kulm	1937	734	Room	2	733	87	1,394	2.15	4.68
Linton	1936	1,602	Room $260	13	2,607	......	6,828	209.76	737.52
Mohall	1937	687	Librarian's salary	7½	2,302	440	2,560	256.41	467.73
Oberon	1938	225	None	4	626	131	1,624	52.33	134.55
[illegible]e	1946	123	Room	3	469	78	1,560	....	....
Pembina	1946	703	$75	3	1,[illegible]60	60	3,500	75.00	[illegible]
Sanish	1928	455	$25	1	877	74	2,860	61.12	72.76

ASSOCIATION LIBRARIES CHARGING FOR SERVICE

Town	Date Established	1940 population	Municipal help	Hours per week	Volumes	Borrowers	Circulation	1944-46 Expenditures Books	1944-46 Expenditures Total
Cando	1902	1,282	....	2	4,000	65	7,631	$188.70	$449.12
Dawson	....	263	Room	3	910	34	2,500	....	....
Edgeley	1912	803	Room	2	2,543	30	3,300	45.90	72.80
Enderlin	1912	1,593	Room	4	3,524	617	9,000	481.96	858.92
Forman	1939	500	Room $100	4	1,403	110	2,290	70.00	214.00
Gackle	1936	537	....	2	625	13	2,000	7.07	9.19
Hansboro	1928	196	$10	3	756	18	1,594	48.37	74.67
Harvey	1909	1,851	Room	3	1,991	46	1,330	29.18	37.12
Hettinger	1912	1,138	Room	3	1,505	200	2,100	....	....
Hope	1910	474	Room	3	1,400	100	3,500	....	....
Langdon	1912	1,546	Room $250	6½	6,924	162	3,000	186.63	585.43
Leeds	1902	782	Room $50	3	2,176	398	1,300	....	....
Lehr	1941	458	Room	2	389	200	2,704	101.88	133.65
New England	1931	895	Room	2	1,799	144	3,300	67.73	77.81
New Rockford	1917	2,017	Room	4	4,000	.....	4,960	....	....
Regent	1935	261	Room	2	879	54	3,560	....	42.50
Rolla	1924	1,008	Room	2	1,493	15	1,878	100.03	229.12
St. Thomas	1917	503	Light, heat & $50	1	2,744	200	7,990	74.76	248.36
Wimbledon	1915	357	Room	2	1,605	22	2,860	20.00	20.00
Zeeland	1946	489	Room	1	363	40	2,600	30.00	33.00

REPORT OF STATE LIBRARY COMMISSION

LIBRARY DIRECTOR

Town	Name of Library	Librarian
Arnegard	Public Library	Mrs. Clifford Sovig
Ashley	Public Library	Mrs. G. H. Hernett
Bathgate	Free Public Library	Mrs. Henry Kane
Beach	Public Library	Mrs. Grace Houck
Beulah	Public Library	Mrs. Robert W. Easton
Bismarck	Public Library	Erana Stadler
Bismarck	State Historical Library	Mrs. Florence Davis
Bottineau	Public Library	Mrs. E. M. Ertresvaag
Bottineau	State Forestry School Library	Valborg Oslund
Bowman	Clara Lincoln Phelan Library	Mrs. Mertie Pond
Cando	Public Library	Lucile Harris
Carrington	City Library	Mrs. Ella Mae Hargrave
Casselton	Public Library	Mrs. Martha B. Correll
Cavalier	Public Library	Mrs. Robert Thacker
Cogswell	Public Library	Olive M. Bartlett
Cooperstown	Public Library	Mrs. S. H. Larson
Crosby	Divide County Library	Mrs. John Shield
Dawson	Public Library	Mrs. Joseph A. Kooker
Devils Lake	Carnegie Library	Mrs. James Barrett
Dickinson	Public Library	Gertrude Voldal
Dickinson	State Teachers College Library	Matilda L. Stoxen
Drake	Public Library	Mrs. John Haldi, Sec.
Drayton	Public Library	Mrs. Albert Charbonneau
Edgeley	Public Library	Mrs. Florence Lee
Elbowoods	Public Library	Alice M. Watson
Ellendale	Public Library	Mrs. Lois L. Brokaw
Ellendale	Normal & Industrial School Library	Kathleen Dooley
Enderlin	Public Library	Mrs. O. H. Schaible
Fargo	Public Library	Inga Rynning
Fargo	State Agricultural College Library	Elliott L. Hardaway
Flaxton	Public Library	Mrs. E. A. Anderson
Forbes	Public Library	Merle Borgen
Forman	Public Library	Patricia Norton
Gackle	Public Library	Mrs. J. M. Hummel
Goodrich	Public Library	Mrs. Ralph N. Leland
Grafton	Public Library	Mrs. Ella Myers
Grand Forks	Public Library	Helen E. Garnaas
Grand Forks	State University Library	Della Mathys
Halliday	Public Library	Mrs. Elmer Goetz
Hamilton	Public Library	Mrs. Andrew Knutson

LIBRARY DIRECTORY

Town	Name of Library	Librarian
Hankinson	Public Library	Bernice Spreckels
Hansboro	Public Library	Mrs. J. O. Funk
Harvey	Public Library	Mrs. A. B. Hannes
Hebron	Public Library	Mrs. W. G. Klick
Hettinger	Public Library	Mrs. Josephine Kirby
Hoople	Public Library	Mary Ann Heder
Hope	Public Library	Mrs. D. J. Gumb
Jamestown	Alfred Dickey Free Library	Mrs. Anna P. Bensch
Jamestown	Jamestown College Library	Dr. Foster St. Clair
Killdeer	Public Library	Mrs. J. O. Severtson
Kulm	Public Library	Mrs. E. E. Orth
Lakota	The A. M. Tofthagen Library	Mrs. Inga Ferris
LaMoure	Public Library	Mrs. James A. Frank
Langdon	Public Library	Mrs. E. J. Donovan
Leeds	Public Library	Mrs. Ben Baglien
Lehr	Public Library	Mrs. Roy Bittner
Leonard	Watts Free Library	Mrs. Elsie Greuel
Lidgerwood	City Library	Mrs. Elizabeth Kings
Linton	Public Library	N. S. Sheffield
Lisbon	Public Library	Dorothy J. Thompson
Mandan	Public Library	Eleanor Trzcinski
Mayville	Public Library	Cora I. Ames
Mayville	State Teachers College Library	Mrs. Hazel W. Byrnes
Minot	Public Library	Mrs. Lois A. Ronning
Minot	State Teachers College Library	Nellie R. Swanson, Acting
Mohall	Public Library	Mrs. John Smith
Mott	Inez Hendrickson Library	Mrs. J. W. Hoye
New England	Public Library	Mrs. E. M. Boucher
New Rockford	Public Library	Mrs. James Donnelly
Northwood	Northwood City Library	Mrs. S. C. Sampson, Sec.
Oakes	Public Library	Jessie M. Robinson
Oberon	Public Library	Mrs. Hazel Carlson
Omemee	Public Library	Mrs. Willis Watson
Park River	Park River Public Library	Vera H. Warner
Petersburg	Public Library	Carrie Barnum
Pembina	Public Library	Mrs. Pauline Brennan
Portal	Public Library	Mrs. W. H. McCauley
Regent	Public Library	Mrs. E. A. Reitan
Rolla	Public Library	Mrs. Clarence Jacobsen
Rugby	Public Library	Mrs. P E. McMahon
St. Thomas	Public Library	Mrs. E. T Thompson
Sanish	Public Library	Mrs. Arvid Olson
Towner	Public Library	Mrs. Joe Harnit, Sec.
	brary	Mrs. John Frey
Valley City	Carnegie Public Library	Mrs. Helen H. Tracy
Valley City	State Teachers College Library	D. W. Ferguson
Verona	Public Library	Mrs. R. Freeman
Wahpeton	Leach Public Library	Mrs. M. Kachelhoffer
Wahpeton	State Science School Library	Patricia Murray
Williston	James Memorial Library	Mrs. Sylvia R. Monson
Wimbledon	Public Library	Mrs. Henry Fehr
Wishek	Public Library	Irene Frank
Zeeland	Public Library	Mrs. August E. Boschee

Twenty-second Biennial Report

of the

State Library Commission

to the

State Board of Administration

FOR THE PERIOD
July 1, 1948 - June 30, 1950

Twenty-second Biennial Report

of the

State Library Commission

to the

State Board of Administration

STATE LIBRARY COMMISSION STAFF
June 30, 1950

Hazel Webster Byrnes..Director and State Librarian
Arlene Stocker ....Assistant to the Director
Wilda Sebastian ....Chief Clerk
Dorothy Bigwood ....Acting Reference Librarian

FOR THE PERIOD
July 1, 1948 - June 30, 1950

TO THE STATE BOARD OF ADMINISTRATION: R. H. Sherman, Chairman, O. A. Braseth, F. A. Foley, Math Dahl, and Garfield B. Nordrum.

The North Dakota State Library Commission has the honor to submit its Twenty-second biennial report, covering the period from July 1, 1948 to June 30, 1950.

HAZEL WEBSTER BYRNES,
Director

REPORT OF THE DIRECTOR, NORTH DAKOTA STATE LIBRARY COMMISSION—1948-1950

We believe that this great state of North Dakota can no more be built without books than the Garrison Dam, which is taking so much thought, attention, and money, can be built without a solid foundation. Books are essential in the economic, educational and cultural development of our state. People respond eagerly to the offer of books, as this report indicates. Service progresses with each period of time. However, we are constantly aware that there is a tremendous task to be accomplished before North Dakota reaches the recommended standards which are so long overdue in this state.

ADMINISTRATIVE ACTIVITIES

PUBLICATIONS AND NEWSCASTS: That the public in general may be made aware of what is taking place in the library picture, the State Library Commission publishes its LIBRARY NOTES AND NEWS. The mailing list for this publication numbers about one thousand and, other than librarians, it includes state institutional and legislative officials, newspapers, out-of-state library agencies and editors of several publications.

Newspapers of this state have been generous in printing library publicity as has the press agency of the state capitol. Library journals, too, have given some commendatory write-ups to North Dakota. Radio also has helped. The KFYR radio station in Bismarck invited the director of the Commission to have time on one of its programs.

Special Publications: BULLETIN NO. 5, NINTH EDITION, in parts I and II, is the work of the State Library Commission. A good part of a year was given to its preparation. Part I is a revision of BULLETIN NO. 5, EIGHTH EDITION, 1937, and its seven supplements. It is a list of books suggested for boys and girls in grades one to eight, for which a Reader's Certificate is issued by the county superintendents. This is as well a recommended list for school purchase. Part II, ORGANIZING THE LIBRARY, is written to assist the teacher, who has had little or no library training, in taking the step-by-step procedures for organizing the elementary school library. Many details have been omitted so that the fundamentals might stand out more clearly.

MEETINGS AND PARTICIPATIONS:

Regional: A new type of meeting, the regional meeting, has shown the value of the library in a larger area. Examples of this type are the Northern Great Plains Library Conference at Great Falls, Montana, 1949, and Billings, Montana, 1950, with representatives from seven states in attendance; the Mountain-Plains Regional Conference at Ft. Collins, Colorado, 1949, and Salt Lake City, Utah, 1950, with six states represented; the Midwest Conference on Rural Life and Education, Lincoln, Nebraska, 1949, and Minot, North Dakota, 1950, with representatives from seven states and two Canadian provinces. North Dakota was represented at all of these meetings, with official representation from the State Library Commission.

National: Other than the above, there are the annual meetings of the American Library Association and the Mid-Winter business sessions, in Chicago, Illinois. At these conferences, the director of the State Library Commission represented North Dakota as the state council member and served as state coordinator for the Federal Relations Program.

State: The meeting of the North Dakota Library Association took place in Minot, 1949, and Fargo, 1950. At the Fargo meeting, the Association gave recognition to North Dakota authors at a dinner in their honor.

Workshops: In connection with the North Dakota Congress of Parents and Teachers, the State Library Commission held a series of workshops in six centers over this state. Problems and projects dealing with various types of libraries were discussed.

Library courses are now being offered in all of the teachers colleges and in the University of North Dakota. During the summer session, the director visited all of these schools and as many of the library classes as possible.

Art Week Exhibit: For the first time, books were featured in the over-all idea of creative art. The State Library Commission prepared and arranged a display of books and photographs of North Dakota authors. Several authors were invited as guest speakers.

CHANGES AND IMPROVEMENTS: The large reading room at the Commission has, in part, been converted into additional and needed office space. Two large desks with swivel chairs give an up-to-date business air. At the same time a new overstuffed davenport and chair offer welcome to the modern reader for whom the clack of typewriters offers no disturbance.

The director's office, opening into the room described above, has a new rounded combination council table and desk. Chair sets to match make for an attractive setting.

One of the improvements of which we are very proud is a new mailing counter with a huge scale placed in the center on the level of the counter. This permits the wrapping of the hundreds of packages and boxes at one end, and the sliding of them onto the scales without lifting them. A new post-a-meter in this department is another much appreciated labor saving device.

DISTINGUISHED VISITORS: Among the guests who have signed our Library Log, some of whom have counseled with us and addressed our meetings, are Miss Helen A. Ridgway, Chief Public Library Specialist, American Library Association; Dr. Ralph E. Ellsworth, Director of Libraries, University of Iowa and member of the American Library Association Executive Committee; Mr. William Easton, Regional Librarian, Reclamation District, United States Department of Interior, Billings, Montana; Miss Mercedes McKay, Secretary and Director, State Library Commission, Pierre, South Dakota; Brigadier General Heber L. Edwards, Fraine Barracks, Bismarck; Mrs. Gertrude E. Flyte, Consultant, National Congress of Parents and Teachers, Chicago, Illinois, and Mrs. Jessie (Ballard) Mackintosh, former director, State Library Commission, Yakima, Washington.

ACCOMPLISHMENTS AND ANTICIPATIONS: The State Library Commission worked hard for the passage of the Public Library Demonstration Bill. All of North Dakota's congressmen voted in favor—an accomplishment of merit for this state. This act as you know, was defeated in the House by only three votes. This discouragement acted only as a spur for plans in the making. At present, 88 public libraries are serving all urban areas of the state. It is therefore the rural areas to which energies are especially directed. The deterrents of distance, scattered population and low property evaluations are for the present, preventing the establishment of county libraries which would anywhere nearly meet standards set up by the American Library Association. Due to these circumstances, the State Library Commission of necessity is the main source of library service to the large rural population. Mail service from the Commission has increased some 20% in the last two years and to every county in the state.

Throughout the state, workshops have been held, visitations made to some forty different libraries, school libraries have been reorganized and public libraries re-opened and organized, and library courses have been encouraged. It sounds like accomplishment, and it is, but a field worker is needed as are additional qualified staff workers at the Commission, and more money must be found for books. Libraries are needing more funds in the form of state aid in order to stimulate more local support, and present services should be developed to approach suggested standards.

An anticipation which does us good is that of a bookmobile to be donated by the Federated Women's Clubs of the state. It is to be used for demonstration. For its operation and personnel we must also appeal to the Legislature for funds.

"Something has been accomplished
Much remains to be done."

MRS. HAZEL WEBSTER BYRNES
Director and State Librarian

DEPARTMENTAL REPORTS

Reference Department

Work in the reference department is varied and harried. The chief duty of the department is the filling of all requests for direct service from individuals, clubs, and libraries throughout the state where local facilities are inadequate. All the books in the main collection are processed in this department. Each book is classified, accessioned, provided with book cards and pockets; the backs are lettered, the books shellacked and then put on the shelves for distribution. During the past two years 2,282 books underwent this handling. This is an increase of almost 1000 over the number of books catalogued during the past biennium.

The library maintains an outstanding file of articles, newspaper clippings, and pamphlets covering topics of present day interest. Out of date material is constantly weeded out of the file and replaced by more recent information. This file is continually expanding and is of great help to the librarian in filling many of her requests. This Vertical File includes an outstanding collection of North Dakota material.

Many of our patrons, particularly those with families, find that they enjoy getting a box of books every month. In order for them to be supplied with books all the time, and to save them the necessity of writing in and requesting new books each month, the library has a service which we call **Books-a-Month.** A file is kept of reading preferences of people indicating a desire to have this service, and each time such a patron returns books, another box is automatically sent without further request.

As a special **service to the club women** of our state, the State Library Commission makes up a selection of interesting topics as suggestions for each year's programs. These are attractively listed and sent out to clubs throughout North Dakota. Topics may be arranged for one meeting only, but topics suited to year programs and part-year programs are also suggested.

A corresponding service supplies material necessary for preparing papers on topics selected by the clubs. Any club wishing this service sends the library a copy of its club program, and asks to be registered. Material for the topics listed is reserved, and without further request from the registered club, it is sent sufficiently in advance of the club meeting for the person scheduled to prepare the paper. This service attracts more women's clubs every year. Last year, the Commission sent out literature to about 84 clubs. Among the most popular of the topics chosen were Alaska, Believe It or Not, Community Projects for Club Women, Our Homes Today, and The United Nations. Topics dealing with North Dakota are always much in demand.

Reading Circle Department

The demand for Reading Circle books has grown steadily since its beginning several years ago. Many rural and consolidated schools make use of this fine service to supplement their inadequate libraries. The Reading Circle collection is composed of books for grade students which are selected by the State Library Commission and approved by the Department of Public Instruction. All pupils who read and report on two of these approved books each month during the year are issued a Reading Certificate by the County Superintendent. For this accomplishment, the teacher is authorized to add 10% of the yearly grade in Reading. This plan is very popular with County Superintendents and also teachers and pupils. We now send books each month to about nine hundred teachers with enrollment of approximately ten thousand students. Needless to say, our budget is inadequate to provide the books necessary to meet the demands of so many schools. More funds for this department are urgently needed.

Traveling Library Department

Activity in the Traveling Library Department continued at high speed during the past biennium. Circulation from this Department is handled by means of fixed collections of from 25 to 40 books, arranged for elementary schools, high schools, public libraries and community centers. Thirty-three new libraries were made ready for circulation, and all of the old collections renovated. A total of 20,912 volumes were sent out in 792 libraries to 464 stations for loan periods of three months, with the privilege of renewing for an additional three months. As in the other departments, the demand for service in this department exceeds the number of libraries available. We hope an increased book budget will remedy this situation.

A PICTORIAL REVIEW

Books added:
- Reference—2,282
- Reading Circle—1,000
- Traveling Library—830

Volumes available:
- Reference—18,189
- Reading Circle—8,500
- Traveling Library—8,750

Circulation—151,499

Requests—15,751

PUBLIC LIBRARIES

Town	Date established	1940 Population	RECEIPTS Tax Appropriation 1948-1949	Tax Appropriation 1949-50	Total Receipts 1948-49	Total Receipts 1949-50
Bismarck	1914	15,496	$19,924.00	$22,985.00	$22,812.04	$26,205.52
Bowman	1916	967	1,456.25	2,807.40	2,572.08	4,517.51
Carrington	1906	1,200	1,200.00	1,500.00	2,645.78	2,736.50
Casselton	1906	1,358	321.30	320.61	956.05	924.92
Devils Lake	1896	6,204	4,440.91	4,405.85	9,862.39	9,119.09
Dickinson	1908	5,839	6,500.00	6,500.00	7,229.41	7,418.47
Ellendale	1912	1,517	850.00	850.00	1,393.25	1,253.10
Fargo	1900	32,580	29,627.64	30,155.95	47,982.81	48,754.43
Grafton	1895	4,070	1,200.00	1,200.00	4,531.24	4,337.65
Grand Forks	1899	20,228	18,000.00	19,000.00	22,865.76	23,050.08
Jamestown	1901	8,790	6,550.00	7,150.00	8,417.57	9,267.15
Lakota	1906	907	532.37	651.22	807.35	929.83
LaMoure	1924	990	750.00	750.00	818.02	844.26
Leonard Township	1912	465	150.00	150.00	153.07	151.69
Lidgerwood	1913	1,042	1,180.00	1,230.66	1,252.36	1,333.58
Lisbon	1915	1,997	1,475.85	1,840.78	4,226.96	4,342.75
Mandan	1896	6,685	3,485.69	4,138.36	5,854.72	6,504.10
Mayville	1900	1,351	875.30	1,000.00	1,363.28	1,361.95
Minot	1908	16,577	13,642.35	14,122.53	24,060.32	24,902.29
Mott	1912	1,220	410.21	338.50	457.05	405.05
Oakes	1905	1,665	1,261.61	1,500.00	2,485.51	2,852.48
Park River	1900	1,408	500.00	500.00	573.41	983.48
Rugby	1912	2,215	1,191.44	1,760.00	2,184.97	2,527.77
Turtle Lake	1926	632	137.70	369.12	231.74	492.33
Valley City	1900	5,917	9,464.90	5,067.40	13,558.62	13,341.71
Wahpeton	....	3,747	2,800.00	5,000.00	4,303.12	5,482.25
Williston	1910	5,790	8,221.47	9,626.95	10,691.59	16,357.22
Wishek	1926	1,112	200.00	200.00	544.50	400.00

PUBLIC LIBRARIES

EXPENDITURES

Town	Salaries 1948-49	Salaries 1949-50	Maintenance 1948-49	Maintenance 1949-50	Books-Periodicals 1948-49	Books-Periodicals 1949-50	Total 1948-49	Total 1949-50
Bismarck	$13,521.29	$16,078.30	$ 3,531.00	$ 4,660.59	$ 4,078.22	$ 3,828.82	$21,130.51	$24,567.71
Bowman	558.60	603.60	121.76	175.71	307.94	280.80	988.30	1,060.11
Carrington	924.00	924.00	42.84	107.55	442.44	430.26	1,409.28	1,461.81
[illegible]on	121.00	107.00	106.10	25.65	148.64	193.15	375.74	325.65
Devils Lake	2,392.75	2,287.00	1,285.16	1,972.26	[illegible]	1,219.01	4,920.76	5,478.27
Dickinson	4,336.35	1,832.35	1,113.50	791.87	1,214.10	1,467.31	6,663.95	7,091.53
Ellendale	609.00	604.00	93.02	167.55	418.18	440.13	1,120.20	1,211.68
Fargo	21,219.44	21,044.47	8,236.37	9,137.04	4,185.74	4,857.01	33,641.55	35,038.52
Grafton	1,350.00	1,443.00	655.47	639.51	399.70	910.43	2,405.17	2,992.94
Grand Forks	11,978.68	12,226.49	4,643.11	4,714.88	3,373.23	3,697.05	19,995.02	20,638.42
Ja[illegible]e t[illegible]wn	4,740.22	1,740.37	1,446.43	2,006.07	1,777.63	1,977.19	7,964.28	8,723.63
Lakota	430.35	480.00	180.76	180.00	31.17	100.38	642.28	760.38
LaMoure	[illegible]	387.50	126.47	147.23	272.54	300.99	786.51	835.72
[illegible]ard [illegible]wnship	96.00	100.00	4.60	18.60	....	5.00	100.60	123.60
Lidgerwood	746.00	675.00	276.57	263.65	167.72	[illegible]	1,190.29	1,250.38
[illegible]bon	794.70	780.00	699.83	787.03	405.46	405.13	1,899.99	1,972.16
Mandan	2,135.00	2,227.92	514.68	650.13	1,025.14	1,024.88	3,674.82	3,902.93
[illegible]ille	470.00	420.00	477.28	640.12	215.39	271.25	1,262.67	1,331.37
Minot	8,582.07	8,571.25	2,578.68	3,716.99	3,135.71	3,623.04	14,296.41	15,911.28
Mott	240.00	245.00	33.48	2.00	265.56	117.10	539.04	364.10
Oakes	850.00	850.00	87.21	62.00	356.60	388.84	1,293.81	1,300.84
Park River	420.00	420.00	9.00	78.61	90.99	109.14	519.99	607.75
Rugby	1,080.00	1,043.28	97.21	132.87	454.44	490.02	1,631.65	1,666.17
Turtle Lake	50.00	50.00	5.50	6.55	61.03	79.74	116.53	136.29
[illegible]ley City	3,206.38	3,243.83	1,224.80	1,042.21	1,134.39	1,115.23	5,565.57	5,401.27
Wahpeton	2,946.44	3,046.51	677.23	[illegible]	541.94	796.97	4,165.61	4,401.37
[illegible]on	2,197.83	3,217.40	936.56	6,400.88	884.55	1,057.88	4,018.94	11,676.16
Wishek	172.55	174.00	14.78	16.00	253.24	[illegible]	440.57	[illegible]

PUBLIC LIBRARIES

Town	(Circulation) 1948-49	1949-50	Total	Volumes	Borrowers	Hours Open a Week	Rural Borrowers
Bismarck	120,370	119,888	240,258	25,029	6,619	66	......
Bowman	2,905	3,111	6,016	7,097	546	14	......
Carrington	8,459	8,681	17,140	6,116	777	25	150
Casselton	4,929	2,561	7,490	3,160	382	4	......
Devils Lake	21,865	28,164	50,029	14,440	3,226	36	......
Dickinson	31,900	37,366	69,266	[illegible]	2,625	40	270
Ellendale	13,440	12,626	26,066	6,338	574	14¼	76
Fargo	169,860	175,026	344,886	53,917	22,006	42	632
Grafton	5,122	6,680	11,802	5,419	474	18	......
Grand Forks	68,084	76,892	144,976	23,079	8,106	69	442
Jamestown	51,809	53,947	105,756	16,782	5,138	48	551
Lakota	2,951	2,965	5,916	5,007	167	9	17
LaMoure	5,583	6,807	12,390	5,793	1,215	12	609
Leonard Township	....	....	....	2,143	35	6	......
Lidgerwood	14,134	10,103	24,237	6,939	838	20	402
Lisbon	9,438	9,856	19,294	3,873	863	18	313
Mandan	16,126	19,992	36,118	5,940	1,563	38	187
Mayville	2,489	2,987	5,476	5,859	64	8	......
Minot	88,648	91,443	180,191	23,134	5,816	63	82
Mott	5,772	6,208	11,980	3,482	181	5	......
Oakes	18,261	20,002	38,263	7,877	802	25	......
Park River	6,656	7,700	14,356	3,298	660	20	120
Rugby	15,635	17,924	33,559	6,456	1,139	30	166
Turtle Lake	532	503	1,035	1,585	75	2	......
Valley City	21,837	23,459	45,296	16,157	2,909	36	403
Wahpeton	18,149	19,098	37,247	12,358	2,141	27	450
Williston	5,974	7,967	13,941	11,613	4,493	30	......
[illegible]	2,076	2,100	4,176	2,900	700	4	150

ASSOCIATION LIBRARIES GIVEN FREE SERVICE

Town	Date Estab-lished	1940 Popu-lation	Municipal Help	Hours Open Week	Volumes	Bor-rowers	Circu-lation	1948-1950 Expenditures Books	1948-1950 Expenditures Total
Ashley	1913	1,345	$250	6	5,341	575	6,240	$ 455.81	$ 961.31
Bathgate	1916	312	None	2	1,363	87	1,144	84.10	141.52
Beach	1912	1,178	Room $300	5½	3,339	675	3,692	485.14	920.55
Beulah	1931	942	Room	2	2,127	241	2,028	170.96	251.71
Bottineau	1915	1,739	None	2	1,503	358	2,756	193.23	208.29
Cavalier	1915	1,105	Room	4	2,920	522	2,860	409.22	790.23
[illegible]n	1945	1,077	$500	6	945	......	1,248	639.92	1,246.22
Crosby	1930	1,404	Room	30	7,319	590	14,976	4,700.00	[illegible]
Drake	1920	654	Room	3	2,502	275	5,460	202.22	303.22
Drayton	1946	688	Room	5	1,089	419	2,912	184.46	353.46
Flaxton	1935	362	Room	2	1,887	70	1,560	....	....
[illegible]	....	....	None	60	1,105	90	2,080	....	....
Forbes	1944	268	Room	6	1,139	128	2,756	201.52	351.94
[illegible]h	1926	475	$50	2	2,232	135	624	....	116.96
Halliday	1937	395	No Report					No Report	
Hankinson	1907	1,420	Room	2	2,035	40	1,820	....	120.00
Hettinger	1912	1,138	Room $350	8	2,150	329	4,784	425.80	871.15
Hoople	1937	346	No Report					No Report	
Hope	1910	474	Room	3	1,500	100	1,300	....	177.01
Kulm	1937	734	Room	2	1,348	138	3,640	109.87	183.34
Leeds	1902	782	Room $100	3	2,577	150	676	80.00	184.00
Linton	1936	1,602	Room, Lib. Sal.	12	3,170	72	2,340	116.00	1,326.27
Northwood	1941	[illegible]	Room	2	876	......	1,040	159.14	204.14
Oberon	1938	225	None	4	752	140	[illegible]	37.45	47.47
Pembina	....	....	Room $75	3	2,000	65	10,400	165.00	280.00
Rolette	1947	460	Room	4	519	150	1,144	131.34	230.48
St. [illegible]as	1917	503	None	2¾	3,000	......	1,040	40.00	[illegible]
Sanish	1928	455	$25	1	1,409	55	1,248	39.56	155.65

ASSOCIATION LIBRARIES CHARGING FOR SERVICE

Town	Date Estab-lished	1940 Popu-lation	Mal Help	Hours Open Week	Volumes	Bor-rowers	Circu-lation	1948-1950 Expenditures Books	Total
Cando	1902	1,282	None	2	4,000	149	15,600	$ 302.45	$ 688.33
Edgeley	1912	803	Room $75	2	2,552	30	1040	....	24.00
Enderlin	1912	1,593	Room	4	3,550	......	3,120	350.00	350.00
Forman	1939	500	Room $100	4	1,458	110	780	....	144.00
Hamilton	1916	255	None	2	2,421	22	1,144	25.00	25.00
Ha hero	1928	196	$10	2½	1,000	65	780	100.00	100.00
Hebron	1938	1,267	Room $100	2	1,394	1,245	728	42.07	188.07
Killdeer	....	650	$25	2	1,764	......	1,820	91.66	131.73
Langdon	1912	1,546	Room $250	7½	6,965	105	7,800	142.21	775.95
Milton	....	....	Room	2	660	30	1,196	105.56	105.56
Mohall	1937	687	Room $200	6	2,734	318	5,876	132.39	932.39
New England	1931	895	Room	2	2,034	100	1,664	69.82	275.48
New Rockford	1917	2,017	Room	8	3,323	152	2,756	322.46	437.31
Regent	1935	261	Room	2	941	33	1,352	14.00	97.87
Rolla	1924	1,008	Room	4	2,084	106	1,612	206.89	228.08
Zeeland	1946	489	Room	1	553	34	4,472	102.40	109.94

STATE OF NORTH DAKOTA

LIBRARY DIRECTORY

Arnegard	Public Library	Mrs. Clifford Sovig
Ashley	Public Library	Mrs. Ben Lang
Bathgate	Free Public Library	Mrs. Scott Park
Beach	Public Library	Mrs. Grace Houck
Beulah	Public Library	Mrs. Robert Easton
Bismarck	Public Library	Erana Stadler
Bismarck	State Historical Society	Margaret Rose
Bottineau	State Forestry School Library	Geo. P. Hynes
Bottineau	Public Library	Mrs. E. M. Ertresvaag
Bowman	Clara Lincoln Phelan Library	Mrs. Mertie Pond
Cando	Public Library	Lucile Harris
Carrington	City Library	Mrs. Ella Mae Hargrave
Casselton	Public Library	Laura Port
Cavalier	Public Library	Mrs. Robert Thacker
Cogswell	Public Library	Olive N. Bartlett
Cooperstown	Public Library	Mrs. W. W. Barr
Crosby	Divide County Library	Mrs. Anna Phelps
Devils Lake	Carnegie Library	Mrs. James Barrett
Dickinson	Public Library	Gertrude Voldal
Dickinson	State Teachers College Library	Matilda L. Stoxen
Drake	Public Library	Mrs. W. H. Halbert
Drayton	Public Library	Mrs. Willis J. Devlin
Edgeley	Public Library	Mrs. Florence Lee
Elbowoods	Public Library	Alice M. Watson
Ellendale	Public Library	Mrs. Maude B. Blumer
Ellendale	Normal and Industrial College Library	Marvella Stubbe
Enderlin	Public Library	Mrs. Thomas Pierce, Jr.
Fargo	Public Library	Inga Rynning
Fargo	State Agricultural College Library	H. Dean Stallings
Flaxton	Public Library	Dora L. Kundiger
Forbes	Public Library	Merle Borgen
Forman	Public Library	Margie Holen
Gackle	Public Library	Mrs. J. M. Hummel
Goodrich	Public Library	Mrs. David Unruh
Grafton	Public Library	Mrs. Hazel Barr
Grand Forks	Public Library	Mrs. Louise Norrell
Grand Forks	State University Library	Della Mathys
Halliday	Public Library	Mrs. Elmer Goetz
Hamilton	Public Library	Mrs. Andrew Knutson
Hankinson	Public Library	Mrs. Geo. Schuett

Hansboro	Public Library	Mrs. P. E. Orton
Harvey	Public Library	Mrs. A. B. Hannes
Hatton	Public Library	Mrs. Carrie Clausen
Hebron	Public Library	Mrs. Theophil Frey
Hettinger	Public Library	Mrs. Mabel Tommerson
Hillsboro	Public Library	Mrs. Anna Henning
Hoople	Public Library	Mrs. Elmer Gryte
Hope	Public Library	Mrs. Frank Sussex
Jamestown	Public Library	Mrs. Anna P. Bensch
Jamestown	Jamestown College Library	Hazel Prytherch
Killdeer	Public Library	Mrs. William Cockborn
Kulm	Public Library	Mrs. E. E. Orth
Lakota	The A.M. Tofthagen Library	Mrs. Inga Ferris
LaMoure	Public Library	Mrs. James A. Frank
Langdon	Public Library	Mrs. E. J. Donovan
Leeds	Public Library	Mrs. Ben Baglien
Lehr	Public Library	Mrs. Roy Bittner
Leonard Twp.	Watts Free Library	Mrs. Elsie Greuel
Lidgerwood	City Library	Mrs. Elizabeth Kings
Linton	Public Library	Mrs. Eva Sheffield
Lisbon	Public Library	Pauline M. Billing
Mandan	Public Library	Mrs. Eleanor Trzcinski
Mayville	Public Library	Sophia Springen
Mayville	State Teachers College Library	Lillian Skalet
Milton	Public Library	Gudrun Goodman
Minot	Public Library	Mrs. Lois A. Ronning
Minot	State Teachers College Library	Nellie R. Swanson
Mohall	Public Library	Mrs. Orville P. Witteman
Mott	Inez Hendrickson Library	Mrs. Virginia Mehrer
New England	Public Library	Mrs. Gudrun Van Fleet
New Rockford	Public Library	Mrs. James Donnelly
Northwood	Northwood City Library	Mrs. West Mutchler
Oakes	Public Library	Mrs. Helene T. Hample
Oberon	Public Library	Mrs. Hazel Carlson
Omemee	Public Library	Mrs. Willis Watson
Park River	Public Library	Vera H. Warner
Petersburg	Public Library	Carrie Barnum
Pembina	Public Library	Mrs. Pauline Brennan
Portal	Public Library	Mrs. W. H. McCauley
Regent	Public Library	Mrs. C. J. Bowers
Rolette	Public Library	Mrs. John Fish
Riverdale	Public Library	Mrs. F. S. Witzigman
Rolla	Public Library	Mrs. Clarence Jacobsen
Rugby	Public Library	Mrs. P. E. McMahon

LIBRARY DIRECTORY—(Continued)

St. Thomas	Public Library	Mrs. Albert Paciseau
Sanish	Public Library	Mrs. W. E. Blatherwick
Steele	Public Library	Ruth Thieling
Turtle Lake	Public Library	Mrs. John Frey
Valley City	Carnegie Public Library	Mrs. Helen H. Tracy
Valley City	State Teachers College Library	D. W. Ferguson
Velva	Public Library	Mrs. H. O. McCoy
Verona	Public Library	Mrs. Louise Laney
Wahpeton	Leach Public Library	Alice Persons
Wahpeton	State Science School Library	Carol Anderson
Westhope	Public Library	Mrs. W. T. Munn
Williston	James Memorial Library	Florence Kearns
Wimbledon	Public Library	Mrs. J. J. Mundt
Wishek	Public Library	Joan Herr
Zeeland	Public Library	Mrs. August Boschee

Twenty-Third Biennial Report

of the

State Library Commission

to the

State Board of Administration

STATE LIBRARY COMMISSION STAFF
June 30, 1952

Hazel Webster Byrnes	Director and State Librarian
Arlene Stocker	Assistant to the Director
Dorothy Bigwood	Head, Reference Department
Winnifred Coyne	Head, School Department
Lorraine LeFleur	Head, Traveling Library Department

FOR THE PERIOD
July 1, 1950 — June 30, 1952

Twenty-Third Biennial Report

of the

State Library Commission

to the

State Board of Administration

STATE LIBRARY COMMISSION STAFF
June 30, 1952

Hazel Webster Byrnes	Director and State Librarian
Arlene Stocker	Assistant to the Director
Dorothy Bigwood	Head, Reference Department
Winnifred Coyne	Head, School Department
Lorraine LeFleur	Head, Traveling Library Department

FOR THE PERIOD
July 1, 1950 — June 30, 1952

1-76360

TO THE STATE BOARD OF ADMINISTRATION: R. H. Sherman, Chairman, O. A. Braseth, F. A. Foley, Math Dahl, and M. F. Peterson.

The North Dakota State Library Commission has the honor to submit its Twenty-Third biennial report, covering the period from July 1, 1950 to June 30, 1952.

HAZEL WEBSTER BYRNES
Director

REPORT OF THE DIRECTOR, NORTH DAKOTA STATE LIBRARY COMMISSION—1950-1952

North Dakota is entering a new era of development. It is probably outrunning many another state in the progress it is making. The evidence offered by the requests which come to the State Library Commission are indicative of the thinking of the people of this state. This attitude of mind means the building of the people at the same time that this building of economic progress is taking place. It is a healthy omen. Cultural and material pursuits should balance each other, lest North Dakota be overtaken by the lopsidedness of basic values found in the world today. Library interests and activities count big in keeping balances, and though results of library service are not measurable in dollars and cents, they are perhaps of as much or more value in measure of worth.

THE STATE LIBRARY COMMISSION AT WORK

While sitting at my desk writing this report, the business office adjoining hums with the clack of typewriters, mimeograph and adding machines. Across the hall the girls are rushing to fill requests, searching in stacks and files for books, periodicals and pamphlets. At the same time a force in the mailing department is packing, wrapping, tying and putting mailing labels on the materials which are brought to them. These services are mostly for the schools and the clubs. Two floors below one sees somewhat similar operations where boxes containing traveling libraries are being sent to communities hither and yon over the state. The Bismarck mail truck official who picks up the boxes and big mail sacks, tells us that he gets from the State Library Commission more parcel post than from the capitol building. Today, October 7, 1952, a typical day, 645 books are being mailed out. These go to rural areas and small towns all over the state. Service is for the areas that have inadequate library service. Since North Dakota is mostly a rural state, it means that every county in the state, without exception, — all 53 of them, have received some service from the State Library Commission. Putting it another way, mail has been directed to 470 towns out of the 615 postoffice towns listed in the atlas for North Dakota. Some 12,000 books per month have gone out during the busiest months. This past biennial period has seen an increase in circulation reaching an all-time high and there is every indication that the figures will increase as time goes on.

Many factors contribute to this upsurge of requests which come to the State Library Commission. One would name as one of the first the general buildup which has come to this state because of new pursuits relating to water power, lignite and oil. This in itself is having the effect of arousing a potent curiosity. Like a mirror in a car, it is serving also to cause a look backward in order to know how to go forward. Books afford the best view and hence best satisfy the curiosity.

Another factor which we feel rates high in promoting library progress, and which will continue to have an even greater effect is the establishment of library courses in all schools of higher education. This has been one of the fond dreams of the director. She has visited these schools not only once, but two and three times and has conferred with the presidents and deans of education and in cases has demonstrated work by conducting library classes. Augmenting this dream was her appointment by the Director of Secondary Education as chairman of Library Standards for the secondary schools of the state. These standards are incorporated in the revised edition of the ADMINISTRATIVE MANUAL FOR NORTH DAKOTA HIGH SCHOOLS. Since the schools of higher education will need to teach the courses which will prepare the teacher-librarian, the circle of library interests is now running throughout the schools. This circle may be thought of as a basic circle from which tangents of library promotion will move in every direction.

Still another factor in library promotion is due to the work done over the state in making people aware of this service given by the state: speeches, many of them, for all sorts of occasions; articles written for magazines, state and national; the regular publication by the State Library Commission, LIBRARY NOTES AND NEWS; workshops in cooperation with the Parent-Teacher Association held in six sections of the state; visitations and again many of them to public libraries, school libraries and to points where there were no libraries but should be. Sometimes a library was organized, or was re-organized, or was otherwise put onto its feet, as it were. The problem to be dealt with might be book selection, or cataloging, or public relations, or building, or securing funds, or legal procedures. Anything and sometimes most unusual things presented themselves. With it all, the people of North Dakota have for the most part given excellent response, but whatever the reaction, the people have become more library conscious and with satisfying and surprising results which are shown by the letters and questions that come our way.

A fourth factor should be mentioned and that resides in the life conditions of the people themselves. As North Dakota enters this new era of its history, the older people who have pioneered, who have assumed the responsibility of raising their families and have had the resourcefulness and the stick-to-it-iveness to come through all manner of discouragements, — these people who have built this state — are now retiring and are wanting to catch up, as it were, on their reading, and make up for what they have missed. They want the better things, the old classics and literature and verse from which their parents often quoted.

And more than this, they want that which they have missed for their children and their children's children. This three-way urge, therefore, first of the grandparents, then their urge that the young folks have reading material, and thirdly that the little ones, too, of preschool age, be not forgotten is also doing its big part in promoting library service.

Tied closely to this factor is the factor that North Dakota appropriates no funds for adult education and no funds for kindergarten. It means that the State Library Commission is the only organized state agency which approaches and contributes to the education of these groups. This would serve as an excellent argument, we feel, — especially in light of the service now given by the State Library Commission, for an appropriation at least ¼ again as large as our present budget. Extension plans to meet growing needs in other phases of the library work could easily take an equal amount.

MOVING AHEAD

COUNTY LIBRARY. Approval for the second county library in North Dakota was noted at the general election, November 4, 1952, for Stutsman County. Jamestown Public Library will become a city-County Library. Mrs. Anna Bensch is librarian. She had much cooperation from the Homemakers Clubs and other organizations.

LIBRARY COURSES IN SCHOOLS OF HIGHER EDUCATION. These courses will provide a basic understanding and appreciation of meaning of books and libraries by those who are training as teacher-librarians in the state.

REVISION OF LIBRARY STANDARDS FOR THE HIGH SCHOOLS OF NORTH DAKOTA. Meeting library standards by the high schools of the state will help to place North Dakota in the educational bracket desired as compared with other states.

PUBLICATIONS. LIBRARY NOTES AND NEWS, the official publication of the State Library Commission. Calls for this have increased our mailing list from some 160 to 1,300. It goes to librarians, state and national; to school librarians, county superintendents, heads of schools, state officials, legislators, and presidents of state organizations.

ARTICLES. The State Library Commission has appeared in the following publications: A.L.A. Bulletin, November, 1951, "From Bookshelves to Mailboxes." A prize winning essay in the American Library Association American Heritage contest. NORTH DAKOTA TEACHER, March, 1952, "Library Commission's Service." LIBRARY JOURNAL, June 1, 1952. "Books in North Dakota." NORTH DAKOTAN, March 1952, Picture in Traveling Library Department. NORTH DAKOTAN, July, 1952. Cultural Advancement in North Dakota Keeping Pace With Industrial Progress."

PROGRAM PARTICIPATIONS. A representative list. American Library Association. Chicago, July 8-14, 1951 and 1952, January 28-February 2, 1952, New York City, June 29-July 3, 1952; North Dakota Library Association. Bismarck, September 27-29, 1951; Congress of Parents and Teachers. Workshops in connection with this organization, June 15-30, 1950, 1951 and 1952. Minot, Dickinson, Valley City, Ellendale, Mayville, Grand Forks, and Fargo. State Convention, Fargo, April 24-26, 1951; Adult Education Association. Columbus, Ohio, May 13-15, 1951; North Dakota Council on Education. Bismarck, November 15, 1951; Iowa Library Association, Iowa City, Iowa, October 11-13, 1951; Delta Kappa Gamma (Education) Mandan, April 19, 1951; National League of American Pen Women, Medora Branch. Dickinson, April 11, 1951; Farmers Union. Jamestown, August 30, 1950 and February 6, 1951; Farm Bureau. Bismarck, March 29, 1951; Cosmos Club. Bismarck, November 3, 1951.

VISITATIONS. When making trips to the larger towns in the different sections of the state, as listed above, the director made it opportune to visit the public and the school libraries in these cities and in neighboring towns. These additional towns visited and given library service by either the director or members of the staff are as follows: Edgeley, Oakes, LaMoure, Ashley, Zeeland, Westhope, Hettinger, Turtle Lake, Mott, Underwood, Riverdale, Garrison, Westhope, Crosby, Kenmare, Mohall, Devils Lake, Bottineau, Lakota, Petersburg, Larimore, Hillsboro and Hatton.

DEPARTMENTAL REPORTS

Reference Department

The Reference Department continues to be mainly concerned with the filling of requests from clubs, high schools, libraries and individuals in areas where adequate library facilities are not available. There were 4,913 separate requests of this kind during the year July, 1951 to June 30, 1952. Included in this number was a large percentage of reference questions that required a good deal of thought and searching for satisfactory material. Since our circulation is almost entirely by mail, the selection of books in most cases is left to the person filling the requests. All of this adds to the interest but also the complications of the department.

The reference librarian has at her disposal in filling the requests a collection of some 20,000 books exclusive of the school collections and the traveling libraries. These are supplemented by a large number of assorted magazines and an outstanding file of pamphlets, and clippings. A special collection of this department is the North Dakota collection.

Our service to the women's club of the state grows with each year. In the spring the Library Commission prepares and sends to the clubs a list of suggested club topics to assist in the preparation of the year's club programs. In connection with this service, the Commission supplies material necessary for preparing program lessons. Any club that wishes to register for regular service, files its program with the Commission.

and without futher request from the club, material is sent out in advance of each meeting on the topic for the program. Our records show that we sent literature to 111 clubs during the past year.

A special service that has meant a great deal to families in the small towns and rural areas of North Dakota away from a local library is the one we call Books-a-Month. Under this plan, a family receives a box of books each month. A file is kept of the reading preferences, the age range and the size of the family registered for this service, and each time a box of books is returned another is sent without further request.

In addition to the reference work, this department handles the cataloging for all the books in the main collection. Books are classified, accessioned, book cards and pockets are made, and the books are lettered and shellacked and put on the shelves for distribution.

SCHOOL DEPARTMENT

Most of the schools in the rural areas of the state have inadequate libraries and insufficient funds to purchase books. In order to supplement the libraries in these schools, the State Library Commission maintains a large school collection. The collection is composed of titles included in Bulletin #5. These are called Reading Circle books, for they are the approved books for which pupils are given a Reading Certificate by the County Superintendent if they read two books each month during the school year. The plan is very popular with the county superintendents, teachers and pupils, and as a result we have an average of 700 to 800 teachers each year who request books each month. It is interesting to note that if we could add to our circulation the possible number of readers for each book while it is in the school, our circulation figure would be several thousand higher each month. The school service has assumed almost gigantic proportions.

TRAVELING LIBRARY DEPARTMENT

Renewed interest in the services of the Traveling Library has all but swamped this Department. We began rejuvenating the library boxes during the summer only to find our need for books far exceeded our supply. Boxes are made up for Grades 1 to 6, 1 to 8, 7 to 9, High School and Adults. These go out for three months at a time, with the privilege of renewal. Our aim is to have the country school or some center in every community which is without library service receive a box or boxes of these books. A cold blizzardy day will be converted into a day of joy with books from the Traveling Library at hand. L. L.

LIBRARY STATISTICS

26.6% of the people in North Dakota have adequate public library facilities

11.1% of the people have public library service available in their towns, but it is far from adequate

62.3% of the people have no public library service, and would be without library service of any kind if it were not for the services of the State Library Commission.

The State Library Commission circulation for this biennial period was 188,568.

PUBLIC LIBRARIES

Town	Date Estab-lished	1950 Popu-lation	RECEIPTS Tax Appropriation 1950-51	1951-52	Total Receipts 1951	1951-52
Bismarck	1914	18,640	$24,511.99	$30,470.00	$26,482.76	$32,347.33
Bowman	1916	1,382	1,574.22	666.76	4,278.68	1,342.53
Carrington	1906	2,101	1,500.00	1,500.00	2,774.69	2,897.87
Casselton	1906	1,373	315.27	325.73	927.54	1,040.05
Devils Lake	[illegible]	6,427	5,595.75	6,162.06	9,156.07	10,317.34
Dickinson	1908	7,469	7,000.00	8,000.00	7,658.09	8,760.51
Ellendale	1912	1,759	1,000.00	1,200.00	1,228.36	1,469.65
Fargo	1900	38,256	32,676.59	40,902.08	53,488.82	61,656.89
Grafton	1895	4,901	1,800.00	1,960.00	3,944.38	3,469.06
Grand Forks	1899	26,836	21,453.00	25,775.00	23,355.53	28,351.23
Jamestown	1901	10,697	8,000.00	7,828.26	12,282.13	11,124.79
Lakota	[illegible]	1,032	1,106.29	1,080.47	1,709.68	1,375.39
LaMoure	1924	1,010	750.00	750.00	945.92	861.20
Leonard Township	1912	469	125.00	....	126.85	....
Lidgerwood	1913	1,147	1,360.00	1,465.00	1,567.54	[illegible]
Lisbon	1915	2,031	2,005.49	1,974.23	6,787.31	6,781.09
Mandan	1896	7,298	4,162.40	4,823.24	7,106.05	7,588.18
Mayville	1900	1,790	903.83	1,439.83	1,281.55	1,747.41
Minot	[illegible]	22,032	17,345.03	17,258.09	27,443.90	28,459.60
Mott	1912	1,583	499.05	[illegible]	[illegible]	578.73
Oakes	1905	1,774	1,332.17	1,472.63	3,056.75	3,174.65
Park River	[illegible]	1,692	500.00	600.00	971.40	1,002.66
Rugby	1912	2,907	[illegible]	1,485.00	2,682.93	2,723.82
Turtle Lake	1926	839	[illegible]	350.00	361.23	604.70
Valley City	1900	6,851	5,789.77	7,040.65	14,015.24	15,983.73
Wahpeton	......	5,125	7,500.00	2,800.00	8,913.84	[illegible]
Williston	1910	7,878	11,223.71	12,234.29	15,908.87	27,959.59
Wishek	1926	1,241	300.00	300.00	302.38	384.78

PUBLIC LIBRARIES

EXPENDITURES

Town	Salaries 1950-51	Salaries 1951-52	Maintenance 1950-51	Maintenance 1951-52	Books-Periodicals 1950-51	Books-Periodicals 1951-52	Total 1950-51	Total 1951-52
Bismarck	$16,421.35	$17,875.45	$ 4,080.18	$ 5,830.72	$ 5,729.01	$ 4,706.00	$26,230.84	$28,[illegible]
Bowman	670.88	528.10	2,691.54	169.67	[illegible]	324.29	3,772.58	1,[illegible]
Carrington	924.00	924.00	102.77	134.34	350.05	239.61	1,376.82	[illegible]
Casselton	128.00	130.15	32.7 2	26.50	88.50	257.49	249.22	625.91
Devils Lake	2,[illegible]	2,312.00	1,735.78	2,345.80	1,428.23	1,232.94	9,456.07	10,317.34
Dickinson	5,260.00	5,467.75	1,219.35	986.38	981.92	1,241.80	7,462.17	7,695.93
Ellendale	604.00	729.20	59.33	84.52	486.43	590.45	[illegible]	1,404.17
Fargo	22,977.57	25,148.78	6,649.21	5,431.68	5,346.34	5,416.50	34,973.12	35,811.75
Grafton	1,262.10	1,540.93	857.05	961.28	[illegible]	[illegible]	2,732.32	2,902.87
Grand Forks	12,859.62	14,790.35	4,379.29	5,404.53	4,880.68	6,100.55	22,119.66	26,296.43
Jamestown	6,279.53	6,749.82	2,763.54	2,715.44	2,110.94	2,264.31	11,154.01	10,599.57
Lakota	[illegible]	432.00	268.86	455.14	58.09	103.63	633.70	990.77
LaMoure	390.00	390.00	229.01	197.13	284.33	261.18	903.34	848.31
Leonard Township	63.00	77.50	30.66	35.50	....	4.25	93.96	117.25
Lidgerwood	780.00	840.00	306.69	302.04	388.83	246.73	1,475.52	1,388.77
Lisbon	820.00	925.18	808.97	954.80	423.05	817.75	2,092.02	2,697.73
Mandan	2,582.50	2,777.00	448.95	698.72	1,500.98	1,385.97	4,532.43	4,861.49
Mayville	420.00	420.00	[illegible]	1,047.87	148.94	[illegible]	1,086.20	1,632.94
Minot	10,[illegible]	10,407.11	2,754.53	2,392.29	4,625.25	5,044.37	17,381.51	17,844.74
Mott	240.00	240.00	10.95	15.30	337.17	199.60	[illegible]	454.90
Oakes	884.25	886.59	166.13	243.67	465.20	387.37	1,515.58	1,517.63
Park River	420.00	419.50	74.76	73.65	143.10	141.47	637.86	634.62
Rugby	1,080.00	1,080.00	59.22	86.54	565.89	682.34	1,705.11	1,848.88
Turtle Lake	50.00	53.00	2.50	18.00	54.03	81.48	106.53	152.48
Valley City	3,368.35	3.399.35	875.80	1,526.57	1,192.79	1,334.45	5,436.94	6,260.87
Wahpeton	3.188.76	3,500.87	2,023.96	747.44	694.44	1,037.61	5,907.16	5,285.87
Williston	4,556.55	5,418.57	4,411.23	2,432.34	1,267.09	1,560.83	10,234.87	10,138.62
Wishek	109.40	108.00	15.06	59.99	97.41	154.54	[illegible]	322.53

PUBLIC LIBRARIES

Town	Circulation 1950-51	Circulation 1951-52	Total	Vol mes	Borrowers	Hours Open a Week	Rural Borrowers
Bismarck	[illegible]	123,589	243,735	26,694	6,861	66	......
Bowman	3,449	3,613	7,062	7,232	592	20	......
Carrington	8,437	8,170	16,607	4,321	680	25	110
Casselton	2,817	2,888	5,705	4,083	384	4	......
Devils Lake	31,312	30,658	63,970	4,725	3,738	36	......
Dickinson	41,764	41,971	83,735	19,886	2,554	36	294
Ellendale	[illegible]	13,722	29,018	6,869	288	14¼	52
Fargo	[illegible]	192,743	372,936	54,151	23,095	72	684
Grafton	5,746	5,916	11,662	5,766	725	19½	......
Grand Forks	91,781	109,166	[illegible]	22,749	7,549	69	525
Jamestown	55,744	57,718	113,462	18,237	5,018	48	650
Lakota	2,045	1,264	3,309	4,715	594	9	......
LaMoure	5,790	6,490	12,280	6,070	1,299	6	649
Leonard Township	....	....	....	2,150	....	5	......
Lidgerwood	9,866	11,495	21,361	7,443	751	20	376
Lisbon	8,973	8,414	7,387	4,357	1,050	15	386
Mandan	17,856	20,305	38,161	5,739	1,582	46	150
Mayville	3,648	4,267	7,915	5,965	56	8	......
Minot	[illegible]	11,223	[illegible]	24,751	6,666	48	90
Mott	2,942	4,779	7,721	3,876	407	5	152
Oakes	20,649	18,919	39,568	7,784	584	25	......
Park River	6,838	5,866	12,704	2,818	665	20	124
Rugby	16,672	17,604	34,276	7,083	1,131	30	222
Turtle Lake	602	865	1467	1,661	77	2	......
Valley City	25,296	26,338	51,634	16,464	3,114	36	419
Walhpeton	17,290	17,668	34,958	3,038	2,164	27	605
Williston	4,721	24,303	39,024	10,153	1,100	36	50
Wishek	3,220	5,640	8,860	2,415	....	4½	......

ASSOCIATION LIBRARIES GIVING FREE SERVICE

Town	Date Established	1950 Population	Municipal Help	Hours Open a Week	Volumes	Borrowers	Circulation	1950-1952 Expenditures Books	1950-1952 Expenditures Total
Ashley	1913	1,423	$500	6	5,559	694	13,752	$ [illegible]	$ 979.35
Bathgate	1916	209	[illegible]	2	1,491	225	2,132	80.39	160.66
Beach	1912	1,461	$600	5½	3,526	650	6,292	449.00	1,034.14
Beulah	1931	1,501	Room	2	2,226	303	3,432	145.21	[illegible]
Bottineau	1915	2,268	None	2	1,655	324	5,876	[illegible]	175.87
Cavalier	1915	1,459	Room $75	4	2,896	730	6,314	[illegible]	[illegible]
Cooperstown	1945	1,189	$993.50	6	1,475	25	4,212	793.17	1,771.52
Crosby	1930	5,967	Room	30	8,169	887	34,860	1,871.81	5,019.81
Drake	1920	831	No Report					No Report	
Drayton	1946	875	Room	5	1,230	255	1,524	174.18	[illegible]
Edgeley	1912	943	Room $225	7	3,363	159	8,330	[illegible]	[illegible]
Elbowoods	....	....	[illegible]	60	338	138	217	....	....
Flaxton	1935	436	Room	3	2,242	60	1,560	....	....
Forbes	1944	204	Room	6	1,198	183	2,236	204.16	374.16
Goodrich	1926	448	Room $50	1	851	......	520	12.23	53.98
Hankinson	1907	[illegible]	Room $144	2	2,000	55	1,640	....	144.00
Hettinger	1912	1,762	Room $700	8	2,434	357	[illegible]	455.15	[illegible]
Hoople	1937	447	No Report					No Report	
Hope	1910	170	Room	2	1,650	......	1,612	100.00	152.00
Kulm	1937	707	Room	2	1,559	126	6,240	110.13	[illegible]
Leeds	1902	778	Room $200	2	2,617	144	2,236	55.00	[illegible]
Linton	1936	1,675	Room $1220	12	3,024	539	6,708	[illegible]	1,331.33
Northwood	1941	1,182	Room	2	992	......	2,444	76.46	[illegible]
Oberon	1938	238	None	4	925	165	2,600	48.86	40.15
Pembina	....	640	No Report					No Report	
Portal	1935	409	Room	2	1,000	......	416	20.00	65.00
Rolette	1947	451	Room	2	634	125	1,716	142.89	142.89
Samish	1928	[illegible]	$50	1	1,456	62	5,824	60.69	112.69
Steele	1950	762	Room	2	459	122	988	4.50	33.27
Velva	1914	1,170	$204.97	2¼	5,718	450	36,400	249.42	310.41
Westhope	1950	575	No Report					No Report	

ASSOCIATION LIBRARIES CHARGING FOR SERVICE

Town	Date Established	1950 Population	Municipal Help	Hours Open a Week	Volumes	Borrowers	Circulation	1950-1952 Expenditures Books	Total
Cando	[illegible]	1,530	None	2	2,904	146	[illegible]	$ [illegible]	$2,204.44
Enderlin	1912	1,504	Room	3	3,766	1,113	6,032	[illegible]	457.32
Forman	1939	466	Room	4	2,207	30	2,120	24.00	252.00
Hamilton	1916	241	None	2	1,267	26	1,040	25.00	25.00
Hansboro	1928	134	Room	2	1,038	81	728	72.89	82.89
Hatton	....	991	Room	1½	382	38	936	224.53	271.31
Hebron	1938	1,412	Room $200	2	1,454	1,285	9,360	....	156.00
Killdeer	....	477	None	2	1,874	......	2,184	65.72	116.67
Langdon	1912	1,838	Room $500	6½	7,101	105	15,600	126.86	176.86
Milton	....	322	Room	2	733	28	2,600	132.53	132.53
Mohall	1937	1,073	Room $400	6	2,889	357	....	100.53	580.53
New England	1931	1,117	Room	2	2,120	91	8,736	56.35	246.35
New Rockford	1917	[illegible]	Room	8	3,633	143	8,996	622.88	[illegible]
Regent	1935	405	Room	2	1,021	42	2,184	....	87.12
Riverdale	1949	....	Room	8	2,102	91	6,240	100.00	[illegible]
Rolla	1924	1,176	Room	2	2,241	87	4,836	249.85	265.01
Underwood	1951	1,061	Room $100	4½	847	119	208	150.42	[illegible]
Zeeland	1946	484	Room $200	1	825	48	9,461	284.45	289.10

STATE OF NORTH DAKOTA
LIBRARY DIRECTORY

Ashley	Public Library	Mrs. Gerald Coyle
Bathgate	Public Library	Mrs. George Brown
Beach	Public Library	Miss Mabel Koehney
Beulah	Public Library	Mrs. Robert Easton
Bismarck	Public Library	Mr. Robert Thomas
Bismarck	State Historical Society Library	Miss Margaret Rose
Bottineau	Public Library	Mrs. E. M. Ertresvaag
Bottineau	State Forestry School Library	Mr. George P. Hynes
Bowman	Clara Lincoln Phelan Library	Mrs. Mertie Pond
Cando	Public Library	Miss Lucile Harris
Carrington	City Library	Mrs. Ella Mae Hargrave
Casselton	Public Library	Miss Laura Port
Cavalier	Public Library	Mrs. Robert Thacker
Cooperstown	Public Library	Mrs. W. W. Barr
Crosby	Divide County Library	Mrs. Anna S. Phelps
Devils Lake	Carnegie Library	Mrs. James Barrett
Dickinson	Public Library	Miss Gertrude Voldal
Dickinson	State Teachers College Library	Miss Matilda Stoxen
Drake	Public Library	Mrs. W W Halbert
Drayton	Public Library	Mrs. Willis J. Devlin
Edgeley	Public Library	Mrs. Ruth Evert
Elbowoods	Public Library	Miss Alice M. Watson
Ellendale	Public Library	Mrs. Maude Blumer
Ellendale	Normal and Industrial College Library	Mr. Robert A. Elftmann
Enderlin	Public Library	Miss Helen Jean Shaw
Fargo	Public Library	Miss Inga Rynning
Fargo	State Agricultural College Library	Mr H. Dean Stallings
Flaxton	Public Library	Miss Dora Kundiger
Forbes	Public Library	Mr. Merle Borgen
Forman	Public Library	Miss Bev. Bommersback
Goodrich	Public Library	Miss Beverly Bodwin
Grafton	Public Library	Mrs. Hazel J. Barr
Grand Forks	Public Library	Mrs. Irene P. Norell
Grand Forks	State University Library	Miss Della Mathys
Hamilton	Public Library	Mrs. Andrew Knutson
Hankinson	Public Library	Mrs. George Schuett
Hansboro	Public Library	Mrs. Walter White
Hatton	Public Library	Mrs. G. J Clauson
Hebron	Public Library	Mrs. Theophil Frey
Hettinger	Public Library	Mrs. Mabel Tommerson
Hoople	Public Library	Mrs. Elmer Gryte

Hope	Public Library	Mrs. Frank Sussex
Jamestown	Public Library	Mrs. Anna P. Bensch
Jamestown	Jamestown College Library	Miss Mary Steele
Killdeer	Public Library	Mrs. Wm. Cockburn
Kulm	Public Library	Mrs. E. E. Orth
Lakota	The A. M. Tofthagen Library	Miss Ann Sjursuth
LaMoure	Public Library	Mrs. James A. Frank
Langdon	Public Library	Mrs. E. J. Donovan
Leeds	Public Library	Mrs. Arne Gregor
Leonard Twp	Watts Free Library	Mrs. Gilbert Elliott
Lidgerwood	City Library	Mrs. Elizabeth Kings
Linton	Public Library	Mrs. N S. Sheffield
Lisbon	Public Library	Miss Pauline M. Billing
Mandan	Public Library	Mrs. Eleanor Trzcinski
Mayville	Public Library	Miss Sophia Springen
Mayville	State Teachers College Library	Miss Clenora Quanbeck
Milton	Public Library	Miss Gudrun Goodman
Minot	Public Library	Mrs. Lois Ronning
Minot	State Teachers College Library	Miss Nellie B. Swanson
Mohall	Public Library	Mrs. Orville P. Witteman
Mott	Inez Hendrickson Library	Mrs. Elmer Wenetandt
New England	Public Library	Mrs. Chester Erickson
New Rockford	Public Library	Mrs. James Donnelly
Northwood	Public Library	Mrs. West Mutchler
Oakes	Public and School Library	Mrs. H. Thomas Hample
Oberon	Public Library	Mrs. Hilda Carlson
Park River	Public Library	Miss Vera H. Warner
Pembina	Public Library	Mrs. Pauline Brennan
Portal	Public Library	Mrs. Harry Rocher
Regent	Public Library	Mrs. H. D. Johnson
Riverdale	Public Library	Miss Mary C. Jackson
Rolette	Public Library	Mrs. G. E. Ellingson
Rolla	Public Library	Mrs. Clarence Jacobsen
Rugby	Public Library	Mrs. P. E. McMahon
Sanish	Public Library	Mrs. Arvid Olson
Steele	Public Library	Miss Ruth Thieling
Turtle Lake	Public Library	Mrs. John Frey
Underwood	Public Library	Mrs. Grant Roseth
Valley City	Public Library	Mrs. Helen H. Tracy
Valley City	State Teachers College Library	Mr. D. W. Ferguson
Velva	Public Library	Mrs. Fred Robinson
Wahpeton	Leach Public Library	Mrs. Hermine Becker

LIBRARY DIRECTORY—(Continued)

Wahpeton	State Science School Library	Mrs. Mildred Larson
Westhope	Public Library	Mrs. W. T. Munn
Williston	James Memorial Library	Mrs. Florence M. Kearns
Wishek	Public Library	Miss Mavis Heinle
Zeeland	Public Library	Mrs. August Boschee

Twenty-Fourth Biennial Report

of the

State Library Commission

to the

Board of Administration

STATE LIBRARY COMMISSION STAFF
June 30, 1954

Hazel Webster Byrnes	Director and State Librarian
Arlene Stocker	Assistant to the Director
Dorothy Bigwood	Head, Reference Department
Winnifred Coyne	Head, School Department
Lorraine LaFleur	Head, Traveling Library Department

For the Period
July 1, 1952 - June 30, 1954

Twenty-Fourth Biennial Report

of the

State Library Commission

to the

Board of Administration

STATE LIBRARY COMMISSION STAFF
June 30, 1954

Hazel Webster Byrnes	Director and State Librarian
Arlene Stocker	Assistant to the Director
Dorothy Bigwood	Head, Reference Department
Winnifred Coyne	Head, School Department
Lorraine LaFleur	Head, Traveling Library Department

For the Period
July 1, 1952 - June 30, 1954

TO THE STATE BOARD OF ADMINISTRATION: R. H. Sherman, Chairman, F. A. Foley, H. H. Joos, M. M. Peterson, and Math Dahl.

The North Dakota State Library Commission has the honor to submit its Twenty-Fourth biennial report, covering the period from July 1, 1952 to June 30, 1954.

Hazel Webster Byrnes
Director

STATE LIBRARY SURVEY

A library survey begun last summer was completed this year under the direction of the State Library Commission.

Mrs. Hazel Webster Byrnes, director, and Miss Anne Haugaard, who for a second summer assisted with the work, have made many visitations to places not visited last year and have made return calls to points where professional help was needed. In some places two or three days of help have been given. Visitations have now included all of the 75 public libraries in the state and many school libraries. Miss Haugaard is school librarian and principal of the High School at Harvey, North Dakota. She is a graduate from the Library School, University of Minnesota.

A brief of the Public Library Survey shows 31 public libraries wholly or partially tax supported, 42 libraries and reading rooms sponsored and supported by clubs and associations, and 2 county libraries (in Divide and Stutsman counties). The annual operating expenditure in North Dakota is 37½ cents per capita as compared to the minimum recommended standard of $1.50 per capita. In terms of population the survey shows that there are public libraries located easy of access to 40.9% of the population. This leaves 59.1% of the population without public libraries easy of access. Although this situation is far from desirable, it is better than it appears, for this 59.1% does have book service from the State Library Commission. Since the State Library Commission is the coordinating agency for all library work in the state, as well as being the public library for all sections of the state not receiving adequate library service, statistics from the Commission offer the following corroborating evidence of the survey findings.

In the last five years the Commission has made a 66% increase in circulation. More schools have enrolled for service, more communities have requested traveling libraries, more clubs have taken advantage of the special service to organizations, and more individuals have called for general help in reference and recreational reading than at any time in the history of the Commission.

Other than this book circulation service, there have been more calls than ever before for assistance in organizing and re-organizing libraries and giving professional help.

The survey shows the urgency for better library housing, for more adequate book collections, for better organized libraries and for additional competent library personnel.

LIBRARY PROGRESS IN NORTH DAKOTA

Only a few years ago 79% of the people were without local public library service. This number has decreased to 59%. Our recent library survey indicated a revision upward in important phases of library work. We have seen the expansion of local libraries through local tax support and the beginnings of new libraries; the establishment of a new county in Stutsman County and the enlargement of the Divide County Library; the introduction and addition of library courses in the institutions of higher education; the formation of standards for school libraries of the state; field work and workshop training over the state, and publication of helpful lists, articles and the official bulletin LIBRARY NOTES AND NEWS, giving library information of state and general nature. Most significant are the increased calls from over the state for library services of all kinds.

The significance of this library progress so far as the State Library Commission is concerned:

The State Library Commission is the directing and cooperative agency for all library work in the state, and gives practical help to individuals, groups and agencies who are interested in extending library service.

Significant also is the fact that for the 59% of the people of North Dakota without access to local public library, the State Library Commission has been the chief source of library material. This 59% is all rural and represents 366,237 of the 619,636 people of the state. Another 69,154 have small libraries in their communities, but depend upon the State Library Commission for a great deal of library service. The needs of these people show a steady increase, and to meet only their book needs, facilities of the State Library Commmission have been increased.

Why is Library Expansion Necessary?

North Dakotans, now faced with new responsibilities in the state, are recognizing to a greater extent the wisdom and the strength to be found in books. They want information. They want the personal enjoyment of reading. They want the privilege of self-education provided through library facilities. They are awakening to the fact that this is the time in the state's history when a cultural program should be provided. There is a strong feeling that there must be a balance in the development of this state,—that if money goes for roads and buildings and livestock programs, it should also be spent for books and libraries and the development of the people themselves.

What Shall We Do for North Dakota's Immediate Future?

A new need is for a Rural Service Librarian to help handle the many calls which come to the State Library Commission which are now beyond the possibility of the Commission to care for with its limited staff and funds. These calls involve setting up local and school libraries, classifying, cataloging and weeding book collections, dealing with such problems of policy, local support and the possible converting to county or regional libraries, and the formation of book stations and other types of extension.

Increased salaries is another important need. Putting members of the State Library Commission on a par with other professional and clerical workers will do much to promote continued interest and less turn-over. Supplies and travel need to be increased to make possible caring for the increased library demands of the people of North Dakota.

To meet the increased demands of North Dakota's people is the problem and the challenge of the State Library Commission.

COUNTY PUBLIC LIBRARIES

County — Hdqrs.	Date Established	1950 County Pop.	RECEIPTS: Tax Appropriation 1952-53	RECEIPTS: Tax Appropriation 1953-54	RECEIPTS: Total Receipts 1952-53	RECEIPTS: Total Receipts 1953-54
Divide — Crosby	1947	5,967	$ 3,985.00	$ 4,000.00	$ 4,445.65	$ 4,700.42
Stutsman — Jamestown	1954	24,158				

PUBLIC LIBRARIES

Town	Date Estab-lished	1950 Popu-lation	RECEIPTS Tax Appropriation 1952-53	1953-54	Total Receipts 1952-53	1953-54
Bismarck	1914	18,640	$36,500.00	$42,286.73	$38,758.11	$44,719.32
Bowman	1916	1,382	1,403.91	1,193.88	1,829.54	2,249.63
Carrington	1906	2,101	1,800.00	2,300.00	3,399.92	3,993.29
Casselton	1906	1,373	322.89	314.34	986.62	1,012.73
Devils Lake	1896	6,427	6,390.36	5,815.38	11,055.66	11,213.44
Dickinson	1908	7,469	9,400.00	8,700.00	10,827.85	10,302.99
Edgeley	1912	943	350.00	750.00	608.66	881.15
Ellendale	1912	1,759	1,200.00	1,200.00	1,466.75	1,358.67
Fargo	1900	38,256	42,314.31	45,799.07	70,339.26	79,612.17
Grafton	1895	4,901	3,299.60	1,812.14	5,083.89	5,987.64
Grand Forks	1899	26,836	28,525.00	30,630.00	30,329.20	30,630.63
Harvey	1952	2,337	1,606.70	2,036.04	1,721.17	3,141.28
Hettinger	1912	1,762	350.00	350.00	516.45	755.61
Jamestown	1901	10,697	9,643.17	10,735.00	13,828.46	19,029.75
Lakota	1906	1,032	1,004.35	447.24	2,992.63	2,604.49
LaMoure	1924	1,010	1,000.00	1,000.00	1,091.00	1,055.89
Lidgerwood	1913	1,147	1,500.00	1,620.00	1,728.90	1,956.67
Linton	1936	1,675	720.00	720.00	804.55	804.10
Lisbon	1915	2,031	2,014.36	1,859.92	4,292.64	5,075.79
Man	1896	7,298	5,611.69	5,262.80	8,852.80	9,370.45
Mayville	1900	1,790	1,170.41	1,613.66	2,088.29	1,714.03
Mot	1908	22,032	18,501.25	19,923.52	30,229.31	32,091.57
Mhall	1937	1,073	200.00	250.00	650.81	1,348.00
Mott	1912	1,583	712.74	1,509.54	882.49	1,723.31
Oakes	1904	1,774	1,852.12	1,674.46	3,698.62	3,878.29
Park River	1900	1,692	800.00	949.34	1,301.48	1,667.55
Rugby	1912	2,907	1,215.00	1,941.00	2,294.07	2,655.53
Turtle Lake	1926	839	300.00	300.00	462.22	496.67
Valley City	1900	6,851	7,022.56	7,088.64	17,807.20	19,417.97
Wahpeton	....	5,125	6,000.00	6,000.00	7,113.42	8,902.05
Williston	1910	7,378	12,968.28	14,716.74	13,505.99	22,140.45
Wishek	1926	1,241	500.00	700.00	580.24	721.01

COUNTY PUBLIC LIBRARIES

Expenditures

County	Salaries 1952-53	Salaries 1953-54	Maintenance 1952-53	Maintenance 1953-54	Books-Periodicals 1952-53	Books-Periodicals 1953-54	Total 1952-53	Total 1953-54
Divide	$ 2,120.00	$ 2,520.00	$ 731.73	$ 412.26	$ 1,237.98	$ 1,312.74	$ 4,089.71	$ 4,245.00
Stutsman	Organized, 1954							

PUBLIC LIBRARIES

Town	Salaries 1952-53	Salaries 1953-54	Maintenance 1952-53	Maintenance 1953-54	Books-Periodicals 1952-53	Books-Periodicals 1953-54	Total 1952-53	Total 1953-54
Bismarck	$20,174.90	$22,824.89	$ 5,760.86	$ 8,818.81	$ 5,470.62	$ 5,240.89	$3[illegible]	$36,884.59
Bowman	573.50	[illegible]	258.26	208.79	119.34	119.06	951.10	859.69
Carrington	924.00	989.00	124.59	251.53	658.04	477.78	1,706.63	1,718.31
Casselton	[illegible]	[illegible]	28.08	138.80	150.35	146.12	308.43	414.92
Devils Lake	2,630.60	3,018.30	2,017.39	2,227.44	1,259.31	1,430.68	5,897.30	5,976.46
Dickinson	5,973.15	6,440.50	1,415.35	1,557.45	2,362.38	1,666.56	9,728.44	9,664.51
Edgeley	250.00	260.00	244.14	129.43	223.42	149.63	717.56	539.60
Ellendale	729.20	729.20	89.22	85.08	639.92	528.40	1,458.34	1,342.68
Fargo	27,309.13	32,301.40	4,837.94	5,407.82	6,692.08	7,024.17	38,839.15	44,608.49
Grafton	1,747.80	1,461.30	1,355.77	609.04	293.70	640.81	3,397.37	2,711.15
Grand Forks	15,639.04	15,454.28	5,149.91	6,676.37	7,995.16	8,499.97	28,780.11	30,630.63
Harvey	255.00	660.75	340.72	404.92	47.88	306.60	643.60	1,372.27
Hettinger	258.00	312.75	47.40	5.58	124.69	252.67	430.09	571.00
Jamestown	7,009.71	7,442.57	1,672.70	5,655.74	2,472.57	2,755.21	11,154.98	15,853.52
Lakota	420.00	318.00	356.61	352.31	78.81	103.97	855.42	774.28
LaMoure	378.25	398.00	508.33	403.91	204.50	218.70	1,091.08	1,053.96
Lidgerwood	840.00	870.00	446.50	292.53	303.55	506.80	1,590.05	1,669.33
Linton	720.00	720.00	17.05	18.83	51.09	50.00	788.14	788.84
Lisbon	1,060.00	1,165.00	673.03	1,973.95	433.44	514.17	2,166.57	3,653.12
Mandan	2,920.00	3,354.55	352.56	575.18	1,758.26	1,952.51	5,030.82	5,882.24
Mayville	432.50	420.00	356.02	787.67	215.26	459.33	2,003.78	1,667.00
Minot	11,938.24	11,380.74	2,584.08	3,111.13	4,712.60	5,610.94	19,234.92	20,671.55
Mohall	240.00	240.00	----------	15.00	102.00	118.00	342.00	373.00
Mott	240.00	249.45	28.93	518.04	446.07	318.22	715.00	1,085.71
Oakes	930.00	936.00	213.64	249.14	511.99	611.49	1,655.63	1,796.73
Park River	420.00	599.25	47.54	112.93	248.76	134.41	716.30	846.59
Rugby	1,080.00	1,080.00	142.80	55.27	561.84	771.83	1,784.64	1,907.10
Turtle Lake	59.50	60.75	3.00	55.00	77.82	171.42	140.32	213.50
Valley City	3,527.25	3,701.25	933.75	2,077.49	1,853.32	1,728.04	6,312.52	7,506.53
Wahpeton	2,975.89	2,962.08	1,441.40	2,497.95	640.80	904.13	5,058.09	6,304.16
Williston	5,585.38	6,702.52	5,142.53	8,058.45	2,794.75	2,357.08	13,522.66	13,547.51
Wishek	125.25	137.55	109.83	45.57	239.32	293.58	474.40	493.53

COUNTY PUBLIC LIBRARIES

County	Circulation 1952-53	Circulation 1953-54	Total	Volumes	Borrowers	Hours Open a week
Divide	18,474	22,252	40,726	9,509	878	42½
Stutsman						

PUBLIC LIBRARIES

Town	Circulation 1952-53	Circulation 1953-54	Total	Volumes	Borrowers	Hours Open a Week	Rural Borrowers
Bismarck	135,811	134,369	270,180	28,836	7,454	66	100
Bowman	3,044	3,214	6,258	7,414	300	18	75
Carrington	8,453	10,448	18,901	4,236	772	27½	150
Casselton	5,408	3,839	9,247	4,088	408	4	......
Devils Lake	28,510	31,312	59,822	14,986	3,180	36	......
Dickinson	44,931	44,402	89,333	18,351	3,065	36	322
Edgeley	9,880	12,333	22,213	4,527	296	7	69
Ellendale	15,215	14,841	30,056	7,176	269	14¼	86
Fargo	204,635	202,995	407,630	58,038	23,589	72	768
Grafton	6,898	5,959	12,857	6,375	730	16½	......
Grand Forks	124,158	131,534	255,692	26,737	9,712	63	700
Harvey	1,144	10,697	11,841	1,988	600	17	50
Hettinger	13,000	....	13,000	2,567	460	18	55
Jamestown	60,247	71,569	131,816	20,399	5,568	48	780
Lakota	984	1,427	2,411	6,378	146	6	......
LaMoure	8,119	6,600	14,719	6,078	1,286	6	643
Lidgerwood	7,444	6,646	14,090	7,835	653	24	304
Milton	3,848	6,225	10,073	3,622	586	9	......
Lisbon	9,627	9,711	19,338	4,832	1,030	15	400
Mandan	22,389	23,208	45,597	6,729	1,970	36	197
Mayville	4,317	4,352	8,669	5,633	2,861	8	20
Minot	120,209	120,681	240,890	26,646	5,678	54	58
Mohall	1,050	1,872	2,922	2,760	325	6	27
Mott	7,791	5,171	12,962	3,454	607	5	263
Oakes	19,388	17,544	36,932	8,431	689	25	......
Park River	4,287	6,284	10,571	3,097	669	12	125
Rugby	17,326	18,701	36,027	7,838	1,211	30	287
Turtle Lake	742	822	1,564	1,814	D1	2	......
Valley City	29,344	32,156	61,500	17,625	2,715	36	260
Wahpeton	17,034	13,992	31,026	13,461	2,369	27	630
Williston	32,830	37,678	70,508	10,592	2,000	42	6
Wishek	6,155	4,985	11,140	2,868	889	4½	......

ASSOCIATION LIBRARIES GIVING REE SERVICE

	Date Estab-lished	1950 Popu-lation	Municipal Help	Hours Open a Week	Volumes	Borrowers	Circu-lation	1952-1954 Expenditures Books	Total
Ashley	1913	1,423	$500	6	5,623	738	12,306	$580.90	$2,697.49
Bathgate	1916	209	None	2	1,071	83	3,328	124.82	281.29
Beach	1912	1,461	$600	5½	.....	552	12,054	583.25	1,122.47
Beulah	1931	1,501	Room	2	2,252	289	3,224	86.24	198.24
Bottineau	1915	2,268	None	2	1,707	357	6,322	295.93	375.93
Cavalier	1915	1,459	Room, $360	4	3,006	565	9,616	342.85	825.81
Cooperstown	1945	1,189	$999.65	6	1,924	.....	5,312	701.43	1,726.21
Drake	1920	831	None	4	2,767	160	7,400	90.80	93.82
Drayton	1946	875	Room	2	1,224	57	2,346	151.93	260.01
Flaxton	1935	436	Room	15	2,342	75	3,820	....	....
Forbes	1944	204	Room	6	1,267	151	6,234	140.00	330.26
Fordville	1952	376	None	2½	640	50	2,624	31.80	70.37
Goodrich	1926	448	No Report					No Report	
Hankinson	1907	1,409	Room	2	2,000	70	....	....	84.00
Hillsboro	1954	1,331	Reorganized					Reorganized	
Hoople	1937	447	No Report					No Report	
Hope	1910	470	Room	3	1,752	.....	2,100	60.75	110.75
Kulm	1937	707	Room	2	1,610	120	8,150	65.87	80.33
Larimore	1954	1,374							
Leeds	1902	778	Room, $250	1½	1,388	.....	3,680	123.56	310.16
Leonard	1912	469	Room	5	1,506	.....	....	....	126.60
New Town	1954	....	Reorganized					Reorganized	
Northwood	1941	1,182	Room	2	1,014	12	832	17.54	152.52
Oberon	1938	238	None	2	963	40	812	53.00	61.00
Pembina	....	640	No Report					No Report	
Portal	1935	409	Room	2	450	80	1,500	28.00	34.00
Rolette	1947	451	Room	2	801	115	2,894	119.23	137.88
St. Thomas	1954	566	Reorganized					Reorganized	
Steele	1950	762	Room	2	505	100	289	....	....
Velva	1914	1,170	Room, $200	3	3,826	415	13,200	722.84	810.35

ASSOCIATION LIBRARIES CHARGING FOR SERVICE

	Date Established	1950 Population	Municipal Help	Hours Open a Week	Volumes	Borrowers	Circulation	1952-1954 Expenditures Books	Total
Cando	1902	1,530	None	2	3,460	120	8,212	$ 335.78	$ 734.08
Enderlin	1912	1,504	Room	3	3,748	580	2,650	232.66	250.21
Finley	1954	671	Room, $50	2	263	------	--------	41.45	51.45
Gackle	1954	604	Reorganized					Reorganized	
Hamilton	1916	241	None	2	727	47	2,450	64.16	107.52
Hansboro	1928	134	Room, $35	2½	1,229	71	2,904	210.93	222.25
Hatton	-------	991	Room	1½	472	------	1,456	95.72	270.88
Hebron	1938	1,412	Room, $200	2	1,526	270	4,370	---------	159.00
Killdeer	-------	477	None	2	1,973	------	1,768	44.32	99.74
Langdon	1912	1,838	Room	6½	6,428	101	10,608	171.33	771.33
Milton	-------	322	Room	2	752	20	1,560	40.16	40.16
New England	1931	1,117	Room	2	1,402	80	1,640	68.57	395.83
New Rockford	1917	2,185	Room	8	3,140	219	5,250	520.01	596.50
Regent	1935	405	Room	2	1,027	23	1,080	---------	49.46
Riverdale	1949	-------	Room	10	2,802	945	12,554	918.68	11,198.92
Rolla	1924	1,176	Room	2	2,433	81	4,128	182.12	193.36
Underwood	1951	1,061	Room	4	1,087	54	2,550	49.03	368.43
Zeeland	1946	484	Room	1	1,102	22	4,140	104.60	120.01

STATE OF NORTH DAKOTA
LIBRARY DIRECTORY

Ashley	Public Library	Mrs. Gerald Coyle
Bathgate	Public Library	Mrs. Fern Yon
Beach	Public Library	Mrs. Mabel Koshney
Beulah	Public Library	Mrs. Robert Easton
Bismarck	Public Library	Mr. Robert Thomas
Bismarck	State Historical Society Library	Miss Margaret Rose
Bottineau	Public Library	Mrs. E. M. Ertresvaag
Bottineau	State Forestry School Library	Mr. George P. Hynes
Bowman	Clara Lincoln Phelan Library	Mrs. Martha Stone
Cando	Public Library	Mrs. V. D. Lord
Carrington	Public Library	Mrs. Ella Mae Hargrave
Casselton	Public Library	Miss Laura Port
Cavalier	Public Library	Mrs. Robert Thacker
Cooperstown	Public Library	Mrs. W. W. Barr
Crosby	Divide County Library	Mrs. Anna S. Phelps
Devils Lake	Carnegie Library	Mrs. Eva Barrett
Dickinson	Public Library	Miss Gertrude Voldal
Dickinson	State Teachers College Library	Miss Matilda Stoxen
Drake	Public Library	Mrs. W. W. Halbert
Drayton	Public Library	Mrs. Vic Walstad
Edgeley	Public Library	Mrs. Ruth Evert
Ellendale	Public Library	Mrs. Maude Blumer
Ellendale	Normal and Industrial College Library	Mr. John Borden
Enderlin	Public Library	Mrs. E. M. Northenscold
Fargo	Public Library	Miss Inga Rynning
Fargo	State Agricultural College Library	Mr. H. Dean Stallings
Finley	Public Library	Mrs. E. C. Gilbertson
Flaxton	Public Library	Miss Dora Kundiger
Forbes	Public Library	Mr. Merle Borgen
Fordville	Public Library	Mrs. Dave Robertson
Gackle	Public Library	Mrs. J. M. Hummel
Goodrich	Public Library	Miss Joyce Unruh
Grafton	Public Library	Mrs. Hazel J. Barr
Grand Forks	Public Library	Mrs. Irene P. Norell
Grand Forks	State University Library	Dr. Jonathan Ashton
Hamilton	Public Library	Mrs. Andrew Knutson
Hankinson	Public Library	Mrs. George Schuett
Hansboro	Public Library	Mrs. L. C. Agarand
Harvey	Public Library	Mrs. Violet Bailey
Hatton	Public Library	Mrs. Herman Iverson
Hebron	Public Library	Mrs. Theophil Frey
Hettinger	Public Library	Mrs. Mabel Tommerson
Hillsboro	Public Library	Mrs. Anne Henning
Hoople	Public Library	Mrs. Elmer Gryte
Hope	Public Library	Mrs. Katie Glumb

Jamestown	City County Library	Mrs. Anna P. Bensch
Jamestown	Jamestown College Library	Miss Mary Steele
Killdeer	Public Library	Mrs. Wm. Cockburn
Kulm	Public Library	Mrs. E. E. Orth
Lakota	City Library	Mrs. Marian Swinland
LaMoure	Public Library	Mrs. James A. Frank
Langdon	Public Library	Mrs. E. J. Donovan
Larimore	Public Library	Mrs. J. F .Ralston
Leeds	Public Library	Miss Oleanna Thompson
Leonard Township	Watts Free Library	Mrs. Gilbert Elliott
Lidgerwood	City Library	Mrs. Elizabeth Kings
Linton	Public Library	Miss Ellen C. Woods
Lisbon	Public Library	Miss Pauline M. Billing
Mandan	Public Library	Mrs. Eleanor Trzcinski
Mayville	Public Library	Mrs. Agnes Skarperud
Mayville	State Teachers College Library	Miss Clenora Quanbeck
Milton	Public Library	Miss Gudrun Goodman
Minot	Public Library	Mrs. Lois Ronning
Minot	State Teachers College Library	Miss Nellie B. Swanson
Mohall	Public Library	Mrs. John Smith
Mott	Inez Hendrickson Library	Mrs. Elmer Wentlandt
New England	Public Library	Mrs. Thomas W. Gallup
New Rockford	Public Library	Mrs. James Donnelly
New Town	Public Library	Mrs. Arvid Olson
Northwood	Public Library	Mrs. West Mutchler
Oakes	Public and School Library	Mrs. H. Thomas Hample
Oberon	Public Library	Mrs. Hilding Carlson
Park River	Public Library	Miss Vera H. Warner
Pembina	Public Library	Mrs. Pauline Brennan
Portal	Public Library	Miss Louise Cummins
Regent	Public Library	Mrs. E. A. Stone
Riverdale	Public Library	Mrs. William Bassett
Rolette	Public Library	Mrs. G. E. Ellingson
Rolla	Public Library	Mrs. Clarence Jacobson
Rugby	Public Library	Miss Kathryn Cruden
St. Thomas	Public Library	Mrs. Walter Felt
Steele	Public Library	Miss Ruth Thieling
Towner	Public Library	Mrs. J. M. Harnit
Turtle Lake	Public Library	Mrs. John Frey
Underwood	Public Library	Mrs. Grant Roseth
Valley City	Public Library	Mrs. Helen H. Tracy
Valley City	State Teachers College Library	Mr. D. W. Ferguson
Velva	Public and School Library	Mrs. Fred Robinson
Wahpeton	Leach Public Library	Mrs. Hermine Becker
Wahpeton	State Science School Library	Mrs. Mildred Larson
Williston	James Memorial Library	Mrs. Florence M. Kearns
Wishek	Public Library	Miss Mavis Heinle
Zeeland	Public Library	Mrs. August Boschee

Twenty-Fifth Biennial Report

of the

State Library Commission

to the

Board of Administration

For the Period
July 1, 1954 - June 30, 1956

Twenty-Fifth Biennial Report

of the

State Library Commission

to the

Board of Administration

STATE LIBRARY COMMISSION STAFF
June 30, 1956

Hazel Webster Byrnes	Director and State Librarian
Arlene Stocker	Assistant to the Director
Dorothy Bigwood	Head, Reference Department
Winnifred Coyne	Head, School Department
Lorraine LaFleur	Head, Traveling Library Department
Gabriella Holkesvik	Chief Clerk

•

For the Period
July 1, 1954 - June 30, 1956

TO THE STATE BOARD OF ADMINISTRATION: R. H. Sherman, Chairman, H. H. Joos, Edwin G. Sailer, M. F. Peterson, and Math Dahl.

The North Dakota State Library Commission has the honor to submit its Twenty-fifth biennial report, covering the period from July 1, 1954 to June 30, 1956.

(Mrs) HAZEL WEBSTER BYRNES
Director

REPORT OF THE DIRECTOR
STATE LIBRARY COMMISSION 1954-1956

The past two years show an all-time high record in accomplishments. We look with satisfaction on this record for it has meant the investments of the best efforts of the State Library Commission. It is a rewarding experience. Well do we realize, however, that sharing in these accomplishments by seeing the importance and realizing the need for greater support of the library movement, are members of the State Board of Administration, Library Planning Board, Budget Board, North Dakota Library Association, and the Legislature.

Expressing the work of the State Library Commission is this quotation published by the Department of Health, Education and Welfare, Office of Education, in the brochure, THE STATE LIBRARIES. 1956.

"No other official agency is so strategically situated to widen the library opportunities for all the people and to continually improve public library services. To local public libraries the public library extension agency occupies a place similar to that of the State Department of Education in relation to local public schools. The post of the chief library extension officer for public libraries is comparable to the post of the chief state school officer for public schools . . ."

Pleased though we may be with past efforts, nevertheless the story of what should be accomplished is just beginning. The Look Ahead holds a cheering promise for North Dakotans. We therefore prefer to let statistics appearing elsewhere in this report help to tell of the past biennium, while we Look Ahead.

THE LOOK AHEAD

Two recent developments in the library field are causing the State Library Commission to take an exciting look ahead.

One of these is the Library Services Act, the other the new Library Standards.

Library Standards

First, let us look at the Standards, since they will offer help in carrying out the provisions of the Library Services Act. These will supercede the Post-War Standards for Public Libraries.

One change and key feature is the idea of "systems" of libraries. "Systems" are explained as "libraries working together, sharing their services and materials to meet the full needs of their readers. The development of systems of libraries does not weaken or eliminate the small community library. On the contrary, it offers that library and its users greatly expanded resources."

Library Services Act

This is federal legislation which will have a far reaching effect in North Dakota.

The Library Services Act, Public Law 597 passed by the 84th session of Congress and signed by President Eisenhower, June 16, 1956, will provide federal funds "to promote the further developments of public library services in rural areas".

The Act authorized Congress to appropriate $7,500,000 a year for each of five years to be allotted to the states on a matching basis. $2,500,000 will be granted for the first year beginning July 1, 1956 to June 30, 1957. This, in effect, means that each state will receive a basic $40,000 with which to begin the work. All funds are to be matched on the basis of the per capita income of the state as compared to the national per capita income.

The North Dakota Library Commission has submitted plans to the Federal authorities and is ready to start the work in this state. This work will be begun after a meeting in Kansas City, Missouri, October 29-31, 1956, where the director of the North Dakota State Library Commission and other representatives of state library agencies in this mid-west area will meet with federal authorities to discuss legal aspects and other problems involved in the administration of the Act. The exact amount of matching funds will also then be announced.

Putting this Act into operation in North Dakota will mean an expansion of the State Library Commission's program—and incidently, the State Library Commission's fondest dream—to reach unserved or inadequately served areas as rapidly as possible so long as demonstrations are in keeping with standards of good service. Although the State Library Commission has now reached the highest record of circulation in its history, it does not and never would be able to give adequate service to the entire rural areas of the state.

These federal funds will provide help to pull North Dakota from the category—1953 statistics—(a) of states which have the greatest percentage of their Population without Local Public Library Service. In order they are:

North Dakota	59.1%
South Dakota	56.5
West Virginia	56.5
Mississippi	55.9
Idaho	51.2

(b) of states having the least amount for Operating Expenditures per capita for Local Public Library Service. The minimum standard is $1.50. In this category are:

West Virginia	$0.19	Virginia	$0.33
Texas	0.26	New Mexico	0.34
Arkansas	0.27	Kentucky	0.34
Alabama	0.28	*North Dakota	0.35
Mississippi	0.30	North Carolina	0.35
Arizona	0.30	South Carolina	0.40
Tennessee	0.31	South Dakota	0.48
Oklahoma	0.32		

*North Dakota's expenditures have in the past three years increased from 35¢ to 45½¢ per capita.

Since the State Library Commission must put into operation the provisions of this Act in North Dakota, the need for increased amounts in the Commission's budget for 1957-1959 becomes the more necessary.

STATE LIBRARY COMMISSION STATISTICAL REPORT

July 1, 1954 - June 30, 1956

Circulation

July 1, 1954 - June 30, 1955	124,524
July 1, 1955 - June 30, 1956	127,811
TOTAL	252,335

Requests

July 1, 1954 - June 30, 1955	11,644
July 1, 1955 - June 30, 1956	13,088
TOTAL	24,732

What the above figures represent—

From the Traveling Library Department

1,922 collections went to 1,246 schools and communities

From the School Department

1,965 teachers received monthly boxes for Reading Circle work in grade schools

From the Reference Department

217 clubs were sent material to prepare 1,057 topics

125 families and individuals received monthly packages under our Books-a-month plan

9,611 requests were filled for high school students doing term papers; mothers wanting to entertain Children; adults looking for information and entertainment; individuals doing research in all fields.

Not included in the circulation figures are 26,205 pieces of first class mail from the various departments and the office of the director.

Book Stock

45,000 volumes

100 subscriptions to leading magazines

50 vertical file drawers of miscellaneous information on many topics in pamphlet or clipping form

Budget

Salary	$ 9,000
Clerkhire	55,000
Postage, supplies, etc.	6,500
Miscellaneous	1,000
Travel	2,000
Aids to Libraries	500
Books	15,000
OASIS	1,000
	$90,000

ENTERPRISING SERVICES AFFILIATED WITH THE STATE LIBRARY COMMISSION

State Library Planning Board

This Board, made up of leaders representing different fields of interest and areas of the state, meets at intervals to help view the library situation and make plans for library betterment and expansion. Working in connection with the State Library Commission, it has reviewed the reports of the field workers; developed plans for the administration of the Library Services Act; considered the budget of the State Library Commission; and offered suggestions regarding coming legislation, and the like.

Field Work

Four young people, all with library training, have worked in various sections over the state. They are enthusiastic over library prospects, and their enthusiasm is contagious. They have not only made visitations, but they have "rolled up their sleeves" and given help where help was needed. Forty-six Public Libraries received help and seventeen school libraries. The length of the stops, which the field workers made, depended on what needed to be done, as well as whom there was to see, for they not only built up libraries, they were looking to the future in preparing for larger library units.

North Dakota Library Association

The State Library Commission has received generous and loyal support from the North Dakota Library Association. The Association has helped with letters to Congressmen and to State Legislators, as well as with publicity for the Trustees' Award for Judge Eugene A. Burdick, and other library pursuits. It has donated funds to assist the Washington ALA Office with the passage of the Library Services Act, also assisted the State Library Commission with funds for special projects, and given funds also to further the promotion of the Citizens for the Library movement. It is now preparing a history giving excerpts from the time of the organization of the North Dakota Library Association in January, 1906, to the present. This will be printed and kept in a permanent file.

Citizens for the Library

Citizens' movements for library promotion are springing up in different parts of the country. North Dakota was one of the early states to develop a most active organization. Calling itself "Citizens for the Library", this movement is dove-tailing with the State Library Commission. It is composed of representatives or "delegates" working through different organizations to give understanding and promotion to the library program. Mrs. Emil Bloedow, starting in her home town of Edgeley, North Dakota, heads this movement which deals with the laymans' phase of work not touched by figures and statistics, but most valuable to any development.

Award to North Dakota Library Trustee

Some splendid publicity for North Dakota resulted because of this award to Judge Eugene A. Burdick, president of the Board of Directors of the James Memorial Library, Williston, North Dakota, who was honored by the American Library Association at its National Conference, Miami Beach, June 19, 1956.

Judge Burdick's citation—one of two annual citations given to trustees in the United States—was for "his distinguished achievements in restoring and developing library service in Williston; . . . his inspiring leadership in promoting public interest in libraries; and his notable contributions to the welfare of public libraries in the state of North Dakota."

Director's "outside-office" Activities

The director has met and addressed local and state groups; attended conferences and committees; and has given direction to library activities in many places. Altogether these number some 35 meetings in various parts of the state. Outside of the state she has participated in the following:

Annual Conference, American Library Association
Philadelphia, Pennsylvania, July 3-9, 1955

Mountain-Plains Library Association (regional)
Jackson, Wyoming, September 15-17, 1955
(also attended by Arlene Stocker of the Commission staff)

National Joint Committee of the National Education Association and the American Library Association
Washington, D.C., October 24-25, 1955

Annual Conference, American Library Association
Miami Beach, Florida, June 17-23, 1956

Publicity

Articles regarding the State Library Commission have appeared in many state newspapers and in the **Minneapolis Tribune** and the **Dakota Farmer**, and stories have also been used by the Associated and United Press for other chain papers.

LIBRARY NOTES AND NEWS is published quarterly under the editorship of the director of the State Library Commission with cooperation of the staff. It has a mailing list of about 2,000. This last year the merit of this publication brought an invitation to the editor to join the North Dakota Press Womens' Association.

The Biennial Report of the State Library Commission is published by the State Board of Administration and is distributed to libraries in the state, to state officials and to designated offices outside of the state.

The director has told the library story over the radio and on television.

Mail

In terms of the mail which goes out and returns to the State Library Commission, this story might be told as follows: Three hundred eighty large boxes from the Traveling Library Department go out and return practically three times every year, and books from the School and Reference Departments, which number up to 80 packages on some days, are circulated on an average of nine times during the year. Day by day these packages from the three departments are piled up so that the outgoing mail often numbers some 40 large sized cartons and numerous small packages, besides the 20 to 40 letters in the first class mail. The Post Office Department repeats to us the fact that day by day the State Library Commission has more parcel post than any department on Capitol Hill.

(Mrs.) HAZEL WEBSTER BYRNES
Director

COUNTY PUBLIC LIBRARIES

COUNTY	CIRCULATION 1954-55	CIRCULATION 1955-56	Total	Volumes	Borrowers	Hours open per week
Divide	25,137	17,331	42,468	9,995	942	39
Stutsman	41,290	51,070	92,360	10,790	2,430	40

PUBLIC LIBRARIES

TOWN	CIRCULATION 1954-55	CIRCULATION 1955-56	[illegible]	[illegible]	Borrowers	Hours open per week	Rural Borrowers
Ashley	7,128	7,649	14,777	5,743	894	6	
Beach	[illegible]	11,756	20,165	4,410	738	5½	220
Bismarck	138,546	148,124	286,670	30,593	7,396	66	225
Bowman	3,423	3,384	6,807	4,650	[illegible]	13	60
Carrington	13,258	13,545	26,803	4,266	575	25	150
Casselton	[illegible]			4,028	414	4	
Cavalier	5,374	5,428	10,802	3,013	593	4	163
Cooperstown	2,882	3,015	5,897	2,327	54	7	56
Devils Lake	31,605	28,753	60,358	15,619	3,120	36	
Dickinson	45,527	48,355	93,882	18,970	3,147	51	325
Edgeley	11,873	12,603	24,476	4,391	446	7	215
Ellendale	13,112	12,977	26,089	6,164	240	14½	
Fargo	234,136	230,931	465,067	59,753	25,414	72	965
Grafton	5,417	5,380	10,797	6,658	911	19½	
Grand Forks	142,241	147,886	290,127	39,015	9,305	69	901
Harvey	8,670	11,670	20,340	3,178	827	13	94
Hebron	585	480	1,065	1,653	68	2	
Hettinger	5,200	4,266	9,466	2,652	483	21	60
Jamestown	76,614	79,152	155,766	23,196	6,292	60	847
[illegible]	[illegible]	1,653	3,600	5,538		6	
LaMoure	7,791	Temporarily Closed Because of Fire					
Langdon	6,240	5,980	12,220	6,661	160	9	
Leeds	1,581	1,106	2,687	1,510	318	2	47
Lidgerwood	8,233	6,557	14,790	8,130	521	19½	190

Linton	8,335	6,527	14,862	3,730	530	15	65
Lisbon	9,208	10,284	19,492	5,354	900	15	400
Mandan	29,265	26,463	55,728	7,301	2,349	36	171
Mayville	3,812	3,964	7,776	5,531	2,962	8	
Mot	123,103	178,924	302,027	31,272	8,575	54	85
Mall	1,575	1,600	3,175	349	303	6	
Mott	5,341	4,253	9,594	3,757	614	5	276
Oakes	21,478	7,165	38,643	8,461	686	32	
Park River	7,914	8,707	16,621	3,309	703	12	167
Rugby	21,018	23,783	44,801	8,255	1,557	30	
St. ffias	1,486	1,369	2,855	1,972	36*	3	
Turtle Lake	870	930	1,800	1,966	128	2	
Valley City	30,443	30,615	61,058	18,549	2,765	36	503
Velva	No record			3,062	450	20	
Wahpeton	12,880	15,570	28,450	13,873	2,568	30	700
'Won	48,991	62,084	111,075	12,902	3.011	43	12
Wishek	5,172	4,959	10,131	3,342	1,338	4½	

*Family cards.

COUNTY PUBLIC LIBRARIES

COUNTY	Headquarters	Date Established	[illegible] Population	Tax Appropriation 1954-55	Tax Appropriation 1955-56	Total Receipts 1954-55	Total Receipts 1955-56
Divide	Crosby	1947	[illegible]	$ 4,580.00	$ 5,264.40	$ 5,030.00	$ 5,776.09
Stutsman	Jamestown	1954	24,158	28,396.92	14,908.50	28,396.92	21,461.92

PUBLIC LIBRARIES

A new definition of a Public Library as given in Public Law 597 passed by the 84th Congress, 1956, has been used in the designation of the libraries in North Dakota. "The term 'public library' means a library that serves free all residents of a community, district, or region, and receives its financial support in whole or in part from public funds."

TOWN	Date Established	1950 Population	Tax Appropriation 1954-55	Tax Appropriation 1955-56	Total Receipts 1954-55	Total Receipts 1955-56
Ashley	1913	1,423	$ 250.00	$ 500.00	$ 1,155.24	$ 1,313.32
Beach	1912	1,461	325.00	[illegible]	679.83	1,822.11
Bismarck	1914	18,640	40,000.00	45,000.00	41,900.87	46,910.94
[illegible]an	1916	1,382	1,188.37	621.63	2,710.94	3,449.47
Carrington	1906	2,101	2,300.00	2,300.00	4,574.98	5,033.18
Casselton	1906	1,373	[illegible]	953.85	1,519.69	2,271.96
Cavalier	1915	1,459	180.00	180.00	573.44	530.05
[illegible]n	1945	1,189	489.88	[illegible]	3,280.43	[illegible]4.01
Devils Lake	1896	6,427	7,335.32	7,462.26	13,037.94	13,996.84
Dickinson	1908	7,469	9,000.00	9,180.00	10,115.60	10,233.54
Edgeley	1912	943	900.00	950.00	1,008.04	1,034.14
Ell[illegible]dale	1912	1,759	1,200.00	1,500.00	1,389.29	1,656.97

Fargo	1900	38,256	31,907.00	48,572.90	69,355.59	88,535.62
Grafton	1895	4,901	2,748.37	3,415.20	5,885.99	6,965.11
Gnd Forks	1899	26,836	33,615.42	35,895.00	33,615.42	35,895.00
Harvey	1952	2,337	1,793.76	3,120.32	3,685.21	1,797.14
Hebron	1938	1,412	100.00	100.00	378.29	307.13
Hettinger	1912	1,762	350.00	350.00	729.36	669.10
Jamestown	1901	10,697	10,815.85	11,500.00	17,565.77	16,950.03
Lakota	1906	1,032	1,087.55	1,450.96	2,641.21	2,334.85
LaMoure	1924	1,010	1,186.44	1,069.91	1,246.07	2,264.56
Langdon	1912	1,838	250.00	350.00	390.85	467.56
Leeds	1902	778		100.00		115.20
Lidgerwood	1913	1,147	1,680.00	1,680.00	1,991.81	2,054.18
Linton	1936	1,675	720.00	720.00	821.83	827.08
Ilion	1915	2,031	1,891.65	2,951.28	3,4 9.32	4,217.21
Mandan	1896	7,298	6,428.68	6,675.39	10,279.48	11,364.46
Mayville	1900	1,790	2,291.63	2,735.22	2,389.52	2,899.82
Mot	1908	22,032	23,730.25	24,994.32	36,413.77	43,536.26
Mhall	1937	1,073	200.00	400.00	1,206.45	1,619.73
Mott	1912	1,583	[illegible]	1,284.06	2,114.89	2,893.02
Oakes	1904	1,774	1,773.54	1,646.37	4,118.32	3,875.52
Park River	1900	1,692	975.00	1,080.00	1,864.08	2,276.75
Rugby	1912	2,907	1,631.51	1,611.00	2,584.89	2,640.39
St. Thomas	1954	566	250.00	100.00	3,124.03	904.22
Turtle Lake	1926	839	177.98	191.25	493.48	504.67
Valley City	1900	6,851	7,545.65	8,134.08	20,543.93	21,817.01
Velva	1914	1,170	100.00	100.00	808.00	928.53
Wahpeton		5,125	6,000.00	5,656.29	8,897.98	8,263.22
Williston	1910	7,378	13,197.68	16,000.00	22,733.89	25,465.08
Wishek	1926	1,241	500.00	500.00	[illegible]	634.05

COUNTY PUBLIC LIBRARIES

Expenditures

COUNTY	SALARIES		MAINTENANCE		BOOKS-PERIODICALS		TOTAL	
	1954-55	1955-56	1954-55	1955-56	1954-55	1955-56	1954-55	1955-56
Divide	$2,520.00	2,520.00	$ 2,038.95	$ 2,184.92	$ 852.11	$ 1,067.52	$ 4,730.96	$ 5,772.44
Stutsman	6,484.82	6,884.87	10,444.85	2,265.39	4,913.82	4,263.10	21,843.49	13,413.36

PUBLIC LIBRARIES

TOWN	SALARIES		MAINTENANCE		BOOKS-PERIODICALS		TOTAL	
	1954-55	1955-56	1954-55	1955-56	1954-55	1955-56	1954-55	1955-56
Ashley	$ 193.91	$ 230.00	$ 649.46	$ 1,147.12	$ 312.87	$ 350.00	$ 1,155.24	$ 1,727.12
Beach	310.00	316.00	39.86	52.70	448.43	577.63	798.29	958.41
Bismarck	23,538.84	25,625.25	6,038.72	4,889.82	5,741.40	5,691.35	35,318.96	36,206.42
Bowman	554.34	559.23	142.42	286.05	192.62	217.41	889.38	1,062.69
Carrington	1,104.00	1,080.00	160.01	485.56	642.79	896.49	1,906.80	2,462.05
[illegible]on	[illegible]		22.20	5.00	56.88	38.49	201.58	43.49
Cavalier	187.00	183.00	14.17	31.31	134.25	122.90	335.92	337.21
Cooperstown	180.00	205.00	325.65	342.02	337.01	339.85	842.66	886.87
Devils Lake	3,461.60	3,558.80	1,498.46	2,878.16	1,720.81	1,923.32	6,680.87	8,360.28
Dickinson	6,666.80	[illegible]	1,136.89	1,685.04	1,786.59	1,429.58	9,590.28	9,689.67
Edgeley	425.00	425.00	82.59	115.69	429.44	388.19	937.03	928.88
[illegible]dale	729.20	733.60	73.10	74.81	574.05	579.18	1,376.35	1,387.59
Fargo	34,103.50	34,798.50	6,039.21	5,553.66	6,808.44	6,928.74	46,951.15	47,280.90

Grafton	1,560.00	1,616.75	1,252.88	1,034.15	[illegible]	931.60	3,199.99	3,582.50
Grand Forks	16,745.74	19,919.07	8,653.56	6,592.82	[illegible]	9,198.22	33,615.42	35,710.11
Harvey	720.00	765.30	530.62	595.90	[illegible]	809.53	1,759.27	[illegible]
Hebron	37.85	58.50			[illegible]	37.58	165.51	96.08
Hettinger	315.00	309.50		6.00	192.10	190.91	407.10	[illegible]
Jamestown	7,830.62	8,718.60	4,540.28	3,182.95	3,402.30	2,984.89	15,773.20	14,887.44
Lakota	[illegible]	301.94	2,175.14	1,319.76	64.61	325.15	2,542.09	1,946.85
LaMoure	410.35	399.60	366.08	393.35	447.67	292.03	1,224.10	1,084.98
Langdon	250.00	250.00			114.52	172.18	516.25	495.18
Leeds	78.00	57.00			100.00	44.00	178.00	112.88
Lidgerwood	875.00	875.00	335.81	435.83	436.01	413.73	1,646.82	1,724.56
Linton	720.00	720.00	36.32	33.73	49.88	60.55	806.20	814.28
Lisbon	1,142.00	[illegible]	706.50	1,004.53	[illegible]	460.34	2,361.83	[illegible]
Mandan	3,874.00	3,837.42	334.91	1,893.42	1,758.35	1,870.76	5,967.26	7,601.60
Mayville	654.60	656.00	1,531.90	1,829.56	[illegible]	425.66	2,357.57	2,911.22
Minot	12,241.72	15,098.22	7,042.83	11,866.42	5,490.41	5,791.28	24,774.96	32,755.92
Mohall		288.20				143.51		
Mott	240.00	306.00	38.99	470.08	289.86	642.52	568.85	1,418.60
Oakes	900.00	950.00	366.54	233.07	827.54	921.43	2,094.08	2,104.50
Park River	600.00	599.50	47.77	[illegible]	116.78	264.78	764.55	931.19
Rugby	1,080.00	1,080.00	153.92	79.71	539.53	738.22	1,773.45	1,897.93
St. Thomas			1,215.04	138.37	81.71	39.85	2,842.55	703.22
Turtle Lake	75.00	86.00	22.66	5.08	140.40	108.54	238.06	199.62
Valley City	4,082.85	4,243.75	1,801.87	2,225.02	1,887.55	2,167.77	7,772.27	8,636.54
Velva					897.35	881.63		
Wahpeton	3,170.59	3,069.05	2,518.84	1,754.51	870.33	[illegible]	6,559.76	5,591.97
Williston	6,722.65	7,988.38	3,767.64	5,127.04	3,108.15	3,763.75	13,598.44	16,879.17
Wishek	140.50	138.75	136.45	77.40	345.64	296.10	622.59	512.25

ASSOCIATION LIBRARIES GIVING FREE SERVICE

	Date Established	1950 Population	Municipal Help	Hours Open a Week	Hes	Borrowers	Circulation	1954 956 EXPENDITURES Books	Total
Bathgate	1916	209	None	2	1,142	101	2,656	$108.21	228.31
Bah	1931	1,501	Room	2	2,429	430	3,746	134.08	278.91
Bteau	1915	2,268	None	2	1,911	163	6,655	234.39	290.05
Drake	1920	831	Room	4	2,620	160	6,512	237.39	261.40
Dton	1946	875		2	1,310	174	798	106.63	202.72
Flaxton	1935	436	None	18	2,516	75	485		
Forbes	1944	204	None	6	1,505	168	6,883	245.70	447.03
Fordville	1952	376	None	2	840	150	2,090	1.00	25.00
Forman	Being re-organized								
Ie	1954	604	None	7	1,064	95	4,169	3296	327.30
Goodrich	1926	448	$75.00	1	894	105	415	None	128.37
Hankinson	1907	1,409	Room	2	2,175	40	140		
Hiro	1954	1,374	No report						
Hoople	1902	778	No report						
Hope	1910	470	Room	3	1,880		1,793	62.00	164.40
Kulm	1937	707	Room	2	1,613	120		43.52	56.50
Larimore	1954	1,374	None	4	1,456	280	1,995		
Lard	112	469	None	5	1,520			9144	20.93
New England	1931	1,117	None	2	1,538	130	2,854	102.51	318.00
New Town	1954		None	1	1,381	50			
Northwood	1941	1,182	None	2	1,264			2.18	61.90
Pembina		640	$75.00	3	1,000		170	220.61	274.61
Portal	1935	409		1	485	125	864	41.00	55.28
Rolette	1947	451		2	949	135	1,890	146.30	160.18
Steele	1950	762	None	2	498	134	411		7.22
Walhalla	1955	1,463		6	1,999	400	425		825.00

CLUB SPONSORED LIBRARIES CHARGING FOR SERVICE

	Date Established	1950 Population	Municipal Help	Hours Open a Week	Volumes	Borrowers	Circulation	1954-1956 EXPENDITURES Books	Total
Cando	1902	1,530	No report						
Enderlin	1912	[illegible]	No report						
Finley	[illegible]	671	None	2	281		100	$ 20.14	$ 23.14
Hamilton	1916	241	No report						
Hansboro	1928	134	None	2½	1,388	64	[illegible]	165.35	198.01
Hatton		991	None	1½	530	35	2,444	53.59	174.59
Killdeer		477	None	2	2,022		2,089	67.33	[illegible]
Milton		322	None	2	756	11	878		16.82
New Rockford	1917	2,185	None	8	3,458		6,137	583.79	596.70
Riverdale	1949		None	10	3,486	465	17,031	367,94	589.63
Rolla	1924	1,176	None	2	2,579	92	3,970	154.26	185.83
Underwood	1951	1,061	Room, $ 100	4	1,255	28	1,555	86.49	191.44
Zeeland	1946	484	No report						

STATE OF NORTH DAKOTA

LIBRARY DIRECTORY

Ashley	Public Library	Mrs. Gerald Coyle
Bathgate	Public Library	Mrs. Fern Yon
Beach	Public Library	Mrs. Mabel Koshney
Beulah	Public Library	Mrs. R. W. Easton
Bismarck	Public Library	Mr. Andrew Hansen
Bismarck	State Historical Society Library	Miss Margaret Rose
Bottineau	Public Library	Mrs. E. M. Ertresvaag
Bottineau	State Forestry School Library	Mr. George P. Hynes
Bowman	Clara Lincoln Phelan Library	Mrs. Martha Stone
Cando	Public Library	Mrs. V. D. Lord
Carrington	Public Library	Mrs. Ella Mae Hargrave
Casselton	Public Library	Miss Laura Port
Cavalier	Public Library	Mrs. Robert Thacker
Columbus	Public Library	Miss Lucille L. Thorndal
Cooperstown	Public Library	Mrs. W. W. Barr
Crosby	Divide County Library	Mrs. Anna S. Phelps
Devils Lake	Carnegie Library	Mrs. Eva Barrett
Dickinson	Public Library	Miss Gertrude Voldal
Dickinson	State Teachers College Library	Miss Matilda Stoxen
Drake	Public Library	Mrs. W. W. Halbert
Drayton	Public Library	Miss Pat McEnrae
Edgeley	Public Library	Mrs. Ruth Evert
Ellendale	Public Library	Mrs. Maude Blumer
Ellendale	Normal and Industrial College Library	Mr. Thomas A. Hunt
Enderlin	Public Library	Mrs. Jerome Martin
Fargo	Public Library	Miss Inga Rynning
Fargo	State Agri. College Library	Mr. H. Dean Stallings
Finley	Public Library	Mrs. Bert Dronen
Flaxton	Public Library	Miss Dora Kundiger
Forbes	Public Library	Mr. Merle Borgen
Fordville	Public Library	Mrs. E. J. Beetz
Forman	Public Library	Mrs. John Spencer
Gackle	Public Library	Mrs. J. M. Hummel
Goodrich	Public Library	Mrs. Harold Jenner
Grafton	Public Library	Mrs. Hazel J. Barr
Grand Forks	Public Library	Miss Mary M. French
Grand Forks	State University Library	Dr. Jonathan Ashton
Hankinson	Public Library	Mrs. George Schuett
Hansboro	Public Library	Mrs. C. O. Nord
Harvey	Public Library	Mrs. Violet Bailey
Hatton	Public Library	Mrs. Vernon Johnson
Hebron	Public Library	Miss Verda Mears
Hettinger	Public Library	Mrs. Mabel Tommerson
Hillsboro	Public Library	Mrs. Anne Henning
Hoople	Public Library	Mrs. Elmer Gryte

Hope	Public Library	Mrs. Katie Gumb
Jamestown	City-County Library	Mrs. Anna P. Bensch
Jamestown	Jamestown College Library	Mr. Gordon Clarke
Killdeer	Public Library	Mrs. W. F. Cockburn
Kulm	Public Library	Mrs. E. E. Orth
Lakota	A. M. Tofthagen Library	Mrs. Marion I Swinland
LaMoure	Public Library	Mrs. Dacotah Harmsen
Langdon	Public Library	Mrs. E. J. Donovan
Larimore	Public Library	Mrs. J. F Ralston
Leeds	Public Library	Miss Mary Ann Johnson
Leonard	Watts Free Library	Mrs. Gilbert Elliott
Lidgerwood	City Library	Mrs. Elizabeth Kings
Linton	Public Library	Mrs. Ellen C. Woods
Lisbon	Public Library	Miss Ada D. Stewart
Maddock	Public Library	Mrs. Vernon Johnson
Mandan	Public Library	Mrs. Eleanor Trzcinski
Mayville	Public Library	Mrs. Leon Skarperud
Mayville	State Teachers College Library	Miss Clenora Quanbeck
Milton	Public Library	Mrs. Oscar Landsem
Minot	Public Library	Mrs. Lois Ronning
Minot	State Teachers College Library	Miss Nellie B. Swanson
Mohall	Public Library	Mrs. John Smith
Mott	Inez Hendrickson Library	Mrs. Elmer Wentlandt
Napoleon	Public Library	Mrs. Ruth S. Wurl
New England	Public Library	Mrs. Thomas W. Gallup
New Rockford	Public Library	Mrs. James Donnelly
New Town	Public Library	Mrs. Arvid Olson
Northwood	Public Library	Mrs. West Mutchler
Oakes	Public Library	Mrs. Helene T Hample
Park River	Public Library	Miss Vera H. Warner
Parshall	Public Library	Mrs. Robert Cordes
Pembina	Public Library	Mrs. Pauline Brennan
Portal	Public Library	Mrs. A. J Lindsay
Riverdale	Public Library	Miss Viola E. Sells
Rolette	Public Library	Mrs. G. E. Ellingson
Rolla	Public Library	Mrs. C. R. Jacobsen
Rugby	Public Library	Miss Kathryn Cruden
St. Thomas	Public Library	Mrs. Walter A. Felt
Steele	Public Library	Miss Ruth Thieling
Towner	Public Library	Mrs. J. M. Harnit
Turtle Lake	Public Library	Mrs. John Frey
Underwood	Public Library	Mrs. Grant Roseth
Valley City	Public Library	Mrs. Helen H. Tracy
Valley City	State Teachers College Library	Mr. D. W. Ferguson
Velva	School and Public Library	Mrs. Ella Robinson
Wahpeton	Leach Public Library	Mrs. Mabel Darner
Wahpeton	State Science School Library	Mrs. Mildred Larson
Walhalla	Public Library	Mrs. Romeo Charbonneau
Williston	James Memorial Library	Mrs. Florence M Kearns
Wishek	Public Library	Miss Margaret Tuchscher
Zeeland	Public Library	Mrs. August Boschee

Twenty-seventh Biennial Report

of the

State Library Commission

to the

State Board of Administration

STATE LIBRARY COMMISSION STAFF

June 30, 1960

Hazel Webster Byrnes	Director and State Librarian and Supervisor, Federal-State Library Project
Arlene Stocker	Assistant to the Director
Leone Morrison	Head, Reference Department
Winnifred Coyne	Head, School Library Department
Lorraine LaFleur	Head, Traveling Library Department
Josephine Davenport	Chief Clerk
Eva Fogderud	Assistant, Federal-State Library Project
Gertrude Funston	Assistant, Federal-State Library Project
Marie Huber	Assistant, Federal-State Library Project
Margaret Anderson Stav	Project Coordinator
Freda Hatten	Field Library Consultant

For the Period

July 1, 1958 - June 30, 1960

BISMARCK TRIBUNE

96274

TO THE STATE BOARD OF ADMINISTRATION: H. H. Joos, chairman, Edwin G. Sailer, Palmer Levin, M. F. Peterson, and Math Dahl.

The North Dakota State Library Commission has the honor to submit its Twenty-Seventh biennial report, covering the period from July 1, 1958 to June 30, 1960.

(Mrs.) HAZEL WEBSTER BYRNES
Director

REPORT OF THE DIRECTOR
STATE LIBRARY COMMISSION 1958-1960

"Suddenly a better-read, better-informed American has become a necessity." This quotation used by National Book Week is aptly used. This country has learned that only a life time of continuing self-education through reading, supplementing formal education, can keep alive our mighty heritage and at the same time make our people alert to what may be happening in the future. North Dakota is keeping pace in this effort to keep Americans "better-read and better-informed." Seventy thousand people, by and large, in this state are receiving library service who have not before received it.

It is obvious as one looks at the figures on the following pages that the budget of the State Library Commission has been augmented by Federal-State funds. The Library Services Act has made this possible. The Congress of the United States affirms the principle of federal support as a shared responsibility with the states in connection with library service. Both major political parties have placed in their platform the support of libraries. The Republican platform declared: "support of library service to extend it to all our people." The Democratic platform pledged to "further federal support of libraries."

The State Legislature matches federal funds proportionately for this purpose. This Federal-State money is used only to start the programs of library service, which once started are continued with local support.

All money for library purposes falls into categories as follows:

Books and Materials

Reference, School, and Traveling Library Departments of the State Library Commission, cooperate in handling requests to give the most effective service. All have benefited by additional books both for general circulation and for reference. The State Library Commission has not only strengthened its own resources, but has been able to help with book service to the various area projects.

Staff

One professional staff member has been added and three whose library training though not complete merits recognition. These additional qualified staff members have been badly needed. Federal-State funds have made it possible to secure their services.

Equipment

Additional book stacks have been placed in strategic places. Space generally is too crowded, but it must also accommodate additional desks, typewriters and reproduction appliances. New fluorescent lighting throughout the library stacks and offices give more easement to the work.

Extension

In dealing with the problem of extension the various states have found that the organization of County and Regional (comprised of two or more counties) Libraries offer the best and most economical service and utilize all libraries, big and little, in those certain areas. Circulation where desirable is by bookmobile.

The Federal-State funds give a start to these projects, after 51% of the voters of a county have indicated through petitions that they wish this library program. These Federal-State funds which begin this program are often called "seed money," for the project once started with the "seed money" is carried on by local county funds. County Commissioners agree to place in the County budget one and up to two mills for library support. House Bill No. 538 passed by the 35th Legislature sets forth these conditions. North Dakota has been commended nationally for the fact that its county and regional libraries have been "started on a firm foundation since a county tax levy is required before a Federal-State grant is made".

Thus far up to June 30, 1960, seven counties in North Dakota have completed development and are supported entirely by local funds. Some of these have united in threes and twos for economy and for better library service. All are operating bookmobiles. One of these — a three county region — is finding that two bookmobiles are profitable. Reports from all counties are most favorable.

County and Regional Libraries

Counties and regions now on their own operated by local funds are as follows: Williams, Mountrail and McKenzie Counties; McLean and Mercer Counties; and LaMoure and Logan Counties. Others are in process of development but that is a story for a later report.

Travel

In previous biennial reports we have endeavored to enumerate the travel given to the library program in this state. The present situation, however, shows field workers and consultants now working in various parts of the state, and the director giving attention here and there, and travel is now too much for enumeration. Suffice it to say that calls are answered for work in individual libraries, including school libraries, as can be arranged, as well as for county and regional libraries. Planning is done at the State Library Commission to coordinate the work of libraries, librarians and trustees in bringing about any new development.

Trips outside the state have taken those directing County and Regional work to a general workshop in Minneapolis. The director, as council member for North Dakota, has attended the Midwinter business meeting in Chicago and has gone to Montreal, Canada, for the first joint meeting of the American Library Association and the Canadian Library Association.

Publications

The State Library Commission puts out a Manual and yearly Supplements for elementary school librarians, and compiles Book Lists for the grades, high school and adult readers. It also sends promotional and informational material to the public libraries over the state; and publishes quarterly a bulletin, LIBRARY NOTES AND NEWS, of which the state librarian is the editor.

Trustees

The first state Trustees' Section was organized at the annual meeting of the North Dakota Library Association in Minot, 1959. This was voted a recognized section of the North Dakota Library Association. A committee was appointed to study and work on a Trustees' manual to be presented for discussion at the annual meeting in Grand Forks, 1960, at which time Mrs. Raymond Young, National President of the American Library Trustees Association, will be present as a dinner speaker and as special consultant for the Trustees' section.

Awards

A trustees' award — one of two in the United States given at each annual meeting of the American Library Association, went to a trustee from North Dakota. (Florida received the other). Mrs. Emil G. Bloedow of Edgeley was the recipient of this award. This is the second time within four years that North Dakota has been the winner of this Trustees' award. In 1956 it went to Judge Eugene Burdick, of Williston. That North Dakota should twice receive this coveted honor within this short time is another indication of the forward movement of library development in this state.

Standards

New standards for libraries — public, college and school — have come off the press in 1959 and 1960. These standards do not come upon us unawares. North Dakota has long recognized that libraries are a necessary part of the total educational resources of any community and has aimed at these goals which are now set forth. The beginnings made by this state are greatly to its credit. We could fill pages with points of achievement and some of these are indicated in the following pages. The standards cannot all be met this year or next, as we are sure is true of many another state, but goals are set and these standards help to raise the level of attainments.

We would call attention to one of the items set forth in the Standards, that of "personal characteristics of the librarian." On this, North Dakota's rating would be high. It can be explained as follows: Many who started the little libraries over this state were born here of pioneer parents who gave them the spirit of books and libraries. Those first librarians with this splendid heritage in their inmost being gave a dedication to unlocking for growing generations the knowledge, enrichment and enjoyment to be obtained from books.

At the present time when it is so necessary to make Democracy work as it has never worked before, we find a renewed effort to give all possible use to books and libraries. This spirit will do much to carry this state far forward toward meeting all points in standards and to keep devoted workers in this most worthy effort.

REPORT OF EXPENDITURES OF FEDERAL-STATE FUNDS FOR BIENNIUM

July 1, 1958 to June 30, 1960

RECEIPTS	STATE	FEDERAL	TOTAL
Matching funds appropriated by the state legislature for the biennial period July 1, 1958 to June 30, 1960	$43,304		
Federal appropriation fiscal 1959 .... for period ending June 30, 1959		$72,079	
Federal appropriation fiscal 1960 .... for period ending June 30, 1960		$84,291	
	$43,304	$156,370	$199.674

EXPENDITURES

West Plains — fiscal 1959		$ 18,150
(Williams, Mountrail & McKenzie Co.)	— fiscal 1960	13,500
	McKenzie County share in operation expense plus $5,000 additional book budget for strengthening service.	
McLean-Mercer	— fiscal 1959	$ 20,000
	— fiscal 1960 additional book budget	5,000
LaMoure-Logan	— fiscal 1959	10,000
	— fiscal 1960	13,000
	Logan county share in operation expense plus $5,000 additional book budget	
Ward County — fiscal 1960 (includes cost of Bookmobile)		22,000
Morton County — fiscal 1960		10,000
Public Library grants (none earned)		5,000
State Library Commission	— fiscal 1959	35,581
	— fiscal 1960	37,443
Unexpended		10,000
		$199,674

NORTH DAKOTA'S STATE PLAN FOR FISCAL 1961

Plan for the use of Federal-State Funds for Rural Library Development.

The appropriation under the Library Services Act for the 1961 fiscal year (July 1 1960 to June 30, 1961) is $7,500.00. The maximum amount is available to each state having the required matching funds. The amount available to North Dakota is $84,291.

State Library Commission

1. Strengthen the State Agency
   a. Additional personnel
   b. Increased book collection
2. Promotion and rural library development
   a. Continue present program of rural library promotion
   b. Provide guidance for areas formed under Library Services program
   c. Continue help to areas through book selection and cataloging services
   d. Library training for staff members — consultations, workshops for library personnel and board members, this to include expenses for travel and per diem.

Ward County Project

Support library service to the rural population of Ward County established during the past fiscal period until tax funds already levied are available.

Morton County Project

Support library service to the rural population of Morton County established during the past fiscal period until tax funds already levied are available.

Area Improvement Project

To increase materials and collections of the established libraries of West Plains, McLean-Mercer, South Central areas.

GENERAL CIRCULATION REPORT

Including Departments of Reference, School and Traveling Library

As North Dakotans become more library-minded each year, the State Library Commission receives an increased number of requests. There were 12,706 requests from July 1, 1958 to June 30, 1959, and 13,700 requests from July 1, 1959 to June 30, 1960. These requests may call for just one book, or many references which will help with study in a special line of work, or for several boxes of Traveling Library books. The requests vary from the timely topics of today to a classic of yesterday. This is ample proof that people are interested in knowing what is happening locally and over our country, as well as throughout the world at large.

The State Library Commission is so organized that all departments function as a unit, so that any person in the state may receive whatever type of library service he or she needs. Small libraries may receive books to supplement their own collections with the very latest of literary productions. Along with the small libraries, various clubs, camps, organizations, and school districts throughout the state as well as individuals are served by the various departments.

The State Library Commission carries an extensive coverage of public library service via the mails. Letters from satisfied patrons continue to pour in and many visitors from other states have commended the service of the State Library Commission.

Biennial Appropriation

Salary	$ 11,000
Clerkhire	60,000
Postage, Supplies, etc.	8,500
Miscellaneous	1,200
Travel	2,500
Aids to Libraries	1,000
Books, Binding and Repair	20,000
Social Security	2,000
OASIS	3,730
	$109,930
Matching Fund for Library Services	$ 43,304

COUNTY AND REGIONAL LIBRARIES

COUNTY	Headquarters	Date Established	1960 County Population	RECEIPTS Tax Appropriations 1958-59	Tax Appropriations 1959-60	Total Receipts 1958-59	Total Receipts 1959-60
Divide	Crosby	197	5,566	$12,037.63	$ 8,500.00	$12,586.44	$ 9,264.65
LaMoure-Logan	Edgeley	197	14,072	....	27,060.44	....	27,176.33
McLean-Mercer	Riverdale	197	20,835	....	20,776.96	....	21,182.10
Stutsman	Jamestown	194	25,137	18,166.15	16,017.44	18,166.15	16,017.44
West Plains Regional Williams, Mountrail and McKenzie Counties	Williston	197	39,424	42,847.33	30,611.36	43,091.36	30,682.30

COUNTY AND REGIONAL LIBRARIES
Expenditures

COUNTY	SALARIES 1958-59	SALARIES 1959-60	MAINTENANCE 1958-59	MAINTENANCE 1959-60	BOOKS-PERIODICALS 1958-59	BOOKS-PERIODICALS 1959-60	TOTAL 1958-59	TOTAL 1959-60
Divide	$ 3,062.86	$ 3,110.40	$ 4,322.24	$ 4,666.71	$ 1,404.09	$ 1,085.77	$ 8,789.19	$ 8,862.88
LaMoure-Logan	1,780.35	8,338.17	144.30	3,8[illegible]6.76	2,218.21	6,831.31	4,142.86	19,165.24
Mercer-McLean	....	9,202.08	....	3,111.67	....	3,749.49	....	16,063.24
Stutsman	7,235.08	8,283.58	6,851.71	4,393.60	5,244.72	4,639.60	19,337.51	17,316.78
West Plns Regional Williams, Mountrail, McKenzie Counties	13,341.25	12.048.22	9,005.44	11,779.23	7,605.61	4,228.11	28,0[illegible]	29,952.30

COUNTY AND REGIONAL LIBRARIES

COUNTY	CIRCULATION 1958-59	CIRCULATION 1959-60	Total	Volumes	Borrowers	Hours Open Per Week
Divide	9,780	21,839	31,619	10,396	1,886	37½
LaMoure-Logan	29,741	37,994	67,745	7,630	3,915	40
McLean-Mercer	....	64,005	64,005	9,201	6,324	40
Stutsman	55,317	63,258	118,575	16,079	3,898	40
West Plains Regional Williams, Mountrail, and McKenzie Counties	69,202	81,519	150,721	13,648	5,350	42½

PUBLIC LIBRARIES

A new definition of a Public Library as given in Public Law 597 passed by the 84th Congress, 1956, has been used in the designation of the libraries in North Dakota. "The term 'public library' means a library that serves free all residents of a community, district, or region, and receives its financial support in whole or in part from public funds."

Town	Date Established	1960 Population	RECEIPTS: Tax Appropriations 1958-59	Tax Appropriations 1959-60	Total Receipts 1958-59	Total Receipts 1959-60
Ashley	1913	1,422	$ 600.00	$ 900.00	$ 1,856.62	$ 933.08
Beach	1912	1,461	600.00	600.00	1,598.77	1,834.87
Bismarck	1914	27,361	51, [illegible]	52,842.03	54,188.43	57,076.25
Bowman	1916	1,703	1,145.44	1,007.52	[illegible]	1,164.60
Carrington	1906	2,447	2,800.00	2,800.00	2,800.00	2,800.00
Casselton	1906	1,380	818.27	784.14	884.27	910.36
Cavalier	1915	1,422	[illegible]	537.54	723.22	590.82
Cooperstown	1945	1,488	517.63	508.89	1,086.27	2,097.25
Devils Lake	1896	6,225	9,268.11	13,436.47	9,483.39	13,812.78
Dickinson	1908	[illegible]	13,913.54	4,736.57	14,593.23	15,507.90
Edgeley	1912	943	1,138.25	[illegible]	3,301.76	2,805.63
Ellendale	1912	1,759	1,500.00	1,500.00	1,682.26	1,713.29
Fargo	1900	46,491	76,339.03	82,687.57	80,346.58	86,702.17

Forman	....	466	334.46	168.20	285.73	531.27
Glen Ullin	1957	1,185	400.00	350.00	436.99	362.70
Grafton	1895	5,875	4,672.02	4,882.66	5,111.61	5,380.66
Grand Forks	1899	34,256	41,873.39	48,236.00	44,983.00	51,185.00
Harvey	1952	2,356	2,103.87	1,989.69	2,209.87	2,105.93
Hettinger	1912	1,759	....	1,572.42	405.96	1,758.16
Jamestown] [illegible]re	1901	14,986	12,975.00	14,460.00	17,292.26	18,891.81
	1924	1,067	1,222.80	....	1,322.12	1,556.46
Langdon	1901	2,141	300.00	300.00	576.00	522.84
Lidgerwood	1913	1,079	1,680.00	1,680.00	1,766.30	1,829.71
[illegible]n	1936	1,831	720.00	720.00	811.04	953.44
Lisbon	1915	2,087	[illegible]99	2,809.99	4,056.14	4,109.05
Mandan	1896	10,474	8,042.92	9,160.68	8,553.94	9,666.07
Mayville	1900	2,112	2,059.81	2,579.29	2,179.38	2,728.72
[illegible]ot	1908	30,277	34,585.14	38,290.00	35,771.92	45,814.64
[illegible]all	1937	1,073	....	....	218.00	....
[illegible]tt	1912	1,453	1,336.00	1,605.31	1,436.63	1,704.22
[illegible] Rockford	1917	2,185	300.00	300.00	599.39	861.22
Oakes	1905	1,639	1,298.53	2,463.13	1,548.71	3,046.16
Park River	1900	1,811	1,646.37	1,412.00	1,812.76	[illegible]0.19
Parshall	....	935	769.01	851.51	1,051.97	871.51
Rugby	1912	2,952	1,[illegible]76	3,894.44	2,291.67	4,234.46
Turtle Lake	1926	839	42.26	429.27	101.04	549.79
Underwood	1951	1,061	....	....	1,158.39	1,271.24
Valley City	1900	7,764	9,475.90	9,901.50	10,083.46	10,743.26
Wahpeton	....	5,788	6,000.00	13,655.92	6,318.56	14,043.68
[illegible]rd City	....	1,145	....	2,000.00	....	2,102.75
Williston	1910	11,766	24,276.46	23,611.63	41,192.70	19,626.81
Wishek	1926	1,288	750.00	900.00	797.35	908.00

PUBLIC LIBRARIES

Expenditures

Town	SALARIES 1958-59	SALARIES 1959-60	MAINTENANCE 1958-59	MAINTENANCE 1959-60	BOOKS-PERIODICALS 1958-59	BOOKS-PERIODICALS 1959-60	TOTAL 1958-59	TOTAL 1959-60
Ashley	$ 300.00	$ 300.00	$ 1,291.67	$ 308.65	$ 258.95	$ 228.77	$ 1,850.62	$ 837.42
Beach	394.00	409.06	451.85	697.25	646.12	708.79	1,491.97	1,815.10
Bismarck	33,582.07	36,406.73	9,691.99	6,756.15	7,644.79	11,024.49	49,745.45	54,187.37
Bowman	654.80	00.02	150.81	413.48	223.34	161.51	1,028.95	1,275.01
Carrington	1,209.00	1,200.00	307.89	324.69	887.92	939.89	2,404.81	2,464.58
Casselton	228.00	225.50	129.90	139.90	775.24	633.88	1,133.14	999.28
Cavalier	405.00	421.00	13.33	11.15	100.23	150.21	518.56	582.36
Cooperstown	274.99	27.00	375.96	672.04	379.24	374.04	1,030.19	1,323.08
Devils Lake	3,539.15	5,816.65	1,569.47	8,725.61	1,722.05	1,589.74	6,830.67	16,132.00
Dickinson	7,867.15	8,121.75	3,945.87	3,926.93	3,170.01	3,462.34	14,983.03	15,511.02
Edgeley	420.00	479.43	2,598.60	1,638.60	137.87	356.42	3,156.47	2,174.80
Ellendale	845.02	841.90	125.35	238.39	623.87	820.16	1,594.24	1,900.45
Fargo	37,726.19	48,516.58	14,698.76	13,899.95	8,213.41	11,142.89	60,638.36	73,559.42
Forman	168.20	175.13	6.54	207.08	85.10	125.06	259.84	507.27
Glen Ullin	....	....	250.58	38.19	277.58	341.50	528.16	379.69
Grafton	1,513.88	1,517.75	770.75	1,594.21	820.20	942.60	3,104.83	4,054.56
Grand Forks	26,499.09	30,910.21	6,826.07	10,773.84	10,623.35	9,376.24	43,948.51	51,060.29
Harvey	1,241.50	1,242.60	623.60	637.07	755.13	398.16	2,620.32	2,277.83
Hettinger	....	282.12	....	128.86	....	279.96	....	690.94
Jamestown	11,386.12	12,781.46	3,431.81	3,700.13	3,362.49	2,715.45	18,180.42	19,197.04

LaMoure	390.00	420.00	153.84	[illegible]	600.71	549.26	1,149.55	1,148.70
Langdon	300.00	....	13.40	11.79	95.92	141.84	409.32	153.63
Lidgerwood	938.81	915.50	439.49	488.96	435.52	477.35	1,813.82	1,881.81
Linton	720.00	720.00	21.56	31.09	62.26	182.67	803.82	[illegible]
Lisbon	1,378.88	1,494.34	1,443.92	2,265.33	778.43	607.45	3,601.23	4,367.12
Mandan	4,544.00	5,226.87	1,772.17	2,237.35	2,144.81	2,096.84	[illegible]	9,561.06
Mayville	[illegible]	608.05	985.25	1,518.51	561.61	519.80	2,182.70	2,646.36
Minot	19,564.21	22,347.14	9,446.80	13,599.59	[illegible]	9,065.80	35,588.63	45,012.53
Mohall	310.00	....	53.51	....	151.39	....	514.90	....
Mott	370.25	366.41	306.78	142.10	969.56	893.32	1,646.59	1,401.83
New Rockf'rd	300.00	300.00	15.45	86.47	262.91	433.94	[illegible]	820.41
Oakes	1,050.07	1,024.08	367.09	717.50	890.04	[illegible]	2,307.20	[illegible]
Park River ..	1,199.25	1,066.20	168.65	247.32	397.51	[illegible]	[illegible]	1,623.18
Parshall	159.00	100.00	161.50	301.99	521.52	1,256.30	842.02	1,658.29
Rugby	1,500.00	2,325.00	282.69	193.92	1,137.86	535.84	2,920.55	3,054.76
Turtle Lake ..	66.00	174.00	2.69	11.17	141.48	89.22	210.17	274.39
Underwood ..	....	250.00	....	219.38	....	599.36	....	[illegible]
Valley City ..	5,338.38	6,064.60	1,657.60	2,180.70	1,967.46	2,174.23	8,963.44	10,419.53
Wahpeton	3,739.98	3,143.55	1,312.07	10,329.06	1,011.86	765.40	6,063.91	14,238.01
Watford City	....	709.00	....	90.70	....	1,094.91	....	1,894.61
Williston	9,985.95	10,477.79	32,368.76	[illegible]	2,217.99	2,092.70	44,572.70	24,246.32
Wishek	212.70	[illegible]	254.12	53.88	490.44	405.32	957.26	736.84

PUBLIC LIBRARIES

	CIRCULATION 1958-59	1959-60	Total	Volumes	Borrowers	Hrs. Open Per Week	Rural Borrowers
Ashley	6,792	7,649	14,441	5,651	1,137	6	....
Beach	9,469	10,600	20,069	5,644	830	7½	228
Bismarck	188,654	204,008	392,662	32,935	2,935	62½	263
Bowman	2,687	2,973	5,660	4,713	125	13½	50
Carrington	15,647	16,600	32,247	4,263	989	25	162
Casselton	5,583	4,232	9,815	3,403	416	6	40
Cavalier	4,063	5,199	9,262	2,741	740	4	187
Cooperstown	2,695	3,673	6,368	3,223	81	10	....
Devils Lake	32,081	36,777	68,858	15,309	2,500	36	550
Dickinson	47,139	56,152	103,291	20,205	3,856	33	356
Edgeley	11,038	14,261	25,299	4,942	778	6	363
Ellendale	13,534	15,620	29,154	6,301	286	14½	....
Fargo	215,913	205,295	421,208	57,233	4,108	69	171
Forman	1,722	2,159	3,881	3,349	136	4	....
Glen Ullin	1,201	1,440	2,641	1,438	218	2	....
Grafton	12,793	16,376	29,169	7,447	1,252	19½	15
Grand Forks	155,266	230,902	386,168	41,194	14,514	69	1,244
Harvey	21,452	32,662	54,114	4,416	1,132	25½	350
Hettinger	....	3,250	3,250	3,558	535	6	38
Jamestown	85,438	95,943	181,381	26,300	7,062	54	851

LaMoure	8,594	8,993	17,587	2,577	772	6	386
Langdon	....	....	....	7,095	160	....	....
Lidgerwood	5,678	4,758	10,436	9,917	505	18	206
Linton	6,460	6,310	12,770	3,835	540	11	72
Lisbon	12,009	14,189	26,198	6,238	900	15	400
Mandan	37,599	38,079	75,678	8,700	2,793	38	254
Mayville	5,095	4,388	9,483	5,759	3,279	8	....
Minot	134,021	383,157	517,178	38,866	12,022	54	108
Mohall	....	....	....	3,720	320	6	....
Mott	4,098	6,392	10,490	5,069	834	6	353
New Rockford	3,524	5,694	9,218	4,000	370	8	....
Oakes	19,722	22,493	42,215	7,954	952	32	....
Park River	9,193	8,479	17,672	3,095	767	12	130
Parshall	3,634	5,095	8,729	2,492	543	6	144
Rugby	32,688	39,028	71,716	11,058	999	40	....
Turtle Lake	2,130	2,469	4,599	1,580	114	2	....
Underwood	....	2,341	2,341	2,341	181	6	49
Valley City	42,162	43,836	85,998	19,490	3,501	36	342
Wahpeton	16,050	20,245	36,295	14,859	1,150	27	180
Watford City	....	....	....	3,179	404	14	....
Williston	65,113	66,419	131,532	14,919	2,713	42	5
Wishek	4,223	9,859	14,082	4,898	1,814	5	514

ASSOCIATION LIBRARIES GIVING FREE SERVICE

	Date Established	1960 Population	Municipal Help	Hours Open Per Week	Volumes	Borrowers	Circulation	1958-1960 EXPENDITURES Books	Total
Bathgate	1916	209	None	2	1,094	89	1,210	80.81	278.47
Beulah	1913	1,310	None	4	2,957	92	4,800	137.68	1,147.13
Bottineau	1915	2,558	None	2	2,350	196	3,055	264.60	349.90
Cando	1902	1,548	No report	....	....	....	....	....	....
Drake	1920	831	$112.79	3	2,908	150	....	....	....
Drayton	1946	875	None	2	1,427	166	230	36.00	121.16
Enderlin	1912	1,570	None	3	4,001	1,183	2,401	232.33	304.38
Finley	1954	671	None	2	....	....	141	....	....
Flaxton	1935	436	None	9	2,804	40	110	....	....
Forbes	1944	204	None	5	1,669	126	3,080	150.00	394.50
Gackle	1954	604	$200	3	1,910	54	1,148	242.84	669.07
Goodrich	1926	448	$50	1	648	58	136	4.95	141.72
Hankinson	1907	1,277	None	2	2,127	72	540	28.36	29.70
Hansboro	1928	134	None	3	1,570	29	512	....	....
Hebron	1938	1,331	$100	2	1,853	....	1,386	60.26	254.26
Hillsboro	1954	1,269	None	2	2,040	56	....	....	....
Hope	1910	470	$200	3	1,633	....	921	....	....
Killdeer	....	477	None	2	2,166	....	568	62.60	153.34
Kulm	1937	707	None	2	1,809	130	....	....	12.00
Lakota	1906	1,070	None	6	2,886	....	2,728	450.64	626.34

Larimore	1954	1,713	None	4	1,945	197	1,230	25.00	28.00
Leeds	1902	778	$200	2	3,500	1,190	1,119	117.00	174.01
Leonard	1912	469	None	5	1,291	....	....	20.00	165.00
Maddock	....	741	None	2	1,902	290	1,518	....	....
Napoleon	....	1,070	No report	...	....	....	....	....	....
New England	1931	1,075	None	....	....	....	....	....	....
New Salem	....	942	None	4	3,000	138	....	60.00	....
New Town	1945	1,549	None	6	1,600	....	....	....	....
Northwood	1941	1,068	$200	2	1,428	....	....	66.95	193.61
Pembina	....	640	None	....	....	....	....	....	....
Portal	1935	409	None	2	755	114	1,340	6.10	32.92
Rolette	1947	451	$25	1	971	....	....	29.55	....
Rolla	1924	1,639	None	3	3,128	76	2,469	333.54	408.15
St. Thomas	1954	566	None	2	2,145	40	511	49.00	143.89
Steele	1950	762	None	3	1,900	....	936	205.00	331.82
Velva	1914	1,312	$100	15	4,690	506	....	1,685.32	1,797.04
Walhalla	1955	1,424	None	10	2,965	400	3,100	....	....
Zeeland	1946	484	None	1½	1,300	63	1,500	20.32	187.41

NORTH DAKOTA LIBRARIES BY COUNTY

Counties and Towns with Libraries	County Population	*Net Assessed Valuation
ADAMS	4,449	$ 10,391,603
Hettinger		
BARNES	16,719	36,995,132
Valley City		
BENSON	9,435	22,938,385
Leeds		
BILLINGS	1,513	5,465,401
BOTTINEAU	11,315	28,060,112
Bottineau		
BOWMAN	4,154	10,215,636
Bowman		
BURKE	5,886	16,050,015
Flaxton, Portal		
BURLEIGH	34,016	55,927,421
Bismarck		
CASS	66,947	136,332,692
Fargo, Casselton, Leonard		
CAVALIER	10,064	28,266,933
Langdon		
DICKEY	8,147	22,810,967
Ellendale, Oakes, Forbes		
DIVIDE	5,566	14,415,943
Crosby		
DUNN	6,350	14,516,157
Killdeer		
EDDY	4,936	13,338,636
New Rockford		
EMMONS	8,462	19,604,746
Linton		
FOSTER	5,361	15,224,961
Carrington		
GOLDEN VALLEY	3,100	9,097,202
Beach		
GRAND FORKS	48,677	81,283,829
Grand Forks, Larimore, Northwood		
GRANT	6,248	13,416,109
GRIGGS	5,023	15,160,129
Cooperstown		
HETTINGER	6,317	13,358,457
Mott, New England		
KIDDER	5,386	16,124,050
Steele		
LaMOURE	8,705	22,604,754
Edgeley, Kulm, LaMoure, South Central Regional — Edgeley		
LOGAN	5,367	11,938,820
Gackle, Napoleon		
McHENRY	11,099	26,314,897
Towner, Velva, Drake		
McINTOSH	6,702	14,929,502
Ashley, Wishek, Zeeland		
McKENZIE	7,296	16,181,438
Watford City		

NORTH DAKOTA LIBRARIES BY COUNTY

Counties and Towns with Libraries	County Population	*Net Assessed Valuation
McLEAN	14,030	23,793,548
McLean - Mercer Regional, Riverdale, Turtle Lake, Underwood		
MERCER	6,805	14,702,490
Beulah		
MORTON	20,992	41,043,435
Mandan, Hebron, Glen Ullin		
Morton County — Mandan		
MOUNTRAIL	10,077	20,062,351
New Town, Parshall		
NELSON	7,034	20,316,419
Lakota		
OLIVER	2,610	7,251,102
PEMBINA	12,946	29,723,883
Pembina, Walhalla, Bathgate, Drayton, St. Thomas, Cavalier		
PIERCE	7,394	19,471,952
Rugby		
RAMSEY	13,443	33,883,961
Devils Lake		
RANSOM	8,078	18,215,160
Lisbon, Enderlin		
RENVILLE	4,698	11,874,646
Mohall		
RICHLAND	18,824	41,119,630
Wahpeton, Hankinson, Lidgerwood		
ROLETTE	10,641	12,925,535
Rolla, Rolette		
SARGENT	6,856	17,885,407
Forman		
SHERIDAN	4,305	10,666,107
Goodrich		
SIOUX	3,662	4,227,080
SLOPE	1,893	6,096,692
STARK	18,451	29,470,872
Dickinson		
STEELE	4,719	15,058,528
Finley, Hope		
STUTSMAN	25,137	52,175,158
City-County Library — Jamestown		
TOWNER	5,624	18,135,753
Hansboro, Cando		
TRAILL	10,583	27,260,105
Mayville, Hillsboro		
WALSH	17,997	36,282,672
Park River, Grafton, Fordville		
WARD	47,072	70,830,700
Minot		
Ward County Library, Minot		
WELLS	9,237	25,535,952
Harvey		
WILLIAMS	22,051	48,751,683
Williston		
West Plains Regional — Williston		

*The tax levy is figured on one-half the assessed valuation given.

STATE OF NORTH DAKOTA
LIBRARY DIRECTORY

Ashley	Public Library	Mrs. Gerald Coyle
Bathgate	Public Library	Mrs. Fern Yon
Beach	Public Library	Mrs. Jennie Spiegelberg
Beulah	Public Library	Mrs. C. A. Thelander
Bismarck	Public Library	Mr. Andrew Hansen
Bismarck	State Historical Society Library	Miss Margaret Rose
Bottineau	Public Library	Mrs. E. M. Ertresvaag
Bottineau	State Forestry School Library	Mr. George P. Hynes
Bowman	Clara Lincoln Phelan Library	Mrs. Martha Stone
Cando	Public Library	Mrs. V. D. Lord
Carrington	Public Library	Mrs. Ella Mae Hargrave
Casselton	Public Library	Miss Laura Port
Cavalier	Public Library	Mrs. Carol Walster
Cooperstown	Public Library	Mrs. S. L. Lemna
Crosby	DIVIDE COUNTY LIBRARY	Mrs. Clovis Ralph
Devils Lake	Carnegie Library	Miss Beatrice Larson
Dickinson	Public Library	Miss Gertrude Voldal
Dickinson	State Teachers College Library	Miss Matilda Stoxen
Drake	Public Library	Mrs. W. H. Halbert
Drayton	Public Library	Miss Barbara Vollmers
Edgeley	Public Library	Mrs. Ruth Evert
Edgeley	South-Central Regional Library	Mrs. Ruth Evert
Ellendale	Public Library	Mrs. Maude Blumer
Ellendale	Normal and Industrial College Library	Mr. Thomas A. Hunt
Enderlin	Public Library	Miss Effie Selvig
Fargo	Public Library	Mr. Donald C. Anthony
Fargo	State Agricultural College Library	Mr. H. Dean Stallings
Finley	Public Library	Miss Joyce Dronen
Flaxton	Public Library	Miss Dora Kundiger
Forbes	Public Library	Mrs. E. W. Bull
Forman	Public Library	Mrs. Clifford Dahl
Gackle	Public Library	Mrs. Irene Bonemeyer
Glen Ullin	Public Library	Mrs. Clara Muggli
Goodrich	Public Library	Mrs. Martha Demke
Grafton	Public Library	Mrs. Willis H. Baird
Grand Forks	Public Library	Mrs. Mary Margaret Frank
Grand Forks	State University Library	Mr. Donald J. Pearce
Hankinson	Public Library	Mrs. George Schuett
Hansboro	Public Library	Mrs. Leonard Groetz

Harvey	Public Library	Mrs. Violet Bailey
Hebron	Public Library	Mrs. Verda Mears
Hettinger	Public Library	Mrs. Bertha Sands
Hillsboro	Public Library	Mrs. J. C. Kopanger
Hope	Public Library	Mrs. L. J. Bowen
Jamestown	CITY-COUNTY LIBRARY	Mrs. Anna P. Bensch
Jamestown	Jamestown College Library	Mr. Norman Clark
Killdeer	Public Library	Mrs. W. F. Cockburn
Kulm	Public Library	Mrs. E. E. Orth
Lakota	A. M. Tofthagen Library	Mrs. H. J. Byrne
LaMoure	Public Library	Mrs. Dacotah Harmsen
Langdon	Public Library	Mrs. E. J. Donovan
Larimore	Public Library	Mrs. J. F. Ralston
Leeds	Public Library	Mrs. Curtis Cowan
Leonard	Leonard Watts Free Library	Mrs. Gilbert Elliot
Lidgerwood	City Library	Mrs. Alice Biewer
Linton	Public Library	Miss Alice Stewart
Lisbon	Public Library	Mrs. Ada D. Stewart
Maddock	Public Library	Mrs. Helen Lysne
Mandan	Morton County Library	Mrs. Borghild Culp
Mandan	Public Library	Mrs. Ruth Schoenhard
Mayville	Public Library	Mrs. Leon Sharperud
Mayville	State Teachers College Library	Miss Clenora Quanbeck
Minot	Public Library	Mrs. Lois Ronning
Minot	State Teachers College Library	Miss Nellie B. Swanson
Minot	Ward County Library	Mrs. Lois Ronning
Mohall	Public Library	Mrs. Ralph Rowe
Mott	Inez Hendrickson Library	Mrs. Richard Furness
Napoleon	Public Library	Mrs. Ruth S. Wurl
New England	Public Library	Mrs. A. P. Zereu
New Rockford	Public Library	Mrs. James Donnelly
New Salem	Public Library	Mrs. Christine Streib
New Town	Public Library	Mrs. Vivian O. Wilson
Northwood	Public Library	Mrs. West Mutchler
Oakes	Public Library	Mrs. Helene T. Hample
Park River	Public Library	Mrs. A. C. Bye
Parshall	Public Library	Miss Claudia Risan
Pembina	Public Library	Miss Milly Kneeshaw
Riverdale	McLean-Mercer Regional Library	Mrs. Doratha Welk
Rolette	Public Library	Mrs. G. E. Ellingson
Rolla	Public Library	Mrs. C. R. Jacobsen
Rugby	Public Library	Miss Kathryn Cruden

St. Thomas	Public Library	Mrs. Walter Afelt
Steele	Public Library	Mrs. George Murphy
Towner	Public Library	Mrs. J. M. Hernit
Turtle Lake	Public Library	Mrs. John Frey
Underwood	Public Library	Mrs. Bernard Thomsen
Valley City	Public Library	Mrs. Helen H. Tracy
Valley City	State Teachers College Library	Mr. D. W. Ferguson
Velva	School and Public Library	Mrs. Ella Robinson
Wahpeton	Leach Public Library	Mrs. F. H. Fleishman
Wahpeton	State Science School Library	Mrs. Mildred Larson
Walhalla	Public Library	Mrs. Leonard Tetrault
Watford City	Public Library	Mrs. T. J. Boe
Williston	James Memorial Library	Mrs. Florence M. Kearns
Williston	West Plains Regional Library	Mrs. Anne Lassey
Wishek	Public Library	Miss Carole Rudolf
Zeeland	Lola Zick Memorial Library	Mrs. August Boschee

Twenty-ninth Biennial Report

of the

State Library Commission

to the

State Board of Administration

For the Period

July 1, 1962 to June 30, 1964

Twenty-ninth Biennial Report

of the

State Library Commission

to the

State Board of Administration

For the Period
July 1, 1962 — June 30, 1964

STATE LIBRARY COMMISSION STAFF

June 30, 1964

Hazel Webster Byrnes	Director and State Librarian and Supervisor, Federal-State Library Project
Arlene Stocker	Assistant to the Director
Leone Morrison	Head, Reference Department
Winnifred Coyne	Head, Children's and Young People's Service
Lorraine LaFleur	Head, Traveling Library Department
Josephine Davenport	Chief Clerk
Eva Fogderud	Assistant, Federal-State Library Project
Marie Huber	Assistant, Federal-State Library Project
Freda Hatten	Field Library Consultant
Nora Mohberg	Field Library Consultant

BISMARCK TRIBUNE
10820

"Buy North Dakota Products"

TO THE STATE BOARD OF ADMINISTRATION: James O. Fine, chairman, Paul A. Dalager, M. F. Peterson, and Math Dahl.

The North Dakota State Library Commission has the honor to submit its Twenty-Ninth biennial report, covering the period from July 1, 1962 to June 30, 1964.

(Mrs.) HAZEL WEBSTER BYRNES
Director

REPORT OF THE DIRECTOR

July 1, 1962 — June 30, 1964

Progress During Past Two Years:

The past two years have been "banner years" for the State Library Commission. The benefits provided with the help of the Library Services Act have during the two years just past become obvious.

Not only has this program helped, first to provide the headquarters of the State Library Commission with better equipped staff members and an increased general budget, all of which have resulted in increased service and a new pride in the work; but also second, it has permitted the added expansion and development work over the state with trained staff members in charge and sufficient budget to carry on this work.

The state is now at a point where it can make a creditable showing in any follow-up of library procedures.

Details in Brief:

Let us look a bit more in detail as to what has brought about this progress of the past two years. The wise use of federal funds supplemented by state appropriations provides much of the answer. As stated, this began a few years earlier with results now showing.

In reviewing the whole library situation, the State Board of Administration under which the State Library Commission functions saw the needs both at Commission headquarters and over the field. It looked at what was right and what was wrong. It decided that the State Library Commission was forced to undertake too much work with too little funds and with not sufficient skilled help. Action therefore was, putting it in greatly simplified terms, as follows:

A. To provide training for library workers in all ranges of work.

B. To build up libraries which might be qualified for expansion.

Therefore, working with librarians, trustees, friends of the library, schools of higher education over the state and library committees, programs of training were established.

(1) To provide a $2,000 study grant for qualified library workers to secure a Master's degree in Librarianship at any accredited library school in the United States and return for two years work in North Dakota. Two have returned with their Master's degree and are working in the state, and three are about to complete their work.

(2) To provide for librarians not at the top level a $15.00 subsidy for each quarter hour credit to become better acquainted with library essentials by taking library courses offered in any school of higher education in our own state and return to library positions in a public library. All state schools of higher education are cooperating in providing these courses, and are now in public libraries in the state.

(3) One of the most important programs in operation is what is termed the Points of Growth program. It provides a $50.00 bonus per point to any public library which meets the prerequisites, if it can show, point by point growth since its last report. This growth must be in such points as better trained librarian, more books, budgets supplied by the city or county, cooperation with other libraries, and the like.

Thousands of dollars have gone into these programs, but the worth cannot be measured in money, but in value to society. At the time when nations are competing in this confused world, public libraries have changed and seem to be regarded anew as most important developments, almost as though they had never before existed.

STATISTICAL SUMMARY

At Headquarters

Books—Approximately 75,000, with valuable reference collections.

Staff—Nineteen, with 11 professional and semi-professionl.

Books circulated at headquarters yearly—119,461.

Requests yearly—15,868.

(If the State Library Commission is not able to supply what is desired, it is obtained on inter-library loan from other libraries and the Bibliographical Center at Denver, in which a membership is maintained, or the Library of Congress, Washington, D. C.)

Book circulation to schools—43,859.

Traveling library collections—463. Sent to 377 stations over the state.

Books selected in part and partially processed for county and regional libraries.

A news letter is published quarterly.

General help to all public libraries and to the eight county and regional libraries (2 and 3 counties.)

Library Services Operation Over the State

Library Services funds have made possible county library demonstrations in Dickey, Barnes, Cass and Kidder counties. Kidder County is about to complete organization of a county library.

By contract, two counties are now under one management—Morton and Sioux.

Two counties have built substations to help care for circulation—Adams and McLean.

New county systems are in beginning stages.

Three new bookmobiles have been ordered.

An area improvement plan continues to work in favor of the counties which have been and are at present organized so that all are making good progress.

Each area has one or two bookmobiles, each circulating about 9,000 books per month.

Public Libraries

Population of state—632,466.

Number of people with public library service—368,958.

Number of people without public library service—263,488.

Amount spent for public library service—$631,927.

Amount per capita served—$1.71

Libraries with a tax levy—45 Public Libraries - Eight County or Regional Libraries.

Book Circulation—2,586,800.

Books circulation per capita served—6.7.

REQUESTS FOR THE FUTURE

The big cry of the State Library Commission now is for more room. This we present with a request for a few changes in the library laws and a few in addition which will permit further advancement. Legislative requests therefore, are as follows:

1. New quarters for the State Library Commision.
2. Amended listing of the powers and duties of the State Library Commission (Sections 54-24-03, 04, 05 and 06.)
3. Certification.
4. Higher tax base for public library support. (Section 40-38-02)
5. Specific terms for public library trustees. (Section 40-38-03)
6. Inter-state compacts for public libraries. (Section 40-38-04)
7. Amended insurance program for public libraries.

STATE LIBRARY COMMISSION

Biennial Appropriation

July 1, 1963 — June 30, 1965

Salary	$ 13,000
Clerkhire	65,998
OASIS and Social Security	4,500
Postage, Supplies, etc.	8,500
Miscellaneous	1,200
Travel	2,500
Aids to Libraries	1,000
Books, Binding and Repair	20,000
Library Services (matching)	23,304
	$140,002

COUNTY AND REGIONAL LIBRARIES

COUNTY	Headquaters	Date Established	1960 County Population	RECEIPTS Tax Appropriations 1962-63	1963-64	Total Receipts 1962-63	1963-64
Adams	Hettinger	1961	4,449	$ 2,905.24	$ 7,095.13	$ 3,111.44	$12,543.61
Stations:							
Reeder							
Divide	Crosby	1946	5,566	8,575.00	9,050.00	8,827.62	9,600.95
LaMoure-Logan	Edgeley	1957	14,074	15,792.95	14,999.60	15,910.88	15,202.37
Stations:							
Napoleon							
Gackle							
McLean-Mercer	Riverdale	1957	20,835	14,234.50	26,584.85	14,654.10	26,983.62
Stations:							
Turtle Lake							
Underwood							
Garrison							
Beulah							
Morton-Sioux	Mandan	1960	24,654	16,168.08	16,687.50	18,816.66	22,732.36
Stations:							
New Salem							
Glen Ullin							
Hebron							
Stutsman	Jamestown	1954	25,137	17,445.31	16,838.53	17,515.31	16,923.53

Ward	Minot	1960	47,072	18,400.00	19,100.00	18,670.55	20,690.59
West Plains Regional	Williston	1957	39,424	34,900.49	34,351.16	35,028.36	34,468.47
Williams, Mountrail and McKenzie Counties							
Stations:							
Tioga							
Parshall							
New Town							

COUNTY AND REGIONAL LIBRARIES

Expenditures

COUNTY	SALARIES 1962-63	SALARIES 1963-64	MAINTENANCE 1962-63	MAINTENANCE 1963-64	BOOKS – PERIODICALS 1962-63	BOOKS – PERIODICALS 1963-64	TOTAL 1962-63	TOTAL 1963-64
Adams	$ 3,755.27	$ 3,165.16	$ 491.33	$ 3,337.10	$ 1,168.17	$ 1,359.59	$ 5,414.77	$ 7,861.85
Stations:								
Reeder								
Divide	4,088.74	3,987.40	1,178.05	2,804.64	1,359.94	2,317.86	6,626.73	9,109.90
LaMoure-Logan	10,475.32	10,685.97	4,727.07	4,614.31	2,855.14	2,576.54	18,057.53	17,876.82
Stations:								
Napoleon								
Gackle								
McLean-Mercer	8,109.97	9,081.63	4,030.80	13,077.73	2,769.92	3,413.37	14,910.69	25,572.73
Stations:								
Turtle Lake								
Underwood								
Garrison								
Beulah								
Morton-Sioux	6,840.50	10,457.50	7,354.57	12,302.30	3,100.37	3,629.35	17,295.44	26,389.15
Stations:								
New Salem								
Glen Ullin								
Hebron								

Stutsman	10,180.40	10,201.67	4,937.75	4,371.64	2,365.49	2,260.64	17,483.64	16,833.95
Ward	10,931.41	11,520.26	2,818.57	2,723.83	4,648.36	4,833.72	18,398.34	19,077.81
West Plains Regional	15,424.52	15,016.70	18,238.62	15,999.86	5,161.54	2,727.63	38,824.68	33,744.19
Williams, Mountrail and McKenzie Counties								
Stations:								
Tioga								
Parshall								
New Town								

COUNTY AND REGIONAL LIBRARIES

COUNTY	CIRCULATION 1962-63	CIRCULATION 1963-64	Total	Volumes	Borrowers	Hours Open Per Week
Adams	18,826	23,447	42,273	11,421	1,506	26
Stations:						
Reeder						
Divide	44,496	29,549	74,045	13,713	1,255	27
[illegible]Logan	98,170	103,017	201,187	19,989	6,100	48
Stations:						
[illegible]						
[illegible]						
McLean-Mercer	96,052	88,717	184,760	16,481	3,044	40
Stations:						
Turtle Lake						
[illegible]rwood						
Garrison						
Beulah						
[illegible]	48,742	61,927	110,669	14,817	6,319	40
Stations:						
New Salem						
Glen Ullin						
Hebron						

Stutsman	69,899	68,178	138,077	20,645	5,006	40
Ward	166,213	178,298	344,511	16,550	4,558	35
West Plains Regional	162,579	162,401	324,980	29,051	6,592	42½
Williams, Mountrail and McKenzie Counties						
Stations:						
Tioga						
Parshall						
New Town						

PUBLIC LIBRARIES

A new definition of a Public Library as given in Public Law 597 by the 84th Congress is "a library that serves free all residents of a community, district, or region, and receives its financial support in whole or in part from public funds."

TOWN	Date Established	1960 Population	RECEIPTS: Tax Appropriations 1962-63	RECEIPTS: Tax Appropriations 1963-64	RECEIPTS: Total Receipts 1962-63	RECEIPTS: Total Receipts 1963-64
Ashley	1913	1,419	$ 600.00	$ 600.00	$ 625.75	$ 682.54
Beach	1912	1,460	600.00	600.00	[illegible]	1,812.80
Bismarck	1914	27,670	61,875.19	64,517.31	65,492.09	71,607.53
Bowman	1916	1,730	768.76	1,429.34	1,104.26	1,589.47
Carrington	1906	2,438	3,000.00	3,000.00	3,000.00	4,187.04
Casselton	1906	1,394	1,125.14	1,507.93	1,223.54	1,622.71
Cavalier	1915	1,423	438.74	597.61	515.29	668.13
Cooperstown	1945	1,488	511.63	478.66	2,079.11	1,795.57
Devils Lake	1896	6,299	12,512.86	13,806.58	13,126.75	14,574.11
Dickinson	1908	9,971	15,237.97	18,828.56	16,161.63	19,821.17
Drake	1920	752	....	681.95	55.61	733.00
Edgeley	1912	992	1,197.59	1,102.68	2,253.88	1,997.14
Ellendale	1912	1,800	2,00000	2,501.44	2,208.09	2,693.85
Enderlin	1912	1,596	....	1,800.00	52.39	2,033.50
Fargo	1900	46,662	124,689.07	128,630.09	131,159.76	133,817.57
Forman	....	530	244.40	395.21	293.67	491.04
Gackle	1954	523	500.00	500.00	676.28	796.62
Glen Ullin	1957	1,210	350.00	350.00	364.40	357.90
Grafton	1895	5,885	5,831.82	5,664.71	6,364.80	6,297.71
Grand Forks	1899	34,451	52,714.78	67,032.00	55,769.00	69,500.00
Harvey	1952	2,365	3,000.00	3,414.00	3,114.50	4,020.80
Jamestown	1901	15,163	18,340.00	19,245.00	27,973.87	23,740.79
Lakota	1906	1,066	....	....	....	....

LaMoure	1924	1,069	1,353.13	1,282.06	1,444.22	1,349.24
Langdon	1901	2,151	300.00	300.00	455.65	4,719.70
Lidgerwood	1913	1,081	1,680.00	1,880.00	1,753.90	1,982.66
[illegible]	1936	1,826	780.00	932.70	793.80	1,213.90
Lisbon	1915	2,093	3,565.32	2,209.27	3,818.02	3,635.17
Mandan	1896	10,525	13,961.56	14,665.06	14,488.88	15,123.53
Mayville	1900	2,168	....	2,628.04	103.07	2,797.72
[illegible]	1908	30,604	54,506.51	61,941.88	56,938.86	64,868.56
[illegible]	1937	956	....	1,470.61	....	1,500.00
[illegible]	1912	1,463	2,250.00	2,500.00	2,324.10	2,588.84
[illegible] Rockford	1917	2,177	760.00	528.00	[illegible]	932.04
Oakes	1905	1,650	1,797.56	2,145.28	1,976.91	[illegible]
Park River	1900	1,813	2,247.44	2,259.92	2,377.86	2,356.57
Parshall	....	1,216	1,058.88	1,151.04	[illegible]	1,213.73
Pembina	....	625	324.45	....	364.00	....
Rolla	1924	1,398	400.00	400.00	498.23	482.16
Rugby	1912	2,972	4,293.02	4,514.36	4,634.52	4,888.89
Stanley	1962	1,795	1,323.65	....	2,300.15	....
Valley City	1900	7,809	10,862.20	10,940.74	11,981.41	12,093.71
Wahpeton	....	5,876	7,178.08	8,617.10	7,530.52	9,025.54
Watford City	....	1,865	2,000.00	2,100.00	2,111.84	2,200.95
Williston	1910	11,866	26,829.01	26,821.69	28,610.03	29,654.44
Wishek	1926	1,290	1,250.00	1,250.00	1,250.00	1,267.85

PUBLIC LIBRARY EXPENDITURES

[illegible]	SALARIES 1962-63	SALARIES 1963-64	MAINTENANCE 1962-63	MAINTENANCE 1963-64	BOOKS – PERIODICALS 1962-63	BOOKS – PERIODICALS 1963-64	TOTAL 1962-63	TOTAL 1963-64
Ashley	$ 338.77	$ 353.80	$ 478.79	$ 551.29	$ 215.19	$ 312.63	$ 1,032.75	$ 1,217.72
[illegible]ch	[illegible]	439.41	463.26	619.14	623.72	638.76	1,597.82	1,697.22
[illegible]k	43,611.69	46,225.65	[illegible]	10,311.93	11,872.01	9,706.16	63,287.37	66,243.74
Bowman	679.35	607.82	312.57	480.43	486.48	239.76	1,478.40	1,328.01
Carrington	1,200.00	1,200.00	303.73	1,688.54	868.18	1,274.30	2,371.91	4,162.84
Casselton	748.00	1,317.65	208.82	46.50	298.15	380.28	1,254.97	1,744.43
[illegible]er	360.00	[illegible]	63.00	16.99	237.61	108.58	660.61	543.07
Cooperstown	[illegible]	429.00	1,068.93	1,038.21	286.51	519.22	1,782.44	1,986.43
Devils Lake	6,863.21	7,483.22	2,145.78	2,247.62	4,087.43	3,646.39	13,096.42	13,377.23
Dickinson	9,570.50	9,590.51	2,420.82	5,609.79	3,337.62	4,292.49	15,328.94	19,492.79
Drake	....	....	31.81	35.41	175.46	270.42	207.27	305.83
Edgeley	400.00	400.00	1,630.91	1,761.21	16.54	40.95	2,047.45	2,202.16
Ellendale	840.00	834.64	189.09	1,097.90	715.65	1,197.26	1,744.74	3,129.80
Enderlin	....	677.40	25.70	535.37	185.43	514.09	[illegible]	1,726.86
Fargo	76,698.96	79,881.25	15,136.93	14,526.42	21,098.95	25,088.54	112,934.84	119,496.21
Forman	176.40	173.46	72.08	223.10	55.87	52.76	[illegible]	449.32
Gackle	180.00	180.00	275.99	259.53	35.65	68.92	491.64	508.45
Glen Ullin	....	....	33.05	28.41	344.75	333.84	377.80	432.81
Grafton	2,714.50	3,117.91	1,575.85	899.90	1,936.18	1,884.49	6,226.53	5,902.30
Grand Forks	35,380.34	38,112.76	8,158.75	10,249.78	9,871.72	12,419.91	53,410.81	60,782.45
Harvey	1,349.52	1,636.89	875.84	1,016.68	824.00	1,472.41	3,049.36	4,125.98
[illegible]wn	14,770.15	15,494.51	3,865.10	3,578.95	3,443.92	3,578.95	22,079.17	22,629.38
Lakota	....	....	....	....	....	....	....	....
LaMoure	664.12	681.12	227.24	67.90	538.20	434.98	1,429.56	1,184.00
Langdon	300.00	600.00	11.79	....	173.27	779.12	485.06	1,379.12

Lidgerwood	993.30	960.00	470.93	463.92	344.44	545.04	1,808.67	1,968.96
Linton	780.00	900.00	44.61	77.27	66.82	134.13	891.43	1,111.40
Lisbon	1,518.27	1,600.20	952.33	3,015.43	533.65	877.11	3,004.25	5,481.74
Mandan	7,205.63	8,529.25	983.88	1,479.74	3,973.07	4,055.34	12,162.58	14,064.33
Mayville	600.00	676.50	10.42	1,545.29	357.57	517.63	967.99	2,739.42
Minot	26,177.93	28,452.13	8,838.82	11,465.19	13,291.42	13,061.50	48,309.17	52,978.82
Mohall	....	445.16	....	177.00	....	551.92	....	1,174.08
Mott	838.11	1,107.66	805.48	231.27	1,356.79	1,334.02	3,000.38	2,672.95
New Rockford	438.00	528.00	34.10	69.85	293.31	375.14	765.41	972.99
Oakes	1,123.04	1,195.15	203.95	120.86	823.35	1,040.91	2,150.34	2,356.92
Park River	1,274.64	1,271.64	197.99	18.20	190.80	171.51	1,663.43	1,461.35
Parshall	100.00	200.00	172.90	5.00	664.66	1,234.85	937.56	1,439.85
Pembina	75.00	....	....	....	35.43	....	110.43	....
Rolla	19.45	47.00	43.81	166.56	363.45	250.92	426.00	464.48
Rugby	2,555.40	2,400.00	135.72	264.65	564.30	597.24	3,255.42	3,261.89
Stanley	507.25	....	501.43	....	35.89	....	1,044.57	....
Valley City	7,043.31	7,738.92	2,067.93	1,421.45	2,287.19	3,048.38	11,398.43	12,208.75
Wahpeton	4,242.83	3,312.29	3,961.66	2,148.38	743.54	982.08	8,948.08	6,442.75
Watford City	1,158.00	1,292.50	391.98	71.67	571.83	819.21	2,111.81	2,183.38
Williston	17,386.92	18,024.24	6,797.09	3,615.54	4,497.26	4,875.25	28,681.27	26,515.03
Wishek	599.68	481.87	254.82	61.83	431.69	454.95	1,286.19	998.65

PUBLIC LIBRARIES

TOWN	Circulation 1962-63	Circulation 1963-64	Total	Volumes	Borrowers	Hours Open Per Week	Rural Borrowers
Ashley	3,912	6,266	0,178	8,021	1,336	6	......
Beach	8,349	9,021	17,370	6,988	746	9½	193
Bismarck	217,928	221,106	439,034	39,120	11,334	65½	338
Bowman	3,938	4,229	8,167	5,128	200	11	50
Carrington	23,300	22,136	45,436	5,469	1,185	22	300
Casselton	11,585	10,461	22,046	4,405	529	28	144
Cavalier	4,797	4,757	9,554	3,096	1,082	4½	......
Cooperstown	6,347	6,314	12,661	5,328	1,092	7	......
Devils Lake	47,577	50,634	98,211	16,203	3,088	48	856
Dickinson	57,690	71,926	129,616	22,726	[illegible]	42	831
Drake	....	....	....	2,864	561	3¾	......
Edgeley	....	....	....	4,922	....	20	......
Ellendale	12,855	10,799	23,654	5,960	384	13½	......
Enderlin	2,797	5,330	8,127	4,021	523	10	......
Fargo	301,810	340,450	642,260	70,000	18,500	69	198
Forman	1,170	1,369	2,539	3,601	....	4	......
Gackle	1,467	1,508	2,975	2,253	....	8	......
Glen Ullin	1,918	2,071	3,989	2,071	369	2	......
Grafton	21,281	28,825	50,106	8,739	1,166	42	32
Grand Forks	235,532	216,925	452,457	51,442	10,733	66½	693
Harvey	28,821	28,297	47,218	6,108	1,483	26	533
Jamestown	103,388	108,824	212,212	29,541	7,914	58	1,018
Lakota	....	....	....	....	....	....	......
LaMoure	9,581	8,146	17,727	4,182	....	6	......
Langdon	....	3,686	3,686	6,887	328	11	......

Lidgerwood	8,573	9,136	17,709	11,593	465	18	126
Linton	8,449	8,473	16,922	6,419	589	11	88
Lisbon	12,545	13,913	26,458	7,268	900	15	400
Mandan	42,442	47,966	90,408	14,537	3,933	51	32
Mayville	7,777	8,025	15,802	6,186	3,300	8	......
Mt	343,575	354,065	697,640	49,694	16,105	54	85
Mohall	[illegible]	9,360	[illegible]	3,732	410	6	......
Mott	7,961	8,625	16,586	7,524	746	12½	194
New Rockford	4,428	[illegible]	8,773	5,411	717	8	......
Oakes	25,094	25,258	50,352	8,115	957	38	......
Park River	6,578	6,146	12,724	3,325	1,050	12	......
Parshall	5,184	5,596	10,780	3,701	829	15	......
Pembina	1,310	....	1,310	1,421	....	3	......
Rolla	5,916	5,487	11,403	4,449	356	3	100
Rugby	41,592	39,918	81,510	11,183	840	39	87
Stanley	....	....	....	1,440	....	....	......
Valley City	47,393	47,758	85,151	21,073	3,695	40	249
Wahpeton	22,459	26,066	48,525	15,514	2,990	25	335
[illegible]d City	7,980	5,989	13,969	5,086	....	14	......
[illegible]on	79,161	77,171	156,332	16,865	3,019	40	3
Wishek	5,180	4,890	10,070	5,641	2,146	10	......

ASSOCIATION LIBRARIES GIVING FREE SERVICE

TOWN	Date Established	1960 Population	Municipal Help	Hours Open Per Week	Volumes	Borrowers	Circulation	1962-64 Expenditures Books	1962-64 Expenditures Total
Bathgate	1916	175	$ None	2	1,275	60	2,180	$ 72.47	$118.83
[illegible]	1913	1,318	None	5	3,916	......	8,371	302.53	566.78
Bottineau	1915	2,613	None	4	3,670	116	....	971.44	1 227.28
[illegible]	1902	1,566	None	2	4,185	200	4,833	171.06	[illegible]
Drayton	1946	940	None	2	1,651	369	1,200	101.31	220.01
Elgin	....	944	No Report	....	....	......	....	....	....
Finley	1954	808	None	2	512	......	315	21.00	79.11
[illegible]	1926	392	No Report	....	....	......	....	....	....
Hankinson	1907	1,285	120.00	2	2,332	120	2,799	271.07	282.07
Hebron	1938	1,340	None	2	2,027	......	699	50.00	144.80
[illegible]	1954	1,278	None	2	2,358	......	....	68.00	192.14
Hope	1910	470	100.00	3	1,720	......	1,077	96.74	234.24
Killdeer	....	765	No Report	....	....	......	....	....	....
Kulm	1937	664	None	2	1,853	76	....	....	17.56
Larimore	1954	1,714	300.00	3½	3,070	182	1,816	84.82	334.30
Leeds	1902	797	200.00	3	4,048	185	2,809	194.89	408.99
Leonard	1912	232	None	5	1,315	......	....	....	....
Maddock	....	740	None	2	2,187	330	1,756	....	....
New England	1931	1,095	No Report	....	....	......	....	....	....
New Salem	....	986	None	4	2,349	323	2,500	43.18	51.93
New Town	1945	1,586	279.26	6	....	......	3,597	165.65	165.65
Northwood	1941	1,195	100.00	2	1,956	......	....	....	....
Portal	1935	351	None	1½	832	321	....	....	14.10
Rolette	1947	524	None	1	1,219	......	832	37.64	81.64
St. Thomas	1954	660	None	2	2,596	......	502	72.67	542.49
[illegible]	1950	847	No Report	....	....	......	....	....	....
[illegible]	....	948	No Report	....	....	......	....	....	....
Turtle Lake	1912	792	[illegible]	4	1,603	......	854	100.60	425.77
[illegible]	1914	1,330	No Report	....	....	......	....	....	....
[illegible]	1955	1,432	None	10	4,969	350	3,625	....	....
Zeeland	1946	427	None	3	1,059	114	....	50.87	75.78

NORTH DAKOTA LIBRARIES BY COUNTY

Counties and Towns with Libraries	County Population	*Net Assessed Valuation
ADAMS	4,449	$ 10,668,196
Adams County - Hettinger, Reeder		
BARNES	16,719	38,042,606
Valley City		
BENSON	9,435	22,578,220
Leeds		
BILLINGS	1,513	5,749,007
BOTTINEAU	11,315	27,267,120
Bottineau		
BOWMAN	4,154	10,595,634
Bowman		
BURKE	5,886	16,984,246
Portal		
BURLEIGH	34,016	64,463,065
Bismarck		
CASS	66,947	148,388,454
Fargo, Casselton, Leonard		
CAVALIER	10,064	27,857,337
Langdon		
DICKEY	8,147	22,656,063
Ellendale, Oakes, Forbes		
DIVIDE	5,566	13,655,108
Divide County - Crosby		
DUNN	6,350	14,795,422
Killdeer		
EDDY	4,936	13,676,324
New Rockford		
EMMONS	8,462	18,580,801
Linton		
FOSTER	5,361	15,630,737
Carrington		
GOLDEN VALLEY	3,100	9,025,931
Beach		
GRAND FORKS	48,677	87,590,634
Grand Forks, Larimore, Northwood		
GRANT	6,248	13,629,648
GRIGGS	5,023	15,323,787
Cooperstown		
HETTINGER	6,317	13,539,266
Mott, New England		
KIDDER	5,386	$ 16,104,731
Kidder County - Steele		

NORTH DAKOTA LIBRARIES BY COUNTY — (Continued)

Counties and Towns with Libraries	Population County	*Net Valuation Assessed
LAMOURE	8,705	22,335,328
Edgeley, Kulm, LaMoure South Central Regional - Edgeley		
LOGAN	5,367	12,144,951
Gackle, Napoleon		
McHENRY	11,099	26,125,219
Towner, Velva, Drake		
McINTOSH	6,702	15,597,926
Ashley, Wishek, Zeeland		
McKENZIE	7,296	16,374,265
Watford City		
McLEAN	14,030	24,417,439
McLean-Mercer Regional - Riverdale Turtle Lake, Underwood, Garrison		
MERCER	6,805	15,522,120
Beulah		
MORTON	20,992	47,054,836
Morton County - Mandan Mandan, Hebron, Glen Ullin, New Salem		
MOUNTRAIL	10,077	20,288,949
New Town, Parshall, Stanley		
NELSON	7,034	20,624,874
Lakota		
OLIVER	2,610	6,927,029
PEMBINA	12,946	29,848,750
Pembina, Walhalla, Bathgate Drayton, St. Thomas, Cavalier		
PIERCE	7,394	18,925,714
Rugby		
RAMSEY	13,443	34,576,371
Devils Lake		
RANSOM	8,078	18,464,438
Lisbon, Enderlin		
RENVILLE	4,698	11,580,807
Mohall		
RICHLAND	18,824	41,380,666
Wahpeton, Hankinson, Lidgerwood		
ROLETTE	10,641	12,913,778
Rolla, Rolette		
SARGENT	6,856	17,780,063
Forman		
SHERIDAN	4,305	10,676,949
Goodrich		
SIOUX	3,662	4,274,339

NORTH DAKOTA LIBRARIES BY COUNTY — (Continued)

Counties and Towns with Libraries	County Population	*Net Assessed Valuation
SLOPE	1,893	6,222,467
STARK	18,451	31,970,729
Dickinson		
STEELE	4,719	14,925,261
Finley, Hope		
STUTSMAN	25,137	52,884,968
Stutsman County - Jamestown Jamestown		
TOWNER	5,624	17,877,326
Cando		
TRAILL	10,583	26,867,386
Mayville, Hillsboro		
WALSH	17,997	35,346,567
Park River, Grafton		
WARD	47,072	80,723,414
Ward County - Minot Minot		
WELLS	9,237	25,835,123
Harvey		
WILLIAMS	22,051	49,754,241
West Plains Regional - Williston, Tioga Williston		

* The tax levy is figured on one-half the assesed valuation given.

STATE OF NORTH DAKOTA
LIBRARY DIRECTORY

PUBLIC, COUNTY and REGIONAL LIBRARIES

Ashley	Public Library	Miss Janice Bender
Bathgate	Public Library	Mrs. Fern Yon
Beach	Public Library	Mrs. Dorothy E. Thompson
Beulah	Public Library	Mrs. C. A. Thelander
Bismarck	Veterans Memorial Public Library	Mr. Richard E. Miller
Bottineau	Public Library	Mrs. E. M. Ertresvaag
Bowman	Clara Lincoln Phelan Memorial Library	Mrs. Martha Stone
Cando	Public Library	Mrs. V. D. Lord
Carrington	Public Library	Mrs. Ella Mae Hargrave
Casselton	Public Library	Miss Laura E. Port
Cavalier	Public Library	Mrs. Carl A. Berg
Cooperstown	Public Library	Mrs. Ethel A. Lemna
Crosby	Divide County Library	Mrs. Clovis Ralph
Devils Lake	Carnegie Library	Miss Beatrice Larson
Dickinson	Public Library	Mrs. Inez M. Caton
Drake	Public Library	Mrs. Ervin Adam
Drayton	Public Library	Mrs. Albert Charbonneau
Edgeley	Public Library	Mrs. Ruth Evert
Edgeley	South Central Regional Library	Mrs. Ruth Evert
Elgin	Public Library	Mrs. Lloyd Ranken
Ellendale	Public Library	Mrs. Janet Bunn
Enderlin	Municipal Library	Mrs. Wayne Wilson
Fargo	Public Library	Mr. Richard Waddington
Finley	Public Library	Mrs. Addie K. Thompson
Forbes	Public-School Library	Mrs. Evelyn Bull
Forman	Public Library	Mrs. Clifford Dahl
Gackle	Public Library	Mrs. Irene H. Bonemeyer
Glen Ullin	Public Library	Mrs. Lena Gartner
Goodrich	Public Library	Mrs. Martha Demke
Grafton	Public Library	Mrs. Willis H. Baird
Grand Forks	Public Library	Mrs. Mary Margaret Frank
Hankinson	Public Library	Mrs. Edwin Roeder
Harvey	Public Library	Mrs. Violet Bailey
Hebron	Public Library	Mrs. Nick Bingert
Hettinger	Adams County Library	Mrs. Geraldine Marion
Hillsboro	Public Library	Mrs. Ruby Engel
Hope	Public Library	Mrs. L. J. Bowen
Jamestown	Alfred Dickey Free Library	Mrs. Jeanne L. Cobb
Jamestown	Stutsman County Library	Mrs. John R. Zimmerman
Killdeer	Public Library	Mrs. Ben Ottmar
Kulm	Public Library	Mrs. Ed. Orth
Lakota	A. M. Tofthagen Library	Mrs. H. J. Byrne
LaMoure	Public Library	Mrs. Dacotah Harmsen
Langdon	Public Library	Mrs. E. J Donovan
Larimore	Edna Ralston Library	Mrs. W. W. Smith
Leeds	Public Library	Mrs. Kirk Cowan
Leonard	Leonard Watts Free Library	Mrs. Gilbert Elliott
Lidgerwood	City Library	Mrs. Alice Biewer
Linton	Public Library	Miss Alice Stewart
Lisbon	Public Library	Mrs. Raymond Stewart

Maddock	Public Library	Mrs. Helen Lysne
Mandan	Public Library	Mrs. Ruth Schoenhard
Mandan	Morton County Library	Mrs. Borghild Culp
Mayville	Public Library	Mrs. Marcus I. Moen
Minot	Public Library	Mrs. Lois Ronning
Minot	Ward County Library	Mrs. Lois Ronning
Mohall	Public Library	Mrs. John Smith
Mott	Inez Hendrickson Library	Mrs. Eleanor Schwartz
New England	Public Library	Mrs. A. P. Zereu
New Rockford	Public Library	Mrs. Roy Brown
New Salem	Public Library	Mrs. Lloyd Just
New Town	Public Library	Mrs. Vivian O. Wilson
Northwood	Public Library	Mrs. West Mutchler
Oakes	Public Library	Mrs. Helene T. Hample
Park River	Public Library	Mrs. A. C. Bye
Parshall	Public Library	Mrs. Claudia R. Risan
Pembina	Public Library	Miss Milly Kneeshaw
Portal	Public Library	Mrs. Evelyn Anderson
Riverdale	McLean-Mercer Regional Library	Mrs. Doratha Welk
Rolette	Public Library	Mrs. Galen Olson
Rolla	Public Library	Mrs. Marlin Kyle
Rugby	Public Library	Miss Kathryn Cruden
St. Thomas	Public Library	Mrs. Erwin Buchholtz
Stanley	Public Library	Mrs. John Klokstad
Steele	Kidder County Library	Mrs. Minnie Albright
Towner	Public Library	Mrs. J. M. Hernit
Turtle Lake	Public Library	Mrs. Walter Clark
Underwood	Public Library	Mrs. Bernard Thomsen
Valley City	Carnegie Public Library	Mrs. Helen H. Tracy
Velva	Public Library	Mrs. Ronald Larson
Wahpeton	Leach Public Library	Mrs. F. H. Fleishman
Walhalla	Public Library	Mrs. Leonard Tetrault
Watford City	Public Library	Mrs. T. J. Boe
Williston	James Memorial Library	Mrs. Florence M. Kearns
Williston	West Plains Regional Library	Mrs. Anne Lassey
Wishek	Public Library	Mrs. John W. Ackerman
Zeeland	Laya Zick Memorial Library	Mrs. August E. Boschee

COLLEGE AND UNIVERSITY LIBRARIES

Bismarck	Bismarck Junior College Library	Mrs. Lois Engler
Bismarck	Mary College Library	Sister Martha Claire
Bottineau	State Forestry School Library	Mr. George P. Hynes
Dickinson	State College Library	Miss Mathilda Stoxen
Ellendale	State College Library	Mr. Thomas A. Hunt
Fargo	N. D. State University Library	Mr. H. Dean Stallings
Grand Forks	University of North Dakota Library	Mr. Donald J. Pearce
Jamestown	Jamestown College Library	Mr. R. W. Witt
Mayville	State College Library	Miss Clenora E. Quanbeck
Minot	State College Library	Mr. Eugene R. Hanson
Valley City	State College Library	Mr. A. H. Partlow
Wahpeton	State School of Science Library	Mrs. Mildred Larson

Thirtieth Biennial Report

of the

State Library Commission

to the

State Board of Administration

For the Period

July 1, [illegible] to June 30, [illegible]

Thirtieth Biennial Report

of the

State Library Commission

to the

State Board of Administration

For the Period
July 1, 1964 to June 30, 1966

STATE LIBRARY COMMISSION STAFF
June 30, 1966

Freda W. Hatten	Director
Arlene Stocker	Business Administration
Leone Morrison	Head, Reference Department
Lorraine LaFleur	Head, Traveling Library Department
Josephine Davenport	Circulation and Mailing Department
Pauline Sadler	Technical Services Department
Duane Crawford	Library Extension
Nora Mohberg	Library Consultant
Mary Femling	Serials Librarian

"Buy North Dakota Products"

BISMARCK TRIBUNE
17263

TO THE STATE BOARD OF ADMINISTRATION: Isak Hystad, Chairman; Paul A. Dalager, E. Odin Sjaastad, M. F. Peterson, and Arne Dahl.

The North Dakota State Library Commission has the honor to submit its Thirtieth biennial report, covering the period from July 1, 1964 to June 30, 1966.

(Mrs.) FREDA W. HATTEN
Director

REPORT OF THE DIRECTOR

July 1, 1964 — June 30, 1966

Many changes in service and personnel have taken place in the past two years.

Mrs. Hazel Webster Byrnes, director of the State Library Commission since 1947, resigned in January, 1965, to accept the position of Assistant Dean in the Institute of Lifetime Learning of the Retired Teachers Association in Long Beach, California. Mrs. Freda W. Hatten was named Acting Director at that time and on March 2, 1966, took the oath of office as Director. Professional librarians were added to the staff in the technical services and library extension departments. A serials librarian was also added.

Changes in service resulted from 1965 state legislation and the federal Library Services and Construction Act of 1964 which added Title II giving aid for public library construction and remodeling.

Legislation:

The state legislation changed the powers and duties of the State Library Commission to include, in addition to other previous items, the following:

1. Coordinate the efforts of librarianship, advise and assist the extension of qualified public libraries into centers of county or regional libraries,
2. Collect and maintain a collection of the publications of the departments and agencies of state government and to distribute copies to the depository libraries throughout the state,
3. Conduct or arrange to have conducted research into conditions of library service to produce written plans for the development of better service,
4. Compile union lists of resources of libraries throughout the state,
5. Establish levels of certification for librarians of the state that will meet recommended American Library Association standards.

Other legislation provided for the establishment of ten state depository libraries and an interstate library compact which allowed cooperation with other states to promote better library services.

The Library Services and Construction Act of 1964 provides funds to North Dakota on a 41% state and local to 59% federal matching basis effective the fiscal year 1965-1966. Previously it had been 36.79% to 63.21% ratio. A further change in this Act is that local funds may also be used as matching funds on approved projects.

State Library Project:

The federal funds have been used by the State Library to hire additional personnel, enrich the reference and general book collections and to purchase equipment. Seven staff members are paid by the federal funds. Major acquisitions which could not have been afforded otherwise were the National Union Catalog and other valuable reference works of more than average cost. Many specialized encyclopedias and bibliographies were acquired.

Area Improvement:

A large portion of the federal funds are used for library extension service. Aid was given to Adams County to help remodel a country schoolhouse as a branch library at Reeder; to West Plains Rural Library to establish a branch at Tioga; to McLean-Mercer Regional Library to establish a branch at Hazen; to Sioux County to aid them in contracting bookmobile service from Morton County Library; to Stutsman County to replace their old and inadequately-sized bookmobile. A large number of books were added to the collections of each of the libraries established under the Library Service program. Two state-owned non-roadworthy bookmobiles were replaced with new ones and a new bookmobile was purchased for the regional library demonstration.

Library Demonstrations:

County library demonstrations were completed in Cass, Dickey and McHenry Counties. Cass County in 1965 succeeded in getting more than the 51% of the voters' signatures on petitions necessary to the establishment of a county library, but the petitions were refused by the County Commissioners. A request in 1966 to reconsider the petitions was likewise refused. A circulation of 60,791 books in one year in McHenry County from the bookmobile indicates a great need for more library service than their present resources provide; and it is hoped that the necessary signatures will yet be obtained to establish county library service. Dickey County failed to get the necessary number of signatures.

The Northern Red River Valley Regional Library Demonstration in the five counties of Pembina, Cavalier, Walsh, Grand Forks and Nelson Counties just got well underway by June, 1965, and will continue to June, 1967. The center is located in Grafton from which two bookmobiles operate to the north and south of the center. Mrs. Nora Mohberg, State Library consultant, was placed in charge of this demonstration. County school superintendents are taking an active part in the temporary library board of this demonstration library. The purpose of this demonstration is to give the people an idea of how a library system operates and how a larger regional library can strengthen the small local libraries, and to indicate the extent that libraries would be used if service were more convenient. The demonstration cannot show the absolute in library service, but it is hoped that it will stimulate thought that will lead to a realization of how good library service can be achieved through cooperation of villages, counties, regions and states. As an indication of the success of the demonstration, we note that all the local libraries operated as before; eight of them borrowed 100 or more books per month for circulation in their communities, and in addition 123,594 books were loaned from the bookmobiles in one year in these five counties with a population served of 62,269.

Study Grants:

The $2,000 study grant program to give aid to qualified persons to obtain a master's degree in librarianship at an accredited library school continues. Four of these graduates have been added to the staff at the State Library; one is librarian at Dickinson State College; and one has accepted a position in Williston. Also still in progress is the $15 per quarter hour subsidy to public librarians for study in library science to meet personnel qualifications while in service.

Construction:

Construction funds available under Title II of the Library Services and Construction Act have been given or promised to three library boards. Minot Public Library received $135,000 toward a $685,000 library building which will open in September. Parshall Public Library received $29,500 toward a $50,000 library that is under construction and will be completed by late fall; and $140,000 to supple-
50,000 ment a ~~$500,000~~ bond issue has been approved for the Fargo Public Library which will begin construction the latter part of 1966.

Depository Libraries:

The ten depository libraries are the State Historical Society, North Dakota State University, University of North Dakota, Minot Public Library, Dickinson State College, Minot State College, James Memorial Library at Williston, Alfred Dickey Free Library at Jamestown, Lake Region Community College at Devils Lake, and the State Library Commission. The state publications are collected by the State Library and sent periodically to the other depository libraries. Twice a year the State Library publishes an indexed listing of the state publications.

Union Catalog:

The proposal for the state union catalog was presented at the North Dakota Library Association conference in Jamestown in 1965 and it received enthusiastic support from the librarians. Twenty-three academic and public libraries compose the participating libraries which allow their books to be borrowed through inter-library loan service anywhere in the state. A microfilmer was rented to film the card catalogs of these libraries. To keep the union catalog up to date, these libraries send one author card of each adult non-fiction book they catalog to the State Library, which is the union catalog center. A microfilm reader with an index attachment and a 72-drawer card cabinet constitute the equipment purchased to implement this project. The union catalog, besides being a library resource center, has other uses. The University of North Dakota obtained duplications of their microfilm to send a record of its holdings to its branches at Ellendale and Williston and to the U. S. Air Base at Grand Forks. The catalog can also be the source for a compilation of the reference resources of these participating libraries.

Library Study:

To conduct research into the conditions of library service throughout the state, Dr. David K. Berninghausen, Director of the Library School, University of Minnesota, was contracted to head a research team to make this study during the summer of 1966. It is to be completed by November 1 of this year. He is to supply printed copies of the study and proposed plan of library development feasible in North Dakota. Federal funds will be used for this project.

LIBRARY STATISTICS

State population — 632,466

	1964-65	1965-66
Circulation from the State Library	119,463	116,224
Circulation from library demonstration bookmobiles	42,723	183,385

It is interesting to note the use of good library services that are readily available. The two current library demonstrations in the introductory year, 1965-1966, circulated 183,385 books to a population of 73,368. This points up the need and value of county and regional library service with a strong state agency to supplement the public library collections and to supply special reference material.

Public Libraries meeting minimum library standards		26
County and Regional Libraries		9
Branches and Stations		16
Population served — 356,129		
Circulation	1,786,472	1,743,913
Libraries not meeting minimum standards and open only from one to nine hours a week		36
Circulation	123,780	107,415
People in the state with no local public library service of any kind		234,402

STATE LIBRARY COMMISSION

Biennial Appropriation

July 1, 1965 — June 30, 1967

Salaries	$109,000
Services	32,000
Supplies	33,002
Total	$174,002

This report is divided into two parts. The first part consists of the statistics of the libraries that meet national minimum requirements. Only these statistics will appear in the national reports. Part two is the statistics of other libraries and reading rooms in the state.

Definition of a Public Library

> Taken from "Library Statistics: A Handbook of Concepts, Definitions and Terminology," prepared by the staff of the Statistics Coordinating Project, American Library Association.

"The definition of a public library must be broad enough to allow for a difference in government, source of income, service area, and nature of collection; but there is also a point at which an agency ceases to be a public library.

"To be included in public library statistics, every agency must offer **free services** to everyone within some stipulated geographical area. Libraries which do not, whether from tradition as old subscription or corporation libraries or from extreme financial pressure, should not be considered public and should not be included."

With regard to the book collection, "it is suggested that unless the agency is a member of a library system, it must meet **all of the following criteria** to be included in public library statistics: (1) Give at least 10 hours of public service per week, (2) Have a book collection of at least 2,000 volumes, (3) Purchase at least 200 volumes per year, and (4) Expend at least $1,000 per year.

"These criteria are not intended to relate to, or to set minimum standards of library service. They merely indicate the **lowest level** at which an agency can be considered a statistical unit. Inclusion of figures for libraries which do not meet all of these criteria negates the concepts of "population served" and "area served," and distorts all total figures of public library resources and services.

"Because data on school-public library combinations often cannot be separated accurately, it is recommended that such libraries be included wholly in either school library statistics or public statistics. If the library is physically located in a school but is established under public library laws, and serves only incidentally the library needs of teachers and pupils, it will be counted as a public library."

STATISTICS OF NORTH DAKOTA PUBLIC LIBRARIES, 1964-66

LIBRARY	Population Served (1960 Census)	Government County or Municipal	Separate Location	Size Square Feet	Hours Open a Week	Volumes	CIRCULATION 1964-65	CIRCULATION 1965-66
1. Adams County, Hettinger	4,449	County	Yes	1,248	20	11,698	26,099	23,495
Reeder, branch								
2. Divide County Library—Crosby	5,566	County	Yes	2,252	27	15,036	30,925	32,769
3. Kidder County Library—Steele	5,286	County	Steele Comm. Building	....	36	4,600	11,671	26,761
4. McLean-Mercer Regional—								
Riverdale	20,835	County	Yes	1,480	40	26,064	91,849	98,310
Beulah, branch				....	....	....	6,148	7,663
Garrison, branch				....	....	....	....	....
Hazen, branch				....	....	....	....	....
Turtle Lake Public, station				....	4	1,708	1,100	....
Underwood Public, station				....	6	5,244	....	6,863
5. Morton County Library—								
Mandan	10,467	County	Mem. Bldg.	602	40	23,130	....	64,735
Glen Ullin Public, station				....	2	2,312	2,186	....
New Salem Public, station				....	4	2,520	3,034	....
Hebron Public, station				....	....	....	....	....
Sioux County, contract	3,662			....	....	....	....	....
6. South Central Area Library—								
Edgeley	14,074	County	Yes	1,460	20	22,385	103,136	97,133
Edgeley Public, station				....	20	5,110	....	....
Gackle Public, station				....	3½	2,375	986	942
Kulm Public, station				....	2	1,877	....	....
7. Stutsman County—Jamestown	9,974	County	Alfred Dickey Free Library	624	24	22,539	69,556	68,448
8. Ward County—Minot	16,468	County	Minot Public Library	....	45	20,538	185,673	193,921
9. West Plains Rural—Williston	27,558	County	Price Office Building	720	20	32,720	157,926	166,266
New Town City, station				....	13	2,754	4,522	5,390
Parshall Public, station				....	8	3,888	5,128	3,942
Tioga, branch				....	....	....	....	....
TOTAL	**118,339**			....	....	**206,498**	**699,939**	**796,638**

RECEIPTS

LIBRARY	TAXES 1964-65	TAXES 1965-66	OTHER 1964-65	OTHER 1965-66	TOTAL 1964-65	TOTAL 1965-66
1. Adams County Library—Hettinger	$ 5,465.30	$ 7,896.23	$ 3,113.71	$ 731.13	$ 8,579.01	$ 8,627.36
Reeder, branch	....	....	....	....	....	....
2. Divide County Library—Crosby	7,625.00	7,500.00	1,008.20	1,030.10	8,633.20	8,530.10
3. Kidder County Library—Steele	....	10,000.00	8,000.00	31.69	8,000.00	10,031.69
4. McLean-Mercer Regional—						
Riverdale	19,379.29	8,330.33	635.80	1,417.74	19,515.09	9,748.07
Beulah, branch	....	....	212.38	....	212.38	....
Garrison, branch	....	....	....	....	....	....
Hazen, branch	....	....	....	....	....	....
Turtle Lake Public, station	262.76	269.61	....	1.83	262.76	271.44
Underwood Public, station	....	850.00	....	73.92	....	923.92
5. Morton County Library—Mandan	....	17,723.23	....	4,191.85	....	21,915.08
Glen Ullin Public, station	350.00	300.00	8.26	8.76	358.26	308.76
New Salem Public, station	....	....	123.39	62.46	123.39	62.46
Hebron Public, station	....	....	....	....	....	....
Sioux County, contract	....	....	....	....	....	....
6. South Central Area Library						
Edgeley	15,272.62	15,721.11	855.73	434.03	16,128.35	16,155.44
Edgeley Public, station	1,126.57	1,241.39	1,327.25	5,220.36	2,453.82	6,461.75
Gackle Public, station	....	500.00	88.89	85.95	88.89	585.95
Kulm Public, station	....	....	....	....	....	....
7. Stutsman County—Jamestown	17,752.57	22,917.13	....	7,637.13	17,752.57	30,554.26

RECEIPTS

LIBRARY	TAXES 1964-65	TAXES 1965-66	OTHER 1964-65	OTHER 1965-66	TOTAL 1964-65	TOTAL 1965-66
8. Ward County—Minot	20,300.00	22,300.00	1,942.17	4,335.83	22,242.17	26,635.83
9. West Plains Rural—Williston	32,952.66	32,694.44	3,032.73	364.05	35,985.39	33,058.49
New Town City, station	503.00	442.83	171.92	375.00	674.92	817.83
Parshall Public, station	1,350.00	1,575.68	251.00	27.29	1,601.00	1,602.97
Tioga, branch	....	....	....	....	....	....
TOTAL	$122,339.77	$150,261.98	$20,771.43	$26,029.12	$142,611.20	$176,291.40

EXPENDITURES

LIBRARY	CAPITAL EXPENDITURES 1964-65	CAPITAL EXPENDITURES 1965-66	SALARIES 1964-65	SALARIES 1965-66	LIBRARY MATERIALS 1964-65	LIBRARY MATERIALS 1965-66	TOTAL 1964-65	TOTAL 1965-66
1. Adams County, Hettinger	$6,017.84	....	$ 3,720.32	$ 4,224.55	$ 1,252.70	$ 1,102.54	$12,183.96	$ 6,362.36
Reeder, branch	....	....	....	....	....	....	....	....
2. Divide County Library —Crosby	279.25	68.62	4,271.98	5,336.09	2,112.02	1,970.05	9,048.00	10,979.93
3. Kidder County Library —Steele	....	56.98	2,815.21	4,549.90	2,012.08	1,691.87	6,571.19	7,490.21
4. McLean-Mercer Regional —Riverdale	694.89	....	13,156.23	13,506.23	3,277.65	2,135.22	19,762.26	18,463.36
Beulah, branch	154.00	....	79.50	....	226.47	....	588.78	....
Garrison, branch	....	....	....	....	....	....	....	....
Hazen, branch	....	....	....	....	....	....	....	....
Turtle Lake Public, station	....	....	162.00	204.90	98.78	45.54	275.07	261.07
Underwood Public, station	....	....	....	....	....	....	....	....
5. Morton County Library —Mandan	14,972.05	3,611.51	10,822.02	11,876.04	6,400.63	7,231.63	34,222.25	25,441.49
Glen Ullin Public, station	....	....	....	....	328.93	288.66	364.89	313.29
New Salem Public, station	....	....	....	....	100.03	46.01	118.00	72.06
Hebron Public, station	....	....	....	....	....	....	....	....
Sioux Co., contract	....	....	....	....	....	....	....	....

EXPENDITURES

LIBRARY	CAPITAL EXPENDITURES 1964-65	CAPITAL EXPENDITURES 1965-66	SALARIES 1964-65	SALARIES 1965-66	LIBRARY MATERIALS 1964-65	LIBRARY MATERIALS 1965-66	TOTAL 1964-65	TOTAL 1965-66
6. South Central Area								
Library Edgeley	85.03	187.20	9,340.86	8,798.54	1,309.22	1,859.43	14,683.11	14,251.03
Edgeley Public, station	33.25	4,114.87	400.00	400.00	52.19	10.40	2,909.82	5,280.51
Gackle Public, station	....	....	191.00	180.00	65.72	86.09	499.77	494.81
Kulm Public, station	....	....	....	....	....	....	....	....
7. Stutsman County—Jamestown	....	6,697.00	10,962.44	10,547.19	2,598.13	2,118.65	17,730.59	23,170.99
8. Ward County—Minot	....	....	12,009.64	13,500.90	4,521.82	4,943.12	20,290.53	22,287.43
9. West Plains Rural—Williston	....	....	16,661.23	20,852.42	4,750.45	2,426.83	38,037.05	34,904.37
New Town City, station	152.32	258.40	....	5.00	747.22	444.21	1,030.13	744.42
Parshall Public, station	200.00	....	200.00	316.87	796.13	1,129.23	1,247.13	1,675.46
Tioga, branch	....	....	....	....	....	....	....	....
TOTALS	$22,588.63	$14,994.58	$84,792.43	$94,298.63	$30,650.17	$27,529.48	$179,562.53	$172,192.79

LIBRARY	Population Served (1960 Census)	Government County or Municipal	Separate Facilities	Size Square Feet	Hours Open a Week	Volumes	CIRCULATION 1964-65	CIRCULATION 1965-66
1. Veterans Memorial Public Library Bismarck	27,670	Municipal	Yes	17,300	66	46,806	201,055	206,262
2. Clara Lincoln Phelan Memorial Library, Bowman	1,730	Municipal	Yes	1,092	11	5,324	3,404	4,450
3. Carrington City Library	2,438	Municipal	Armory	1,110	24	6,126	24,997	30,150
4. Casselton Public Library	1,394	Municipal	City Hall	....	28	5,147	9,758	9,052
5. Cooperstown Public Library	1,424	Municipal	Security Trust Co.	....	10	6,082	7,884	6,973
6. Carnegie Library, Devils Lake	6,299	Municipal	Yes	3,458	56	17,659	47,237	46,369
7. Dickinson Public Library	9,971	Municipal	Yes	2,750	39	34,030	70,514	70,290
8. Ellendale Public Library	1,800	Municipal	City Hall	720	18	6,253	11,167	18,499
9. Enderlin Municipal Library	1,596	Municipal	City Hall	504	11	4,252	6,628	5,613
10. Fargo Public Library	46,662	Municipal	Yes	....	....	78,945	363,499	366,467
11. Grafton Public Library	5,885	Municipal	Yes	1,152	42	9,775	32,671	34,792
12. Grand Forks Public Library	34,451	Municipal	Yes	7,750	66½	56,875	216,405	177,870
13. Harvey Public Library	2,365	Municipal	Yes	1,300	29	6,898	24,690	24,881
14. Alfred Dickey Free Library, Jamestown	15,163	Municipal	Yes	8,929	58	30,523	104,660	105,809
15. Lidgerwood City Library	1,081	Municipal	Yes	1,000	18	11,970	9,078	9,970
16. Lisbon Public Library	2,093	Municipal	Yes	3,456	15	7,668	14,247	14,179
17. Mandan Public Library	10,525	Municipal	Yes	4,660	48	18,610	58,916	63,524
18. Minot Public Library	36,604	Municipal	Yes	....	66	56,059	376,906	371,989
19. Inez Hendrickson Library, Mott	1,463	Municipal	City Hall	850	12½	7,108	7,572	7,364
20. Rolla Public Library	1,398	Municipal	City Hall	450	10	7,795	7,436	....
21. Rugby Public Library	2,972	Municipal	City Hall	810	39½	11,813	41,247	31,295
22. Carnegie Public Library Valley City	7,809	Municipal	Yes	3,248	34	21,129	47,132	42,342
23. Leach Public Library, Wahpeton	5,876	Municipal	Yes	....	28	15,718	21,020	20,589
24. Watford City Public Library	1,865	Municipal	Civic Center	336	17	5,448	5,419	5,450
25. James Memorial Library, Williston	11,866	Municipal	Yes	....	44	17,403	68,496	66,235
26. Wishek Public Library	1,290	Municipal	City Hall	....	10	6,261	4,434	3,499
TOTAL	237,690	Municipal	Yes	....	....	491,677	1,786,472	1,743,913

RECEIPTS

LIBRARY	TAXES 1964-65	TAXES 1965-66	OTHER 1964-65	OTHER 1965-66	TOTAL 1964-65	TOTAL 1965-66
1. Bismarck	$ 69,450.00	$ 91,986.00	$ 6,374.79	$ 9,060.54	$ 75,824.79	$101,046.91
2. Bowman	973.00	1,173.71	160.75	292.62	1,265.62	1,466.33
3. Carrington	3,000.00	3,000.00	475.00	....	3,475.00	3,000.00
4. Casselton	1,846.68	2,002.85	493.62	89.00	2,340.30	2,091.85
5. Cooperstown	1,339.69	1,509.03	2,313.60	934.29	3,653.27	2,443.32
6. Devils Lake	12,451.47	13,975.93	648.50	757.62	13,099.97	14,733.55
7. Dickinson	19,776.06	19,732.27	1,724.03	2,679.25	21,500.09	22,411.52
8. Ellendale	2,000.00	2,500.00	717.64	206.23	2,717.64	2,706.22
9. Enderlin	1,600.00	1,800.00	701.80	246.14	2,301.80	2,046.14
10. Fargo	131,789.40	137,001.41	57,814.61	56,148.07	189,604.01	193,149.48
11. Grafton	5,645.22	5,835.86	391.00	891.00	6,639.22	6,726.86
12. Grand Forks	76,453.79	61,235.86	2,546.21	13,728.00	91,619.00	74,963.86
13. Harvey	2,900.00	4,017.80	622.00	607.36	3,522.00	4,625.16
14. Jamestown	20,200.00	22,000.00	19,560.20	5,669.22	39,706.20	27,669.22
15. Lidgerwood	1,920.00	1,920.00	104.57	60.74	2,024.57	1,980.74
16. Lisbon	2,011.36	2,918.77	843.82	311.90	2,855.18	3,230.67
17. Mandan	15,450.41	16,273.11	2,261.68	755.97	17,712.09	17,029.08
18. Minot	65,861.93	516,427.39	11,808.46	139,769.20	77,670.39	656,196.59
19. Mott	2,500.00	2,500.00	606.18	290.37	3,106.18	2,790.37
20. Rolla	....	1,153.91	986.15	74.73	896.15	1,228.64
21. Rugby	4,632.83	4,772.68	711.64	424.88	5,344.47	5,197.56
22. Valley City	10,556.60	11,663.20	1,823.18	1,134.35	12,379.78	12,797.55
23. Wahpeton	1,800.00	9,500.00	310.34	404.63	2,263.00	9,904.63
24. Watford City	1,990.25	2,061.57	342.05	397.79	2,332.30	2,459.36
25. Williston	26,453.51	32,958.90	12,304.43	1,491.72	27,683.94	34,450.62
26. Wishek	1,250.00	1,275.00	20.00	....	1,270.00	1,275.00
TOTAL	$483,852.20	$971,195.25	$126,612.25	$236,425.62	$612,706.96	$1,207,621.23

EXPENDITURES

LIBRARY	Capital Expenditures 1964-65	Capital Expenditures 1965-66	Salaries 1964-65	Salaries 1965-66	Library Materials 1964-65	Library Materials 1965-66	TOTAL 1964-65	TOTAL 1965-66
1. Bismarck	$ 500.00	$..........	$ 45,780.00	$ 51,021.90	$ 10,676.02	$ 13,678.91	$ 75,555.00	$ 73,713.32
2. Bowman	....	....	630.32	623.58	401.33	358.89	1,278.17	1,226.00
3. Carrington	454.33	118.95	1,200.00	1,594.85	1,007.05	1,436.26	2,857.13	3,457.90
4. Casselton	....	....	469.41	1,235.19	268.15	292.52	2,073.75	1,613.21
5. Cooperstown	....	120.00	620.00	701.00	900.00	500.32	2,916.81	2,413.82
6. Devils Lake	137.00	....	8,162.88	8,475.53	3,861.30	3,766.94	14,123.27	14,336.06
7. Dickinson	....	....	12,898.84	14,127.11	3,559.13	3,308.15	21,500.87	19,947.47
8. Ellendale	116.17	....	917.75	1,072.97	1,611.08	1,281.33	2,795.15	2,442.79
9. Enderlin	240.77	143.13	863.84	958.00	416.61	751.73	1,655.13	2,180.95
10. Fargo	1,399.44	315.35	83,808.87	87,632.43	32,044.57	24,085.82	133,691.44	128,660.75
11. Grafton	....	....	1,505.64	4,853.72	2,182.17	2,173.14	8,738.04	8,482.16
12. Grand Forks	195.00	....	36,820.92	40,567.06	12,293.13	12,484.32	59,951.81	64,259.86
13. Harvey	155.00	....	1,957.00	2,538.97	1,166.73	949.98	3,656.30	4,010.43
14. [illegible]n	1,105.18	84.65	1,435.62	14,626.81	3,434.77	3,840.13	22,427.02	21,464.96
15. Lidgerwood	....	....	960.00	1,163.98	631.90	604.88	2,040.26	1,945.28
16. Lisbon	....	198.76	1,528.66	1,464.81	602.67	889.82	3,043.12	3,915.38
17. Mandan	15.30	....	8,243.59	8,740.40	4,848.41	5,358.73	15,332.20	17,422.41
18. Mot	2,181.75	589,114.62	31,764.51	36,140.00	20,097.59	19,060.88	78,143.65	652,983.30
19. Mott	187.30	....	1,069.85	1,074.01	1,595.38	1,381.64	2,970.48	2,698.14
20. Rolla	36.96	....	886.00	863.74	444.37	440.58	1,523.54	1,372.86
21. Rugby	....	....	2,536.20	2,974.50	979.36	951.96	3,777.16	1,050.96
22. Valley City	724.07	349.10	7,551.32	7,903.41	2,407.97	2,713.67	12,358.72	12,680.09
23. Wahpeton	....	....	2,894.55	3,516.99	1,022.81	1,019.39	7,188.56	6,707.15
24. Watford City	....	....	1,214.31	1,271.70	756.80	822.57	2,016.15	2,153.30
25. Williston	3,316.91	....	17,997.09	19,298.81	3,977.38	3,665.62	30,813.22	28,560.28
26. Wishek	197.61	....	522.10	569.81	438.58	475.65	1,269.98	1,073.16
[illegible]LS	$10,962.79	$590,444.56	$290,939.27	$315,011.28	$111,625.26	$106,363.83	$493,696.93	$1,083,771.99

These libraries have not met all of the minimum standards indicated for public libraries. See Definition at beginning of this Section.

LIBRARY	Population (Served) (1960 Census)	Government Municipal or Association	Separate Facilities	Size Square Feet	Hours Open A Week	Volumes	CIRCULATION 1964-65	CIRCULATION 1965-66
1 Ashley	1,419	Association	Yes	512	6	8,197	6,061	4,856
2. Beach	1,460	Association	American Legion Hall	4,866	9½	7,388	9,570	8,214
3. Bottineau	2,613	Association	....	....	....	....	....	....
4. Cando	1,566	Association	Yes	....	2	4,825	5,204	....
5. Cavalier	1,423	Municipal	Yes	....	5	3,253	4,510	....
6. Drake	752	Association	Public School	....	4	3,280	....	....
7. Drayton	940	....	City Hall	....	2	1,400	2,080	3,120
8. Finley	808	Association	....	....	....	....	....	....
9. Forman	530	Association	Yes	....	4	3,872	2,000	1,967
10. Goodrich	392	....		....	....	....	....	....
11. Hankinson	1,285	Municipal	City Hall	....	2	2,407	2,556	1,598
12. Hillsboro	1,278	Association	City Hall	....	2	2,435	....	....
13. Hope	390	Municipal	City Hall	....	3½	2,044	795	761
14. Killdeer	765	Association	Yes	508	1½	2,609	611	650
15. Lakota	1,066	Municipal	A. M. Tofthagen Museum	....	....	....	....	....
16. LaMoure	1,068	Municipal	Community Building	....	6	4,627	7,791	9,731
17. Langdon	2,151	Association	Memorial Court House	....	9	6,787	10,400	13,000
18. Larimore	1,714	Association	City Hall	322	6	3,122	3,192	3,404
19. Leeds	797	Association	City Hall	....	3	4,192	2,109	1,284
20. Leonard	232	....	....	....	....	....	....	....
21. Linton	1,081	Municipal	City Hall	1,225	12	6,908	7,507	4,324
22. Maddock	740	Association	City Hall	....	....	....	....	....
23. Mayville	2,168	Municipal	Yes	1,854	8	6,527	7,623	5,617
24. Mohall	956	Municipal	City Hall	....	6	4,207	7,400	8,633
25. New England	1,095	Association	Memorial Hall	540	2	1,911	....	1,783

26. New Rockford	2,177	Association	Yes	......	10	6,055	4,505	4,545
27. Northwood	1,195	Association	City Hall	......	2	2,130	......	......
28. Oakes	1,650	Municipal	Public School	1,560	47	8,568	28,656	27,215
29. Park River	1,813	Municipal	City Auditorium	380	12	3,454	6,731	6,316
30. Pembina	625	Municipal	City Hall	......	....	......	......	......
31. Rolette	524	Association	Memorial Hall	......	1	1,329	379	397
32. St. Thomas	660	Association	Yes	......	....	......	......	......
33. Stanley	1,795	Municipal	Mem. Bldg.	......	12	2,122	......	......
34. Towner	948	Association	Fire Hall	......	....	......	......	......
35. Walhalla	1,432	Municipal	City Hall	......	10	4,973	4,100	......
36. Zeeland	427	Association	Bank Building	166	4	1,231	......	......
TOTAL	41,935			......	....	109,853	123,780	107,415

RECEIPTS

LIBRARY	TAXES 1964-65	TAXES 1965-66	OTHER 1964-65	OTHER 1965-66	TOTAL 1964-65	TOTAL 1965-66
1. Ashley	$ 800.00	$ 800.00	$ 77.03	$ 53.70	$ 877.03	$ 853.70
2. Beach	600.00	600.00	1,348.91	91.18	1,948.82	691.18
3. Bottineau (no report)	....	....	....	....	....	....
4. Cando	....	....	339.15	....	339.15	....
5. Cavalier	166.08	....	400.95	....	567.03	....
6. Drake	356.02	117.92	37.33	34.75	393.35	152.67
7. Drayton	....	....	65.00	58.97	65.00	58.97
8. Finley (no report)	....	....	....	....	....	....
9. Forman	....	322.14	....	69.55	....	391.69
10. Goodrich (no report)	....	....	....	....	....	....
11. Hankinson	490.00	50.00	....	1.00	490.00	51.00
12. Hillsboro	....	....	....	....	....	....
13. Hope	100.00	100.00	211.00	9.21	311.00	109.21
14. Killdeer	....	....	41.95	14.65	41.95	14.65
15. Lakota (no report)	....	....	....	....	....	....
16. LaMoure	1,396.48	1,361.82	60.02	52.29	1,456.50	1,414.11
17. Langdon	300.00	1,920.00	540.00	516.00	840.00	2,436.00
18. Larimore	300.00	300.00	61.00	524.77	361.00	824.77
19. Leeds	200.00	200.00	27.80	23.55	227.80	223.55
20. Leonard (no report)	....	....	....	....	....	....
21. Linton	1,050.00	....	552.90	619.00	1,602.90	619.00
22. Maddock (no report)	....	....	....	....	....	....
23. Mayville	800.00	1,959.43	576.40	654.96	1,376.40	2,614.39
24. Mohall	....	1,995.81	....	35.00	....	2,030.81
25. New England	500.00	500.00	34.21	44.21	534.21	544.21

26. New Rockford	350.00	1,070.00	501.71	461.82	851.71	1,631.82
27. Northwood (no report)	....	....	....	....	....	....
28. Oakes	2,188.57	2,832.56	616.99	644.86	2,805.56	3,477.42
29. Park River	2,083.04	1,811.65	98.25	103.20	2,181.29	1,914.85
30. Pembina (no report)	....	....	....	....	....	....
31. Rolette	....	....	6.00	125.00	6.00	125.00
32. St. Thomas (no report)	....	....	....	....	....	....
33. Stanley	1,335.84	....	10.00	20.00	1,345.84	....
34. Towner (no report)	....	....	....	....	....	....
35. Walhalla	....	....	....	....	....	....
36. Zeeland	....	100.00	....	103.87	....	203.87
TOTALS	$13,016.03	$16,041.33	$5,606.60	$4,261.54	$18,622.54	$20,382.87

EXPENDITURES

LIBRARY	CAPITAL EXPENDITURES 1964-65	CAPITAL EXPENDITURES 1965-66	SALARIES 1964-65	SALARIES 1965-66	LIBRARY MATERIALS 1964-65	LIBRARY MATERIALS 1965-66	TOTAL 1964-65	TOTAL 1965-66
1. Ashley	....	.... $	389.83 $	340.47 $	207.32 $	155.01 $	819.14 $	870.07
2. Beach	....	....	622.74	....	805.12	....	2,160.15	46.09
3. Bottineau (no report)	....	....	....	....	....	....	....	....
4. Cando	....	....	91.00	....	36.25	....	343.61	....
5. Cavalier	....	....	430.00	....	136.39	....	582.99	....
6. Drake	....	....	....	....	323.28	268.63	388.77	316.57
7. Drayton	....	....	55.00	55.00	12.88	14.34	76.29	69.34
8. Finley (no report)	....	....	....	....	....	....	....	....
9. Forman	....	....	176.40	179.20	98.89	68.08	317.06	406.70
10. Goodrich (no report)	....	....	....	....	....	....	....	....
11. Hankinson	....	....	....	....	60.00	51.00	291.24	52.50
12. Hillsboro	....	....	120.00	120.00	53.63	82.74	173,63	209.00
13. Hope	....	....	76.50	74.50	1.38	152.77	79.77	227.27
14. Killdeer	....	....	....	30.72	6.12	....	71.84	30.72
15. Lakota (no report)	....	....	....	....	....	....	....	....
16. LaMoure	....	....	663.32	332.46	845.92	515.66	1,591.72	1,258.20
17. Langdon	....	....	900.00	900.00	279.80	185.75	1,179.80	1,805.75
18. Larimore	....	....	249.00	323.48	154.50	91.06	448.50	471.69
19. Leeds	....	....	128.25	128.25	47.54	28.53	183.59	158.78
20. Leonard (no report)	....	....	....	....	....	....	....	....
21. Linton	67.55	....	1,075.00	....	395.64	185.75	1,670.22	253.26
22. Maddock (no report)	....	....	....	....	....	....	....	....
23. Mayville	91.33	....	647.50	797.91	793.38	737.84	2,275.16	2,739.89
24. Mohall	....	....	468.02	730.57	597.90	640.89	1,100.19	1,403.06
25. New England	....	....	67.00	104.00	281.39	134.02	468.34	378.10
26. New Rockford	....	210.74	534.00	720.00	555.02	720.00	1,178.58	1,686.44

27. Northwood (no report)	....	....	....	....	....	....	....	....
28. Oakes	....	....	1,037.07	1,105.34	953.98	1,671.24	2,260.93	3,046.63
29. Park River	....	....	1,280.63	1,279.67	404.66	152.93	1,712.90	1,502.72
30. Pembina (no report)	....	....	....	....	....	....	....	....
31. Rolette	....	....	....	....	30.28	100.00	43.89	100.00
32. St. Thomas (no report)	....	....	....	....	....	....	....	....
33. Stanley	....	....	611.67	....	75.76	....	1,067.12	....
34. Towner (no report)	....	....	....	....	....	....	....	....
35. Walhalla	....	....	....	....	....	....	....	....
36. Zeeland	....	....	....	....	....	1.00	....	49.20
TOTALS	$158.88	$210.74	$9,622.93	$7,221.57	$7,157.03	$5,957.24	$20,485.43	$17,081.98

NORTH DAKOTA LIBRARIES BY COUNTY

Counties and Towns with Libraries	County Popoulation (1960 Census)
ADAMS	4,449
Adams County — Hettinger Reeder	
BARNES	16,719
Valley City	
BENSON	9,425
Leeds, Maddock	
BILLINGS	1,513
BOTTINEAU	11,315
Bottineau	
BOWMAN	4,154
Bowman	
BURKE	5,886
BURLEIGH	34,016
Bismarck	
CASS	66,947
Casselton, Fargo Leonard	
CAVALIER	10,064
Langdon	
DICKEY	8,147
Ellendale, Oakes	
DIVIDE	5,566
Divide County—Crosby	
DUNN	6,350
Killdeer	
EDDY	4,936
New Rockford	
EMMONS	8,462
Linton	
FOSTER	5,361
Carrington	
GOLDEN VALLEY	3,100
Beach	
GRAND FORKS	48,677
Grand Forks, Larimore Northwood	
GRANT	6,248
GRIGGS	5,023
Cooperstown	
HETTINGER	6,317
Mott, New England	
KIDDER	5,386
Kidder County—Steele	
LAMOURE	8,705
Edgeley, Kulm, LaMoure South Central Regional — Edgeley	
LOGAN	5,367
Gackle	
McHENRY	11,099
Drake, Towner	
McINTOSH	6,702
Ashley, Wishek, Zeeland	
McKENZIE	7,296
Watford City	
McLEAN	14,030
Turtle Lake, Underwood McLean-Mercer Regional—Riverdale	
MERCER	6,805
Beulah	
MORTON	20,992
Glen Ullin, Hebron, Mandan, New Salem Morton County—Mandan	
MOUNTRAIL	10,077
New Town, Parshall, Stanley	
NELSON	7,034
Lakota	
OLIVER	2,610
PEMBINA	12,946
Cavalier, Drayton, Pembina, St. Thomas, Walhalla	
PIERCE	7,394
Rugby	
RAMSEY	13,443
Devils Lake	
RANSOM	8,078
Enderlin, Lisbon	
RENVILLE	4,698
Mohall	

NORTH DAKOTA LIBRARIES BY COUNTY (Continued)

Counties and Towns with Libraries	County Popoulation (1960 Census)
RICHLAND	18,824
Hankinson, Lidgerwood Wahpeton	
ROLETTE	10,641
Rolla, Rolette	
SARGENT	6,856
Forman	
SHERIDAN	4,305
Goodrich	
SIOUX	3,662
SLOPE	1,893
STARK	18,451
Dickinson	
STEELE	4,719
Finley, Hope	
STUTSMAN	25,137
Jamestown Stutsman County— Jamestown	
TOWNER	5,624
Cando	
TRAILL	10,583
Hillsboro, Mayville	
WALSH	17,997
Grafton, Park River	
WARD	47,072
Minot Ward County—Minot	
WELLS	9,237
Harvey	
WILLIAMS	22,051
Williston West Plains Regional— Williston	

STATE OF NORTH DAKOTA
LIBRARY DIRECTORY
Public, County and Regional Libraries, and Reading Rooms

LOCATION	Zip Code	LIBRARY	LIBRARIAN
Ashley	58413	Public Library	Mrs. Bob Johnson
Beach	58621	Public Library	Mrs. J. Spiegelberg
Beulah	58523	Public Library	Mrs. T. P. Herman
Bismarck	58501	Veterans Memorial Public Library	
Bottineau	58318	Public Library	Mrs. Alice Marsden
Bowman	58623	Clara Lincoln Phelan Memorial Library	Mrs. Martha Stone
Cando	58324	Public Library	Mrs. V. D. Lord
Carrington	58421	Public Library	Mrs. Ella Mae Hargrave
Casselton	58012	Public Library	Miss Laura Port
Cavalier	58220	Public Library	Mrs. Carl A. Berg
Cooperstown	58425	Public Library	Mrs. John E. Erickson
Crosby	58730	Divide County Library	Mrs. Ruth Ralph
Devils Lake	58301	Carnegie Library	Miss Beatrice Larson
Dickinson	58601	Public Library	Mr. Ivan F. Opp
Drake	58736	Public Library	Mrs. Ervin Adam
Drayton	58225	Public Library	Mrs. Lloyd Myster
Edgeley	58433	Public Library	Mrs. Ruth Evert
Edgeley	58433	South Central Regional Library	Mrs. Ruth Evert
Ellendale	58436	Public Library	Mrs. Agnes Martinson
Enderlin	58027	Municipal Library	Mrs. ~~John Olson~~ Wayne Will
Fargo	58102	Public Library	Mr. Richard C. Waddington
Finley	58230	Public Library	Mrs. G. Washburn
Forman	58032	Public Library	Mrs. Clifford Dahl
Gackle	58442	Public Library	Mrs. Alvin Hummel
Glen Ullin	58631	Public Library	Mrs. Lena Gartner
Goodrich	58444	Public Library	Mrs. Rose Jenner
Grafton	58237	Public Library	Mrs. Willis H. Baird
Grand Forks	58201	Public Library	Mrs. Mary Margaret Frank
Hankinson	58041	Public Library	Mrs. Edwin Roeder
Harvey	58341	Public Library	Mrs. Violet Bailey
Hebron	58638	Public Library	Mrs. Nick Bingert
Hettinger	58639	Adams County Library	Mrs. Claude Marion
Hillsboro	58045	Public Library	Mrs. Herbert Engel
Hope	58046	Public Library	Mrs. C. C. Hawley
Jamestown	58401	Alfred Dickey Free Library	Mrs. Jeanne L. Cobb

STATE OF NORTH DAKOTA
LIBRARY DIRECTORY

Public, County and Regional Libraries

LOCATION	Zip Code	LIBRARY	LIBRARIAN
Jamestown	58401	Stutsman County Library	Mrs. John R. Zimmerman
Killdeer	58640	Public Library	Mrs. David Tabor
Kulm	58456	Public Library	Mrs. Richard Stadler
Lakota	58344	A. M. Tofthagen Library	Mrs. H. J. Byrne
LaMoure	58458	Public Library	Mrs. Dacotah Harmsen
Langdon	58249	Public Library	Mrs. E. J. Donovan
Larimore	58251	Edna Ralston Library	Mrs. William Eastgate
Leeds	58346	Public Library	Mrs. Kirk Cowan
Leonard	58052	Leonard Watts Free Library	Mrs. Gilbert Elliott
Lidgerwood	58053	City Library	Mrs. Alice Biewer
Linton	58552	Public Library	Mrs. Albert Wenzel
Lisbon	58054	Public Library	Mrs. Raymond Stewart
Maddock	58348	Public Library	Mrs. Helen Lysne
Mandan	58554	Public Library	Mrs. Jake Geiss
Mandan	58554	Morton County Library	Mrs. Jennie Salveson
Mayville	58257	Public Library	Mrs. Marcus I. Moen
Minot	58701	Public Library	Mrs. Lois Ronning
Minot	58701	Ward County Library	Mrs. Lois Ronning
Mohall	58761	Public Library	Mrs. John Smith
Mott	58646	Inez Hendrickson Library	Mrs. Eleanor Schwartz
New England	58647	Public Library	Mrs. Ron Bender
New Rockford	58356	Public Library	Mrs. Roy Brown
New Salem	58563	Public Library	Mrs. Lloyd Just
New Town	58763	Public Library	Mrs. Lilian O. Wilson
Northwood	58646	Public Library	Mrs. Art Nelson
Oakes	58474	School-Public Library	Mrs. Helene Thomas Hample
Park River	58270	Public Library	Mrs. A. C. Bye
Parshall	58770	Public Library	Mrs. John Risan
Pembina	58271	Public Library	Mr. Lloyd B. Parker
Riverdale	58565	McLean-Mercer Regional Library	Mrs. Charles R. Halbert
Rolette	58366	Public Library	Mrs. Inez E. Ellingson
Rolla	58367	Public Library	Mrs. Marlin Kyle
Rugby	58484	Public Library	Miss Kathryn Cruden
St. Thomas	58276	Public Library	Mrs. Edwin Buchholtz
Stanley	58784	Public Library	Mrs. R. J. Ellis

STATE OF NORTH DAKOTA
LIBRARY DIRECTORY
Public, County and Regional Libraries

LOCATION	Zip Code	LIBRARY	LIBRARIAN
Steele	58482	Kidder County Libraray	Mrs. Minnie Albright
Towner	58788	Public Library	Mrs. J. N. Harnit
Turtle Lake	58575	Public Library	Mrs. Walter Clark
Underwood	58756	Public Library	Mrs. Bernard Thomsen
Valley City	58072	Carnegie Public Library	Mrs. Helen H. Tracy
Wahpeton	58075	Leach Public Library	Mrs. F. H. Fleischman
Walhalla	58282	Public Library	Mrs. Leonard Tetrault
Watford City	58854	Public Library	Mrs. Fred Piper
Williston	58801	James Memorial Library	Miss Linda Engberg
Williston	58801	West Plains Regional Library	Mrs. J. E. Lassey
Wishek	58495	Public Library	Miss Noreen Weisser
Zeeland	58581	Laya Zick Memorial Library	Miss Sheila Reede

College and University Libraries

LOCATION	Zip Code	LIBRARY	LIBRARIAN
Bismarck	58501	Bismarck Junior College Library	Mrs. Lois Engler
Bismarck	58501	Mary College Library	Sister Martha Clare, O.S.B.
Bottineau	58318	State Forestry School Library	Mr. Wendal J. Cushing
Devils Lake	58301	Lake Region Community College Library	Miss Beatrice Larson
Dickinson	58601	State College Library	Mr. Bernnett J. Reinke
Ellendale	58436	UND Ellendale Branch Library	Mr. Thomas A. Hunt
Fargo	58101	N. D. State University Library	Miss Barbara Wetterstrom
Grand Forks	58202	UND Chester Fritz Library	Mr. Donald J. Pearce
Jamestown	58401	Jamestown College Library	Mr. R. W. Witt
Mayville	58257	State College Library	Miss Clenora E. Quanbeck
Minot	58701	State College Library	Mr. Eugene R. Hanson
Valley City	58072	State College Library	Mrs. Lillian Jacobson
Wahpeton	58075	State School of Science Library	Mrs. Mildred Larsson
Williston	58801	UND Williston Center Library	Miss Mary L. Endsley

STATE LIBRARY COMMISSION—PAYROLL REPORT

Payroll Report		1964-65	1965-66
STATE PAYROLL			
Freda W. Hatten	18 mo.	3,069.00	9,000.00
Arlene Stocker		4,775.00	6,000.00
Lorraine LaFleur		4,145.00	4,320.00
Josephine Davenport		3,410.00	3,480.00
Betty Sprynczynatyk		3,365.00	3,420.00
Lawrence Ringuette		2,705.00	2,700.00
Leone Morrison		5,465.00	6,000.00
Inez Crimmins		3,065.00	3,120.00
Thelma Buchert		....	3,120.00
Marshall Conner		....	3,180.00
Sheila Saufferer	6 mo.	....	1,350.00
Pauline Sadler	2 mo.	....	1,000.00
Clara Knoepfle	part time	2,190.00	....
Hazel W. Byrnes	6 mo.	3,355.00	....
Winnifred Coyne		4,145.00	1,005.00
Julie Hunze	2 mo.	....	580.00
Sharon Johnson	2 mo.	....	1,000.00
Myrtle Sidener	2 mo.	....	362.00
FEDERAL PAYROLL			
Duane Crawford	5 mo.	$...............	$ 2,675.00
Mary Femling	8 mo.	....	2,313.00
Julie Hunze	20 mo.	1,988.00	2,660.00
Techla Knoll	part time	1,690.00	1,979.00
Lois Mertz	15 mo.	1,200.00	2,025.00
Marshall Conner		3,305.00	....
Thelma Buchert		3,065.00	....
Freda Hatten	6 mo.	2,443.00	....
Sheila Saufferer	4 mo.	458.00	400.00
Sharon Johnson	22 mo.	4,925.00	4,325.00
Clara Knoepfle	part time	....	99.00
Eva Fogderud	part time	3,240.00	117.00
Marie Huber		3,305.00	3,080.00
Judye Anderson		977.00	2,307.00
Dorothy Hoff	Temporary	245.00	450.00
Kathryn Zins	Temporary	175.00	307.00
Euvagh Wenzel	Temporary	....	152.00
Gary DeKrey	Temporary	....	27.00
Judy Munsch	Temporary	....	347.00
Eugene Nielson	Temporary	....	53.00
Shirley Eisenbarth	Temporary	....	200.00
Linda Chambers	Temporary	....	225.00
Guner Unger	Temporary	24.00	....
Marjo Hewitson	Temporary	295.00	
Helen Sailer	Temporary	62.00	
Lois Ude	Temporary	52.00	
Nora Mohberg	Temporary	1,310.00	
Myrtle Sidener	Temporary	117.00	
Alfred Riskedahl	Temporary	90.00	

Thirty-First Biennial Report

of the

STATE LIBRARY COMMISSION

to the

STATE BOARD OF ADMINISTRATION

For the Period Beginning July 1, 1966
and Ending June 30, 1968

Thirty-First Biennial Report

of the

STATE LIBRARY COMMISSION

to the

STATE BOARD OF ADMINISTRATION

FOR THE PERIOD

July 1, 1966 to June 30, 1968

STATE LIBRARY COMMISSION STAFF

1968-1969

Leone Morrison	*Acting Director*
Arlene Stocker	*Business Administrator*
Josephine Davenport	*Circulation and Mailing Department*
Pauline Sadler	*Coordinator*
Ruth Schoenhard	*Union Catalog*
Thomas W. Nielsen	*Serials Librarian*
Nora Mohberg	*Demonstrations Administrator*

TO THE STATE BOARD OF ADMINISTRATION:

Isak Hystad, Chairman;

Paul A. Dalager, E. Odin Sjaastad, M. F. Peterson, and Arne Dahl.

The North Dakota State Library Commission has the honor to submit its Thirty-first biennial report, covering the period from July 1, 1966 to June 30, 1968.

(MRS.) LEONE MORRISON
Acting Director

REPORT OF THE DIRECTOR

July 1, 1966 - June 30, 1968

The growth and development of the library program has been part of the general progress in the state. The following statement is a brief resume of this library picture over the past biennial period.

The State Library Commission has assisted the public, school, special and state agency libraries in an advisory capacity as well as with reference materials via the Union Catalog. One of the powers and duties of the Library Commission (54-24-03) is "to promote and assist by counsel and encouragement the formation of libraries and improvement of those already established." The Library Services and Construction Act funds have made monetary help available through the state agency for the improvement of library materials in the libraries serving small and large communities. In areas where there are no local public library facilities or only minimal service through libraries open but a few hours a week, the State Library Commission has provided library service by mail directly to the individual. In spite of great strides in library development in the past several years, this group still represents one third of the population of the state.

The State Library Commission assisted with library programs, such as the National Library Week program under the direction of Mrs. Pauline Sadler. The 1968 National Library Week award will be presented to the North Dakota Library Association by Mr. Peter S. Jennison, Director of the National Book Committee, at the NDLA Convention at the University of North Dakota Student Union, Grand Forks, September 29, 1968. North Dakota is the fifth state to win the annual $1,000 award for library promotion activities. The Governor's Conference on Libraries was the highlight of National Library Week in the state.

GOVERNOR'S CONFERENCE ON LIBRARIES

The first North Dakota Governor's Conference on Libraries was held April 22, 1968, at the Holiday Inn, Bismarck, North Dakota. Governor William L. Guy gave the keynote address; Story Birdseye, Judge of the Superior Court, State of Washington, and Dr. David K. Berninghausen, Professor and Director of the Library School, University of Minnesota, spoke on the role of the citizen and today's library needs. Two hundred fifty delegates from all over the state attended the successful one-day meeting on "Libraries—A Citizen's Necessity." The purpose of the Conference was to show the role that school, public, college and special libraries can continue to play in serving the educational needs of the communities. Twelve Regional Governor's Conferences on Libraries are to be held throughout the state to bring to the attention of the public the library's place in the growth of the educational and cultural development of the state of North Dakota.

UNION CATALOG AND UNION LIST OF SERIALS

One significant service of the State Library Commission is the Union Catalog. Instituted in 1965 through a federal grant, it has grown and is supplying untold service to the people of the state. Requests for interlibrary loans through the Union Catalog have increased 30% in this second year. Extending the service of the Union Catalog is a Union List of Serials of 40 North Dakota libraries and 14 South Dakota college libraries. Copy has been prepared and is currently in the data processing center. The serials catalog will be supplied to school and public libraries in the state and to others on request.

LIBRARY DEMONSTRATIONS

The Northern Red River Valley Regional Library Demonstration of the past biennial period was a big 4/5th's successful. Only one of the five counties of the demonstration did not levy to support regional service. This Northeastern Dakota Bookmobile Library consists of Walsh, Cavalier, Pembina and Nelson Counties. Mrs. Charles Stewart is the librarian. It is gratifying to know that citizens of these communities have cooperated in order to improve library services. Participating in the regional system are Grafton, Park River, Langdon, Cavalier, Drayton, Pembina, St. Thomas, Walhalla and Lakota.

Mrs. Nora Mohberg, demonstration administrator, has extended the demonstration in the northeastern area to include Ramsey, Steele, Griggs and Traill Counties and will initiate service through two bookmobiles out of Mayville in November, 1968. The demonstration will operate for a two-year period after which the counties will be expected to levy for local support.

LIBRARY BUILDING DEVELOPMENTS

A public library building was constructed at **Parshall** in the spring of 1967. Construction of the **Fargo Public Library** was completed and the new building was dedicated May 20, 1968. Children's rooms were added to the **Grafton Public Library** and to the **Adams County Library** at Hettinger. **Pierce County** and the city of Rugby formed a city-county library. A building is being constructed in **Rugby** through local, federal and private funds. The city of **Cooperstown** has purchased a building to be used as a library. **Harvey Public Library** is adding on to their building.

LIBRARY STUDY GRANTS

There are three study grants awarded in the 1966-68 biennial period: Miss Lonnie Newman attended the University of Denver Library School on a $2,000 grant; Mrs. Ora Stewart of Grafton accepted a grant and will finish during the summer of 1969. At the present time she is librarian of the Northeastern Dakota Bookmobile

Library. Miss Carolyn Snyder, Pembina, is attending the Graduate School of Librarianship, University of Denver, on a grant. She will receive her degree in June, 1969. Subsidies in the amount of $1,712.50 were paid to 16 persons for library credit earned. The grant is $15 for each quarter hour.

LIBRARY SERVICES AND CONSTRUCTION ACT TITLES III & IV

Federal funds were made available in the spring of 1968 for interlibrary cooperation and library services to the handicapped and disadvantaged. Title III (Interlibrary Cooperation) and Title I (Library Services) grants have made it possible to finance a demonstration of library cooperation in eleven counties in the northwestern part of the state with headquarters at the Minot Public Library. Mr. Everett Foster, coordinator for the project, has contracted with fourteen libraries for services including the rotation of new fiction and non-fiction collections, book processing, interlibrary loan and copy service, borrower's cards good in all libraries, in-service training, 16mm film service, publicity, subject specialists and speakers' bureau. At the end of a two-year trial period, if the project is accepted, the financial support will be determined by the libraries involved.

Under Title IV, which is intended to improve state institutional libraries and to give library service to the physically handicapped who cannot use regular library facilities, books were purchased for institutions and are being sent out on a rotating basis to the State Industrial School, the State Penitentiary, the State Hospital, Grafton State School, the Tuberculosis Sanatorium, and the Soldiers' Home. In addition, materials were purchased for the State Industrial School, the School for the Deaf, the State Penitentiary, and the State Hospital which will be kept at these institutions. A grant of $2,400 was made to the Division of Vocational Rehabilitation for extended services to the blind, and grants of $1,000 and $5,000 respectively to Valley City and Minot for services to the handicapped in the area.

The State Library Commission now approaches the legislative period with trepidation. Without a substantial raise in the $87,200 annual state appropriation, the state would not be in a position to accept all of the federal funds available to North Dakota. In addition to library extension under Title I of the Library Services and Construction Act, and construction under Title II, there is available to the state $105,118 under Titles III and IVa and IVb for interlibrary cooperation and library services to the state institutions and the physically handicapped. State funds for matching are necessary because local matching for Titles III and IV are almost nonexistent.

STATE LIBRARY FACILITIES

An item to match federal funds for construction was included in the 1967-69 budget and has again been included in the 1969-71 budget for a new state library building. Without adequate facilities the State Library Commission cannot function to the fullest extent and cannot satisfactorily supply the library needs of the state.

PERSONNEL CHANGES

Mrs. Freda Hatten resigned as Director of the State Library Commission July 31, 1968, and has taken the position of Serials Cataloger at North Dakota State University, Fargo. Mr. Duane Crawford, Head of the Union Catalog, has resigned and accepted a position at Valley City State College. There has been an overload of work which all of the staff has undertaken to do to continue library development. Mrs. Leone Morrison is now Acting Director of the State Library Commission.

THE CURRENT PUBLIC LIBRARY PICTURE.

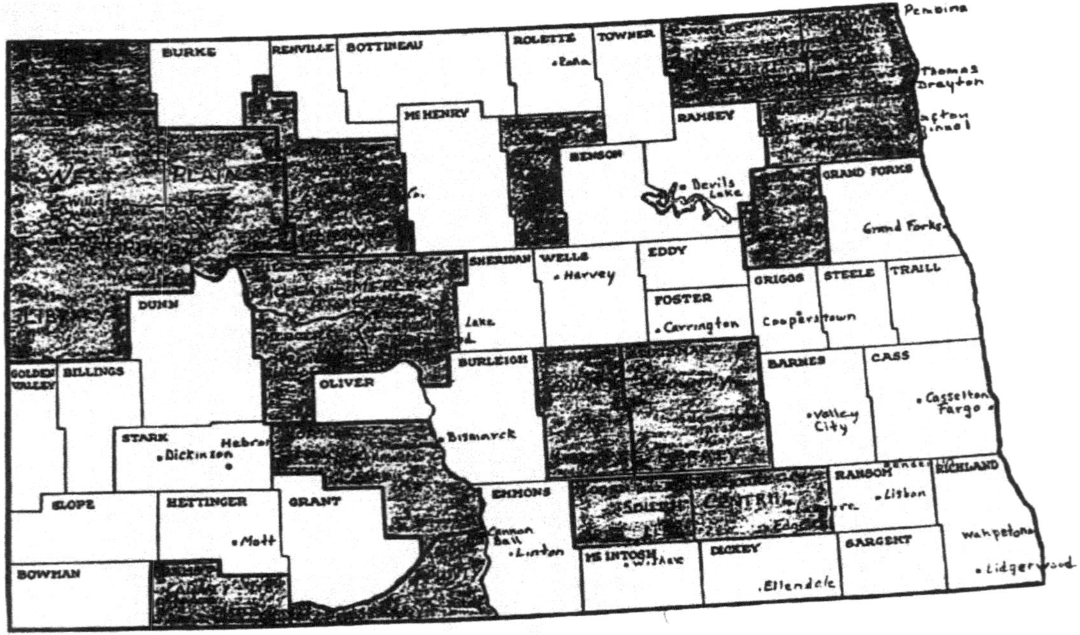

County and regional libraries and their branches

Public libraries

STATE LIBRARY COMMISSION

BIENNIAL APPROPRIATION

1967-1969

Salaries	$178,200
Services	41,000
Supplies	80,000
Equipment	24,200
Grants	700,000

Of the above $174,400 represents state funds and $849,000 federal funds. Titles III and IV of the Library Services and Construction Act have made available to the state an additional $207,301.

Grants were made as follows during the period of the report:

1966-1967

Sioux County		$ 2,800
Northern Red River Valley Regional Library Demonstration		55,000
McLean Mercer Regional Library		12,692
South Central Area Library		10,792
James Memorial Library		6,000
Minot Public Library		5,000
Divide County Library		1,500
West Plains Regional		10,915
Veterans Memorial Library		25,000
Library Survey		7,880
Study Grants		2,000
Subsidies		970
Construction		114,452
Parshall	$29,452	
Minot	50,000	
Fargo	35,000	

1967-1968

Northern Red River Valley Regional Library Demon.	$ 47,000
Adams County Library	4,295
McLean-Mercer Regional	9,350
Sioux County	3,000
South Central Area	3,500
Stutsman County	4,515
West Plains Rural	1,200
Veterans Memorial	5,075
Carrington Public	900
Fargo Public	10,000
Dickinson Public	950
Grafton Public	7,000

Harvey Public	3,500
Mandan Public	6,300
Minot Public	10,000
Valley City Public	1,000
Wahpeton Public	1,000
James Memorial	7,200
Northeastern Dakota Bookmobile Library	18,000
Grants	1,000
Subsidies	682
Construction — Fargo	140,187

Titles III & IV

Northwestern Federation	10,815
Vocational Rehabilitation	2,400
Valley City Public	1,000
Minot Public	5,000

This report is divided into two parts. The first part consists of the statistics of the libraries that meet national minimum requirements. Only these statistics will appear in the national reports. Part two is the statistics of other libraries and reading rooms in the state.

DEFINITION OF A PUBLIC LIBRARY

Taken from "Library Statistics: A Handbook of Concepts, Definitions and Terminology," prepared by the staff of the Statistics Coordinating Project, American Library Association.

"The definition of a public library must be broad enough to allow for a difference in government, source of income, service area, and nature of collection; but there is also a point at which an agency ceases to be a public library.

"To be included in public library statistics, every agency must offer **free services** to everyone within some stipulated geographical area. Libraries which do not, whether from tradition as old subscription or corporation libraries or from extreme financial pressure, should not be considered public and should not be included."

With regard to book collection, "it is suggested that unless the agency is a member of a library system, it must meet **all of the following criteria** to be included in public library statistics: (1) Give at least 10 hours of public service per week, (2) Have a book collection of at least 2,000 volumes, (3) Purchase at least 200 volumes per year, and (4) Expend at least $1,000 per year.

"These criteria are not intended to relate to, or to set minimum standards of library service, They merely indicate the **lowest level** at which an agency can be considered a statistical unit. Inclusion of figures for libraries which do not meet all of these criteria negates the concepts of "population served" and "area served," and distorts all total figures of public library resources and services.

"Because data on school-public library combinations often cannot be separated accurately, it is recommended that such libraries be included wholly in either school library statistics or public statistics. If the library is physically located in a school but is established under public library laws, and serves only incidentally the library needs of teachers and pupils, it will be counted as a public library."

Statistics of North Dakota Public Libraries, 1966-68

COUNTY AND REGIONAL LIBRARIES

Library	Population Served (1960 Census)	Separate Location	Size Square Feet	Hours Open per Week	Staff Number	Volumes	Circulation 1966-67	Circulation 1967-68
Adams County, Hettinger	4,449	Yes	1,248	20	7	13,146	20,092	17,729
Reeder, branch								
Divide County, Crosby	5,566	Yes	1,152	27	2	16,921	40,051	43,688
Fortuna, station								
Noonan, station								
Kidder County, Steele	5,386	Steele Comm. Building	352	8	1	6,105	28,310	27,049
McLean-Mercer Regional, Riverdale	20,835	Yes	4,860	17	9	29,493	101,917	103,178
[illegible], branch								
Garrison, branch								
Hazen, branch								
Turtle Lake, station		City Hall	208	4	1	800		
Underwood, station								
Morton County, Mandan	10,467	Mem. Building	602	40	5	24,251	62,725	54,249
Glen Ullin Public, branch		Legion Theatre		2	Volunteers	2,644		
Hebron Public, branch								
New Salem Public, branch		City Auditorium	748	4	1	2,664		
Northeastern Dakota Bookmobile Library, Grafton	62,267	Yes	1,670	48	8	26,638		105,423
Cavalier Public, branch								
Grafton Public, branch		Yes	1,622	42	2	11,247	31,256	30,568
A. M. [illegible], [illegible]akota, branch								
Langdon Public, branch		Cavalier Co. Court House		9		6,660	13,936	14,540

Statistics of North Dakota Public Libraries, 1966-68

COUNTY AND REGIONAL LIBRARIES

Library	Population Served (1960 Census)	Separate Location	Size Square Feet	Hours Open per Wk	Staff Number	Volumes	Circulation 1966-67	Circulation 1967-68
Park River Public, branch		Bures Building	1,128	12	1	3,068		6,656
Pembina Public, branch		City Hall	168		Volunteers			
St. Thomas Memorial, branch		Yes	300	2	Volunteers		432	350
Rugby Public	7,394	City Hall	610		1	12,164	29,919	
Sioux County, Fort Yates	3,662	Yes			1	1,000		1,020
[illegible]l, station								
Selfridge, station								
South Central Area, Edgeley	14,300	Yes	1,460	20	5	24,198	102,202	102,074
Edgeley Public, branch				20	5	5,137		
[illegible]le Public, branch		Yes	540	3½	1	2,536	1,582	1,567
Kulm Public, station								
Napoleon Public, station								
Stutsman County, Jamestown	9,974	Alfred Dickey Free Library	1,024	24	4	25,795	66,631	60,735
Ward County Bookmobile, Minot	16,468	Minot Public Library	2,400	56	3	24,134	164,487	183,436
West Plains Rural, Williston	27,558	Price Office Building	1,400	35	8	34,421	167,314	162,950
New Town Public branch		New Town Health Center	480	9	1	3,386	5,880	5,205
Parshall Public, branch		Yes	750	13	2	4,748	4,243	4,293
Tioga Public, branch								
TOTAL	188,326					281,156	840,977	924,710

RECEIPTS

Library	Taxes 1966-67	Taxes 1967-68	Other 1966-67	Other 1967-68	Total 1966-67	Total 1967-68
Adams County, Hettinger	$ 7,660.75	6,690.01	457.11	4,570.14	8,117.86	11,260.15
Divide County, Crosby	8,625.00	12,675.00	1,867.26	712.85	10,492.26	13,387.85
Kidder County, Steele	5,000.00	7,898.97			5,000.00	7,898.97
McLean-Mercer Regional,						
Riverdale	22,277.02	27,462.45	14,330.22	9,992.90	33,607.24	37,455.35
Turtle Lake, branch	9 308.33	264.64	1.23	278.00	309.56	542 64
Morton County Mandan	17,089.04	17,105.20	3,487.50	530.43	20,576.54	17,635.63
Glen Ullin, branch	300.00	300.00	11.75	43.05	311.75	346.05
New Salem, branch			82.14	79.85	82.14	79.85
Northeastern Dakota						
Bookmobile, Grafton				47,000.00		47,000.00
Grafton, branch	7,000.00	7,629.75	1,008.00	7,857.00	8,008.00	15,486.75
Langdon, branch	900.00	400.00	368.50	394.90	1.268.50	794.90
Park River, branch	2,194.27	2,312.58	101.20	1,586.42	2,295.47	3,899.00
Pembina	533.76				533.76	
St. Thomas			250.00		250.00	
Rugby Public	4,725.57	10,760.82	378.57	316.38	5,104.14	11,077.20
Sioux County, Fort Yates		4,152.35		1,800.00		5.952.35
South Central Area, Edgeley	15,604.37	15,761.17	19,393.84	5,121.44	34,998.21	20,882.51
Edgeley Public, branch	1,211.75		1,299.90		2,511.65	
Gackle Public, branch	500.00	500.00	29.34	9.77	529.34	509.77
Stutsman County, Jamestown	19,154.00	18,352.97	16.54	4,515.00	19,170.54	22,867.97
Ward County Bookmobile, Minot	27,800.00	28,520.00	414.49	355.00	28,214.49	28,875.00
West Plains Rural, Williston	48,297.27	40,720.10	254.42	12,602.67	48,551.69	53,322.77
New Town Public, branch	1.010.38	1,002.66	100.50		1,110.88	1,002.66
Parshall Public, branch	22,088.00	1,944.81	29,527.38	343.03	51,615.38	2,292.84
TOTAL	$212,279.51	204,453.43	73,379.89	98,116.33	285,659.40	302,570.31

EXPENDITURES

Library	Capital Expenditures 1966-67	Capital Expenditures 1967-68	Salaries 1966-67	Salaries 967-68	Library Materials 1966-67	Library Materials 1967-68	Total 1966-67	Total 1967-68
Adams County	$	5,152.73	3,812.68	3,615.56	1,053.94	1,029.40	5,815.00	10,802.58
Divide County	1,101.19	386.03	5,782.81	7,248.95	[illegible]	1,968.87	11,070.54	11,896.50
Kidder County	108.30		4,433.89	4,765.74	2,195.21	1,678.25	[illegible]	7,729.16
McLean-Mercer								
Regional	13,152.41	4,881.49	15,948.19	17,250.95	5,097.93	5,021.02	37,207.74	30,997.85
Turtle Lake	247.09	99.93	112.36	220.28	39.66		399.11	320.21
Morton County	339.49	69.62	13,244.08	13,070.50	2,735.19	3,234.58	18,950.78	18,839.89
Glen Ullin					[illegible]	241.82	[illegible]	315.22
New Salem					85.80	61.99	91.36	66.87
Northeastern Dakota								
[illegible]				34,895.17		4 168.21		43,838.[illegible]
Grafton Public		5,000.00	4,638.98	5,555.53	2,090.99	2,488.01	7,527.47	14,152.63
Langdon			900.00	955.55	43.00	9.45	943.00	965.00
Park River		172.37	1,778.80	1,634.46	197.60	754.81	[illegible]	3,431.20
Pembina	480.00						512.00	
St. Thomas							100.00	
Rugby Public		4,250.00	3,017.66	3,081.25	903.89	[illegible]	[illegible]	8,503.24
Sioux County				724.30		1,967.66		4,836.28
South Central Area	15,376.35	60.15	10,819.54	10,957.49	3 682,01	2,796.46	33,797.19	17,839.85
Edgeley Public	274.90		260.00		[illegible]		1,847.72	
Gackle			180.00	263.75	44.70	[illegible]	[illegible]	687.07
Stutsman County		2,084.41	11,250.00	11,431.12	1,500.00	3,769.57	13,165.70	24,247.01
Ward County								
Bookmobile			12,452.54	15,587.88	5,668.44	6,721.53	27,790.66	28,515.62
West Plain Rural		18,500.00	22,367.80	30,649.23	2,534.58	3,633.02	37,648.37	64,160.01
New Town			213.00	302.50	422.70	549.22	660.42	851.72
Parshall	50,015.01	230.00	456.00	450.00	805.29	587.85	51,276.30	1,768.82
TOTAL	$31,095.24	40,886.73	111,668.33	162,710.21	32,585.57	41,820.45	268,767.04	300,766.40

PUBLIC LIBRARIES

Library	Population Served (1960 Census)	Separate Location	Size Square Feet	Hours Open per Week	Staff Number	Volumes	Circulation 1966-67	Circulation 1967-68
Veterans Memorial, Bismarck	27,670	Yes	15,000	66	12	48, 06	96, 89	190,102
Clara Lincoln Phelan, Bowman	1,30	Yes	1,092	11	1	5, 92	4,896	4,880
Carrington City	2 438	Armory	1,152	24	1	6 6[illegible]	30 000	30,000
Casselton Public	[illegible]4	City Hall	660	18	2	5, 59	10,385	11,108
Cooperstown Public	1,[illegible]4	Farmers and Merchants Bank	1,000	13	1	6,623	6,674	8,323
[illegible]ie Library, Devils Lake	6,299	Yes	3,518	36	2	18, 01	38, 69	39,110
Dickinson Public	9,971	Yes	2,750	44	4	25, 83	61, 04	49, 99
Ellendale Public	1,800	City Hall	720	21	1	6, 89	18, 95	16, 89
Enderlin Municipal	1,596	City Hall	504	12	1	4,418	5, 87	5, 30
Fargo Public	46,662	Yes	32,000	69	22	83,160	83, 65	303,014
[illegible]d Forks Public	34,451	Yes	7,750	69	12	59,759	178 201	202, 63
Harvey Public	2,365	Yes	1,200	33	3	7,795	[illegible]0,307	21, 89
Alfred Dickey Free, Jamestown	15,163	Yes	8,928	58	5	32, 53	122,307	123 525
Lidgerwood City	1,081	Yes	1,763	18	1	12,464	10, 07	9,305
Linton Public	1, 86	City Hall	1,225	12	1	7, 83	3, 86	6,600
Lisbon Public	2 09[illegible]	Yes	3,456	17	1	8,391	11, 95	12, 55
Mandan Public	10 525	Yes	4,660	48	[illegible]	21,700	62, 31	65 209
Min[illegible] Public	36,604	Yes	18,500	68	15	61, 86	412, 54	85 275
Mott Public	[illegible]	City Hall	850	17	1	7,778	6, 86	7,313
Rolla Public	1,39[illegible]	City Hall	450	12	1	3,251		
Carnegie Public, Valley City	17 [illegible]00	Yes	2,600	34	4	21,976	41 418	36 379
Le[illegible]ch Public, Wahpeton	5,876	Yes		23	[illegible]	15 [illegible]	13 151	2[illegible],412
Watford City Public	1 865	Civic Center	333	17	2	5 806	6 83	6,822
James Memorial, Williston	11,866	Yes		59	4	23 220	53 731	60 225
Wishek Public	1,[illegible]90	City Hall		10	1	7,749	2 332	3 241
TOTAL	245,850					511,[illegible]4	1,708,373	1, 8,188

RECEIPTS

Library	Taxes 1966-67	Taxes 1967-68	Other 1966-67	Other 1967-68	Total 1966-67	Total 1967-68
[illegible]	$ 95,765.08	100,502.02	7,347.80	36,625.63	103,112.88	137,127.65
Bowman	1,196.51	40.17	191.10	200.61	1,387.61	640.78
[illegible]	[illegible]	3,000.00	44.02	1,005.05	3,044.02	[illegible]05.05
[illegible]	1,977.67	2,289.30	86.58	100.99	2,064.25	2,390.29
[illegible]		1,453.03	1,298.02	1,398.52	1,298.02	2,851.55
[illegible]	13,008.59	14,381.15	545.81	576.72	13,554.40	[illegible]57.87
[illegible]	22,693.33	24,855.00	1,050.58	2,161.84	23,743.[illegible]	27,016.84
[illegible]	2,500.00	2,[illegible]00.00	23.32	121.40	2,773.32	2,621.40
[illegible]	2,650.00	2,[illegible]5.00	[illegible]7.79	118.25	2,807.79	3,083.25
Fargo	143,[illegible]4.16	152,[illegible]50.71	6,103.73	16,342.93	149,747.89	168,893.64
Grand Forks	80,272.50	106,[illegible]0.96	2,427.50	3,961.00	82,700.00	110,191.96
Harvey	3,450.33	4,[illegible]46.70	82.56	3,616.61	3,832.89	8,033.31
Jamestown	21,336.99	26,[illegible]5.91	6,606.77	7,298.28	27,943.76	34,254.19
Lidgerwood	1,920.00	1,[illegible]0.00	93.54	8.93	2,013.51	1,928.98
Linton	1,000.00	1,[illegible]0.00	[illegible]5.00	270.00	1,365.00	1,570.00
Lisbon	3,156.87	4[illegible]0.27	[illegible]2.64	306.84	3,8[illegible]9.51	4,[illegible]47.11
Mandan	20,755.70	[illegible]2.16	1[illegible]79.93	7,627.99	22,535.63	29,610.15
Minot	78,993.27	[illegible]5.37	1[illegible]1.53	26,607.82	89,374.80	111,023.19
Mott	2,700.00	2,[illegible]4.16	48.85	153.00	2,[illegible]48.85	2,877.16
Rolla	3,207.10	3,[illegible]3.16	42.98	93.0[illegible]	3,250.03	3,576.22
Valley City	16,017.62	16,894.85	1,155.80	2,958.20	17,173.51	19,853.05
Wahpeton	6,[illegible]00.00	3,750.00	[illegible]1.72	1,334.13	6,351.72	5,084.13
Watford City	2,191.20	2,146.49	[illegible]3.86	151.90	2,355.06	2,298.39
Williston	35,669.71	37,305.85	7,274.79	9,307.51	42,[illegible]44.50	46,613.36
Wishek	1,275.00	1,275.00	4.00		1,279.00	1,275.00
TOTAL	$552,973.63	623,97[illegible]7.26	48,640.31	122,347.26	613,321.9[illegible]	746,324.52

EXPENDITURES

Library	Capital Expenditures 1966-67	Capital Expenditures 1967-68	Salaries 1966-67	Salaries 1967-68	Library Materials 1966-67	Library Materials 1967-68	Total 1[illegible]67	Total 1967-68
Bismarck	$14,661.55	10,224.32	58,830.09	62,363.93	14,396.45	39,226.36	[illegible]8	128,374.23
Bowman			635.17	885.87	405.88	320.03	1,244.72	2,253.41
[illegible]ton	953.83	629.57	1,500.00	1,967.20	1,069.97	1,294.60	3,631.89	4,030.61
[illegible]h	458.80		1,322.67	1,602.59	490.77	614.00	2,282.24	2,277.84
[illegible]n	163.60		650.00	832.50	523.28	1,050.52	2,276.50	2,926.91
[illegible]s Lake	912.00	175.00	6,837.33	9,033.59	3,143.90	3,340.74	13,318.15	14,811.88
[illegible]h		420.93	15,524.97	17,567.15	3,801.71	5,089.97	24,946.30	25,791.28
[illegible]le	140.06		1,234.20	1,361.40	1,302.03	915.29	2,718.14	2,750.90
[illegible]h			1,[illegible]27.10	1,[illegible]01.40	659.30	[illegible]8.18	2,169.12	2,443.39
Fargo	541.47	873,625.23	93,[illegible]92.65	107,193.35	25,687.53	28,157.18	137,[illegible]40.76	1,[illegible]61,690.06
Grand Forks			42,[illegible]85.18	51,243.98	12,939.04	14,618.30	[illegible]81.81	80,409.35
Harvey		4,922.55	2,[illegible]91.17	3,403.52	767.18	[illegible]82.59	4,196.30	9,751.05
Jamestown	4,637.88	1,749.01	18,[illegible]35.15	20,053.34	4,189.94	5,[illegible]38.33	29,[illegible]02.35	30,114.84
Lidgerwood			1,173.64	1,202.09	688.00	[illegible]55.87	[illegible]39.29	1,940.95
Linton	30.00		1,000.00	1,000.00	258.38	[illegible]80.10	1,345.62	1,627.35
Lisbon	91.41		1,582.20	2,211.29	727.84	[illegible]82.69	3,296.52	4,427.94
Mandan	635.25	2,214.88	15,920.38	12,283.19	5,152.66	14,754.68	31,483.27	34,064.94
Minot		4,552.72	43,344.13	58,748.94	21,830.66	23,139.01	92,679.77	109,[illegible]94.14
Mott	400.00	400.00	1,102.45	[illegible]96	1,136.09	946.78	2,804.64	2,[illegible]85.90
Rolla	99.52		837.03	1,030.07	565.41	[illegible]41.68	1,588.60	2,448.19
Valley City	386.87		7,637.61	7,447.15	3,051.81	3,325.72	[illegible]9	13,[illegible]36.16
Wahpeton			3,810.43	4,093.27	754.75	1,817.33	6,407.73	6,[illegible]80.57
Watford City	49.75	175.00	1,347.00	1,283.60	769.45	[illegible]82.83	2,308.37	2,[illegible]84.34
Williston	342.40	3,685.12	20,440.68	21,140.40	[illegible]94	6,660.29	[illegible]84	37,515.24
Wishek			511.97	524.90	599.34	418.87	1,194.50	976.58
TOTAL	$24,504.39	902,774.33	343,333.50	391,365.98	114,072.71	155,962.24	589,667.60	1,555,088.35

READING ROOMS

Library	Population Served (1960 [illegible])	Government: Municipal or Association	Separate Location	Size Square Feet	Hours Open per Week	Staff Number	Volumes	Circulation 1966-67	Circulation 1967-68
Ashley Public	1,419	Association	Yes	512	6	1	8,375	4,000	4,369
Beach Public	1,460	Association	American Leg. Hall	4,866		1		7,196	
Bottineau Public	No Report								
Cando Public	No [illegible]								
Drake Public	752	Association	Public School	212	4	Volunteer	3,579		
Forman Public	530	Association	Yes		4	1	4,100	2,200	1,981
Hankinson Public	1,285	Association	City Hall		2	Volunteer	2,645	2,626	2,410
Hope City	390	Municipal	City Hall		2	1	2,095	496	452
Kildeer Public	[illegible]	Association	Yes	508	1½	Volunteer	2,645	2,626	2,410
A. M. Tofthagen, Lakota	No Report								
LaMoure Public	1,068	Municipal	Community Building		6	1	5,191	9,116	8,518
Edna Ralston, Larimore	[illegible]	Municipal	City Hall	322				3,237	
Leeds Public	797	[illegible]	[illegible]		2	1	4,361	793	529
Mayville Public	2,168	[illegible]	Yes	1,854	8	1	6,780	5,222	5,140
Mohall Public	956	[illegible]	[illegible]		6	1		7,450	
New England Public	1,095	[illegible]	Memorial Hall	540	2	1		1,503	
New Rockford Public	[illegible]	[illegible]	Yes		10	Volunteer	6,524	4,158	3,594
Oakes Public	[illegible]	[illegible]	[illegible] School	1,560	45	1	7,675	29,178	24,170
Towner Public	[illegible]		Fire Hall		2				1,200
Laya Zick Memorial, Zeeland	427	[illegible]	Bank Building	166	4	Volunteer	1,273		
TOTAL	20,085						61,042	77,850	51,838

RECEIPTS

Library	Taxes 1966-67	Taxes 1967-68	Other 1966-67	Other 1967-68	Total 1966-67	Total 1967-68
Ashley	$ 700.00	700.00	74.85	71.65	774.85	771.65
Beach			1,953.43		1,953.43	
Bottineau						
Cando						
Drake	400.00	400.00	39.73	30.07	439.73	430.07
Forman	221.60	222.00	169.86	46.45	391.46	268.45
Hankinson	100.00	100.00	6.25	461.35	106.25	561.35
Hope	100.00	100.00	8.68	7.86	108.68	107.86
Killdeer			32.39	38.16	32.39	38.16
Lakota						
Lamoure	1,361.82	1,427.63	65.44	72.34	1,427.26	1,499.97
LaMoure	300.00		256.88		556.88	
Leeds	200.00	200.00	18.00	18.80	218.00	218.80
Mayville	1,208.09	1,539.64	[illegible]	105.10	1,408.13	1,644.74
Mohall	1,649.05				1,649.05	
New England	250.00		26.91		276.91	
New Rockford	300.00	300.00	487.05	405.42	787.05	705.42
Oakes	2,992.83	3,292.47	649.95	513.92	3,642.78	3,806.39
Towner						105.73
Zeeland				9.59		9.59
TOTAL	$ 9,783.39	8,281.74	3,989.46	1,780.71	13,772.85	10,062.45

EXPENDITURES

Library	Capital Expenditures 1966-67	Capital Expenditures 1967-68	Salaries 1966-67	Salaries 1967-68	Library Materials 1966-67	Library Materials 1967-68	Total 1966-67	Total 1967-68
Ashley	$		350.79	388.20	340.60	221.97	792.39	718.10
Beach			570.46		618.03		2,059.21	
Bottineau								
Cando								
Drake					303.66	310.35	347.12	352.42
Forman			183.60	180.00	73.39	130.37	298.88	[illegible]
Hankinson					103.65	550.00	105.61	555.57
Hope			74.50	74.50	53.39	59.43	127.89	133.93
Killdeer			30.78	30.96			30.78	30.96
Lakota								
LaMoure			657.60	674.10	595.00	815.12	1,306.44	1,533.44
Larimore			325.20		138.28		485.48	
Leeds			105.00	105.00	135.29	79.38	264.32	204.80
Mayville			922.41	944.41	571.08	765.23	1,590.70	1,815.50
Mohall			984.98		446.37		4[illegible]1.35	
New England			105.00		169.17		320.25	
New Rockford			21.00	100.55	392.20	414.61	446.22	515.16
Oakes			1,029.49	1,187.53	1,508.41	1,384.68	2,910.64	2,786.82
Towner				54.50		55.91		110.41
Zeeland								24.90
TOTAL	$		5,360.81	3,685.25	5,448.52	4,731.14	12,517.28	9,035.75

NORTH DAKOTA LIBRARIES BY COUNTY

Counties and Towns with Libraries	Population County (1960 Census)
ADAMS	4,449
Adams County—Hettinger, Reeder	
BARNES	16,719
Valley City	
BENSON	9,425
Leeds	
BILLINGS	1,513
BOTTINEAU	11,315
BOWMAN	4,154
Bowman	
BURKE	5,886
BURLEIGH	34,016
Bismarck	
CASS	66,947
Casselton, Fargo	
CAVALIER	10,064
Langdon	
DICKEY	8,147
Ellendale, Oakes	
DIVIDE	5,566
Divide County—Crosby, Fortuna, Noonan	
DUNN	6,350
Killdeer	
EDDY	4,936
New Rockford	
EMMONS	8,462
Linton	
FOSTER	5,361
Carrington	
GOLDEN VALLEY	3,100
Beach	
GRAND FORKS	48,677
Grand Forks, Larimore	
GRANT	6,248
GRIGGS	5,023
Cooperstown	
HETTINGER	6,317
Mott, New England	
KIDDER	5,386
Kidder County—Steele	
LAMOURE	8,705
Edgeley, Kulm, LaMoure, South Central Area—Edgeley	
LOGAN	5,367
Gackle, Napoleon	
McHENRY	11,099
Drake, Towner	
McINTOSH	6,702
Ashley, Wishek, Zeeland	
McKENZIE	7,296
Watford City	
McLEAN	14,030
Garrison, Turtle Lake, Underwood, McLean-Mercer Regional—Riverdale	
MERCER	6,805
Beulah, Hazen	
MORTON	20,992
Glen Ullin, Hebron, Mandan, New Salem, Morton County—Mandan	
MOUNTRAIL	10,077
New Town, Parshall, Stanley	
NELSON	7,034
Lakota	
OLIVER	2,610
PEMBINA	12,946
Cavalier, Drayton, Pembina, St. Thomas, Walhalla	
PIERCE	7,394
Rugby	
RAMSEY	13,443
Devils Lake	
RANSOM	8,078
Enderlin, Lisbon	
RENVILLE	4,698
Mohall	
RICHLAND	18,824
Hankinson, Lidgerwood, Wahpeton	
ROLETTE	10,641
Rolette, Rolla	
SARGENT	6,856
Forman	
SHERIDAN	4,305
Goodrich	
SIOUX	3,662
Cannonball, Selfridge, Sioux County—Fort Yates	
SLOPE	1,893
STARK	18,451
Dickinson	
STEELE	4,719
Finley, Hope	
STUTSMAN	25,137
Jamestown, Stutsman County—Jamestown	

NORTH DAKOTA LIBRARIES BY COUNTY

Counties and Towns with Libraries	Population County (1960 Census)	Counties and Towns with Libraries	(1960 Census)
TOWNER	5,624	Minot, Ward County— Minot	
TRAILL	10,583	WELLS	9,237
Mayville		Harvey	
WALSH	17,997	WILLIAMS	22,051
Grafton, Northeastern Dakota Bookmobile— Grafton, Park River		Tioga, Williston, West Plains Rural— Williston	
WARD	47,072		

STATE OF NORTH DAKOTA LIBRARY DIRECTORY

Public, County and Regional Libraries, and Reading Rooms

Location	Zip Code	Library	Telephone	Librarian
Ashley	58413	Ashley Public Library	288-3616*	Mrs. Bruce McShane
Beach	58621	Beach Public Library	872-3988*	Mrs. Frank Kress
Beulah	58523	Beulah Public Library	873-5210*	Mrs. T. P. Herman
Bismarck	58501	[illegible]ns Memorial Library	223-4267	Mr. Richard J. Wolfert
Bottineau	58318	Bottineau Public Library	228-2016*	Mrs. Alice [illegible]
Bowman	58623	Clara Lincoln Phelan Library	523-2311*	Mrs. Martha [illegible]
Carrington	58421	Carrington City Library	652-3921	Mrs. Ella Mae Hargrave
Casselton	58012	Casselton Public Library	672-4861	Miss Laura Port
Cavalier	58220	Cavalier Public Library	265-8952*	Mrs. Carl A. Berg
Cooperstown	58425	Cooperstown Public Library	4464*	Mrs. Marjorie Larson
Crosby	58730	Divide County Library	965-6305	Mrs. Ruth [illegible]
Devils Lake	58301	[illegible]gie Library	662-2220	Miss Merle McIntyre
Dickinson	58601	Dickinson Public Library	225-2162	Miss Dorothea Booke
Drake	58736	Drake Public Library	465-2816*	Mrs. Ervin [illegible]
Drayton	58225	Drayton Public Library	454-3317*	Mrs. Lloyd Myster
Edgeley	58433	Edgeley Public Library		Mrs. Ruth Evert
		South Central Area Library	3711	Mrs. Ruth Evert
Ellendale	58436	Ellendale Public Library	None	Mrs. Don [illegible]
Enderlin	58027	Enderlin Municipal Library	49911	Mrs. [illegible] Wilson
Fargo	58102	Fargo Public Library	235-7567	Mr. Richard Waddington
Finley	58230	Finley Public Library	5841*	Mrs. Marie E. [illegible]
Foorman	58032	Forman Public Library	724-3681*	Mrs. [illegible] Dahl
Fort Yates	58538	Sioux County Library	422-5691*	Mrs. Donald Port
Gackle	58442	Gackle Public Library	485-3229*	Shields, N. Dak.
Glen Ullin	58631	Glen Ullin Public Library	8731*	Mrs. [illegible]
Goodrich	58444	Goodrich Public Library	None	Mrs. [illegible] Muggli
Grafton	58237	Grafton Public Library	352-2745	Mrs. [illegible] Demke
		Northeastern Dakota Bookmobile Library	352-2011	Mrs. Alice Baird Mrs. Ora Stewart

STATE OF NORTH DAKOTA LIBRARY DIRECTORY

Public, County and Regional Libraries, and Reading Rooms

Location	Zip Code	Librarian	Telephone	Librarian
Grand Forks	58201	Grand Forks Public Library	[illegible]61	Mr. Dennis N. Page
Hankinson	58041	Hankinson Public Library	None	Mrs. [illegible]
Harvey	58341	Harvey Public Library	324-2156	Mrs. Violet Bailey
Hazen	58638	Hazen Public Library	752*	Mrs. Nick Bingert
Hettinger	58639	Adams County Library	567-2741	Mrs. Geraldine Marion
Hope	58046	Hope City Library	945-2461	Mrs. C. C. [illegible]ey
Jamestown	58401	Alfred Dickey Free Library	252-2990	Mrs. Jeanne L. Cobb
		Stutsman County Library	252-1531	Mrs. Ella Zimmerman
Killdeer	58640	Killdeer Public Library	932-5236*	Mrs. David Tabor
Lakota	58344	A. M. [illegible]	247-2565*	Mrs. H. J. Byrne
LaMoure	58458	LaMoure Public Library	6509*	Mrs. [illegible]
Langdon	58249	Langdon Public Library	256-2725*	Mrs. E. J. Donovan
Larimore	58251	Edna Ralston Library	343-2650*	Mrs. William [illegible]
Leeds	58346	Leeds Public Library	466-2234*	Mrs. Kirk [illegible]
Lidgerwood	58053	Lidgerwood City Library	6552*	Mrs. [illegible]
Linton	58552	Linton Public Library	254-6651*	Mrs. [illegible] Wenzel
Lisbon	58054	Lisbon Public Library	683-4208*	Mrs. Ada Stewart
Mandan	58554	Mandan Public Library	663-3255	Mrs. Frances [illegible]
		Morton County Library	663-6133	Mrs. [illegible] Salveson
Mayville	58257	Mayville Public Library	786-2941*	Mrs. [illegible]
Minot	58701	Minot Public Library	838-7045	Mr. Everett Foster
		Ward County Mobile Library	838-7045	Mrs. C Dean [illegible]
Mohall	58761	Mohall Public Library	756-6692*	Mrs John Smith
Mott	58646	Mott Public Library	824-2163	Mrs [illegible] Schwartz
New England	58647	New England Public Library	579-4576*	Mrs Ron Bender
New Rockford	58356	New Rockford Public Library	947-2744*	Mrs. Roy Brown
New Salem	58563	New Salem Public Library	553*	Mrs. William Becker
New Town	58763	New Town Public Library	627-4741	Mrs. Lilian O. Wilson
Oakes	58474	Oakes Public Library	742-2251*	Mrs. Helene Hample

Park River	58270	Park River Public Library	284-6116	Mrs. Art Erick
Parshall	58770	Parshall Public Library	862-4466*	Mrs. Aldia R. Risan
Pembina	58271	Pembina Public Library	825-6625	Mr. Lloyd B. Parker
Portal	58772	Portal Public Library	3371*	Mrs. Wile Kramer
Powers Lake	58773	Notre Dame Public-School Library	None	Miss Myrtle Pfeifer
Riverdale	58565	McLean-Mercer Regional Library	7521	Mrs. Vera DeTienne
Rolette	58366	Rolette Public Library	246-3372*	Mrs. Inez Ellingson
Rolla	58367	Rolla Public Library	5791*	Mrs. Hazel E. Kyle
Rugby	58368	Rugby Public Library	776-6181	Miss Kathryn Cruden
St. Thomas	58276	St. Thomas Memorial Library	257-6616*	Miss Billie Grant
Stanley	58784	Stanley Public Library	628-2939*	Mrs. R. J. Ellis
Steele	58482	Kidder County Library	475-2806*	Mrs. Minnie Albright
Tioga	58788	Tioga Public Library	537-3435*	Mrs. Ella J. Jones
Turtle Lake	58575	Turtle Lake Public Library	448-6825*	Mrs. Jessie Gikk
Underwood	58576	Underwood Public Library	3521*	Mrs. Bernard Thomsen
Valley City	58072	Carnegie Public Library	845-3821	Mrs. Helen H. Tracy
Wimbledon	58075	Wimbledon Public Library	642-5732	Mrs. Helen Fleischman
Walhalla	58282	Walhalla Public Library	549-2531*	Mrs. Leonard Tetrault
Watford City	58854	Watford City Public Library	4911	Mrs. Lilian G. Piper
Williston	58801	James Memorial Library	572-9751	Mrs. Suzanne Smith
		West Williams Rural Library	572-2811	Mrs. Anne Lassey
Wishek	58495	Wishek Public Library	None	Miss Susan Miller
Zeeland	58581	Anna Zick Memorial Library	2031*	Mrs. August Boschee

College and University Libraries:

Bismarck	58501	Bismarck Junior College	223-4500	Mrs. Lois N. Engler
		Mary College	255-1520	Sister Martha Clare, OSB
Bottineau	58318	State School of Forestry	228-2278	Mr. Wendal J. Cushing
Devils Lake	58301	Lake Region Junior College	662-4951	Miss Beatrice Larson
Dickinson	58601	Dickinson State College	225-6092	Mr. Bernnett Reinke
Ellendale	58436	Fred J. Graham Library UND—Ellendale Branch	349-3427	Mr. Thomas A. Hunt
Fargo	58101	North Dakota State University	237-7811	Mr. Kilbourn Janacek
Grand Forks	58202	Chester Fritz Library, University of North Dakota	777-2617	Mr. Donald J. Pearce

STATE OF NORTH DAKOTA LIBRARY DIRECTORY

Public, County and Regional Libraries, and Reading Rooms

Location	Zip Code	Library	Telephone	Library
Jamestown	58401	Jamestown College	252-4331 Ext. 260	Mr. R. W. Witt
Mayville	58257	Mayville State College	[illegible]16	Miss Clenora Quanbeck
Minot	58701	Minot State College	[illegible]01	Mr. Clyde Kiang
		Northwest Bible College	839-5920	Miss Lillian Van de Trol
Richardton	58652	Assumption College	974-3315	
Valley City	58072	Allen Memorial Library, Valley City State College	845-3318	Brother Paul Nyquist, OSB
Wahpeton	58075	State School of Science	642-6671 Ext. 294	Mrs. Lillian Jacobson Mrs. Mildren Larsson
Williston	58801	UND—Williston Branch	572-5834	Miss Mary L. Endsley

* No phone at library, librarian's home phone number listed.

STATE LIBRARY COMMISSION

Payroll Report		1966-67	1967-68
State Payroll			
Freda W. Hatten	24 mo.	$9,000	$9,480
Arlene Stocker	24 mo.	6,000	6,240
Josephine Davenport	24 mo	3,900	3,978
Betty Sprynczynatyk	24 mo.	3,420	3,564
Leone Morrison	24 mo.	6,300	6,426
Inez Crimmins	24 mo.	3,180	3,240
Thelma Buchert	24 mo.	3,180	3,555
Marshall Conner	24 mo.	3,240	3,240
Sheila Saufferer	24 mo.	3,120	3,420
Pauline Sadler	24 mo.	6,000	6,420
Federal Payroll			
Duane Crawford	24 mo.	6,240	6,360
Lois Mertz	24 mo.	3,030	3,360
Mildred Johnson	22 mo.	2,150	2,820
Ruth Schoenhard	18 mo.	2,700	5,520
Thomas W. Nielsen	14 mo.	886	6,120
Shirley Ziegler	17 mo.	1,138	2,850
Alice Schafer	3 mo.		675
Paulette Gion	1 mo.		200
Mildred Nelson (part-time)			1,720
Mary Lou Norton	2 mo.		407
Paul Ellingson (part-time)			356
Renee Clarice West (temporary)			717
Carolyn Snyder (temporary)			1,350
Linda Elaine Chambers (part-time)		1,822	675
No longer employed:			
Lorraine LaFleur	14 mo.	4,404	537
Lawrence Ringuette	14 mo.	2,697	301
Mary Femling	10 mo.	3,825	
Judith Kay Munsch	5 mo.	720	457
Techla Knoll	14 mo.	2,484	360
Julie Hunze	5 mo.	1,363	
Shirley Ann Eisenbarth	6 mo.	1,164	
Clara Knoepfle (part-time)		134	
Hazel Leinhart	1 mo.	150	
Dennis Page (part-time)	3 mo.	1,272	
Michael Miller (part-time)	3 mo.	450	

1973/75

THIRTY-FIFTH

BIENNIAL REPORT

OF THE

DIRECTOR
STATE LIBRARY COMMISSION

TO THE

GOVERNOR

AND TO THE

DIRECTOR OF INSTITUTIONS

FOR THE PERIOD BEGINNING
July 1, 1973 and Ending June 30, 1975

STATE LIBRARY COMMISSION
Bismarck, N.D. 58505

RICHARD J. WOLFERT
State Librarian

November 1, 1975

Honorable Arthur A. Link
Governor
State Capitol
Bismarck, North Dakota

Mr. Edward J. Klecker
Director of Institutions
State Capitol
Bismarck, North Dakota

Dear Governor Link and Mr. Klecker:

In accordance with NDCC 54-24-03 (7), I hereby submit the Thirty-fifth Report of the Director of the State Library Commission to the Governor and to the Director of Institutions, which constitutes the State Library Commission, for the period July 1, 1973 to June 30, 1975.

Respectfully,

RICHARD J. WOLFERT
Director

INTRODUCTION

While the federal role in the support of library service still remains somewhat unclear, state support of the operations of the State Library has become firm.

The State Library is no longer dependent upon the availability of federal funds for its operation. However, funding for the improvement or development of local public library service is still entirely dependent upon federal library funds.

At this time, the federal library program is under study by the Congress, the Administration, and the library profession. Many changes are being proposed, and it remains to be seen what will emerge from the various conflicting philosophies about federal-state-local relationships and responsibilities in the provision of library service.

I. Authorization, Programs, and Responsibilities of the State Library.

The Thirty-third Report detailed the authorization, programs, and responsibilities of the State Library. No significant changes have been made, and thus, they will not be repeated in this report.

II. State Library Publications.

A complete listing of all State Library publications during this reporting period may be found in **North Dakota State Publications**, Nos. 17, 18, 19 and 20.

III. State Plan for Library Development.

The federal Library Services and Construction Act requires the submission of a State Plan each fiscal year to the U.S. Office of Education. The State Plan is published each year as an issue of **North Dakota Library Notes**. Minor changes have been made each year in the Plan.

IV. Advisory Council on Libraries.

In accordance with LSCA regulations, Governor Link appointed fifteen persons to the North Dakota Advisory Council on Libraries. The Council provides advice and counsel to the Governor, Director of Institutions, and the State Librarian on matters of policy and programs pertaining to statewide library service and development.

A comprehensive report on the status of North Dakota libraries and recommendations for improvement is to be filed with the Governor by the Advisory Council before December 31, 1976.

Minutes of the Council meetings have been published in **Flickertale Newsletter**.

V. State Library Building.

Upon completion of the new Heritage Center building in 1979, the State Historical Society will vacate the Liberty Memorial Building. The Legislative Council Budget Committee "C" is conducting a space needs study of the various state agencies. The Director of the State Library Commission prepared a report for this committee detailing the space needs of the State Library. One recommendation could be the assignment of the Liberty Memorial Building to the State Library Commission in 1979.

The present space of the State Library has been satisfactory except for the lack of proximity to the Capitol Building. It is a priority of the State Library Commission to expand and improve information and library service to state officials and employees.

VI. Talking Book Service.

Since August 1973, the Talking Book Service for North Dakota residents who are certified as blind or physically handicapped has been provided by contract from the South Dakota State Library in Pierre. Certification of eligibility and distribution of machines remains the responsibility of Division of Vocational Education, Special Services for the Blind, Grand Forks.

The State Library provides supplementary service to the certified persons through loans of large print books and tape cassettes not available through a Talking Book Service.

VII. State Document Depository.

The volume of state documents received amounts to 1,300 items each year. Each item is indexed by agency name and by the title of the publication. The indexing information is transferred to machine readable tape and stored by the State Central Data Processing Center. Monthly print-outs of new additions are prepared each month and accompanies the shipment of depository items to the designated depository libraries around the state and to the Library of Congress. Semi-annual compilations are published and distributed to North Dakota libraries. All documents are microfilmed at the end of the year, and duplicate reels are available for sale. An annual index to the microfilm reels is also published.

A "Keyword-out-of-Context" subject index was published for the years 1965-1974, and an agency and title index was published for the years 1965-1973.

VIII. State Government Service.

The Governmental Affairs section of the State Library has developed a simple computer program (LC-5) to index its materials pertaining to state government. Like other State Library computer programs, the data entered can be arranged in many ways and appropriate print-outs produced to fill the needs of the users of the system.

A cooperative project has been developed with the Supreme Court to add materials in the Court Administrator's library to the LC-5 computer indexing program. The Bureau of Governmental Affairs, University of North Dakota, has expressed willingness to add its extensive collection of library materials to the system.

There are other collections in the Capitol and elsewhere that could also be added to this system.

The nature of this material is that it consists of short reports or articles, usually not listed in usual bibliographic indexes and therefore elusive. In traditional library procedures, this type of material is not indexed and therefore difficult to retrieve.

The goal of this project is a union listing of materials physically located in several different locations. It is expected that the union listing will facilitate researchers locating their needed materials on governmental affairs.

IX. Constitutional Convention Publications.

A four volume 1,993 page book, the **North Dakota Constitutional Con-**

vention, 1971-1972; A Newspaper Account, was published by the State Library in 1974. One hundred copies were printed, and copies are for sale for $40.00 each.

Senate Bill 2074, introduced by Senator Frank Wenstrom, President of the Constitutional Convention, was passed by the 1975 Legislature. This Bill transferred the remaining copies of the Constitutional Convention **Journal and Debates** to the State Library from the Secretary of State for sale to interested persons and for a reserve supply for safe keeping.

X. Legislation.

Legislation introduced and acted upon by the 1975 Legislature was summarized in the **Flickertale Newsletter** of May 15, 1975.

House Bill 1499 changed municipal library board appointments from the school district board to the city council or commission. Senate Bill 2137 expanded the powers of contract by library boards to include municipalities and counties in adjoining states. Senate Concurrent Resolution 4005, pertaining to a Legislative Council study of library service, again failed to pass.

XI. Statewide Library Service Statistics.

Public library and academic library statistics for the fiscal years 1973 and 1974 were published in separate issues of **North Dakota Library Notes.** School library/media center statistics are available from the State Department of Public Instruction.

XII. Research Commissioned.

Several research projects were commissioned during the biennial period.

The Lewis and Clark 1805 Regional Planning Council and the Lake Agassiz Regional Planning Council each conducted studies in their region to determine library and information needs, attitudes, resources, services, and finances, and to recommend a plan for improvement.

The Law School of the University of North Dakota conducted a study of the financial and legal aspects of public library service in North Dakota.

Ronald Rudser, Minot State College Library, conducted a survey of the Devils Lake Public Library. He was assisted by Dennis Page, Grand Forks Public Library, and Ora Stewart, Carnegie Bookmobile Library, Grafton.

The North Dakota Public Library Planning Council was awarded a grant to facilitate a series of planning meetings. A report was submitted to the State Advisory Council on Libraries.

XIII. ABM Impact Funds for Library Service.

The State Library was again instrumental in securing Department of Defense funds for the provision of public library service to the ABM installation area. The funds are channeled through the State Library to the Carnegie Bookmobile Library, a four-county operation with headquarters in Grafton.

XIV. Workshops.

Statewide workshops were held during this reporting period:

Carrington, November 29-30, 1973 (Fall Frolic)

Bismarck, May 16-17, 1974 (Spring Frolic)
Bismarck, May 28-31, 1974 (Management)
Aberdeen, S.D., April 11-12, 1975 (Information and Referral)
Bismarck, April 22, 1975 (Teletype)

XV. Minimum Wage Rates.

State Minimum Wage Order was extended to persons employed in public libraries on March 7, 1974. The minimum wage was set at $2.00 per hour.

The federal minimum wage was also extended to public libraries. The federal minimum wage was set at $2.00 per hour.

XVI. Use of State Computer.

The State Library has made extensive use of the IBM 370/145 computer facilities located on the Capitol Grounds. There are four separate on-going programs:

LC-2 cataloging state documents
LC-3 cataloging monographic materials
LC-4 cataloging audio-visual materials
LC-5 cataloging governmental affairs materials

The cataloging data in each of these programs can be manipulated to produce print-outs by author, title, subject, and classification number. The data in each program, however, cannot be intermixed.

Fifteen subject catalogs have been produced, published, and distributed to libraries. Microfiche editions will be published in 1976, making the process from computer tape to user catalog much faster and cheaper. It is expected that increased use of the State Library resources will result from this project.

Utilizing the LC-3 program, a catalog of the complete holdings of the McLean-Mercer Regional Library (28,000 titles) was produced and distributed to branch libraries and to the bookmobile.

Mary College has also been transferring its cataloging data to the LC-3 program, and joint State Library Commission and Mary College catalogs will be produced.

XVII. Revenue Sharing.

Public libraries are eligible to receive federal revenue sharing funds through their city or county government. During the 1973 calendar year twenty-eight libraries received a total of $170,232.00 in revenue sharing funds. During the 1974 calendar year twenty-nine libraries received a total of $180,333.00. Regretably, about fifty percent of the libraries failed to even request any of these funds from their city or county government.

XVIII. Public Library Construction.

Public library construction during this reporting period included:

A. Jamestown, Alfred Dickey Library: an addition of 1,600 square feet, $53,924.00

B. Dickinson Public Library: an addition of 4,400 square feet, $218,857.00

C. Watford City Public Library: a new building of 1,600 square feet, $41,561.00

D. West Fargo: a new building of 5,000 square feet, $147,240.00

XIX. MINITEX Service.

The State Library Commission signed a one-year agreement with the Minnesota Higher Education Coordinating Commission to provide North Dakota residents, through their local libraries, improved library and information services.

The agreement provides for MINITEX (which is operated by the Minnesota Higher Education Coordinating Commission) to provide access to Minnesota library and information resources via the North Dakota State Library Commission. This access includes loan of books and documents, and photocopies of periodical articles.

Three North Dakota libraries have been designated as access points to MINITEX: The State Library, Bismarck; The Chester Fritz Library, University of North Dakota; The Library, North Dakota State University, Fargo. All other North Dakota libraries channel their requests for service through the State Library unless special arrangements have been made with University of North Dakota or North Dakota State University.

The agreement requires that North Dakota library resources must first be exhausted before contacting MINITEX. Thus, all requests for books must be cleared through the State Library Union Catalog to be sure that the material is not available in North Dakota. Periodical requests must be filled within the state whenever possible before referring to MINITEX. Access libraries are using TWX to transmit MINITEX requests in a designated format and verified in accepted bibliographic tools.

The agreement also provides for MINITEX to produce a new edition of the North Dakota Union List of Serials. Fifty libraries are participating in the new edition. MINITEX has recently published the Minnesota Union List of Serials. It is expected that the North Dakota List would be published in late 1975 by the State Library Commission. In addition to the statewide list, area-wide lists, or type of library lists can also be produced.

XX. State Library Use and Service Patterns.

The biennial period contained a continuation of long-term trends in patterns of service from the State Library.

A. The utilization of juvenile books has continued to decline as have the Traveling Library and Reading Circle services. Schools have accounted for the bulk of the circulation of these special collections. As schools establish and build up their own libraries their dependence upon the State Library diminishes.

LOANS 1975

	1975	1974	1973	1972	1971
Juvenile books	4,171	4,618	7,307	14,719	14,972
Reading Circle	-0-	706	4,917	5,228	7,190
Traveling Libraries	7,179	10,939	10,448	9,970	10,439

B. Adult readers' use of information books has increased. The State Library has emphasized its role as a statewide information center. The changing nature is reflected in the statistics. Much fiction and other "popular" reading material previously supplied at the state level is now being provided at the regional level. A more sophisticated State Library collection fills a need for this type of material, but the utilization is less than a popular collection. The objective is to place lesser used material at one location in the state—the State Library—with access to all.

LOANS

	1975	1974	1973	1972	1971
Adult Information Books	23,328	20,670	22,184	20,068	18,165

C. The circulation of State Library books of adult fiction has declined, except for the 1975 year.

LOANS

	1975	1974	1973	1972	1971
Adult Fiction Books	5,886	4,694	5,514	5,424	6,227

D. Audio-visual materials, such as tape cassettes and filmstrips are in great demand by individuals, schools, and for adult listening groups. The State Library has greatly expanded its collection of these popular and instructive items during the biennium to meet the growing need. The collection of phonograph records has been discontinued and tape cassettes substituted because of their mailing ease.

LOANS

	1975	1974	1973	1972	1971
Tape Cassettes	11,838	8,274	8,324	3,898	679
Phonograph Records	-0-	68	589	644	896
Filmstrips	7,854	2,543	2,573	603	149
8 mm Films	958	-0-	-0-	-0-	-0-
Slides	-0-	-0-	-0-	-0-	302
Other	260	118	-0-	180	117

E. Other printed materials.

LOANS

	1975	1974	1973	1972	1971
Other Printed Materials	7,105	3,642	6,947	6,752	10,232

F. Total Loans of Materials.

	1975	1974	1973	1972	1971
Total Loans	68,579	56,272	69,756	67,486	69,368

G. Service to state government officials and employees has increased as we have promoted this service. Selected appropriate material has been added to the collection.

LOANS

	1975	1974	1973	1972	1971
State Officials and Employees	3,128	1,992	2,257	2,603	1,280

H. Book loans to college and university libraries have also increased. The increase can be attributed to the State Library collection becoming more academically useful as it builds its non-fiction collection.

LOANS

	1975	1974	1973	1972	1971
College and University Libraries	2,312	1,639	1,444	894	370

I. Use of the State Library by individuals without local library service has declined, except in 1975, while loans to libraries have increased. This pattern is a result of channeling requests for service through local and regional libraries. In this way libraries close to patrons supply requests for most popular materials, and generally only requests for more sophisticated and specialized material are now being filled from the State Library collection.

LOANS

	1975	1974	1973	1972	1971
Individuals	27,414	22,926	32,616	29,472	37,536
Public Libraries	9,662	6,201	6,036	6,324	3,835

J. Service requests from high schools have increased for material not available in the school library media center. Such items include photocopies, filmstrips, tape cassettes, and many adult level books. This increase is in contrast to the decline in requests for the "pre-packaged" Reading Circle and Traveling Library collections which contain mostly books for younger school children.

LOANS

	1975	1974	1973	1972	1971
Schools	18,247	11,560	11,712	12,753	8,334

K. State institutions. Service to the seven state supported institutions has increased. Increased usage has been for both staff and resident use.

LOANS

	1975	1974	1973	1972	1971
State institutions	637	309	326	242	384

L. Service on the "Network for Knowledge" has increased. The Network is a teletype-telephone-mail communication system coordinating and improving the services of all North Dakota libraries. The headquarters is at the State Library and contains a listing of all books and periodicals in the twenty-six larger libraries of the state. The provision of information and reading material through the Network makes the total resources of the state's libraries available to all its citizens.

NETWORK TRANSACTIONS

1975	1974	1973	1972	1971
21,541	18,443	15,230	10,122	6,192

NORTH DAKOTA NETWORK FOR KNOWLEDGE REPORT *
Fiscal 1974

Library	Requests Rec'd From	Requests Filled By: State Library	Within State	Other	Total	Requests Not Filled	Requests Filled By Library
Bismarck JC	97	29	50	1	80	17	93
Bismarck PL	787	323	230	6	559	228	316
Bottineau SF	48	22	19		41	7	25
Devils Lake PL	139	73	43		116	23	17
Dickinson PL	331	160	90		250	81	60
Dickinson St. Col	469	113	187	6	306	163	245
Fargo PL	280	146	51		197	83	158
Grand Forks PL	537	180	180	4	364	173	229
Jamestown Col.	319	60	135	1	196	123	121
James Memorial-W	195	101	55	5	161	34	41
Jamestown PL	335	196	63		259	76	36
Lake Region JC	76	21	34		55	21	17
Mandan PL	283	135	77	7	219	64	218
Mary College L	742	435	147	8	590	152	105
Minot PL	1,582	530	478	10	1,018	564	87
Minot State Col	264	76	104	1	181	83	359
Mayville St. Col	82	10	44		54	28	66
NDSU Library	281	53	84	1	138	143	721
Other N.D. PL	3,665	2,098	932	14	3,044	621	8
State Lib. Comm	431		344	8	352	79	10,253
St. Sch. of Science	132	26	62	3	91	41	129
Univ. of N.D.	1,233	191	383	40	614	619	743
UND-Medical L.	6	6			6		4
UND-Williston Br	185	47	71	1	119	66	37
Valley City PL	124	44	38	2	84	40	74
Valley City St. Col	353	127	98	2	227	126	244
W. Plains—Williston	191	95	41		136	55	9
High Schools	4,531	4,229	107		4,336	195	
Elem. Schools	731	713	3		716	15	
Other (Out-of-State)	14	14			14		120
TOTAL	18,443	10,253	4,150	120	14,523	3,920	14,523

*Includes only requests received by the State Library Commission, and does not include requests sent directly from one library to another.

NORTH DAKOTA NETWORK FOR KNOWLEDGE REPORT*
Fiscal 1975

Name of Library	Requests Rec'd From	Requests Filled By: State Library	Within State	Minitex	Other	Total	Requests Not Filled	Requests Filled By Library
Minitex								1,224
Bismarck JC	71	21	34		2	57	14	91
Bismarck Mary Col.	578	261	115	36	7	419	159	208
Bismarck Public	776	276	252	14	9	551	225	317
Bismarck State Lib	1,023		744	97	34	875	148	10,991
Bottineau SF	47	12	28			40	7	43
Devils Lake Col	68	19	32			51	17	13
Devils Lake Pub	347	174	111			285	62	23
Dickinson Public	262	103	77	3	4	187	75	75
Dickinson State	636	241	179	19		439	197	253
Fargo Public	461	223	81	16	1	321	140	185
N.D.S.U.	577	72	178		4	254	323	845
Grafton CB (4-1-75 +)	87	46	20			66	21	
Grand Forks Public	546	171	166	24	7	368	178	269
U.N.D., Grand Forks	1,903	139	427	668	132	1,366	537	811
UND—Medical Lib.	2		2			2		74
Jamestown Col.	424	119	157	8	8	292	132	146
Jamestown Public	437	268	62		1	331	106	52
Mandan Public	654	302	118	2	2	424	230	138
Mayville State	144	20	61	37		118	26	42
Minot Public	1,553	618	438	1	11	1,068	485	89
Minot State Col	605	67	138	267	37	509	96	420

Network (Continued)

Name of Library	Requests Rec'd From	Requests Filled By: State Library	Within State	Minitex	Other	Total	Requests Not Filled	Requests Filled By Library
Valley City Public	198	118	31		1	150	48	61
Valley City State	234	73	69	6	2	150	84	224
Wahpeton S. of Sci.	131	53	38		1	94	37	138
Williston James M	675	267	192	8	4	471	204	70
Williston—UND	62	17	21	3	2	43	19	30
Other ND Libraries	4,096	2,480	782	13	16	3,291	805	
High Schools	4,479	4,249	60			4,309	170	
Elem. Schools	592	561	3			564	28	
Other (out-of-state)	23	21	1			22	1	285
TOTAL	21,691	10,991	4,617	1,224	285	17,117	4,574	17,117

*Includes only requests received by the State Library Commission, and does not include requests sent directly from one library to another.

XXI STATE LIBRARY COLLECTION

	Added 1974	Added 1975	Withdrawn 1974	Withdrawn 1975	Total (6-30-75)
Adult information books	2,961	4,030	809	433	51,272
Adult fiction books	181	191	899	15	6,229
Juvenile books	-0-	-0-	1,940	346	3,715
Tape Cassettes	1,895	1,875	-0-	29	8,614
8MM Films	445	446	-0-	-0-	891
16MM Films	-0-	20	-0-	-0-	20
Filmstrips	573	267	-0-	-0-	1,080
Microfilm Reels					1,622
Microfiche Cards					4,227
Reading Circle	-0-	-0-	8,445	-0-	-0-
Traveling Library	-0-	-0-	4,856	-0-	8,128
TOTALS	6,055	6,829	16,949	823	85,798

XXII STATE LIBRARY STAFF

The State Library has 17 authorized state funded positions, and each one has been classified in the newly created state personnel system:

Name	Position
1. Bailey, Cheryl	Librarian III
2. Beckler, Terry	Library Technician
3. Bina, Leeila	Librarian II
4. Buchert, Thelma	Clerk I
5. Guttromson, Marilyn	Librarian I
6. Hetler, Dawn	Library Technician
7. Johnson, Mildred	Library Technician
8. Mertz, Lois	Clerk Typist II
9. Nelson, Mildred	Clerk I
10. Norton, Mary Lou	Clerk I
11. Parkman, Bea	Clerk II
12. Schafer, Alice	Library Technician
13. Sprynczynatyk, Betty	Librarian I

Library Staff (Continued)

Name	Position
14. Stocker, Arlene	Library Technician
15. Wald, Donald	Administrative Officer III
16. Wolfert, Richard	State Librarian
17. Ziegler, Shirley	Secretary I

Federally funded: 1. Stenstrom, Ralph Library Consultant
Temporary Positions: 1. Dewald, Alice
2. Schneider, Susan
3. Steinwand, Pamela
4. Wingenbach, Joyce

NORTH DAKOTA STATE LIBRARY
Expenditures 7-1-73 — 6-30-75

	FY-1974	FY-1975	Biennial Total
Salaries & Wages	$136,299	$188,105	$324,404
Fees & Services			
Travel	$ 4,664	$ 8,020	$ 12,684
Utilities	3,583	4,228	7,811
Rents	38,043	37,850	75,893
Communications	2,374	5,884	8,258
Repairs	5,919	2,732	8,651
Data Processing	7,338	31,861	39,199
Professional Fees	3,581	5,583	9,164
Research Projects RC & D	10,483	-0-	10,483
Blind Service—South Dakota	-0-	24,000	24,000
Minitex	-0-	42,500	42,500
Insurance	642	620	1,262
Miscellaneous	3,927	4,997	8,924
TOTAL	$80,554	$168,275	$248,829
Supplies & Materials			
Office Supplies	$ 4,915	$13,983	$18,898
Printing	5,071	9,527	14,598
Books	21,396	29,909	51,305
Audio Visual	87,369	31,659	119,028
Periodicals	5,893	2,836	8,729
Miscellaneous	840	1,528	2,368
TOTAL	$125,484	$ 89,442	$214,926
Equipment	$12,958	$ 10,140	$ 23,098
Grants	$301,322	$361,398	$662,720
TOTAL	$656,617	$817,360	$1,473,977

NORTH DAKOTA STATE LIBRARY
Library Services and Construction Act Grants

Library	FY-1974	FY-1975	Biennial Total
Title I Library Services			
Physically Handicapped			
Service to the Blind & Physically Handicapped			
State School for the Blind	$ 2,878	$1,295	$ 4,173
South Dakota State Library	22,000	(note)	22,000
TOTAL	$24,878	$1,295	$26,173

Note—1975-South Dakota Contract Expense paid through Fees and Services of the State Library Appropriation.

Library Services and Construction Act Grants

Library	FY-1974	FY-1975	Biennial Total
Wide-Area Library Service			
Service to the surrounding trade area free of charge			
Devils Lake Public	$ 2,228	$ -0-	$2,228
Dickinson Public	2,500	2,028	4,528
Fargo Public	12,750	19,610	32,360
Harvey Public	2,000	-0-	2,000
Jamestown—Alfred Dickey	2,760	2,016	4,776
Lisbon Public	1,500	-0-	1,500
Mandan Public	2,000	-0-	2,000
Minot Public	6,720	16,866	23,586
Mott Public	1,500	-0-	1,500
Valley City Public	2,000	-0-	2,000
Wahpeton—Leach Public	2,500	-0-	2,500
Williston—James Memorial	3,360	-0-	3,360
TOTAL	$41,818	$40,520	$82,338
Groups of Persons			
Service to special, ethnic, and shut-in groups			
Bismarck—Veterans Memorial	$ -0-	$10,255	$10,255
Dickinson Public	1,000	500	1,500
Divide County	500	-0-	500
Fargo Public	32,750	-0-	32,750
Grafton—Carnegie Bookmobile	2,500	2,000	4,500
Jamestown—Alfred Dickey	2,000	1,000	3,000
Lisbon Public	2,000	-0-	2,000
Mandan Public	500	5,000	5,500
Minot Public	9,000	-0-	9,000
Stutsman County	500	-0-	500
Valley City	500	500	1,000
Williston—James Memorial	3,000	-0-	3,000
Williston—West Plains Rural	14,870	2,500	17,370
TOTAL	$69,120	$21,755	$90,875
Demonstration—Development			
Bismarck—Veterans Memorial	$15,442	$19,886	$35,328
Cooperstown—Griggs County	-0-	10,000	10,000
Divide County	4,500	-0-	4,500
Grafton—Carnegie Bookmobile	15,000	1,730	16,730
Grand Forks Public	-0-	4,000	4,000
Linton Public	-0-	4,000	4,000
McLean—Mercer	-0-	3,697	3,697
Minot Public	25,000	6,200	31,200
Stutsman County	1,200	-0-	1,200
Wahpeton—Leach Public	9,000	-0-	9,000
Ward County	-0-	4,000	4,000
Fargo Public	-0-	19,390	19,390
TOTAL	$70,142	$72,903	$143,045
Institutional Library Service			
Service to state Institutions			
N.D. State Hospital	$ 7,000	$ 6,278	$13,278
State Industrial School	7,000	6,278	13,278
School for the Deaf	5,000	6,279	11,279
Grafton State School	3,000	3,165	6,165
TOTAL	$22,000	$22,000	$44,000
Planning Education & Research Grants			
Grants to Individuals	$1,114	$ 180	$ 1,294
Bismarck—Veterans Memorial	10,450	-0-	10,450
UND—Law School	7,500	-0-	7,500
TOTAL	$19,064	$ 180	$19,244

Title II Construction			
Dickinson	$ -0-	$77,476	$77,476
Grafton	9,900	-0-	9,900
Grand Forks	32,400	5,400	37,800
Jamestown	12,000	-0-	12,000
Watford City	-0-	24,000	24,000
West Fargo	-0-	70,869	70,869
TOTAL	$54,300	$177,745	$232,045
A B M Impact Grant	$ -0-	$25,000	$25,000
TOTAL GRANTS	$301,322	$361,398	$662,720

REPORT COVERING THE ACTIVITIES OF THE LIBRARY SERVICES AND CONSTRUCTION ACT FOR THE FISCAL YEAR JULY 1, 1973-JUNE 30, 1974.
Submitted to the Office of Libraries and Learning Resources, Washington, D.C.

INTRODUCTION

Funds for the federal Library Services and Construction Act were subject to unusual stresses and strains during the 1974 fiscal year, and they were reflected in the difficulties of administering the State Plan.

When the Administration planned an abrupt termination of the Library Services and Construction Act by eliminating all funding for FY-1974, the State Legislature did (after much consternation) appropriate sufficient funds for the State Library to continue statewide services, albeit at a reduced level.

It should be noted, however, that the increased state funding was contingent upon the termination of Library Services and Construction Act funds. When Library Services and Construction Act funds were restored by Congressional action, the increased state funds reverted back to the state general fund.

As in the 1971/73 and the 1973/75 biennial budget requests, the State Library Commission has submitted a state budget document detailing the need and justification for state funds to operate statewide library service. The federal Library Services and Construction Act funds are to be used for public library development, coordination of all types of libraries, and providing special library services to groups of persons such as the blind and physically handicapped, institutionalized, senior citizens, etc. At this time the State Legislature has not completed action upon the budget request for the 1975/77 biennium. Should the Library Services and Construction Act program terminate, as the Administration plans, or should Library Services and Construction Act be amended to prohibit the substitution of federal funds for state funds, then the State Library will, by necessity, be state funded.

ADVISORY COUNCIL—

Governor Arthur A. Link established a new Advisory Council on Libraries to supersede the Council that served under former Governor William L. Guy. The new Council has received the instruction from Governor Link to submit to him a detailed report on the status of North Dakota libraries (academic, school, public, and special) and to make recommendations for the development and coordination of the resources and services of these libraries.

To assist the Council, planning committees have been appointed in the academic, school, and public library areas. These committees, consisting of professionals in their respective fields, are to report to the Council with their detailed findings and recommendations. The State Librarian serves as executive secretary to the Council and he or his representative also serves as ex-officio on each of the planning committees.

TITLE I, PROJECT 1, ADMINISTRATION OF THE STATE PLAN

The administrative staff consists of the State Librarian, an administrative officer, a secretary, and a part-time bookkeeper. Administrative costs also include space rental, utilities, and travel.

No administrative changes were made during FY-1974. Project costs are estimated at $25,000. This amount is about five percent of the total funds administered by the State Library.

TITLE I, PROJECT 2, STATE INSTITUTIONAL LIBRARY SERVICE

Grants were made to the following state supported institutions for staff, materials, or equipment:

School for the Deaf, Devils Lake	$ 5,000.00
School for the Mentally Retarded, Grafton	3,000.00
State Hospital, Jamestown	7,000.00
State Industrial School, Mandan	7,000.00
	$22,000.00

Each of these institutions has greatly benefited from this project since 1967 when Library Services and Construction Act funds became available for state institutional service. While much more needs to be accomplished, some of these libraries have reached a reasonable level of service. Others lack even a minimal level of service. In FY-1975, a survey of the state institutional libraries is being completed and a report with recommendations will be filed with the Advisory Council.

The state institutions regularly borrow material from the State Library. Consultant services are available to each institution upon request.

TITLE I, PROJECT 3, STATEWIDE LIBRARY SERVICES TO THE BLIND AND PHYSICALLY HANDICAPPED.

Talking Book Service to North Dakota residents is provided by contract from the South Dakota State Library, Pierre.

The North Dakota State Library provides supplementary library service with large print books and tape cassettes of material not available through the Talking Book Service.

This contractual service arrangement with South Dakota and supplemental service from the State Library is satisfactory at this time.

Talking Book machine distribution and certification of eligible persons is under the control of the Division of Special Services to the Blind, Department of Vocational Rehabilitation, Grand Forks.

A grant was made to the School for the Blind, Grand Forks, for the purchase of library materials and equipment.

Contractual Expenditures:

South Dakota State Library	$22,000.00
School for the Blind, Grand Forks	2,878.00
	$24,878.00

(TITLE I,) PROJECT 4, LIBRARY SERVICE TO STATE GOVERNMENT

This project is entirely state funded and consists of information and consultant service to state government personnel.

It is included in this report because it is an integral part of the State Plan.

TITLE I, PROJECT 5, STATEWIDE INFORMATION AND LIBRARY SERVICE

The State Library continued its supportive role in the supplementary provision of library materials to local libraries and in the provision of direct library service to the population which does not have access to local library service.

Library materials were expanded to include tape cassettes, sound filmstrips, and 8mm recreational films. Many computer produced catalogs of the newer media material were distributed to libraries and to individuals.

Consultant service to local public libraries is provided by the State Library staff.

A large portion of the Library Services and Construction Act funds have been expended in this program, because of insufficient state appropriations and because of the lack of viable public library service over two-thirds of the state.

Wide Area Service grants continue to be made to selected local public libraries. Libraries that meet certain standards are granted Library Services and Construction Act funds to extend their services to their surrounding trade area. A statewide library card is a goal of this project. In addition to the loan of library materials, reference and information service, photocopy service, and interlibrary loan service are also provided. Many areas of the state and large segments of the population are provided with free public library service for the first time under this project.

Wide Area Service Contractual Agreements.

Devils Lake Public Library	$ 2,228.00
Dickinson Public Library	2,500,00
Fargo Public Library	12,750.00
Harvey Public Library	2,000.00
Jamestown Public Library (Alfred Dickey)	2,760.00
Lisbon Public Library	1,500.00
Mandan Public Library	2,000.00
Minot Public Library	6,720.00
Mott Public Library	1,500.00
Valley City Public Library	2,000.00
Wahpeton Leach Public Library	2,500.00
Williston (James Memorial) Public Library	3,360.00
	$41,818.00

TITLE I, PROJECT 6, LIBRARY SERVICES TO SPECIAL GROUPS OF PERSONS

Emphasis was again given to the improvement of library services for senior citizens, homebound, and institutionalized persons, as well as other groups needing special attention.

Collections of suitable library materials were placed in senior citizens centers, rest homes, hospitals, and jails. In some areas, transportation was provided to visit the library by those persons who could not do so under their own circumstances. Volunteers were often the chief means of bringing library materials to homebound and institutionalized.

Contractual Agreements.

Service to Senior Citizens—

Fargo Public Library (for 14 rural communities)	$30,000.00
Lisbon Public Library	2,000.00
Mandan Public Library	500.00
Stutsman County Library	500.00
Valley City Public Library	500.00
West Plains Rural Library, Williston (for 5 rural communities)	12,700.00
	$46,200.00

Service to Special Groups (includes senior citizens, homebound, institutionalized)—

Dickinson Public Library	$ 1,000.00
Divide County Library	500.00
Carnegie Bookmobile Library, Grafton (for communities in 4 counties)	2,500.00
Alfred Dickey Public Library, Jamestown	2,000.00
Minot Public Library	5,810.00
James Memorial Public Library, Williston	3,000.00
	$14,810.00

Disadvantaged—

A grant was made to the Minot Public Library to continue a special paperback reading service via a bookmobile to low income families in the city.

Minot Public Library	$ 3,190.00

Indians—

Grants were made to the Fargo Public Library and the West Plains Rural Library, Williston, for special library services to Indians in their surrounding areas.

The grant to Fargo was for the purchase of library materials to be housed in the Fargo-Moorhead Indian Club.

The Williston grant was for the purchase of library materials to be housed in Indian day care centers located in Mountrail County.

Fargo Public Library	$ 2,750.00
West Plains Rural Library, Williston	2,170.00
	$ 4,920.00
Total Contractual Agreements for Project 6	$69,120.00

TITLE I, PROJECT 7, DEVELOPMENT OF PUBLIC LIBRARY SERVICE

Divide County Library received a grant to hire additional staff and for travel expenses to permit the county librarian to develop extended service programs from the combined school media/county library located in a new building.

Divide County Library .... $ 4,500.00

Carnegie Bookmobile Library, Grafton, received a grant to demonstrate improved multi-county library service through rapid communication systems (IN-WATS from local library to headquarters library, and TWP from headquarters library to the State Library); consultant staff for local library improvements; added library materials.

Carnegie Bookmobile Library, Grafton $15,000.00

Minot Public Library received a grant to develop an Area Referral and Information Service. A directory of services is being compiled and will be published for the seven-county area. Telephone and in-person service is available from service center.

Minot Public Library $25,000.00

Bismarck Public Library received a grant for publishing an Area Referral and Information Service directory for a ten-county area. The directory had been previously compiled.

Bismarck Public Library .... $ 8,442.00

The Wahpeton Public Library received a grant for equipment and library materials to demonstrate improved community service in the areas of reference and a community meeting room.

Wahpeton Public Library .... $ 9,000.00

Stutsman County received a grant for the installation of a two-way radio in their bookmobile to expedite service by providing reference service and interlibrary loans. Blizzard warnings during the winter months are also a vehicle staff benefit.

Stutsman County Library .... $ 1,200.00

The Bismarck Public Library received a grant to improve service by integrating its two book classification systems into one classification.

Bismarck Public Library .... $ 7,000.00

Total Contractual Agreements for Project 7 .... $70,142.00

Community Library Service—

While no funds were granted this fiscal year, activities from previous years continued at the local level. This project provides for public library service in small communities which do not have a public library by extending the services of the school media center to the community.

The Velva Public and School Library activity was a success and has been allocated an increase in local funds and is supplemented by federal revenue sharing funds. A research report on this activity has been published by the State Library. The Divide County Library in Crosby has merged with the school media center in a new school building in Crosby. Several other communities have this library service arrangement under consideration.

TITLE I, PROJECT 8, PLANNING, RESEARCH, AND EDUCATION

Educational grants were made for undergraduate library courses taken at North Dakota colleges or by correspondence courses by library staff members throughout the state. Courses in management were also offered through the business department of a local college.

Library conferences brought technical administrative assistance as well as technical procedural information to North Dakota librarians through the use of professional speakers and evaluation teams.

Total education costs ....$ 3,798.00

Planning and research grants were made on local, regional and statewide basis. The final results of these studies are not yet available. However, the ultimate goal of the three level approach is to determine the problem areas as well as the potential resources available throughout the state.

Planning and research grants for FY-1974 are as follows:

One for local planning—	
Bismarck Public Library	$ 6,010.00
Two for regional planning—	
Lake Agassiz Regional Planning Council	5,483.00
Lewis & Clark Regional Planning Council	5,000.00
Two for statewide planning—	
Law School, University of North Dakota	7,500.00
Bismarck Public Library as agent for the Public Library Planning Council	4,440.00
	$32,231.00

TITLE I, PROJECT 9, GRANTS-IN-AID FOR IMPROVED PUBLIC LIBRARY SERVICE

No grants were made in this category during this fiscal year.

TITLE III, PROJECT 1, NORTH DAKOTA NETWORK FOR KNOWLEDGE

The State Library continued to operate the North Dakota Network for Knowledge. This Network is a teletype-telephone-mail communications system with headquarters in the State Library and includes a union catalog of books, periodicals, and A-V materials in the twenty-six largest libraries in the state. Out-of-state searching is also done at the State Library. Negotiations are presently underway with the Minnesota Higher Education Coordinating Commission for the extension of MINITEX library and information services to North Dakota. A joint two-state Union List of Serials and document delivery service would be a feature of the proposed bi-state relationship.

A planning and coordinating director has been added to the staff. His responsibility will be to work with the Advisory Council and with regional and local planning bodies. He will also update the State Plan as required.

ABM IMPACT GRANT

The Carnegie Bookmobile Library, a four-county operation serving the ABM impacted area, received a $25,000.00 Department of Defense grant via the State Library Commission. These funds were used to operate an additional bookmobile in the impacted area and to provide additional staff and library materials.

REPORT COVERING THE ACTIVITIES OF THE LIBRARY SERVICES AND CONSTRUCTION ACT FOR THE FISCAL YEAR JULY 1, 1974-JUNE 30, 1975
Submitted to the Office of Libraries and Learning Resources, Washington, D.C.

INTRODUCTION

Funds for the federal Library Services and Construction Act were again subject to what has become the usual stresses and strains during the 1975 fiscal year. Difficulties of administering the State Plan were minimized because of the carry-over provision of the "Tydings Amendment" which allowed the State Agencies another year to expend the funds. However, the lack of support by the administration causes great difficulties for effective state-level planning.

ADVISORY COUNCIL

The North Dakota Advisory Council on Libraries, appointed by Governor A. Link, has met 5 times during the fiscal year and is preparing a detailed report on the status of North Dakota libraries (academic, school, public, and special) and will make recommendations for the development and coordination of the resources and services of these libraries.

To assist the Council, planning committees have been appointed in the academic, school, and public library areas. These committees, consisting of professionals in their respective fields, report to the Council with their detailed findings and recommendations. The State Librarian serves as executive secretary to the Council and he or his representative also serves as ex-officio on each of the planning committees.

The minutes of the Council meetings have been published in the Flickertale Newsletter.

TITLE I, PROJECT 1, ADMINISTRATION OF THE STATE PLAN

The administrative staff consists of the State Librarian, an administrative officer, a secretary, and a part-time account clerk. Administrative costs also include space rental, utilities, and travel.

No administrative changes were made during FY-1975. Administrative costs are estimated at $25,000. This amount is about seven percent of the total federal funds administered by the State Library.

TITLE I, PROJECT 2, STATE INSTITUTIONAL LIBRARY SERVICE

Grants were made to the following state supported institutions for staff, materials, or equipment:

School for the Deaf, Devils Lake	$ 6,279.00
School for the Mentally Retarded, Grafton	3,165.00
State Hospital, Jamestown	6,278.00
State Industrial School, Mandan	6,278.00
	$22,000.00

Each of these institutions has greatly benefited from this project since 1967 when Library Services and Construction Act funds became available for state institutional service. While much more needs to be accomplished, some of these libraries have reached a reasonable level of service. Others lack even a minimal level of service. A survey of the state institutional libraries has been completed and a report with recommendations will be filed with the Advisory Council.

Each of the state institutions regularly borrows library materials from the State Library. Consultant services are available to each institution upon request.

TITLE I, PROJECT 3, STATEWIDE LIBRARY SERVICES TO THE BLIND AND PHYSICALLY HANDICAPPED

Talking Book Service to North Dakota residents is provided by contract from the South Dakota State Library, Pierre.

The North Dakota State Library provides supplementary library service with large print books and tape cassettes of material not available through Talking Book Service.

Talking Book machine distribution and certification of eligible persons is under the control of the Division of Special Services to the Blind, Department of Vocational Rehabilitation, Grand Forks.

A grant was made to the School for the Blind, Grand Forks, for the purchase of library materials and equipment.

Contractual Expenditures

South Dakota State Library	$24,000.00
School for the Blind, Grand Forks	1,295.00
	$25,295.00

(TITLE I,) PROJECT 4, LIBRARY SERVICE TO STATE GOVERNMENT

This project is entirely state funded and consists of reference, information and consultant service to state government personnel.

It is included in this report because it is an integral part of the State Plan.

TITLE I, PROJECT 5, STATEWIDE INFORMATION AND LIBRARY SERVICE

The State Library continued its supportive role in the supplementary provision of library materials to local libraries and in the provision of direct library service to the population which does not have access to local library service.

Library materials were again expanded to include tape cassettes, sound filmstrips, and 8mm recreational films. Many computer produced catalogs of the newer media and books were distributed to libraries and to individuals. (See list of publications at end of this report.)

Consultant service to local public libraries is provided by the State Library staff.

A smaller portion of the Library Services and Construction Act funds have been expended in this program than in previous years, because of increased state appropriations for this service.

Wide Area Service grants continue to be made to selected local public libraries. Libraries that meet certain standards are granted Library Services and Construction Act funds to extend their services to their surround ing trade area. A statewide library card is a goal of this project. In addition to the loan of library materials, reference and information service, photocopy service, and interlibrary loan service are also provided. Many areas of the state and large segments of the population are provided with free public library service for the first time under this project.

Wide Area Service Contractual Agreements

Dickinson Public Library	$ 2,028.00
Fargo Public Library	19,610.00
Jamestown Public Library (Alfred Dickey)	2,016.00
Minot Public Library	16,866.00
	$40,520.00

TITLE I, PROJECT 6, LIBRARY SERVICES TO SPECIAL GROUPS OF PERSONS

Emphasis was again given to the improvement of library services for senior citizens, homebound, and institutionalized persons, as well as other groups needing special attention.

Collections of suitable library materials were placed in senior citizens centers, rest homes, hospitals, and jails. In some areas, transportation was provided to visit the library by those persons who could not do so under their own circumstances. Volunteers were often the chief means of bringing library materials to persons homebound or institutionalized.

Contractual Agreements

Dickinson Public Library	$ 500.00
Mandan Public Library	5,000.00
Carnegie Bookmobile Library, Grafton (for communities in 4 counties)	2,000.00
Alfred Dickey Public Library, Jamestown	1,000.00
Valley City Public Library	500.00
	$ 9,000.00

Disadvantaged Groups

In addition to the senior citizens (the largest numerical disadvantaged group in the state), the homebound and the institutionalized, special projects were developed for Native Americans and for other low-income concentrations of population.

A grant was made to the West Plains Rural Library in Williston for the purchase of library materials to be used by children at several Indian Day Care Centers in rural communities.

The State Library, as part of its Project 5—Statewide Information and Library Service, has strengthened its collection of materials on Native Americans and has published a 328 page catalog of these materials and distributed it to libraries in the state.

The United Tribes Training Center located in Bismarck has made extensive use of the State Library collection in their educational and cultural programs.

Sioux County, which contains the North Dakota portion of the Standing Rock Indian Reservation, was a project area to provide improved bookmobile service through an upgraded materials collection, a refurbished bookmobile, professional direction, consultant service, and interlibrary loan services. The project was under contract with the Bismarck Public Library.

West Plains Rural Library, Williston	$ 2,500.00
Bismarck Public Library	10,255.00
	$12,755.00

TITLE I, PROJECT 7, DEVELOPMENT OF PUBLIC LIBRARY SERVICE
Grants were made to the following libraries:

$19,866	**Bismarck Public Library** (to demonstrate library service to Burleigh County via bookmobile, deposit collections and walk-in service)
$ 4,000	**Ward County, Minot** (to help equip a new branch library in Kenmare as part of the Ward County Library)
$ 6,200	**Minot Public Library** (to publish and distribute an "Area Information and Referral Service" directory for a seven county area)
$ 1,730	**Carnegie Bookmobile Library, Grafton** (to demonstrate improved library service in smaller communities in four rural counties)
$10,000	**Griggs County Library** (to consolidate the city and county library into one administrative and service unit)
$ 3,697	**McLean-Mercer Regional Library** (to produce a book catalog of library materials for distribution to branches and bookmobile. The data processing is being done by the State Library Commission at an additional estimated cost of $7,500.00.)
$ 4,000	**Linton Public Library** (to help equip a new library construction as part of a community center)
$ 4,000	**Grand Forks Public Library**) to establish clearinghouse of audio-visual resources in the City of Grand Forks)
$19,390	**Fargo Public Library** (in Region V, to provide free library borrowers cards and mail service to residents and supplemental library service to public libraries; provide consultant service to Region V; administer grants for participating public libraries)
$72,903	Total

In addition, the State Library Commission purchased filmstrip/cassette projectors (Dukane) to promote local public library use of the State Library Commission collection of sound filmstrips. These projectors were loaned to public libraries.

Kodak super 8 film projectors were also purchased by the State Library Commission to promote local public library use of the State Library Commission collection of super 8 films. These projectors were loaned to public libraries.

Lightning Source UK Ltd.
Milton Keynes UK
UKHW011541040119
334726UK00008B/300/P

9 780265 94275